SOCIAL WORK AND SOCIAL WELFARE

An Introduction

THIRD EDITION

SOCIAL WORK AND SOCIAL WELFARE

An Introduction

JOSEPH HEFFERNAN
University of Texas at Austin

GUY SHUTTLESWORTH
University of Texas at Austin

ROSALIE AMBROSINO
University of Texas at Austin

West Publishing Company
Minneapolis/St. Paul   New York   Los Angeles   San Francisco

TO OUR STUDENTS

Production Credits

Cover Image: Jacob Lawrence, *Men Exist for the Sake of One Another. Teach Them Then or Bear with Them.* National Museum of American Art, Smithsonian Institution, gift of the Container Corporation of America./Art Resource, New York.
Text Design: Maureen McCutcheon Design
Copyediting: Christianne Thillen
Artwork: Alice Thiede and Will Thiede, Carto-Graphics
Composition: Parkwood Composition Services, Inc.
Index: Schroeder Indexing Services
Production, Prepress, Printing and Binding: West Publishing Company
Photo credits follow the index.

WEST'S COMMITMENT TO THE ENVIRONMENT

In 1906, West Publishing Company began recycling materials left over from the production of books. This began a tradition of efficient and responsible use of resources. Today, 100% of our legal bound volumes are printed on acid-free, recycled paper consisting of 50% new fibers. West recycles nearly 27,700,000 pounds of scrap paper annually—the equivalent of 229,300 trees. Since the 1960s, West has devised ways to capture and recycle waste inks, solvents, oils, and vapors created in the printing process. We also recycle plastics of all kinds, wood, glass, corrugated cardboard, and batteries, and have eliminated the use of polystyrene book packaging. We at West are proud of the longevity and the scope of our commitment to the environment.

West pocket parts and advance sheets are printed on recyclable paper and can be collected and recycled with newspapers. Staples do not have to be removed. Bound volumes can be recycled after removing the cover.

PRINTED ON 10% POST CONSUMER RECYCLED PAPER

British Library Cataloguing-in-Publication Data. A catalogue record for this book is available from the British Library.

04 03 02 01 00 99 98 97   8 7 6 5 4 3 2 1 0
Library of Congress Cataloging-in-Publication Data

Heffernan, W. Joseph, 1932–
    Social work and social welfare : an introduction / by Joseph Heffernan, Guy Shuttlesworth, Rosalie Ambrosino. —3rd ed.
        p.   cm.
    Includes bibliographical references and index.
    ISBN 0-314-06715-9 (hard : alk. paper)
    1. Social services—United States.   2. Public welfare—United States.   I. Shuttlesworth, Guy.   II. Ambrosino, Rosalie.   III. Title.
HV91.H424 1997
361.3′2—dc20
                                                            96-14990
                                                            CIP

BRIEF CONTENTS

v

CONTENTS

CHAPTER 3

The Systems/Ecological Perspective: Understanding Social Work and Social Welfare 64

CHAPTER 4

Diversity and Social Equality: The Impact of Race, Ethnicity, and Gender 102

PART TWO

SOCIAL WORK: METHODS OF INTERVENTION   130

CHAPTER 5

Direct Practice: Social Work with Individuals and Families   134

CHAPTER 6

Direct Practice: Social Work with Groups and the Community   154

CHAPTER 7

Social Agency Administration   172

CHAPTER 8

Research and Practice   192

CHAPTER 11

Health Care 296

CHAPTER 14

Criminal Justice   442

CHAPTER 15

Occupational Social Work   460

CHAPTER 16

Social Work in Rural Settings 500

CHAPTER 17

Older Adulthood: Issues, Problems, and Services 522

PREFACE

The third edition of this book is written at a critical time for the United States in addressing its domestic social policy issues. It is also a critical time for social workers as they advocate for policies and programs they believe will most effectively address these issues, and also provide services and support to those vulnerable populations most likely to be affected by rapidly changing social policies and programs. Just as social welfare needs are diverse, so is the social work profession. This book is about the many social welfare issues facing the United States today and the many roles that social work professionals play in responding to those issues.

Approaches to social welfare have changed over the decades; however, the needs to which the social work profession responds remain much the same. These needs remain, not because the social work profession has been ineffective, but because as society advances, so do the ways that we address social needs. Thomas Merton has suggested that in a community of saints, sin needs to be redefined—so, too, with social needs and social responses. There is a rhythm of social responses to social welfare problems. At this time, poverty, homelessness, AIDS, substance abuse, child abuse and neglect, teen pregnancy, youth crime, and inadequacies of health care stand high on the social agenda. At other times, these problems are barely perceived as problems at all, while other problems demand the limelight and receive the bulk of public attention. It is our intent that this text will help students develop a frame of reference to understand social welfare and an approach to address social issues which will serve them well in times of commitment and retrenchment.

This is a collaborative work among three colleagues. Where consensus was possible we sought it; where it was not possible we sought to identify the diverse views that exist about the established wisdom of social work. Each of us contributed the perspectives of our own education: child development, education, and psychology in the case of Ambrosino; sociology and history in the case of Shuttlesworth; political science and economics in the case of Heffernan; and social work for all three authors. The text is interdisciplinary in this sense, but it is disciplined by the continuity and the certainty of unresolved social issues to which social work skills are relevant.

Four "referent" groups played an important role in strengthening this book: our families, our students, our colleagues in Austin, and our colleagues in the profession. We owe our gratitude to our families—Jean, Bob, Megan, Will A., Will C., Catie, and Coleman—for their support and understanding when the book took priority over them. We also thank our colleagues at the University of Texas School of Social Work for their critique and for assuming tasks for us at times when we were trying to meet deadlines: Joyce Hunter, Melissa Waelder, Steve Onken, and Yolanda Padilla.

We also personally thank the diverse group of reviewers whose comments significantly contributed to the quality of this third edition:

Kenneth Green, *St. Francis Medical Center, Cape Girardeau, Missouri*

Ernest W. Kachingwe, *University of Nebraska at Kearney*

Stephen Anderson, *University of Oklahoma*

Gene Daniels, *California State University—Northridge*

Richard Enos, *University of North Texas*

Bennie C. Robinson, *Kentucky State University*

Phyllis Schiller, *Northern Arizona University*

We very much appreciate the thoughtful guidance they provided to us in making revisions from the second edition.

The referent group of greatest relevance has been our students. Their comments in classes over our collective seventy years of teaching helped shape our views of what they wanted and needed to know in order to become better social workers and citizens in our complex society. The most rewarding part of teaching is watching our students begin to see connections between the many complex factors that shape social welfare issues and their differential effects on the diverse populations within the United States. We especially appreciate their critique of the second edition and their enthusiastic suggestions for changes. We have incorporated many of their ideas into the third edition.

Last but not least, we express our gratitude to our acquisition editor, Bob Jucca, for his persistence and encouragement in the book preparation and publication. Also, a very special thanks to the production guidance and abilities—and the patience—of Jana Otto Hiller of West Publishing Company and to all those who helped with this publication along the way.

We hope that a number of you using this text will be persuaded, or have your choices reinforced, to join the social work profession. We urge those of you considering a career in social work to talk with your course instructors about the BSW degree. We also recommend that you visit social agencies and complete some volunteer experience in conjunction with your course. Most importantly, however, we hope this book in some way contributes to your social conscience no matter what career you choose and encourages you to recognize social work as a dynamic, challenging profession.

Rosalie Ambrosino
Joe Heffernan
Guy Shuttlesworth

PART ONE

UNDERSTANDING SOCIAL WELFARE AND SOCIAL WORK

Key Concepts and Perspectives

The beginning part of this book introduces you to the nature of social welfare and social work: what social welfare encompasses and what social workers who function in social welfare settings do. Historical and theoretical contexts also are provided that can be used as a framework for understanding subsequent chapters in the book.

In Chapter 1, "Social Welfare, Past and Present," we discuss the historical context of social welfare to help you understand how the past has shaped present-day social welfare problems and society's views toward people in need. We examine selected historical welfare policies that have influenced the structure and format of our contemporary social welfare institutions, and we explore the evolution of social welfare.

In Chapter 2, "Social Work and Other Helping Professions," we examine the relationships between social welfare as a broad system intended to maintain the well-being of individuals within a society and the profession of social work. We explore the diverse roles and functions of social work professionals, and we contrast the profession of social work with other helping professions. We also explore ways that related professionals are used by social workers as resources in helping clients. We portray the social welfare system and the profession of social work as challenging and dynamic arenas for those of you interested in careers in one of the helping professions.

In Chapter 3, "The Systems/Ecological Perspective: Understanding Social Work and Social Welfare," we provide a theoretical framework that can be used to understand content presented in subsequent chapters. We introduce the social work profession's use of a systems/ecological perspective for viewing individuals within the broader context of their environment. We discuss this framework from a broad societal perspective, a family perspective, and an individual perspective to help you begin to see how the framework is applied by social work practitioners. We also introduce generalist social work practice and the strengths perspective to help you begin to see how these perspectives fit together within a systems/ecological context to form the comprehensive body of knowledge that social workers use in addressing social welfare issues at all levels of the environment.

In Chapter 4, "Diversity and Social Equality: The Impact of Race, Ethnicity, and Gender," we discuss the ways that racism, sexism, homophobia, and other forms of oppression and discrimination disenfranchise vulnerable groups in our society. We use specific examples to explore the long-range effects of social injustice experienced at the individual, group, organizational, community, and societal levels because of color, gender, and sexual orientation. We also address the roles of the social work profession in promoting social and economic justice and working toward eliminating oppression at all levels of the environment.

These chapters introduce you to the major concepts upon which the profession of social work is based, and they lay the groundwork for content addressed in the remaining chapters of the book. They are intended as an overview. Many of the ideas presented may be new to you, and we do not expect you to immediately understand in depth what they all mean or how they all fit together in the context of the social work profession. As you continue in this text and in your classwork, these ideas and concepts will become more clear to you. And if you are majoring in social work, by the time you graduate they will be second nature; you will use them daily, probably without even realizing it.

As you read the chapters in Part 2, in which you will learn about the methods of intervention used by social workers, and Part 3, in which you learn about fields of practice and populations with which social workers are involved, you will be considering the issues raised in these parts within the context of the broad perspective of social welfare, the nature of the social work profession, the systems/ecological framework, and the impact of oppression and social and economic injustice on at-risk populations. ■

CHAPTER I

SOCIAL WELFARE, PAST AND PRESENT

Just over three decades ago, during the economic boom of the 1960s, a rough consensus existed on the future of the American welfare state. Strengthening the Social Security system and even declaring "war on poverty" were in the mainstream of American politics. It was widely believed that the national government in our federal system should assume the lead in accepting responsibility for the well-being of all citizens, including their civil rights, their economic security, their economic opportunity, their mental health, and their access to quality medical care without regard to their age or income. The Republican presidential aspirant of the time, Barry Goldwater, issued cautionary notes on all these endeavors and was widely portrayed as being out of step and out of touch with his times. ∎

Now no consensus exists regarding the nature, focus, and development of social policy or the responsibility—if any—that the government has in developing programs to assist those in need. In the following discussion we identify some of the more salient factors related to developing a comprehensive approach to social welfare in the United States. But first, a few basic questions are in order: What is social welfare? Who gets it? Who pays for it? Does it create dependency? Why is our social welfare system organized as it is? *Social welfare* in our society long has been a matter of dispute and controversy. Often the controversy surrounding the topic of social welfare results from a misunderstanding of the policies that govern social welfare as well as misinformation about people who are entitled to receive benefits. Clients who receive public assistance (commonly called "welfare") often are viewed as ne'er-do-wells who are too lazy to work and are willing to live off the labor of others. Others identify them as victims of a rapidly changing society who lack necessary employment skills. Some view poverty, mental illness, unemployment, broken homes, lack of income in old age, and related problems as matters of personal failure or personal neglect. It is understandable, then, that people who hold divergent views would have different opinions about the nature of social welfare programs and the people served by them.

Determining who is in need has always been a problem in our society. This is particularly true in relation to providing assistance for those who are poor but appear to be able to work. This concern has resulted in analyses that are often incorrect and ill-founded. Does it seem reasonable to assume that individuals who are poor choose a life of poverty? Why, then, does the problem persist? Assessments which conclude that the poor have elected such a lifestyle, are lazy, or lack motivation often fail to consider how changing social systems contribute to outcomes that result in poverty for a substantial portion of the population. Frequently, a distinction is made between the needy poor and the undeserving poor. Many individuals are more accepting of the needs of the aged, disabled, and chronically ill than those of seemingly able-bodied persons. In this chapter we examine selected historical welfare policies that have influenced the structure and format of our contemporary social welfare institutions. ∎

A DEFINITION OF SOCIAL WELFARE AND ITS RELATIONSHIP TO SOCIAL WORK

What is social welfare? Definitions invariably reflect the definer's knowledge and value base. A broad definition of what constitutes social welfare may well include all organized societal responses that promote the social well-being of a population. This definition would include, at least, education, health, rehabilitation, protective services for adults and children, public assistance, social insurance, services for persons with physical and mental disabilities, job training programs, marriage counseling, psychotherapy, pregnancy counseling, adoption, and a myriad of related activities designed to promote social well-being. P. Nelson Reid, in the newest edition of the *Encyclopedia of Social Work,* states:

> Social welfare . . . is perhaps best understood as an idea, that idea being one of a decent society that provides opportunities for work and human meaning, provides reasonable security from want and assault, promotes fairness and evaluation based on individual merit, and is economically productive and stable. The idea of social welfare is based on the assumption that human society can be organized and governed to produce and provide these things, and because it is feasible to do so, the society has a moral obligation to bring it to fruition. (Reid 1995, 2206)

The term **social welfare,** then, is commonly used to refer to the full range of organized activities of public and voluntary agencies that seek to prevent, alleviate, or contribute to the solution of a selected set of social problems. The length and breadth of that list of social welfare problems depends on the perspective of the person compiling the list. What is included on the list may reflect a conscious social choice, as well as other factors such as the background of the person compiling the list, the historical time that the list is developed, and the perceived economic resources available to meet the social welfare problems listed. Regardless of what exactly gets listed as a social welfare program, it is clear that there is no one social welfare program in this country but, in fact, thousands.

Social work is the primary profession that works within the social welfare system and with those served by the system, although individuals from a variety of other professions are also involved. The roles of social work professionals and other helping professions in the social welfare system are discussed in Chapter 2.

THE VALUE BASE OF SOCIAL WELFARE

Any discussion of social welfare and the development of social welfare organizations would be incomplete without identifying the value context within which they occur. **Values** are assumptions, convictions, or beliefs about the way people should behave and the principles that should govern behavior. Since values are beliefs, they may vary with socialization experiences. Many values are dominant and are supported by the majority of the population. For example, life is viewed as sacred; killing with malicious intent or wanton disregard for another person's life is viewed as a criminal offense by rich and poor alike. On the other hand, support of capital punishment is a value around which our society is divided.

The history of the development of social welfare reflects differences in values as they relate to social responsibility for making provisions for the needy. Values, however, are not the sole determinant of social policy. Availability of resources, coupled with economic, religious, and political influences, results in an evolving policy of social responsibility for the vulnerable members of a society. One dominant value that has guided the development of our social welfare system is humanitarianism, which is derived in large part from the Judeo-Christian base upon which the United States was established. The social application of humanitarianism, however, often is obscured by the resolve to find the most efficient and effective way to help those with unmet needs.

Our society also is influenced largely by the economic doctrine of **laissez faire,** which stresses limited government involvement, individualism, and motivation. From this perspective, government welfare programs are viewed as a threat to those cherished and desirable ends. Problems of the poor and the disenfranchised are perceived as a matter of personal failure that would only be perpetuated by government welfare programs. Social responsibility for the vulnerable members of society, from the laissez faire point of view, would be carried out through volunteerism aimed at encouraging those in need to become self-sufficient. From this perspective, work is considered the only justifiable means of self-maintenance, since it contributes to the productive effort of society.

Another values perspective maintains that we all are members of society and, by virtue of that membership, are entitled to share in its productive effort. This belief argues that people become poor or needy as a result of inefficient social institutions. For example, the continually changing economic system results in layoffs, unemployment, obsolescent jobs, and transiency. Individuals do not cause these conditions; rather, they are victimized by them. Members of some ethnic groups, for example, may face barriers such as inferior educational resources, limited (and usually menial) job opportunities, poor housing, and less than adequate health resources. An analysis from this perspective would not lay blame for these conditions upon individual group members, but would identify such reasons as institutional discrimination and oppression as causal factors.

When considering these value positions, the reader can readily understand that there are wide variations regarding societal responsibility for vulnerable members of our society. As you follow our discussion of the historical influences that have converged to shape our present social welfare structure, see if you can identify the value positions that have contributed to the formulation of social policy.

◤ OUR ENGLISH HERITAGE

In England, prior to the period of mercantilism, care for the poor was primarily a function of the church. By extending themselves through charitable efforts to those in need, parishioners fulfilled a required sacred function. The resources of the church usually were sufficient to provide the relief that was made available to the poor. The feudal system itself provided a structure that met the needs of most of the population. The only significant government legislation that existed during this time was passed as a result of the so-called Black Death—bubonic plague—which began in 1348 and resulted in the death of approximately two-thirds of the English population within two years. In 1349, King Edward III mandated the Statute of Laborers Act, which made it mandatory that all able-bodied persons accept any type of employment within their parish. Furthermore, it laid the groundwork for residency requirements, which later became an intrinsic part of American social welfare legislation, by forbidding able-bodied persons from leaving their parish.

Some 150 years later, with the breakdown of the feudal system and the division of the church during the Reformation, organized religious efforts no longer could provide for the increasing numbers of poor. Without the church or the feudal manor to rely on in times of need, the poor were left to their own means of survival. This often meant malnutrition, transiency, poor health, broken families, and even death.

Many of the poor found their way into cities, where they were unwanted. Employment was always a problem, since most of the poor were illiterate, and their skills generally were related to agricultural backgrounds. Many turned to begging. Local officials were pressed to find suitable solutions for the problem. As Europe struggled with the transition from an agricultural society to an industrial one, the numbers of dislodged persons increased. National practices differed, but in England, legislation originated in parishes throughout the country to deal with problems of the homeless, the poor, and dependent children.

Overseers were appointed by magistrates to assume responsibility for the poor residing in the various parishes. The overseer assessed the needs of the poor and made judicious responses to those needs. The role played by overseers was important, since it usually was their judgment alone that determined the fate of the poor.

Analyses of the situation invariably led to the conclusion that problems were of an individual nature and most likely resulted from the economic transition. Unfortunately, legislation often had punitive overtones, which added to the burden of the poor and left them hopelessly entwined in impoverished conditions with little opportunity to find a way out. In response to these alarming conditions, the Elizabethan **Poor Law** [Elizabeth 43] was passed in 1601. This legislation is significant in that it attempted to codify earlier legislation and establish a national policy for the poor. The Poor Law established "categories" of assistance, a practice found in our current social welfare legislation.

The first of two categories was designed for individuals considered to be "worthy," since there was little doubt that their impoverishment was not a fraudulent attempt to secure assistance. These included the aged, the chronically ill, the disabled, and orphaned children. Those eligible typically were placed in almshouses (poorhouses), where the physically able assisted the ill and disabled. This practice was referred to as **indoor relief,** since it provided services to the poor by placing them in institutions. In some instances, children were placed with families and often were required to work for their keep.

The second category included the able-bodied poor. Here, programs were less humane. Some of the able bodied were placed in prisons, others were sent to workhouses, and many were indentured to local factories or farms as slave laborers. Unlike the worthy poor, the able-bodied poor were assumed to be malingerers or ne'er-do-wells who lacked the motivation to secure employment. The treatment they received was designed to deter others, as well as to punish them for their transiency and idleness.

This act was to be of crucial significance because it established the guiding philosophy of public assistance legislation in England until 1834 and in the United States until 1935. The important aspects of the law (Axinn & Levin 1982, 10) in relation to U.S. policies toward the poor are the establishment of

1. Clear government responsibility for those in need

2. Government authority to force people to work

3. Government enforcement of family responsibility

4. Responsibility to be exercised at the local level

5. Residence requirements

The Elizabethan Poor Law was enacted less out of altruism and concern for the poor than as an orderly process of standardizing the way in which they were to be managed. It established a precedent for subsequent social legislation in the United Kingdom as well as the United States.

The Poor Law Reform Act of 1834 was passed as a reaction to concerns that the Poor Law of 1601 was not being implemented as intended and that liberalized supervision of the programs for the poor had served as a disincentive for work and had, in effect, created dependency on the program. The Poor Law Reform Act mandated that all forms of "outdoor" relief (assistance given to people in their home) be abolished and that the full intention of the provisions of the Poor Law of 1601 be rigidly enforced. Furthermore, it established "the principle of least eligibility," which prescribed that no assistance be provided in an amount that rendered the recipient better off than the lowest-paid worker. This principle also served as a basic tenet of early American social welfare legislation.

◤ SPEENHAMLAND

Although the Poor Law remained the dominant legislation under which services to the poor were administered, attempts were made to create labor laws that would serve as an incentive for the poor to engage in employment. One such effort took the form of "minimum wage" legislation and was enacted in Speenhamland in 1795. Motivated by a desire to induce large numbers of the poor into the labor market, the Speenhamland Act provided for the payment of minimum wages to workers and their families. Wages were adjusted according to family size, thereby assuring minimally adequate income even for the largest of families. Employers were encouraged to pay minimum wages, and where this was not possible, the government made up the difference. It was anticipated that business would be stimulated to produce more commodities through the added incentives provided by the government subsidy, which in turn would create a need for more workers. Unfortunately, the effect of the subsidy program was to drive wages down, and employers then turned to the government to make up the difference.

The Speenhamland Act was not designed specifically to be a social welfare reform measure, although it did have implications for the working poor, the unemployed, and the impoverished. In effect, it was a work incentive program. Although important symbolically, the Speenhamland Act had little impact. Ultimately rejected by employers, it proved expensive for the government and was never applied uniformly. It did establish the principle of government subsidy for private employers, a practice that is relatively widespread in our society today.

◤ SOCIAL WELFARE IN COLONIAL AMERICA

Early American settlers brought a religious heritage that emphasized charity and the mutual interdependence of people. They also brought with them the heritage of the English Poor Law. America, in the early days, was a land of vast natural resources, and settlers found it essential to work hard in order to survive. When neighbors became needy through illness or death, church members usually were quick to respond. No formal government network for providing assistance existed on any significant basis. Later, as the population increased, many colonies passed laws requiring that immigrants demonstrate their ability to sustain themselves, or in the absence of such ability, sponsors were required to pledge support for new arrivals. Transients were "warned out" and often returned to their place of residence (Federico 1938, 98). In some instances, the homeless and unemployed were returned to England. Times were difficult, the Puritan work ethic was embedded deeply, and with little surplus to redistribute to those in need, assistance often was inadequate. The practice of posting names of habitual paupers at the town house was a routine procedure in many towns and villages.

It is difficult to obtain reliable estimates of the magnitude of public welfare in colonial America. One important fact was that the presence of the indentured servant system rekindled in this country a replica of feudal welfare. In the indentured system of the middle colonies and the slavery system of the southern colonies, there was a clear lack of freedom for the pauper class. Often overlooked, however, was the existence of a set of harsh laws—reasonably enforced up until the time of independence—that required masters to meet the basic survival needs of servants and slaves. (Almost half of all colonists came to the country as indentured servants.) Ironically, as the economy matured from plantation to artisan and became preindustrial in character, economic uncertainty also increased. Consequently, public relief was the largest expenditure in the public budgets of most major cities at the time of the American Revolution.

Concomitantly, a rigid restraint of the Poor Law philosophy was thoroughly consistent with the fact that the colonial economy was one of extreme scarcity. Colonial law stressed the provision of indoor relief, by which paupers could be conveniently segregated within almshouses and put to tasks that at least paid for their meager keep. The apprenticeship of children reflected a belief in family controls for children and stressed work and training for productive employment. Also, the deification of the work ethic and the belief that pauperism was a visible symbol of sin permitted a harsh response to those in need, as a means of saving their souls.

CHANGING PATTERNS AFTER THE REVOLUTION

Between the American Revolution and the Civil War, several broad patterns of welfare emerged, all of which were thoroughly consistent with the basic tenets of the Elizabethan Poor Law. The American separation of church and state forced a severance of the connection between parish and local welfare office. Nevertheless, many states—most, in fact—retained a religious connection, with the requirement that at least one member of the welfare board must be a "licensed preacher." Local governments accepted grudgingly the role of welfare caretaker and adopted rigid residency requirements.

The most important shift in this period was from indoor to **outdoor relief.** Outdoor aid, with its reliance on in-kind aid and work-relief projects, was most adaptable to the volatile economics of the first half of the nineteenth century. This led some to see early American welfare as principally an instrument for the regulation of the supply of labor. The contrary evidence, that it essentially is a fiscal choice, stems from the observation that the shift to outdoor relief occurred within places of both labor shortage and labor surplus.

Another significant movement before the Civil War was the shift away from public sector to private sector welfare, or voluntary welfare. The responsibility for welfare therefore was left to charitable institutions rather than remaining a public concern.

CARING FOR THE URBAN POOR

As the new nation grew, cities began to appear on the eastern seaboard. With immigrants arriving regularly, jobs often were difficult to find, and a large population of displaced poor began to emerge. Persons interested in those less fortunate sought avenues for meeting the needs of the poor. Although attaching the poor to subsistence-level employment usually was the goal, there was concern over assuring that basic needs were met until income could be derived through employment. Although almshouses often were used to care for the chronic poor, outdoor relief found increased acceptance as a suitable way of caring for the poor, including the practice of providing cash assistance to persons who remained in their own homes. Differing segments of the population found cause for alarm in the practices of both indoor and outdoor relief.

One of the earlier major organizations to seek solutions to problems of poverty was the New York Society for the Prevention of Pauperism, established in 1817. This society sought to identify and remedy the causes of poverty. Following the precedent established by Thomas Chalmers in England, the society divided the city into districts and assigned "friendly visitors" to each district to assess and respond to the needs of the poor (Friedlander & Apte 1974, 21). Later, in 1843, the Association for Improving the Conditions of the Poor was established in New York City to coordinate relief efforts for the unemployed. One significant technique introduced by the association was the requirement that relief could not be disbursed until the individual's needs were assessed so that agencies providing relief could do so more effectively.

Perhaps the most effective relief organization for the poor was Buffalo's Charity Organization Society (COS). A private organization modeled after London's COS, it was founded by wealthy citizens who embraced the work ethic yet had compassion for the deserving poor. The COS sought to add efficiency and economy to programs serving the poor, as well as to organize charities in an effort to prevent duplication of services and reduce dependency on charitable efforts. Like the Association for Improving Conditions of the Poor, which preceded it, the COS emphasized the necessity for assessing the condition of the poor and added the dimension of engaging "friendly visitors" with clients in an effort to guide, rehabilitate, and assist them in preparing for self-sufficiency. The COS had little sympathy for chronic beggars and viewed them essentially as hopeless derelicts.

◪ CARING FOR SPECIFIC POPULATIONS

During these early years, many other private charities emerged to address special problem areas, such as the Orphan's Home Movement, which gave institutional care to children left alone as the result of the death of their parents. Other institutional services began to appear throughout the country to provide care for the deaf, blind, and mentally ill. These services largely were sponsored by state or local governments. There was often grave concern regarding the treatment received by inmates. Dorothea Dix, a philanthropist and social reformer, traveled the United States observing the care given the "insane" and was appalled by horrid conditions and inhumane care. Dix sought to convince President Franklin Pierce to allocate federal and land-grant monies for establishing federal institutions to care for the mentally ill. Her plea was blocked by Congress, which believed such matters to be the state's responsibility. Resources allocated for institutional care by states were limited. The results were poor conditions and limited treatment.

Toward the latter part of the nineteenth century, a number of states developed centralized agencies following the precedent by state boards of charities, agencies that had been organized in several states to oversee the activities of charitable institutions. State charity agencies sought to ensure a better quality of care for institutional inmates, as well as to seek greater efficiency and economy in the provision of poor relief. With the federal government assuming only limited responsibility for selected groups (veterans, for example), state agencies became the primary public resource for addressing the problems of the poor and debilitated (Leiby 1978, 130–31).

A new wave of immigrants from southern Europe entering this country in the late 1800s and early 1900s further added to the burden of unemployment, homelessness, and poverty. Reacting to the problems experienced by immigrants in coping with the new culture, Jane Addams, a social worker, was instrumental in anchoring the settlement house movement as a resource for dealing with problems of assimilation and in preparing immigrants to live in a new society. Education was emphasized for adults and children alike. In Chicago, Hull House, established by Addams in 1869, sparked the initiative for similar movements in other cities. It also sought needed social reforms to improve the quality of life and opportunity structure for all new citizens. By addressing the problems of poor housing, low wages, child labor, and disease, Hull House and other settlement houses became major social action agencies.

During the 1800s more clearly defined parameters of public versus private welfare programs were established. Public welfare benefit programs relied on taxation for funding. Private welfare programs were funded through the voluntary contributions of individuals or philanthropic organizations. No clearly defined limits determined what types of benefits would be offered by either public or private (voluntary) agencies. As a result, services often overlapped. Public agencies were administered by government agencies at the local, state, or federal levels. Private agencies often had religious or philanthropic sponsorship or received contributions from citizens.

Following World War I, the nation entered a period of great social change and prosperity. The economy was improving, and the nation experienced a sense of euphoria. In 1929 this euphoria ended with the economic downturn that led to the Great Depression. In short order, conditions were grave. Businesses considered to be stable ceased their production, banks declared bankruptcy, and thousands of workers lost their jobs. Although this nation had experienced recessions and depressions before, none was quite as devastating to the economic security of Americans as the Great Depression.

◢ THE NEW DEAL

Today, it is difficult for us to comprehend the effects the Great Depression had on Americans. Savings were lost as banks collapsed, and many were left penniless, homeless, and without resources as unemployment increased. Jobs became scarce, and the unemployed had nowhere to turn. Organized charities quickly exhausted their limited resources. Pessimism and despair were rampant, and many experienced a sense of

Jane Addams, one of the first social workers in the United States and the founder of Hull House in Chicago, advocated for social reforms to improve the lives of immigrants.

hopelessness. Unemployment insurance was nonexistent, and no federal guarantees existed for monies lost in bank failures. The economic disaster produced a state of chaos never experienced before on American soil. As conditions worsened, homes were lost through foreclosed mortgages.

State and local governments responded to the extent that resources permitted; however, many of the poor states lacked resources to provide relief even of a temporary nature. In the state of New York, an Emergency Relief Act was passed providing public employment, in-kind relief (food, clothing, and shelter), and limited cash benefits. This act later served as a model for federal relief programs.

Following the earlier constitutional interpretation of federal and state roles by President Pierce, subsequent administrations through the Hoover administration reinforced the position that federal involvement in relief programs was not mandatory but rather a matter that should be delegated to the states. Although sympathetic with those victimized by the Depression, President Hoover was convinced that the most effective solution to the Depression and its consequences was to offer incentives for business to regain its footing, expand, and provide jobs for the jobless.

The critical nature of the Depression was manifested in starvation, deprivation, and the suffering of millions of Americans and required an immediate response. Under these conditions, Franklin Delano Roosevelt, the former governor of New York, was elected president in 1932.

One of President Roosevelt's initial actions was to institute emergency legislation that provided assistance for the jobless and poor. Not only did this legislation mark the first time the federal government engaged itself directly in providing relief, it also invoked an interpretation of the health and welfare provisions of the Constitution that established a historical precedent. The result mandated the federal government to assume health and welfare responsibility for its citizens. The statement was clear: citizens were first and foremost citizens of the United States and, second, residents of specific states. This policy opened the door for later federal legislation in the areas of civil rights, fair employment practices, school busing, public assistance, and a variety of other social programs.

One of the first attempts to supply relief for depression victims was the Federal Emergency Relief Act (FERA). Modeled after the New York Emergency Relief Act, it provided food, clothing, and shelter allowances for the homeless and displaced. In a cooperative relationship with states, the federal government made monies available to states to administer the relief programs. States were responsible for establishing agencies for that purpose and also were required to contribute state funds, where possible, for the purpose of broadening the resource base available to those in need. This established the precedent for "matching grants," which later became an integral requirement for public assistance programs.

Additional federal emergency legislation was enacted to provide public employment for the unemployed. In 1935 the Works Progress Administration (WPA) was created to provide public service jobs. Although resisted by private contractors, the WPA ultimately employed approximately 8 million workers over the duration of the Depression. States and local governments identified needed projects and supplied necessary materials for laborers, who were paid by the WPA. Many public schools, streets, parks, post office buildings, state college buildings, and related public projects were constructed under the auspices of the WPA. It was anticipated that as the private business sector expanded, WPA workers would secure employment in the private sector.

Youth programs also were established. Perhaps the most noteworthy was the Civilian Conservation Corps, which was designed to protect natural resources and to improve and develop public recreational areas. Primarily a forest camp activity, the CCC provided young men between the ages of seventeen and twenty-three with jobs, food, clothing, and shelter. Wages were nominal (around twenty-five dollars per month), and the major portion of the wages (twenty dollars per month) was conscripted and sent home to help support families. Many national parks were improved and developed by CCC labor. The National Youth Administration, also established under the WPA, gave work-study assistance to high school and college youth as an incentive to remain in school. In addition, the NYA provided part-time jobs for out-of-school students to learn job skills and increase their employability (Friedlander & Apte 1974, 113).

Low-interest loans to farmers and small business operators also were extended through FERA programs as a means of enabling those activities to survive and become sources of employment for the unemployed.

In retrospect, it is clear that the Depression legislation was designed to be temporary in nature and had as its main focus the creation of work activities that enabled individuals to earn their income rather than become objects of charity. It also was anticipated that the private economic business sector would prosper and emergency relief employment would no longer be needed.

The Depression legislation offered a temporary solution to the crisis generated by the Great Depression. The jobless found jobs, the hungry were fed, and the homeless were given shelter. Perhaps of more importance, the nation felt the full impact of system changes. The issue of blaming poverty on idleness and laziness was put to rest at least temporarily.

◪ THE SOCIAL SECURITY ACT

The **Social Security Act** was passed by Congress and signed into law by President Roosevelt on August 4, 1935. Even today this act remains the most significant piece of social legislation yet enacted in the United States. It also paved the way for greater federal involvement in health and welfare. The act reflected a realization that our economic system was subject to vacillations that would invariably leave many people without resources due to unemployment in an ever-shifting economic marketplace. It also acknowledged that older adults needed income security as an incentive to retire. This act was designed to be a permanent resource system administered by the federal government. The provisions of the act were outlined under three major categories. Chapter 9 covers these categories in greater depth. Briefly, the provisions of the act were social insurance, public assistance, and health and welfare services.

Social Insurance

Social insurance, commonly referred to as **Social Security,** consisted of two important benefit programs. The first (and most widely known) consisted of three categories: Old Age, Survivors, and Disability Insurance (OASDI; see Chapter 9). These programs were based on taxes deducted from employees' wages and matched by employer contributions. Eligibility was based on participation earned through employment. The second type of insurance program was unemployment insurance, with the funds contributed by employers. The purpose of the unemployment benefit program was to provide a source of income security for covered workers who had lost their jobs.

Benefits derived from these programs were considered to be a matter of right in that the recipients and their employers had paid "premiums" for the benefits they would receive. In many ways, social insurance was similar to private insurance, for which entitlement to benefits is directly related to beneficiary participation through contributions.

Public Assistance

Public assistance was based on "need" and was not established as a right earned through employment. This program was administered by states with monies made available by states and matched by the federal government (matching grants). Public assistance consisted of three categories: Old Age Assistance, Aid to Dependent Children, and Aid to the Blind. In 1955, the category of Aid to the Permanently and Totally Disabled was added. Benefits under each of these categories were invariably low and varied among the states according to each state's willingness to "match" federal funds. Eligibility requirements were rigid and rigorously enforced. Participation further was based on a "means" test, a test that required applicants to demonstrate that they were hopelessly without resources. The private lives of recipients were opened to the scrutiny of welfare workers in an attempt to minimize fraud and to assure that benefit levels did not exceed budgeted needs. Perhaps the most controversial assistance program was Aid to Dependent Children (ADC). This program made limited funds available to mothers with dependent children where no man was present in the home. Since benefit levels were adjusted for family size (to a maximum of four children), there was concern that promiscuity and illegitimacy would be rewarded by increasing benefits as the family size increased. Rigid cohabitation policies were instituted mandating that mothers guilty of cohabitation would lose their grant funds entirely. Since most ADC recipients were able-bodied, there was also concern that welfare payments were a disincentive for meeting their needs through gainful employment. In may ways, ADC recipients were treated as the "unworthy" poor and, as a consequence, were often dealt with in a punitive manner.

Public assistance generally is referred to as *welfare* by the public. Since benefits are based on impoverishment and not earned through employment, participation in the program carries a stigma of personal imprudence, ineptness, or failure.

Health and Welfare Services

Programs authorized under **health and welfare services** provided for maternal and child care services, vocational rehabilitation, public health, and services for physically impaired children. The provision of services was emphasized. Services authorized under this title are discussed more fully in Chapters 10, 11, 12, and 13.

In the ensuing years, amendments to the Social Security Act extended each of these titles and included more people in their coverage. Social insurance later added health insurance (Medicare), and a health assistance program (Medicaid) was instituted for public assistance recipients. The ADC assistance category was redefined as Aid to Families with Dependent Children (AFDC) so that states could assist families under limited circumstances when an employable unemployed man was in the home (AFDC-UP/AFDC-Unemployed Parent). Only a few states adopted the AFDC-UP provisions. As requirements for participation in these programs became less stringent in the 1960s and 1970s, welfare rolls increased dramatically.

◪ SOCIAL WELFARE: THE POST–SOCIAL SECURITY ERA

Establishing well-focused comprehensive social welfare programs in the United States has been problematic because of differing values, vacillations of the economy, and fluctuations in resources available to meet the needs of an expanding population. The period since passage of the Social Security Act has been tumultuous, with three wars, a long-standing cold war (now coming to an end), and periods of economic upswings as well as recessions and depressions. Unemployment has varied from 12 percent of the work force in 1979 to 6.1 percent in 1990. Among other things, the divorce rate has increased dramatically since the 1940s, single-parent families are more common, the population is growing older, and diseases have become more costly to treat. All of these factors affect how the government responds to social needs. In the following paragraphs, we discuss some of the more significant governmental attempts to address the need for support services.

The Great Society Programs

Attempts to broaden the activities of government in securing the rights of citizens and providing for personal, social, and economic development were introduced through social reform measures enacted during the Lyndon Johnson administration (1963–1968). The so-called **Great Society** legislation extended benefits of many existing programs and services designed to help the poor, the disabled, and the aged. The Social Security Act was amended to provide for health care benefits to the aged under the Health Insurance Program (Medicare) and to public assistance recipients through the Health Assistance Program (Medicaid). New legislation also was designed to meet needs not specifically addressed through existing resources. The Older Americans Act (1965) established a legal base for developing senior luncheon programs, health screening, transportation, meals-on-wheels programs, and recreational activities. The Civil Rights Act (1964) sought to end discrimination in employment and in the use of public business facilities. It also was targeted toward nondiscriminatory extension of credit. Education bills were passed that sought to rectify many of the educational disadvantages experienced by children of the poor.

Perhaps the most significant—and controversial—effort to achieve social reform came through the Economic Opportunities Act (1964), dubbed the War on Poverty. The objective of this act was to "eliminate poverty" through institutional change. Poverty was viewed traditionally as an individual matter, and its causes generally were thought to be the result of personal failure, the lack of motivation, or personal choice. Poverty program designers came to a different conclusion. Poverty was considered to be the result of inadequate social institutions that failed to provide opportunities for all citizens. Traditional approaches to solving the problems of poverty were considered unsuccessful. Changing the status of the poor would come not through working with them on an individual basis but rather through the modification of institutions that produced the problems in the first place. Hence, Economic Opportunities Act programs were structured to assure the poor a greater likelihood of success by creating opportunities for decision making and participation. Educational programs such as Head Start, Enable, and Catch-up sought to extend relevant learning experiences to educationally disadvantaged children. Community Action Agencies encouraged the poor to become more vocal in community affairs and to organize efforts for community betterment. Special employment incentives were generated to teach job skills. Youth job corps programs provided public service jobs contingent upon remaining in school, thus assuring greater potential for employment upon graduation. Job Corps centers taught teenage dropouts employment skills. Small-business loans were made to individuals with potential for developing businesses. Rural programs extended health and social services for the poor in rural areas.

In a nation that boasted the highest standard of living in the world, it was believed that the scourge of poverty could be eliminated forever. The euphemism of "War on Poverty" was selected to rally the population to a full-scale commitment to assure that the enemy, poverty, would be overcome. Social action advocates found the climate produced by the Economic Opportunities Act favorable for their efforts. It was a heyday for the expansion of social programs, with spending often outstripping planning. The War on Poverty was short-lived because federal funds were channeled to the war in Vietnam. Social legislation is invariably affected by the political climate. As government resources and attention were diverted to the Vietnam War, the domestic "war" was soon neglected and ultimately terminated.

Conservatism in the Mid-Sixties and Seventies

The period from the mid-1960s through the mid-1970s was one of both domestic and foreign conflict. While the Vietnam War was raging, the antiestablishment movement in the United States was well under way, rioting was occurring in the Watts section of Los Angeles and in Detroit, Martin Luther King was championing the cause of disenfranchised

Americans, and inflation was depleting the buying power of those who were working.

In reaction to these disconcerting changes, many middle-class Americans initiated a wave of conservatism that led to an effort to dismantle many of the social programs enacted during the New Deal and expanded through the Great Society programs. The welfare "establishment" was viewed as being costly, ineffective, and counterproductive. The conservatives maintained that the federal government was much too large and cumbersome and that many functions, including social welfare, could be assumed by the states. Although federal involvement in welfare had emerged largely because states had lacked sufficient resources to provide supports, conservatives were convinced that states and localities were better suited to determine policies and administer social programs. One result was the reorganization—and eventual termination—of the federal poverty program. Several popular programs, such as Head Start and job-training programs, were transferred to other government agencies. Under the Nixon administration, a major welfare reform measure, the Family Assistance Program (FAP), was submitted for congressional approval as House Bill 1. Although never enacted into law, the reform would have eliminated the public assistance program and substituted in its place a proposal that was designed to provide incentives for recipients to work without losing all of the their government benefits. The level of defined need, $1,600 per year for a family of four, was far below benefit levels already in existence in the higher-paying states but higher than the benefits in over half the states. Table 1.1 illustrates the differences in the level of defined need from 1970 to 1994 for a three-person family in the various states.

The Family Assistance Act failed, but on a more positive note, public assistance programs for the aged, disabled, and blind were combined by the enactment of the Supplemental Security Income (SSI) Act in 1974. SSI increased benefit levels for millions of recipients. Since the AFDC category, which would have been abolished by the Family Assistance Act, failed to pass, AFDC continues to be funded and implemented under the federal-state arrangements already in effect. Thus, AFDC benefits continue to vary appreciably from state to state.

Welfare Reform and the Late Seventies

The policymakers of the mid-1970s inherited a welfare system that had no positive constituency. Recipients, social workers, public officials, and tax-conscious groups agreed only on the inadequacy of the existing system. Each of the four constituencies had initiated a welfare reform effort, and each constituency had failed to achieve its reform, largely because of the opposition of the others. Because of the political costs that had come to be associated with welfare reform efforts, no knights-errant were ready to champion a new welfare reform effort. The problems that had drawn such attention in earlier decades persisted. The rapidly expanding welfare costs in the Nixon and Ford years, in juxtaposition to the intractability of poverty, made welfare reform an urgent but unpleasant necessity. Likewise, welfare reform will remain a necessity into the 1996 elections.

Thus, welfare reform again became an issue. The Carter administration proposed that $8.8 billion be appropriated to create up to 1.4 million public service jobs. It was expected that 2 million persons would hold such jobs in a given year, as they were processed through these jobs on their way to regular employment in the public or private sector. According to the proposal, most of these jobs would pay a minimum wage (projected to be $3.30 in 1980) and would be full-time, full-year jobs, thus yielding an annual income of $6,600.

In addition, a family would receive an income supplement. The size of the supplement would be geared to family size. The jobs would not be eligible for the earned income tax credit. A worker would always have an income incentive to move from the public job to regular employment in the public or private sector. Those eligible for such jobs would be those adults—one per family—in the "expected to work" category of the second part of the program who could not find employment in the regular economy. Care was to be taken to assure that these jobs would not replace ordinary public jobs, thus removing the objections to the plan from the labor unions. However, Carter's proposal was not adopted, and debate about the most effective way to overhaul the welfare system continued.

Cutbacks in the Reagan-Bush Years

The 1980s were characterized by relentless efforts to reduce and eliminate social entitlement programs. Public expenditures for welfare were viewed as antithetical to economic progress. Mounting inflation was considered to be the result of federal domestic spending. The sad state of our economy was considered the work of social progressives who had engineered welfare expansionism and, as a result, had caused the economy to falter. Many social support programs were reduced dramatically or eliminated. Funds supporting Title XX of the Social Security Act— which provided a wide range of benefits, upgraded the quality of the social service delivery system, and provided services to the aged, children and other populations at risk—were reduced drastically. Many transportation and job-training programs were discontinued.

The administration during the Reagan years promoted a policy of social and income assistance programs to be administered by states through block grants. The effect of this program would have been to decentralize government and return it to the pre–New Deal era, when states assumed responsibility for their own social problems. An unlikely coalition of conservative governors and liberal mayors joined efforts to defeat the Reagan initiative of welfare reform.

As part of his State of the Union message in 1982, President Reagan proposed his version of welfare reform. It went under the title *New Federalism.* The centerpiece was a plan whereby the states would assume financial and administrative responsibility for food stamps and AFDC, while the federal government would assume responsibility for the Medicaid program. The program was dubbed the Welfare Swap. The plan went through a number of variations before it was dropped by the administration as politically infeasible. The problem was that neither

TABLE 1.1

AFDC DEFINED NEED STANDARD FOR A THREE-PERSON FAMILY BY STATE FOR SELECTED YEARS[1]

	July 1970[2]	July 1975	July 1980	January 1985[3]
Alabama	$148	$180	$192	$384
Alaska	350	350	457	719
Arizona	212	233	233	233
Arkansas	149	245	234	234
California	351	316	480	555
Colorado	193	217	290	421
Connecticut	283	346	475	546
Delaware	245	245	266	287
District of Columbia	229	286	394	654
Florida	189	195	195	400
Georgia	177	193	193	366
Hawaii	226	428	468	468
Idaho	238	345	371	554
Illinois	232	261	288	657
Indiana	272	307	307	307
Iowa	247	309	360	497
Kansas	243	321	345	373
Kentucky	208	185	188	197
Louisiana	172	164	402	538
Maine	277	277	415	510
Maryland	249	259	270	433
Massachusetts	268	259	379	439
Michigan (Washtenaw County)	NA	NA	NA	592
Michigan (Wayne County)	219	333	425	557
Minnesota	256	330	417	524
Mississippi	202	241	220	286
Missouri	285	325	312	312
Montana	221	201	259	401
Nebraska	281	279	310	350
Nevada	269	279	285	285
New Hampshire	262	308	346	378
New Jersey	302	310	360	385
New Mexico	167	197	220	258
New York (Suffolk County)	NA	NA	NA	579
New York (New York City)	279	332	394	474
North Carolina	168	183	192	446

January 1988[3]	January 1989[3]	January 1990[3]	January 1991[3]	January 1992[3]	January 1993[3]	January 1994[3]
$384	$571	$578	$ 603	$ 637	$ 673	$ 673
779	809	846	891	924	923	975
621	621	621	621	928	964	964
695	705	705	705	705	705	705
633	663	694	694	694	703	715
421	421	421	421	421	421	421
601	623	649	680	680	680	680
319	333	333	338	338	338	338
712	712	712	712	712	712	712
775	807	838	880	928	965	991
366	376	414	424	424	424	424
515	557	964	1,012	1,067	1,109	1,140
554	554	554	554	554	554	991
713	740	777	811	844	867	890
320	320	320	320	320	320	320
497	497	497	497	849	849	849
409	427	409	409	422	429	429
207	218	526	526	526	526	526
632	658	658	658	658	658	658
573	632	652	652	573	553	553
497	522	548	562	522	497	507
510	539	539	539	539	539	579
576	608	611	622	587	587	587
540	572	575	586	551	551	551
532	532	532	532	532	532	532
368	368	368	368	368	368	368
312	312	312	312	312	312	846
434	434	434	453	478	497	511
350	364	364	364	364	364	364
550	550	550	550	620	620	699
486	496	506	516	516	1,513	1,648
424	424	424	424	424	985	985
264	264	264	310	324	324	357
665	665	703	703	703	703	703
539	539	577	577	577	577	577
532	532	544	544	544	544	544

continued

TABLE 1.1

concluded

	July 1970[2]	July 1975	July 1980	January 1985[3]
North Dakota	232	283	334	371
Ohio	207	346	346	627
Oklahoma	179	217	282	282
Oregon	229	369	282	386
Pennsylvania	265	296	332	614
Rhode Island	229	278	340	479
South Carolina	162	178	187	187
South Dakota	264	289	321	329
Tennessee	179	179	179	246
Texas	198	155	155	494
Utah	223	327	480	685
Vermont	287	402	670	852
Virginia	240	298	344	363
Washington	258	315	458	768
West Virginia	220	275	275	275
Wisconsin	214	383	522	628
Wyoming	246	240	315	360
Guam	NA	NA	261	265
Puerto Rico	108	108	102	180
Virgin Islands	NA	131	209	209
Median State[4]	232	279	321	401

conservative governors nor liberal mayors liked the idea. Following his reelection in 1984, President Reagan began again to push for reshaping welfare responsibilities among the various layers of government. A presidential task force was appointed, and it was to issue its report after the congressional elections in 1986. That election resulted in a Democratic landslide, and the responsibility for welfare reform has now shifted from the White House to Capitol Hill.

The Bush administration continued to be influenced by a conservative view of welfare and welfare reform. With the winding down of the cold war, progressives held hopes that monies appropriated for defense spending could be directed toward domestic programs. Meanwhile, welfare costs continued to go up. Table 1.2 shows the costs and growth rates for the major welfare programs. In 1988, the Democratic Congress passed the Family Support Act. It was hailed by proponents of welfare reform as the most significant piece of domestic legislation since the Social Security Act in 1935, but is now in jeopardy of being eliminated due to the current Republican Congress. The Family Support Act man-

January 1988[3]	January 1989[3]	January 1990[3]	January 1991[3]	January 1992[3]	January 1993[3]	January 1994[3]
371	386	386	401	401	401	409
685	712	739	776	817	853	879
471	471	471	471	471	471	471
412	420	432	444	460	460	460
614	614	614	614	614	614	614
503	517	543	554	554	554	554
388	403	419	440	440	440	440
366	366	377	385	404	476	491
353	365	387	412	426	426	426
574	574	574	574	574	574	574
693	502	516	537	537	537	552
889	930	973	1,029	1,112	1,122	1,124
393	393	393	393	393	393	393
835	872	907	983	1,014	1,125	1,158
497	497	497	497	497	497	497
647	647	647	647	647	647	647
360	360	360	674	674	674	674
265	265	330	330	330	330	330
180	180	180	180	160	360	360
209	300	300	300	300	300	300
503	522	539	544	544	554	579

[1]The defined standard of need, used to develop AFDC payments, is usually a percentage of the amount it is estimated a family needs to survive and varies by state. It is important to note that the standard and the AFDC payments are rarely the same; for example, while the 1993 standard for Texas is $574 per month for a family of three, the average AFDC payment is $159 per month (see Chapter 9 for the average AFDC payments by state).

[2]Data on 3-person families were not published or reported before 1975. Thus, the 1970 data were derived by reducing the reported 4-person need standard by the proportional difference between 3- and 4-person AFDC need standards as shown in the July 1995 DHEW reports.
[3]CRS survey data.
[4]Among 50 States and the District of Columbia.
NA—Not available.

Note: Table compiled by the Congressional Research Service (CRS) on the basis of data from the Department of Health and Human Services and, where noted, from CRS itself.

Source: U.S. Congress, House, Committee on Ways and Means, *Overview of Entitlement Programs*, 103rd Cong., 2nd Session, Committee Print 103–27 (Washington, D.C.: U.S. Government Printing Office, 1994), 371–3.

dates that states provide job opportunities and basic skills (JOBS) programs for most AFDC recipients (some, such as those with very young children or health problems, are exempt from participation).

The act also provides transitional benefits, including up to twelve months of Medicaid (health care) and child care after recipients find jobs to give them a chance to move from welfare to work without loss of income. The act also mandates that states provide AFDC-UP

TABLE 1.2	WAYS AND MEANS PROGRAM OUTLAYS COMPARED WITH TOTAL FEDERAL GOVERNMENT OUTLAYS, IN NOMINAL DOLLARS, AND AVERAGE ANNUAL GROWTH RATES FOR SELECTED YEARS

	FISCAL YEAR					
	1970	1975	1980	1985	1990	1995
	In Nominal Dollars (Billions)					
Social Security[1]	29.6	63.6	117.1	186.4	246.5	334.8
Medicare[1]	6.8	14.1	34.0	69.7	107.4	177.3
Unemployment compensation and trade adjustment assistance[1]	2.8	12.0	15.7	16.0	17.5	24.8
Public assistance and social services (Family Support Administration, SSI, Title XX, EITC, and Foster Care)	5.1	13.5	17.8	23.3	32.0	60.5
Nondefense discretionary spending and other entitlements	−55.5	117.8	219.6	270.6	306.0	446.1
Deposit insurance	−0.5	0.5	−0.4	−2.2	58.1	−12
National defense	81.9	87.6	134.6	253.1	300.1	273
Net interest	14.4	23.2	52.5	129.5	184.2	213.5
Total	195.6	332.3	590.9	946.4	1,251.8	1,518
Memo: CPI-XI (1987 = 100)	40.3	54.2	80.2	106.7	128.8	151.6
	AVERAGE ANNUAL GROWTH RATES					
	1970– 75	1975– 80	1980– 85	1985– 90	1990– 95	
Social Security[1]	16.5	13.0	9.7	5.7	6.3	
Medicare[1]	15.7	19.2	15.4	9.0	10.5	
Unemployment compensation and trade adjustment assistance[1]	33.8	5.5	.4	1.8	7.2	
Public assistance and social services (Family Support Administration, SSI, Title XX, EITC, and Foster Care)	21.5	5.7	5.5	6.6	13.6	
Nondefense discretionary spending and other entitlements	16.2	13.3	4.3	2.5	7.8	
Deposit insurance	NA	NA	NA	NA	NA	
National defense	1.4	9.0	13.5	3.5	−1.9	
Net interest	10.0	17.7	19.8	7.3	3.0	
Total	11.2	12.2	9.9	5.8	3.9	
Memo: CPI–XI	5.8	8.0	5.6	3.8	3.2	

[1]Includes entitlement spending only.

Note: All growth rates were calculated using the LOTUS 1-2-3 formula @Rate $= (Y/A)^{1/n} = r$.

Source: U.S. Congress, House, Committee on Ways and Means, *Overview of Entitlement Programs,* 103rd Cong., 2nd Session, Committee Print 103–27 (Washington, D.C.: U.S. Government Printing Office, 1994), 1261.

(unemployed parents) benefits for a limited time to those families with previously employed males who are unable to find employment. The act also requires stronger enforcement of child support payments by absent parents. Parts of the act were not required to be implemented by states until 1992.

The Clinton Years

By 1992, the political coloration of the welfare reform agenda had shifted again. The Democratic presidential candidate was a "New Democrat" who had been instrumental, as governor of Arkansas, in support of the Family Support Act of 1988. As a presidential candidate, Clinton had sought a wider role for the states in the design of federal welfare programs. More significantly, he sought to distance himself from "liberal Democratic reform" that had also been instrumental in the passage of the 1988 legislation as yet then largely unimplemented.

As a candidate, Clinton promised to "end welfare as we know it," but gave few specifics other than a vague endorsement of the principles of the 1988 legislation. The goal of the reform was to make welfare "a second Chance, not a second Choice." Employment readiness, parental responsibility, and state discretion were portrayed as the keystones of Clinton's reform agenda.

Welfare-to-work programs have been tried without significant success in the past. There was much greater pressure behind this new welfare reform effort. Lawmakers at all levels of government and of both parties were now demanding that welfare recipients be required to take more responsibility for ending, or at least easing, their dependence on public support. The demand for such change was being driven by a variety of factors, among them a significant shift to the right in public mood and a much-increased effort to reduce the federal deficit. The General Accounting Office, a congressional agency that monitors federal programs, reports the number of unmarried mothers on welfare rose from 380,000 in 1976 to more than 1.5 million in 1992 (Demott 1994). Charles Murray, in a report for the Heritage Foundation, a Republican think tank in Washington, D.C., concluded that

> the current welfare system bribes individuals into behavior—such as not marrying, and having children out of wedlock—which is self-defeating to the individual, a tragic handicap for children, and, because it contributes to every other social pathology, is increasingly a threat to society. (Should the system 1994, 21)

This view was not new; it had long been a theme of right-wing critics of welfare. What was different was that this view now represented mainstream thought.

The view that the welfare system has failed both those who finance it and those supported by it is shared by liberals who were long its strongest proponents. Clinton's Health and Human Services Secretary, Donna Shalala, said more and more Americans are seeing "an unfairness" in the difference between "those who get up in the morning and go to work at entry-level jobs and those who stay on the welfare system" (Demott 1994, 18). Mary Jo Bane, her assistant secretary for children and families, told *Nation's Business* that

> the welfare system doesn't help recipients move into the labor market. It's in the wrong business. The welfare system is in the business of writing checks and filling out forms. It's not in the business of getting people to work. (Demott 1994, 18)

In the Clinton administration there was a debate over what would constitute genuine welfare reform. The critical choice was the White House's decision in 1994 to push for health care reform (discussed in Chapter 11) and then deal with welfare reform. This decision was based partially on the reasoning that many families received public assistance, or got off programs such as AFDC but then were forced to return to the AFDC rolls, because of health-related problems and the unavailability of adequate health care. The health care reform failed.

Following that failure, the Republicans won both houses of Congress in the 1994 national elections. They celebrated their electoral victory with the Contract with America. Many reform measures were introduced in the 104th session by various coalitions and individual members of Congress. Nearly all would limit stays on welfare, restrict the right to welfare of unmarried mothers under the age of 18, and impose far more stringent work requirements. Perhaps most disturbing to members of the social work community are the efforts to end AFDC as a national government entitlement program and replace it with fifty-one different programs: one for each state and the District of Columbia.

SUMMARY

Welfare, like all domestic policy, is in a constant state of evolution. We have preference for but not a knowledge of what it is evolving to. Always, policies and practice have emerged from a set of choices, national or state, governmental or voluntary, expanding or restrictive. Welfare in America will never be satisfactory to a concerned minority that will believe we have made the wrong choices. Sometimes the minority will be on the left and sometimes on the right. Welfare policy can never escape the contradictions in its dual goals: to respond compassionately to those in need but to structure the compassion in such a way that the natural tendencies of people to work, to save, and to care for their own are not eroded.

KEY TERMS

Great Society
health and welfare services
indoor relief
laissez faire
outdoor relief
Poor Law

public assistance
social insurance
Social Security
Social Security Act
social welfare
values

DISCUSSION QUESTIONS

1. Of what significance was the Elizabethan Poor Law to the subsequent development of public welfare in the United States?

2. How did the Speenhamland Act of 1795 differ from the Elizabethan Poor Law? What effect did the Speenhamland Act have on resolving the problems of the poor?

3. Argue the case that the Social Security Act has been the most significant social legislation passed in the United States.

4. What were the goals of the Economic Opportunities Act? How successful was this act in reducing poverty? Why was it discontinued?

5. Contrast President Johnson's Great Society programs with Presidents Nixon's and Reagan's positions on social welfare.

6. Compare the views on social welfare and plans to assist people in poverty held by the Clinton administration and the Republican Contract with America.

7. Identify at least two social factors that have influenced social legislation in the past twenty years; in the past five years.

REFERENCES

Axinn, June, and Herman Levin. 1982. *Social welfare: A history of the American response to need.* 2d ed. New York: Harper and Row.

Berkowitz, Edward D. 1991. *America's welfare state: From Roosevelt to Reagan.* Baltimore: Johns Hopkins Press.

Demott, J. 1994. Welfare reform could work. *Nation's Business* 82(18):18–23.

Ehrenreich, John H. 1985. *The altruistic imagination: A history of social work and social policy in the U.S.* Ithaca, N.Y.: Cornell University Press.

Federico, Ronald D. 1983. *The social welfare institution.* 4th ed. Lexington, Mass.: Heath.

Friedlander, Walter, and Robert Z. Apte. 1974. *Introduction to social welfare.* 4th ed. Englewood Cliffs, N.J.: Prentice-Hall.

Katz, Michael B. 1986. *In the shadow of the poorhouse.* New York: Basic Books.

Leiby, James. 1978. *A history of social welfare and social work in the U.S.* New York: Columbia University Press.

Reid, P. N. 1995. *Encyclopedia of Social Work,* vol. 3, 2206–2225. Washington, D.C.: NASW Press.

Should the system be abolished? Interview with Charles Murray. *Nation's Business* 82(18):21.

Trattner, Walter I. 1994. *From Poor Law to welfare state.* New York: Free Press.

SUGGESTED FURTHER READINGS

On the Right

Kaus, Mickey. 1992. *The end of equality.* New York: A New Republic Book.
Mead, Lawrence. 1992. *The new politics of poverty.* New York: Basic Books.
Phillips, Kevin. 1993. *Boiling point.* New York: Random House.

In the Center

Danziger, S. and P. Gottschalk. 1995. *America unequal.* Cambridge, Mass.: Harvard University Press.
Rochefort, David A. 1986. *American social welfare policy.* Boulder, Colo.: WestView Press.

On the Left

Ellwood, David. 1988. *Poor support: Poverty in the American family.* New York: Basic Books.
Wilson, William Julius. 1987. *The truly disadvantaged.* Chicago: University of Chicago Press.

Other

Chatterjee, P. 1996. *Approaches to the welfare state.* Washington, D.C.: NASW Press.
Howell, Joseph T. 1973. *Hard living on Clay Street.* Garden City, N.J.: Anchor Books.
Ryan, William. 1971. *Blaming the victim.* New York: Vintage Books.
Trattner, Walter. 1982. *From poor law to welfare state: A history of social welfare in America.* 4th ed. New York: Free Press.

CHAPTER 2

SOCIAL WORK AND THE OTHER HELPING PROFESSIONS

Carmen Castillo, a school social worker for the local intermediate school, has recently called a case conference to coordinate efforts to assist the Wright family. Ms. Wright is a single parent who has two children: Frank, age 13 (who is developmentally disabled), and Janice, age 5. Jill Turner, a social worker at the local Family Service Association, has been working with Ms. Wright to help her develop more effective parenting skills. Charles Johnson, a social worker for the Department of Human Services, has worked with Ms. Wright in completing her application for Aid to Families With Dependent Children (AFDC) and has initiated contact with Ms. Wright's ex-husband in soliciting child support payments. Nina Clark, a social worker for the local child care center, is attempting to arrange for Janice's enrollment at and transportation to the center while Ms. Wright attends a job skills training program.

Carmen Castillo, who is serving as case manager for the Wright family, has called the meeting of Ms. Wright and the social workers assisting her to evaluate the progress being made and to establish goals and priorities for future interventions. ▪

The Wright Case, just described, represents only a few of the broad and diverse activities that encompass social work practice. Social workers are employed by a wide variety of local, state, and federal agencies as professionals who engage clients in seeking solutions to unmet needs. In this book, our aim is to give you, the reader, an understanding of the goals and objectives of professional social work practice, the nature of the profession, and the types of needs that social workers help their clients address. Social work practice demands from its practitioners the utmost in intellect, creativity, skill, and knowledge. It is an exciting, challenging profession. Students who have the aptitude and desire to prepare for a career in the helping professions may find social work well suited to their needs and interests.

In this chapter, we examine the professional culture, activities, knowledge base, and skills incorporated into social work practice. The broader field of social welfare, of which professional social work practice is the major discipline, is also reviewed. But first, we examine why people have unresolved problems and why they need professional assistance in seeking solutions to them. ∎

WHY DO PEOPLE HAVE PROBLEMS?

It may sound trite, but all human beings have problems. Problems can be thought of as representing either an unsettled question or a source of concern or perplexity. Not all of us have the same types of problems, nor do problems affect us in the same ways. What constitutes a problem for one person may not be viewed as such by another. Some see problems as a challenge to be resolved; others are often overcome by them and see no avenues for their solution. Decision making for some individuals comes only with great difficulty, whereas others seem to have little trouble in making choices.

Social workers deal with problems that inhibit optimal functioning for individuals and groups, or those that result in dysfunctional behavior. Poverty, marital conflict, parent-child relationship problems, delinquency, abuse and neglect, substance abuse, and mental/emotional stress are among the many problems that professional social workers help people address.

Why do individuals develop problems so great that outside assistance is needed? There is no simple answer. Obviously, no rational person plans to have debilitating problems. No child plans to spend a life in poverty, nor does an adolescent choose a life of mental illness. What newly married couple, much in love and looking forward to the future together, plans for marital disharmony, family violence, or divorce? Why, then, do these problems emerge? Why do some individuals experience happy, satisfying marriages, whereas others move from marriage to marriage without finding satisfaction? Why are some people prosperous and readily move up the occupational and income ladders, whereas others remain deeply enmeshed in poverty? A matter of personal choice? Of course not! Problems of social functioning result from a mix of many factors. Briefly, we need to examine the factors that contribute to adaptation.

Genetics and Heredity

From the biological standpoint, people are born with many of the physiological characteristics of their ancestors. Some people have a tendency to be tall, others short; some are lean, others heavy; some are physically attractive, others less attractive; and so on. Undoubtedly, many people have greater intellectual potential than others; some are more agile, others less so. To a certain degree these characteristics affect adaptation and, indeed, opportunities throughout life. For example, regardless of skill or ability, it is virtually impossible for a 5'6" young man to become a professional basketball player. Regardless of desire or skill, opportunity is affected by physical characteristics. We encourage you to think of other examples in which genetic and/or hereditary factors might impose limitations on social behavior or opportunities.

Abnormal, or psychopathological, behavior is often attributed to biochemical types of genetic disorders. **Psycho-biological** approaches to behavioral dysfunctions focus on identifying the nature of body chemistry anomalies and how environmental stress converges with those anomalies to produce maladaptive behavior. Behavioral dysfunctions such as schizophrenia, depression, chronic anxiety, somatoform disorders, and others are often believed to be genetically linked.

Socialization

Whatever limits may be imposed by heredity, individuals develop as social beings through the process of **socialization.** Social behavior is learned behavior acquired through interacting with other human beings. Parents are the primary source of early socialization experiences. Family culture has a significant impact on the development of values, priorities, and role prescriptions. Families, of course, are not the only source of our social development. Neighbors, playmates, and acquaintances from school and other community institutions also play a part. Lower-income parents and wealthy ones may socialize their children in different ways, because resources and problem-solving opportunities vary so much. Thus, as children develop, their behaviors are shaped by the particular learning opportunities available to them. The thoughts people have and the mental attitudes they develop are as much a product of learning as are the skills they develop. Children who grow up in dysfunctional families often learn inappropriate techniques of problem solving.

Cultural Differences

Cultural differences may also serve to create behaviors that appear to be in conflict with broader societal norms and expectations. Traditional customs and behaviors may vary conversely with the majority group's requirements and create dissonance, which results in interpreting behavior as maladaptive or dysfunctional. The United States takes pride in and has been enriched by immigrants from around the world. The adaptation and assimilation of these immigrants, while problematic, are expected (even though they may not necessarily be viewed as desirable by the immigrants). Language differences and cultural traits often result in stereotyping and categorizing individuals as "out-group" members as well as in imposing barriers to social opportunities.

Environmental Factors

Geography, climate, and resources all affect quality of life and opportunities available for satisfactory growth and development. These factors vary throughout the land. Added to this are the economic and political forces that largely determine the availability of opportunities and resources around which people seek to organize their lives. Smog-infested, polluted areas contribute to a variety of health problems. Unpredictable economic trends may result in many workers losing their jobs. Discrimination limits opportunities for career development and impedes adequate employment. The environment is a major element in the opportunity structure. It can serve as a stimulus for producing life's satisfactions or become a major source of the problems people experience.

The Opportunity Structure

Obviously, genetics and heredity, socialization and cultural differences, and environmental factors are important in understanding why people have problems. All of these factors shape an individual's **opportunity structure,** that is, the accessibility of opportunities for an individual within that individual's environment. For example, a person may have physical traits and characteristics that are valued by society, a good educational background, a stable and supportive family, work-oriented values, and a desire to work, yet have no job because of a recession or depression. In spite of suitable preparation, this person may remain unemployed for some time, with all the problems associated with lack of income. Or, we might consider an individual who was born into a poor family, was abused as a child, did not receive the encouragement or incentives to complete school, and had poorly developed social skills because of inadequate parenting. Even if jobs were plentiful, this person would be able to compete for only the lowest-paying positions, if at all.

Other illustrations relate to genetic endowment. Gender, race and ethnicity often result in discrimination and unequal treatment in both job opportunities and the amount of remuneration a person will receive on the job. Women, African Americans, and Hispanics, for example, are not afforded equal opportunity in the job market even when all other factors are equal.

◪ SOCIAL WORK DEFINED

In the minds of many, **social workers** are often identified as "welfare" workers who are engaged in public assistance programs. Obviously, this is a false premise since social workers are involved in many different practice settings that offer a wide range of service. Social welfare literally means "social well-being." In the sense that this term is used in our society, it generally refers to the provision of institutional programs for the needy. **Social work,** on the other hand, is one of the professions that is instrumental in administering planned change activities prescribed by our social welfare institutions.

We must keep in mind, too, that the opportunity structure consists not only of what is available in the environment but also of inner resources such as cognitive development and personality structure. Furthermore, many problems that individuals, families, and groups experience result from the way society is organized and the limited choices that are available to some people.

Because social workers are actively involved in wide-ranging tasks, devising a specific, all-inclusive definition of *social work* is difficult. Unfortunately, this has resulted in definitions that are so general that they fail to relate appropriately all of the activities encompassed by the profession. For example, Box 2.1 lists some of the roles played by social workers today. The National Association of Social Workers (NASW) definition states that social work is

> the professional activity of helping individuals, groups or communities enhance or restore their capacity for social functioning and creating societal conditions favorable to that goal. (NASW 1973, 4)

Social work is viewed as an activity that seeks to remediate human problems by helping individuals, groups, or communities engage resources that will alleviate those problems. In addition, social work is concerned with enabling clients to develop capacities and strengths that will improve their social functioning. As this definition indicates, social work is an active, "doing" profession that brings about positive change in problem situations through problem solving or prevention. The social work profession is also committed to effecting changes in societal values and policies that limit or prohibit the free and full participation of individuals. Social workers have a professional responsibility to work for changes in discriminatory or otherwise restrictive practices that limit opportunities and prevent maximal social functioning.

◪ THE EARLY YEARS

Professional social work developed slowly over the years as a result of efforts to refine and improve its knowledge and skill base. As discussed in

---

BOX 2.1

ROLES FOR SOCIAL WORKERS

Outreach worker: A social worker who identifies and detects individuals, groups or communities who are having difficulty (in crisis) or are in danger of becoming vulnerable (at risk) works as an outreach worker.

Broker: The social worker who steers people toward existing services that may be of service to them is called a broker in the same way that a stockbroker steers prospective buyers toward stocks which may be useful to them.

Advocate: A social worker who fights for the rights and dignity of people in need of help advocates their cause.

Evaluator: A social worker who gathers information, assesses problems and makes decisions for action is, among other things, an evaluator.

Mobilizer: A social worker who assembles, energizes and organizes existing or new groups takes the role of mobilizer. This is most often a community organization role, although not always.

Teacher: A social worker whose main task is to convey and impart information and knowledge and to develop skills is a teacher. This role may or may not be played in a formal classroom situation.

Behavior changer: A social worker who works to bring about change in behavior patterns, habits and perception of individuals or groups is a behavior changer.

Consultant: A social worker who works with other workers or other agencies to help them increase their skills and solve clients' problems is a consultant.

Community planner: A social worker who works with neighborhood groups, agencies, community agents or government in the development of community programs is called a community planner.

Data manager: A social worker who collects, classifies and analyzes data generated within the welfare environment is a data manager. This role may be performed by a supervisor, administrator, or it may be carried out by a clerical person with the necessary skills.

Administrator: A social worker who manages an agency, a facility, or a small unit is operating in the role of administrator.

Care giver: A social worker who provides ongoing care—physical, custodial, financial—for whatever reason is acting as a care giver.

Source: From Betty J. Piccard: *An Introduction to Social Work: A Primer*, 4th ed., pp. 27–28. Homewood, Ill.: The Dorsey Press, 1988. Reprinted by permission of Wadsworth, Inc.

Chapter 1, the early administration of relief to the needy was accomplished by a wide variety of individuals: overseers of the poor, friends and neighbors, church members, the clergy, philanthropists, and friendly visitors, among others. As early as 1814 in Scotland, the Reverend Thomas Chalmers expressed concern over wasteful and inefficient approaches used by relief programs and sought to encourage the development of a more humane and effective system for providing services and support. Chalmers emphasized the need for a more personalized involvement with the needy. He devised a system wherein his parish was divided into districts, with a deacon assigned to investigate each case in order to determine the causes of problems. If the resultant analysis indicated that self-sufficiency was not possible, an attempt was made to engage family, friends, neighbors, or wealthy citizens to provide the necessary assistance for the needy. As a last resort, the congregation was asked to provide assistance (Pumphrey and Pumphrey 1961).

Later, in the United States, the Association for Improving the Conditions of the Poor (New York City) and the Charity Organization Society (Buffalo, New York City, and Philadelphia) used similar approaches when organizing activities to help the poor. The **Charity Organization Society (COS)** had a profound effect on establishing social work as a specialized practice. The COS promoted "scientific philanthropy," emphasizing that charity was more than almsgiving and had as its "long-run goal . . . to restore the recipient of charity to the dignity of as much self-sufficiency and responsibility as he could manage" (Leiby 1978, 111–12). Furthermore, the COS stressed the importance of individual assessment and a coordinated plan of service. The COS was the first relief organization to pay personnel to investigate requests for assistance and to refer eligible applicants to one or more existing agencies for intensive aid and supervision. Special emphasis was given to "following up" on the recipients of assistance, and efforts were made to secure someone to establish friendly relationships with them (Leiby 1978, 112–35).

Just as "friendly visiting" was encouraged, attention was also given to data collection and assessment. It was believed that a more structured, informed, and skillful approach would increase efficiency, discourage dependence on charity, lead to personal development and self-sufficiency, and reduce the practice of providing relief for chronic beggars.

The settlement house movement also emerged as a viable means for providing a variety of community services and advocacy for the poor and disenfranchised during the late 1800s. Perhaps the most noteworthy of the settlements was Hull House, established in 1889 by Jane Addams, a pioneer social worker. The success of this venture was immediate, and the programs offered by Hull House captured the imagination of both philanthropic helpers and the needy. The settlements maintained a strong family focus, provided socialization experiences, and, through advocacy efforts, sought to influence the community to correct the dismal social conditions under which the poor were living.

This structured approach to managing charitable efforts quickly resulted in the need for trained workers. Mary Richmond, a major contributor to the COS movement (and considered by many to be the founder of the professional social work movement), inaugurated the first training program for social workers at the New York School of Applied Philanthropy, the forerunner of schools of social work. Richmond also formulated the concept and base for **social casework,** a practice method designed to "develop personality through adjustments consciously effected, individual by individual, between [persons] and their environment" (Richmond 1922, 9). She also maintained a keen interest in personality and family development and stressed the environmental influence within which interpersonal interactions transpired. Believing that environmental factors were significant contributors to personal as well as family dysfunctions, she maintained a strong interest in social reform that would promote a better quality of life for individuals (Leiby 1978, 124). Richmond was convinced that this task should be included in the social worker's sphere of responsibility. In her classic work, *Social Diagnosis* (1917), she laid the framework for social casework practice.

Under the impetus provided by Richmond, Jane Addams, and other early social work pioneers, a profession was born.

Schools of social work began to emerge along the eastern seaboard and in large cities of the Midwest, emphasizing direct social work practice (casework). Many were influenced by newly developing psychological perspectives, most notably those of Sigmund Freud and Otto Rank. Schools adopting Freudian psychology were more prevalent and became identified as "diagnostic" schools. Schools incorporating Rankian theory were known as "functional" schools. Shaping of curriculum around psychological theories increased the scientific knowledge base for social work practice.

By the late 1920s, **social group work** had gained visibility as a method of social intervention, rather than "treatment" per se. Learning and social development were believed to be enhanced through structured group interactions. This technique soon became popular in settlement houses and in work with street gangs, organized recreational clubs, and residents of institutions. Social group work became well entrenched as a viable helping method and later was adopted as a social work method.

Community organization had its roots in the New York Society for the Prevention of Pauperism, the Association for Improving Conditions of the Poor, and the Charity Organization Society. It became prominent as a resource development method by the late 1930s. Dealing largely with community development and stressing the importance of citizen participation and environmental change, community organizers plied their skills in identifying unmet human needs and working toward the development of community resources to meet those needs. Skills in needs assessment, planning, public relations, organizing, influencing, and resource development were among the prerequisites for community organizers.

By the 1950s, social casework, group work, and community organization were all considered methods of social work practice. In 1955, the various associations established to promote and develop each separate method merged and became known as the **National Association of Social Workers (NASW).** NASW continues to serve as the main professional organization for social workers today, with over 100,000 members. NASW seeks to promote quality in practice, stimulates political participation and social action, maintains standards of eligibility for membership in the association, and publishes several journals, including *Social Work.* Each state has an NASW chapter with a designated headquarters, and local membership units are active in all major cities.

UNDERPINNINGS OF THE PROFESSION

Social work practice is based on values, ethics, knowledge of human behavior, practice skills, and planned change. Each of these attributes is important to professional social workers.

Values

Social workers are committed to the dignity, worth, and value of all human beings, regardless of social class, race, color, creed, gender, or age. The value of human life transcends all other values, and the best interest of human beings merits a humane and helpful response from society. People with problems, regardless of the nature of those problems, are not to be judged, condemned, or demeaned. Social workers emphasize that nonjudgmental attitudes are essential for maintaining clients' dignity and privacy, and that clients must be accepted as they are, with no strings attached. Furthermore, clients (or the **client system,** which may include more than one individual, such as a family or a group of retarded adults) have the right to autonomy, that is, the right to determine courses of action that will affect their lives. Likewise, groups and communities hold these fundamental rights.

Ethics

Ethics (i.e., moral duty) is a product of values. Professional ethics, therefore, relates to the moral principles of practice. Social work values provide the basis for the social worker's beliefs about individuals and society, while ethics defines the framework for what should be done in specific situations. Both value and ethical dilemmas and conflicts are common. Social workers, like their clients, have personal reference groups whose values may often conflict with those of others. For example, a client may belong to a religious group that forbids and censures the use of professional medical intervention in cases of illness. The social worker may strongly favor medical intervention in those cases. Noting the value differences, what is the social worker's moral (ethical) duty in such cases? How can the best interests of the client be served where value conflicts are present? Do clients have the right to self-determination in such cases? As you ponder these questions, ask yourself what you would do. You will discover that responses to these types of situations are seldom easily achieved.

Later in this chapter (see Box 2.3), we present a summary of the National Association of Social Workers Code of Ethics. Review this code to see if it helps you arrive at appropriate ethical behavior in assisting the client discussed in the preceding paragraph.

Knowledge

Social work practice is derived from theories of human behavior as well as experiential knowledge related to practice. Research is an integrally important contributor to understanding individual, group, and community behavior. Research also is a method of identifying more effective interventive techniques. Students of social work are expected to have an understanding of the life cycle, as well as personality development, social dysfunction, developmental processes, group dynamics, effects of discrimination, social policy formulation, research methods, and community environments. Schools of social work encourage students to become familiar with a wide range of social and behavioral science theories that serve as a basis for understanding how client systems adapt and cope with client needs, and how theory guides planned social intervention. This knowledge undergirds the social worker's practice competence.

Practice Skills

Social workers are familiar with techniques related to direct practice with individuals (casework) and groups (group work), as well as communities (community organization). Organizing, planning, and administration also are included as areas of specialization for many social work practitioners. Research skills are essential for evaluating practice effectiveness, too.

Planned Change

Professional social work intervention is based on a process of planned change. Change is indicated when client systems present dysfunctional problems that go unresolved. Planned change is an orderly approach to addressing client needs and is based on assessment, knowledge of the client system's capacity for change, and focused intervention. The social worker functions as a change agent in this process. Planned change is characterized by purpose and a greater likelihood of predictable outcomes derived from the change effort. Box 2.2 presents a statement of the purpose of social work formulated by social workers.

These underpinnings of the profession (values, knowledge, practice skills, and planned change) are discussed in greater detail in Chapters 5 through 8.

 # SOCIAL WORK METHODS

Social workers are committed to the process of planned change. In their role, they become agents of change, who focus on improving the conditions that adversely affect the functioning of clients (or client systems). Change efforts may be geared toward assisting individuals, groups, or communities (or all three), and appropriate methods of intervention for achieving problem solutions are engaged. Practice methods incorporate social work values, principles, and techniques in

- Helping people obtain resources
- Conducting counseling and psychotherapy with individuals or groups
- Helping communities or groups provide or improve social and health services
- Participating in relevant legislative processes that affect the quality of life for all citizens

A variety of social work practice methods exist, as discussed in the following sections and described more extensively in Part II.

Direct Practice with Individuals and Families

When the social worker's effort is focused on working directly with individuals or families, the process is called **direct practice** (casework). This type of method is geared toward helping individuals and families

---

BOX 2.2

WORKING STATEMENT ON THE PURPOSE OF SOCIAL WORK

The purpose of social work is to promote or restore a mutually beneficial interaction between individuals and society in order to improve the quality of life for everyone. Social workers hold the following beliefs:

- The environment (social, physical, organizational) should provide the opportunity and resources for the maximum realization of the potential and aspirations of all individuals, and should provide for their common human needs and for the alleviation of distress and suffering.
- Individuals should contribute as effectively as they can to their own well-being and to the social welfare of others in their immediate environment as well as to the collective society.
- Transactions between individuals and others in their environment should enhance the dignity, individuality, and self-determination of everyone. People should be treated humanely and with justice.

Clients of social workers may be an individual, a family, a group, a community, or an organization.

OBJECTIVES

Social workers focus on person-and-environment in interaction. To carry out their purpose, they work with people to achieve the following objectives:

- Help people enlarge their competence and increase their problem-solving and coping abilities.
- Help people obtain resources.
- Make organizations responsive to people.
- Facilitate interaction between individuals and others in their environment.
- Influence social and environmental policy.

To achieve these objectives, social workers work with other people. At different times, the target of change varies—it may be the client, others in the environment, or both.

Source: Copyright 1981, National Association of Social Workers, Inc., *Social Work* 26(1):6. Reprinted with permission.

---

identify solutions to personal or other problems related to difficulty in social functioning. In many instances, problems related to social inadequacy, emotional conflict, interpersonal loss, social stress, or the lack of familiarity with resources create dysfunction for individuals. Practitioners are skilled in assessment and know how to intervene strategically in providing assistance for those problems. Direct practice is often considered to be therapeutic in nature.

Direct Practice with Groups (Group Work)

Group work techniques seek to enrich the lives of individuals through planned group experiences. Group work stresses the value of self-development through structured interaction with other group members. This process is based on theories of group dynamics and encourages personal growth through active participation as a group member. Groups may be natural (already formed), such as street gangs, or formed purposefully at the group work setting, such as support groups. In either instance, the value of participation, democratic goal setting, freedom of expression, ac-

Social workers take on many roles in working with people. Here, a group of teens participates in a group counseling session with a social worker.

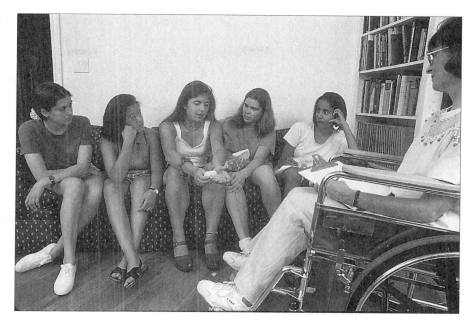

ceptance, and the development of positive attitudes through sharing is stressed. Group work generally is not considered therapeutic, and it should not be confused with group therapy, which also utilizes group processes. Group therapy is designed to be therapeutic in that it seeks to alter or diminish dysfunctional behavior through the dynamic use of group interaction. Members of therapeutic groups often share common emotionally distressing experiences (e.g., a group of recent divorcées) and through focused discussion develop options for more adaptive behaviors.

Community Organization

Social workers who practice at the community level utilize techniques of community organization to promote change. Recognizing that citizen awareness and support are vital to the development of resources in generating a more healthy and constructive environment for all citizens, community organizers work with established organizations within the community (such as Lions and Kiwanis clubs, city governments, welfare organizations, the Junior League, political groups, social action groups, and other citizens' organizations) in order to gain support for needed services and to secure funding for their maintenance. Social workers who intervene at this level may be employed by city governments, planning agencies, councils of social agencies, or related community agencies.

Social Work Research

Although all social workers use research, many social workers specialize in social work research. This serves to increase both the knowledge base of practice and the effectiveness of intervention. Research also provides an empirical base upon which more focused policy formulation may be designed. Social research is essential in the process of establishing a scientific framework for solving problems and refining social work practice methods. Evaluative research enables agencies as well as practitioners to gain a better understanding of the effectiveness of efforts designed to meet goals and objectives around which practice efforts are focused. Competent social work practitioners keep abreast of the professional research and utilize research findings in their practice.

Social Work Administration and Planning

Administration and planning is a social work method that seeks to maximize the effective use of agency resources in problem solving. Administrators must be skilled in organizing, planning, and management techniques, as well as have knowledge about social work practice. Many social agency administrators begin their careers as direct practitioners, subsequently become supervisors, and then move into administrative roles. Social planning also is seen as a social work role, which is discussed in Chapter 7.

◪ PROFESSIONAL ISSUES IN SOCIAL WORK

Social work, like professional fields such as nursing and public administration, has experienced resistance in being acknowledged as a profession. To the extent that this is an important question, one really needs to ask, what are the characteristics of a profession?

Ernest Greenwood (1957) suggests that a profession is identified by the following characteristics:

- A systematic body of theory
- Professional authority
- Sanction of the community
- A regulative code of ethics
- A professional culture

The attributes outlined by Greenwood have long characterized social work, which has emerged as one of the more significant helping professions. For example, education for social work practice is predicated on the foundations of social and behavioral sciences, as well as theory and knowledge produced by social work research and years of experimental practice. The social worker's authority is acknowledged by the community and clients who are involved with the profession. Authority presumes the social worker's expertise, including assessment capabilities as well as knowledge about appropriate interventions designed to alleviate problems. Community sanction for social work practice has become more evident within recent years through state laws requiring registration, certification, or licensing of social workers. The National

Association of Social Workers has established a code of ethics (Box 2.3) for its members, and a strong professional culture has developed and is expressed through the state and national associations (such as NASW) of social work practitioners. The increasing number of social workers engaged in private practice also contributes to the recognition of social work's professional status. All evidence suggests that social work meets the standards identified by Greenwald for professional status.

◪ THE SOCIAL AGENCY

The majority of social workers perform their professional functions through the auspices of a social agency. **Social agencies** are organizations that have been formed by communities to address social problems experienced by a significant number of citizens. Agencies may be *public* (funded by taxes), *voluntary* (funded through contributions), or, in increasing numbers, *proprietary* (profit-oriented). The typical social agency is headed by a board of directors of local citizens. It meets regularly to review the agency's activities and to establish policy that governs agency services. Many larger agencies have an administrator who has sole responsibility for supervising the agency's activities. In many smaller agencies, the administrator also may be involved in assisting clients with their needs.

Agencies are community resources that stand ready to assist in addressing needs that make day-by-day functioning difficult. Social workers are employed to carry out the mission of the agency. Many agencies do not charge fees for the services they provide. In some instances, however, agencies employ a ''sliding-fee scale'' and adjust the fee to the client's ability to pay. All clients, regardless of ability to pay, are afforded the same quality of service.

Typically, agencies cooperate in meeting human needs. Referrals are often made when clients have needs that can be addressed more effectively by another agency. Interagency coordination is a helpful process, maximizing community resources to meet unaddressed needs.

◪ EDUCATION AND LEVELS OF SOCIAL WORK PRACTICE

Professional social workers are involved in assisting clients with a large variety of unmet needs. As a consequence, the nature and degree of skills necessary for addressing unmet needs vary with the complexities of the needs encountered. Recognizing that professional competence is a right clients have in seeking assistance, regardless of how difficult meeting their needs might be, the social work profession has established three different levels of practice for meeting these divergent needs. The profession has also established the **Council on Social Work Education (CSWE)** which, through its division of standards and accreditation,

BOX 2.3

CODE OF ETHICS, NATIONAL ASSOCIATION OF SOCIAL WORKERS

PREAMBLE

This code is intended to serve as a guide to the everyday conduct of members of the social work profession and as a basis for the adjudication of issues in ethics when the conduct of social workers is alleged to deviate from the standards expressed or implied in this code. It represents standards of ethical behavior for social workers in professional relationships with those served, with colleagues, with employers, with other individuals and professions, and with the community and society as a whole. It also embodies standards of ethical behavior governing individual conduct to the extent that such conduct is associated with an individual's status and identity as a social worker.

This code is based on the fundamental values of the social work profession that include the worth, dignity, and uniqueness of all persons as well as their rights and opportunities. It is also based on the nature of social work, which fosters conditions that promote these values.

In subscribing to and abiding by this code, the social worker is expected to view ethical responsibility in as inclusive a context as each situation demands and within which ethical judgement is required. The social worker is expected to take into consideration all the principles in this code that have a bearing upon any situation in which ethical judgement is to be exercised and professional intervention or conduct is planned. The course of action that the social worker chooses is expected to be consistent with the spirit as well as the letter of this code.

In itself, this code does not represent a set of rules that will prescribe all the behaviors of social workers in all the complexities of professional life. Rather, it offers general principles to guide conduct, and the judicious appraisal of conduct, in situations that have ethical implications. It provides the basis for making judgements about ethical actions before and after they occur. Frequently, the particular situation determines the ethical principles that apply and the manner of their application. In such cases, not only the particular ethical principles are taken into immediate consideration, but also the entire code and its spirit. Specific applications of ethical principles must be judged within the context in which they are being considered. Ethical behavior in a given situation must satisfy not only the judgement of the individual social worker, but also the judgement of an unbiased jury of professional peers.

This code should not be used as an instrument to deprive any social worker of the opportunity or freedom to practice with complete professional integrity; nor should any disciplinary action be taken on the basis of this code without maximum provision for safeguarding the rights of the social worker affected.

The ethical behavior of social workers results not from edict, but from a personal commitment of the individual. This code is offered to affirm the will and zeal of all social workers to be ethical and to act ethically in all that they do as social workers.

The following codified ethical principles should guide social workers in the various roles and relationships and at the various levels of responsibility in which they function professionally. These principles also serve as a basis for the adjudication by the National Association of Social Workers of issues in ethics.

In subscribing to this code, social workers are required to cooperate in its implementation and abide by any disciplinary rulings based on it. They should also take adequate measures to discourage, prevent, expose, and correct the unethical conduct of colleagues. Finally, social workers should be equally ready to defend and assist colleagues unjustly charged with unethical conduct.

SUMMARY OF MAJOR PRINCIPLES

　I. The Social Worker's Conduct and Comportment as a Social Worker

Propriety. The social worker should maintain high standards of personal conduct in the capacity or identity as social worker.

Competence and Professional Development. The social worker should strive to become and remain proficient in professional practice and the performance of professional functions.

Service. The social worker should regard as primary the service obligation of the social work profession.

Integrity. The social worker should act in accordance with the highest standards of professional integrity.

Scholarship and Research. The social worker engaged in study and research should be guided by the conventions of scholarly inquiry.

II. The Social Worker's Ethical Responsibility to Clients

Primacy of Clients' Interests. The social worker's primary responsibility is to clients.

Rights and Prerogatives of Clients. The social worker should make every effort to foster maximum self-determination on the part of clients.

Confidentiality and Privacy. The social worker should respect the privacy of clients and hold in confidence all information obtained in the course of professional service.

Fees. When setting fees, the social worker should ensure that they are fair, reasonable, considerate, and commensurate with the service performed and with due regard for the clients' ability to pay.

III. The Social Worker's Ethical Responsibility to Colleagues

Respect, Fairness, and Courtesy. The social worker should treat colleagues with respect, courtesy, fairness, and good faith.

Dealing with Colleagues' Clients. The social worker has the responsibility to relate to the clients of colleagues with full professional consideration.

IV. The Social Worker's Ethical Responsibility to Employers and Employing Organizations

Commitments to Employing Organizations. The social worker should adhere to commitments made to the employing organizations.

V. The Social Worker's Ethical Responsibility to the Social Work Profession

Maintaining the Integrity of the Profession. The social worker should uphold and advance the values, ethics, knowledge, and mission of the profession.

Community Service. The social worker should assist the profession in making social services available to the general public.

Development of Knowledge. The social worker should take responsibility for identifying, developing, and fully utilizing knowledge for professional practice.

VI. The Social Worker's Ethical Responsibility to Society

Promoting the General Welfare. The social worker should promote the general welfare of society.

A revision of this code will be voted upon at the meeting of the NASW Delegate Assembly in August 1996. We suggest you obtain a copy of the revised code either from your instructor or local NASW chapter as it is an important professional document, which will be discussed in your future social work classes.

Source: Copyright 1993, National Association of Social Workers, Inc. NASW Code of Ethics. Reprinted with permission.

serves as the accrediting body for professional educational programs at the BSW and MSW levels.

Bachelor of Social Work: BSW

The entry level for professional social work practice is the bachelor (BSW) degree. Social work practitioners entering practice at this level must complete the educational requirements for an undergraduate social work program accredited by the Council on Social Work Education. Although professional social work educational programs offered by colleges and universities may vary, CSWE mandates that each must provide basic education in human growth and behavior, social policy, research, practice methods, social and economic justice, cultural diversity, understanding at-risk populations, and social work values as a minimum requirement for meeting accreditation standards. All students who graduate from an accredited BSW program must complete 480 clock hours of field experience in a social work or related setting under the supervision of a social work practitioner. Students are placed in settings such as senior citizens' centers, battered women's shelters, child welfare agencies, residential treatment centers, juvenile and adult probation programs, public schools, health clinics, hospitals, industries, and mental health agencies.

The educational curriculum for baccalaureate-level practice is developed around the generalist method of practice. Typically, the generalist practitioner is knowledgeable about the systems/ecological approach (see Chapter 3 for a complete discussion) to practice and is skillful in needs assessment, interviewing, resource development, case management, use of community resources, establishment of intervention objectives with clients, and problem solving. Baer and Federico have outlined **competencies,** skills necessary to perform certain functions, that undergird social work practice at the BSW level:

1. Identify and assess situations where the relationship between people and social institutions needs to be initiated, enhanced, restored, protected, or terminated.

2. Develop and implement a plan for improving the well-being of people based on problem assessment and the exploration of obtainable goals and available options.

3. Enhance the problem-solving, coping, and developmental capacities of people.

4. Link people with systems that provide them with resources, services, and opportunities.

5. Intervene effectively on behalf of populations most vulnerable and discriminated against.

6. Promote the effective and humane operation of the systems that provide people with services, resources, and opportunities.

7. Actively participate with others in creating new, modified, or improved service, resource, opportunity systems that are more equitable, just, and responsive to consumers of services, and work with others to eliminate those systems that are unjust.

8. Evaluate the extent to which the objectives of intervention were achieved.

9. Continually evaluate one's own professional growth and development through assessment of practice behaviors and skills.

10. Contribute to the improvement of service delivery by adding to the knowledge base of the profession as appropriate and by supporting and upholding the standards and ethics of the profession. (1978, 86–89)

Entry-level social workers are employed by agencies offering a wide spectrum of services. As direct practice workers, they may perform professional activities as eligibility workers for state human services departments; work with children and families as protective services (protecting children from abuse and neglect) workers; serve as youth or adult probation workers; work in institutional care agencies that provide services for children or adults, especially the aged; engage in school social work; act as program workers or planners for areawide agencies on aging; work in mental health outreach centers or institutions; serve as family assistance workers in industry; or perform their professional tasks in many other agencies providing human services. It is not uncommon for baccalaureate-level professionals with experience and demonstrated competence to be promoted to supervisory and administrative positions.

Social work professionals at the BSW level of practice are eligible for full membership in the NASW. The professional activities they perform in helping clients are challenging and rewarding. Many social workers prefer to practice at this level throughout their careers. For others, an advanced degree in social work is desirable and opens up areas of practice that are not typically in the domain of the baccalaureate (BSW) practitioner. For those who have completed their undergraduate social work education from an accredited college or university, advanced standing may be granted by the school of social work to which they apply. Although not all graduate schools accept advanced-standing students, the CSWE provides a listing of those that do. Advanced-standing students, when admitted to a graduate program, are able to shorten the time required to secure the masters degree without diluting the quality of their educational experience. Advanced practice in social work is predicated upon the master's degree in social work (MSW).

Master of Social Work: Advanced Practice

Slightly more than one hundred colleges and universities in the United States have accredited graduate schools of social work (CSWE 1995). Students in these programs are engaged in an educational curriculum that is more specialized than the BSW curriculum. Students may specialize in direct services (casework or group work), community organization, administration, planning, or research. All students master a common core of basic knowledge, including human growth and behavior, social policy, research, and practice methods related to their area of specialization. Many graduate programs also offer fields of specialization, such as social work with the aged, child welfare, medical social work, industrial social work, mental health, or social work with the developmentally disabled. The two-year master's degree program (MSW) is balanced between classroom learning and clinical (field) practice. Graduates seek employment in such specialized settings as Veterans Administration hospitals, family and children's service agencies, counseling centers, and related settings that require specialized professional education.

Doctorate in Social Work: DSW and PhD

Professional social workers interested in social work education, highly advanced clinical practice, research, planning, or administration often seek advanced study in programs offering the Doctor of Social Work (DSW) or the Doctor of Philosophy in Social Work (PhD). A number of graduate schools of social work offer education at this level. Students admitted tend to be seasoned social work practitioners, although this is not a prerequisite for admission to all schools. Education at this level stresses research, advanced clinical practice, advanced theory, administration, and social policy. Graduates usually seek employment on the faculty of schools of social work or in the administration of social welfare agencies, or with increasing frequency, in private clinical practice.

◤ SOCIAL WORK CAREERS

The number of employed social service workers grew rapidly from 95,000 in 1960 to well over 350,000 by 1995. However, based on current federal and state funding, it is unlikely that the rate of growth will increase dramatically in the near future. But this should not discourage students interested in a social work career. New positions are being created in addition to the vacancies created through attrition. Some fields of practice with a vast potential for growth are beginning to emerge. For example, the fields of health care, aging, and substance abuse are experiencing a great need for professional social workers.

Social work is an ideal profession for individuals interested in working with people and helping them address their needs. These broad interests are the heart of the social work profession. Positions in a wide variety of areas continue to attract social workers at all levels of practice, such as child welfare, health, corrections, developmental disabilities, family counseling, substance abuse, and public assistance programs.

Wages in social work usually are adequate, and increases are based on skill and experience. Baccalaureate-level workers typically earn less than the more specialized master's degree workers. Entrance salaries may range from $18,000 to $30,000 per year, depending on experience, degree, location, and agency sponsorship. A few social workers earn upwards of $75,000 after extensive experience. Mobility often is a valuable asset to the worker looking for an initial social work job. Rural areas often experience shortages of workers, whereas some metropolitan areas have a tighter employment market. Employment vacancies often are listed with college placement services, state employment commissions, professional associations, state agencies, or local newspapers.

In recent years, more social workers with advanced degrees in social work have engaged in **private practice.** Unlike more traditionally employed social workers, private practitioners must rely on fees from their clients to support their practice. Often, social workers spend most of their time employed by a social agency and see clients in private practice on a part-time basis. Others may devote full time to their practice. Generally, private practice focuses on clients in need of counseling or group therapy. Private practitioners are governed by the NASW Code of Ethics and the social work value base. They extend their services to clients who often would not seek assistance through traditional agency networks.

THE OTHER HELPING PROFESSIONALS

Social workers are not alone in assisting people who are experiencing problems. Social workers often find that the unique skills of other helping professionals are beneficial in addressing needs that are beyond the scope of the social worker's skill and knowledge base or are otherwise inappropriate for social work intervention. Frequently, social workers are members of a collaborative effort with other professionals in assisting individuals, families, groups, or communities in finding solutions to troubling problems or in establishing problem-prevention programs. For example, a school social worker, guidance counselor, clinical psychologist, and school nurse might combine their professional expertise in developing a program designed to prevent teenage pregnancy. Or, a social worker might work with a pastoral counselor and psychiatrist to help a former mental patient become reestablished into community life. Although there are many instances in which professional teamwork enhances the opportunities of clients and furthers the opportunities for successful intervention, it is the social worker's responsibility to guard the integrity of the referral process when seeking the expertise of resources to whom they refer their clients.

In the following paragraphs, we include a brief overview of the more prominent community professionals who practice in the area of human services.

Psychiatrists

Psychiatry is a specialized field of medical practice that focuses on mental and emotional dysfunction. While psychiatrists typically treat clients experiencing some form of psychopathology, many help with other problems of social dysfunction and interpersonal relationships. For example, a psychiatrist may counsel couples experiencing marital discord, assist adolescents with problems in adaptation, use play therapy with children whose social development has been retarded, counsel individuals and couples who experience sexual dysfunctions, and so on. Unlike other professionals who assist with psychological and emotional problems as well as those of social dysfunction, psychiatrists can provide medications where physiological symptoms indicate the need for them. Because psychiatrists are physicians (with a medical degree), they have at their disposal a wide array of medical interventions as well as their expertise in treating problems of a mental and emotional nature.

Psychiatrists practice in a variety of settings. Hospitals established for the treatment of the mentally ill constitute the most frequent employment sites. Many psychiatrists establish private practices in major metropolitan areas. Others are either employed full-time or serve as treatment consultants in residential treatment centers, children's agencies, centers designed for the treatment of specialized problems such as family violence or alcohol or substance abuse, or suicide prevention centers. Some also assist other agencies that provide specialized services to the emotionally disturbed.

Like other helping professionals, psychiatrists are educated in various programs that emphasize different theoretical and methodological approaches to problem solving. Some embrace Freudian psychology, others Adlerian or Jungian, while still others incorporate Sullivanian theories into their practice, all of which are "insight therapies." In recent times, many psychiatrists have adopted learning theory approaches (behavior modification) as well as reality therapy, rational emotive therapy, transactional analysis, and related approaches. Psychiatrists typically are well educated within their specialty and constitute a significant and important resource for treating problems of the mentally ill and emotionally disturbed.

Psychologists

Coon (1982) has identified thirty-four subspecialties in the field of **psychology.** The majority of these specialties do not involve special preparation in counseling or psychotherapy. According to Coon, over one-half of all psychologists are employed by educational institutions, another 15 percent work in hospitals or clinics, 10 percent are in government service or research, 7 percent are in private practice, and 6 percent are employed by public or private schools. In terms of the focus of their employment, 29 percent engage in clinical practice; 10 percent are experimental psychologists; 19 percent are educational or school psychologists; 9 percent are developmental, social, and personality psychologists; 8 percent are general, engineering, and other industrial specialists; 3 percent are involved in testing as a subspecialty; and 1 percent are environmental psychologists (Coon 1982, 18).

Without some awareness of the differences in specialty areas, it might be difficult to identify the appropriate resource for problem solving. Unlike psychiatrists, professional psychologists are not physicians. Those who engage in practice designed to assist with psychological and emotional problems generally are referred to as *clinical* or *counseling* psychologists. Like psychiatrists, psychologists are educated in universities and professional schools that emphasize a wide variety of theoretical and methodological approaches to practice. Again, like psychiatrists, many have developed skills in psychotherapy and psychoanalysis. Others prefer methodological approaches that reflect a behavior modification, cognitive therapy, Gestalt therapy, or related practice modality. Psychologists treat clients with deep-rooted emotional conflict, faulty personality development, interpersonal problems represented in marriage and family conflict, substance abuse, and various psychological and behavioral disorders. Psychologists typically use various forms of **psychometric instruments** (testing) in diagnosing a problem. These instruments are designed to provide information about clients and their functioning that often is not readily observable during a client interview. Tests also may be used as a basis for establishing a personality profile for clients. Tests can be useful in providing insights into the client's abilities to handle stress and areas where the client is vulnerable. Tests, however, are only one of many sources of evidence needed to assess clients' problems.

Many psychologists are skilled in group therapy as well as individual practice. In recent years group psychotherapy and group treatment have emerged as significant treatment techniques in helping clients with similar problems resolve those problems through the use of group dynamics and the skillful intervention of the group therapist.

Psychologists engaging in psychometry are often called on as consultants to test clients in social service agencies and educational institutions. This service is often very helpful in gaining better insights into clients and establishing appropriate treatment and intervention plans.

Sociologists

Sociologists are experts in the study of society, its organization, and the phenomena arising out of the group relations of human beings. As such, professionals in this area contribute much to our awareness of human interaction, including the establishment of norms, values, social organization, patterns of behavior, and social institutions. Sociologists are skilled in research techniques and methodologies. Like other professionals, they may focus on a subspecialty such as the family, deviancy, industrial sociology, symbolic interaction, bureaucracy and related forms of social organization, and the sociology of knowledge and social problems.

The majority of sociologists are employed at institutions of higher education and related educational institutions, although a growing number are entering the field of clinical, or applied, sociology. Professionals engaging in clinical sociology seek to apply the knowledge and principles gleaned from sociological theory to identify or enrich the understanding of organizational or interactional relationships, with the goal of resolving problems. Sociologists using this approach may function as family counselors, group therapists, industrial consultants, problem analysts, or program planners. The contribution of sociology to the understanding of the impact of environment and group membership on behavior has proven immeasurable.

Pastoral Counselors

Perhaps no other single source of contact by persons experiencing problems is sought out more often than religious leaders. Priests, pastors, ministers, rabbis, and other persons in positions of spiritual leadership are called on readily by members of their congregations and others in trouble. Religious leaders are placed in a unique and valued position by the laity. As spiritual leaders, they are presumed to have an extraordinary understanding of human frailty and a special ability to communicate with supernatural powers. Just as congregations vary in size and sophistication, so do the educational background and experience of religious leaders as problem solvers. Many receive extensive theological education coupled with a subspecialty in counseling. Others become counselors by demand, with little academic and supervised practical instruction to do so. Still others are relatively uneducated and hold their positions by what they perceive as a unique calling from God. In most instances, they are committed to helping their parishioners find solutions to problems within the context of a religious belief system.

Professional **pastoral counselors** are most often educated at schools of theology offering specializations in counseling. Typically, these programs offer classroom theory and a practicum that utilizes various psychological approaches to intervention and problem solving. Many religious leaders complete their theological education and enter graduate schools in clinical or counseling psychology, social work, or guidance and counseling programs. Larger congregations frequently employ a pastoral counselor to supplement the overall pastoral ministry.

Pastoral counselors may assist parishioners with marriage and family problems, developmental problems, social problems, difficulties with interpersonal relationships, and a myriad of other problems. Individuals experiencing inner conflict with respect to spiritual problems are frequently given assistance and support by the pastoral counselor. Skilled practitioners also may form groups to work on specific problems. Pastoral counselors also are engaged in various educational activities designed either to enrich the awareness and understanding of the congregation or to prevent problems. Like other human service professionals, pastoral counselors must develop an awareness of the limits of their professional skills and make referrals, where necessary, to assure that the best interests of the client are served.

Guidance Counselors

Most guidance counselors are educated in public schoolteacher educational programs and certified by state educational agencies. They are generally required to have classroom teaching experience before they are eligible for certification as guidance counselors. Guidance counselors specialize in assisting students with educationally related problems and in locating educational resources best suited to their individual interests. Students with behavioral problems, as well as those with academic difficulties, often are referred to the guidance counselor for assistance. Although guidance counselors focus on academically related concerns, they often become engaged in a therapeutic relationship with students who are experiencing adaptive or emotionally related problems. Guidance counselors also may assist the school psychologist in administering tests to students and, in smaller school systems, may assume primary responsibility for the testing program. They are called on to provide essential information to classroom teachers about the performance of students and, in collaboration with them, to develop an educational plan for students experiencing difficulty with their academic progression. Guidance counselors occasionally find themselves in the role of ombudsman as they seek to assist students and teachers or administrators in resolving conflicts in their interaction. They may work with the school social worker where truancy or family problems are related significantly to the student's academic performance. The guidance counselor's specialized awareness of educational processes and resource alternatives can be valuable to students needing information or an awareness of options available to them.

Guidance counselors are not all assigned to public school systems, however. Many are employed in correctional systems, where they help inmates assess attitudes and skills needed to obtain productive employment after release from prison. This type of intervention generally requires collaboration with other members of the correctional team, for example, with specialists in vocational education and/or related areas. Correctional counselors also often network with the inmates' families as well as community social service agencies. Experience has demonstrated that many prisoners have never had an adequate opportunity structure within which productive learning and job opportunities were available. The correctional counselor attempts to equip inmates with personal, social, and job-related skills that will enable them to use their time more creatively while in prison and to make a smoother, better-prepared transition back into society when discharged. Under most circumstances, each released inmate is assigned to a parole officer, who will continue to provide counseling and assistance with job opportunities and family-related problems.

Rehabilitation counseling is yet another form of guidance counseling. Most states have established agencies to help individuals with physical or mental disabilities in identifying competencies and securing academic or vocational training that will enable them to find employment. These counselors may also help clients get specialized medical treatment for enhancement of physical, mental, and social capacities. Rehabilitation counselors are, by the nature of their specialization, heavily involved in teamwork and networking with other human and vocational service workers in securing resources that will assist their clients in achieving their productive potential. If successful, the client's level of independence will increase along with greater self-esteem and employability.

Guidance counselors usually are required to have an advanced degree as well as specialized coursework. In general, required coursework does not prepare the counselor for psychotherapy or long-term counseling.

Employment Counselors

Professionals who focus on assisting clients in locating employment, assessing their skill levels, and enrolling in educational courses designed to prepare them for skill development and ultimate employment often are identified as "employment counselors." Their specialized knowledge of the employment market and unique skills in matching clients seeking work with the needs of employers are designed to improve the probabilities of securing satisfaction with a job as well as competence in performance on the job. Employment counselors are skilled at interpreting various tests used to determine a client's aptitude for various positions. Not only do employment counselors assist persons needing a position or those maladapted in the positions they hold to find employment of the most suitable nature, they also are available to assist them with locating the essential supports to maintain involvement on the job. For example, transportation or child care could represent barriers for an individual who otherwise needs work. Locating and referring the client to an appropriate resource may resolve those problems and produce a more favorable arrangement for meeting the demands of the job.

Employment counselors work with the business community in identifying employment needs and the skill requirements that will be necessary to provide optimum benefit for the business as well as the worker. Feedback and monitoring systems may be established as mechanisms for fine-tuning the job referral process.

Vocational education programs abound in the United States and provide instruction in a variety of areas: cosmetology, aircraft maintenance, welding, carpentry, computer technology, auto mechanics, heavy machine operations, office management, hotel administration, and many other specialty areas. Workers who are dissatisfied in their current employment or whose jobs have disappeared because of changing technology, persons reentering the job market, or new workers entering employment often find vocational education beneficial in learning and strengthening skills. Persons with disabilities also find vocational education an invaluable resource in adapting their abilities to marketable skills. Employment counselors typically are influential in helping clients use vocational educational programs that enhance development of job-related skills.

Nurses

In recent years the role of nurses has changed dramatically. Traditionally viewed as "doctors' helpers" or as pseudo-professionals whose primary responsibility was to see that the doctor's orders were dutifully carried out, contemporary nurses have emerged as professionals in their own right. Schools of nursing now focus on the psychosocial aspects of services to debilitated or hospitalized clients as well as mastery of the basic skills related to patient care. Like other professionals, nurses may specialize in a variety of areas such as pediatrics, gerontolgy, psychiatry and mental health, oncology, and other related areas. The body of knowledge required to be a professional nurse today is far different than in past decades. Emphasis on the therapeutic use of relationships and psychosocial adaptation has enhanced the nurse's ability to engage the client in the healing process. Nurses are involved in counseling roles ranging from handling stress-related illnesses to counseling with families of ill patients and collaborating with other specialists in seeking the best therapeutic treatment approaches for their clients.

Professional nurses typically receive their education from colleges or universities that have accredited schools of nursing. They earn a bachelor's degree in nursing and, after successfully passing the state board examinations, become registered nurses, or RNs. Many pursue a master's degree in nursing, and larger numbers are enrolling in PhD programs.

Other nurses may opt to pursue the licensed vocational nurses (LVN) certification. Nurses, at whatever level, play a vital role in the delivery of physical care as well as human services.

Attorneys-at-Law

Lawyers are professionals who engage in both criminal and civil matters to assist individuals in securing their rights under the law. Most communities, large or small, have practicing attorneys. Law, like other professional areas, has many subspecialties. Many lawyers are employed by large corporations and deal with contracts and their interpretation, assessing legal specifications relative to business practices and providing legal expertise essential for corporate ventures. Others are in private practice, with many handling primarily civil matters such as lawsuits, divorces, property settlements, deeds, estate management, wills, and similar civil matters. Lawyers are educated in graduate schools of law throughout the country. As professionals, they encounter a myriad of problems that have legal consequences. In some cases, such as that of divorce or child custody, the lawyer often becomes involved in a counseling role. Although many lawyers lack the appropriate educational background and expertise, clients often seek their assistance with emotional as well as legal problems. Lawyers also make referrals to appropriate agencies or other professionals when indicated.

Many of the larger communities have established legal aid clinics, which specialize in offering legal counsel to the poor or near poor. The poor, as well as the nonpoor, encounter many problems that need the attention of a legal expert, such as divorce, child custody, property settlements, and adequate defense in a court of law. Legal aid clinics are an invaluable resource for the poor. Many lawyers are employed as full-time legal counselors at the clinics, while others work part-time or volunteer their time. Legal aid clinics seek to promote justice for the poor as well as for those in better financial circumstances. Typically, law firms assign a portion of their staff time to *pro bono* ("for the public good") efforts, often representing indigent clients.

Lawyers constitute a valuable resource to the problem-solving process. Indeed, a number of social work students enter law school after receiving their BSW degree. Matters that need legal attention often are a source of stress and are responsive to the skillful intervention of the legal profession.

◢ THE NEED FOR PROFESSIONAL DIVERSITY

Although the brief discussion of selected professions is by no means complete, it does encompass the primary disciplinary areas in the human service field. Social workers and others in the helping professions need to develop an awareness of the expertise available in their practice arena. Many problems require the attention of experts from diverse areas of practice in order to move toward resolution. It also is requisite that all professionals develop an awareness of their limitations as well as strengths, if clients are to maximize the benefits they receive from those assisting them in meeting their needs.

In our complex, highly technological society, the emergence of a variety of specialists is a necessity. With the explosion of knowledge and our understanding of human needs, it would be impossible for any one person to master it all. Just as society is complex, so, we have learned, are human beings. Values vary, as do the many diverse groups with whom we hold an identity. Specialty areas have emerged in response to such diverse needs and to the understanding of the theoretical explanations of behavior. Life is a problem-solving process, and our ability to respond appropriately to those problems involves not only our personality makeup but knowledge, awareness, resources, and sensitivities as well. Invariably, all of us will at times encounter problems for which there appear no ready solutions. Often, the friendly advice of a neighbor, spouse, or confidant is sufficient in providing the perspective that will lead to an acceptable solution. At other times, professional assistance is essential in achieving a satisfactory resolution of the problem.

A question often raised relates to the likenesses and differences among the professions. What, for example, does a psychiatrist do with clients that is different from what a psychologist would do? Or a social worker? Or a pastoral counselor? And so on. All, for example, might engage in marital counseling or assist a family struggling with the behavioral problems of an adolescent. To an uninformed observer, the professional response to those problems may appear to be approximately the same. Clients see the professional for an hour or so per week, the content of the interaction consists primarily of verbal interaction, and generally the client is given specific tasks to work on until the next visit. The professionals may contact other social systems related to the client's functioning, such as the school system or employment system. What, then, constitutes the difference? In part, although not exclusively, the differences may lie in the theoretical perspective that the professional brings to bear on the problem. The specialized emphasis on individual psychodynamics as reflected in psychiatry and psychology often varies with social work's emphasis on the systems/ecological framework and the relationship between the person and the environment within which the person functions. Also, social work's mastery of and emphasis on utilizing community resources are distinct from the typical approaches used in psychiatry and psychology.

Social work emphasizes a holistic approach that focuses on enhancing the strengths of the client. Recognizing that stress may be generated by the lack of resources as well as intrapsychic conflict, social workers also may help their clients with concrete resources, such as locating a job, adequate housing, health care services, child care, or other needed services. The various roles that the social worker plays, such as advocate, broker, enabler, case manager, and intervener, often are essential to creating an environment in which clients can move toward addressing their own needs.

The cooperative relationship and respect that exist among the helping professions are necessary if the optimum helping environment is to be attained. Social workers have clients who need psychiatric treatment, or the special services provided by a clinical or counseling psychologist or pastoral counselor. Many clients are assisted by referrals to the employment counselor, and students experiencing difficulty in school adaptation benefit by referrals to the school guidance counselor. Positive interaction and collaboration among these professionals enrich the service systems and increase the probabilities of securing a better quality of intervention for clients in need. Each profession has its own distinct professional culture, and an awareness of these varying cultures should promote more appropriate referrals.

THE BACCALAUREATE SOCIAL WORKER AND OTHER PROFESSIONS

Baccalaureate social workers (BSWs) typically function as generalist practitioners and hold a unique position in the professional community. Their attention to a great variety of human needs demands skills as counselors, resource finders, case managers, evaluators, advocates, brokers, enablers, and problem solvers. The BSW's awareness of community resources and the ability to use them skillfully in the problem-solving process are particularly valuable in securing the needed assistance for clients. BSWs work in varied social service agencies and community settings.

In cases representing a myriad of problems, the BSW may become engaged as a case manager, with a focus on securing referrals to appropriate resources. The worker may also become involved in providing the necessary supports to insure that the clients use the services. In this role, the BSW would continue to monitor and coordinate the treatment effort, with all of the intervention system components cooperating.

The BSW may serve as a vital link between community professionals. The special knowledge related to individual, family, and community functioning within the systems/ecological framework helps the BSW identify the appropriate referral resources, engage them, and become an essential component of the helping process.

SUMMARY

Social work is a complex profession. It relies on a strong value base and code of ethics, the development of practice skills in direct practice, community organization, and research as well as in administration and planning. All social work practice is based on knowledge of human behavior and social organizations. In this chapter, we discussed the attributes of the profession and clarified the definition of social work as a distinctive profession.

We also examined why people have problems. Problems stem from heredity and genetics, socialization, cultural differences, environmental factors, and deficiencies in the opportunity structure. The brief history of the development of social work included in this chapter should give the reader a basis for understanding factors that led to the emergence of the profession and the need it fulfills in the community. We also briefly discussed the levels of social work education and career opportunities available for individuals interested in entering the helping professions. In subsequent chapters, we will explain each aspect of social work methodology in greater detail.

Other prominent community professionals seek to help clients with problems of adaptation. We attempted to identify similarities and differences among the professions. The need for interprofessional collaboration was examined in relation to obtaining the greatest expertise for clients in the intervention process.

KEY TERMS

Charity Organization Society
client system
community organization
competencies
Council on Social Work
  Education (CSWE)
direct practice
ethics
National Association of Social
  Workers (NASW)
opportunity structure
pastoral counselor

private practice
psychiatry
psycho-biology
psychology
psychometric instruments
social agencies
social casework
social group work
social work
social worker
socialization
sociologist

DISCUSSION QUESTIONS

1. Identify the factors that contribute to social problems and provide an illustration for each factor.

2. Discuss why values and ethics are important in the practice of social work.

3. Identify the various methods of social work practice and illustrate how those methods are both alike and different.

4. Justify the history of the social work profession in relationship to its contribution to society.

5. What distinguishes BSW and MSW levels of social work practice?

6. What is the purpose of a code of ethics for a profession? To the individual social worker?

7. What is the baccalaureate social worker's role in working with other professionals in addressing client needs?

REFERENCES

Baer, Betty L., and Ronald Federico. 1978. *Educating the baccalaureate social worker.* Cambridge: Ballinger.

Coon, Dennis, 1982. *Essentials of psychology.* 2d ed. St. Paul, Minn.: West.

Council on Social Work Education. 1995. *Statistics on social work education in the United States: 1994.* Washington, D.C.: Author.

Greenwood, Ernest. 1957. Attributes of a profession. *Social Work* 2 (3): 44–45.

Leiby, James. 1978. *A history of social welfare and social work in the United States.* New York: Columbia University Press.

National Association of Social Workers. 1973. *Standards for social service manpower.* New York: Author.

Piccard, Betty J. 1988. *An introduction to social work: A primer.* Homewood, Ill.: Dorsey.

Pumphrey, Ralph E., and Muriel W. Pumphrey. 1961. *The heritage of American social work.* New York: Columbia University Press.

Richmond, Mary. 1917. *Social diagnosis.* New York: Russell Sage.

———. 1922. *What is social casework?* New York: Russell Sage.

U.S. Department of Labor. 1982. *Occupational outlook handbook. 1982–83.* Washington, D.C.: GPO.

———. 1986. *Occupational outlook handbook, 1986–87.* Washington, D.C.: GPO.

Zastrow, Charles, 1986. *Introduction to social welfare institutions.* 3d ed. Chicago: Dorsey.

SUGGESTED FURTHER READINGS

Bell, Winfred. *Contemporary social work practice.* 2d ed. New York: Macmillan.

Dubois, Brenda, and Karla K. Miley. 1990. *Social work: An empowering profession.* Boston: Allyn and Bacon.

Epstein, Laura. 1980. *Helping people: The task-centered approach.* St. Louis: Mosby.

Goldstein, H. 1990. The knowledge base of social work practice: Theory, wisdom, analogue, or art? *Families in Society,* 71: 32–43.

Hyslop, J. H. 1988. Causes of poverty. *The Charities Review,* 7: 383–9.

Johnson, L. 1989. *Social work practice: A generalist approach.* Boston: Allyn and Bacon.

Lowenberg, F., and R. Dolgoff. 1988. *Ethical decisions for social work practice.* 3rd ed. Itasca, IL: F. E. Peacock.

Macarov, D. 1995. *Social welfare: Structure and practice.* Thousand Oaks, CA: Sage.

Moxley, D. P. 1989. *The practice of case management.* Newberry Park, CA: Sage.

National Association of Social Workers. 1981. *Standards for the classification of social work practice: Policy statement 4.* Silver Springs, Md.: NASW Task Force on Sector Classification.

Norback, Craig. 1980. *Careers encyclopedia.* Homewood, IL: Dow Jones-Irwin.

Wells, C. 1989. *Social work: Day to day.* 2d ed. New York: Longman.

CHAPTER 3

THE SYSTEMS/ECOLOGICAL PERSPECTIVE

Understanding Social Work and Social Welfare

Juan, a 12-year-old Mexican American boy, is in the seventh grade in an urban school in California. His teachers are concerned about him and are recommending to Christina Herrera, the school social worker, that he be enrolled in the school's dropout prevention program. Recently, Juan has been socializing during school with a group of much older students who are members of a local gang. He has been skipping classes, not completing class assignments, fighting with other students, and arguing with his teachers when they confront him about his behavior. During the past two weeks, he has been caught smoking marijuana and pulling a knife on a classmate. Ms. Herrera has talked with both Juan and his mother. She has suggested that Juan participate in a school support group and has referred Juan and his mother to the local teen/parent outreach center for counseling as soon as a counseling slot is available. Juan's mother is very concerned about him. But she also has indicated to Ms. Herrera that she is under a great deal of stress and is angry that Juan is adding to it.

Juan lives in a one-bedroom apartment with his mother and his younger brother, who is 5 years old. Six months ago, Juan's parents divorced, and his father moved to a neighboring state 300 miles away. Juan always had a fairly close relationship with both his parents. Although he knew that they fought a lot and that his father drank and lost his job, he was surprised when his parents told him that they were getting a divorce.

When Juan's father moved out, his mother had to get an extra job to make ends meet. The family also had to move into a small apartment in another part of the city. Juan's mother's relatives and friends, all devout Catholics, were very much against the divorce and have not been at all supportive. When she is not working, Juan's mother spends much of her time crying or sleeping. At first, Juan tried hard to be supportive of his mother, cooking meals, cleaning the house, and taking care of his little brother. But at times he doesn't cook or clean exactly the way his mother wants him to. When his brother gets noisy, Juan gets in trouble for not keeping him quiet. Lately, Juan's mother has begun yelling at or hitting Juan when this happens. Because she was abused as a child, Juan's mother feels guilty when she gets so angry at Juan, but she cannot understand why he can't be more supportive when she is trying so hard to keep the family together.

Juan has felt abandoned by everyone since the divorce. His mother is usually angry at him, and his two long-time friends, who come from two-parent families, seem less friendly to him. When they do ask him to do things with them, he usually can't anyway because he has to take care of his younger brother or he doesn't have any money. Transportation is also a problem, since Juan's friends live across town in his former neighborhood. Although he used to do well in school, Juan has lost interest in his classes. He can't get used to the new school, and he doesn't know any of the teachers there. But he has several new friends who seem to accept him. They are older, and their interest in him makes him feel important. Juan is excited that they want him to be a member of their gang. As long as school is so boring, he can spend time with them during the day and still take care of his brother after school. But he is seriously considering running away from home and moving in with one of the gang members, who lives with his older brother. The friend's older brother recently got out of prison and has promised that Juan can make a lot of money as a drug runner for him. ■

Juan's case illustrates the many factors that influence how people react to what is going on in their lives. Juan's present situation is affected by his developmental needs as he enters adolescence; his relationships with his mother, father, younger brother, friends, and school personnel; his father's alcoholism and unemployment; his parents' divorce; the fact that his mother was abused as a child; his family's tenuous economic situation; the lack of positive social support available from relatives, friends, the workplace, the school, the church, and the neighborhood to the members of Juan's family; the lack of programs available to divorced parents and teens in Juan's community; Juan's cultural and ethnic background; and community and societal attitudes about divorce, female-headed households, and intervention in family matters. From Juan's perspective, the family system, the economic system, the political system, the religious system, the educational system, and the social welfare system have not been there to meet his needs. Yet he continually interacts with all of these individuals, groups, and social structures and also depends on all of them in some way.

In this chapter we explore frameworks used by social workers to understand social problems and issues faced by individuals and families in today's world. The **systems/ecological framework** is an umbrella framework used by generalist social work practitioners with Bachelor of Social Work (BSW) degrees to understand both social welfare problems and individual problems and guide the various interventions social workers use when helping clients.   ■

◩ THE IMPACT OF THEORETICAL FRAMEWORKS ON INTERVENTION

All individuals perceive what is going on in their lives and in the world somewhat differently. For example, an argument between a parent and a teenager over almost any topic usually is perceived quite differently by the parent and the teenager. People view their environments and the forces that shape them differently depending on many things: biological factors, such as their own heredity and intelligence; personal life experiences, including their childhood; ethnicity and culture; and level and type of education. How people perceive their world determines to a large extent how involved they are in it and how they interact with it. Women who perceive themselves as unimportant and powerless may continue to let their partners beat them and may not be successful at stopping the abuse or being self-sufficient if they decide to leave the batterer. On the other hand, women who perceive that they have some control over their lives and feel better about themselves may get into a counseling program and get a job at which they can be successful.

Professionals from different disciplines also view the world somewhat differently. A physicist, for example, is likely to have a different explanation about how the world began than a philosopher or a minister. A law enforcement officer and a social worker may disagree about how best to handle young teens who join gangs and harass the elderly. A physician may treat a patient who complains of headaches by meeting the patient's physical needs, whereas a psychologist may treat the person's emotional needs through individual counseling to ascertain how the individual can better cope. The way professionals who work with people perceive the world largely determines the type of intervention they use in helping people.

Worldview is an important aspect for social workers, for two reasons. Not only do they continually have to be aware of their own worldviews and how this affects their choices of intervention in helping people, they also must be aware of the worldviews of others. Some worldviews have more influence on world, national, state, and local policies and the ways our society at all levels is structured than others. One key to being an effective social worker is to understand those influences and how they have shaped current policies and systems and how those influences have affected at-risk and diverse populations. An important aspect of social work is to help people find their voices to advocate for themselves and to be allies for them when they cannot (Shriver 1995, 15–16).

Joe Shriver, a social work educator, suggests the following criteria for analyzing worldviews, or ways of thinking (1995, 7–8):

- Does this perspective contribute to preserving and restoring human dignity?

- Does this perspective recognize the benefits of, and does it celebrate, human diversity?

- Does this perspective assist us in transforming ourselves and our society so that we welcome the voices, the strengths, the ways of knowing, the energies of us all?

- Does this perspective help us all (ourselves and the people with whom we work) to reach our fullest potential?

- Does the perspective or theory reflect the participation and experiences of males and females, economically well-off and poor; white people and people of color; gay men, lesbians, bi-sexuals, and heterosexuals; old and young; temporarily able-bodied people and people with disabilities?

Worldviews are sometimes called paradigms or frameworks. In our society many individuals are currently rethinking ways to view critical social issues such as poverty and health care. The profession of social work needs a framework that helps it understand how and why such views are changing and how to work for social change during this shift in viewpoints.

The Difference between Causal Relationships and Association

In the past, many professionals who dealt with human problems tended to look at those problems in terms of **cause and effect.** A cause-and-effect relationship suggests that if x causes y, then by eliminating x, we also eliminate y. For example, if we say that smoking is the sole cause of lung cancer, then eliminating smoking would mean eliminating lung cancer. This limited worldview presents problems for many reasons. First, even in relation to smoking, we know that it does not always cause lung cancer, and sometimes people who do not smoke get lung cancer. The relationship between smoking and lung cancer is also not always unidimensional. Other intervening variables or factors, such as living in a city with heavy smog, also increase a person's chances of getting lung cancer. The chances of getting lung cancer are more than twice as great for a person who smokes and lives in a city with heavy smog than for someone who does neither. The causal relationship viewpoint is not usually appropriate when examining social welfare problems.

Juan's case definitely cannot be discussed in terms of a cause-and-effect relationship. Are the situations Juan is experiencing caused by the abuse his mother suffered as a child, by the divorce, by his father's drinking too much, by his mother's worries about money, by his use of marijuana, by his association with gang members, by the limited social support system available, or by discrimination because he and his family are Mexican American? It is unlikely that one of these factors caused Juan's present situation, but they all probably contributed to it in some way. In looking at factors related to social welfare problems, it is more appropriate to view them in **association** with the problem, meaning that all factors are connected to or relate to the problem, rather than saying that one isolated factor, or even several factors, *directly* causes a social problem.

The Need: A Conceptual Framework for Understanding Social Welfare Problems

The fact that there are obviously many factors associated with or that contribute to social welfare problems suggests the need for a broad theory or framework to understand them. First, it is useful to define theory and to discuss why theories are important. A **theory** is a way of clearly and logically organizing a set of facts or ideas.

All of us use theories in our daily lives. We are continually taking in facts, or information, from our environment and trying to order them in some way to make sense about what is going on around us. Although some of our theories may be relatively unimportant to everyone else, they are useful to us in being able to describe, understand, and predict our environment. Most important, theories are useful in helping us to change either the environment or the ways we relate to it. For example, a college student has a roommate who always turns up the compact disc player to full volume whenever the student gets a telephone call. Over the year that they have shared a room, the student has gathered a great deal of information about when this happens. She is now able to articulate a theory she has based on this information to describe the situation, to understand why it happens, and to be able to predict when her roommate will exhibit this behavior. Making sense of the facts in this situation has made it easier for her to deal with this trying behavior and try to change it. What theories might you suggest to understand why this roommate situation is occurring? A theory can be relatively insignificant, such as the one just described, or it can have major importance to many people.

A theory can be used to describe something, such as Juan's family situation; to explain or to understand something, such as why a family in crisis would exhibit some of the behaviors of Juan's family; to predict something, such as what behaviors another family in a similar situation might experience; or to change something, such as Juan's ability to get his needs met from his environment in a more healthy way. The same set of facts can be ordered in different ways, depending on who is doing the ordering and the worldview of that person or group. If you think of facts as individual bricks, and a theory as a way of ordering the bricks so that they make sense, you can visualize several different theories from the same set of facts, just as you can visualize a number of different structures built from the same set of bricks.

A good theory must have three attributes, if it is to be widely used. First, it must be **inclusive,** or able to explain consistently the same event in the same way. The more inclusive a theory is, the better able it is to explain facts in exactly the same way each time an event occurs. For example, if the person in the roommate situation could describe, explain, or predict the roommate's behavior exactly the same way every single time the telephone rang, she would have a highly inclusive theory.

A good theory must also be **generalizable.** This means that one must be able to generalize what happens in one situation to other similar situations. Even though the person may be able to explain the facts about her roommate in a highly inclusive way, it is not likely that exactly the same situation would occur with all roommates in the same university, much less in the same city, the United States, or the world. The more a theory can be generalized beyond the single situation it is describing or explaining, the better it is as theory.

Finally, a good theory must be **testable.** This means that we must be able to measure it in some way to ensure that it is accurate and valid. This is the major reason why we have very limited theory in understanding and predicting social welfare problems and human behavior. Only limited measures have been developed relating to what goes on inside people's minds, their attitudes, and their behaviors. How do we measure, for example, behavior change such as child abuse, particularly when it most often happens behind closed doors? Can we give psychological tests to measure attitudes that would lead to abuse, or can we measure community factors such as unemployment to predict child abuse? Any time we try to measure human behavior or environmental influences, we have difficulty doing so. This does not mean that we should stop doing research or trying to develop higher-level theories. In fact, this is an exciting area of social work, and the problems merely point out the need to develop skilled social work practitioners and researchers who can devote more attention to the development of good social work theory.

Because social work draws its knowledge base from many disciplines, many theories are applicable to social work. These include psychological theories such as Freud's theory of psychoanalysis and its derivatives, economic and political theories, sociological theories such as Durkheim's theory relating to suicide, and developmental theories such as Jean Piaget's. All of these theoretical perspectives are relevant to social work and an understanding of social welfare problems, but looking at only one limits understanding and, in turn, intervention. Thus, it is important to focus on a framework or perspective that allows us to view social problems and appropriate responses that incorporate a multitude of factors and a multitude of possible responses.

◢ THE SYSTEMS/ECOLOGICAL FRAMEWORK

Social workers, more than any other group of professionals, have focused both on the individual and beyond the individual to the broader environment since the professional casework of the Charity Organization Societies and the settlement house reform movements of Jane Addams (Germain and Gitterman 1995). Consider the definitions of social work discussed in Chapter 2. All focus on enhancing social functioning of the individual or in some way addressing the relationships, the interactions, and the interdependence between persons and their environments. This is exemplified by the many roles social workers play within the social welfare system. True generalists, they advocate for changing living conditions of the mentally ill and obtaining welfare reform legislation that enables the poor to succeed in obtaining employment and economic self-sufficiency; empower clients to advocate for themselves to reduce violence in their communities; lead groups of children who have experienced divorce; educate the community about parenting, AIDS, and child abuse; and provide individual, family, and group counseling to clients. The profession needs a broad framework that allows for identifying all of the diverse, complex factors associated with a social welfare problem or an individual problem; understanding how all of the factors interact to contribute to the situation; and determining an intervention strategy or strategies, which can range from intervention with a single individual to an entire society and can incorporate a variety of roles. Such a framework must account for individual differences, cultural diversity, and growth and change at the individual, organizational, community, and societal levels.

The generalist foundation of social work is based on a systems framework, which also incorporates an ecological perspective. The authors choose to use the term *systems/ecological framework* rather than *theory* because the systems/ecological perspective is much broader and more loosely constructed than a theory. It is most useful in understanding social welfare problems and situations and determining specific theories that are appropriate for intervention. Additionally, whereas various systems (see for example, works by Talcott Parsons, Max Siporin, Allen Pincus, and Anne Minahan) and ecological approaches (see for example, works by Uri Bronfenbrenner, James Garbarino, Carel Germain, Alex Gitterman, and Carol Meyer) have been extensively described in the literature, they have not been tested or delineated with enough specificity to be considered theories. A number of advocates of the systems/ecological framework, in fact, refer to it as a metatheory, or an umbrella framework that can be used as a base from which to incorporate additional theories.

A general systems framework has been discussed in the literature of many disciplines—medicine, biology, anthropology, psychology, economics, political science, sociology, and education—for many years, and has been used somewhat differently in each discipline. Its principles, as well as similar principles associated with social systems, or systems associated with living things, have been incorporated into the social work literature since the beginning of social work. Mary Richmond, the social work pioneer discussed in Chapter 2, wrote in 1922, ''The worker is no more occupied with abnormalities in the individual than in the environment, is no more able to neglect the one than the other'' (98–99). Since then, many social work proponents, such as Hearn, Pincus and Minahan, Siporin, Perlman, and Bartlett, have developed specific approaches or explored varying aspects of social work from within the boundaries of the systems/ecological framework.

More recently, other social work theorists such as Germain, Gitterman, and Meyer have advocated an ecological perspective, which incorporates many of the same concepts as the systems framework. It should be noted that some social work theorists (Meyer 1983) clearly separate the systems perspective and the ecological perspective, and consider them two distinct frameworks. These theorists view the systems framework as largely relating to the *structure*, or the systemic properties of cases, which helps us to focus on how variables are related and to order systems within the environment according to complexity. In contrast, they view the ecological perspective as one that focuses more on *relationships* of person and environment, with greater emphasis on interactions and transactions than on structure. Others (Compton and Galaway 1994) incorporate the very similar concepts of both and refer to one framework, the systems/ecological framework. This is the approach taken in this text. Rather than get confused over semantics, readers should focus on the broad definitions and principles of the various frameworks discussed and their commonalities rather than their differences. We emphasize these important points in understanding a systems/ecological perspective and its significant contributions to social work.

The Perspective of Systems Theory

Systems theory was first used to explain the functioning of the human body, which was seen as a major system that incorporated a number of smaller systems: the skeletal system, the muscular system, the endocrine system, the circulatory system, and so on. Medical practitioners, even ones in ancient Greece, realized that when one aspect of the human body failed to function effectively, it also affected the way that other systems within the body functioned and, in turn, affected the way the human body as a whole functioned. This led to further exploration of the relationships between subparts of living organisms. (For example, Lewis Thomas's *The Life of a Cell* clearly articulates the intricate interrelations among the many complex parts of a single cell that enable the cell to maintain itself and to reproduce.)

System

Von Bertalanffy (1968, 38) defines a **system** as ''a set of units with relationships among them.'' A system can also be defined as a whole, an entity composed of separate but interacting and interdependent parts. The early Greek physicians, for example, viewed the body as the larger system and the body's various smaller systems as interacting and interdependent parts. A family can be viewed as a system composed of separate but interdependent and interacting individual family members.

From a global perspective, the world can be viewed as a system composed of separate but interdependent and interacting nations. One advantage of the systems/ecological framework is that it is a conceptual framework and can be applied in many different ways to many different situations.

Synergy

The contribution from biology to systems theory is the emphasis on the concept that the whole is greater than the sum of its parts—that is, when all of the smaller systems or subsystems of an organism function in tandem, they produce a larger system that is far more grand and significant than the combination of those smaller systems working independently. The larger system, when it functions optimally, is said to achieve **synergy,** or the combined energy from the smaller parts that is greater than the total if those parts functioned separately. Imagine for a moment that your instructor for this course gives you an exam on the chapters you have covered thus far in this text. Each student takes the exam separately, and scores of each student are listed. The lowest score is 50; the highest is 85. Now, suppose that your instructor decides to let the entire class take the exam together. Each person in the class now functions as part of the total group, together solving each exam question. As a class, your score on the exam is 100. Your class has demonstrated the concept of the whole being greater than the sum of its parts, or synergy.

Boundaries

An important aspect of a system is the concept of **boundary.** A system can be almost anything; but by its definition, it usually is given some sort of boundary or point at which one system ends and another begins. The system's environment encompasses everything beyond this boundary. For example, the human body can be seen as a system, as discussed earlier, with the skin as a boundary and the various body subsystems as smaller components of the larger system. From a different perspective, the human mind can be seen as a system, with Freud's id, ego, and superego as components within that system that interact to form a whole greater than any of the three components alone: the human mind.

An individual can also be part of a larger system; for example, a family system might include one or two parents, a child, and the family dog. We might wish to expand the boundaries of the family system and include the grandparents and the aunts and uncles. We can establish larger systems, such as school systems, communities, cities, states, or nations, and focus on their interactions and interdependence with each other. We can also look at a political system, an economic system, a religious system, and a social welfare system and the ways that those broader systems interact with each other.

The important thing to remember when using a systems perspective is that the systems that we define and the boundaries that we give those systems are conceptual; that is, we can define them in whatever ways make the most sense in looking at the broad social welfare or the more narrow individual problem that we are addressing. For example, if we were to conceptualize Juan's family as a social system, we could include within its boundaries his mother, his younger brother, and Juan. We may also choose to include Juan's father as part of his family system (even though he is out of the home, he is still part of Juan's life, and his absence is a major emotional issue for Juan). We could also include grandparents or other extended family members, because although they are not actively involved either physically or emotionally in any supportive way with the family, they are a possible source of support since they have been very involved in the past (see Figure 3.1). If we were looking at another family system, however, we might well include a larger number of other members. The systems/ecological framework is a useful way to organize data to help understand a situation, and its flexibility allows us to define systems and their boundaries in a number of ways.

Open and Closed Systems

While we can draw boundaries wherever it seems appropriate when using a systems/ecological framework, it is also important that we be able to ascertain how permeable those boundaries are. Some systems

FIGURE 3.1   **USING AN ECO-MAP TO UNDERSTAND JUAN'S FAMILY SITUATION**

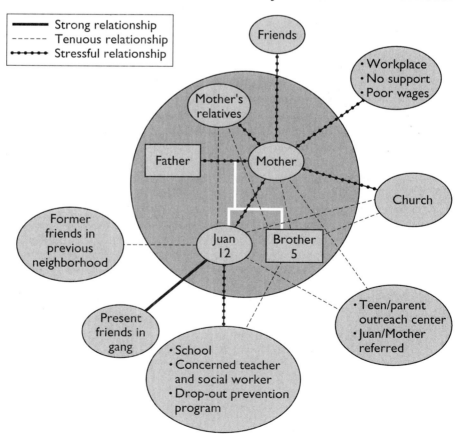

have easily permeated boundaries between units (e.g., people) in the system and those outside; we call those systems **open systems.** Some families exemplify open systems. Those are the families that readily incorporate others; when someone rings the doorbell at dinnertime, a plate is always added. A cousin or a friend may live with the family for a short or a long time period, and it is often difficult to tell exactly who is a family member and who is not. There are internal boundaries within systems as well. Sometimes boundaries can be too open. For example, in some families members become overly involved in each others' lives. In other families parents do not set consistent limits for their children and there are no clear boundaries between the parents and the children. Unclear boundaries within systems can lead to family problems, such as incest. But healthy open systems with clear boundaries are likely to achieve synergy because of their members' willingness to accept new energy from their interactions with the broader environment.

On the other hand, some families represent **closed systems;** they have extremely closed boundaries and are very tightly knit. Although they might get along well with each other, they are isolated and rarely incorporate other individuals into their system. They may have special traditions that are for family members only. Sometimes boundaries can be too closed. For example, an abusive husband may not allow his wife to go anywhere unless he goes along.

Before Juan's father began drinking heavily, his family was a fairly open system. Although his family did many activities together just as a family, they also socialized a great deal with friends and relatives. If Juan's friends were playing at his house, they were often invited to have dinner or to participate in family activities. When Juan's father's drinking increased, his family system became more closed. Juan's mother tried to limit his father's drinking by limiting the family social activities. When relatives became more critical of his drinking, Juan's family stopped socializing with them to avoid being confronted about the problem. Because Juan's father lost his temper easily when he drank, Juan stopped inviting his friends over and began playing at their houses instead. The family became more isolated. The isolation continued, and the family system remained closed when Juan's father left and his parents divorced.

Organizations also may be open or closed systems. Some organizations welcome new members and readily expand their activities to meet new interests. Others are very closed and do not encourage new members, making those that try to enter the organization feel unwelcome and shunning new ideas. Communities and other social structures can also be viewed as open or closed. Juan's new school, for example, is a somewhat closed system, which has made his making friends and feeling as if he fits in difficult.

Usually, the more closed a system is, the less able it is to derive positive energy from other systems. Over time, closed systems tend to use up their own energy and to develop **entropy,** which means that they tend to lose their ability to function and can eventually stagnate and die. The more isolated Juan's family becomes, the less energy it takes in from the environment, the less energy there then is within the family system for family members, and the less able the family is to function. The family system becomes more and more lethargic and will eventually either change or die, with the family separating and members becoming part of other family systems. If, for example, Juan's mother were to become extremely abusive and Juan were to become involved in the gang and serious criminal activities, his brother might be placed in foster care and Juan in a correctional facility for youth.

Interactions and Interrelations

Boundaries and open and closed systems are *structural* aspects of systems. An additional feature of the systems/ecological framework is its emphasis on the *interactions and interrelations* between units rather than on the systems or subsystems themselves. This lends itself well to the need for focusing on associations among large numbers of factors rather than on cause-and-effect relationships between two factors. The interactions and interrelatedness between systems suggest constant motion, fluidity, and change. The relatedness and interactions also incorporate the concept that a change or movement in one part of the system, or in one system, will have an impact on the larger system, or other systems, as well. Imagine a room full of constantly moving Ping-Pong balls, each representing a system or a subsystem of a larger system. Hitting one Ping-Pong ball across the room will change the movement of the other balls. Similarly, a change in the economic system (for example, inflation) will result in changes in other systems: the educational system could be affected because fewer students could afford to go to college; the social welfare system could be affected because more people would have financial difficulties and need public assistance and social services; the criminal justice system could be affected because more persons might turn to crime; and the political system could be affected because the dissatisfied populace might not reelect the party in office.

The results of interactions and interrelatedness between systems can also be seen when viewing Juan's family. His father's drinking led to his job loss, which then resulted in an increased pattern of drinking. Both of these factors affected his parents' relationships with each other, or the marital system; the parents' relationships with Juan and his younger brother, or the parent-child system; the communication patterns between the family as a system; and relationships between Juan's family system and other systems beyond the family, such as his father's workplace, his family's church, and Juan's school.

Such interactions and interrelatedness occur continually. There are usually constant flows of energy within and across systems. This creates natural tensions, which are viewed as healthy if communication is open, because the energy flow creates growth and change. Feedback among systems is an important part of the systems/ecological perspective, which emphasizes communication. It is important that social workers and others who work within and across various systems understand the goals of those systems and their communication patterns. In unhealthy systems, for example, the various members of the system may be communicating in certain ways and may have certain unspoken goals that maintain the system because its members are afraid to change the system or the system is in some way productive for them. In a family such as Juan's where a parent is an alcoholic, the other parent or an older child may perpetuate the alcoholism and unconsciously try to keep the family system as it is because the nonalcoholic may see his or her role as one of caretaking—keeping the family together and protecting the younger children from the alcoholism. If the family system changes, the nonalcoholic parent or older child will no longer be able to maintain that role and thus may try to force the system back to the way it once was.

Steady State

Another important concept of the systems/ecological framework is that of **steady state,** in which systems are not static but are steadily moving. The concept of steady state means that the system is constantly adjusting to move toward its goal while maintaining a certain amount of order and stability, giving and receiving energy in fairly equal amounts to maintain equilibrium. A healthy system, then, may be viewed as one that is not in upheaval but is always ebbing and flowing to achieve both stability and growth. If Juan and his family receive counseling and other support from the broader environment, his family system should achieve equilibrium. The system will not stop changing but will move toward its goals in a less disruptive manner.

Equifinality

One last concept of the systems/ecological framework is that of **equifinality,** or the concept that the final state of a system can be achieved in many different ways. Because there are many ways to interpret a given situation, there are usually many options for dealing with it. A number of alternatives can be considered, for example, when working with Juan and his family to help them function better as individuals and as a family unit. Options could include individual and family counseling, support or therapeutic groups for Juan and his mother, a child care program for his younger brother, increasing interactions between Juan and his father, enrollment in a chemical dependency program for Juan's father, enrollment in a job-training program for Juan's mother and/or father, involvement in positive recreational programs for Juan, and membership in a supportive church. Although not all of these options might be realistic for Juan and his family, various combinations of them could lead to the same positive results. The concept of equifinality is especially important to social workers because their role is to help clients determine what is best for them, and clients' choices are as diverse as the clients themselves.

Critiques of the Systems/Ecological Framework

One criticism of the systems/ecological framework in social work is that it encompasses the broad environment yet ignores the psychosocial and the intrapsychic aspects of the individual. Proponents of the systems/ecological framework argue, however, that the individual is perceived as a highly valued system itself, and that intrapsychic aspects and psychosocial aspects, which incorporate the individual's capacity and motivation for change, are parts of any system involving individuals that cannot and should not be ignored. The framework's inclusiveness incorporates the biological, psychological, sociological, and cultural aspects of developing individuals and their interactions with the broader environment. In fact, the systems/ecological framework is often referred to as a bio-psycho-social-cultural framework.

Another criticism of the systems/ecological framework is that, because it incorporates everything, it is too complicated, making it easy to miss important aspects of a situation. The ecological perspective articulated by social scientists Uri Bronfenbrenner and James Garbarino attempts to address this concern. Bronfenbrenner and Garbarino incorporate individual developmental aspects into the systems perspective of the broader environment, but they break the system into different levels, or layers of the environment. They suggest that for all individuals, both risks and opportunities exist at each of these environmental levels. Opportunities within the environment encourage an individual to meet needs and to develop as a healthy, well-functioning person. Risks are either direct threats to healthy development or the absence of opportunities that facilitate healthy individual development.

Levels of the Environment

Bronfenbrenner (1979) and Garbarino (1992) suggest that risks and opportunities can be found at all levels of the environment. They describe these levels as being like a series of Russian eggs, with a large egg cut in half that opens to reveal a smaller egg, that also opens to reveal a still smaller egg, that opens to reveal a still smaller egg (see Figure 3.2 and Table 3.1). They suggest that we consider the tiniest egg to be the **microsystem level,** which includes the individual and all persons and groups that incorporate the individual's day-to-day environment. The focus at this level would incorporate the individual's level of functioning, intellectual and emotional capacities, and motivation; the impact of life experiences; and the interactions and connections between that individual and others in the immediate environment. Also, the focus at this level would be on whether the relationships are positive or negative, whether the messages and regard for the individual are consistent across individuals and groups, and whether the individual is valued and respected. Juan's microsystem level, for example, includes all of his own personal characteristics such as his biological makeup and intelligence, and his culture and gender, as well as his interactions and connections with his mother, brother, father, teachers, and friends. His mother and his old friends, as well as the social worker, could be viewed as providing opportunity to Juan, while his new friends could be viewed as providing both opportunity through peer support and risk through drug use and skipping of school.

The next level of the system is termed the **mesosystem level.** A mesosystem involves the relationship between two microsystems that are linked by some person who exists in both microsystems. For example, because Juan is part of his family and his school, he provides the link between these two microsystems. The interactions in one microsystem influence the interactions of the others. For example, the conflicting messages to Juan from his school and family settings versus his peer setting had an impact on Juan and can be seen as environmental risks. While his mother and school personnel advocated against skipping school and experimenting with marijuana, his new peers encouraged him to become involved in these activities. His mother's involvement with the school social worker, however, can be viewed as a mesosystem opportunity for Juan.

The third level is the **exosystem level.** This level includes community-level factors that may not relate directly to the individual but affect the

---

FIGURE 3.2   **THE LEVELS OF THE ECOLOGICAL SYSTEM**

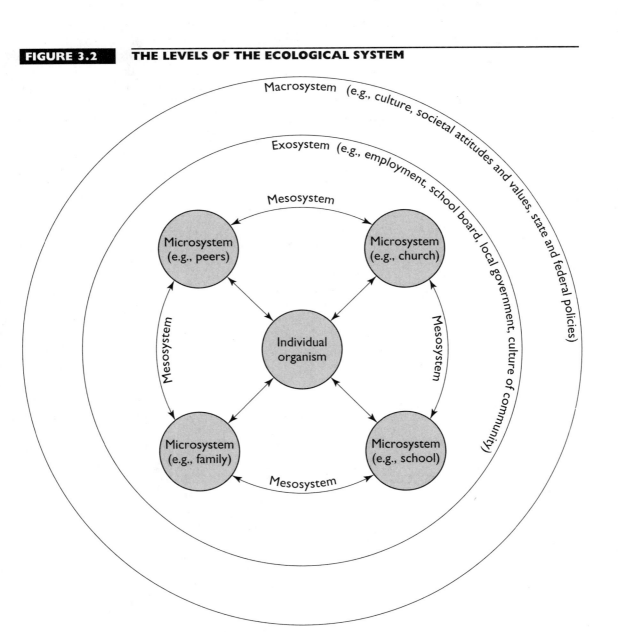

TABLE 3.1   **HOW LEVELS OF THE ENVIRONMENT AFFECT THE INDIVIDUAL**

Ecological Level	Definition	Examples	Issues Affecting Person
Microsystem	Situations in which the person has face-to-face contact with influential others	Family, school, workplace, peer group, church	Is the person regarded positively? Is the person accepted? Is the person reinforced for competent behavior? Is the person exposed to enough diversity in roles and relationship? Are the person's culture and ethnicity valued and positively affirmed? Is the person given an active role in reciprocal relationships?
Mesosystem	Relationships between microsystems; the connections between situations	Home-school, home-workplace, home-church, school-neighborhood	Do settings respect each other? Are cultural factors respected between settings? Do settings present basic consistency in values?
Exosystem	Settings in which the person does not participate but in which significant decisions are made affecting the person or others who interact directly with the person	Place of employment of others in the person's microsystem, school board, local government, peer groups of others in the person's microsystem	Are decisions made with the interests of the person and the family in mind? How well do supports for families balance stresses for parents and children? Is diversity considered when decisions are made?
Macrosystem	"Blueprints" for defining and organizing the institutional life of the society	Ideology, social policy, shared assumptions about human nature, the "social contract"	Are some groups valued at the expense of others? Are some groups oppressed (e.g., sexism, racism)? Is there an individualistic or a collectivistic orientation? Is violence a norm?

Source: Garbarino, James. *Children and Families in the Social Environment.* 2nd Edition. (New York: Aldine de Gruyter). Copyright © 1992 Walter de Gruyter, Inc., New York.

way the individual functions. This includes factors such as the workplace policies of the parents (if they cannot take sick leave when the child is sick, for example, this has an impact on the child), school board and community policies, community attitudes and values, and economic and social factors that exist within the neighborhood and community. For Juan's family, exosystem risk factors include the lack of jobs that pay well for persons with his mother's skill level, lack of affordable child care for Juan's younger brother, and community attitudes toward divorce, Mexican Americans, and single parenting. The teen/family outreach center provides an exosystem opportunity for Juan, if it is not too overloaded with other clients.

The final level is the **macrosystem level.** This level includes societal factors such as the cultural attitudes and values of the society (for example, attitudes toward women, people of color, the poor, and violence); the role of the media in addressing or promoting social problems (some suggest, for example, that the media promotes violence and teen pregnancy); and federal legislation and other social policies that affect a given individual. Lack of governmental programs for single parents and potential school dropouts, societal attitudes toward divorce and single parents, discrimination toward Hispanics, and the media's glamorization

The systems/ecological framework allows social workers and their clients to identify both risks and opportunities in the environment that can be used to address client needs. Programs at the community level, such as Habitat for Humanity, bring together diverse groups of individuals to build homes for those who cannot otherwise afford them. The future homeowners and their families are also involved extensively.

of gangs and violence all contribute to Juan's current life situation and can be viewed as environmental risks. But in spite of these risks there are opportunities for Juan, such as democracy, freedom of religion, and education, that might not be found within other macrosystems.

Many advocates of the ecological framework as conceptualized by Bronfenbrenner and Garbarino agree that it is a derivation of systems theory and another way of defining boundaries of systems. They suggest that it is advantageous to use because it allows us to see the interdependence and interaction across levels from the microsystem level to the macrosystem level and also allows us to target intervention at a variety of levels to address social problems and individual needs. For example, we could provide individual counseling to Juan, counsel his family, and help him develop a new network of friends at the microlevel; work with Juan's mother, teachers, and peers to help them become more consistent in the messages they are conveying to Juan at the mesolevel; advocate for the establishment of a community program to assist teens who experience family problems and of low-cost child care for working parents at the exolevel; and lobby for legislation to develop national media programs that educate the public about gangs, drugs, and the working poor at the macrolevel.

Note that this framework is a guide to be used to understand how systems interact with and are shaped by the broader environment. It may not always be exactly clear at which level of the environment a factor fits, and some factors may fit at more than one level of the environment. For example, in Juan's situation, religion and the church can fit at all levels, depending on how they are conceptualized. If Juan has an individual relationship with a higher power/spiritual being, that relationship could be viewed as a microsystem relationship. Juan's interactions with individual members of his church—his priest, for example—could also be viewed as microsystem relationships. The church and Juan's family could be viewed as a mesosystem relationship, since Juan is part of both of these microsystems. The church can also be viewed at the exo level of the environment, since the attitudes, values, and policies of the church at the community level have a definite impact on how Juan and his family are perceived in the community, especially after the divorce. And likewise, the church plays a major role in shaping the norms, attitudes, and values about divorce and other issues at the societal level, and can also be a macro-level factor that shapes Juan's development. It is not as important to focus on where in the environment each factor fits as it is to focus on the interdependence and interactions between the different levels of the environment and how they influence and are influenced by the developing system being viewed (Garbarino 1992).

Problems in Living

Social workers Carel Germain and Alex Gitterman (1995) incorporate the ecological perspective somewhat differently in their approach, adding still another important way of viewing individuals within their environments. They suggest that all persons have problems at some point in their lives, or what they term "problems in living." The first problem area they discuss includes those problems associated with life transitions—marriage, the birth of a first child, movement into middle age, movement of children out of the family, and so forth. They suggest that all individuals go through such transitions, and that as a person moves from one life stage to another, transitional problems and needs develop that may need social work intervention. Juan's family, for example, is experiencing the transitions of divorce and a child moving into adolescence.

The second area Germain and Gitterman identify includes problems associated with tasks in using and influencing elements of the environment (1995). Juan's mother has had difficulty locating affordable child care for her youngest son, and Juan is having difficulty adjusting to a new school setting. The limited social networks available to Juan and his family suggest the need for intervention in this area.

A final area of focus suggested by Germain and Gitterman is that of maladaptive interpersonal problems and needs in families and groups. Juan's family, for example, has developed some of the unproductive communication patterns typically found in families where alcoholism is a problem. Although these patterns maintained the family as an intact unit for many years, they will continue to stifle individual and family growth unless they change. Germain and Gitterman reinforce the need to incorporate the transactional patterns between persons and their environment when planning any social work intervention.

In summary, a systems/ecological framework emphasizes that our lives are shaped by the choices we make, and that the environment shapes our choices, while our choices shape the way we interact with our environment. This continual interaction and cyclical perspective suggest that we cannot discuss the individual without focusing on the environment, nor the environment without considering the strong forces that individuals play in its formulation. The individual and the environment are continually adapting to each other. The primary role of the social worker is to ensure that this adaptation is mutually supportive to both the individual and the environment.

The Utility of the Systems/Ecological Framework

The systems/ecological framework is intended to be used as a mechanism to order facts about social welfare problems or individual needs in such a way that appropriate theories can be identified to further explore the problems and needs or to determine interventions. Box 3.1 examines some ways the framework aids social workers. It is useful to think of this framework as a way to "map the territory" or gather and fit together pieces of a puzzle to understand a situation. When dealing with a problem such as poverty, for example, which is addressed in Chapter 9, many individuals may have unidimensional ways of explaining the problem—it is because people are lazy, for example, or the victims of their own circumstance. A systems/ecological perspective would identify many factors—a large, complex territory and a puzzle with many pieces. Individual factors, family factors, community factors, and societal factors such as the impact of the economic system and of unemployment, racism, sexism, and so forth—all contribute to poverty in some way. Table

BOX 3.1

VALUE OF SYSTEMS/ECOLOGICAL PERSPECTIVE TO SOCIAL WELFARE PROBLEMS AND SOCIAL WORK PRACTICE

The systems/ecological perspective makes a number of valuable contributions as an organizing framework for social work practice.

1. The systems/ecological perspective allows one to deal with far more data than other models and to bring order to these large amounts of data from a variety of disciplines.

2. The concepts relating to systems are equally applicable to the wide range of clients served by social workers, including individuals, families, groups, organizations, communities, and society.

3. The systems/ecological framework allows for identifying the wide range of factors that have an impact on social welfare problems, their interrelationships, and the ways that a change in one factor affects other factors.

4. The systems/ecological framework shifts attention from characteristics of individuals or the environment to the transactions between systems and their communication patterns.

5. The systems/ecological framework views persons as actively involved with their environments, capable of adaptation and change.

6. The systems/ecological framework views systems as goal-oriented, supporting client self-determination and the client's participation in the change process.

7. If systems require constant transactions with each other to survive, the purpose of the social worker is to provide and maintain such opportunities for transactions for all populations and to work to reduce isolation of individuals and systems.

8. Social workers need to work to ensure that change and tension are not resisted in systems and to remove the notions that change and conflict are pathological.

9. Social workers need to be aware of the systems within which they work and how change within those systems affects the whole. This means that social workers must choose points of intervention with care.

10. Social workers are a social system and components of a social systems network.

Source: From *Social Work Processes* by B. Compton and B. Galaway. Copyright © 1994, 1989 Wadsworth Publishing Company; © 1984, 1979, 1975 The Dorsey Press. By permission of Brooks/Cole Publishing Company, Pacific Grove, CA 93950, a division of International Thomson Publishing Inc.

3.2 lists just some of the factors that shape the interactions between individuals and their environments.

Once the territory is mapped out or all of the puzzle pieces (or as many as possible) are obtained, then the systems/ecological framework can also allow for further exploration of certain factors, parts of the terrain, or pieces of the puzzle. This perspective also allows for individualization and diversity, which also means that cultural and gender differences are readily accounted for (see Table 3.2). Once the larger picture is obtained, we can better ascertain where to focus; whether more information is needed and in what areas; and if intervention is required, at what level and within which system or systems within the environment. One or more additional theories or frameworks can then be used to obtain more information or

TABLE 3.2	FACTORS THAT SHAPE INDIVIDUAL FUNCTIONING AND RELATIONSHIP WITH THE ENVIRONMENT

Personal Factors	Community Factors
Level of prenatal care received	Social class compared to rest of community
Intellectual capacity/ability	Ethnic/cultural/class diversity/attitudes and values
Emotional capacity/mental health	Social roles available within community
Level of social functioning	Community support
Physical health	Economic conditions
Age	Employment opportunities
Ethnicity/culture	Educational opportunities
Motivation	Environmental stress
Life stage/transitional period	
Crisis level	
Family Factors	**Societal Factors**
Support systems/availability of significant others	Societal attitudes and values
Family patterns/structure/values	Racism, sexism, poverty levels
Economic level/employment	Supportive or lack of supportive legislation/programs/policies
Level of functioning/family crisis	Media role

to guide intervention. The advantage of the systems/ecological perspective is that we are less likely to miss a major aspect of a situation or intervene inappropriately.

The Utility of Other Theories and Frameworks

Other more limiting theories and frameworks are used by social workers in their professional practice under the umbrella of the systems/ecological framework. Two useful types of frameworks include psychosocial frameworks and cognitive/behavioral frameworks (Whittaker and Tracy 1988). These and other frameworks commonly used by social workers are discussed in greater depth in Chapter 5.

Psychosocial Frameworks
Psychosocial frameworks include psychoanalytic theory, ego psychology, and life-span development frameworks. These frameworks are often used together and are not always viewed as mutually exclusive.

Psychoanalytic Theory   Psychoanalytic theory, based largely on the works of Sigmund Freud, is built on the premise that children are born with biologically rooted functions, termed "drives," that dictate individual functioning. These drives are primarily related to sexual expression and aggression. Psychoanalytic theory is also a stage or developmental framework, since its premise is that persons cope with different changes in biological, psychological, and social functioning at different stages of their lives. This framework focuses on both conscious and unconscious drives and on internal interactions within an individual between the person's id, ego, and superego. The focus on interaction between the individual and the broader environment is more limited than it is in many other theories, although the psychoanalytic theory includes attention to the impact of life experiences, primarily during early childhood; on later functioning; and on the development of internal defense mechanisms to cope with the environment, such as denial and rationalization. If Juan's situation were to be viewed from this framework, his sexual drives during preadolescence and the impact of his father leaving during this time would be major focal points. This framework is complex and based largely on individual psychopathology, or emotional illness. If one uses this framework for persons who have problems, the suggested intervention is individual psychoanalysis to work through intrapsychic conflicts.

Ego Psychology and Life-Span Development Frameworks Ego psychology stems from psychoanalytic theory but focuses mainly on the development of a strong ego as opposed to interactions between the id, ego, and superego. The ego psychology perspective also focuses more on the transactions between the person and environment and the impact of the environment in shaping the development of a healthy ego (Erikson 1959). The impact of Juan's family situation during his childhood would be explored, and ways to help Juan feel better about himself and to increase his self-esteem would be major issues for intervention within this framework.

Both psychoanalytic and ego psychology are life-span development frameworks. These frameworks suggest that individuals interact with their environments in different ways to meet different needs at different points in the life cycle, and the ways that needs are met in previous stages shape individual functioning and later development. Like psychoanalytic theory, there is a strong emphasis on ways that early life experiences shape later behavior. However, the emphasis is much more on the ways that the environment shapes the resolution of these issues. For example, using a life-span development framework developed by Erik Erikson, an individual addresses issues of basic trust versus basic mistrust during the first year of life. If an infant is placed in an environment where his or her basic needs (such as feeding or nurturing) are not met, or are met inconsistently, the child does not develop a sense of trust. If trust is not developed later, the child has difficulty in other stages of life, for example, in developing intimate relationships during young adulthood. Within this framework, Juan's developmental needs involve developing a sense of identity, primarily through peer relationships. Thus, for example, the gang members are filling a major developmental need for Juan that he does not feel can be met in other ways.

Although important and useful to social workers, these frameworks are more limiting than the systems/ecological framework. They place more emphasis on early life experiences than later experiences and less emphasis on interactions and transactions among broader levels of the environment and the impact on the individual. Finally, they suggest intervention primarily at the individual level.

Cognitive/Behavioral Frameworks

A second set of frameworks can be termed "cognitive/behavioral frameworks." These frameworks place little emphasis on life experiences or biological aspects of an individual. Their premise is that environment, and not heredity, largely determines behavior. These frameworks focus primarily on the present and on shaping individual thinking and behavior within the person's immediate environment. The goal is to shape behavior, not to change personality. For example, Juan may have developed a series of self-messages that suggest he is not competent. These repeated messages have led to his poor schoolwork and his attempts to seek competence in other areas, such as drug use and illegal activities. If Juan is helped to change his self-messages to positive affirmations about himself, he will begin to see himself as competent and begin reengaging in school. The interventions within these frameworks are largely at the individual level, and there is much greater emphasis on the present and the environment. Cognitive/behavioral frameworks, however, are extremely useful to social workers. They can help individuals not only to understand ways that unproductive thought patterns shape behaviors but also to develop new thought patterns and behaviors that can lead to healthier functioning.

Social workers often use these frameworks, as well as other frameworks, in a variety of ways and often in tandem with each other. Although the systems/ecological perspective can also be used when intervening with an individual or the broader environment, it is almost always used by social workers as the major framework for understanding a given situation/ problem. However, once the problem is understood and the broad terrain is mapped out using this framework, other frameworks may be used for further assessment as well as intervention.

The Systems/Ecological Framework and Professional Practice

Because the generalist model of social work incorporates all different levels of the environment and the interactions and interdependence within and between levels, the systems/ecological framework is especially useful as an organizing framework for professional practice. Specifically, the framework:

1. Allows the social worker to deal with large amounts of information from many different areas and to bring order to that information

2. Includes concepts that are applicable to the full range of clients served by social workers, including individuals, couples, families, groups, organizations, communities, and broader societal systems

3. Incorporates not only the structures of the social units involved, but the interrelatedness and interactions within and between units

4. Shifts attention away from the characteristics of units to the transactions and interactions between them

5. Views individuals as active participants in their environments, capable of change and adaptation, including shifting to new environments

6. Incorporates the concept of client self-determination and recognizes that multiple approaches can be effective in facilitating change

7. Focuses social workers on the need to provide and maintain continual transactions between persons and their environments for all populations and to monitor social systems heading for isolation

8. Provides a constant reminder to social workers that change is healthy and necessary for systems to grow but that systems often resist change

9. Places both the social worker and the agency within the client's environment

10. Reminds social workers that since a change in one level of the system creates changes at other levels, interventions must be thought through and chosen with care (Compton and Galaway 1994, 130–31)

Applying the Systems/Ecological Framework: The Social Welfare System and Poverty

The systems/ecological framework is especially useful in understanding the complexities of large systems within our environment, such as the social welfare system. The social welfare system in place at any given moment is the product of the interactions and interrelatedness of historical, economic, and political forces. As a large system, it is constantly reshaped by changes in societal values and events beyond its boundaries. Changes in societal values, for example, result in increased public acceptance of programs for battered women and child care for children of working mothers. An economic recession results in extensive cutbacks in social welfare services.

The scope of social welfare systems in the United States is not as broad, comprehensive, and integrated as most social workers would like, nor is it as constrained and limited as some others would contend. In a sense, it is not a formal system at all, but rather a collection of ad hoc programs developed in diverse and special political circumstances. Thus, although we have programs for the aged, the disabled, the blind, and dependent children, each program has its own political history and its own political constituency.

As a matter of practice, if not of principle, the target populations of social agencies are those subgroups in our society that are not adequately served by the primary social systems in our society (the economic system, the political system, the family system, the religious system, the health system, and the educational system). Typically, the social welfare system comes into play as a result of family breakdown, problems in income distribution, and institutional failure in the religious, education, health, and/or business sectors.

While each of us would probably give a somewhat different statement of mission for an ideal social welfare system, at a minimum we would probably all agree that such a system should guarantee to each person a socially defined minimum standard of well-being. In meeting this standard, the social welfare system interacts with primary social systems within our society: the family system, the economic system, and the political system. Each of these primary systems, in its turn, has a principal function as illustrated in Table 3.3. The social welfare system is most frequently perceived as a residual social system that comes into play when there is a failure in the primary system, or when the primary system generates undesirable consequences. (Wilensky and Lebeaux 1975).

The organized social welfare system, composed of numerous and varied social services and institutions, is designed to help individuals and groups attain satisfying standards of life and health. This view implies recurrent failure in other social systems. It assumes that individuals sometimes need outside help in coping with a complex social order. Social welfare institutions that make up the social welfare system assist in time of crisis of the individual, but since recurrent and random crisis is the ordinary condition of social life, a structured set of social agencies needs to stand ready to respond to crises and failures—to overcome the crisis; enhance problem-solving and coping skills of communities, groups, families, and individuals; and empower these entities to create social change so that crisis is less frequent.

In this view, the social welfare system is seen as the structured set of responses developed to deal with the dysfunction of other systems. For

TABLE 3.3   SOCIAL SYSTEMS

Systems	Functions
Primary	
Family	The primary personal care and mutual assistance system between parents and children, between adults and elderly
Political	The authoritative allocation of public social goals and values
Economic	The allocation and distribution of scarce resources to competing entities
Secondary	
Other goal-specific systems (i.e., education system, health care system, defense system)	The list and functions of secondary systems are dependent on individual choice. What would you include?
Social Welfare System	To respond to failure and/or dysfunction in primary and secondary systems

example, the family system is intended to meet the physical and emotional needs of children. But at times, the primary family system fails and is unable to serve this function. At that point, the social welfare system provides child welfare services, such as respite child care, foster care, and services to abused and neglected children. When the social welfare system functions to assist or replace the family in its child care roles, this exemplifies a social welfare system response to a primary system failure. A second example of a social welfare system response to a primary system dysfunction can be seen in relation to the economic system. We know that the economic system distributes income unevenly, leaving some people poor. Thus, we have generated an income security system to provide various income guarantees to specific classes of persons in need.

Objectively speaking, an overview of American social welfare institutions and social work practice reveals an incredible range of public and voluntary agencies seeking to respond to social problems. For some problem areas, the response is well conceptualized and generous; for others the response is hasty and scanty; still other social problems invoke no response at all. A major problem with our social welfare system is that each problem is usually treated as a separate issue, rather than an interactive and interdependent part of a larger issue. Seldom, for example, is attention given to how a response to problem A is related to its impact on problem B. The passage of recent welfare reform legislation, for example, was intended to help large numbers of individuals receiving public assistance become self-sufficient through gainful employment. But the staff of employment and training programs established to work with clients as part of the legislation quickly learned that many clients cannot read and write well. This has resulted in a tremendous and often unanticipated overload of the education system, which is being asked to provide remedial education programs for this group of clients. The original legislation unfortunately did not allow for allocation of additional resources to the education system.

A second example of the interrelatedness between systems and social problems can be seen in the area of health care. In a number of states in the past five years, state legislators, concerned about costs being paid for health care for the poor, reduced the funds allocated in this area rather than raise taxes. Unfortunately, they have overlooked the fact that most of these state dollars are used to provide the match for federal dollars allocated to states for health care. For every dollar that a state contributes, the federal government matches the amount with federal money. The reduction in dollars by the states has limited the amount of federal money coming into the states, seriously reducing the number of clients that could be served by state public assistance health programs. No longer served by these health programs, the states' poor do not seek health care until they are desperate, and when they do, they come to local hospitals as indigent (unpaying) patients. This means that local hospitals have to foot these bills, now higher than they might have been if care had been sought earlier. It also means that all of the higher costs in these states are footed by local taxpayers who all pay local taxes to support hospitals. Thus, what the legislators ultimately intended as a money-saving measure for their states' citizens has turned out to be far more costly.

The systems/ecological framework can be used to help understand issues at every level of the environment and across levels. The framework can also be used to determine types of intervention at all levels of the environment once the complex issues are understood.

THE GENERALIST MODEL

The generalist model of social work practice taught at the BSW level suggests the use of multiple interventions in working with clients at the individual, family, group, organizational, community, or societal level. Generalist practice focuses on the interface between systems,

> with equal emphasis on the goals of social justice, humanizing systems, and improving the well-being of people. It uses a multilevel methodology that can be focused on varying levels of the environment, depending on the needs of the client system. Generalist practice incorporates a knowledge, value and skills base that is transferable between and among diverse contexts and locations. (Schatz, Jenkins, and Sheafor 1990, 223)

The central theme of most generalist practice is the systems/ecological framework. Generalist practice is based on the idea that there needs to be congruency, or a positive fit between the person and his/her environment, and that the role of social work is to promote, strengthen, and restore—if necessary—that positive fit. **Person-environment fit** is the actual fit between the person or group's needs, rights, goals, and capacities and the physical and social environment within which the person or group operates. The fit can be favorable, adequate, or unfavorable. When exchanges with the environment over time are inadequate, the healthy development of the individual might be affected negatively, or the environment might be damaged (Germain and Gitterman 1995, 817).

The Strengths Perspective

Generalist social work practice is directed toward identifying the strengths of a system and using those strengths to modify the environment with which that system interacts to increase the level of person-environment fit. Generalist practice requires social work knowledge and skills in working with individuals, families, groups, organizations, and communities, including advocacy, to empower individuals to change their environments. This focus views the client as the expert, with the role of the social worker to build on the strengths of individuals to facilitate their ability to change their environment, or their coping mechanisms in interacting with it. The generalist social work strengths perspective can be contrasted with what is commonly referred to as the "medical model," which focuses on the client as having some type of illness or weakness and the helper as the expert who determines and provides the treatment. Table 3.4 compares the generalist social work strengths perspective and the medical model.

TABLE 3.4   **COMPARISON OF GENERALIST SOCIAL WORK STRENGTHS PERSPECTIVE AND MEDICAL MODEL**

Generalist Practice/Strengths Perspective	Medical Model
Lack of goodness of fit between person and environment; needs not being met.	Problem with individual/weakness of individual; person is labeled as sick/deviant, given diagnosis.
Client and environment present strengths/opportunities and barriers/risks; building on strengths can motivate clients to change themselves/perceptions/and/or their environment.	Client has problems/needs; sick clients need help in changing their world views to fit with the norm.
Client is expert about his/her life and needs; social worker is facilitator to help client discover needs and identify possible resources to get them met.	Helper is expert who diagnoses client and prescribes treatment; expert is in charge of treatment; client is expected to cooperate.
Client can be empowered to get needs met/use or learn new skills and resources.	Client needs expert helper to help change; needs to be dependent on experts for help.

Source: Adapted from *The Integration of Social Work Practice* by R. J. Parsons, J. D. Jorgensen, and S. H. Hernández. Copyright © 1994 Brooks/Cole Publishing Company, Pacific Grove, CA 93950, a division of International Thomson Publishing Inc. By permission of the publisher.

All individuals have strengths, and they are much more likely to grow and change when their strengths, rather than their deficiencies, are emphasized. In his book *The Strengths Perspective in Social Work Practice,* Dennis Saleeby, a social work educator at the University of Kansas, delineates six basic principles upon which the **strengths perspective** is based (1992, 6–7):

- Respecting clients' strengths—Social work practice is guided first *and* foremost by a profound awareness of, and respect for, clients' positive attributes and abilities, talents and resources, desires and aspirations. . . .

- Clients have many strengths—Individuals and groups have vast, often untapped and frequently unappreciated reservoirs of physical, emotional, cognitive, interpersonal, social and spiritual energies, resources and competencies. . . .

- Client motivation is based on fostering client strengths—Individuals and groups are more likely to continue autonomous development and growth when it is funded by the coin of their capacities, knowledge, and skills. . . .

- The social worker is a collaborator with the client—The role of "expert" or "professional" may not provide the best vantage point from which to appreciate client strengths. . . .

- Avoiding the victim mindset—Emphasizing and orienting the work of helping around clients' strengths can help to avoid "blaming the victim" (Ryan, 1976). . . .

• Any environment is full of resources—In every environment there are individuals and institutions who have something to give, something that others may desperately need . . . and for the most part, they are untapped and unsolicited. . . .

Empowerment

Another key aspect of generalist social work practice is **empowerment,** the "process of increasing personal, interpersonal, or political power so individuals can take action to improve their life situation" (Gutierrez 1990, 149). Many of the individuals with whom social workers work are members of at-risk populations who face barriers at all levels of the environment that often limit their functioning. Such individuals often lack the power and resources to change their environments, or may be in situations where they perceive themselves as powerless, incompetent, and/or lacking in resources. Rather than "fixing" problems, which often reinforces such feelings, social workers help clients see that they can create change. People who are empowered can make changes at the individual, family, group, neighborhood, organizational, community, state, national, or international levels.

As Ms. Herrera continued to emphasize Juan's strengths, he realized that he had more power over his life than he had thought. He was able to talk with his mother and negotiate more time with friends. He also felt empowered to say no to his peers who were pressuring him to join the gang. And, realizing that there were other teens in situations similar to his, he became active in a school leadership program and a key member of a community group that helped to establish a youth center.

Empowering clients like Juan gives them hope and helps them to see that they have a sense of control over their lives. Empowerment leads to continual growth and change and increased feelings of competence.

Social and Economic Justice

The systems/ecological framework also is useful in applying the social work profession's commitment to the promotion of **social and economic justice,** which includes fairness and equity in regard to basic civil and human rights, protections, resources and opportunities, and social benefits. How resources are distributed at every level of the environment, who has access to those resources and opportunities, and how policies at all levels of society affect human development shape social work practice and types and levels of intervention. Juan and his family, because they were Mexican American, poor, and in a family situation involving divorce, faced social and economic injustice at all levels of the environment.

Social workers advocate for social and economic justice by working to expand individual access to resources and opportunities at all levels of the environment, including adequate education; food, clothing, and shelter; employment; health care; and participation in local, state, and national political processes. Social workers also have a commitment to

The promotion of social and economic justice is a primary mission of the social work profession. How resources are distributed, who has access to resources and opportunities, and the differential treatment of people because of factors such as ethnicity affect individual development throughout the life cycle.

alleviate social and economic injustice and its resulting oppression and discrimination. Some of the possible types of oppression that can result from social and economic injustice are shown in Table 3.5.

The Helping Process

The beginning generalist social work professional is seen as a "change agent" who can assist client systems in identifying needed change, developing strategies to make the change with those client systems, empowering and assisting client systems to implement those strategies, and monitoring and evaluating throughout the process to ensure that the desired change is taking place. Note that the term *client system* is used rather than *client* since social work intervention is often directed at a level of the environment beyond the individual. A **client system** can include individuals, families, groups, organizations, or communities, or it can include larger social entities at which intervention is directed. BSW social workers are trained to use a generalist approach, which can be used to address individual needs that are a part of everyday life as well as to help larger client systems. No matter what level of the environment the social worker selects as an intervention point, the generalist approach can be a useful tool in bringing about planned change.

Although there are many variations used when delineating the stages of the helping process from a generalist social work perspective, all use the systems/ecological framework as a base. Miley, O'Melia, and DuBois (1995, 90) incorporate the framework with a strengths/empowerment perspective in their identification of three stages:

TABLE 3.5	COMMON FORMS OF OPPRESSION	
Institutional		**Cultural**
Housing		Values/norms
Employment		Language
Education		Standards of behavior
Media		Holidays
Religion		Roles
Health services		Logic system
Government		Societal expressions
Legal services		The arts
Transportation		
Recreation		

Source: A. Condeluci, *Interdependence: The Route to Community* (Delray Beach, Fla.: St. Lucie Press, 1991), 18.

- Dialogue
  - Share and establish collaborative relationships with clients
  - Clarify client perspectives and social worker perspectives regarding strengths, challenges, and needs
- Discovery
  - Search and explore resources and strengths clients may not know they have
  - Assess and explore feelings and determine needs
  - Develop plans and frame solutions
- Development
  - Strengthen and help clients get what they need
  - Activate resources, including personal resources of clients
  - Recognize success and reinforce strengths
  - Build new resources and competencies

Social work educators Compton and Galaway (1994, 385–386) and others take a somewhat more traditional view, delineating what is referred to as a problem-solving approach, but suggest similar stages when working with client systems:

- Contact or engagement
  - Develop a relationship with the client system
  - Define the problem
  - Identify preliminary goals
  - Obtain as much information as possible to develop an intervention strategy
- Contract
  - Assess and evaluate the needs of the client system
  - Formulate an action plan

- Determine what resources are needed for the plan to be successful
- Action
  - Carry out the plan
  - Monitor and adjust it as needed
  - Terminate
  - Evaluate

Note the similarities between these stages and those with a greater emphasis on the strengths and empowerment of the client system.

In moving through these stages with a client system regardless of the specific model used, the social worker and the client address the following issues:

- Who has the power?
- What connections does the client have?
- What connections are working?
- What connections are not working?
- What connections are missing?
- Is this the way things should be? What would the client like to see changed?
- What connections can be used as resources to facilitate the change?
- What about the big picture? How do all the pieces of the system fit together? (Miley et al. 1995, 293)

As you can see from the phases and issues addressed, the systems/ecological framework is the organizing framework used, and intervention is from a generalist practice perspective, which incorporates the strengths of the client and the broader environment, empowerment and the promotion of social and economic justice. A large part of generalist social work practice is often directed toward mediating between systems to strengthen their connections to each other.

After reviewing the phases of the helping process, it is easy to see the "goodness of fit" between this process and the systems/ecological framework and the many ways that the two are related. Ms. Herrera's involvement with Juan and his family can be used to demonstrate how this framework can be applied to understand or to intervene at various levels of the environment.

Applications with Juan and His Family

During the contact/engagement or dialogue phase of the helping process, Ms. Herrera, the school social worker, used all of the concepts of the systems/ecological framework. In developing an initial relationship with Juan and his mother, she used preliminary knowledge about areas such as twelve-year-old boys and their developmental needs during this preadolescence stage, single-parent women and their special needs, the Mexican American culture, and ways that preadolescents and parents might view a professional from an authoritative organization such as a school. She empathized with Juan and his mother as she realized how they might view life from their day-to-day reality. As she continued to get to know Juan, Ms. Herrera allowed him to be the "expert," telling her what his life was like and what his needs were. She emphasized his strengths and helped him realize he had many on which to draw.

As Juan and Ms. Herrera began the contract or discovery phase, Ms. Herrera gathered information about Juan from his mother, his teachers, his friends, and others within his environment who could help them obtain as holistic a picture of Juan and his needs as possible. Ms. Herrera and Juan looked not only at the characteristics of Juan, his mother, his teachers, and his friends, but also their interactions with Juan and with each other. They focused not only on needs but also on strengths. They realized that both Juan and his mother were motivated to change, and that his teachers were very committed to helping him. Ms. Herrera incorporated information she learned about Juan's family with her knowledge about the dynamics of a family in which substance abuse had been a problem, about long-term effects of child maltreatment on parents, about gangs and peer relationships when adolescents feel lonely and isolated, and about Juan's family's church, Juan's mother's jobs, and the community and its attitudes toward Juan and his family. She was especially concerned about the lack of resources in the community and the lack of support for young adolescent males and single-parent mothers.

As she discovered more about Juan's situation, Ms. Herrera and Juan began to explore possible resources available to help Juan get his needs met. Ms. Herrera set up a meeting with Juan and his mother to clarify needs and to establish preliminary goals based on the information they had gathered. The three of them agreed that three initial needs were to reduce Juan's responsibility at home, to address his sense of loss over his father's leaving and anger because he had left, and to help Juan create a positive peer support group. They identified goals that focused on reducing the pressure from Juan's mother to take care of his brother and do so much at home, helping Juan deal with his feelings about the divorce, and helping Juan develop a positive peer support group. The three of them agreed that, although the initial referral related to Juan's school behavior and performance, these underlying needs were more critical and would, in fact, most likely improve his school performance if they were addressed.

After these three goals were identified, Juan and Ms. Herrera began meeting, sometimes separately and sometimes with his mother. They considered all possible options regarding how these goals might be met, listing potential resources available that might be helpful. Some resources, such as more financial help from Juan's father and Juan's mother quitting her job and going on public assistance, were rejected for various reasons. Finally, the three of them developed a contractual agreement that specified how Juan's needs would be addressed.

During the action or development phase, Ms. Herrera referred Juan's mother to the local human services agency, where she was able to qualify for low-income child care for her youngest child. Juan's mother also asked for information about a job-training program to upgrade her skills so that she could get a higher-paying job and be able to work one job instead of two. This would allow her to spend more time with Juan and his brother. With Ms. Herrera's help, Juan and his mother negotiated specific tasks Juan would do at home and agreed that he would have two hours after school every day to spend time with friends. They also agreed to rules regarding how he could spend his time with them. Juan and his mother also agreed that if Juan followed the rules and completed his chores, he could spend time weekly with his previous friends in his old neighborhood. In addition, Juan agreed to participate in a school support group for seventh-grade boys whose parents have experienced divorce. Ms. Herrera felt that this would not only help Juan work through some of his feelings about the divorce, but also develop a new set of peers with whom he could become socially involved. Juan and his mother also began counseling at the local teen/parent center, and the counselor and Ms. Herrera conferred regularly about his progress there. Ms. Herrera, while maintaining confidentiality about Juan's specific family issues, communicated with Juan's teachers, and they agreed to help Juan feel more accepted in his new school and to provide opportunities for him to get to know other students.

After three months, Juan's teachers reported that he was coming to class, participating in class discussions, handing in his homework, and no longer exhibiting behavior problems. His grades also improved significantly. Juan began to feel more empowered, and he dropped his friends who were gang members and formed several solid friendships with his classmates at his new school. Two of his friends were from the support group. Although the group was terminated after eight weeks, Ms. Herrera still met with Juan every two weeks or so to be sure that he was doing well. Juan spent a great deal of time in the group talking about the divorce and his feelings about his father. He visited his father twice and was looking forward to seeing him during his spring vacation. Juan and his mother, and sometimes his younger brother, also participated in family counseling sessions at the teen/parent center. Juan's mother developed a new set of friends and a support system through her youngest son's child care center, where there were also many other single parents. She enrolled in a computer-programming training course and was looking forward to the opportunity to upgrade her skills.

As the positive changes in one system occurred, they had a positive impact in other systems as well. The fact that Juan's mother was able to obtain child care, for example, reduced her stress and enabled her to interact more positively with Juan. Ms. Herrera's talking with Juan's teachers and helping them to understand his needs for acceptance also enabled them to view Juan more positively. This, in turn, reduced some of the pressure on him, increased his self-esteem, and gave him the needed confidence to seek out new friendships and find more positive ways to gain acceptance. Juan became involved in a school leadership program and helped develop an outreach program for new students.

Although she felt that she was able to make a difference when helping Juan and his mother, Ms. Herrera was increasingly frustrated about the large number of students she had who were like Juan. She had referrals on her desk for twelve more students in similar situations. She decided that it would be a more productive use of her time to develop additional resources at other levels of the environment than to deal with each student on a case-by-case basis. Ms. Herrera contacted the head of the counseling center and a number of other individuals in the community who were also concerned. A group of fifteen community representatives, including Juan as the teen representative from the school, began developing plans for a comprehensive program that would help teens and their families. The plan called for staff from the counseling center to come to the school weekly to lead additional support groups, for outreach efforts to be made to local businesses to locate adult mentors to work on a one-to-one basis with teens in need of additional adult support, and for the development of a teen center with after-school, evening, and weekend recreational programs. The group also decided to work with a state legislative group to advocate for additional funding for adolescent services and for single-parent families.

SUMMARY

Social welfare needs involve many complex and interrelated factors. These factors may be ordered in a number of ways to describe social welfare needs, to understand them, and to predict when they will occur and under what conditions. Because the needs are so complex and involve human behaviors and environmental influences that are difficult to measure, as well as a variety of disciplines, there is no theory that can be used to address all social welfare or human needs. However, the systems/ecological framework, which incorporates the concept that an individual may be seen as part of a larger environment with whom he or she continually interacts and is an interdependent part of that environment, is useful in organizing information to determine what else is needed and to develop an appropriate intervention strategy. This framework incorporates factors at the individual, family, group, organizational, community, and societal levels and allows for a variety of interventions at one or more levels. The framework is also congruent with the generalist practice approach and its focus on client strengths, empowerment, and the promotion of social and economic justice.

KEY TERMS

association
boundary
cause-effect relationship
client system
closed system
empowerment
entropy
equifinality
exosystem level

generalizable
inclusive
macrosystem level
mesosystem level
microsystem level
open system
person-environment fit
social and economic justice
steady state

strengths perspective
synergy
system

systems/ecological framework
testable
theory

DISCUSSION QUESTIONS

1. Why is it difficult to develop good theory to address social welfare needs?

2. Briefly identify the key components of the systems/ecological perspective. Compare and contrast open and closed systems, and static and steady state systems.

3. Using a systems/ecological perspective, identify the systems that currently affect Juan's life.

4. Using the ecological perspective as delineated by Bronfenbrenner and Garbarino, identify at least one strategy you might use if you were a social worker to help Juan and his family at each of the four levels of the environment: the microsystem, the mesosystem, the exosystem, and the macrosystem.

5. Identify at least four advantages of using the systems/ecological perspective to understand social welfare needs.

6. Briefly describe the helping process and its advantages to social workers within social welfare institutions. What type of intervention plan would you suggest if you were the school social worker assigned to work with Juan?

7. Show how the concepts of empowerment, client strengths, and social and economic justice are congruent with the systems/ecological framework.

REFERENCES

Bronfenbrenner, U. 1979. *The ecology of human development.* Cambridge Mass.: Harvard University Press.

Compton, B., and B. Galaway. 1994. *Social work processes.* 5th ed. Pacific Grove, Calif.: Brooks/Cole.

Condeluci, A. 1991. *Interdependence: The route to community.* Delray Beach, Fla.: St. Lucie Press.

Erikson, E. 1959. Identity and the life cycle: Psychological issues. Monograph no. 1. New York: International Universities Press.

Garbarino, J. 1992. *Children and families in the social environment.* New York: Aldine.

Germain, C., and A. Gitterman. 1995. Ecological perspective. *Encyclopedia of social work,* vol. 1, 816–824. Washington, D.C.: NASW Press.

Gutierrez, L. M. 1990. Working with a woman of color. *Social Work* 35:149–153.

Hartman, A. Diagrammatic assessment of family relationships. *Social Casework* 59 (October 1978):8.

Meyer, C. 1983. *Clinical social work in an eco-systems perspective.* New York: Columbia University Press.

Miley, K., M. O'Melia, and B. DuBois. 1995. *Generalist social work practice: An empowering approach.* Boston: Allyn and Bacon.

Parsons, R., J. Jorgensen, and S. Hernández. 1994. *The integration of social work practice.* Pacific Grove, Calif.: Brooks/Cole.

Richmond, M. 1922. *What is social casework?* New York: Russell Sage.

Saleeby, D. 1992. *The strengths perspective in social work practice.* New York: Longman.

Schatz, M., L. Jenkins, and B. Scheafor. 1990. Milford redefined: A model of initial and advanced generalist social work. *Journal of Education for Social Work* 26(3):217–231.

Shriver, J. 1995. *Human behavior and the social environment.* Boston: Allyn and Bacon.

Von Bertalanffy, L. 1968. *General system theory.* New York: Braziller.

Whittaker, J., and E. Tracy. 1988. The search for coherence. In *Clinical social work in the eco-systems perspective,* ed. C. Meyer. New York: Columbia University Press, 5–34.

Wilensky, H., and C. Lebeaux. 1965. *Industrial society and social welfare.* New York: Free Press.

SUGGESTED FURTHER READINGS

Anderson, R., and I. Carter. 1984. *Human behavior in the social environment: A social systems approach.* New York: Aldine.

Bronfenbrenner, U. 1979. *The ecology of human development.* Cambridge Mass.: Harvard University Press.

Buckley, W., ed. 1968. *Modern systems research for the behavioral scientist.* Hawthorne, N.Y.: Aldine.

Council on Social Work Education. 1982. *Curriculum policy for the master's degree and baccalaureate degree programs in social work education.* New York: Author.

Garbarino, J. 1982. *Children and families in the social environment.* New York: Aldine Press.

Germain, C. 1979. *Social work practice: People and environments.* New York: Columbia University Press.

Martin, P., and G. O'Connor. 1989. *The social environment: Open systems applications.* New York: Longman.

Ryan, W. 1976. *Blaming the victim.* New York: Vintage Books.

Zastrow, C., and K. Kirst-Ashman. 1994. *Understanding human behavior in the social environment.* Chicago: Nelson-Hall.

CHAPTER 4

DIVERSITY AND SOCIAL EQUALITY

The Impact of Race, Ethnicity, and Gender

Frances Philpott was valedictorian of her high school's graduating class, attended a major northeastern university where she obtained a degree in finance and administration, and graduated summa cum laude. Later, she obtained a master's degree in administration and earned several credits toward a doctorate. Her education was interrupted by marriage to Frank, an attorney.

Frances obtained employment with a large chemical corporation, where she performed in an exemplary manner. Within eight years, she was promoted to a mid-management position. Frances was recognized as an unusually astute and capable manager whose concept of the corporation's mission, organization, and growth potential was superior to that of her peers. After twelve years of employment with the corporation, Frances learned that the position of chief executive officer had become vacant. Feeling that her performance record and qualifications were consistent with those sought for the position, she applied. Although the board of directors unanimously agreed that Frances was highly qualified, she was not offered the position. She was told that her skills were much too valuable in the position that she held and that they viewed her as irreplaceable. Frances is a 43-year-old Mexican American woman. ▪

Like Frances, many individuals seek fulfillment and opportunity only to find that social barriers may hamper the achievement of those goals. Frances may well exemplify such a case. The evidence suggests that she had been a superior employee for over twelve years, and had graduated with honors in administration and management. All agreed that her management skills and perspective on the corporation's mission were faultless. Why, then, was she passed over for the position? Could it have been because she is a woman? Or because she is Mexican American? The limited information in the short case history gives us little basis for conjecture. If we are confident that Frances was at least as well qualified as other applicants, is it possible that her gender, her ethnic affiliation, or both underlie the decision not to offer her the position? Since the corporation's board argued her irreplaceability in the position she currently holds, we might infer that they are not willing to advance a woman (and a Mexican American woman in particular) to the role of chief executive officer. Even if Frances suspects that gender or ethnicity (or both) was a factor in the corporate board's decision, it would be difficult for her to prove.

Unfortunately, Frances represents only one of millions of Americans who find that social and economic justice are not necessarily achieved through hard work and top job performance. All too often, social mobility and opportunity are not available equally to all who aspire to achieve the American dream. Women and people of color long have been denied opportunities in business and social life that white men have come to expect and take for granted. Under the subtle guise of institutional sexism and racism, the rights to free and full participation in our social and economic institutions are denied to individuals who fail to meet dominant group criteria. In Frances' case, it is possible that the corporation's board felt justified for not offering her the position because of a long-standing tradition of having white men in that position. Rationalizing their position, the officials may have believed that males are best suited for the position of chief executive officer; or, more subtly, that women should not hold chief executive positions. Whatever their rationale, the decision effectively served to exclude Frances from achieving that position.

In this chapter we examine the characteristics of social inequality implicit in racism and sexism in more detail. The effects of social inequality are not always equal between people of color and women. It is somewhat ironic that white women, the targets of gender inequality, often discriminate against people of color. To understand better the differential effects of institutional racism and sexism, each is reviewed separately. Keep in mind that both lead to a life of second-class citizenship in our society. The ways that prejudice and discrimination are directed toward gays and lesbians are also discussed. ■

PREJUDICE AND DISCRIMINATION

Social inequality is partly a result of prejudice and discrimination. **Prejudice** is a value learned through the process of socialization. Prejudices are internalized and become a dimension of an individual's value system. People who are prejudiced generally do not consider themselves so. The objects of prejudice are presumed to possess behavioral characteristics that the holders of prejudice find objectionable. Through the process of **stereotyping,** women and people of color all are assumed to hold behavior traits that justify their exclusion from free and full participation in the social roles of society. Stereotypes are beliefs that members of certain groups always or generally behave in specific ways. Hence the belief that women are not as intelligent as men, lack decision-making ability, are prone to be emotional, and are better nurturers; that African Americans are lazy and lack initiative; that Mexican Americans prefer the slower pace of an agrarian life; or that Jews are elitist and money hungry—these are among many of the stereotypes associated with groups. Dominant group members often behave toward members of minority groups as though the stereotypes were true. To illustrate better how prejudice affects decision making, consider this example paraphrased from the work of M. Sirkin in his article, "Resisting Cultural Meltdown":

> A traditional Jewish family had an older daughter who had moved to Albuquerque, commenced dating her non–Jewish employer, and, in spite of long-standing Jewish traditions against intermarriage and strong family pressure not to do so, subsequently married her employer. As a consequence, her parents as well as her sisters discontinued contact with her. In effect, intermarriage tore this family apart. (1994, 51)

In this case, strong in-group values and traditions that had become institutionalized and affirmed as a matter of faith and practice were violated by the older daughter. There was little doubt that her husband was of impeccable character, a hard worker, an outstanding citizen, a man of faith, and a loving and caring husband. Those qualities from the family's perspective were necessary but not sufficient for their blessing and acceptance of the newlyweds into the family. Indeed, from the parents' perspective no non-Jewish male would have been acceptable as a marriage partner for their daughter. While most people hold deep respect for traditions and strongly held values, one can readily understand how prejudgement can ensue.

Like the family just described, dominant group members in society have long-standing values, attitudes, customs, and beliefs related to women and people of color. These beliefs often result in the erection of social barriers that preclude or limit women and people of color from living in a socially just society. Social distance is invariably a mirror of prejudice, just as discrimination serves as a vehicle to ensure social distance. Prejudice is the presumption, without the benefit of facts, that certain behaviors are characteristic of all members of a minority group. As a consequence, members of the dominant group may demean members of a minority group by assuming that assigned behaviors in fact are true, and by then relating to individual members through the filter of prejudice.

Although the target of prejudice may vary, the paradox is that virtually no one is free from prejudice. For example, prejudice may not be directed toward gender, race, ethnicity, or creed—it may even be directed toward people who are themselves prejudiced.

Prejudice is a psychological construct that may result in discrimination. Although prejudice can exist without discrimination (and discrimination without prejudice, for that matter), they usually coexist (Yinger 1970). Prejudice fuels the fires and provides the justification for discrimination. If it is falsely believed (an axiom for prejudice) that people of certain groups are less intelligent, incapable of equal participation, or would threaten traditional practices, differential treatment (an axiom for discrimination) may occur, thereby placing the erroneously feared threat at some distance. Denying women, people of color, the elderly, gays and lesbians, and other social groups the right to equal social participation limits the opportunity structures through which the desired behavioral characteristics could be acquired. A viscious, self-perpetuating cycle is then set in motion. Discrimination is the action that maintains and supports prejudice. Zastrow observes that

> individuals who are targets of discrimination are excluded from certain types of employment, educational and recreational opportunities, certain residential housing areas, membership in certain religious and social organizations, certain political activities, access to community services, and so on. (1986, 379)

Institutional discrimination and the resultant differential treatment have been codified in administrative rules and regulations and are thereby "intrinsic" to the mores of a society. Discrimination is reinforced through the social practices of dominant group members, who may be oblivious to the effects of their actions. Institutionalized racism is based on a person's color, whereas institutionalized sexism results in the denial of rights or opportunities for participation on the basis of gender. In both instances, free and full participation is denied on the basis of group membership.

WOMEN AND SOCIAL INEQUALITY

In the book *The Compleat Chauvinist*, Edgar Bergman, a physician in Maryland (1982, 185), raises the question, "What would our Neanderthal forefathers have thought of our succumbing to the outrageous myth of sexual equality?'' In buttressing his antiegalitarian views, he refers to comments made by Marvin Harris, a professor of anthropology at Columbia University, who is quoted as saying:

> Feminists are wailing in the wind if they think they're going to abolish sexism by raising consciousness. There is not a shred of evidence—historical or contemporary—to support the existence of a single society in which women controlled the political and economic lives of men.

Bergman offers a number of illustrations in defense of the position that men are clearly superior to women in decision making. To the detriment of social equality, Bergman's views and arguments are not new. Women have experienced social inequality throughout recorded history. Invariably, inequality was—and is—justified on the basis of the biological superiority of men, despite no evidence to support that premise. In the social sciences, social inequality is viewed as a product of human interaction and social organization (Perrucci and Knudsen 1983).

In spite of advances made during the past several decades, women in our society experience discrimination. Perhaps sex-biased discrimination is more visible in the occupational market and economic areas than in other aspects of social participation. Zastrow has identified a few of the more salient roles played by women:

> Women tend to be concentrated in the lower paying, lower status positions of secretaries, child care workers, receptionists, typists, nurses, hairdressers, bank tellers, cashiers, and file clerks. Men tend to be concentrated in higher paying positions: lawyers, judges, engineers, accountants, college teachers, physicians, dentists, and sales managers. (1986, 392)

Although some progress has been made, many male-dominated job positions have remained virtually unobtainable to qualified women. Management and administrative positions at the upper levels continue to be held mostly by men.

Income

From 1890 to 1986, the proportion of all white women who were in the labor force increased from 14.9 percent to 66.3 percent, and the proportion of nonwhite women who were in the labor force increased from 38.4 percent to 66.4 percent (Presser 1987). These increases ushered in a number of conflicts and issues related to women's participation in the labor market. Chief among the issues was the concept of "comparable worth."

> Comparable worth has radical implications because it initiates an end to women's economic dependency and questions the market basis of wages. In doing so, it exposes the way gender hierarchy is incorporated into the organization of the economy, the traditional strategies of the labor movement, and the ideologies of gender in the United States; it provides the basis for an attack on the sexual division of labor and gender hierarchy; and it lays the foundation for reordering of gender relations throughout social life. (Feldberg 1984, 312–13)

Comparable worth is a concept often best understood by the phrase "equal pay for equal work." Much of the income disparity between men and women, however, is largely attributable to differences in occupational positions, which have changed little over the past decade. As Matthews and Rodin note, "Although women have entered the labor force in tremendous numbers since 1970, they are still by and large entering occupations that are dominated by women" (1989, 1391). Income differences exist primarily because men are employed in positions of leadership or in technical fields, whereas women are disproportionately employed in the lower-paying clerical and service fields. Even when women hold positions similar to those of men, their income is less. Seniority or related factors do not always account for these differences, and employers generally concede that, for a given type of position, men get a higher income than do women.

Notwithstanding traditional notions that incomes produced by women are less essential for family maintenance than those generated by men, the practice of channeling women into lower-level positions, with the resultant limited career choices and lower incomes, represents an institutionalized policy of sex-based discrimination. Although efforts recently have been made to provide equal employment opportunities for women, social roles continue to be gender typed and are passed down from generation to generation through the process of socialization.

It is interesting to note that women continue to be less well represented in business administration, engineering, law, medicine, and dentistry, while they are overrepresented in the fields of fine arts, social work, and nursing. When women are excluded or limited from participating in these arenas of job opportunities, educational preparation programs are also affected because women are forced to make career (and consequently educational) choices on the basis of opportunities for employment and advancement.

Education

Ironically, men hold leadership positions in professions that predominantly employ women, such as public education and social work. In a study of Texas public school administrators it was found that

> administration and school leadership at all levels are dominated by males. During 1967–1977 less than 1 percent of the superintendents' positions were filled by women. In 1977, the year of the largest number of women appointed to administrative positions, women held only 7 out of 1106 superintendent positions, 607 out of 4471 principalships and 360 out of 2030 assistant principalships. (Shuttlesworth 1978)

These findings suggest that a career-oriented woman entering the educational system would have greater difficulty in securing promotion to an administrative position than a similarly qualified man. As a result, women are relegated to the lower-paying, less prestigious position of classroom teacher throughout their careers. Although nondiscrimination policies exist, qualified women educators who seek promotion to administration are confronted with the task of penetrating a gender-biased tradition of assigning men to those roles in the public school system. Although the study just cited is based on data that is seventeen years old, there is little current evidence that any substantial change has occurred in the numbers and percentages of women holding administrative positions in Texas public school systems. Opening the opportunity structure to accommodate all qualified professionals, regardless of gender, appears to be a slow, arduous process.

In 1988, women earned 50 percent of the bachelors and masters degrees awarded and 35 percent of academic doctoral degrees. During that year, women were awarded 40 percent of the law degrees earned, 31 percent of the medical doctor degrees, and only 23 percent of the dental doctorates. Although larger numbers of women are now engaged in the educational process at both undergraduate and graduate levels, men continue to dominate the doctoral degree market in academic as well as professional schools.

Social Work

Historically, most social work professionals have been women. Dressel reported that as of 1987 two-thirds of all social work practitioners were women (1987, 297). In a field that has long championed equal rights for women (as well as one that is predominantly female), it is ironic that leadership roles are primarily held by men. Fanshel reports that men are represented disproportionately in administrative and managerial roles, and, as a group, receive higher salaries than women (1976, 448–53). To that extent, the social work profession—despite its advocacy of women's rights—reflects the tendency of other professions as well as the business community.

Religion

In organized religion, where women are more active participants, less than 5 percent are ordained to the clergy (Perrucci and Knudsen 1983). In very few instances do women hold the position of primary leadership in churches, and even less often are they employed in higher levels of administration in religious associations. Many religious groups base their male-biased pastoral leadership roles on the "holy writ," thereby effectively excluding women from appointments to significant leadership responsibilities in those bodies.

Politics

In 1991, only 29 of 435 U.S. representatives and 2 of 100 U.S. senators were women (Congressional Quarterly Weekly Report 1990). Only 3 of the 50 governors were women. These figures reflect the subordinate role that women continue to play in the legislative process. Male bias is ever present in legislative debates in those areas where laws directly affect women.

▨ INSTITUTIONAL SEXISM

The discussion and illustrations just presented indicate the strong gender bias in administrative and managerial positions. Women *are* treated differently in the professions and business. Their status as women negatively influences the opportunity to move into those prominent roles *regardless* of their competence or ability. In effect, women are discriminated against in the marketplace solely because they are women. This practice, called **sexism,** is a result of the values and practices embodied in our social institutions. Children are taught by their parents that boys are to be aggressive and dominant and that girls are to be nurturing and submissive. Parents often model these attributes in family interaction, where father assumes the roles of rule maker, disciplinarian, and decision maker and mother assumes responsibility for the nurturing roles of caring for the children and the household.

Performance differences between men and women invariably reflect societal attitudes and values far more than any inherent physical or psychological variances in maleness or femaleness. In modern society few roles exist that could not be performed by either men or women, although throughout the life cycle sex-role distinctions are made and differences are emphasized. These distinctions become entrenched in societal values, thus hindering women from "crossing over" into roles considered masculine. Hence, an aggressive, goal-oriented, intelligent woman may be viewed as masculine and censured for departing from prescribed female role behavior.

Societal values and practices continue to result in a gender-segregated division of labor. Although some progress has been made in identifying roles as "asexual" (neither male nor female), roles in general are gender typed. Women have great difficulty gaining access to roles identified as appropriate for men only. Gender differentiation also is observed in opportunities to secure credit, purchase homes, negotiate contracts, and obtain credit cards, where men typically have the advantage.

In the past decade, the issue of "sexual harassment" has received considerable attention as a problem that women must contend with in the workplace. While definitions of sexual harassment may vary, it is generally agreed that unsolicited sexual suggestions, pinching, patting, hugging, kissing, or sexual relations constitute harassment. It is highly likely that much sexually harassing behavior goes unreported by employees for fear that their jobs might be placed in jeopardy. While some progress has been made in reporting and eradicating these behaviors, it still poses a significant problem for working women.

▨ THE ABORTION DILEMMA

One of the more emotionally charged issues that epitomizes the conflict between feminist and traditional values is abortion. In reality, abortion consists of three central concerns: (1) the legal issue, (2) the medical issue, and (3) the value issue.

The Legal Issue

The legal precedent for abortion was established in 1973 by the *Roe v. Wade* decision. In effect, the U.S. Supreme Court maintained that a woman has the constitutional right to seek an abortion, if she so desires. This decision defined abortion as a personal decision rather than one to be determined by government policy. Although the Court's interpretation was straightforward and clear, attempts were made to cut funds from family planning agencies that gave abortion counseling and references. The lack of acceptance of the Court's ruling did not, however, close the door on the controversy. More recently, states have been delegated the power to determine abortion policy. A 1989 policy established by Florida imposed strict requirements on abortions, so that legal abortions could be performed only when a pregnancy resulted from rape or when the health of the mother would be in jeopardy, should the pregnancy continue. In 1990, Louisiana sought to pass similar legislation. In spite of *Roe v. Wade*, there is no uniform code that mandates "abortion on demand" across the states. It is estimated, however, that approximately 1.5 million abortions are performed in the United States each year.

The Medical Issue

From a medical perspective, abortion, during the first trimester of a pregnancy, is a relatively simple, uncomplicated procedure. Although there is risk involved with any medical intervention, abortion is generally not considered a high-risk procedure, even during the second trimester. The majority of abortions are performed during the first trimester and very few during the last trimester. Assessing women's psychological preparedness for an abortion can be difficult. Most abortion clinics require a psychological assessment and counseling as prerequisites for an abortion. Few studies have attempted to assess postabortion adaptation, and their results have, for the most part, provided limited insight.

The Values Issue

Perhaps the most emotionally charged aspect of abortion involves values. Members of the antiabortion (right-to-life) movement base their resistance to abortion on the conviction that life begins at conception. Consequently, they view abortion (termination of the fetus) as murder. Members of pro-choice groups, on the other hand, argue that life begins at birth, and they further insist that a woman has the constitutionally granted right to decide whether she wishes to continue her pregnancy or terminate it. Antiabortion groups seek the government's protection of the life (and rights) of the fetus in the same sense that children and adults merit the protection of the law from injury or injustice. Within each of the groups there is some variance of value positions. For example, while arguing that life begins at conception, some antiabortion groups take the position that abortion is acceptable and justified in instances of rape or where the mother's health would be jeopardized.

Other antiabortion groups oppose abortion under any circumstance, arguing that taking the life of the fetus is not acceptable under any circumstance.

Abortion is not solely a women's problem. However, only women become pregnant and have the legal right to decide whether a pregnancy will be carried to its full term or terminated. The law remains unusually silent concerning the role of men in matters of conception and pregnancy. Fathers are referred to as "alleged fathers," and they have no legal right to affect a woman's decision to abort a pregnancy.

We have included this discussion to illustrate further the problem of differential treatment of women in our society. Social workers must be especially attuned to such treatment and to the views surrounding abortion. Although they may have personal views that would preclude their participation in abortion counseling, they have a professional responsibility to assure that referrals are made in order to protect the rights of the client. Zastrow clearly outlines the profession's position as follows:

> Our premise is that social work as a profession must view abortion as a legal right of every client, should she make this choice, and must therefore sublimate personal beliefs to that end. It is the practitioner's responsibility to facilitate intelligent, rational, and unanimous decision making on the part of the individual client, and to support that decision, whatever it may be. (1986)

While professional social workers may agree with the preceding statement, we must not conclude that all social workers support the prochoice position. Social workers, like other professionals, vary greatly in their personal values, and this is certainly true regarding the abortion controversy.

SOCIAL REFORM: THE FEMINIST MOVEMENT AND SOCIAL ACTION

Women have pursued equal social treatment since this nation's inception. Some of the more noteworthy leaders were Elizabeth Stanton (1815–1902), who petitioned for a property rights law for women in New York (1845); Lucretia Mott (1793–1880), who organized the first women's rights convention in New York; Susan B. Anthony (1820–1906), who helped to form the National Women's Suffrage Association in 1869; and Lucy Stone (1818–1893), who formed the National American Women's Suffrage Association. Carrie Catt (1859–1947), a political activist, founded the International Women's Suffrage Alliance and later, following World War I, the League of Women Voters, an organization that today wields significant political influence. Ms. Catt's efforts were largely responsible for the enactment of the Nineteenth Amendment to the Constitution, which extended voting rights to women in 1920 (Macksey 1976).

In more recent times, women's groups have intensified their efforts to secure equal rights. The Civil Rights Act of 1964 addressed the problems of discrimination due to gender as well as race. A major attempt to secure women's rights was embodied in the **Equal Rights Amendment (ERA).** Bitterly opposed by organized labor, the John Birch

Society, the Christian Crusade, and the Moral Majority, and over the protest of Senator Sam Ervin (D–North Carolina), who castigated the proposed amendment, the bill was passed by Congress in 1972 and remanded to the states for ratification. Pro-ERA forces, including the National Organization for Women (NOW), the League of Women Voters, and the National Women's Political Caucus, lobbied the states to seek ratification for the amendment. Anti-ERA spokespersons lobbied the states against ratification and argued that all women would be sent into combat, subjected to unisex public facilities, and required to secure jobs (Deckard 1983) if the amendment passed. The Carter administration, favorable to passage of the ERA, had little influence on the states in encouraging its adoption. The Reagan administration opposed the measure. The unratified amendment died in June 1982.

SOCIAL WORK RIGHTS FOR WOMEN

Although the profession of social work has advocated for the abolition of societal barriers that deny equal treatment of women, it has not been in the forefront in providing leadership for the more significant feminist movements. During the 1960s, however, women's equality was established as a major priority for the profession. Both the National Association of Social Workers (NASW) and the Council on Social Work Education (CSWE) initiated policies committing the profession to promotion of social and economic equality for women (Zastrow 1986). Social workers were encouraged to advocate for women's rights and to treat all their clients equally. The abolition of sexism within the profession has been vigorously pursued, and evidence suggests that sex-biased career opportunities are being eliminated.

GAYS, LESBIANS, AND SOCIAL INEQUALITY

According to reliable data, 10 percent of the U.S. population is homosexual. Within the past decade, considerable attention has been directed to the prejudice and discrimination that characterize societal responses toward homosexual men and women. Although a person's sexual persuasion is considered to be a personal and private matter not related to free and full participation in our society, such has not been the case for homosexuals. As Dulaney and Kelly have noted, the intense negative emotional reaction to the homosexual community is a result of "deep-rooted fear and accompanying hatred of homosexual lifestyles and individuals" (1982, 178), a state of psychological conditioning known as **homophobia.** Although it is not known what percentage of the American population is homophobic, Irwin and Thompson (1977, 107–121) found that one-fourth of the respondents to a research inquiry believed that homosexuals should be banned from teaching in colleges and universities. This attitude appears to permeate the business community and carries over to other aspects of social life as well. Acquired immunodeficiency syndrome (AIDS) has further promoted anxiety and fear toward homosexual relationships.

The rejection of homosexual practices, with its consequent nurturance of prejudice and discrimination, has been bolstered in fundamentalist religions as well as the more traditional psychologies. For example, the Moral Majority and Christian Voice movements, which strongly argue that homosexual practices are sinful, have condemned homosexuals along with deviants, pornographers, and athiests (Young 1982). Irving Beiber, a psychoanalyst, in his classic work titled *Homosexuality* (1962), clearly describes traditional psychoanalysts' view that homosexuality is nonnormative and that it can be cured through psychotherapy. These (and other) "authoritative" sources reinforce the biases and prejudices that have long existed in the general population.

Twenty-five states currently have laws designed to prohibit specified sexual acts between consenting adults, with ten states classifying such behaviors as misdemeanors and the remaining fifteen, as felonies. These are laws that are generally used to restrict (or punish) homosexual behavior. Only two states (Wisconsin and Massachusetts) have passed legislation to protect the rights of gays and lesbians (Knopp 1990).

Although experts disagree as to whether sexual orientation is determined by genetics or is a product of socialization, the general public continues to view homosexuality as a matter of choice. Some gays and lesbians have become more vocal and have sought legal redress for discriminatory practices, whereas others, fearing loss of jobs, intimidation, and harassment, have opted to remain "in the closet." In 1973 the American Psychiatric Association removed "functional homosexuality" from its list of behavior disorders, and as a result, mental health professionals no longer view homosexuality as a form of mental illness. One might conclude, however, that a large segment of the public maintains the perspective that gay and lesbian relationships are a form of perversion and that social contact with homosexuals should be avoided. Although some progress has been made in securing legal rights for members of the gay community, discrimination and prejudice continue to undergird public responses to them.

The homosexual life-style has not been without advocates. One of the earlier groups to support the rights of gays and lesbians was the Chicago Society for Human Rights (1924). In 1950, the Mattachine Society was founded to further rights for and acceptance of same-sex-oriented individuals. Currently, the Gay Liberation Front has established itself as a political organization promoting passage of legislation that would provide for nondiscriminatory practices against homosexuals, including recognition of same-sex marriages as well as adoption rights.

Unfortunately, in spite of the enlightenment regarding same-sex orientation, many professionals find it difficult to overcome their own biases and prejudices when helping homosexual clients. Dulaney and Kelly (1982, 178) report that

social work is most sensitive to contemporary social pressures because of its sources of funding and orientation to community service. This sensitivity has led to a conflict in the profession regarding sexual issues and gay and lesbian clients that reflects society's dual value system, which consists of one set of values for heterosexuals and another for homosexuals.

De Crescenzo and McGill (1978) found that homophobia was far more prevalent among social workers than among psychologists and psychiatrists. Although there may be a variety of explanations as to why social workers tend to be more homophobic than other professionals, a primary reason may be that social workers' lack of skill and intense discomfort in dealing with gay and lesbian clients are largely attributable to the fact that many social work students receive almost no training regarding homosexuality in their formal education (Dulaney and Kelly 1982, 179).

Since the majority of the U.S. population is heterosexually oriented, homosexuals experience prejudice and discrimination much like that faced by other minority group members. Stereotypical thinking based on erroneous information guides most heterosexuals' reactions to the gay community. Thus, same-sex-oriented individuals are often denied freedom of expression and access to an opportunity structure that is available for heterosexuals.

Clearly, social work and related professions need to address more forcefully the prejudices and biases toward homosexuality as yet pervasive within the professions. In spite of the acknowledged reticence that exists, considerable progress has been made in the preparation of social workers for engaging clients who are gay or lesbian. Accreditation standards for schools of social work require that course content address the needs of divergent populations, including gays and lesbians. Advocacy on behalf of the homosexual population directed toward the enforcement of anti-discrimination legislation has become a priority of the profession.

Unfortunately, until the fear and apprehensions concerning homosexual behavior are dispelled through public enlightenment, prejudice and discrimination will continue to remain barriers to social and economic justice for the gay and lesbian community.

◪ SOCIAL INEQUALITY AND MINORITY GROUP MEMBERSHIP

What constitutes minority group status? According to Wirth, a **minority group** "is a category of people distinguished by special physical or cultural traits which are used to single them out for differential and unequal treatment" (Wirth 1938). The assignment to a minority status may be made on the basis of "race, nationality, religion or ethnicity" (Perrucci and Knudsen 1983). Hence, African Americans, Mexican Americans, other Hispanics, Asian Americans, Moslems, Lithuanians, Iranians, or Vietnamese, among others, are defined by the dominant (majority) group as minorities. The concept of race suggests that marked, distinct genetic differences are present. The term, in reality, is a social definition, since few genetic differences are found to exist among homo sapiens. Race is commonly used to classify members of groups who have similar physical characteristics such as color or facial features. Behavioral traits are attributed to physical differences rather than to socialization experiences. Conversely, ethnic groups tend to be classified by language differences or cultural patterns that vary from those of the dominant group. Both racial and ethnic groups are viewed as "different" by the dominant group, and prejudice and discrimination are often the result.

PLURALISM

Complete integration of all groups in society would result in the loss of racial or ethnic identity. Many people of color find this prospect objectionable. In recent years, ethnic and racial pride has been given considerable attention by minority group members. Although complete integration (assimilation) theoretically would result in the erosion of racial and ethnic discrimination patterns, it probably will not occur. Many people argue that the contributions of our divergent ethnic and racial groups enrich our culture.

An alternative, **cultural pluralism** (i.e., cultural diversity), the co-existence of various ethnic groups whose cultural differences are respected as equally valid (Perrucci and Knudsen 1983), is difficult to achieve without some vestige of discrimination. Dominant groups demand adherence to their values. Pluralism is difficult to achieve within the matrix of prejudice, discrimination, and cultural differences. Recently, people of color have tried to create and promote cultural pride, yet less-than-equal coexistence continues to characterize their relationship with the dominant group.

Ironically, most immigrant populations have suffered the results of prejudice and discrimination as each new group settled in the United States—the Irish, Italians, Swedes, Germans, French, and others. The irony is, of course, that with the exception of Native Americans, all of us are descendants of immigrants. How quickly groups move from the role of the persecuted to that of persecutors. It is even more ironic that prejudices and discrimination persist and become institutionalized by members of a society that values its Judeo-Christian heritage and provides equal constitutional rights and privileges for all. In recent years some progress has been made in opening up avenues for social and economic participation; however, members of minority groups still must cope with differential treatment and limited opportunities. In the following discussion, we identify some of the issues and problems that confront minority groups and examine antidiscrimination efforts designed to neutralize racial, cultural, and ethnic prejudices.

African Americans

All minority groups have experienced discrimination, but perhaps none more visibly than our African American population. Emerging from slavery, where they were considered chattel (property) and nonpersons, African Americans have continually found societally imposed constraints peding their progress toward the achievement of social equality. During the "Jim Crow" days, for example, blacks could not dine at public restaurants used by whites, could use only specially marked public restrooms and drinking fountains, had to ride in the rear of buses, had to attend segregated schools, faced expectations of subservient behavior in the presence of whites, and could get only lower-paying domestic or manual labor jobs. Few could achieve justice before the law or gain acceptance as equals to even the lowest-class whites. Although the prescribed behaviors that characterized "Jim Crowism" represented an extreme manifestation of discrimination, all minority groups have experienced social inequality in its more subtle forms.

Today, the results of past and present discrimination are best reflected in the characteristics of African Americans, who represent about 11 percent of our total population. They earn only 60 percent as much income as whites, unemployment is particularly high among young African American adults (30 percent), and black families are three times more likely than whites to have incomes below the poverty line. Although, numerically, more whites receive public assistance in one form or another, blacks are proportionally overrepresented on welfare rolls. Educationally, whites complete high school in greater proportions than blacks, and blacks are underrepresented in the fields of law, medicine, dentistry, and business and overrepresented in occupations that require hard manual labor. These data reflect the differential opportunity structure available to the African American population in this country.

Hispanic Populations

Approximately 22 million people of Hispanic origin live in the United States, constituting 9 percent of the total population. Our Hispanic population came to this country from 26 nations. The largest group are Mexican Americans (see Table 4.1).

People of Mexican descent constitute the second largest minority population in the United States. Although most live in major urban areas of the West and Southwest, many continue to reside in rural areas. The Mexican American population is a diverse group. The urban population tends to be better educated, and the effects of acculturation are more

TABLE 4.1   HISPANIC POPULATIONS

Group	Percentage of Population
Mexican	60
Puerto Ricans	12
Cubans	5
Other	23

Source: U.S. Bureau of the Census, *Census of Population, General Population Characteristics, United States,* CP-1-1 (Washington, D.C.: Author, 1990).

visible among them. Those living in rural areas are more likely to be less acculturated, continue to use Spanish as a primary language, and to work in lower-paying jobs often related to harvesting of farm crops. This population group is rapidly growing as "undocumented immigrants" continue to flow across the border into the southwestern states and California. Cultural pride is greatly emphasized and is best reflected in the retention of Spanish as a first language. Bilingual education programs have been designed in some public school systems to enable Mexican American children to progress educationally, although dropout rates continue to be much higher than for the dominant group population. In general, people of Mexican ancestry have experienced the consequences of discrimination in that they hold lower-paying jobs, are underrepresented in politics, live in de facto segregated neighborhoods, and are viewed as being "different" by the dominant group. Upward mobility has been painfully slow in coming, although some progress has been made. Ethnic organizations such as La Raza and LULAC (League of United Latin American Citizens) have sought to unite Spanish-speaking populations to promote favorable social change and to provide greater visibility to the issues and problems that impede the achievement of social equality.

Puerto Ricans and Cubans constitute the largest other Hispanic populations. Approximately two-thirds of the Puerto Rican population reside in the New York City area, while the Cuban population has settled primarily in Florida. The social and economic progress of these groups is similar to that of the Mexican American group. Housing is often inferior, jobs tend to be menial and lower paying, the school dropout rate is high, and access to services and support systems is difficult. Social progress has been considerably greater for the Cuban population due, in part, to its higher educational level. As has been the case with newly migrated Mexicans, other Hispanics came to the United States with the hopes of being able to achieve a higher-quality life, only to find that prejudice and discrimination presented barriers to achieving that dream. Cultural and language barriers continue to make them "different" and more visible targets for differential treatment.

Asian Americans

Asian American immigrants have divergent cultural traits and physical characteristics that separate them from the dominant group. Although they represent less than 2 percent of the United States population, the number of Asian immigrants has increased in recent years. Chinese immigration dates back to the mid-nineteenth century, and they represent the greatest percentage of Asian immigrants (see Table 4.2).

Japanese immigration began around the turn of the twentieth century, the Korean population in the mid-twentieth century, and the Vietnamese in the 1960s and 1970s. The aggregate total of all Asian Americans in the United States is approximately 7.3 million people.

While all of the nationalities constituting the Asian American population have experienced differential treatment, many have been able to achieve a relatively high standard of living in spite of social barriers. The Chinese have been noted for their in-group living patterns; the "China-

Here, a young woman celebrates Dia de los Muertos (Day of the Dead), a time to remember deceased family members and friends, and a holiday that incorporates aspects of Aztec, Mexican, and Catholic traditions. When Mexico and parts of the United States were first controlled by European Catholics, celebration of this holiday was forbidden because it was considered pagan.

towns'' in San Francisco, Los Angeles, New York, and other large cities encourage the preservation of the Chinese cultural heritage. Prejudice and discrimination continue to be among the more significant obstacles for Asian Americans in achieving social and economic progress. Because of their physical characteristics, language and cultural heritage, they continue to be viewed by many as ''foreigners.'' The internment of the Japanese population in ''holding'' camps during World War II is one example of how Japanese citizens, many native born, were viewed as foreigners with presumptive allegiance to Japan rather than the United States. Ironically, German and Italian Americans were not treated in this manner even though Germany and Italy were, along with Japan, the Axis powers.

TABLE 4.2	ASIAN AMERICAN POPULATION BY NATIONALITY

Nationality	Percentage of Asian Americans
Chinese	22.6
Filipino	19.3
Japanese	11.6
Asian Indian	11.2
Korean	11.0
Vietnamese	8.4
Other	15.9

Source: U.S. Bureau of the Census, *Census of Population, General Population Characteristics, United States*, CP-1-1 (Washington, D.C.: Author, 1990).

More recently the Vietnamese have been the target for discrimination, which has been reflected in the difficulty they have experienced in securing housing, employment, and acceptance in American communities. In addition to physical characteristics, language barriers have intensified "differences," resulting in closed avenues for social and economic participation.

Native Americans

Numerically the smallest minority group, Native Americans (American Indians) have over the years been consistently among the most oppressed. Native Americans, who prior to colonialization were free to establish their villages and roam the countryside, lost all rights and privileges once conquered. Considered savages (less than human), most were relegated to reservations where they found oppressive limits on their behaviors and freedom of movement. The responsibility for overseeing these reservations was given to the Bureau of Indian Affairs, a governmental agency that more often was a barrier rather than a help. The effects of differential treatment and limited opportunity are reflected in the fact that the average education for Native Americans age 25 or over is 9.6 years—the lowest of any ethnic group in the United States. Nearly one-third are illiterate, and only one out of five has a high school education.

Although they were the first "Americans," Native Americans seldom have been able to experience free and full involvement in society. Currently, large numbers continue to live on reservations, which further segregates them from interaction with the dominant group and limits their opportunity structure. Reservations represent the most overt form of purposeful discrimination. Although the plight of Native Americans has improved somewhat in recent years (with higher levels of education and commercial development on the reservations), many barriers to free and full social participation remain.

Valuing cultural traditions is an important part of one's ethnic identity. Too often, Native Americans and other groups have been given the message that they must reject their traditions to be accepted and viewed as successful. Fortunately, today many young people are learning to have pride in themselves and their heritage, while older members of ethnic groups are valuing the opportunity to pass down customs and traditions that are important to them and their culture.

Like other minority groups, not all Native Americans share the same values and traditions. Life-styles as well as opportunities vary from tribe to tribe (there are 300 tribes in the United States); many have migrated into cities in search of employment and more optimum resources. The increase of Native Americans in urban areas has created identity problems for many; discriminated against, they don't always fit in well in city environments, yet because they have left their reservation, they also have difficulty being accepted if they return to their homeland (La-Framboise and Bigfoot, 1989).

◢ EFFORTS TO PRODUCE SOCIAL EQUALITY FOR MINORITY GROUPS

Bringing an end to institutional racism and discrimination is not an easy task. Prejudices have lingered over several generations and are difficult to extinguish, in spite of efforts to enlighten the public about the consequences of maintaining false beliefs and practices. Little progress was made in dismantling segregation until the government initiated action to do so. Until President Truman ordered the cessation of segregation in the Armed Forces (1948), most government agencies supported separation of the races (Perrucci and Knudsen 1983).

School Desegregation

The catalyst for ending separate public school education was the Supreme Court decision *Brown v. Board of Education* (1954), which mandated an end to segregation in public schools. Ruling that "separate was not equal," the Court ordered public schools integrated and opened to children of all races and ethnic groups. Because of de facto housing patterns, members of minority groups lived in common neighborhoods and their children attended neighborhood schools. In order to implement the Court's decision, busing became necessary, which resulted in strong resistance by the white population. White citizens' councils emerged in the South and Midwest to resist school integration.

Many state governments questioned the constitutionality of the Court's decision and resisted taking appropriate action to hasten the integration process. "Evidence" was sought to support the position that integration of schools would have catastrophic effects on the educational achievement of all children of all races. In a 1962 report ("The Biology of the Race Problem") Wesley C. George, a biologist commissioned by the governor of Alabama, attempted to offer scientific proof that blacks were innately inferior to whites and would not be able to compete with whites in the classroom. Other racist, white supremacist groups, such as the Ku Klux Klan, joined in efforts to prevent school integration.

In spite of all organized resistance, school busing became commonplace and school integration a technical reality. General public acceptance, however, has been equivocal. In the 1980s and 1990s, movement to return to neighborhood schools has been strong and was supported by the Reagan administration. Charles Murray's book *The Bell Curve* (1994) was a rallying point for many to urge the elimination of busing and a return to neighborhood schools. Although advocates for neighborhood schools have argued that these schools could be more culturally relevant to students and their families, in many instances schools in nonwhite neighborhoods have seen a significant loss of resources when busing has been eliminated.

Major Legislation

During the 1960s, significant progress was made in eliminating segregationist policies and controlling the effects of discrimination. President Johnson's Great Society programs sought to eradicate segregation entirely and to make discrimination an offense punishable under the law. In 1964, the **Civil Rights Act** was passed. This act, amended in 1965, sought to ban discrimination based on race, religion, color, or ethnicity in public facilities, government-operated programs, or employment. A similar act, passed in 1968, made illegal the practice of discrimination in advertising and the purchase or rental of residential property or its financing.

Under the new legal sanctions for desegregation, a groundswell of support mounted among disenfranchised people of color and sympathetic dominant group members. The Reverend Martin Luther King, Jr. and organized freedom marchers sought to raise the consciousness of society regarding the obscenities of segregationist policies. King's nonviolent movement provided great visibility to the injustices of discrimination and served to stimulate and influence policies for change. Other significant organizations, such as the Southern Christian Leadership Conference (SCLC), the National Urban League, the National Association for the Advancement of Colored People (NAACP), La Raza, and the League of United Latin American Citizens (LULAC), were actively pursuing social and economic justice for people of color during this period. As the new civil rights legislation was implemented, an air of hope prevailed that discrimination would soon become a matter of history. School busing facilitated public school integration, public facilities were opened to people of color, and the employment market became more accepting of minority applicants. Further advances were made under the influence of the Economic Opportunities Act of 1964. Neighborhoods were organized, and their residents registered to vote. This movement was furthered by the Voting Rights Act of 1965, which prohibited the imposition of voting qualification requirements based on race, color, age, or minority status. The impact of the civil rights movement was far reaching in gaining ground in the struggle for full and equal participation by minorities in the social and economic areas of our society.

Erosion of Progress

The rapid pace of the change effort was short lived. By the late 1970s, racial polarization had increased with a new wave of conservatism. Whites were much more prone to attribute the "lack of progress" among the African American population to the African Americans themselves, rather than to discrimination, thus supporting the position that discrimination was no longer a problem for "motivated" African Americans. By the late 1970s, it was clear that racial and minority issues were not among the top priorities for the white majority. Instead,

> national defense, energy supplies, and inflation have readily replaced minority concerns as priority issues during the last decade, and that shift in attention has been accompanied by a shift of resources away from minorities. Fostered by this contraction of resources the most intense overt conflicts over resources now occur not between the majority and minority groups, but among minority groups. (Walters 1982, 26)

The outlook for a well-articulated and implemented program to eliminate prejudice and discrimination during the 1990s appears bleak. The effort to creatively and forcefully address this issue has waned since the mid-70s and continues to receive only a token effort from the current administration. Currently, the preoccupation with balancing the budget by scaling down government programs and services tends to overshadow concerted and focused efforts to dismantle the institutional barriers that result in differential treatment for minority groups.

Although efforts to achieve minority equality are still intact, government commitment has waned. **Affirmative action** programs, which once mandated the selection of qualified minority group members for publicly operated business and education, appear to have been downgraded. In 1995, affirmative action directives are under close scrutiny by the Congress as well as the White House. The concept of affirmative action was derived from the civil rights acts of the 1960s and was, in part, an attempt to initiate actions that would equalize the social and economic playing field for all people and ultimately break the barriers of discrimination for those who had long been oppressed by established values, policies, and practices.

Compensatory justice, an underlying axiom for affirmative action directives, provided the impetus for eliminating institutionalized barriers to employment, education, and social intercourse in general. It requires that women and people of color be hired, or admitted to educational institutions and professional schools, on an equal basis with that of white males. Public reaction to what was considered to be a "quota system" resulted in cries of "reverse discrimination." Apparently, Congress has been attentive to public outcries and is seriously pondering legislation that would remove the substantive force of affirmative action programs, if not abolish the programs altogether.

There is little doubt that affirmative action programs have opened up opportunities for the oppressed. Although "tokenism" has been a major concern, many women, African Americans, Hispanics, and other members of minority groups have been able to achieve higher educational status, secure jobs, and achieve vertical mobility in the employment arena as a result of efforts to right historical wrongs. Many view the downgrading of government efforts in the area of affirmative action as a return to past discriminatory practices. On the other hand, proponents of downgrading these programs feel that they have not been effective, have resulted in reverse discrimination and, in the final analysis, all populations will be better served if positions are awarded on competency and merit rather than arbitrarily mandated by social legislation.

Social Work and the Civil Rights Movement

Inherent in social work's identity is its commitment to social action directed toward the elimination of barriers that deny equal rights and full participation to all members of society. Since the early days, when social workers assisted in assimilating new immigrants into our culture and sought to improve social conditions for them, the profession has engaged the citizenry in working toward social equality and an equal opportunity structure. The National Association of Social Workers, as well as the Council on Social Work Education, has given high priority to incorporating content about vulnerable populations, including women, gays and lesbians, and people of color, into professional social work practice and social work education. Social work practitioners strive to be mindful of the consequences of minority group status and familiar with the racial and cultural backgrounds of their clients when assisting them in achieving solutions to problems. Through social action, efforts are made to change community attitudes, policies, and practices that disadvantage members of vulnerable populations. As advocates, social workers seek to modify rules and regulations that deny equal treatment to those assigned to a minority status. As organizers, they work with leaders from minority groups in identifying priorities, gaining community support, and facilitating change through the democratic process.

Social workers are active in organized public efforts to abolish discriminatory practices. As citizens (as well as professionals), they support political candidates who are openly committed to working for social equality. They are involved in public education designed to dispel prejudice and to promote productive interaction among divergent racial and ethnic groups. In a public climate where the pursuit of social and economic equality has lessened, social workers have the responsibility to maintain a vigilant pursuit of equality.

Social workers should view the concept of **social justice** not as rhetorical verbiage, but as a variable that is inherent as a mandate for the social work profession. In fact, since the profession's inception, social justice has been a basic axiom for practice. Social justice—that is, achieving a society in which all members have access to the same rights and privileges without regard to gender, race, ethnic affiliation, creed, age, sexual orientation, or physical and mental capacities—is essential for the establishment of a nondiscriminatory society. Only when that goal is achieved can social and economic equality prevail.

A fundamental avenue through which social justice is achieved is by empowering disenfranchised and oppressed individuals and groups. **Empowerment** is both a process and a goal, through which individuals and groups gain mastery over their lives, become active participants, and make decisions, that is, gain control over their lives and the environment in which they interact (Swift and Levin 1987). Disempowered populations can only react to the norms and mandates of others, which can lead to the perpetuation of discriminatory practices.

SUMMARY

Few observers would deny that the United States has experienced a major sexual revolution during the past few decades. As part of the human rights movement, many advances have been made in reducing sexism in our society. Opportunities for economic and social participation of women are greater now than they have been before in the history of this country. Although there have been reversals, such as the failure to ratify the ERA, societal pressures to assure equal treatment and opportunities for women continue.

Social inequality also has characterized the treatment of racial and ethnic minorities and homosexuals in the United States. Although some progress has been made toward more favorable treatment, full participation rights have not yet been achieved. Discrimination and differential treatment of women, people of color, and homosexuals continue to restrict their achievement of social and economic progress. Although legislation has served as a catalyst for removing long-standing practices that denied equal rights, in recent years the conservative movement has lowered the priorities for attaining social equality for women and people of color. Even less attention has been given to social equality for homosexuals. Social work has a long tradition of promoting social equality, and the commitment of the profession to continue pressing for this will be greater as the societal thrust to do so declines.

Over the past decade the euphemism "politically correct" has gained popularity among those who question the validity and viability of certain attitudes or practices that are directed toward oppressed or disenfranchised groups. Hence the notion that certain words, phrases, or actions (i.e., politically correct responses) have become, for many, substitutes for "correct" responses. Unfortunately, the concept of political correctness invokes negativism for (in many instances) positive actions taken. For example, a person may behave in a certain manner because it is the politically correct thing to do—not necessarily the right (or decent) thing to do. In reality, many (not all) politically correct responses are socially responsible ones. As indicated earlier in this chapter, it is quite possible for persons who are prejudiced to behave in a socially responsible manner even though their intentions are simply to be politically correct. Unfortunately, some may use the guise of political correctness for fear that a true and honest response may place them in jeopardy of losing an advantage they treasure. Social workers should not be overly concerned with being politically correct. The value base of the profession and commitment of social work practitioners to genuineness that is characteristic of socially responsible behavior should always be paramount when intervening with clients or serving as advocates on their behalf.

In this chapter we did not seek to provide an in-depth analysis of the parameters of disenfranchised and oppressed groups in America. Rather, we designed the text to make you aware that institutional discrimination has long existed, and that its victims continue to suffer the consequences of differential treatment and limited opportunity. Although advocacy groups have been able to effect positive political changes, and public attitudes have improved, much has yet to be accomplished to establish social equality for all groups in America. Prejudice and discrimination are the products of social interaction. As social constructs, they can be replaced by values that respect the dignity and worth of all human beings and result in a society that promotes equal treatment for all.

KEY TERMS

affirmative action
Civil Rights Act
comparable worth
cultural pluralism
empowerment
Equal Rights Amendment (ERA)
homophobia

minority group
prejudice
sexism
social inequality
social justice
stereotyping

DISCUSSION QUESTIONS

1. Discuss the factors that produce prejudice and discrimination. How do those factors contribute to institutional sexism and racism?

2. Trace the early efforts to produce social equality for women.

3. Define cultural pluralism. What problems are inherent in achieving social justice for all groups in a pluralistic society?

4. How would you assess the progress that has been made in achieving social equality for minority groups? As a social worker, what would you suggest as a feasible plan for eradicating discrimination?

5. How do you explain public reaction to same-sex partners? As a social worker, how do you explain the concerns that many social workers are homophobic? What suggestions would you make to alleviate the problems of prejudice and discrimination towards gays and lesbians?

6. Identify the role of social work in the civil rights movement. What role do you plan to play to promote social and economic justice?

REFERENCES

Beiber, Irving, ed. 1962. *Homosexuality.* New York: Basic Books.

Bergman, Edgar. 1982. *The compleat chauvinist.* New York: Macmillan.

Deckard, Barbara S. 1983. *The women's movement: Political and psychological issues.* New York: Harper & Row.

De Crescenzo, Teresa, and Christine McGill. 1978. Homophobia: A study of the attitudes of mental health professionals toward homosexuality. Master's thesis, University of Southern California, School of Social Work.

Dressel, P. 1987. Patriarchy and social welfare work. *Social Problems* 34: 294–309.

Dulaney, Diane D., and James Kelly, 1982. Improving services to gay and lesbian clients. *Social Work* 27(2): 178–83.

Fanshel, David. 1976. Status differentials: Men and women in social work. *Social Work* 21(6): 448–53.

Feldberg, R. C. 1984. Comparable worth: Toward theory and practice in the United States. *Signs* 10: 311–28.

George, Wesley C. 1962. *The biology of the race problem.* Report prepared by Commission of the Governor of Alabama.

Irwin, Patrick, and Norman C. Thompson. 1977. Acceptance of the rights of homosexuals: A social profile. *Journal of Homosexuality* 3 (Winter): 107–21.

Knopp, L. 1990. Social consequences of homosexuality. *Geographical Magazine* (May): 20–25.

LaFramboise, T., and D. S. Bigfoot. 1989. Cultural and cognitive considerations in the prevention of American adolescent suicide. *Journal of Adolescence* 11: 139–53.

Macksey, Joan. 1976. *The book of women's achievements.* New York: Stein & Day.

Matthews, Karen A., and Judith Rodin. 1989. Women's changing work roles. *Journal of the American Psychological Association* 11(44): 1389–93.

Murray, Charles. 1994. *The bell curve.* Washington, D.C.: The New Republic.

Perrucci, Robert, and Dean D. Knudsen. 1983. *Sociology.* St. Paul, Minn.: West.

Presser, H. B. 1987. Recent changes in women's employment. Paper presented at the John D. and Catherine T. McArthur Foundation Workshop, Women, Work and Health: The Impact of Changing Roles in Women's Health and the Family. Hilton Head, South Carolina.

Shuttlesworth, Verla. 1978. Women in administration in public schools of Texas. Ph.D. diss., Baylor University.

Sirkin, M. 1994. Resisting cultural meltdown. *The Family Therapy Networker* 18, no. 4 (July/August): 48–52.

Swift, C., and G. Levin. 1987. Empowerment: An emerging mental health technology. *Journal of Primary Prevention* 8: 71–94.

U.S. Bureau of the Census. 1990. *Census of Population, General Population Characteristics, United States.* CP-1-1. Washington, D.C.: Author.

U.S. Government. 1990. *Congressional Quarterly Weekly Report.* (Nov. 10): 36–38. Washington, D.C.: GPO.

Walters, Ronald W. 1982. Race, resources, conflict. *Social Work* 27(1): 24–29.

Wirth, Louis. 1938. Urbanism as a way of life. *American Journal of Sociology* 44 (July): 3–24.

Yinger, J. Milton. 1970. *The scientific study of religion.* New York: Macmillan.

Young, P. 1982. *God's bullies.* New York: Holt, Rinehart & Winston.

Zastrow, Charles. 1986. *Introduction to social welfare institutions.* 3d ed. Homewood, Ill.: Dorsey.

SUGGESTED FURTHER READINGS

Abramovitz, M. 1988. *Regulating the lives of women.* Boston: South End.

Bean, F. D., and M. Tienda. 1987. *The Hispanic population of the United States.* New York: Russell Sage.

Chau, K. C. 1990. Social work practice: Towards a cross-cultural model. *Journal of Applied Social Sciences* 14(2): 249–74.

Cochran, J. W., D. Langston, and C. Woodward, eds. 1988. *Changing our power: An introduction to women's studies.* Dubuque, Ia.: Kendall Hunt.

Davis, L., and E. Proctor. 1989. *Race, gender and class.* Englewood Cliffs, N.J.: Prentice-Hall.

DeVere, W., and E. G. Schlesinger. 1987. *Ethnic sensitive social work practice.* 2d ed. Colombus, Oh.: Merrill Publishing Co.

Goldberg, G. S., and E. Kremen, eds. 1990. *The feminization of poverty: Only in America?* New York: Praeger.

Gould, K. 1988. Asian and Pacific Islanders: Myth and reality. *Social Work* 33: 142–47.

Herek, G. M. 1984. Attitudes towards lesbians and gay men: A factor analysis study. *Journal of homosexuality* 10: 52–67.

Jacobsen, J. L. 1992. *Gender bias: Roadblock to sustainable development.* Washington, D.C.: Worldwatch Institute.

Kitano, H. L., and R. Daniels. 1988. *Asian Americans.* Englewood Cliffs, N.J.: Prentice Hall.

Logan, S., E. Freeman, and R. McRoy, eds. 1990. *Social work practice with black families.* New York: Longman.

Olson, J. S., and R. Wilson. 1984. *Native Americans in the twentieth century.* Provo, Ut.: Brigham Young University Press.

Weyr, T. 1988. *Hispanic USA: Breaking the melting pot.* New York: Harper & Row.

PART TWO

SOCIAL WORK
Methods of Intervention

In this part of the book, you will be learning about methods of intervention used by social workers. In Chapter 5, "Direct Practice: Social Work with Individuals and Families," you will explore the most prevalent method in professional social work practice, intervention by the social worker with individuals and families who are experiencing difficulties interacting within their environment. You will learn about theories and techniques used by social workers in assisting individuals and families to build on their strengths and identify strategies to meet their needs and improve their social functioning or the environment in which they function.

In Chapter 6, "Direct Practice: Social Work with Groups and the Community," we examine methods used in working with clients in groups, an effective method of intervention that is receiving increased attention both because of its effectiveness with many populations and because it is often seen as more cost-effective than working with clients individually. We review relevant theories related to working with groups and identify a variety of groups in which individuals interact. We also describe important factors to consider when social workers form groups, the importance of group process when working with groups; and different methods social workers use when working with groups. Because the exosystem—or community—level of the environment has such a major impact on individual and family functioning, one of the major ways that social workers can address client needs is by working within the community to develop or strengthen programs and policies, advocate for client needs, and empower community members to advocate for themselves and develop interventions that address their needs. In Chapter 6, we also explore the importance of the community in working with clients and various methods of community organization and community intervention commonly used by social workers to create individual and social change.

In Chapter 7, "Social Agency Administration," we look at the myriads of essential tasks used by social workers to bring together the resources, opportunities, roles, and objectives of social welfare agencies to meet human needs. We explore various strategies of leadership, administration, and management as requisites for increasing the efficiency and effectiveness of human service agencies. As social welfare needs continue to grow, while at the same time resources to address these needs are reduced, managing social welfare programs efficiently and effectively and demonstrating that you have done so are increasingly critical for the survival of the agency.

In the final chapter of this part, Chapter 8, "Research and Practice," we focus on the interdependence of social work practice and research and the use of social research as an integral part of the problem-solving process. We discuss the vital role of research in policy and practice to continually buttress practice with data gained from research findings. This role is critical so that we can continue to develop new knowledge about ways to more effectively address social welfare issues and work with client systems, and so that we can demonstrate our effectiveness in order to receive the resources necessary to address the many social welfare needs that exist today.

As you learn about the methods of social work intervention used by social work practitioners in Part 2, ask yourself questions that draw from what you learned in Part 1. For example, as you read the chapter on individuals and families, ask yourself questions such as: How do past and present social welfare perspectives and policies shape the ways people view individuals and families today, the types of needs individuals and families might be likely to have as a result, and the methods of intervention that might be used in working with individuals and families to address these needs? How can the systems/ecological framework help us to understand issues relating to individuals and families and the impact of the broader environment on their functioning? How might these issues be addressed using the methods of intervention discussed in this section of the book? What are the relationships between factors such as race and ethnicity, gender, age, and sexual orientation on individual and family functioning, and how would social workers consider these factors when working with individuals and families in practice settings? ■

CHAPTER 5

DIRECT PRACTICE
Social Work with Individuals and Families

Sam, his wife Karen, and their two children, Teresa (age 8) and Clark (age 6), were considered by all to be an ideal family. Sam was a carpenter who worked for a small construction company and Karen worked part-time at a local McDonald's. All seemed well until it was discovered that Karen had breast cancer, needed chemo and radiation therapy, and could no longer work. Neither Sam nor Karen were covered by health insurance, and medical bills quickly mounted. Sam found a second job in an attempt to generate funds to pay the bills. As a result, Sam was away from home frequently while Karen was too ill to manage the children and assist with household matters. The stress around family finances, deteriorating household management, and unattended children was creating dysfunctional family interaction.

Kelly, a family service social worker, learned of the family's dilemma and arranged for a homemaker to visit the home three times a week to help the family with household maintenance needs. Kelly regularly visited with Sam and Karen to ascertain needs and progress. Kelly also arranged for Terri, a medical social worker, to assist in planning with Karen for her treatment needs and arranged with health care providers a repayment plan that could be managed within the family budget. Terri also collaborated with Norris, the school social worker, to arrange after-school care for Teresa and Clark during those periods in which Karen was receiving treatment. As soon as Karen was physically ready, Terri arranged for Karen to attend a group session for cancer patients.

As a result of the collaborative efforts of the family and the social workers involved, family tension was relieved and the family moved toward more functional family interaction. ■

The society and world in which we live are characterized by rapid transition, change, and uncertainty. The technological revolution has contributed to sweeping modifications of life-styles, increased mobility, and shifting values. As the capacity to create new products has increased, the shifting job market has required new skills and more adaptable employees. Relationships among individuals have become tenuous and short lived. As a result, a sense of roots in the community is becoming increasingly difficult to achieve. Family life has been affected by social and job-related pressures and upward mobility. The pursuit of success has conflicted with long-cherished values regarding the sanctity of family-first goals. These changes, which began in the 1960s, have given rise to an emphasis on individuation and happiness as contrasted with strong family commitments. Broken families have become commonplace as marriages are being terminated with ever-increasing frequency.

Emotionally disturbed children, the illicit use of drugs by both adults and children, an increasing burden of caring for older adults, and two-career marriages have created demands on individuals and families that often leave them disrupted, confused, tense, and frustrated.

These and many other social pressures generated by our rapidly changing society are experienced by virtually all of us at one time or another. It is neither an unusual response nor a sign of weakness for individuals and families in stressful situations to seek professional help with the hope of alleviating stress and its **dysfunctional** consequences. All of us have needed the steady guidance of a respected friend or professional at some time. When problems become increasingly stressful and self-help efforts fail to produce solutions, professional assistance may be needed. *Direct practice social work,* as defined in Chapter 2, is a method of providing that assistance.

Direct practice with individuals, families, and groups is the oldest social work practice method (traditionally referred to as casework, as noted in Chapter 2). As we indicated in Chapter 2, it had its formal developmental roots in the Charity Organization Society Movement, when "scientific charity" was emphasized and the need for trained professional workers became a fundamental prerequisite to a more studied approach in working with client populations. The distinguishing characteristic of **direct practice** (as contrasted with other social work methods) is its face-to-face involvement with individuals, families, and small groups in helping them seek solutions to perplexing problems.

In this chapter, we identify the components and characteristics of direct practice methods that are used with individuals and families. Direct practice with groups and the community is explored in the following chapter. Be aware that the purpose of these direct practice chapters is to enable you to acquire a beginning-level acquaintance with the social work process and method as well as with the theories that undergird direct practice. As you progress through the social work curriculum, more in-depth analyses of methods, processes, and theory will be examined. ∎

◤ DIRECT PRACTICE: A DEFINITION

A social work direct practitioner assists clients in a change process that focuses on producing a higher level of social functioning. Direct practice is both a process and a method. As a process, it involves a more or less orderly sequence of progressive stages in engaging the client in activities and actions that promote the achievement of agreed-upon therapeutic goals. As a method, it entails the creative use of techniques and knowledge that guide intervention activities designed by the direct practitioner. Direct practice also is an art that utilizes scientific knowledge about human behavior and the skillful use of relationships to enable the client to activate or develop interpersonal and, if necessary, community resources to achieve a more positive balance with his or her environment. Direct practice seeks to improve, restore, maintain, or enhance the client's social functioning. The key converging elements in direct practice are that it

- Is an art—that is, it involves a skill that results from experience or training
- Involves the application of knowledge about human behavior
- Is based on client involvement in developing options designed to resolve problems
- Emphasizes the use of the client's resources (psychological and physical) as well as those extant in the community to meet client needs
- Is based on an orderly helping process
- Is based on planned change efforts
- Focuses on solutions

Although the basis for direct practice was grounded in the philosophy and wisdom of early social work pioneers such as Mary Richmond, Gordon Hamilton, Helen Harris Perlman, Florence Hollis, and others, many changes in practice have occurred over the years. As greater knowledge of human development, ecology, economics, organizational behavior, stress management, social change, and more effective intervention techniques have emerged, direct practice has been enriched and offers a more scientifically buttressed model for intervention. The face-to-face relationship between the social worker and the client has maintained its integrity as a fundamental prerequisite for intervention, as has the emphasis on process (study, assessment, intervention objectives, intervention, evaluation, and follow-up). Democratic decision making and the belief in the dignity, worth, and value of the client system continue to undergird direct practice philosophy. The client's right to self-determination and confidentiality are fundamental practice values in the helping process. These values and practice principles form the fundamental concepts and interventive practice techniques that are identified with direct practice.

PREPARATION FOR DIRECT PRACTICE

Earlier in this chapter, we indicated that a requisite for direct practice is an understanding of factors that affect human behavior. The practitioner must not only be armed with an understanding of personality theory and a knowledge of the life cycle but must also be able to assess the effects of the social systems context within which behavior occurs. Factors such as race, gender, ethnicity, religion, social class, sexual orientation, physical condition, occupation, family structure, health, age, income, and educational achievement are among many of the contributing variables that converge to account for behavior within different social contexts. Practitioners obviously cannot master all knowledge related to behavior, but theories allow us to make guided assumptions about behavior from which we can make logical estimates of factors associated with the client's unmet needs. The direct practitioner is able to arrive at probable causes of dysfunction and to establish theoretically plausible interventive activities that will assist client systems in addressing needs.

THE DIRECT PRACTICE PROCESS

The orderly process of direct practice consists of social study, assessment, intervention, and evaluation. Each step in this process is guided by the application of theory and knowledge of human behavior.

Social Study

The social study consists of obtaining relevant information about the client system and perceived needs. The client's perception of needs and problems, their antecedents, ways they are affecting life satisfaction and performance, attempts at life management, and outcome goals are important parts of the social study. The practitioner also obtains information regarding the client's ability to function in a variety of roles and collects data that enhance the practitioner's ability to initiate the process of making initial judgments about probable causes and potential actions that might lead to resolution. The social study responds to such questions as: Who is the client? What is the nature of the needs and problems as the client sees and experiences them? What has the client done to alleviate these needs and problems? How effective were the efforts? What other individuals or groups are affected by the needs and problems, and how is the client related or associated with them? What are the client's strengths and weaknesses? How motivated is the client to work toward solutions to address these needs and problems?

Assessment

Assessment is the process of making tentative judgments about how the information derived from the social study affects the client system in its behaviors as well as in the meaning of those behaviors. As DuBois and Miley (1992) suggest, "the purpose of assessment is to understand the problem and determine how to reduce its impact" (252). As such, assessment provides the basis for initiating and establishing intervention objectives and formally engaging the client system in the interventive process. It is at this stage of the direct practice process that the perceived reality of client behaviors is filtered through the matrix of practice theory and a basic understanding of human behavior in order to arrive at potential sources of the problem(s).

Accurate assessment is the catalyst for establishing goals and objectives with the client and is an essential precursor for focused interventive efforts. For that reason, assessment is a dynamic process that is modified and updated as the worker gains more insight, information, and experience in working with the client system, including estimates of how the client is using the helping process in addressing identified needs. In addition, a meaningful assessment always reflects the ethnic, gender, racial, and cultural context of the client system.

At the most rudimentary level, assessment seeks to answer such questions as: What factors are contributing to the client's unmet needs? What systems are involved? What is the effect of the client's behavior on interacting systems (and vice versa)? What is the potential for initiating a successful change effort?

Goal Setting

Goal setting is the process in which the client and practitioner ascertain intervention options that have the potential to address identified needs based on the client's abilities and capacities. Short-term and long-term goals are developed after reviewing all options and determining which are most appropriate for the particular client, need, and situation.

The responsibility for goal setting evolves as a product of mutual exploration between the social worker and the client. Effective goal setting can serve as a therapeutic "jump-start" for the client as an initial commitment to engage in the change process. Goals always should be realistically achievable, organized around specific targets for change, and related to the client's capacity to engage in behaviors that will move in the direction of positive change. As a practical matter, the least emotionally charged goals should be addressed first since they are more likely to be achieved. As a consequence of successful achievement, the client's confidence is embellished and enthusiasm for the change effort is more likely to occur.

Contracting

In **contracting,** the practitioner and the client agree to work toward the identified intervention goals. To facilitate and clarify the commitment implied by the contract, the role of the practitioner is identified explicitly, and the client agrees to perform tasks related to addressing identified needs and problems. The contract makes visible the agreement both parties have reached and serves as a framework from which they may periodically assess intervention progress. Contracts may be renegotiated or altered during the course of intervention, as more viable goals become apparent. Contracts also help to maintain the focus of intervention.

Intervention

The focus of direct practice intervention is derived from the social study and assessment and sanctioned by the contract between the practitioner and client. The implementation phase of intervention focuses on meeting established goals and may involve such activities as counseling, role playing, engaging other community resources, establishing support groups, developing resources, finding alternative-care resources, encouraging family involvement, offering play therapy, or employing related strategies. The goal of **intervention** is to assist the clients toward an acceptable resolution of problems and to address their unmet needs. The practitioner must skillfully involve the client throughout the intervention process by providing not only regular feedback and support but also an honest appraisal of the problem-solving efforts.

Evaluation

Clients are not likely to remain in the intervention process unless they feel some positive movement has been made toward meeting their needs. **Evaluation** is an ongoing process in which the practitioner and client review intervention activities·and assess the impact on the client's problem situation. Both must intensively examine their behavior, with the goal of understanding the impact on intervention goals. What has changed? What has not changed? Why? How does the client view identified needs and problems at this time? Has social functioning improved? Become less functional? What is the overall level of progress? Are different interventions needed? Evaluation within this context becomes a self-, as well as a joint, assessment process. Based on the evaluation, intervention may continue along the same lines or be modified as implied by the evaluative process.

THE DIRECT PRACTICE RELATIONSHIP

The direct practice relationship is the conduit through which assistance is extended by the social worker and received and acted upon by the client. The principles and values underpinning the relationship are much more than a mere catechism to be learned by the worker. They must be experienced by the client in interacting with the worker. It is essential that the worker be genuine and approachable if the client is to feel enabled to share problems and to develop confidence and trust in the worker and in the helping process. As the client "tests the waters" by investing time and energy in the problem-solving process, trust (an underlying axiom for an effective helping relationship) will be established only if the relationship principles and values are a distinctive aspect of client-worker interaction.

Social work practice principles are derived from the profession's value base and reflected in the Code of Ethics. Historically, professional social workers have been committed to the following principles as basic for the establishment of a helping relationship with client systems:

• **Self-determinism:** Social work practitioners respect their clients' rights to make choices that affect their lives. On occasion, those choices may not appear to be in the best interests of the client; however, the role of the practitioner in such an instance would be to point out the potentially dysfunctional aspects of the choices. Of course, this does not preclude or limit the practitioner's effort to assist the client in making more appropriate choices. However, it does indicate that exerting undue influence or belittling the client is unacceptable behavior in "bringing the client around" to more appropriate choices. Social work is based on a democratic process, in which self-determinism is a fundamental part.

• **Confidentiality:** The client's right to privacy is guarded by the principle of confidentiality. It is based on the notion that information shared between the client and practitioner is privileged. The client must not be compromised by making public the content of information disclosed in the intervention process. Confidentiality assures the client that feelings, attitudes, and statements made during intervention sessions will not be misused. This principle also commits the practitioner to using client information only for professional purposes in working with the client.

• **Individualization and Acceptance:** Regardless of the nature of the client's problems, each client has the right to be treated as an individual with needs, desires, strengths, and weaknesses different from those of anyone else. Acceptance is the ability to recognize the dignity and value inherent in all clients, in spite of the complex array of problems and needs that characterize their behavior.

• **Nonjudgmental Attitude:** Recognizing that all human beings have strengths and weaknesses, experience difficult problems, make improper choices, become angry and frustrated, and often act inappropriately, the practitioner maintains a neutral attitude toward the client's behavior. To judge clients and their behaviors is to erect implicitly a barrier that may block communication with them. From the clients' perspective, judgmentalism places the caseworker in the same category as others who may be making negative judgments about them. Nonjudgmentalism does not limit the right of the caseworker to confront the client with inappropriate behaviors. It does suggest that the client should not be condemned because of them.

• **Freedom of Expression:** The client's need to express feelings and emotions is encouraged. Often, pent-up emotions become disabling to the client and result in more problematic behaviors. The client should be encouraged to engage in free and unfettered self-expression within the safety of the direct practice relationship.

THE DEVELOPMENT OF PRACTICE SKILLS

Social workers can develop competency in using the direct practice method through study, role playing, and supervised practice. Since direct practice involves the application of knowledge, it is an effective method of problem solving only if employed skillfully. As in other applied professions, skill is an "art" that is enriched and refined continually through controlled and thoughtful interaction with clients. Just as you might assume that the skill of a surgeon increases with time and experience, those same principles apply to the development of direct practice skills. We now examine some of the more significant skill areas that are essential for effective direct practice.

Conceptual Skills

The ability to understand the interrelationships of various dimensions of the client's life experiences and behaviors and to place them within an appropriate perspective provides a framework from which intervention

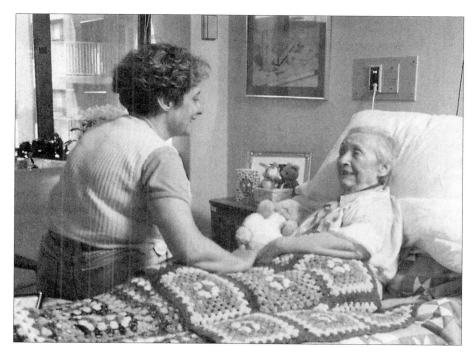

Many social workers function in direct practice settings. Here, an elderly woman in a nursing home receives counseling to help her adjust to her new residence and cope with her failing health.

goals may be established. Conceptual skills enable the worker to view the many incidents and interactions of the client not as discrete entities within themselves, but as interacting parts of the client's behavioral repertoire. Without conceptual skills, social study data have little meaning, and assessment may become less accurate. Conceptual skills also involve an ability to place the client's needs within a theoretical framework and to arrive at appropriate intervention strategies directed toward addressing those needs.

Interviewing Skills

The interview is more than just a conversation with the client. It is a focused, goal-directed activity used to assist clients with their problems. Communication skills are essential in assuring that the interview will be productive. The practitioner must assume the responsibility for maintaining the professional purposes of the interview. Sensitivity to both the client's statements and feelings is necessary. Putting the client at ease, asking questions that enable the client to share observations and experiences, and being a sensitive listener enhance the productivity of the interview. The worker's sensitivity to the client's feelings and the ability to communicate an awareness of those feelings not only strengthen the helping relationship but also encourage and support the client. Empathy, or the ability to "put oneself in the client's shoes," is a benchmark quality of the helping relationship. Clients who feel that the worker really understands their needs are able to feel more relaxed and hopeful that they will be able to work together to find ways to address their needs.

Not all interviews are conducted for the same purpose. Zastrow (1989) identifies three types of interviews that are used to facilitate the helping process in social work.

- *Informational interviews* are used primarily to obtain a client history that relates to the needs and problems currently experienced. The history-collecting process should not be concerned with all of the life experiences of the client, but with only selected information that may have an impact on current social functioning.

- The *diagnostic* (assessment) *interview* has a more clinical focus, in that it elicits responses that clarify the client's reactions to needs and problems and establishes some sequential ordering of events that enables the practitioner to make initial judgments about events that affect client behaviors.

- *Therapeutic interviews* are designed to help clients make changes in their life situations that will help them function more effectively. Not only are the client's feelings and emotions shared in these interviews, but problem-solving options are developed and efforts at change reviewed.

Recording

Maintaining case records that provide insightful information into the client's background (social study data), judgments about the nature of needs and problems (assessment), and client-worker activity are essential in maintaining the focus of ongoing activities with the client. Practitioners typically carry a large caseload, with many clients over a long period of time. Properly maintained records enable the worker to review the nature of the situation, objectives, and progress in each case before appointments. In many instances, cases are transferred both inside and outside of the agency, and the case record gives an up-to-date accounting of the client's problems and activities directed toward their resolution. Case records also are useful for research purposes. Properly maintained records strengthen the direct practice process. If viewed within this context, record keeping becomes less of an irrelevant chore and more of a vital tool for effective service delivery.

Beginning social workers should be informed that not all client systems are equally motivated to become engaged in a process designed to help them resolve problems. Even voluntary clients (i.e., those who take the initial steps to seek help) are not always strongly committed, although all are motivated to some extent. Involuntary clients (those who are mandated to seek help, such as criminal offenders) may or may not be motivated to engage in the change effort. Workers must be aware that although they cannot motivate their clients (motivation comes from within), they may be able to provide the incentives that will result in the client's becoming motivated to work on problems.

PRACTICE THEORY

Over the years, a number of theoretical approaches to direct practice have emerged. Practitioners have adopted various models, and many use an eclectic approach; that is, they integrate different aspects of several theories as a framework for practice. Some often find that one particular theoretical model is viable for one type of situation, whereas another may have greater utility in other situations. For example, a caseworker may use behavior therapy with children and ego psychology with adults. The point is that there are many different approaches to practice, each offering the practitioner a theoretical framework for intervention. In the following paragraphs, we include a brief synopsis of the more widely accepted direct practice theories.

Systems/Ecological Framework

This framework for practice, discussed extensively in Chapter 3, is based on the observation that individuals and their environment are in a continual state of interaction and that problematic behavior is the result of disequilibrium between these entities (i.e., the individual and the environment). Since people live in a constantly changing environment, adaptive skills are required in order to maintain coping abilities consonant with environmental demands. Adequate coping skills are predicated upon the abilities of individuals, families, and groups to both integrate the consequences of environmental forces into their adaptive response repertoires and to influence (and change) those environmental factors involved in creating dysfunctional stress. As Brieland, Costin, and Atherton (1985, 145) state:

> The human being and the environment shape each other. Styles of coping with stress emerge from their perceptions of environmental demands and their capabilities for response. The "ecological" model seeks a match between personal and adaptive needs and the qualities of the environment.

The systems/ecological framework focuses the social worker's attention on the interacting systems within which the client system lives, as well as providing a theoretical framework for understanding the rationale related to the system's adaptive responses. As an assessment tool, this framework enables the social worker to identify both functional and dysfunctional responses to environmental demands and stresses. Once these have been identified, the social worker can focus on the processes of social work intervention and goal setting with the client system.

Ego Psychology

Often referred to as psychosocial treatment theory, **ego psychology** stresses the interplay between the individual's internal state and the external environment. The individual's developmental experiences, fears, hostilities, failures, successes, and feelings of love and acceptance all converge to form an estimate of self through which life experiences are filtered and responded to. A main feature of this theory deals with the individual's ability to cope with external pressures and to respond in such a way as to produce satisfaction and feelings of security and self-worth. Often, internal stress results from the inability to solve problems of a mental or physical nature. Inappropriate or underdeveloped coping skills aggravate and intensify the problems, thus causing the person to become apprehensive, insecure, unwilling to risk, anxious, or in extreme cases, mentally ill.

Ego psychology also is concerned with environmental factors that affect the individual's adaptive abilities. Job loss, immobility, death, divorce, poverty, discrimination, and child-management difficulties are among many potentially stressful conditions that may overextend coping capacities. Because stress is experienced individually, practitioners must give individualized consideration to the client and his or her specific situation. Knowledge of stress management, personality organization, and effective coping mechanisms is essential in the assessment process. Ego psychology is an "insight" therapy. Help comes to clients through developing an awareness of their unmet needs and problems and their reactions to them, and then learning to develop more adaptive coping skills.

Perhaps the key principle associated with using ego psychology as a treatment therapy is that of enabling the individual to develop more adaptive coping skills. The result should be the reduction of internal stress, more satisfactory role performance, and greater life satisfaction.

Problem-Solving Approach

One of the more widely used approaches in social work practice is identified as the **problem-solving approach.** This approach, developed by Perlman (1959), emphasizes that successful intervention is based on the motivation, capacity, and opportunity of the client systems for change. Recognizing that problems often immobilize the client, that the abilities of the client then are neutralized or applied inappropriately, and that opportunities for problem solutions are not engaged, this approach stresses the need to "free up" the client system so that the client can work toward solving the problem. The problem-solving approach requires that the client do more than just identify and talk about problems— although both are necessary. The client must begin to move toward taking action (within his or her capacity to do so) to resolve or alleviate the discomfort produced by those problems. Often this requires that resources (the opportunity structure) be tapped to achieve these goals. Generally, opportunity resources include those of the agency involved in the helping process, although they may extend to other community resources.

Conceptually, the problem-solving approach is based on the premise that without *motivation* (or the will or desire to change), only limited progress can be made with the client. Motivation is often stymied as a result of stress experienced through dysfunctional or unresolved problems. Social workers often experience the client's doubts through statements such as "I know it will not do any good to try," "it has not worked out in the past," or "nothing ever turns out right for me." In such instances the social worker must provide inducements that will enable the client to risk taking steps toward problem resolution, with the social worker's assistance. As successful problem solving occurs, motivation is likely to increase.

In the problem-solving process the social worker must be aware of other issues, too. *Capacity* addresses the limits (or ability) of the client to change and includes physical as well as psychological characteristics. For example, a client functioning at a sixth-grade level probably could not become an electrical engineer, but he or she could possibly attend a vocational training program and thereby develop skills that would enhance job opportunities.

Opportunity relates to possibilities within the environmental milieu in which the client interacts on a daily basis. As indicated in the preceding paragraph, a client might attend a vocational school if one is available within the client's locale. If the client had to travel fifty miles, however, transportation and finances might serve as deterrents, and the client thus might not have opportunity to participate. Optimal problem solving can be achieved only if the three components—motivation, capacity, and opportunity—are engaged in the process.

Cognitive-Behavioral Approaches

Cognitive-behavioral theories fall into the general category of behavioral intervention, which emphasizes the responsibility of the client to actively engage in behaviors that are designed to reduce or eliminate problems.

Behavior Modification

Social learning theory undergirds behavior modification therapy. Based on the assumption that all behavior (adaptive as well as maladaptive) is learned, **behavior modification** is an "action" therapy (see Box 5.1). Developmental processes that contribute to the acquisition of positive human responses also are responsible for the development of inappropriate or dysfunctional ones. Since behavior is learned, it is possible to assist the client in discarding faulty behaviors and acquiring new and more appropriate response patterns. Recognizing that external events and internal processing result in specific behaviors, change is effected by modifying one's actions, which will result in changing thought patterns. Any attempt to change the internal process (i.e., helping the client develop insight into the problem apart from directly addressing behavior changes) is considered largely ineffective.

Based on these general principles, the practitioner using behavior modification approaches intervention with the following organizing framework:

- In a social study, only information that is directly related to the current problem is essential for intervention. Antecedent factors are pertinent, such as when the problem began, the circumstances that contribute to the problem behavior, and the client's efforts at problem resolution.

- Intervention must focus on specific problems, not the entire range of problems, that the client experiences. The practitioner assists clients in resolving each problem in an independent manner rather than treating them in total.

- Although the client's "feelings" are considered an important factor, the behavioral act is the target, not intrapsychic dynamics. The practitioner assists the client in developing specific techniques and learning more appropriate behavioral responses, as opposed to altering thought processes related to the problem and its effect. Thought processes are considered to be the results, not causes, of behaviors.

Behavior modification treats the objective, definable dimensions of human response patterns. To facilitate engaging the intervention process, the practitioner and client must agree on the problem to be addressed, contract to work on that problem, agree on the responsibility each will assume in the change effort, specify goals and objectives, discuss the techniques to be employed, and commit themselves to the treatment effort. As with other therapies, monitoring and evaluation are important dimensions of the process. As more functional and acceptable behavior evolves, it is reinforced by more adaptive functioning. Dysfunctional responses are discarded as they become less functional and rewarding for the client.

Reality Therapy

Reality therapy is based on the assumption that individuals are responsible for their behavior. Maladaptive behavior is viewed as the

BOX 5.1

BEHAVIOR MODIFICATION

Shortly after Fred and Mary Chapman accepted 3-year-old Tonya into their home for foster care, their 6-year-old son, Frank, became enuretic. Neither Fred nor Mary could identify the reason(s) for Frank's bed-wetting behavior, since his last episode had been over three years back. In an effort to help Frank control this behavior, Fred and Mary reduced his liquid intake before bedtime, withheld privileges, and, in their frustration, scolded him—all to no avail.

The problem was discussed with the foster care social worker, who suggested that Frank's behavior may have resulted from Tonya's placement in their home—Frank felt displaced! Fred and Mary agreed that they had been overly solicitous of Tonya in their attempt to make her feel safe, wanted, and secure. Following the so-

cial worker's cue, they began spending more time with Frank alone and included him as an important family member in helping Tonya feel more secure. Within two weeks, Frank's enuretic episodes had ended.

Dramatic family changes such as the one described here can be very threatening to a child, as Frank's behavior demonstrated. His involuntary enuresis was a reflection of insecurity prompted by the arrival and attention given to Tonya. As a 6-year-old child, Frank lacked the insight and maturity to verbalize his feelings. As a consequence, regressive behavior took the form of enuresis. When his parents directed more attention to him and included him in planning for Tonya, his fears of displacement were abated and the consequent enuresis ceased.

product of an identity deficiency. Identity, a basic psychological need of all human beings, is successfully achieved through experiencing love and a sense of self-worth. Individuals who have been deprived of love fail to experience a sense of worth and, as a consequence, develop a poor self-concept. Change is effected by confronting clients with their irresponsible behaviors and encouraging them to accept responsibility for their behavior. It is assumed that clients cannot develop a sense of self-worth while engaging in irresponsible behaviors.

Since **self-concept** is a person's internal reaction to the perception of how others see him or her, the practitioner's role in establishing a warm, friendly, accepting relationship becomes an important factor in the intervention process. As with the case of behavior modification, the focus of intervention is on the client's actions, as opposed to feelings. Confrontation with inappropriate behaviors is emphasized, as is the rejection of rationalizations (excuses). Many practitioners elect reality therapy as an intervention framework because of its straightforward application and the more informal, relaxed role of the therapist.

Task-Centered Casework

The **task-centered casework** method exemplifies a short-term therapeutic approach to problem solving (Reid and Epstein 1972). This approach stresses the selection and establishment of specific tasks to be worked on within a limited time. Although different models of intervention may be used (such as the ones previously discussed), the emphasis on setting brief time limits for problem solutions is an integral therapeutic ingredient. By "compacting" the agreed-upon time limits to work on problems, the client must focus his or her attention and energy on the problem, and tasks for achieving resolution must be adopted quickly. The task-centered approach is an action model that is designed to engage the client quickly and meaningfully in identifying, confronting, and acting on problems.

Family Practice

Social workers have long recognized that the family unit provides physical and emotional support for its members and shapes their identity. As mentioned in Chapter 2, socialization of the young is a basic task of the family. When problems occur, all of the family members are affected. For example, when a father loses his job, the income available for food, clothing, shelter, and family recreation becomes limited, thus altering the family's daily patterns. The father may become depressed, which affects relationships with his wife and children. Or, a teenager may experience emotional problems, have difficulty with schoolwork, and in turn become slovenly with home-maintenance responsibilities. Again, all family members are affected by this problem. These (and, of course, a myriad of related problems) are problems with which we can all identify. We have experienced times in our family when disruption occurred, and we have witnessed the stress and tension that resulted.

Social workers often focus on the family as a unit of intervention. Recognizing that all members of a family are affected by the problems of any one member, intervention is keyed to treating the family system. This approach recognizes that the attitudes and emotions of each family member are significant components in moving the family toward more healthy functioning. Family therapy (or intervention) does not preclude any individual member from specialized treatment. It does, however, require that all members be included in the treatment process, since everyone in a family unit both contributes to and is affected by ongoing problems within the unit.

Other Approaches

In addition to the theoretical approaches identified in the preceding paragraphs, practitioners may elect to use other approaches. Rational emotive therapy focuses on "self-talk" as a target for change. Role therapy examines both prescriptive and descriptive roles played by clients and identifies incongruities in role expectations as well as dysfunctional role behaviors. Its purpose is to guide the client toward more functional and appropriate role performance.

Throughout their careers, social workers develop a deeper and more complete awareness of intervention theories. As new knowledge and understanding of human behavior evolves, social workers must remain vigilant and open to incorporating new theoretical concepts into practice modalities.

Practice Effectiveness

Students who are just beginning to explore social work as a helping profession, and experienced social workers, may well be interested in the extent to which direct practice is successful in helping clients with their problems. Research over the past two decades has, to a large extent, produced mixed results. One researcher, however, studied a number of practice approaches and found that practice using problem-solving models and task-centered methods has resulted in positive outcomes (Rubin 1985, 474). In general, researchers have established that accurate assessment of problems is related to the effectiveness of outcomes where strategic application of interventive techniques was employed. On the whole, recent research has been encouraging with respect to the effectiveness of direct practice with clients. As techniques are refined through practice and as knowledge accrues through research, the direct practice social worker should continue to be more effective in helping clients meet their needs.

Direct Practice Supervision

Supervision is typically thought of as a management function—that of overseeing and assuring that employees are fulfilling the purpose and goals of an agency or organization. Although this function may be one of the responsibilities of the social work supervisor, he or she must do much more through supervision. The social work supervisor provides enrichment to practitioners by helping them to develop practice skills through periodic feedback and discussion of cases. The supervisor regulates the flow of cases assigned to workers and utilizes the unique skills of workers through selective case assignment. The supervisor is at times an educator, a listener, an enabler, and a resource for identifying alternative techniques for addressing problems. In their management functions, supervisors present the need for resources to agency executives and maintain standards for excellence in worker performance. Supervisors play a vital role in helping an agency achieve its purposes.

DIRECT PRACTICE AND THE MSW SOCIAL WORKER

Direct practice is the primary method used by social workers, although contemporary practice requires that the worker become involved in other aspects of social work practice as well. MSW (Master of Social Work) practitioners may specialize in community organization, social policy, research, social planning, or social administration as well as direct practice. At the master's level, **specialization** may occur within direct practice. Many MSW workers are employed in highly therapeutic environments, such as psychiatric or family service settings, in criminal justice settings, at centers serving AIDS patients, or in related fields of practice requiring specialized knowledge and skill. Others may work at agencies such as a department of human resources, serving people with less specialized problems. Competence in the use of all social work methods enhances the effectiveness of the worker in helping client systems seek solutions to problems at all levels of the environment. As discussed in Chapter 2, private practice has increased in recent years; this kind of practice typically calls for competence in psychotherapeutic and intensive counseling skills. Practitioners continue to develop resources that will enable clients to achieve a more satisfactory level of adaptation regardless of the setting in which social work is practiced.

◤ THE BACCALAUREATE SOCIAL WORKER IN DIRECT PRACTICE

Education for social work at the BSW level (Bachelor of Social Work) is geared toward enabling the student to become skilled in generalist social work practice. Guidelines for curricular content are established by the Council on Social Work Education, which also serves as the accrediting body for undergraduate social work programs.

As **generalist** social workers, practitioners at the baccalaureate level typically find employment in social agencies specializing in direct practice. An appreciation of the nature of client needs and problems in such settings is enhanced by a generalist background and focus. Direct practice with individuals does not always demand in-depth psychotherapeutic treatment. Although interviewing and assessment skills are always essential in establishing intervention goals, the BSW worker need not be concerned with those skills required for intensive psychotherapy. It is important to remember that direct practice with individuals extends far beyond psychotherapeutic involvement. The case presented at the opening of this chapter is a good example. The BSW worker could be involved as a case manager in helping identify needed resources for reducing stress and linking with other appropriate resources to ensure that needs were being addressed. The interviewing and counseling skills of the BSW worker would be useful in providing an opportunity to identify needs and problems and explore resources necessary for resolving them.

The skill of the BSW practitioner in articulating community resources in the problem-solving process must not be underestimated. The knowledge of resources and the preparation of clients to use those resources are paramount in problem resolution. BSW practitioners are employed in a variety of direct practice settings. Among the many opportunities are agencies such as state departments of human resources (or public welfare), mental health and mental retardation programs, children's service agencies (child welfare and child care institutions), halfway houses, nursing homes, areawide agencies on aging, agencies serving battered women, rape crisis centers, and child-care centers.

SUMMARY

Social work is a multifaceted profession requiring that its practitioners be familiar with theories of human behavior and social intervention as well as have knowledge of the logic of the social work process. Professional values serve as the basic underpinning for the relationship that social workers establish with their client systems. They are also the catalyst for promoting societal change designed for the enrichment of the lives of our populace. The goal of direct practice is to empower client systems to take charge of their lives and to act on their environment in such a way as to produce positive change for themselves and those with whom they interact.

As we have suggested in this chapter, social work practice must encompass far more than counseling skills in order to be an effective change agent. Generalist social workers engage a variety of social systems to facilitate positive change for their clients. This requires not only interpersonal skills but conceptual, planning, and evaluative ones as well. Social work practice, in order to become effective, requires the skillful application (an art) of scientific knowledge in the problem-solving process.

In this chapter, we have defined direct practice with individuals and families and have examined the components of the direct practice process, skills essential for practice, and theoretical models that serve to structure intervention. Direct practice has been identified as a direct services process that assists individuals and families through a therapeutic problem-solving process.

KEY TERMS

assessment
behavior modification
contracting
direct practice
dysfunctional
ego psychology
evaluation
generalist

goal setting
intervention
problem-solving approach
reality therapy
self-concept
specialization
task-centered casework

DISCUSSION QUESTIONS

1. What is direct practice? What are the components of direct practice methodology?

2. How does generalist practice differ from specialized? What skills must a generalist practitioner acquire?

3. Why are theories essential for effective practice? How do social workers elect theoretical approaches to practice?

4. Why are values an important component in social work intervention? How do they guide the interventive process?

5. Identify the elements of the direct practice process. How does the process facilitate problem solving?

REFERENCES

Brieland, Donald, Lela B. Costin, and Charles R. Atherton. 1985. *Contemporary social work.* New York: McGraw-Hill.

Dubois, B., and Miley, K. K. 1992. *Social work: An empowering profession.* Boston: Allyn & Bacon.

Perlman, Helen Harris. 1959. *Social casework: The problem solving process.* Chicago: University of Chicago Press.

Reid, William J., and Laura Epstein. 1972. *Task-centered casework.* New York: Columbia University Press.

Rubin, Allen. 1985. Practice effectiveness: More grounds for optimism. *Social work* 30, no. 6 (Nov.–Dec.): 469–75.

Zastrow, Charles. 1989. *The practice of social work.* Homewood, Ill.: Dorsey.

SUGGESTED FURTHER READINGS

Compton, B. R., and B. Galaway. 1989. *Social work processes.* Homewood, Ill.: Dorsey.

Goldstein, H. 1990. The knowledge base of social work: Theory, wisdom, analogue or art? *Families in Society* 71: 32–43.

Hepworth, D. H., and J. A. Larsen. 1990. *Direct social work practice.* 3rd ed. Belmont, Calif.: Wadsworth.

Hollis, F. 1964. *Casework: A psychosocial therapy.* New York: Random House.

Johnson, L. 1989. *Social work practice: A generalist approach.* 3rd ed. Boston: Allyn & Bacon.

Lowenberg, F., and R. Dolgoff. 1988. *Ethical decisions for social work practice.* 3rd ed. Itasca, Ill.: F. E. Peacock.

Morales, A., and B. Shaefor. 1989. *Social work: A profession of many faces.* 5th ed. Boston: Allyn & Bacon.

National Association of Social Workers. *Careers in social work.* Silver Springs, Md.: Author.

Paniagua, F. A. 1994. Assessing and treating culturally diverse clients. *Multicultural aspects of counseling series.* Thousand Oaks, Calif.: Sage Publications.

Pincus, A., and A. Minihan. 1973. *Social work practice: Model and method.* Itasca, Ill.: F. E. Peacock.

CHAPTER 6

DIRECT PRACTICE
Social Work with Groups and the Community

Traci was twenty-eight before she decided that something had to change in her life. All of her life, she had felt that she was out of control. She remembered that she was always very shy, would become very anxious when interacting with other people, would never speak up in groups, and was never successful in dating behavior—no one ever asked her out for a second date. She believed that she compensated for her shyness by being overly studious in school (she was nicknamed the "bookworm"), where her performance was superior, and later as a computer technician. She felt unfulfilled in her personal life and had very few close friends. Thoughts of having more self-confidence, more effective interpersonal skills, and the ability to be more assertive were always in her mind.

A friend suggested that she talk with Heather, a social worker. Traci agreed, met with Heather, and felt very comfortable in sharing her concerns with her. After several visits, Heather encouraged Traci to participate in an agency-sponsored encounter group. Heather reassured Traci that the group was small, and that the group members all shared many of the same concerns. Traci was reluctant at first, but had confidence in Heather and agreed to participate. Several times before the first group meeting, Traci found excuses not to attend, but she was able to garner her strengths and forced herself to go. She was greeted by Sally, a group worker for the agency, whom she had met before the group meeting. Sally introduced Traci to each of the members before the start of the meeting.

As the meeting opened, Sally urged members to feel free to express themselves and to ask questions. She encouraged each member to identify one stressful event that they had experienced that day, and then asked the group to offer suggestions as to how that event could be managed. Sally listened and then gave feedback regarding what had been discussed and assisted the group in assessing whether the proposed solutions might be achievable.

During ensuing sessions, Traci became more comfortable with herself in the group and offered as well as received suggestions without undue feelings of anxiety. She found that she could be confrontational as well as being confronted as she became more relaxed in the group. As time progressed, Traci commenced dating a colleague and felt more secure in investing herself in close relationships. Traci identified the one behavior that she was most proud of achieving— her willingness to risk—which for her was a giant step forward. ▪

Reflecting on Traci's experience, what would you view as the overall purpose of the group? From your perspective, do you feel that the group approach to assisting Traci is more effective than a one-on-one counseling experience would have been? If so, why? If not, why not? What considerations do you feel were made by Heather (the social worker) in referring Traci to the encounter group? What methods and processes did the group worker, Sally, have to master in order to help the group (and the individuals who composed it) achieve its objectives?

Group work is a method of direct social work practice that fosters personal development through the mechanism of group process. Many of the problems encountered by clients or client systems can be more effectively addressed and resolved through the group work process. As a generalist practitioner, the BSW recognizes first, the importance of groups in achieving intervention goals, and second, the utility of group methods in effective problem solving. In this chapter we will examine social group work, as well as community work, as social work methods that assist individuals, groups, and communities in problem solving. ▪

◢ SOCIAL GROUPS: A DEFINITION

Social groups are formed for many purposes. The most common type is the **natural group,** in which members participate as a result of common interests, shared experiences, similar backgrounds and values, and personal satisfactions derived from interaction with other group members. A street gang or neighborhood group of individuals who "hang out" together is a natural group. Such groups are further characterized by face-to-face interactions and an emotional investment in the role of the group member. Natural groups are seldom formed purposefully to meet specific objectives. All of us are members of natural groups, and seldom is our membership in those groups the result of a planned effort to become involved. In natural groups, a leader often emerges without premeditation or election by group members but rather because one member possesses behavioral attributes or resources that are highly valued by the other group members. Like all groups, natural groups tend to be transitory, with old members exiting and new ones entering throughout the group's life cycle.

Other groups are formed purposefully for a specific reason. For example, apartment residents may organize to seek building repairs and better living conditions, or a church or synagogue may organize a softball team. Established agencies, such as the YMCA or YWCA, might organize recreational groups within the city. A common characteristic of each of these groups is that they are developed to fulfill a specific purpose.

Before attempting to understand the components and process of direct practice with groups, it is helpful to have a basic understanding of what is meant by a **group.** While many definitions exist, we feel the interpretation offered by Chess and Norlin (1991, 119) best serves to guide our discussions.

> Social Group: A form of social organization comprised of two or more members who identify and interact with one another on a personal basis as individuals, possess a shared sense of the group as a social entity, are affected by the group-related actions of members, and in which expressive (natural) actions dominate.

The type of group with whom the direct practitioner works is called a *primary group*—that is, a group in which there is face-to-face interaction with group members. Regardless of the reasons why a group is formed (i.e., a natural or planned group), the group work method may be used to assist group members in achieving personal growth through the democratic process.

◢ GOALS OF SOCIAL GROUP WORK

Group work is a process and an activity that seeks to stimulate and support more adaptive personal functioning and social skills of individuals through structured group interaction. Euster (1975) and Konopka (1954) emphasize the development of communication competency, adaptive coping skills, and effective problem-solving techniques as goals of the group work experience. Group work techniques can be used more effectively when goals and objectives are related to the needs of group members. Effective group work capitalizes on the dynamics of interaction among members of the group. Members are encouraged to participate in making decisions, questioning, sharing, and contributing their efforts toward the achievement of agreed-upon goals and objectives.

GROUP FOCUS

Social workers engage in practice with groups to accomplish a variety of tasks. Generally, groups may be classified in terms of a specific purpose. Several of the more common types of groups are identified and discussed in Box 6.1.

Group work is both a process and an activity that seeks to stimulate and support more adaptive personal functioning and social skill development of individuals through structured group interaction. As a significant functional product of group work, its goals are directed toward helping individuals achieve communication competency, more effective adaptive coping skills, and more efficient problem-solving options as a result of the group experience.

Recreation Groups

The primary objective of **recreation groups** is to provide for the entertainment, enjoyment, and experience of participants. Activities such as athletic games or table games are typical recreational outlets. Community centers, YMCAs and YWCAs, and settlement houses routinely provide this type of group activity, as do senior centers for older adults. Participation provides opportunities for shared interaction, interdependence, and social exchange. Group recreational activities also provide constructive outlets for individuals in a monitored environment. Group workers must be sensitive to scheduling arrangements and willing to develop activities that are of interest to prospective participants.

Recreation-Skill Groups

As differentiated from recreation groups, the purpose of the **recreation-skill group** is to promote development of a skill within a recreational or enjoyment context. Ordinarily, a resource person with appropriate expertise teaches participants the essential skills necessary to develop greater competency in a craft, game, or sport. Tasks are emphasized, and instruction is provided by the resource person (e.g., a coach).

Educational Groups

Educational groups are formed for the purpose of transmitting knowledge and enabling participants to acquire more complex skills. Although educational groups may take on a classroom appearance, emphasis is given to group task assignments, and opportunities for interaction

---

BOX 6.1

ILLUSTRATIONS OF DIFFERENT TYPES OF GROUPS, THEIR FOCUS AND MEMBERSHIP

- **Recreation Group:** A YWCA organizes and promotes dominos, cards (bridge, etc.), basketball, and volleyball groups for interested community residents of all ages.

- **Recreation-Skill Groups:** The extension division of a local community college offers courses in the manual arts, golf, swimming, volleyball, sewing, and pottery making for community residents who wish to develop skill in those areas. Task development is emphasized, and mutual interaction is encouraged in the learning process.

- **Educational Groups:** A local family service agency offers a group of middle-aged adults opportunities to learn more about the aging process and how to cope with needs of their aged parents. At the same time, the agency sponsors a group on parenting skills for pregnant women and their husbands. In both groups, discussion is emphasized and group members are encouraged to identify their specific concerns for group reaction and discussion.

- **Socialization Groups:** A halfway house serving delinquent adolescents develops a weekly group meeting for its residents. Discussion focuses on specific problems experienced by group members. Activities are introduced that require cooperative interaction among group members for successful completion (e.g., yard maintenance, household chores). Emphasis is

given to democratic participation and personal decision making.

- **Self-Help Groups:** An Alcoholics Anonymous group is formed by individuals wanting to overcome an alcohol addiction. The purpose of the group is to provide support and reassurance to group members in dealing with alcohol-related problems, with the goal of helping members stay sober.

- **Therapeutic Groups:** These groups may consist of individuals who have difficulty in dealing with emotional problems associated with divorce, interpersonal loss, alcohol- and drug-related problems, mental health problems, difficulties in parent-child relationships, or other areas in which dysfunctional behavior results. Typically, emotional problems are related significantly to the problems in day-to-day living being experienced by group members.

- **Encounter Groups:** A group is organized by a local service agency to help young men and women who lack assertiveness, are self-deprecating, and feel inadequate. Members are encouraged to be self-expressive, learn to risk, gain insight into their own and others' feelings, provide mutual support, and establish meaningful relationships. A safe, nonjudgmental environment is essential for the successful participation of members.

---

and idea exchange buttress didactic presentations. Educational groups vary in purpose, from learning to repair an automobile to learning the most effective ways to cope with a family member who has Alzheimer's disease. Group leaders usually are persons with professional expertise in the area of interest for which the group was formed.

Socialization Groups

From a more traditional perspective, **socialization groups** typify the purposes and goals of social group work in that they seek to stimulate behavior change, increase social skills and self-confidence, and encourage motivation (Euster 1975, 220). The group focuses on helping participants develop socially acceptable behavior and behavioral competency. Personal decision making and self-determinism are emphasized as integral aspects of the group process. Typically, socialization groups may consist of runaway youth, predelinquents, or people with developmental disabilities (Zastrow 1989). Leadership is provided by a social worker familiar with group dynamics and knowledgeable about the problem area experienced by the participants.

Self-Help Groups

The underlying motivation for individuals who join **self-help groups** is to resolve a personal or social problem that they find perplexing, continually stressful, and unrelenting. Membership in self-help groups is usually a matter of choice, and the prospective group member may become aware of the group through acquaintances, friends, or related sources. In some instances, participation in self-help groups may be mandated. An abusive parent may be required by the court to participate in Parents Anonymous, or a person charged with driving while intoxicated may be required to participate in Alcoholics Anonymous meetings. It is common for members of the self-help groups to have "given up" on attempting to resolve the problem through their own efforts, through counseling, or through other traditional agency approaches.

As members of a self-help group, individuals are expected to make a strong personal commitment to the group, its members, and its goals. Self-help groups emphasize mutual aid and interdependence, personal involvement, face-to-face interaction, and an active role in responding to the needs of other group members. Typically, self-help groups elect their own convenor and mutually decide on the format for meetings. Ordinarily, professional group workers are not employed to assist the group with process or goal setting. Self-help groups may, however, invite "experts" to meet with them to share information about specific problems.

Self-help groups (often identified as support groups) are formed for many different purposes: for recovery and growth, as in the case of Alcoholics Anonymous, Al-Anon, or Synanon; advocacy, such as pro-life groups, women's liberation groups, or MADD (Mothers Against Drunk Driving); or a combination of personal growth and advocacy, such as Parents Without Partners or Parents Anonymous (Zastrow 1989).

Self-help groups do not always seek professional leadership. Effective efforts to resolve problems are based on personal involvement and a willingness to assist fellow members in learning to cope and develop adaptive skills. Since members have experienced the same problem, they may be more empathetic, insightful, and able to respond with more understanding.

Therapeutic Groups

Therapeutic groups require skilled professional leadership. Group members typically have intensive personal or emotional problems that require the expertise of a well-trained professional, such as a master's degree-level social worker, a clinical psychologist, or other professional counselor. Problems typically addressed in therapeutic groups range from interpersonal loss (death, divorce, abandonment), physically disabling injuries, terminal diseases, and marital or family conflict to psychopathology or other emotionally distressing dysfunctional behaviors. Consider the following case:

> Alice (age 35) recently became a widow when her husband, Carlos, was killed in an automobile accident. Alice has two children, Tina (age 6) and Sean (age 3). She had not worked outside the home since the birth of her children. As time passed since Carlo's death, Alice became more depressed, immobilized, and unable to care for her children. The local mental health outreach center arranged for Alice to be placed in a therapeutic group consisting of ten persons who were also experiencing interpersonal loss.

Monitoring group interaction and its effects on members is an essential requirement for the group leader. Various therapy approaches may be used to promote therapeutic interaction directed toward behavioral change. Therapeutic groups may also be supplemented by individual treatment.

Encounter Groups

Remember the case of Traci presented at the beginning of this chapter? Traci became involved in an **encounter group** that is oriented toward assisting individuals in developing more self-awareness and interpersonal skills. Such groups are characterized by a secure environment in which members can be openly expressive, develop a sense of trust, receive candid feedback, and develop sensitivity to their own and others' feelings and emotions. Assertiveness and confidence resulting from heightened self-acceptance and self-awareness promote more genuine relationships and enhance the quality of interpersonal communication. Encounter groups are identified by many different titles: T (training) groups, sensitivity groups, and personal growth groups.

◪ EFFECTIVE GROUP DEVELOPMENT

The achievement of desired outcomes of the group process is dependent on several key considerations. *Purposefulness* is an essential characteristic for maximum effectiveness of the group work process. Purposefulness involves the establishment of specific goals and objectives and access to their achievement by the group. Purposefulness provides the direction or intent for each group session and supplies a framework for monitoring and evaluating the group's progress.

Leadership is essential in helping the group maintain its focus and in encouraging maximum participation of members. The group worker may play an active or passive role in the group, depending on the needs of the group as it moves toward the established goals and objectives. The leader must be skilled in group processes and able to perform a variety of roles in supporting the accomplishment of tasks necessary to maintain group integrity and continuing progress. Zastrow (1989) has identified a wide range of role responses that may be required of a group leader, such as "executive, policy maker, planner, expert, external group representative, controller of internal relations, purveyor of rewards and punishments, arbitrator and mediator, exemplar, ideologist, and scapegoat."

Effective leadership is essential to successfully achieving the group's purposes. The methods that a leader may use to accomplish group goals should be consistent with the values and purposes of social work practice. Wilson and Ryland (1949, 60–99) have identified five leadership styles, four of which are not compatible with social work goals:

- The *dictatorial* or *authoritarian* method in which the leader orders and the members obey

- The *personification* method, in which members seek to imitate the group worker and attempt to be like him or her, but they do not explore and find their own abilities

- The *perceptive* method, in which the worker gives instructions, and the group members carry them out and learn skills, although they are not detecting their own resources and capacities

- The *manipulative* method, in which the group worker goes with the group through a phase of planning and decision making, but the group is only accepting a prearranged program of the leader and is deceived into believing that the group itself came to the decision

- The *enabling* method, in which the group worker helps the members participate with full responsibility in the life of the group, in its planning and program; in developing their own ideas, skills, and personal attitudes; and in making their own decisions regarding the purposes and actions of the group

Only the enabling method fully embraces the principles of democratic process and encourages individual responsibility and risk sharing as products of group interaction and decision making. The success of group process and goal attainment is related to a large extent to effective group leadership. Needless to say, the group leader is accountable for group maintenance and the success (or failure) of the group in achieving its purposes.

The *selection of group members* is an important factor in achieving group cohesion. In composing groups, the group worker must accurately assess each individual's needs, capacity for social functioning, interests, and willingness to assume an active role as a group member. Although diversity of background and experience may enhance alternatives for achieving the group's purposes, homogeneous (similar) motives are essential to the formation of the group and identification as a group member. Members with few common interests often have more difficulty in becoming involved in group activities. Age and/or gender may be critical factors, depending on the purposes of the group and the activities designed to achieve those purposes. Individuals with severe emotional problems or behavior disorders may be disruptive to the group process; thus, careful consideration should be given to including them as group members. Members should have the ability to focus on group tasks. Systematic disruptive behavior is not only disconcerting but may lead to group disintegration. The type of group being formed (e.g., recreational, educational) will determine the criteria for the selection of members. In all instances, selection should be based on the "principle of maximum profit" (individuals with specific needs that would be most likely to achieve the greatest benefit from the group). The assessment of individuals for group membership is enhanced by a personal interview prior to inclusion in the group.

The *size of a group* is to a large extent determined by its purposes. To determine in advance that four, six, or fifteen members is the "ideal" size of a group has little validity. It is more effective to examine the goals and purposes of the proposed group when determining group size. If, for example, anonymity (or the ability to "lose" oneself) is a desirable end, a larger number of members may be indicated, thus assuring more limited interaction and group fragmentation (i.e., the emergence of subgroups). Smaller groups, by definition, demand more intimate interaction, and group pressures typically are intensified. Absenteeism affects group process and task accomplishment more in small groups than large ones. Small groups may function more informally than larger ones, which usually require a structured format. The role of the group leader also varies with the size of the group. The democratic process can be achieved in both large and small groups, although it is more difficult in the former. The principles and techniques of social group work are effective with large and small groups alike.

The number of members selected for the group depends on the desired effect on its individual members, the needs of the members, and their capacity to participate and support group purposes. Generally, a small group may be composed of four to nine members, whereas a large group may consist of ten to twenty members.

◤ THEORY FOR GROUP WORK PRACTICE

Social group work is a direct social work practice method requiring the social worker to be familiar with theories related to group behavior. Group theory provides a framework for promoting guided change through group interaction. The discipline of social psychology has contributed much to our understanding of group formation, roles, norms, values, group dynamics, and cohesion. Sherif and Sherif's (1956) contribution to the understanding of group formation, maintenance, and conflict resolution; Lewin's (1951) conceptualization of field theory; and Moreno's (1953) insights into group configurations have been helpful in gaining greater awareness of how groups function. Early social group work pioneers also contributed valuable experiential and theoretical insights that added to the knowledge base from which an informed approach to working with groups can be employed.

Social group work can be distinguished as a professional social work method by the informed application of theory in helping groups achieve their objectives and goals. Since groups vary extensively in their composition, types, and purposes, the worker also must have a broad-based understanding of the life cycle, emotional reactions to stress, and maladaptive behavior. Group workers must have skill in working with the group and sensitivity in helping the group move toward achieving its goals.

◢ GROUP WORK SETTINGS

Traditionally, social group work was practiced in recreational settings, such as the YWCA or YMCA, settlement houses, and community centers. With the growing popularity of group work, along with the redefinition of the scope of social work practice, group work has become a valuable practice method within most direct-service agencies. For example, a family service agency might form a group of prospective adoptive parents to orient them to the adoptive process. A treatment center might compose a group of adolescent substance abusers to assist them in learning to identify and manage stress and interpersonal problems. A recreational center might sponsor athletic teams for middle school youth. Older adults living in a nursing home could constitute a "re-motivation" group.

Working with groups not only promotes growth and change through the interaction of the members but also enables the agency and workers to serve a greater number of clients. Although some group members may need the resources of a caseworker in addition to the group experience, in most instances, the group activity is sufficient for personal growth. When direct practice with individuals is not provided by the agency offering the group, referrals are made to an appropriate agency, and a cooperative relationship between the service providers assures the client of maximum assistance with problems.

◢ EVALUATION

Professional practice with individuals and groups must include an evaluative process. Evaluation is always focused on the extent to which the group is able to achieve its objectives. Evaluation may be an ongoing process as well as an assessment of the total group process, which comes at the termination of the group. In the former instance, the worker continually "monitors" group behavior, in order to enable the group to focus on its goals. Monitoring also may help the group redefine its purpose and goals, should it become evident that the original ones are unachievable. Monitoring consists of a critical assessment of the group's output.

Evaluation includes an assessment of all activities and behaviors related to the group's performance. Factors such as group leadership, resources, attendance at sessions, changes in group structure, dysfunctional behaviors, characteristics of group members, group norms, and agency support, among others, all are reviewed in relation to the achievement of personal and group goals and objectives. Evaluation has the potential of providing a basis for answering such questions as: What could have increased group productivity? What were the positive achievements of the group? What implications for change are suggested? Efficiency and better quality of service are likely when rigorous evaluative standards are maintained.

◢ GROUP TERMINATION

Groups are terminated when the purposes for which they were established are achieved. Although many groups are initiated with a predetermined expiration period, termination usually is related to meeting group goals and personal goals of the members. Occasionally, a group is aborted when it becomes obvious that its goals are unattainable or when dysfunctional behavior of one or more group members continually disrupts the group's activities.

The worker must be sensitive to the needs of group members at the time of termination and assist them in phasing out their attachment to the group. Often resistance to termination becomes highly emotional and vocal. Frustration, anger, withdrawal, and grief are among the more common reactions to the loss of the close ties that have developed among members throughout the life of the group. By helping the group assess its accomplishments and plan alternatives, the worker can help members develop a more adaptive transition.

◢ SOCIAL GROUP WORK AS A PRACTICE

As we indicated previously, group work is directed toward the enrichment of an individual's life through a group existence. Coyle (1959, 88–105) observes that the group experience may provide assistance to individuals as

1. A maturing process
2. A supplement to other relationships
3. Preparation for active citizenship
4. A corrective for social disorganization
5. Treatment of intrapsychic maladjustment

Although it is unlikely that group members derive equal benefit from the group experience, all can be expected to experience growth in one or more of these areas. Positive group work is a planned-change effort. Change is predicated on benefits derived from group process and interaction. The worker is responsible for assuring that the principles governing social work practice are included in the process. Euster (1975, 232) identifies those principles as follows:

1. Assuring the dignity, worth, uniqueness, and autonomy of all members
2. A clear working agreement between the worker and the group and an articulated understanding of the group's purpose

3. An assessment of the problems and needs of individual group members and special support by the social worker when the need is indicated

4. Individualization of the group, which reflects its unique character, set of relationships, and needs

5. Strong communications networks, which permit the expression of feelings and emotions of members

6. Relevant program activities, around which constructive interaction, assessment of group process, and the advancement of the group's purpose can be made

7. Preparation for termination

Each group also has its own life cycle, characterized by developmental stages. Stanford and Roark (1974) identify the stages of a group's development as follows:

1. Beginning—basic orientation and getting acquainted
2. Norm development—establishing ground rules for operation
3. Conflict phase—members asserting individual ideas
4. Transition—replacing initial conflicts with acceptance of others
5. Production—sharing of leadership, tasks, and trust
6. Affection—appreciation for the group
7. Actualization—flexibility, consensus, and decision making

An awareness of these stages is helpful in monitoring the progress of the group as it moves toward greater cohesion and effectiveness. Dysfunctional "blocking" at any stage (the conflict phase), once identified, can be addressed and resolved by the group, and the developmental progress can continue. Allowed to continue unchecked, the unresolved blockage may result in group dissolution.

Skill in working with groups is an important aspect of social work practice. The efficiency and effectiveness of the group work process have resulted in personal enhancement, skill development, and problem reduction.

SOCIAL WORK WITH COMMUNITIES

Social work with communities is a direct-practice method that enables individuals and groups to achieve a more desirable level of life satisfaction as well as more effective levels of adaptation. As presented in the following discussion, community social work may take a variety of forms. The following case vignette characterizes one type of situation that is commonly managed by the BSW practitioner:

Norma Carlson, a BSW social worker, has been working with Brenda Bostwick for several months. Brenda, age 16, is a single parent who aspired to complete her high school education in hopes that she could find a good job and better provide for her child. It was difficult for her to concentrate on her schoolwork because she often had to miss school to care for her baby. School officials had suspended her for absences on several occasions, and she was becoming more discouraged every day. With Brenda's consent, Norma visited with the school officials in order to engage them in working out a special educational program for Brenda so that she would not fall behind in her studies. Norma also contacted a local child-care center and arranged for Brenda's child to be cared for while Brenda was in class. She was also successful in securing reduced-rate transportation with the local bus company, which agreed that Brenda should be supported in her determination to work toward her educational goals. Norma was assigned to work with other teen parents, and she realized there were no resources in the community that worked specifically with teen parents. She helped organize a network of interested social workers and school officials. Together, network members secured reduced child-care and transportation rates for all teen parents in the community so they could attend school regularly.

Successful social work intervention, as in the case of Brenda, often requires that the social worker engage community agencies and organizations in the process. It is doubtful whether Brenda, without Norma's knowledge and skill, could have made the arrangements that resulted in a positive solution to her need to complete her high school education. Clients are often unaware of available resources or the process through which successful solutions can be achieved. In some instances, they may not have the self-confidence to pursue alternatives that result in goal achievement. Also, needed resources may not be available in their communities. Social workers in direct practice find that work with the community often becomes an essential ingredient in the problem-solving process. In this section of the chapter, we discuss the concepts and principles of social work with the community.

What Is a Community?

Community is a descriptive term that has many meanings. Communities may be defined as groups of people who live within certain incorporated limits, such as Philadelphia, Pennsylvania; Boise, Idaho; or Mena, Arkansas. Or, others may speak of a "religious community," which refers to a group of people who share common religious values. A community may also be a subunit of a larger metropolitan area, such as Watts in Los Angeles or Shadyside in Pittsburgh. Members of an ethnic group who live close together are often referred to as a community. Illustrations are endless, and our purpose here is to identify the ambiguity of the concept. How, then, do we arrive at a usable definition that enables us to understand the focus of social work with communities? It is obvious from the preceding illustrations that "communities" vary considerably in organization, resources, values, and purpose. It is also obvious that a client may well be a member of several communities—for example, an incorporated city or town, a religious group, an ethnic group, and a well-defined neighborhood. Social workers need to be familiar with the community systems that serve as behavioral contexts for their

Many social workers practice at the community level. To be effective, agencies must develop partnerships with institutions seen as important to various cultural groups.

clients. Keeping these definitional variations in mind, we will, for our purposes, consider **community** as *a group of individuals who live in close proximity to one another, who share a common environment, including public and private resources, and who identify themselves with that community.*

Social workers often feel overwhelmed by the concept of working with the community. Perhaps a better perspective could allay some of these fears: If we consider that the community consists of interacting individuals, then work with the community would consist of working with the individuals and groups who interact. As Zastrow has indicated, "the most basic skill needed in community practice is to be able to work effectively with people [and such practice] . . . primarily involves working with individuals and groups" (1989). As indicated earlier, generalist social work practitioners constantly engage in community practice.

Social work with the community may focus on a wide range of problems and issues. The case illustration with which we initiated this discussion is only one example. Social workers may, as in the case of Brenda, serve as a **broker** with several agencies in order to obtain sources necessary for the achievement of treatment goals. In the broker role, the social worker helps clients plow through the maze of different agencies in locating resources that are most appropriate to problem resolution. In addition to the active role of negotiation with agencies, the worker also gathers and transmits information between client systems and action systems.

At other times, the social worker in community practice may serve as an **enabler** in seeking to help people identify and clarify their problems (assessment) and in supporting and stimulating the group to unite in their efforts to secure change. For example, a group of tenants in a rat-infested tenement might be encouraged to unite and confront the owners or landlords with the problem and seek redress for those conditions. At other times, the social worker in community practice may function in the role of *advocate* for a client system in confronting unresponsive representatives of community institutions. In the advocate role, the social worker is clearly aligned with the client system in seeking to nudge unresponsive institutions to take action. A worker may, for example, represent the client system in increasing police protection in high-risk neighborhoods. Finally, a social work community practitioner might serve as an *activist* who seeks change in institutional response patterns. For example, a worker may serve as an activist in seeking modification of discriminatory hiring practices or in trying to secure the rights of disenfranchised groups.

As indicated earlier, generalist social work practitioners are constantly engaged in community practice as they work with various organizations to address specific needs of their clients, or the populace in general. As was illustrated in the case of Brenda, it was necessary for the social worker to engage the school system, a child-care center, and the local transportation company in order to establish an effective solution for Brenda's dilemma and for teen parents in similar situations.

◪ COMMUNITY PRACTICE APPROACHES

Social work with the community, like other methods of social work practice, is based on planned change and assumes familiarity, skill, and expertise on the part of the worker, including the basic social work skills of problem identification, data collection, assessment, analysis (or interpretation), and the development of planned intervention. Social workers who routinely practice with communities generally use a "social action, social planning or community development" approach. The **social action** strategy was popularized by Saul Alinsky (1969) and was used extensively by oppressed groups in the 1960s "War on Poverty" programs. This approach stresses organization and group cohesion in confrontational approaches geared to modify or eliminate institutional power bases that negatively affect the group. **Social planning** emphasizes modification of institutional practices through the application of knowledge, values, and theory—a practical, rational approach to problem solving that assumes well-intentioned people will be responsive to sound arguments. The **community development** approach considers and respects the diversity of the population and uses those differences as strengths in achieving community betterment for all citizens. Often citizens become polarized as an action group when "superordinate goals" are identified, requiring concerted community efforts for a satisfactory resolution.

Social workers with advanced degrees (the MSW) often specialize in community organization as a basic practice method as well as a field of practice. Workers at this level may be employed by community councils, the United Way, community development centers, administrators of state or federal programs; as directors of agencies; or by a variety of related community organizations. A main objective of the community practitioner is to engage in planning and development that assures an adequate resource base and implementation structure that is directed toward improving the quality of life for populations in need as well as the citizenry in general. In their capacity as community planners, workers often engage in the development of social policy proposals or provide their expertise to city councils, state and federal legislatures, or other policy-formulating groups.

As you are also well aware, many negatives affect the quality of life in communities—crime, substance abuse, discrimination, riots, and disorder. Social work has a long tradition and mandate to apply its workers' skills in addressing dysfunctional forces and vulnerable populations, with the goal of instituting change efforts that move the community toward solving its own problems. Direct practice with communities is an integral practice role for generalist as well as specialized social workers. It is an essential, rewarding, and challenging activity that requires an awareness of theory, knowledge, and practice skills if intervention is to be successful.

SOCIAL WORK WITH GROUPS AND THE COMMUNITY

The baccalaureate social worker, or BSW, has developed familiarity with and a beginning competency in working with groups and the community as part of the generic educational program. Both theory and practice in working with groups and in the community are required by accredited BSW programs. Many opportunities exist for work with groups and the community at the BSW level. Most agencies use the group and community methods as part of their practice modalities. Agencies such as family service agencies, state departments of human services, hospitals, correctional centers, mental health and mental retardation agencies, school social services, youth organizations, and a variety of related service delivery organizations use group and community practice methodologies. It should also be noted that social workers with advanced degrees (the MSW) are also often employed as community organization workers, sometimes specializing in that area as a field of practice. At this level, they may serve as administrators of state or federal programs, as department heads in a city's human services division, or as directors of agencies.

SUMMARY

Social work with groups and social work with the community are social work methods that promote the personal growth of individual members (group work) and enhance the capacity of the community to better serve the needs of its diverse members (community practice). Groups may be identified by their purpose: recreational, recreational-skill, educational, socialization, encounter, self-help, and therapy. Community change efforts are facilitated through social action, social planning, and community development approaches. In all of these, members of the group or community establish goals and objectives, and the facilitator helps the members achieve their goals. Democratic decision making is important to the process. Monitoring and evaluation are major activities used to help the group and community achieve their goals and to enrich practice methods.

KEY TERMS

broker
community
community development
educational group
enabler
encounter group
group
group work

natural group
recreation group
recreation skill group
self-help group
social action
social planning
socialization group
therapeutic group

DISCUSSION QUESTIONS

1. Identify the ways in which natural groups and organized groups differ. Give an example of each group.
2. How does a direct-practice worker assist groups in achieving their goals? How does the group process facilitate goal achievement?
3. Compare and contrast the purposes and goals of the planned-change groups discussed in this chapter.
4. Define community practice. Identify the multiple roles of the community practitioner.
5. Provide illustrations of the various ways in which the generalist social worker engages the community to assist client systems in meeting their needs.

REFERENCES

Alinsky, Saul. 1969. *Reveille for radicals.* New York: Basic Books.
Chess, Wayne A., and Julia M. Norlin. 1991. *Human behavior and the social environment.* 2d ed. Boston: Allyn & Bacon.
Coyle, Grace. 1959. Some basic assumptions about social group work. In *The social group work method in social work education,* ed. Marjorie Murphy, pp. 88–105. New York: Council on Social Work Education.
Euster, Gerald L. 1975. Services to groups. Chap. 13 in *Contemporary social work,* ed. Donald Brieland, Lela B. Costin, and Charles R. Atherton. New York: McGraw-Hill.
Konopka, Gisela. 1954. *Group work in the institution.* New York. Whiteside.

Lewin, Kurt. 1951. *Field theory in social science: Selected theoretical papers.* Ed. D. Cartwright. New York: Harper & Row.

Moreno, J. L. 1953. *Who shall survive?* Rev. ed. New York: Beacon.

Sherif, Muzafer, and Carolyn Sherif. 1956. *An outline of social psychology.* New York: Harper & Row.

Stanford, Gene, and Albert E. Roark. 1974. *Human interaction in education.* Boston: Allyn & Bacon.

Wilson, Gertrude, and Gladys Ryland. 1949. *Social group work practice.* Cambridge: Houghton Mifflin.

Zastrow, Charles. 1989. *Introduction to social welfare institutions.* 3rd ed. Chicago: Dorsey.

SUGGESTED FURTHER READINGS

Boulette, T. R. 1985. Group therapy with low income Mexican Americans. *Social Work* (September): 403–4.

Cox, F. M., J. L. Erlich, J. Rothman, and J. E. Troppman, eds. 1991. *Strategies of community organization: Macro practice.* 4th ed. Itasca, Ill.: F. E. Peacock.

Fellin, P. 1995. *The community social worker.* Itasca, Ill.: F. E. Peacock.

Martinez-Brawley, E. E. 1990. *Perspectives on the small community.* Silver Springs, Md.: National Association of Social Workers Press.

Roberts, R. W., and H. Northern. 1976. *Theories of social work with groups.* New York: Columbia University Press.

Rothman, B., and C. P. Papell. 1988. Social work as a clinical paradigm. In *Paradigms for clinical social work,* ed. R. W. Dorfman, pp. 149–78. New York: Brunner/Mazel.

Shulman, L. 1979. *The skills of helping individuals and groups.* Itasca, Ill.: F. E. Peacock.

Simons, R., and S. M. Aigner. 1985. *Practice principles: A problem-solving approach to social work.* New York: Macmillan.

Walker, J. 1988. The place of group work in organizations. In *New management in human services,* ed. P. R. Keys and L. H. Ginsburg, pp. 102–15. Silver Springs, Md.: National Association of Social Workers Press.

CHAPTER 7

SOCIAL AGENCY ADMINISTRATION

In ancient times, alchemists believed in the existence of a philosopher's stone, which would provide the key to the universe. The quest for coordination may be the next century's equivalent. If we find the right formula for coordination, we can reconcile the irreconcilable, harmonize competing and wholly divergent interests, overcome irrationalities in our government structures, and promote the self-interest of private structures. The need is to understand how to blend the essential ingredients of complex public programs into now fragmented service delivery systems and overcome the specialized concerns of disparate organizations. The perfect pattern of coordination and the right mix of public, voluntary, and market-oriented service delivery systems will surely be as elusive as the philosopher's stone. As the search for the stone helped philosophers to ask better questions, an examination of service delivery will help us to know what is right and what is wrong in current service delivery. ■

The development of *effective*[1] and *efficient*[2] strategies for the delivery of social service is based on an understanding of the characteristics of clients and the agency environment. Social work administrators can increase service by designing the service delivery system to better fit the needs of those they serve, and by rationing expensive resources so that they might have their greatest impacts.

Research relating to the administrative aspects of social service agencies shows that the pattern of use is the result of interactions between clients, social workers, and the delivery system itself. Effective and efficient utilization design requires (1) knowing how clients identify their needs and make the decision to seek services, (2) the knowledge base of the social workers, and (3) knowledge of how clients interact with specific structures.

The central assumption regarding the service structure design is that service involves "an exchange of values between consumers and providers" (Moore et al. 1991).

The services pattern emerges from characteristics of consumers, and from the characteristics of the service delivery system. The availability of the service, the provider of that service, and the allocation of the service costs are similarly a complex pattern that emerges from historical precedents, political consideration, and other socioeconomic variables.

Service utilization research emphasizes the need to understand the nature of the interaction between service providers and service users. If programs are to be client driven, then service providers should begin by understanding who the client is, and by specifying the target population that experiences a certain need. Some services are donor driven. Convicted felons, for example, may have only a vague awareness of their own "need" to be reformed. In both cases the service structure needs to begin, to use an old saw, where the client is.

The social work agency is many things to many people. It is a place where people go for help when problems occur and a place society holds responsible for addressing specific problems. It is also a place of employment for some and a setting for voluntary action by others. With the multiple motives of multiple actors, there is no single purpose of the social agency but rather a myriad of

---

1. *Effective* refers to the ratio of target populations reached to the entire target population.
2. *Efficient* refers to the ratio of valued output to valued input.

purposes. Above all else, the major task of the administrator of a social agency is to bring resources, opportunities, and goals together in such a way that a variety of social missions are accomplished. The focus of this chapter is on the management activities and the administrative processes of the local agency. Management activities are not the sole responsibility of agency executive directors and their assistants. All workers in the agency, the members of the board of directors, and the clients play vital roles in the administrative process.

The dominant view of agency administration used to be "organizational rationality." The notion was that the agency director, responsive to the board of directors, identified cost-efficient means of attaining the board's ends, indicated the costs and benefits of the various alternatives, and then implemented their choice. This view met with criticism from proponents of two positions. First, theories of politics demonstrated that organizations do not have single rational goals but multiple goals emanating from many sources. Second, social workers and other professionals viewed organizational decisions as the product of many forces, of which goal-directed rationality is but one (Grummer 1990).   ■

◪ ADMINISTRATIVE STRATEGY

The administrative processes of an agency can be thought of first as a strategic task. **Strategy** is ongoing, dynamic thinking formulated to analyze problems and to establish specific objectives. This process may best be described as a cycle of administrative activity (see Figure 7.1). The parts of the cycle are as follows:

1. **Strategic Formulation:** Analysis of problems and of objectives with input from staff, community leaders, those with funding authority, clients served, and the media.

2. **Planning and Budgeting Implementation:** Development of specific budgets, resource budgets, fiscal budgets, and time budgets, and deployment of these resources.

3. **Control and Management:** Direction of activities, which are constantly evaluated, establishing a feedback loop back to strategic formulation.

To be effective, the cycle must be completed so that analysis of the data generated by those working directly with clients and community groups leads back to a more precise problem formulation at the highest level of the organization. It is typical to think of strategic formulation as the first phase of the administrative process. But at any point in time, strategic formulation is also the product of many previous administrative cycles.

As an example, since the late 1980s, the Episcopal Community Service Agency of North Fork, Nebraska, has been expected to devise a strategy to deal with AIDS, child and substance abuse, suicides, crime, and other social problems linked to the many farm foreclosures in River

FIGURE 7.1   **THE ADMINISTRATIVE CYCLE**

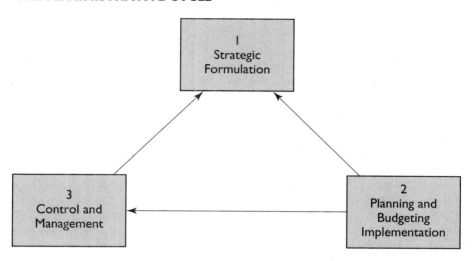

Fork County. The agency was created in the 1940s to provide social and chaplain services to the residents of the county poor farm. It was established by wealthy farmers whose descendants now face the loss of their family farms. How the agency functions today is related to many earlier decisions. For example, the agency provides a food pantry and thrift shop, as well as traditional marriage counseling by a parish priest. In developing the strategic plan to meet current social problems, the staff must review the agency's traditional role within the community as well as factors in the current environment, such as the following:

- **Economic forces:** What are the most likely sources of funds to address current problems?

- **Government policies:** What are state, local, and national governments going to do that will alleviate or exacerbate the problems?

- **The current social structure of the agency:** Specifically, what are the talents and dispositions of the current staff? This is most often the strongest force in strategic planning.

APPLYING A SYSTEMS/ECOLOGICAL PERSPECTIVE

A key aspect of strategic planning is the recognition that the problems addressed lie far beyond the control of any given agency. As the board members, with the assistance of the executive director, contemplate these problems and the appropriate responses, they find that opportunities, risks, resources, and responsibilities interact and reverberate along the way. A systems/ecological perspective suggests that an agency's resources and its goals overlap and interact. Clearly, the goals specified influence the capacity to generate resources, just as the manner in which resources are obtained and the nature of those resources affect and change the goals of the agency (Anthony and Herzlinger 1975).

Perlman and Gurin (1972) suggest that there are five types of resources to which the local social agency manager needs to respond (see Table 7.1):

- A supply of clients, who expect to receive from the agency some valued product or service. These clients may seek the service/product on their own accord, or the service/product may be imposed upon the client, as in the criminal justice system.

- Financial resources, which are made available to the agency by a system of grants, taxation, fees for service, and/or voluntary contributions.

- A social work method, by which the financial resources are transformed into the service/product sought by its clients. The technology of the social work agency typically is one or more of the social work processes: direct practice, client advocacy, and so on.

- The people, or human resources, who make up the agency staff. These paid or volunteer workers are the ones on the front line, who interact directly with the clients to provide the service/product.

- A continuing mandate to operate. The mandate may be in the form of a license, a legislative directive, or a charter of some sort.

In administering any social agency, five essential elements must be considered: the agency, its clients, its product, its goals, and its staff. A specific agency has a set of social programs related to its service or product and its goals. The fit between the agency's product and its goals is one way the agency is judged. An essential administrative task is to achieve an optimal fit between the product and the goal. Similarly, the product and the staff must have some degree of congruence, if the agency is to operate efficiently. The staff members clearly need the training and competency to deliver the service effectively or to produce the product. Since social agencies tend to be labor-intensive organizations, assuring such staff readiness is a crucial aspect of administering an agency.

TABLE 7.1   **ORGANIZING PRINCIPLES OF SOCIAL AGENCIES**

Resource Base	Some Examples
Clients	Children, delinquents, workers with disabilities, retired persons
Fiscal base	Public, private, voluntary funds
Social work method	Direct practice, case management, advocacy
Human resources	Paid staff, volunteer staff, mixed staff
Mandate	Legislative mandate, United Way charter, license to practice

Pairing these five essential elements in various combinations, as indicated in Figure 7.2, dictates the specific administrative tasks that must be performed successfully. There are ten essential pairs or choices to be made. Each choice affects the other choices, so the agency can be understood as a system. Three of the most important pairs are discussed in the following paragraphs.

Goal and Product

An organization provides a product, and although that product is the end stage in the organization's directly visible activities, the product is provided in pursuit of stated, manifest, or latent organizational goals. A retail store sells a particular product, presumably to make a profit for the store owners. It is not the purpose of the bookstore at the local mall to provide employment to its workers or to make first-class literature easily available to potential readers, even though it may serve those ends. For the retail store, the ultimate purpose is profits, and failure to produce profits will cause the enterprise to cease.

In the absence of a profit motive to guide choices, the administrator of a social agency faces several questions: If profit, defined as total revenues minus total costs, is not to be maximized, what should be—the number of people served, the quality of service to those who are served, or some appropriate combination of these? Attempts to answer such questions will force the administrator to think about some of the other pairwise considerations.

Staff and Product

The agency director has to identify staff or position needs, recruit and retain qualified persons to fill those positions, and promote an effective, task-centered work environment. An agency requires human resources,

FIGURE 7.2   **TEN PAIRWISE FACTORS OF A SOCIAL AGENCY THAT MUST BE CONSIDERED FOR THE AGENCY TO BE SUCCESSFUL**

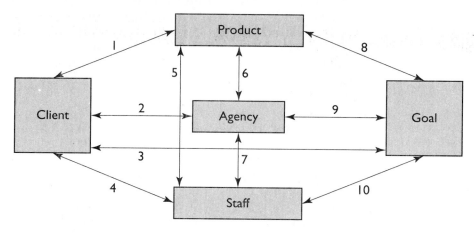

including professional and technical staff members as well as volunteers. Board members, who help to ensure that the links between the community and the agency are sustained and current, also need to be recruited and retained. The nurturing and development of staff, volunteers, and board members are sufficiently complex to be the subject of specialized graduate-level courses. However, some general principles are of interest to other students.

Staff management must begin with clear specification of staffing requirements. The specific objectives of developing staffing standards are

- Determine the requirements of the specific task essential to organizational maintenance and goal attainment.

- Determine the qualities, abilities, knowledge, and skills required to perform these tasks successfully.

- Develop a pattern of task assignments so that staff members are neither underutilized nor expected to accomplish tasks beyond their skill levels.

With a chart of staff needs and staff availability, the agency administrator can specify position requirements and expectations. This task-oriented staff structure needs to address a number of elements. For example, a pattern of supervisory controls must be specified; that is, the nature, extent, and procedure for reviews of task performance and the means available to correct and respond to substandard performance must be addressed. Also needed are ways to measure accountability, review, coordination, and perhaps most important, the ways in which agency services help clients meet the needs that led them to seek help.

Product and Client

The identification and specification of needs call for organized intervention, which involves a political process rather than a rational, technical one. With some problems, such as crime, little conflict exists regarding goals. But various groups strongly disagree about what legitimate social interventions to employ in controlling crime. In another area, such as child care for children of working parents, conflict exists over the desirability of intervention itself. Some see quality child care as benefiting children and allowing parents—especially single parents— to become self-supporting; others see child care simply as a way to watch the "kids" while both parents work. Still other groups oppose child care and view it as a significant factor in the decline of the American family. Clearly, political ideologies constitute the core by which individuals judge the nature of social problems and the propriety of social intervention.

A social work credo suggests that the agency needs to be responsive to the clients served. But the clientele directly served are not the only interest group that affects the resource base of the agency. For example, who is served by a public housing project? Is it the people who live there, the real estate interests, or the building trade unions and construction companies who completed the facility? As you can see, depending on the degree of cynicism, it is possible to specify a myriad of legitimate interests involved in implementing public housing policy—or any other policy.

Weighing the Client's Best Interests

Pluralistic politics do not give the administrator any set of substantive rules for specifying the appropriate product of the agency. Social service agencies that represent clients with little or no political power have very special problems. Too much concern with the wants and desires of the clients directly served clearly can erode the economic and political support necessary for the very existence of the agency. But too little concern will result in exploitation of the clients the agency purports to serve. The very fact that the social agency typically is accused of both errors reflects the delicate balance that an agency administrator faces, and this is only one of many critical administrative choices.

One very specific concern is who makes what choices? Children, the mentally ill, the mentally retarded, and others may not know what is in their own best interest. The phrase "caveat emptor" (let the buyer beware) implies that the customer in a store knows and can best judge his or her own self-interest. For example, a bookstore clerk is not expected to help a customer decide between the hardback or the paperback edition of a book. Presumably, the ethical responsibilities of the firm are satisfied when the client knows of the availability of both books. However, problems become more complicated as choices become more complicated. A surgeon, for instance, is expected to guide a patient through a decision about having an operation or getting chemotherapy when each has different costs and different benefits and, most particularly,

It is essential for agency administrators to keep in touch with client needs. Here, the administrator of a health clinic shares a meal with an elderly client as she tells him about her health problems and her experiences at the clinic.

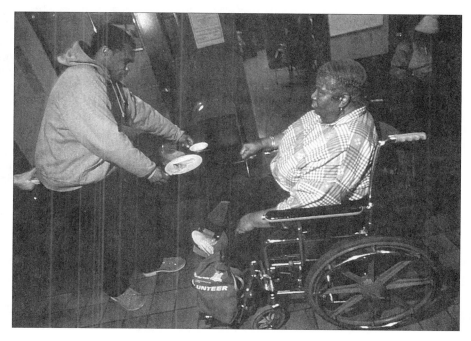

different probabilities of being effective. The problem becomes most acute when the client being served directly cannot choose his or her own best interest.

The professional social worker in the service agency needs to steer between two dangers. On the one hand, rigid adherence to the rules that benefit the agency or the taxpayers who fund the service agency can quickly result in a subtle but debilitating form of tyranny. On the other hand, the agency has a responsibility not to become captives of its clientele or to surrender to its clients the power to determine the structure and nature of the services being offered. When interests are in conflict, there is no one correct way to resolve that conflict. The problem becomes particularly acute in the social agency in which the social worker has to represent the interests of clients incapable of knowing just what their own best interests may be.

IMPLEMENTATION

Failure in strategic thought or process can render a social program, however well intended, useless—or worse. Even brilliant strategy has to be put into effective operation. **Implementation** involves deciding on the actions and coordinating them. It is a process of turning general thoughts into specific actions, through which real people are charged with things they must do within established time frames. Implementation involves selecting the tactics required to carry out the strategy. Further, patterns of communication need to be designed, systems of monitoring and accountability instituted to ensure that activities have been put into place, and the necessary staff recruited and trained.

The key to success in the implementation phase is getting staff and volunteers to understand and support the selected objectives and pattern of attainment. The process is sure to fail if the human aspects of the implementation process are not addressed adequately. The old division between **public sector,** or government agencies, and **voluntary sector,** or nongovernment not-for-profit agencies, has been replaced by a patchwork in which public and private, profit and nonprofit, sectarian and nonsectarian agencies coexist and overlap as avenues for social welfare service delivery. Nonpublic social workers tend to be found in one of four types of settings: (1) traditional voluntary agencies, (2) human services programs within the corporate sector, (3) human service corporations (as employees, stockholders, or directors), or (4) private practice.

Today, public agencies often contract with private agencies to perform essential services, which means that private agencies often receive the majority of their funding from government contracts. The private-practice programs may charge either public or private insurance companies for client services. Added to that are the many profit-oriented human service corporations that directly run hospitals, prisons, and nursing homes. The days when there was a strict separation of public agencies (funded by taxes) and nonprofit private agencies (funded by foundations and charitable contributions) have long since become history.

◢ SOCIAL WELFARE SERVICES: A HISTORICAL OVERVIEW

Since early in American history, the responsibility for providing social welfare services has been split between government and the **private sector,** nongovernment agencies that may be either not-for-profit or for-profit agencies. The government was not expected, indeed not able, to deal with the diverse circumstances associated with human needs. As discussed in Chapter 1, the Poor Law inherited from England provided that the government supply meager help as a last resort. The historian Daniel Boorstin notes that in the new nation "communities existed before governments were there to care for public needs" (1985, 121). Without a tradition of centralized religious or public responsibility for welfare, the responsibility fell to ad hoc sources of assistance and to local churches' organized efforts.

In Chapter 1 we described the history of American social welfare institutions. An overview at the turn of the century would have revealed a neat compartmentalization of social welfare and social service responsibilities (see Table 7.2). The public sector, or the government, accepted the responsibility for addressing long-term dependency through poor houses, which were funded and administered at the local level. The government, typically at the state level, also accepted responsibility for those social services that intrinsically required the use of sovereign authority, such as child welfare programs, the criminal justice system, and the confinement of mentally ill persons. Even today such services would be in violation of civil liberties were it not for the courts granting to the state the "right" to treat children, the insane, and criminals as dependent persons. Sometimes, however, the state oversteps this line by treating the aged and the widowed as if they, too, have somehow lost their civil rights.

Private sector agencies generally were administered at the local level and often by sectarian, or church-related, groups. They provided the more intensely personal social services, such as those in orphanages, nursing homes, adoption agencies, and family counseling centers. The churches very jealously protected their right to provide these personal social services, and social workers as a professional group vigorously defended the notion that the government should stay out of the private

| TABLE 7.2 | WELFARE RESPONSIBILITIES DATED ABOUT 1900 |

Public	Private
State	**Sectarian**
Chronically mentally ill	Moral supervision
Prisoners	Orphan homes
Child welfare	
Aged	**Nonsectarian**
Local	Advocacy
	Settlement houses
Outdoor relief to widows and half-orphans	

social service sector. The division of responsibilities is indicated in Table 7.2. In the twentieth century, this neat compartmentalization of responsibilities disappeared.

◪ THE LINKING OF PUBLIC AND PRIVATE EFFORTS

A historical summary of the relationship between voluntary and public welfare shows that the single constant is that the two exist in a kind of dynamic tension. A good part of voluntary welfare has been an organized effort to force governments to act. Sometimes public and private agencies have been rivals; sometimes unwilling partners. The historical constant is that the shape and structure of one at any point in time cannot be understood without reference to the other. The primacy of the voluntary effort in the nineteenth century was challenged by the social reform movement of the progressive era (1890 to 1920). The reform effort was split irrevocably following Woodrow Wilson's administration. State responsibility was for cash aid to the deserving poor, and the provision of social services was the responsibility of voluntary efforts. A significant school of thought in the first third of this century held that cash public aid was less risky and less humiliating than private charity. Following the Great Depression, government public assistance and social insurance programs replaced the previously provided cash aid function. The voluntary sector jealously guarded its independence from government.

The spirit of earlier cooperation resumed on a small scale in the 1950s, when voluntary agencies began to accept grants and contracts to deliver highly specific child welfare services. This relationship mushroomed in the mid-1960s, when Great Society programs funded "old" social work agencies to provide many of their "new" activities. Not so gradually, public funds began to play the dominant role in the total budget for private voluntary agencies. Some social workers in the private sector raised questions about whether the heavy reliance on public dollars would affect the autonomy and integrity of the private agency. Paradoxically, this period (1965 to 1980) saw the growth of advocacy organizations engaged in monitoring the performance of public actions and working to influence the quantity and quality of public funded social service expenditures by direct lobbying, grassroots organizing, electioneering, and particularly litigation. No doubt, these activities contributed to the significant rise in public spending for social services.

The tables have now turned nearly 180 degrees: there is debate over the proper function of the voluntary sector. The Reagan administration eliminated much federal support for legal aid, social services, and organizing activities. The Bush administration, with its "Thousand Points of Light" programs, encouraged returning direct social service functions to private charity. Both conservative administrations argued that private charity can and should meet the needs for service assistance that are being created by the curtailment of publicly funded social programs. The Clinton administration and Congress have substantial disagreements, but both agree there will be growth in the voluntary sector. In light of the almost certain restructuring of public programs after the 1996 elections, growth in both voluntary and for-profit social services almost certainly will be necessary.

CONTEMPORARY STRUCTURE

Today, organized social service activities clearly are not limited to those provided directly by governments or sectarian agencies. A significant share of social service expenditures (a precise estimate is dependent on the assumptions made) comes from and/or is spent by the little-understood **private nonprofit social agency.** The private nonprofit sector of the social services system employs a majority of the social workers engaged in direct practice to individuals, groups, neighborhoods, and communities. The private nonprofit agency is private in charter and organization but public in function. Neither the economic model of the private firm nor the public finance constructs of the public enterprises quite catches the essence of its operations. The nonprofit social services agencies are a diverse lot of 40,000 entities, which employ 675,000 persons and collectively spend $15 billion to accomplish rather imprecise goals. The nonprofit agencies provide a host of services ranging from prenatal to bereavement programs for individuals, groups, neighborhoods, and communities. They also serve as an organizing entity and conduit for charitable funds and voluntary efforts, with tax dollars commingled and channeled to specific projects.

Three interdependent parts make up the social service portion of nonprofit agencies. A specific agency can represent one or all three parts:

- Agencies that serve public and charitable purposes but serve principally for fund raising and planning, such as the United Way agencies

- Advocacy organizations, which bring together a group of like-minded persons who seek to generate government funding or promote public understanding and support of a specific social problem area or a specific class of persons deemed to be in need, such as the aged or persons with disabilities (advocacy organizations are in essence political interest groups that attempt to garner support, including public spending, for their causes)

- Direct service agencies that deal with particular clients with specific or multiple problems of social functioning

Despite the importance, relevance, and resources of the private sector social agency, there is no uniform explanation for its very existence, much less an agreed-upon explanation of its vitality and durability. Nevertheless, three main explanations exist, namely, historical, administrative, and economic perspectives of private sector social agencies.

Historical Explanation

The first of these three explanations, most completely developed by historian John Leiby (1978), stresses simple historical antecedents. American society, particularly on the frontier, developed in a context of almost nonexistent government. Lacking public institutions to address the problems of collective needs, the frontier society turned to formal and informal voluntary associations, which took roots and maintained their own integrity once governments were vibrant. Even then, according to this explanation, people on the frontier maintained a healthy distrust of government. The famed French social philosopher Alexis de Tocqueville, writing in the mid-1800s, described this tendency of Americans to form nonprofit, nongovernmental associations to accomplish public tasks as characteristic of the new nation:

> Americans of all ages, all stations of life, and all types of disposition are forever forming associations . . . to give fetes, found seminaries, build churches, distribute books and send missionaries to the Antipodes. . . . In every case, at the head of any new undertaking, where in France you would find the government or in England some territorial magnate, in the United States you are sure a find a voluntary association. (Alexis de Tocqueville, *Democracy in America,* as quoted in Palmer and Sawhill 1984, 263)

Administrative Explanation

The second explanation, the administrative one, is considerably more prosaic, although it builds on the first and adds a contemporary focus. The argument is made that during periods of expansion, public officials can more quickly provide a newly mandated service by contracting with private vendors than by launching a full-scale public program. Equally important in the mind of public officials is that a service highly sought today may be seen as an encumbrance or luxury tomorrow. It is far easier administratively and politically to cancel a contract with a vendor than it is to dismantle a fully operative program. Thus, during periods of expansion and contraction of social service spending, public officials have an incentive to purchase service contracts with nonpublic entities. The private nonprofit agencies, in turn, find their fund-raising and maintenance requirements more easily met by offering to contract to provide a particular social service.

Economic Explanation

The third explanation focuses attention on the interaction between economic and political factors in the social service marketplace. This can be visualized by assuming an oversimplified world. Suppose that only three groups competed for spending on a social work service. One group wanted to spend $6 billion, another $8 billion, and the third $10 billion. The $8 billion group, by threatening to form a coalition with either of the other groups, can get the remaining group to agree to its preference. The $8 billion dollar amount is between the two extremes. Where the compromise actually is reached depends on many factors; the critical point is that the group that wants the most certainly will be dissatisfied. If the public institutions spend only $8 billion on, say, AIDS research, and a group wants society to spend $10 billion, money for that program can be collected from the marketplace through donations. This happens all the time. Social workers convince concerned citizens to give money to do things the government ought to do but is not doing. The voluntary sector is a kind of private voluntary government. The situation has been compounded by the fact that many American citizens believe, rightly or not, that government programs are inherently inefficient. In the late 1980s and the early 1990s these dissatisfactions prompted a renewed interest in the privatization of social services. This interest has continued in the 1996 election campaigns.

To understand the organizational auspices of a social service delivery system we can no longer usefully think in terms of the public-private dichotomy. Instead, we need to look at the funding sources and charter of the delivery agency. We thus find many types of public, private, and voluntary agencies, as indicated in Table 7.3. From pure publicly funded and publicly run child protective services agencies (represented in cell 1 of the table) to profit-seeking child care centers with all their users paying their own way (cell 11), social service programs come in many forms. Most agencies would be classified as one of the types represented by the numbers in bold type (i.e., cells 1, 6, 7, and 11). In practice, all combinations can be found. The critical point is that agencies need to be classified on the basis of both their charter and their principal source of funding.

◢ CHARACTERISTICS OF TRADITIONAL VOLUNTARY AGENCIES

First, voluntary agencies represent special interest groups' concern for specific problems. This is expressed in (1) a commitment to deliver a specialized service to a client or constituent group, (2) a commitment to try to influence public policy on behalf of that specialized client population, and (3) a desire to educate a nonattentive public about the service needs, potential, and special attributes of the group of clients to be served.

TABLE 7.3	TYPES OF SOCIAL SERVICE DELIVERY MODELS			
	SOURCE OF FUNDS			
Charter	**Taxes**	**Gifts and Grants**	**Payments for Service**	**Mixed**
Public	1	2	3	4
Private, nonprofit	5	6	7	8
Private, for-profit	9	10	11	12

1—An example of a public agency funded by taxes would be a prison or a child protective services agency.

6—An example of a private, nonprofit agency funded by gifts and grants is a child and family services agency or a child guidance center.

7—An example of a private, nonprofit agency funded by payments for service is a church-operated child care program.

11—An example of a private, for-profit agency funded by payments for service is the Kindercare Childcare Corporation's centers, located throughout the United States.

Note: Public agencies, except hospitals, seldom receive payments for services from persons served.

Second, voluntary agencies have a considerable degree of discretion in their allocation of agency resources since, unlike a public entity, they do not have narrow legislative mandates, nor do their clients have specific legal claims on agency resources. Consequently, voluntary agencies have the freedom to choose which clients to serve and how to serve them. This provides maximum freedom to professional social workers, who often see employment in the voluntary agency as a way to escape bureaucratic constraints. But serving a particular group in a particular way becomes institutionalized over time. Voluntary agencies acquire traditions and obligations that limit their freedom. This often leads to splinter agencies spinning off from the older agencies, which can become as ossified as public ones.

Third, because of their small size, unique history, discretionary power, and freedom (in the short run) from bureaucratic and legal constraints, voluntary agencies depend heavily on the quality of their executive leadership.

Voluntary agencies play a special role in the three-sector (i.e., public, private nonprofit, private for-profit) social service economy. They are bounded on both sides—on one side by the private, profit-oriented approach of the free market, and on the other by a politically driven public sector. Governed by neither marketplace nor voting booth, voluntary agencies can be creative and innovative. But they are also vulnerable to their own excesses and to the expansionary drive of both profit and public enterprises. Thus, any agency may exist only briefly. Much like business firms, there are few—very few—venerable agencies (i.e., those that have existed for a hundred years or more), a small number of agencies in their middle years, and a whole rash of new agencies (i.e., those less than ten years old). A survey conducted by Lester Solomon and Michael Gutowski (1986) found that only 40 percent of the agencies in place that year had existed ten years earlier.

There is a great deal of romantic fantasy about the voluntary approach. Conservative administrations pledged to restore the American spirit of voluntary service and of cooperation between private and community initiatives. Former President Reagan lauded the spirit of the free and vigorous voluntary way, in which communities, out of love, rebuilt the barn and cared for the victims of disaster in a warm, heartfelt, caring way. Conservatives listened to his message and feared the loss of a world that never was. Liberals listened to his message and recognized it for what it was—a historical inaccuracy. We cannot return to a voluntary way, not only because today the world is more complex, but principally because the voluntary spirit, then as now, responded only to a small section of the total problem.

The voluntary agency, in fact, has expanded as the public sector has expanded. Today, only a small segment of our social welfare problems is responded to by the voluntary sector. Firms historically have given about 1 percent of their pretax profits to all of the voluntary sector agencies. Families have contributed about 2 percent of their pretax income to "churches and charities." Between 1969 and 1979, private family giving as a share of the GNP dropped from 2.1 percent to 1.8 percent. The decline continued, although less dramatically, throughout the 1980s and into the 1990s. Tax law accelerated this decline. An increasing share of the voluntary budget now comes from grants, contracts, and purchases of service agreements from the public sector.

THE STATUS OF SOCIAL WORK IN SHAPING SOCIAL WELFARE AGENCIES

The social work profession has shared key roles in the shaping of social welfare agencies with a number of other groups, including politicians, economists, psychologists, educators, attorneys, and increasingly, lobbyists for various constituent groups. To strengthen its relationship with these other entities and its roles as a key shaper of social welfare policies and programs, the profession has continued to seek new ways to maintain credibility in an increasingly technological and politicized society. One way the profession has increased its status has been through state and national licensing and certification programs.

Social workers' status as professionals depends on the presence of two conditions:

- A recognized body of knowledge that can be transmitted
- A defined and legitimized (often certified) area of activity

Certification as a professional by the state serves a general and a specific purpose. Its general purpose is to protect the public from unwarranted claims by individual purveyors of a service. Its specific purpose is to protect the property rights, in this case the intellectual property, of a person trained and educated to perform the service. Technologies change rapidly and are often shared across professional boundaries. This aspect is conspicuous in direct practice, where there is shared theoretical knowledge. In the field of mental health, for example, a member of the public would have difficulty distinguishing between the modes of intervention of a psychiatric social worker, a clinical psychologist, and an educational counselor or a person certified to function as counselor in a specific area such as drug or alcohol abuse.

It is often difficult to discern whether the real political purpose behind the certification of a professional is to protect an unsuspecting public, or to protect the practice rights of a politically powerful professional group. Each professional group seeks to enlarge its own domain of practice, and each professional group seeks to make more restrictive the rights to operate within that domain. Each professional group seeks to justify its expansive and protective stance with the ethic of client interest. Social work professionals are not exempted from this generalization.

Social workers have been and are the implementers of social welfare programs. This fact has not made social work central to social welfare in the shaping of policies. As a professional group, economists have staked that principal claim as the persons with the technical facilities required for program design and evaluation. Social workers' very role as implementers has often reduced them to performing fairly bureaucratic street-level delivery roles with little say in promoting new policy directions and innovations. Increasingly, social workers are saying that their practice wisdom is highly relevant to policy development. To date, however, this policy-practice perspective has not been highly developed in either professional schools of social work or, more importantly, in the states and in the national capitol. A clear challenge for the immediate future is to find ways to make the practice knowledge, the street-level bureaucratic wisdom, a central part of policy development.

The University of Tilburg in the Netherlands has established a new program in social policy and management, open to social workers of the European Community nations. The Department of Social Policy and Social Work at the University of Tampere, Finland, has an MA in comparative social welfare that seeks to blend not only policy, management, and practice perspective but also policy perspectives across national lines. Each nation does not have to start fresh to design policy initiatives, nor can any nation simply borrow the perspective of another nation. These are signs of a new professional commitment to training in policy practice.

The making of social welfare policy is the result of a political process. In the main, the social work literature has neglected a methodology for intervention in that process, relying instead on teaching policy development from a case or historical perspective. Traditionally, policy analysis has used frames of reference to answer questions about who is covered by the policy, what benefits are provided, the form of delivery, and the financial source (for example, Gilbert and Specht 1986). This is changing. Analyses of the dynamics of policy—legislative, judicial, and administrative processes—are finding their way into social work writings.

Hard choices are to be made in the next decade: Should state or national governments play the lead role in the delivery and funding of social welfare programs? Should unwed mothers less than 18 be eligible for direct AFDC support? To what extent, if at all, should the right to a publicly supported abortion be abridged? To what extent can a cultural group deviate from the general standards of child welfare? These are tough questions, and they involve technical, political, and value considerations.

Regardless of the auspices of the social agencies in which they work, social workers must maintain a strong professional presence in both the policy and practice arenas at community, state, and national levels.

SUMMARY

A majority of Americans view voluntary agencies as innovative and flexible vanguards of social service technology and delivery patterns. In point of fact, in recent years it is the public sector that has often been the vanguard. Essentially, voluntary and public agencies are created in particular historical circumstances. The mixture of public, voluntary, and private agency practices and the way they are funded may once have made sense, but adaptation to current needs has been slow. Often the patterns of practice do not fit well with current realities and problems.

A number of hypotheses have been advanced concerning the origins, growth, and functions of voluntary agencies. They have been studied extensively by social psychologists, sociologists, economists, and political scientists. In fact, all of the explanations about the voluntary sector are flawed in one way or another, and more research needs to be done. Basically, the public, voluntary, and even profit-oriented agencies are rapidly becoming more similar to one another, with administrators facing similar issues regardless of the type of agency they oversee.

The cited readings at the end of the chapter give the beginning student access to the many considerations and strategies that are likely to be considered as the process of social agency administration moves into the next century.

KEY TERMS

implementation	public sector
private nonprofit social agency	strategy
private sector	voluntary sector

DISCUSSION QUESTIONS

1. What are some of the factors that need to be considered when shaping the direction an agency takes in developing and implementing new programs?

2. How many social services agencies in your community are public? How many are voluntary? Are there ones for which you are not sure?

3. Discuss the differences between the public and the voluntary social service agencies in your community.

4. Which of the local agencies do you think ought to be voluntary and which ought to be public? Explain why for each one.

5. What principle of separation into public and voluntary would you use an ideal for social services agencies in the United States? What principle of separation appears to operate in practice?

6. What roles should the social work profession play in the development and administration of social welfare programs?

REFERENCES

Anthony, Robert, and Regina Herzlinger. 1975. *Management control in nonprofit organizations.* Homewood, Ill.: Irwin.

Boorstin, D. J. 1985. *The Americans: The national experience.* New York: Random House.

Gilbert, Neil, Harry Sprecht, and Paul Terrell. 1993. *Dimensions of social policy,* 3d ed. Englewood Cliffs, N.J.: Prentice-Hall.

Grummer, Burton. 1990. *The politics of social administration.* Englewood Cliffs, N.J.: Prentice-Hall.

Leiby, John. 1978. *A history of social welfare and social work in the United States.* New York: Columbia University Press.

Moore, S. T., J. Poertner, E. A. Cowdy, and M. Habacker. 1991. Performance guidance system in social work practice: A team-focused approach. *Community Alternatives: International Journal of Family Care* 3: 19–33.

Palmer, John, and Isabel Sawhill. 1984. *The Reagan record.* Cambridge: Ballinger.

Perlman, Robert, and Arnold Gurin. 1972. *Community organization and social planning.* New York: Wiley.

Solomon, Lester M., and M. F. Gutowski. 1986. *The invisible sector.* Washington, D.C.: Urban Institute.

SUGGESTED FURTHER READINGS

Children's Defense Fund. 1992. Child care under the Family Support Act. Washington, D.C.: Author.

Flynn, J. 1992. *Social agency policy: Analysis and presentation for community practice.* Chicago: Nelson-Hall.

Haynes, Karen S. 1986. Affecting change: Social workers in the political arena. New York: Longman.

Heffernan, W. J. 1992. *Social welfare policy: A research and action strategy.* New York: Longman.

Johnson, H., and D. Broder. 1996. *The system.* Boston: Little Brown.

Kleinkauf, C. 1989. Analyzing social welfare legislation. *Social Work* 34: 179–81.

Specht, H. 1990. Social work and the popular psychotherapies. *Social Service Review* 64: 345–57.

Wakefield, J. C. 1988. Psychotherapy, distributive justice and social work. Part 1: Distributive justice as a conceptual framework for social work. *Social Service Review* 62: 187–210.

Wellford, W. Harrison. 1987. *The role of the nonprofit human services organizations.* Washington, D. C.: National Association of Health and Social Welfare Organizations.

Wyers, N. 1991. Policy-practice in social work: Models and Issues. *Journal of Social Work Education* 27: 241–50.

CHAPTER 8

RESEARCH AND PRACTICE

Because of a budget crisis, the directors of the human resources agency in a northwestern state were considering a policy change that would reduce **AFDC** payments. They asked a policy analyst from the agency to determine the probable impact of such reductions. The analyst concluded that the state, rather than saving money, would actually spend more because of having to pick up emergency relief and indigent health care costs for families who could not survive without **AFDC** and Medicaid, both of which are largely federally subsidized. Based on this information and other data the analyst provided, the agency directors increased funding for low-income child care and employment training to reduce the number of **AFDC** recipients, but they did not reduce the actual payments. ■

Research, in its most general sense, refers to any disciplined strategy of inquiry. The term sometimes elicits an image of a white-coated individual in a sterile laboratory, but this conception is unduly restrictive for our purposes. On the other hand, research is sometimes equated with the mere gathering of facts. For our purposes, this concept is too broad. Research within a profession such as social work has many manifestations, but in this chapter we focus on three reasonably specific modes, or forms, of research: (1) disciplinary research, (2) policy research, and (3) evaluative research.

All three modes are scientific in that all depend on the scientific method. All three are objective in that the investigator is required to conform to established canons of logical reasoning and formal rules of evidence. Further, all three are ethically neutral in that the investigator does not take sides on issues of moral or ethical significance. Each mode seeks to generate a proposition, or set of propositions, capable of falsification. Although similar in their demand for objectivity, each of the modes has its own specific intents. ■

◢ DISCIPLINARY RESEARCH

Disciplinary research is the term used to distinguish investigations designed to expand the body of knowledge of a particular discipline. In the social sciences that means to expand or modify the understanding of social and psychological processes so that social behavior can be explained. The intent is explanation for its own sake. This is sometimes called pure, as opposed to applied, research. Disciplinary research begins with a paradigm. The paradigm is a perspective, perhaps a school of thought, that structures the research, the research goals, and hence the research methods that are seen as appropriate in the analysis of a particular topic. The paradigm directs the investigator as to where and how to seek evidence. Complex social behavior cannot be explained except in terms of a paradigm. The political scientist, the economist, and the sociologist each would describe, analyze, and explain identical phenomena in different ways. No single one is right and the others wrong; rather, each paradigm generalizes its own special insight into the problem at hand. Social workers use all of these paradigms in their efforts to identify a pragmatic method of intervention.

The desire to understand the intergenerational transmission of poverty and dependency can be used as an illustration. Investigators do not disagree about whether psychological immaturity, social isolation, or the lack of economic alternatives produces multigenerational welfare. Investigators know that they all do and that when all three are present, the likelihood of multigenerational poverty becomes very large. In science, for the most part, explanations are seen as additive. The economist might think of intergenerational poverty in terms of the job structure or the lack of job opportunities. The social psychologist may explore the problem in terms of role models or the lack of them. The nutritionist will explore food consumption patterns and cognitive development, school failure, and dependency. There is no one route to poverty and dependency.

The social investigator is interested in providing an explanation of why something happened. The first requirement then is to identify a dependent variable (that which we wish to explain) and show how it is related to one or more independent variables (those factors that produce changes in the dependent variable.) In the physical sciences we know that as the temperature falls, or rises, changes occur in the way we see H_2O—as ice, water, or steam. Complex molecular theories are used to explain that simple observable phenomenon. Similarly, as changes in economic circumstances occur, observable changes in employment opportunities occur. Just establishing the direction of causality can be a profound problem. Careful selection of variables, careful use of both inductive and deductive reasoning, and precise application of the established rules of evidence are required to produce correct inferences about relationships. This is what is meant by an explanation.

The glue that holds together a disciplinary investigation is theory. A **theory** is a set of logically related, empirically verifiable generalizations that intend to explain relationships clearly. Since the process of theory building and research is cyclical and constitutes a single feedback loop, we can break into the process at any point.

In science, theory and research interact; in practice, observation and generalization interact. Together they form the whole of an investigation process. The normal presentation is that of a circle, as depicted in Figure 8.1. A theory is derived from a set of generalizations. The theory, in turn, sparks a **hypothesis,** which focuses attention on certain observations, which then yield more carefully phrased empirical generalizations.

The economist, the sociologist, and the psychologist would give widely different explanations for the shifts in family structure associated with shifts in general economic conditions. No one theory is right or wrong; some are more useful to practice patterns than others.

Sometimes the research process begins with observation. For example, the renowned nineteenth-century French sociologist Émile Durkheim looked at crude data on suicides and found that suicide rates were lower for Catholics, married persons, and people in rural areas. The common feature of these correlates was a sense of social involvement. This led him to articulate the theory of linking a lack of social integration—which he called "anomie," or the sense of being without norms and standards—and suicide. Legions of scholars have deduced various hypotheses from Durkheim's groundbreaking work, which led to a number of empirical generalizations about the social consequences of

FIGURE 8.1   **THE INVESTIGATION PROCESS**

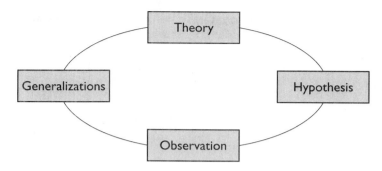

anomie. These have been adopted into practice modes to reduce the sense of anomie via specific practice methods. These, in turn, ultimately are used to expand, modify, and sharpen Durkheim's original theory.

POLICY RESEARCH

Policy planners and policy advocates frequently use specific research methods as they ply their craft. A political decision maker who needs to resolve uncertainties before making a policy choice often seeks the aid of policy research. In deciding whether to expand maximum-security cells or dormitory-type rooms, the individual prison official will want to know more about the effectiveness of various ways of housing prisoners and the reliability of these predictions regarding their postconfinement behavior. Using scientific methods to reduce, or at least minimize, uncertainty is part of the social worker's task.

Policy research is a specialized form of inquiry whose purpose is the provision of reliable, valid, and relevant knowledge for public officials, agency managers, and others in the decision-making processes of government. It is used (or misused) at all levels of government and at all bureaucratic strata. Research studies employ techniques that vary from the simple collection and collation of available data to the design of sophisticated econometric models and social experiments.

Scientific research does not guide or control policy choices. History is replete with examples of public officials rejecting the advice of the research community. The rejection of research findings does not inevitably lead to negative results, nor does the acceptance of the recommendations of the research community always yield the intended beneficial results. Deciding on the contribution to and limits of the research to public decision making is a complex topic that has been treated extensively in other books (e.g., Haveman 1987). For example, if welfare benefits are to be raised and if eligibility standards are to be broadened, then there will be certain obvious consequences. There will also be less obvious, and perhaps even uncertain, consequences. Identifying or at least reducing the policy uncertainty is a central task of policy research. How a society uses this knowledge once it is generated is a political issue.

The answer clearly depends not on what we know but on how our knowledge is related to the various social conditions and how that information is congruent—or incongruent—with particular ideologies and political belief systems. Conservative and liberal actors on the political scene will often select the theory that best fits the ends or goals they seek. Just as expert medical testimony is used, and often misused, by both prosecution and defense attorneys in the same case, so also, social science is used and misused for larger political gain.

Today, almost all graduate schools of social work have created policy tracks or concentrations designed to prepare the professional social worker to assist in the formulation and analysis of policy alternatives in specialized areas, such as social work, public health, city management, or education. The use of research methods to discover and delineate means available to government to respond to problems is a practice as old as government. But specialized education in research procedures, especially structured to policy choice, is a recent development.

Problems arise in the design, execution, and interpretation of research for specific policy choices that are not encountered in disciplinary research. Policy analysis frequently is expected to produce specific kinds of information in a short time on a limited budget. Policy and disciplinary research differ in other ways as well. Both policy research and disciplinary research are governed by the canons of scientific methodology. Disciplinary research is structured to develop theoretically relevant explanations of social phenomena. But policy research is structured to identify, assess, and evaluate public strategies used to produce public ends. As described by Majchrzak (1984), policy research is both an artistic and a scientific process, whereby the solution specifies a desirable relationship between manipulable means and obtainable ends. That is, the investigator directs the social worker to identify the best use of limited but available means to analyze those ends or goals that are realistic in light of what we know about the problem at hand.

Adequately executed social science research often is an inadequate guide to policy choice, because it often fails to be timely or is structured in a way that is unusable to the public official or agency manager. On the other hand, practitioners in the field have often failed to use the most elementary forms of inquiry before instituting a policy action. The connection between scientific demand on inquiry and political demands on action needs to be appraised.

◢ EVALUATIVE RESEARCH

Policy evaluation is a specific kind of policy research. The ordinary **evaluative research** method used to develop a policy perspective on an anticipated change in a program is to review the literature generally available. When this is done, the social worker typically has a mass of written documents, all of which are generally relevant but none of which is precisely related. One useful way to begin is with a particularly influential report, such as a study by the federal government or perhaps

Professionals at all levels in the social welfare system rely on many types of research to help them develop new programs and policies. Here, a researcher conducts a focus group of community residents to determine how they think recent funding given to the area to address youth crime should be spent.

a study done in a state similar to your own. Then the social worker can examine all of the principal bibliographies for relevant references for the new topic. Few social problems are brand new, and even a cursory examination of how other governments deal with similar problems is a valuable way to use existing knowledge to choose among policy options. Sometimes the investigation is very specific, such as what happens to emergency room use when a particular payment method is introduced. Sometimes it is very general, such as how applications for food stamps fluctuate with shifts in the economy. The social worker who serves as an advisor to policymakers needs to be alert to methods of dealing with such questions.

Evaluation, when competently done, measures the extent to which a program attains its goals. The evaluative process helps the practitioner specify, from the multiplicity of objectives, the set of objectives by which the program will be judged; declare that some observable phenomena will be the basis for judging the program successful; and explain how the favorable outcome, if there is one, is the result of the policy action or program under consideration. In evaluative research the practitioner seeks to use the scientific method as the basic analytic tool in determining the program's impact. Because real-world conditions do not have the experimental purity of controlled laboratory conditions, specific research designs are used to maximize the likelihood of determining what the results of a program were. Because of the difficulties inherent in each phase of the process, the results are "known" only within a range of certainty. The principal task of the policy evaluator is not just to show success or failure, but to indicate the range of certainty with which that judgment is made.

In addition to evaluating the effectiveness of social work programs, social workers also evaluate the effectiveness of their direct work with clients. **Single-subject designs,** research designs that evaluate the impact of interventions or policy changes on a single client or case, are often used by social workers in clinical settings.

Identifying Goals

The evaluative process begins with an identification of the goals to be evaluated. This seems obvious, but in fact is an inordinately value-laden undertaking. Initially, there is the problem of ranking goals in an effort to indicate which ones are intended, and their order of importance, and which are desirable but unintended consequences of the policy action or program. Second, the evaluator needs to state clearly the goals that will be measured. Sometimes there is confusion and conflict—possibly political—over goals. Social work research needs to be precise about which goals are being evaluated. Third, the evaluator must frankly and honestly deal with the dysfunctional or undesirable consequences that occur because of the policy action or program. Social science methodology often is overwhelmed by attempts to measure many goals simultaneously, yet the false specification of a program to a too-small set of objectives may mask the good points of a program and expose the bad points. Care in goal identification is a critical first step in devising a policy-relevant evaluation plan.

Formulating Operational Definitions

The second critical step is the selection of valid and reliable measures of the positive and negative outcomes of programs. To be evaluated objectively, such outcomes must be defined in measurable terms; that is, operational definitions that define specific concepts and terms to be studied, for example, work effort, must be formulated. Once that is done, appropriate measures must be identified. A valid measure is one that does in fact measure what it is supposed to; for example, the number of hours worked in a week is thought to be one valid measure of work effort. Reliable measures are dependable and not subject to memory loss or other distortions in observation and reporting. In the example of measuring work effort, a timekeeper's job records typically are more valid and reliable indicators than a worker's memory, although clearly this is not always the case. In social work programs the evaluator has the responsibility of demonstrating that the "observed" changes are valid and reliable estimates of the object of the policy action or program. The test of program success must stand up to criticism from the scientific and political communities. Thus, attention must be paid to the permanency of the impact, the reproducibility of the observation of success, and the reliability of the observation.

Demonstrating a Causal Connection

It is insufficient to report that a favorable outcome occurred while a program was in place. The evaluator has to demonstrate that the outcome reasonably can be attributed to the policy action or program. The basic argument of causal connection was developed by the nineteenth-century philosopher and economist John Stuart Mill, and remains the foundation of social science theories of causation. His approach rests on two methods, known as the positive and negative canons.

Positive Canon
The positive canon, called the sufficient condition, states that for a result, X, to occur, there has been an element, Y, previously. That is to say, whenever Y is observed, X always follows. Y thus is a sufficient condition of X.

Elements of Situation 1:
A, B, Y → produce → X

Elements of Situation 2:
D, E, Y → produce → X

Elements of Situation N:
M, N, Y → produce → X

Negative Canon
To say that Y is a sufficient condition is not to say, however, that it is a cause. The negative canon, or necessary condition, states that the absence of Y always is associated with the absence of X.

Elements of Situation 3:
F, G, non-Y → produce → non-X

Elements of Situation 4:
H, I, non-Y → produce → non-X

Elements of Situation M:
M, N, non-Y → produce → non-X

Thus, if we observed all theoretically possible connections and then found that when Y was present X followed, and that whenever Y was absent X did not occur, we could say that Y causes X.

Now try to think of an example. Whenever we find a broken optic nerve, we find blindness. Broken optic nerves are a sufficient condition for blindness, but not necessarily a cause, since we find blindness occurring as a result of other factors. When there are unbroken optic nerves, we sometimes observe blindness. When we find fire, we find oxygen; when we remove oxygen, we never find fire. Therefore, oxygen is a necessary condition of fire, but not a cause, for we find oxygen and the absence of fire.

Social science evaluation uses both the positive and negative canons. This is the classical experimental design and is called the "method of difference." The inference is then made that *Y* causes *X*. This inference is subject to criticism, however, on the grounds that both *Y* and *X* could result from some more fundamental but unobserved factor; or that *Y* is associated with *X* only when some other factor is present (that is, *Y* and *X* were observed in the fashion noted, but this was a fortuitous occurrence).

Elements of Situation 5:

A, B, Y → produce → X

Elements of Situation 6:

A, B, non-Y → produce → non-X

In the classical design, the evaluator uses both theory and probability to increase the likelihood that the observed relationship is in fact a causal relationship. Theory is used to select the observations to be made. We observe *A, B,* and on through *N* cases when there are compelling, logical reasons to believe that there is a causal connection. We exclude observations where there is no particular reason for investigations. Theories thus guide observations and lead investigators closer to a realistic understanding of the relationship between observed outcome and the program or policy action. The real understanding depends on the adequacy of the theory.

Second, we trust to the rules of chance. If we note an occurrence, by resorting to various statistical manipulations, we can calculate the probability that the observation would occur merely because of random factors. If we give one set of parents a course in child nutrition and, as far as we know, withhold that information from a second set of parents, then test the nutrition adequacy of their children's packed lunch both before and after the course on a score of 1 to 100, we find results such as those in Table 8.1. We can calculate the experimental impact as (*B–A*) minus (*D–C*), with *D–C* being the change attributable to nonexperimental factors that occurred. Of course, we do not know what in the program caused the change, but if (*B–A*) minus (*D–D*) is significantly different from what we would expect to occur by any random process, it certainly is reasonable to behave as if nutritional education and nutritional performance are causally connected. If the goal is better nutritional performance, nutritional education appears to be one way of achieving it.

Obviously, an evaluator who clearly identified the most relevant goal, selected the most appropriate units of evaluation, structured the relationship with the most finely tuned of theories, and tested the results with the most sophisticated statistical test still could not prove that program *Y* is the best way of achieving goal *X*. He or she could show only

TABLE 8.1   NUTRITION SCORES OF PARENTS

	Nutrition Score Before	Nutrition Score After
Parents given course	A	B
Parents not given course	C	D

that Y is a reasonable way. Thus, social science evaluation can be used to help decision makers reject bad policy, but it cannot help them select with certainty the "best policy." Causal relationships that seem clear on the basis of logic are often difficult to test in the real world.

In this section we have used the term *experimental* impact in a technical way, but not strictly in regards to the rigorous rules of formal experimental design. Also, we have not tried to deal with the many complex problems associated with the choice of research methods—surveys, field observations, field experiments, classical laboratory experiments, intensive case studies and single-subject designs, and so on. All of these might be used to establish causal connections. The important point here is that social workers need to back their beliefs about a program's success or failure with both theory and valid, reliable observations. In the following section we explore the fact that connections between cause and effect—between program interventions and policy results or between social work interventions and clinical observations— are made at many levels of abstraction and scientific rigor.

PRACTICE RESEARCH

The practitioner-researcher problem-solving process consists of four phases, or levels, of research activity. Each level of inquiry builds on the levels that precede it, as illustrated in Table 8.2.

Level 1

Level 1 research is undertaken to acquire familiarity with a topic. This may be necessary because the investigator is exploring either an old topic for the first time or a new interest, or because the subject itself is new or unstudied. The purpose of level 1 research is to seek out the facts and develop a structure for thinking about the various aspects of the problem.

As an example, suppose you are interested in the topic of family violence. As a student, you would want to know several things: How is family violence to be defined? How extensive is the problem? Is there an increase in the actual incidence of family violence, or is the increase only apparent because of better reporting of incidents? Do any important subcategories of family violence need to be studied separately? You would want to read the contemporary and classic literature on the topic, check the figures being reported, interview social workers and volunteers working at crisis centers, and perhaps talk with survivors of incidents of family violence and even perpetrators. In exploratory research the procedures of inquiry are relatively unsystematic. It is a first effort to see what is going on.

You might find, for example, that low-income families are treated in clinics, whereas other groups are treated by private physicians; and that clinic doctors, for whatever reason, are more likely to report suspicious injuries. If such is the case, the relationship between socioeconomic status and family violence is apparent, but not necessarily real. You

TABLE 8.2	FORMS OF RESEARCH BY LEVEL OF RESEARCH AND INTENT OF INQUIRY

Level of Research	INTENT OF INQUIRY			
	Distinguish Concepts and Identify Significant Variables	Describe and Measure Interaction of Variables	Establish Logically Connected and Verifiable Causal Paths among Variables	Locate and Isolate Manageable Variables to Alter Outcome
Level 1: Exploratory	Case studies X			
Level 2: Descriptive	X	Cross-case comparisons and surveys X		
Level 3: Explanatory	X	X	Field experiments and statistical tests X	
Level 4: Perspective	X	X	X	Practice research X

might find that class is linked to verbal skills, and verbal skills are inversely linked to family violence. This tells you that the real association between class and violence is only indicative of a more fundamental (yet harder to observe) association.

After the initial review of the literature, exploratory studies tend to become somewhat more focused. Essentially, the purpose of exploratory study is to focus attention, to learn what the important questions are. Exploratory studies most typically are done for one of two interrelated purposes: (1) to satisfy an initial curiosity or a desire for a better understanding, or (2) to lay groundwork for more careful inquiry at levels 2, 3, or 4.

In this first level of study an effort is made to define the central concepts of inquiry. Returning to the example of family violence, as a researcher you would have considerable difficulty using the same conceptual definition for legal, educational, practice, and policy purposes. Also, investigators disagree on points such as whether to include spanking in the concept of family violence. In fact, it is more appropriate to recognize that the inclusion or exclusion of spanking as a category of family violence depends on the conceptual level and the purpose of the specific inquiry.

Level 2

Inquiry at this level seeks to establish the presence or absence of empirical regularities in the problem area. How is socioeconomic class associated with family violence? Are shifts observed in the reported incidence of family violence from one social class to the next? Is the observed change an artifact of the reporting of incidents, or does the actual rate of incidents shift? An evaluator's first general question is: Does the appearance of an association reflect a real association? Do people who differ from one another on social class lines differ from one another in regard to the dependent problem—in this example, the incidence of violence within the family?

Level 3

Once a relationship has been established, level 3 research commences, and the researcher seeks to show not only an empirical regularity but a causal connection. At this point, a formal logical model is required. A causal connection requires a causal chain of events, such as the association between education and communication skills and family violence. A formal theory is stated that links educational attainment to communication skills and communication skills to family violence. If this were established, there would be not only an explanation of why family and educational levels are connected but also of what could change the situation. The practitioner cannot easily change educational level. But it is possible to provide instruction and information on communication skills and thus break the links between education and family violence.

Level 4

The goal of practice research is the assessment and redirection of practice. Knowledge is gained not for its own sake but for direct use in the day-to-day activities of the social worker. Practice research has been criticized as being too subservient to theory, yet insufficiently based in theory. On one side is the assertion that practice models have developed from very highly specialized theoretical frameworks that are of limited use. They are distorted when applied to the range of client problems encountered by the social worker (Muller 1979). Others assert that practice is eclectic, and that models of intervention are chosen intuitively and thus are not sufficiently based in theory to allow broad guidelines for action (Brier 1979). A third critique is that practice models are fixed and closed, unchanged from one generation of users to the next.

These three very diverse critiques appear to be true simultaneously. This occurs because until very recently, practice wisdom and social work research developed as separate spheres. Only a narrow overlap existed between research and practice. In recent years, social workers in practice have begun to expand that overlap, particularly with evaluative research (Rubin and Babbie 1993).

SUMMARY

In this chapter we introduce the student to the wide range of activities that constitute social work research. We review the specific steps in the research process and show how each step builds on previous ones. If there is one message of this chapter, it is that research and practice are not separate spheres but interrelated domains, each fundamentally dependent on the other. All social workers need to be involved in evaluating their efforts and continuing to generate new knowledge that can be used to strengthen social welfare policies and services.

KEY TERMS

disciplinary research
evaluation
evaluative research
hypothesis

policy research
single-subject designs
theory

DISCUSSION QUESTIONS

1. To what extent do you think the practice of social work research helps efforts to assist a client?

2. Can you think of an example in which the research process and the practice process actually reinforce one another?

3. Select a social work-related topic of interest to you. What are some research questions you might address at each of the four levels of research discussed in this chapter?

REFERENCES

Brier, Scott. 1979. Toward the integration of theory and practice. Paper read at the Conference on Social Work Research, San Antonio, Texas, October.

Haveman, Robert. 1987. *Poverty policy and policy research.* Madison: Univ. of Wisconsin Press.

Majchrzak, Ann. 1984. *Methods for policy research.* Beverly Hills, Calif.: Sage Publications.

Melanson, P. H. 1978. *Knowledge, politics and public policy.* Cambridge: Winthrop.

Muller, Edward H. 1979. Evaluating the empirical base of clinical
    circles. Paper read at the Conference on Social Work Research,
    San Antonio, Texas, October.
Rubin, Allen, and Earl Babbie. 1993. *Research methods for social work.*
    Belmont, Calif.: Wadsworth.

SUGGESTED FURTHER READINGS

Kuhn, Thomas S. 1962. *The structure of scientific revolutions.* Chicago:
    Univ. of Chicago Press.
Rubin, Allen, and Earl Babbie. 1993. *Research methods for social work.*
    Belmont, Calif.: Wadsworth.
Schoor, Lisbeth. 1988. *Within our reach: Breaking the cycle of dependency.*
    New York: Doubleday.

PART THREE

FIELDS OF PRACTICE AND POPULATIONS SERVED BY SOCIAL WORKERS

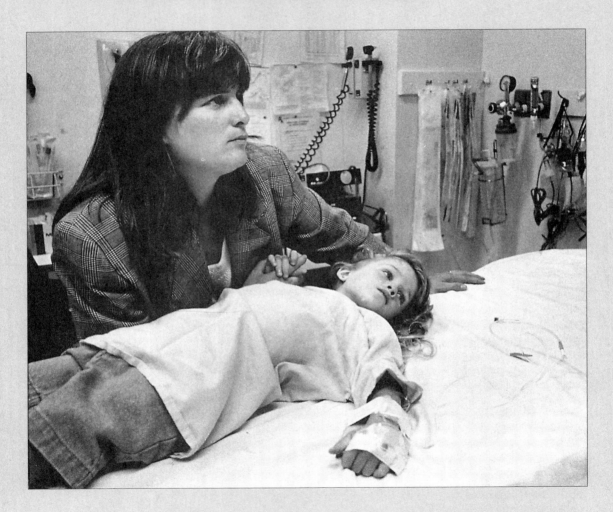

In this part of the book, you will explore many of the settings in which social workers practice and the special populations they serve. While not all settings and special populations can be presented in the limited space in this text, this part gives you an overview of the major social issues and populations that are the domain of the social welfare system and social work practitioners. Each chapter presents a broad systems/ecological perspective to help you understand the issues social work practitioners face in addressing the specific social issue or special population. You will also explore the specific roles and functions that social workers play in dealing with each field of practice and population served, so you will have an idea of what types of social work jobs are available in that field of practice, and what the nature of those jobs entails.

In Chapter 9, "Poverty and Income Assistance," we focus on how poverty is defined, why people are poor, who is poor in the United States, and what types of policies and programs exist to help reduce poverty levels in the United States. We also discuss the roles social workers play in the fight against poverty.

In Chapter 10, "Mental Health, Substance Abuse, and Developmental Disabilities," we explore definitional issues concerning mental health, mental illness, and developmental disabilities. We discuss historical and contemporary incidents that have shaped the way mental health problems are viewed and the types of mental health services available. We highlight several critical current mental health issues, including substance abuse and homelessness. We also explore the many functions that social workers, who constitute the majority of mental health professionals in the United States, provide in this field of practice.

In Chapter 11, "Health Care," we offer an explanation of the present health care system in the United States, the problems it faces, and the types of health care policies and programs available. We also highlight a number of health issues, including increased costs of care, ethical decisions when balancing available technology with costs and needs, and AIDS. Health care is the fastest-growing area of employment for social workers today, and we also explore career opportunities for social workers in this setting.

Chapter 12, "The Needs of Children, Youth, and Families," gives you an overview of the diverse types of families that exist today and the many issues even the healthiest of families face in our contemporary society. We also explore those factors found among healthy families, as well as those that place families more are risk to experience social problems. Finally, we focus on some of the issues families experience that may place individual family members at varying levels of risk, including divorce, alcoholism and other types of drug abuse, child abuse and neglect, and family violence. We also discuss issues more likely to be associated with at-risk adolescents, including teenage pregnancy, gang membership, and youth crime.

In Chapter 13, "Services to Children, Youth, and Families," we focus on current policies and programs that attempt to prevent or alleviate the needs discussed in Chapter 12. We highlight the present service delivery focus on family preservation and other programs and policies whose goal is to keep families together. We also give you a chance to explore the diverse activities that social workers provide in serving children, youth, and families, including child protective services and school social work.

In Chapter 14, "Criminal Justice," we discuss the nature of crime and the criminal justice system, including the roles of law enforcement, the courts, and the prison system. We have included a special section that gives you the opportunity to learn about the juvenile justice system and differences in treatment of adult and juvenile offenders. We also examine the roles that social workers, including probation and parole officers, play in providing services in the criminal justice system.

In Chapter 15, "Occupational Social Work" we explore a field of social work that is resurging and gaining popularity today. We consider changes in workplace demographics and the implications of those changes for employers and their families. We also discuss the importance of considering both the impact of the family setting and the work setting in understanding individual functioning and needs, and what social workers in the workplace do to help employees function better both in the workplace and beyond.

In Chapter 16, "Social Work in Rural Settings," we focus on an important segment of social work that is not often addressed. In this chapter, you will learn about important differences between rural and urban life and the implications for social workers who choose to practice in rural settings.

In Chapter 17, "Older Adulthood: Issues, Problems, and Services," we discuss a special population that increasingly needs attention from the social welfare system and social work practitioners. In this chapter, we examine issues and needs that an older population creates for society, and we identify resources developed to provide physical and social support systems to meet their needs. Social work for the aged is a rapidly growing field, as more people fit this age category. Thus, you will also explore the types of activities in which social workers who assist this population are engaged.

As you learn about the fields of practice and populations with which social workers are involved in Part 3, ask yourself questions that draw from Parts 1 and 2. For example, as you read the chapter on poverty, ask yourself questions such as: How do past and present social welfare perspectives and policies shape the ways people view poverty today and the ways poverty might be viewed in the future? What are the various roles the social work profession has played in addressing poverty? What types of social work intervention have been used to address clients who are affected by poverty? What types of intervention might be most effective in addressing client needs related to this issue? How can the systems/ecological framework help us in understanding issues relating to poverty, including who is more likely to be poor and why, the impact of poverty on individuals and families, and the impact of community, state, and national attitudes, policies and programs that address—or fail to address—poverty? At what levels of the environment might it be most effective to intervene in reducing the numbers of individuals and families who are poor, and why? What are the relationships between factors such as race and ethnicity; gender, age, and sexual orientation; and living in poverty—and why?

POVERTY AND INCOME ASSISTANCE

Robert and Robin Warren, both aged sixty-five, have just retired from very satisfying jobs. Their three children are well established with families and jobs. By any standard the Warrens are well off, emotionally and physically. Financially their retirement was planned around social insurance. Their Social Security Insurance benefits raise their annual retirement income from $45,000 to just over $60,000. This, along with income derived from savings, means their retirement income is actually larger than their income during their working years. Neither Robert nor Robin thinks of their old-age benefits or their Medicare benefits as a form of welfare because, in their view, they paid for these through taxes while working. Robert wrote his congressman to complain about a tax to fund supplemental nursing care insurance, because they are already covered by a private plan. During their working years the social insurance system provided much-needed cash during brief periods of unemployment. Now the social insurance system has provided them with both security and income. While very happy with their income, both worry about cuts to Medicare, on which they are also dependent.

Mary Smith, widowed and aged seventy-two, is a more typical recipient of social insurance. Her $684-a-month Social Security check provides 80 percent of her income. The remaining amount is from the invested income received from the sale of her home six years ago. She lives in a pleasant apartment and with public old-age health insurance, or Medicare, she is covered for major illness and hospitalization. She is not covered for the more immediate threat of a long stay in a nursing home. Her investment income and Social Security payments are not sufficient for the monthly fees, which run to over $2,500.

Maria and Joe Saldana live in an inner-city area in a large northern city. Both in their early thirties, they have five children, ranging in age from two to fourteen. Joe works on construction when he can, and Maria works as a maid at a local hotel when she can find child care for her younger children. Joe and Maria have a combined income of $18,000—well below the poverty level for a family of seven (roughly $23,000). The rent for their two-bedroom house is $450 a month. Money spent for bus fare, utilities, and other necessities often leaves the Saldanas with no money for food at the end of the month. Last year the children often had to miss school during the winter because they didn't have any warm clothes. Neither of the Saldanas works at a job that provides health insurance, which means that the family usually goes without medical care when someone is sick. Both of the Saldanas grew up living in poverty, and both quit school in junior high school to earn money to help their parents provide for their brothers and sisters. Although they have a strong value system and are hard workers, they find it difficult to get jobs with adequate pay and benefits because of their limited education. Maria became sick after the birth of their last child, and shortly after that, Joe lost his job. When his unemployment benefits ran out, he couldn't find another job. Because Joe had a substantial work history and had looked hard for a job, the Saldanas qualified for AFDC. As of 1995, under the Family Support Act, 20 percent of those on AFDC were to have job placement assistance through federally mandated employment programs in their state. However, Joe found a construction job before the placement assistance was needed. Because of income limits the Saldanas are now no longer eligible to receive AFDC. During the transition from AFDC to full-time employment, the family retained eligibility for Medicaid and still qualifies for food stamps. However, Joe and Maria worry about plans to give the states more options in addressing problems of unemployment and poverty. All the talk of change makes them fearful. ■

Over the past twenty years, expenditures on antipoverty programs have increased—but so has the number of persons who are poor. This profoundly frustrating fact helps to explain why revision of our welfare strategies is such a large item on the domestic political agenda. The experts who have studied the issue give reasons for the paradox of higher spending and higher poverty. Some of these explanations are quite complex, and most involve assumptions about people and how they behave. First, although spending has increased overall, inflation-adjusted spending followed a different course (see Table 9.1). Second, antipoverty programs sometimes (how often is a matter of dispute) discourage desirable individual behavior like working, saving, and caring for one's own family. Third, even when working well, many antipoverty programs are not designed to carry a person across the poverty line but rather to reduce the ravages of poverty on the person. Fourth, our economy has not worked well over the past twenty years, and in particular it has not worked well for those at the bottom of the economic ladder. Finally, as a society we are uncertain about the relative weights we wish to put on explanations of poverty linked to the person and explanations of poverty linked to the social system. Even when there is agreement that individual responsibility needs to be enhanced, we debate between a strategy of deterrence and a strategy of compassion. ■

◢ MANY VIEWS ON HOW TO HELP

Virtually no one is indifferent to poverty in America. There are, however, very diverse ideas about how to help the poorest in our society. We all, except for a very few on the fringe, want successful and efficient antipoverty programs. Some persons would like to transfer the public program responsibility to state governments, while others believe that federal leadership is both an economic and political necessity. Some prefer giving the poor cash; others want to restrict spending by providing aid as goods-in-kind. Still others want to give service and training. Most people believe that a proper policy is some mix of cash, in-kind benefits, service, and training. Some want to limit the duration of federal assistance; others disparage that approach. Some prefer a "tough love" approach that would limit and direct assistance to very young unmarried mothers. Others feel that idea is out of touch with the real causes of poverty, dependency, and the rise in illegitimacy. Poverty and dependency are linked in the public mind. While some worry about the stagnation of the poverty rate and the declines in real benefits of the poor,

TABLE 9.1   **NUMBER OF PERSONS POOR AND EXPENDITURES ON ANTIPOVERTY PROGRAMS (1975–1995)**

Year	Poor (in millions)	Nominal Dollars (in billions)	Constant 1988 Dollars (in billions)
1975	25.9	$ 75.80	$139.85
1980	29.3	96.00	119.70
1985	33.1	104.50	97.94
1990	33.6	151.20	117.39
1995	36.7	295.90	195.18

Source: Data from U.S. Social Security Administration, *Social Security Bulletin*, 1985 and 1995 (Washington, D.C.: Author); calculations of constant 1988 dollars by authors.

others disparage the growth of dependency and blame the antipoverty programs for that growth.

Nathan Cohen, in a 1956 volume of the journal *Social Work,* wrote that "one of the differences between the A.M.A. and the N.A.S.W. is that doctors lobby for the vested interest of their membership whereas we lobby for the interest of those we serve" (Steiner 1966). Few social workers today would make such a self-congratulatory assertion. *The resolution of the poverty problem requires an awareness that those with diverse ideas must have respect for the integrity and decency of those with distinct and different ideas about how best to solve the problem.*

WHAT DO POVERTY PROGRAMS DO?

Suppose that before being born, you are given a set of choices:

- Do you wish to be endowed with a native intelligence (whatever that is) above the normal range?

- Do you wish that your parents be married when you are born; and that they both love you and each other?

- Do you wish that one or both of your parents have a marketable skill before you are born?

To ask these questions is to answer them. For, with these three "opportunities," you are born to economic advantage. If one, two, or three of these opportunities are absent, you become increasingly more likely to be poor for significant periods of your life. Antipoverty programs are designed to overcome or compensate for those disadvantages. In our society, your endowment, your family, and your employment opportunities influence most fundamentally your efforts to avoid poverty. Unfortunately, welfare policy can do little with respect to any of these three variables.

As the controversy over the recent book, *The Bell Curve* (Herrnstein and Murray 1994) demonstrates, identifying—much less measuring—endowment is a daunting task. We do not know how much of the endowment is nature and how much is nurture; we do not know how much is immutable and how much is changeable. Few doubt, however, that verbal and mathematical skills are the strongest individual antipoverty weapons. *Poverty is concentrated among those who lack these skills.* Endowment, however, is not enough; it must be nurtured. In our society, nurturing has been the role of the family. In 1993 sixty-seven percent of the children less than 1 year old on welfare had been born to mothers who were not married. Many of these mothers were not only without the educational skills, but also without the support systems necessary to provide economically and emotionally for their families because they themselves came from at-risk families. Thus, many end up in "dead-end" jobs without health care and unable to afford child care, making welfare an often reluctant necessity. If a child from birth to age 18 lives with a parent (or parents) who is continually employed, the chances that the child will experience involuntary poverty at any time in his or her entire life are very low. *Employment has an impact not only on current poverty but also on poverty in the future.*

The best antipoverty programs are preventive programs, and our society does try—with varying levels of success—to provide for full employment at a high wage. From 1960 to 1973, real wages went up by 73 percent and poverty fell by 56 percent. Since 1973, the vicissitudes of the world economy and domestic politics have stymied the efforts of six presidential administrations to bring about a steady rise in real incomes for most Americans. When we look at median wage as an indicator of the health of the economy, we find a close correlation in changes in real wages and changes in real poverty. This is shown in Table 9.2.

In every year except 1969–1970, 1978–1979, and 1982–1983, the direction of change in real incomes and the real poverty rate have had opposite signs. Few deny the basic premise that a growing and dynamic economy is the best way to reduce the scourge of poverty.

WELFARE REFORM

A major goal of welfare reform is to provide greater incentives and opportunity for persons in poverty who receive public assistance, to assist them in moving from public assistance to self-sufficiency. The basic reform strategy is to increase work incentives by raising the amount that a low-income family can gain by working and to provide recipients with the skills that are marketable in the current economy. Three distinct tasks are involved in applying this strategy.

One task is to reform Aid to Families with Dependent Children (AFDC) so that after child care costs are paid and health insurance purchased to replace Medicaid, the family still has a higher income when off welfare. *Work must pay off for the poor, too.* Families qualifying for AFDC have always faced strong work disincentives. Since 1982, after three months on public assistance, the benefit-reduction rate for AFDC has been 100 percent. Each dollar of earnings beyond $90 per month reduces AFDC benefits (net of child care costs) by a full dollar. These strong work disincentives are common knowledge to experts and recipients. To lower the benefit-reduction rate is costly. If we simply lowered the rate at which benefits fall in response to other income, it would increase the number of working households qualifying for AFDC. Since there are many people just above the eligibility line to receive public assistance benefits, such a change would increase, by a geometric rate, the cost to the program. This at a time when there is no political incentive to increase welfare spending.

A second task is to give low-income workers the skills and access to jobs that allow them to become self-sufficient. *A job incentive without a job opportunity is not a job incentive.* Training welfare recipients for low-income jobs is denigrated by some, but training recipients for higher-income jobs is very expensive and might encourage some people to go on public assistance to get the training. A third perplexing task is to find explanations for and ways to help some recipients change behaviors that are seen by the rest of society as antisocial and self-destructive. The time has come for liberals to learn that some welfare programs are harmful to some of the people, and for conservatives to learn that no welfare programs are harmful to all of the people. A small segment of the

TABLE 9.2 **CHANGES IN REAL INCOME AND POVERTY RATES FOR ALL FAMILIES WITH AND WITHOUT CHILDREN**

Year	Poverty Rate	Median Income (in 1993 dollars)
1968	11.3	$33,086
	—	+
1969	10.4	34,596
	+	+
1970	10.9	35,523
	—	—
1971	10.8	34,482
	—	+
1972	10.3	36,177
	—	+
1973	9.7	36,893
	+	—
1974	9.9	35,922
	+	—
1975	10.9	35,274
	—	+
1976	10.3	36,388
	—	+
1977	10.2	36,603
	—	+
1978	10.0	37,763
	+	+
1979	10.2	38,248
	+	—
1980	11.5	36,912
	+	—
1981	12.5	35,905
	+	—
1982	13.6	35,419
	+	+
1983	13.9	35,661
	—	+
1984	13.1	36,762
	—	+
1985	12.6	37,246
	—	+
1986	12.0	38,838
	insig.	+
1987	12.0	39,394
	—	insig.
1988	11.6	39,320
	—	+
1989	11.5	39,869
	+	—
1990	12.0	39,086
	+	—
1991	12.8	38,129
	+	—
1992	13.3	37,668
	+	—
1993	13.6	36,959
	—	+
1994	13.0	38,782

Sources: Data for 1968 through 1993 from U.S. Bureau of the Census, *Income and Poverty, 1993* (Washington, D.C.: Author), Tables F-1 and F-2; data for 1994 from U.S. Bureau of the Census World Wide Web site at http://www.census.gov (cited 11 July 1996).

While debates over what to do about the increasing numbers of individuals living in poverty continue, the number of people who are poor continues to rise. To get out of poverty those who are poor often face many barriers, including substandard housing and unsafe living conditions, inadequate transportation, lack of job training programs and jobs that pay above the minimum wage, and access to child care and health care.

population receiving public assistance, labeled or mislabeled as the underclass, presents a very large problem in the design and adoption of welfare reform (Heffernan and Vickland 1994; Mincy 1995).

To modify the work behavior of those who are long-term dependents is a complex problem. The transmission of dependency across generations is a problem that must be addressed and must be frankly faced somewhere between the denial of individual responsibility and the denial of social responsibility.

The readings in Box 9.1 are given to those of you who want to examine this question in greater depth.

◢ THE CONCEPT OF POVERTY

The concept of poverty is elusive. **Poverty** generally means that a household's income is inadequate as judged by a specific standard. The translation of this concept into practical terms produces technical as well as ideological debate. Even defining *household* for a census count is not simple. Is the unit to be composed of only the nuclear family, or do we count elders, boarders, roommates, foster children, and others who share the dwelling? Similarly, income is elusive. Should it include gifts or in-kind benefits provided by the employer or the government? Should income consider goods and services traded in barter? What

---

BOX 9.1

READINGS ON THE ECONOMICS OF POVERTY

Edelman, Peter B. 1993. Toward a comprehensive antipoverty strategy. *Georgetown Law Journal* 81(5): 1697–1755.

Gueron, Judith M. 1993. Welfare and poverty: The elements of reform. *Yale Law & Policy Review* 11(1): 113–25.

Haveman, Robert H. 1994. Transfers, taxes, and welfare reform. *National Tax Journal* 47(2): 417–34.

Moffitt, Robert. 1993. Welfare reform: An economist's perspective. *Yale Law & Policy Review* 11(1): 126–46.

Sachs, Maria L. 1994. The prospects for ending welfare as we know it. *Stanford Law & Policy Review* 5(2): 99–114.

Unsigned. 1994. Dethroning the welfare queen: The rhetoric of reform. *Harvard Law Review* 107(8): 2013–30.

---

should the time frame be? How do we address the problem of wealth as opposed to income? Does volition enter into the notion? Should the Jesuit priest or Carmelite nun be considered poor? After all, they have vowed to be poor. What ought the standard be? As each question is confronted, the problem of definition becomes more complex. As each question is given a specific answer, the numbers of persons thought to be poor changes.

The Standard

When the federal government began measuring poverty in the early 1960s, the continued existence of poor people in an "Affluent Society" was seen as an anomaly. One idea favored by academics was to look at the distribution of income and make measurements in terms of **relative poverty.** By this notion, after adjustments for family size are made, the lowest one-third, one-quarter, or one-fifth would be considered poor. The trouble with this notion is that, by definition, the proportion of the population poor would be constant. Another measure of progress against poverty is in terms of the relative income of the lowest income class. Measured in this way, our progress against poverty is not very good. After technical adjustments for family size, the lowest fifth's share went down by 1.1 percent while the share of income to the richest fifth went up by 2.0 percent (see Table 9.3).

It is conceivable that the lower-income classes could lose in terms of their relative share but be better off in real purchasing power. Suppose you had a $10,000 income and your neighbor had one of $50,000; if your neighbor's inflation-adjusted income doubled while yours increased by only 150 percent, your share of the income pool fell by 3.6 percent but your purchasing power is up by half. Would you consider yourself better or worse off? In fact, in 1993 the wage, property, and transfer income of the lowest fifth fell by $805 from $6,061 while that income for the highest fifth went up $7,123 from $66,364 (U.S. Congress 1994). The poor in America in the last two decades have become more poor in both absolute and relative terms.

TABLE 9.3	SHARES OF PRETAX ADJUSTED FAMILY INCOME (AFI) BY FAMILY TYPE AND INCOME QUINTILE, 1967, 1973, 1979, 1989, AND 1992

Family Type and Quintile	1967	1973	1979	1989	1992
All Families					
Lowest	5.2	5.5	5.1	4.3	4.1
Second	11.6	11.8	11.6	10.5	10.4
Middle	16.9	17.1	17.3	16.5	16.6
Fourth	23.7	23.9	24.3	24.0	24.3
Highest	42.6	41.7	41.7	44.6	44.6
All Families with Children					
Lowest	6.2	6.0	5.4	4.4	4.1
Second	12.8	12.8	12.5	11.1	10.8
Middle	17.8	18.0	18.2	17.4	17.3
Fourth	23.7	24.1	24.6	24.5	25.0
Highest	39.7	39.0	39.3	42.6	42.9
Married Couples with Children					
Lowest	7.1	7.3	6.9	6.0	5.8
Second	13.2	13.5	13.4	12.3	12.2
Middle	17.7	18.0	18.2	17.6	17.7
Fourth	23.3	23.5	24.0	23.8	24.1
Highest	38.7	37.7	37.5	40.3	40.1
Single Mothers with Children					
Lowest	3.5	4.6	4.1	3.0	3.0
Second	9.9	10.1	9.4	7.9	7.7
Middle	15.3	14.7	15.3	13.9	14.0
Fourth	24.4	23.7	25.3	24.7	25.0
Highest	46.8	46.8	45.9	50.5	50.3

Source: U.S. Congress, House, Committee on Ways and Means, *Overview of Entitlement Programs*, 103rd Cong., 2nd Session, Committee Print 103–27 (Washington, D.C.: U.S. Government Printing Office, 1994), 1200.

The Market Basket

To counter this problem, public officials want to use a definition of poverty based on a **market basket concept.** The relative definitions speak to the distribution of incomes. The officials want to know what public programs have produced in the alleviation of "want" as defined by a fixed standard. Mollie Orshansky (1965) developed the market basket concept by some relatively simple calculations. She used one survey that showed the cost of a minimum adequate nutritional diet for families of different sizes. She used another survey that established that families generally spent one third of their income on food. Orshansky then multiplied the diet number by three, so that a family could purchase the minimum diet and still have twice that amount left over for all other purchases.

Since 1969, the poverty thresholds are adjusted by taking into account the changes in the CPI (consumer price index). The CPI is an index number used to adjust the prices of goods and services for inflation. The poverty thresholds for various-sized families for various years are given in Table 9.4.

The Orshansky or "official definition" counts income from wages, salary, and self-employed income plus interest, dividends, and cash grants from government. The definition does not estimate or consider the value of food stamps, the Medicaid card, or public housing subsidy. To count this would lower the numbers of those considered poor. The calculation of the poverty line is made before taxes are paid or tax credits to be received are calculated. The wealth available to the household is counted for the real interest it produces, but not for its purchasing potential. If, for example, you worked for a full year, saved your money, and went to school full time the next year without working, the number crunchers would count you very rich for one year and very poor for the next. The household is defined as a group of not necessarily related persons who share a domicile and share income and responsibilities for those in that domicile. There is no economist's line in the sand that could account for the real dynamics of family incomes. It is nonetheless this line, and the proportion of the population under this line, that are used in calculating the proportion of our society that is poor.

◪ DEMOGRAPHICS OF THE POOR ARE CHANGING

As indicated, many factors interact to determine who is poor in the United States. Four factors, however, predominate in affecting poverty demographics:

- Shifts in the overall performance of the economy
- Shifts in the composition of households within the nation (for example, more single-parent households headed by women)
- Shifts in the levels of expenditure of social programs
- Shifts in the types of programs implemented and the effectiveness of those programs

The first factor significantly influences the other factors. If the free market economy cannot provide jobs that keep everyone above the poverty line, groups of individuals will be locked out of the opportunity structure that enables them to be self-sufficient, some for short time periods until they are able to find adequate gainful employment with health care benefits, and others for much longer time periods.

Although most people's stereotype of a poor family is an African American single mother on welfare with three or more children living in an inner-city ghetto, the poor are a very diverse group. The majority

TABLE 9.4   **WEIGHTED AVERAGE POVERTY THRESHOLDS FOR NONFARM FAMILIES OF SPECIFIED SIZE, SELECTED YEARS (1959–1992)**

| | UNRELATED INDIVIDUALS | | |
Calendar Year	All Ages	Under Age 65	Aged 65 or Older
1959	$1,467	$1,503	$1,397
1960	1,490	1,526	1,418
1965	1,582	1,626	1,512
1970	1,954	2,010	1,861
1975	2,724	1,797	2,581
1980	4,190	4,290	3,949
1981	4,620	4,729	4,359
1982	4,901	5,019	4,626
1983	5,061	5,180	4,775
1984	5,278	5,400	4,979
1985	5,469	5,593	5,156
1986	5,572	5,702	5,255
1987	5,778	5,909	5,447
1988	6,024	6,155	5,674
1989	6,311	6,452	5,947
1990	6,652	6,800	6,268
1991	6,932	7,086	6,532
1992	7,143	7,229	6,729
1993	7,363	7,518	6,930
1994	7,547	7,710	7,108

of people in the United States living in poverty are white, and many live in two-parent families. Twenty-five percent of children under 6 are living in poverty. Of those children, almost 40 percent live in two-parent families, often with both of their parents working full-time. Most women who go on AFDC stay on it less than two years, although an increasing number are returning to AFDC after losing jobs as the economy changes. More and more workplaces are downsizing and restructuring, transferring work to other countries, requiring their employees to possess greater technological knowledge and skills, or closing completely.

Although these environmental factors often result in different sets of living conditions for many, people of color and women and their children are much more likely to be at the bottom of the income structure in the United States. As Table 9.5 indicates, a person is less likely to be poor today than 35 years or so ago if white, and more likely to be poor

FAMILIES OF 2 OR MORE PERSONS

| | 2 Persons | | | | | | |
All Ages	Head Under Age 65	Head Aged 65 or Older	3 Persons	4 Persons	5 Persons	6 Persons	7 Persons or More
$1,894	$1,952	$1,761	$ 2,324	$ 2,973	$ 3,506	$ 3,944	$ 4,849
1,924	1,982	1,788	2,359	3,022	3,560	4,002	4,921
2,048	2,114	1,906	2,514	3,223	3,797	4,264	5,248
2,525	2,604	2,348	3,099	3,968	4,680	5,260	6,468
3,506	3,617	3,257	4,293	5,500	6,499	7,316	9,022
5,363	5,537	4,983	6,565	8,414	9,966	11,269	[1]12,761
5,917	6,111	5,498	7,250	9,287	11,007	12,449	[1]14,110
6,281	6,487	5,836	7,693	9,862	11,684	13,207	[1]15,036
6,483	6,697	6,023	7,938	10,178	12,049	13,630	[1]15,500
6,762	6,983	6,282	8,277	10,609	12,566	14,207	[1]16,096
6,998	7,231	6,503	8,573	10,989	13,007	14,696	[1]16,656
7,138	7,372	6,630	8,737	11,203	13,259	14,986	[1]17,049
7,397	7,641	6,872	9,056	11,611	13,737	15,509	[1]17,649
7,704	7,958	7,158	9,435	12,092	14,305	16,149	[1]18,248
8,076	8,343	7,501	9,885	12,675	14,990	16,921	[1]19,162
8,509	8,794	7,905	10,419	13,359	15,792	17,839	[1]20,241
8,865	9,165	8,241	10,860	13,924	16,456	18,587	[1]21,058
9,137	9,443	8,487	11,186	14,335	16,592	19,137	[1]21,594
9,414	9,728	8,740	11,522	14,763	17,449	19,718	22,383
9,661	9,976	8,967	11,821	15,141	17,900	20,235	22,923

[1]Poverty threshold for 7 persons, not 7 persons or more.

Sources: Data for 1959 through 1992 from Bureau of the Census, technical papers, as appeared in the U.S. Congress, House, Committee on Ways and Means, *Overview of Entitlement Programs*, 103rd Cong., 2nd Session, Committee Print 103–27 (Washington, D.C.: U.S. Government Printing Office, 1994), 1155; data for 1993 through 1994 from Bureau of the Census, *Income and Poverty* (Washington, D.C.: Author, 1996), CD-ROM.

if African American, Hispanic, Native American, or in a female-headed family. In addition to external factors, psychological factors based on how one views his/her environment also contribute to poverty. Lack of access to opportunity can lead to hopelessness and feelings of low self-worth, depression, anger, beliefs that one has no power or control over one's life, and dependency on others. Programs targeted at eliminating poverty, especially among those persons who have lived in persistent poverty for their entire lifetime, must also address these factors.

Progress against poverty is uneven for different groups. While poverty rates have decreased somewhat among the elderly, who are somewhat less likely to be tied to the fluctuating state of the economy than

CHAPTER 9 Poverty and Income Assistance   **221**

TABLE 9.5   PROFILE OF THE POVERTY POPULATION (1960–1990)

	PERCENTAGE OF THE POOR POPULATION				PERCENTAGE POOR			
	1960	1970	1980	1990	1960	1970	1980	1990
All Persons	100.0%	100.0%	100.0%	100.0%	22.2%	12.6%	13.0%	13.5%
Race/Ethnicity								
White	71.0	68.5	67.3	66.5	17.8	9.9	10.2	10.7
Black[a]	29.0	30.0	29.3	29.3	55.9	33.5	32.5	31.9
Asian or Pacific Islander[b]	—	—	2.4	2.6	—	—	17.2	12.2
American Indian, Eskimo, or Aleut[c]	—	1.2	1.2	1.9	—	38.3	27.5	30.9
Hispanic[d]	—	8.5	11.9	17.9	—	24.3	25.7	28.1
Family Structure								
In all families	87.6	80.0	77.2	75.1	20.7	10.9	11.5	12.0
In families with a female householder, no spouse present	18.2	29.5	34.6	37.5	48.9	38.1	36.7	37.2
Unrelated individuals	12.4	20.0	21.3	22.2	45.2	32.9	22.9	20.7
Young and Old								
Related children under 18	43.4	40.3	38.0	37.9	26.5	14.9	17.9	19.9
Adults 65 and over	14.1[e]	18.5	13.2	10.9	35.2	24.5	15.7	12.2
Residence								
Nonfarm	81.0	92.4	96.6	98.4	19.6	12.2	12.9	13.6
Farm	19.0	7.6	3.4	1.6	51.3	21.1	17.5	11.2
In metropolitan areas	43.9[e]	52.4	61.6	73.0	15.3	10.2	11.9	12.7
In central cities	26.9[e]	32.0	36.4	42.4	18.3	14.3	17.2	19.0
In suburbs	17.0[e]	20.4	25.2	30.5	12.2	7.1	8.2	8.7
Outside metropolitan areas	56.1[e]	47.6	38.4	27.0	33.2	17.0	15.4	16.3

Note: Data from the Current Population Survey (CPS), U.S. Bureau of the Census, Current Population Report Services, except where noted. Population characteristics are as of March of the subsequent year.

[a]Negro and other races in 1960.

[b]Not computed as separate category from the CPS until 1990. Decennial census figures are presented for 1979.

[c]Decennial census figures for the previous year. The geographic distribution of their poverty is important to note: in 1979, 41.3 percent of American Indians, Eskimos, and Aleuts living on reservations, in native villages, or on trust lands were poor; in 1989, 50.7 percent were poor.

[d]Hispanics may be of any race: comparable statistics on non-Hispanics are not available.

[e]Decennial census figures from 1959.

Source: From *Confronting Poverty: Prescriptions for Change*, ed. Sheldon H. Danziger, Gary D. Sandefur, and Daniel H. Weinberg. Copyright © 1994 by the President and Fellows of Harvard College. Reprinted by permission of Harvard University Press.

members of other groups, the numbers of poor children, including those from two-parent working families, have continued to increase. No matter how poverty is defined or measured, the central political question remains: Who shall have their income maintained, at what level, and for what reasons?

◪ ANTIPOVERTY PROGRAMS AND INCOME SUPPORT PROGRAMS

Five types of programs exist to combat poverty that occurs despite our best efforts to prevent it through sound macroeconomic policies:

- Cash support
- Direct provision of basic necessities such as food, shelter, and medical care
- Compensatory job-searching help for people at risk
- Attempts to restructure existing institutions so as to produce a greater equality of economic opportunity
- Efforts to help the poor learn new skills and empower them to feel more in control of their own lives

Most persons now agree that all five strategies have their place in a comprehensive program to combat American poverty. Most also agree that all five strategies can be misused and result in making things worse. For the most part, the poverty policy debate is about the mix of strategies and the appropriate place for each strategy. No one mix is correct. For one subpopulation of the poor, one mix of strategies might be more effective, but not effective for a second group. The ''best'' mix to help the aged poor may be, and probably is, a rather ineffective and inefficient mix for helping poor children.

◪ CASH SUPPORT: TWO FORMS OF HELP

Income support programs are the main form of help to the poor. Because poverty is usually defined as the lack of adequate income, cash subsidies attack it most directly. A problem with cash support is that targeting the poor alone for payments is difficult, and payments may have perverse incentives. Payments to employable persons may reduce the incentive to seek work or stay on the job; payments to single parents may encourage family splitting or the failure to form a family at the time of the birth of the first child. Higher support payments to families as the number of children grows responds to obvious need, but could encourage families to have more children—a pro-natal effect.

Both facts and public opinion play a significant role: the pro-natal impacts may be minuscule, the work disincentive may be very small, and the rise in family breakups and single-parent families may be more properly attributed to factors other than the cash-income support. Facts do matter, but so does public opinion. The public wants to have income support programs, but they want the income support programs structured in such a way that the incentives to work, to save, and to care for one's own are not diminished. A poll in the *New York Times*, 3 January 1995, showed that most Americans did not believe the welfare programs in place were giving them that.

Most of the cash that government gives to people does not go to those who are poor. Cash-giving by government is done in two ways: by social insurance and social assistance. In the former, a wide variety of trust funds are established to pay for income falls associated with involuntary unemployment, retirement, disability, or the death of a wage earner while dependent children are still at home. The benefit is a matter of right; it is established by law, and it goes to needy as well as non-needy persons. In fact, most persons who experience retirement, short-term unemployment, or disability do not become poor, even though their income may drop. A portion of these insurance payments (the estimates vary) bring people above the poverty line, but the programs are judged as income maintenance programs rather than antipoverty programs.

In contrast, cash assistance benefits are designed to aid people who become poor for a wide variety of reasons. These people simply do not have enough money. The benefits are funded from general revenues and are provided on the basis that the applicant proves to be in need and fits into the category of persons targeted for help. The benefit amount is usually not enough to bring a person above the poverty line, only up to a standard that is established for his or her particular program. The standards vary widely across programs and across states within particular programs, as shown in Table 9.6. AFDC benefits in combination with food stamp benefits are structured to provide a cash and food stamp guarantee above the poverty line in only two states. Many poor—in fact most—do not receive any cash welfare benefits.

There is a sense in which insurance programs are seen as going to a more worthy population than the benefits that flow to recipients of assistance programs. The reasons for this perception are complex and ideologically loaded. The political reality is that the two aided populations are different, are seen as different, and are treated differently. In the last fiscal year, federal spending was $360 billion for cash insurance programs, as compared to $60 billion for cash assistance programs (U.S. Congress 1994). The welfare debate is focused most sharply on cash assistance programs rather than the broader social insurance programs, which also provide cash benefits.

Welfare policy requires an understanding of the relationship between market forces and the total social welfare system. It is useful to think of poverty as those left behind after the market, social insurance, and welfare programs have "done their job." Table 9.7 (p. 230) and Figure 9.1 (p. 231) list the numbers and percentages of persons left poor after these factors have been accounted for. The first defense against poverty is a market and family system structured to provide full employment at wages sufficient to bring the worker and his or her family out of poverty. Within the family, work and child care are to be integrated in some way so that children are cared for and jobs are done. Neither the market system nor family system is designed to eliminate poverty. Both have larger social goals, as we indicated in Chapter 3. The second line of defense against poverty is a social insurance system that provides retirement income to supplement private pensions and savings of aged and disabled persons and their survivors. The social insurance system is structured for income security to all income classes, not just the poor. The third line of defense is a system of social assistance to those whose family system has fallen apart, and to those who have limited or no wage income. These persons are helped by assistance-cash grants distinguished by a category of need, such as dependent children (AFDC) or persons who are poor, aged, disabled, or blind **(Supplemental Security Income—SSI).** The final line of defense is a complex system of in-kind benefits and tax credits.

The official poverty line is roughly equal to the line left poor after cash assistance payments. This went up by 25 percent in the years 1979 to 1993. If we look at how the market economy distributed income in 1979, we find that 43.4 million Americans would have been poor. In 1979, the social welfare programs of assistance and insurance removed 36.8 percent of the market poor from poverty. In 1993 they worked only somewhat less well, removing 34.7 percent. The persistence of poverty does not reflect a failed welfare and social insurance system. It reflects the fact that market and family forces left 23 percent poor in 1993 where it left only 19 percent poor in 1979.

Only part of the problem is the failure to provide enough well-paying jobs. Part of the increase in pretransfer poverty (poverty before insurance or assistance benefits are received) is the increase in the number and share of single-parent households. The increase in single-parent households is the result of many forces (McLanahan and Sandefur 1995); but one of its clear consequences is an increase in the number of poor households. Some critics assert that the programs designed to respond to the pressures on the single-person household have the unintended impact of actually producing the condition to which they are designed to respond. Wisdom is on both sides of this argument. The readings in Box 9.2 (p. 232) provide three distinct views of the dynamics of American poverty from a sociological, political, and economic perspective.

The major cash social assistance programs are **Aid to Families with Dependent Children** (AFDC), **Supplemental Security Income** (SSI), and **Earned Income Tax Credit** (EITC). The major programs of social insurance programs are **Old Age Survivors and Disability Insurance** (OASDI), **Medicare** (HI), and **Unemployment Compensation** (UEC). The poor receive their health benefits through **Medicaid.** Most OASDI and SSI recipients have health insurance through Medicare. A number of other disparate social assistance programs, principally food stamps, public housing, Head Start, and the social services, also provide aid to the poor in kind. The spending for all of these programs is shown in Table 9.8 (p. 232).

| TABLE 9.6 | **GROSS INCOME LIMIT, NEED STANDARD, AND MAXIMUM MONTHLY POTENTIAL BENEFITS, AFDC AND FOOD STAMPS, ONE-PARENT FAMILY[1] OF THREE PERSONS, JANUARY 1994** |

State	Gross Income Limit (185 Percent of Need Standard)	100 Percent of "Need"
Alabama	$1,245	$ 673
Alaska	1,804	975
Arizona	1,783	964
Arkansas	1,304	705
California	1,323	715
Colorado	779	421
Connecticut	1,258	680
Delaware	625	338
District of Columbia	1,317	712
Florida	1,833	991
Georgia	784	424
Hawaii	2,109	1,140
Idaho	1,833	991
Illinois	1,647	890
Indiana	592	320
Iowa	1,571	849
Kansas	794	429
Kentucky	973	526
Louisiana	1,217	658
Maine	1,023	553
Maryland	938	507
Massachusetts	1,071	579
Michigan (Washtenaw County)	1,086	587
Michigan (Wayne County)	1,019	551
Minnesota	984	532
Mississippi	681	368
Missouri	1,565	846
Montana	945	511
Nebraska	673	364
Nevada	1,293	699

Maximum AFDC Grant[2]	Food Stamp Benefit[3]	Combined Benefits	Combined Benefits as a Percent of 1993 Poverty Threshold[4]	AFDC Benefits as a Percent of 1993 Poverty Threshold[4]
$164	$295	$ 459	48	17
923	285	1,208	101	77
347	292	639	67	36
204	295	499	52	21
607	214	821	86	63
356	289	645	67	37
680	192	872	91	71
338	295	633	66	35
420	270	690	72	44
303	295	598	62	32
280	295	575	60	29
712	422	1,134	103	65
317	295	612	64	33
[5]367	291	658	69	38
288	295	583	61	30
426	268	694	72	44
[5]429	284	713	74	45
228	295	523	55	24
190	295	485	51	20
418	271	689	72	44
[5]366	295	661	69	38
579	222	801	83	60
[5]489	249	738	77	51
[5]459	258	717	75	48
[5]532	236	768	80	55
120	295	415	43	13
292	295	587	61	30
401	276	677	71	42
364	287	651	68	38
348	292	640	67	36

continued

TABLE 9.6

concluded

State	Gross Income Limit (185 Percent of Need Standard)	100 Percent of "Need"
New Hampshire	3,049	1,648
New Jersey	1,822	985
New Mexico	660	357
New York (Suffolk County)	1,301	703
New York (New York City)	1,067	577
North Carolina	1,006	544
North Dakota	757	409
Ohio	1,626	879
Oklahoma	871	471
Oregon	851	460
Pennsylvania	1,136	614
Rhode Island	1,025	554
South Carolina	814	440
South Dakota	908	491
Tennessee	788	426
Texas	1,062	574
Utah	1,021	552
Vermont	2,079	1,124
Virginia	727	393
Washington	2,142	1,158
West Virginia	919	497
Wisconsin	1,197	647
Wyoming	1,247	674
Guam	611	330
Puerto Rico	666	360
Virgin Islands	555	300
Median AFDC State[6]	938	507

[1] In most States these benefit amounts apply also to 2-parent families of 3 (where the second parent is incapacitated or unemployed). Some, however, increase benefits for such families.

[2] In States with area differentials, figure shown is for area with highest benefit.

[3] Food stamp benefits are based on maximum AFDC benefits shown and assume deductions of $338 monthly ($131 standard household deduction plus $207 maximum allowable deduction for excess shelter cost) in the 48 contiguous States and D.C. In the remaining four jurisdictions these maximum allowable food stamp deductions are assumed: Alaska, $582; Hawaii, $480; Guam, $513; and Virgin Islands, $267. If only the standard deduction were assumed, food stamp benefits would drop by about $62 monthly in most of the 48 contiguous States and D.C. Maximum food stamp benefits from October 1993 through September 1994 are $295 for a family of three except in these 4 jurisdictions, where they are as follows: Alaska, $388; Hawaii, $492; Gaum, $436; and Virgin Islands, $380.

[4] Except for Alaska and Hawaii, this column is based on the Census Bureau's 1993 poverty threshold for a family of three persons, $11,521, converted to a monthly rate of $960. For Alaska, this threshold was increased by 25 percent; for Hawaii, by 15 percent.

Maximum AFDC Grant[2]	Food Stamp Benefit[3]	Combined Benefits	Combined Benefits as a Percent of 1993 Poverty Threshold[4]	AFDC Benefits as a Percent of 1993 Poverty Threshold[4]
550	231	781	81	57
[5]424	276	700	73	44
357	289	646	67	37
[5]703	201	904	94	73
[5]577	239	816	85	60
272	295	567	59	28
409	273	682	71	43
[5]341	295	636	66	36
324	295	619	65	34
[5]460	293	753	78	48
421	270	691	72	44
[5]554	268	822	86	58
200	295	495	52	21
417	271	688	72	43
185	295	480	50	19
184	295	479	50	19
414	272	686	72	43
638	205	843	88	67
354	290	644	67	37
[5]546	258	804	84	57
249	295	544	57	26
517	241	758	79	54
360	288	648	68	38
330	436	766	80	34
180	0	180	NA	19
240	380	620	65	25
366	295	661	69	38

[5]In these States part of the AFDC cash payment has been designated as energy aid and is disregarded by the State in calculating food stamp benefits. Illinois disregards $18. Kansas disregards $57. Maryland disregards $43. New Jersey disregards $25. New York disregards $53. Ohio disregards $14. Oregon disregards $118. Rhode Island disregards $127.85. Washington disregards $86.

[6]With respect to maximum AFDC benefit among 50 States and D.C.

Note: Puerto Rico does not have a food stamp program, instead a cash nutritional assistance payment is given to recipients.

Source: Table prepared by CRS from information provided by a telephone survey of the States, as appeared in the U.S. Congress, House, Committee on Ways and Means, *Overview of Entitlement Programs*, 103rd Cong., 2nd Session, Committee Print 103–27 (Washington, D.C.: U.S. Government Printing Office, 1994), 366–67.

TABLE 9.7   NUMBERS OF PERSONS LEFT POOR BY YEAR AND CATEGORY

THOSE LEFT POOR (IN MILLIONS) BY YEAR AND BY CATEGORY				
Year	Market[1]	Insurance[2]	Assistance[3]	Real[4]
1979	43.4	28.8	26.1	22.7
1983	53.1	37.3	35.3	33.9
1989	49.9	35.0	32.4	29.8
1993	60.5	39.3	39.3	35.3
PERCENTAGE LEFT POOR BY YEAR AND CATEGORY				
Year	Market[1]	Insurance[2]	Assistance[3]	Real[4]
1979	19%	13%	12%	10%
1983	23	16	15	15
1989	20	14	13	12
1993	23	15	15	14

[1]Market—the number of poor before welfare benefits are counted.

[2]Insurance—the number of poor after social insurance is counted.

[3]Assistance—the number of poor after assistance benefits such as AFDC are counted.

[4]Real—the number of poor after tax credits and in-kind benefits are counted.

Source: Calculations by Wendel Primus from materials in the U.S. Congress, House, Committee on Ways and Means, *Overview of Entitlement Programs*, Committee Print (Washington, D.C.: U.S. Government Printing Office, 1994 and 1995).

◪ WELFARE AS WE KNOW IT

In the paragraphs below, brief sketches of the major welfare programs in the U.S. are provided.

AFDC

At the core of the welfare debate is the Aid to Families with Dependent Children—or AFDC, as it is typically known. AFDC provides cash benefits in amounts that vary from state to state to single parent mothers and their children. (A very limited number of single parent fathers, usually with disabilities, also receive AFDC.) The 1988 Family Support Act mandated that all states also develop Aid to Families with Dependent Children–Unemployed Parent (AFDC-UP), programs that provide cash benefits to two-parent families with unemployed fathers. These benefits are available only to families with male heads-of-household who have extensive previous work histories, lose their jobs, and cannot find employment. States have the option to provide AFDC-UP benefits for either six or twelve months and must provide help in finding employment during that time period. The AFDC expenditures alone are relatively modest compared to the other programs in the social welfare system, as shown in Table 9.8. Nonetheless, the program has grown a great deal over the past two decades (see Table 9.9).

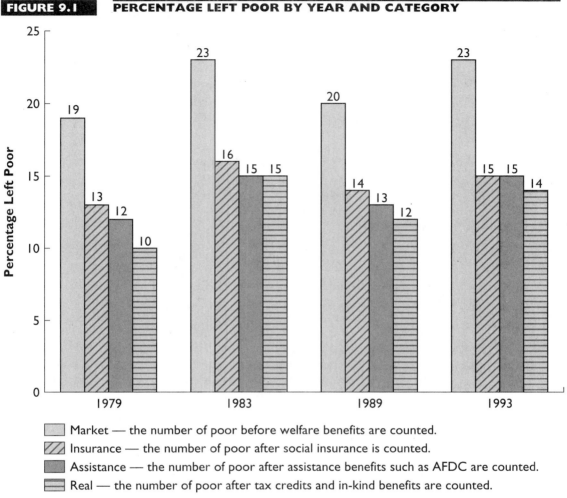

FIGURE 9.1   **PERCENTAGE LEFT POOR BY YEAR AND CATEGORY**

☐ Market — the number of poor before welfare benefits are counted.

▨ Insurance — the number of poor after social insurance is counted.

■ Assistance — the number of poor after assistance benefits such as AFDC are counted.

▤ Real — the number of poor after tax credits and in-kind benefits are counted.

Source: Calculations by Wendel Primus from materials in the U.S. Congress, House, Committee on Ways and Means, *Overview of Entitlement Programs,* Committee Print (Washington, D.C.: U.S. Government Printing Office, 1994 and 1995).

Over the years, the AFDC program has shifted from one concerned with cash benefits alone (1935–1961) to one that provided a number of services to those who wanted the help to become self-sufficient (1962–1981) to one in which behavioral changes are being demanded as a condition of future assistance (1982 to the present). Maryland reduces benefits to parents who fail to ensure that their preschoolers get health care or that their older children attend school regularly. Wisconsin cut grants to mothers whose children did not attend school. The real purchasing value of AFDC has declined because of inflation and because of lagging increases. Nevertheless, some states are considering limiting benefits to mothers who have additional children, or further cutting benefits in other ways. The most dramatic proposal was that of Newt Gingrich, the new Republican speaker of the house, to end AFDC for young mothers without husbands and place the children in child care centers euphemistically called orphanages. This debate is more symbolic

BOX 9.2

READINGS ON THE DYNAMICS OF DEPENDENCY

Bane, Mary Jo, and David Ellwood. 1994. *Welfare realities.* Cambridge: Harvard University Press.

Mead, Lawrence M. 1992. *The new politics of*

poverty. New York: Basic Books.

Danziger, Sheldon, Gary Sandefur, and Daniel Weinberg, eds. 1995. *Confronting poverty.* Cambridge: Harvard University Press.

than substantive and in fact has drawn attention away from the real issue of what is right and what is wrong with AFDC as we know it.

SSI

Federal-state programs were enacted for old-age assistance and aid to the blind as part of the Social Security Act of 1935. Aid to the Permanently and Totally Disabled was added in 1950. In 1974 the means-tested, federally administered SSI replaced these state-administered programs and provides minimum national monthly cash payments indexed to the consumer price index (CPI) with uniform, nationwide eligibility requirements to needy aged, blind, and disabled people. People with disabilities have become the primary recipients of SSI, whose recipients are viewed as the "deserving poor," whereas the recipients of AFDC are more often viewed as the "undeserving poor." Modifications of the SSI program are not seen as a major part of the welfare debate.

General Assistance

General assistance is provided in 32 states by state and local governments without federal funds. Such aid may be furnished to needy people or those with disabilities who are ineligible for federal categorical programs. Eligibility criteria and benefit levels vary by state and often

TABLE 9.8   **SPENDING ON MAJOR SOCIAL WELFARE PROGRAMS IN BILLIONS OF NOMINAL DOLLARS, SELECTED YEARS**

	WELFARE PROGRAM						
Year	OASDI	HI	Medicaid	SSI	AFDC	EITC	Poor in Kind*
1975	$ 63.6	$ 14.1	$ 12.6	$14.9	$ 8.2	$ .9	$39.20
1980	117.1	34.0	25.7	13.5	11.5	1.3	44.00
1985	186.4	69.7	40.9	15.4	14.6	1.5	32.10
1990	246.5	107.4	72.5	17.8	18.5	5.3	37.10
1995	334.8	177.3	168.8	23.8	22.8	21.0	59.50

*Federal spending only on in-kind programs, except Medicaid.

Source: Data from U.S. Social Security Administration, *Social Security Bulletin,* 1985 and 1995 (Washington, D.C.: Author).

| TABLE 9.9 | **TOTAL, FEDERAL, AND STATE AFDC EXPENDITURES: FISCAL YEARS 1970 TO 1999** (In millions of dollars) |

FISCAL YEAR	FEDERAL SHARE		STATE SHARE		TOTAL	
	Benefits	Administrative	Benefits	Administrative	Benefits	Administrative
1970	$ 2,187	$ 572[1]	$ 1,443	$ 186	$ 4,082	$ 881[1]
1971	3,008	271	2,469	254	5,477	525
1972	3,612	240[2]	2,942	241	6,554	NA
1973	3,865	313	3,138	296	7,003	610
1974	4,071	379	3,300	362	7,371	740
1975	4,625	552	3,787	529	8,412	1,082
1976	5,258	541	4,418	527	9,676	1,069
1977	5,626	595	4,762	583	10,388	1,177
1978	5,701	631	4,890	617	10,591	1,248
1979	5,825	683	4,954	668	10,779	1,350
1980	6,448	750	5,508	729	11,956	1,479
1981	6,928	835	5,917	814	12,845	1,648
1982	6,922	878	5,934	878	12,857	1,756
1983	7,332	915	6,275	915	13,607	1,830
1984	7,707	876	6,664	822	14,371	1,698
1985	7,817	890	6,763	889	14,580	1,779
1986	8,239	993	6,996	967	15,235	1,960
1987	8,914	1,081	7,409	1,052	15,323	2,133
1988	9,125	1,194	7,538	1,159	16,663	2,353
1989	9,433	1,211	7,807	1,206	17,240	2,417
1990	10,149	1,358	8,390	1,303	18,539	2,661
1991	11,165	1,373	9,191	1,300	20,356	2,673
1992	12,252	1,422	9,988	1,342	22,240	2,764
1993	12,270	1,518	10,016	1,438	22,286	2,956
1994[3]	12,470	1,564	10,215	1,493	22,685	3,057
1995[3]	12,756	1,597	10,441	1,558	23,197	3,155
1996[3]	13,160	1,637	10,771	1,619	23,931	3,256
1997[3]	13,631	1,682	11,157	1,682	24,788	3,365
1998[3]	14,097	1,741	11,539	1,741	25,636	3,483
1999[3]	14,629	1,802	11,974	1,802	26,603	3,605

[1]Includes expenditures for services.

[2]Administrative expenditures only.

[3]Administrative projection under current law.

NA—Not available.

Note: Benefits do not include emergency assistance payments or reimbursement from child support enforcement collections. Foster care payments are included from 1971 to 1980. Beginning in fiscal year 1984, the cost of certifying AFDC households for food stamps are shown in the food stamp appropriation, U.S. Department of Agriculture. Administrative costs include Child Care administration, Work Program, ADP, FAMIS, Fraud Control, SAVE and other State and local administrative expenditures.

Source: Office of Financial Management, Administration for Children and Families, as appeared in the U.S. Congress, House, Committee on Ways and Means, *Overview of Entitlement Programs,* 103rd Cong., 2nd Session, Committee Print 103–27 (Washington, D.C.: U.S. Government Printing Office, 1994), 389.

within states. Payments are at low levels and for short durations. Benefits range from cash payments to groceries and shelter. During 1990 there were on average 1.2 million recipients a month.

Emergency Assistance

Thirty-two states provide emergency assistance for specified emergencies to adults eligible for SSI and to destitute families with children under age 21. Eligible adults must experience sudden emergencies that deprive them of the means to stay alive and healthy. Benefits are in cash, in kind, or in voucher form. Emergency assistance programs in 1993 served an average monthly caseload of 54,869 families (U.S. Congress 1994).

Assistance in Kind

In addition to the previously mentioned income programs, the public assistance system also includes public and subsidized housing; Medicaid; food stamps; public housing; school lunches; the Supplemental Food Program for Women, Infants, and Children (WIC); and the Low-Income Energy Assistance program. Social services include child care, adoptions, foster and protective care, family planning, and services for the disabled, juvenile delinquents, unmarried parents, and drug and alcohol abusers. Only a portion of such social services are targeted exclusively to the poor.

The spending for the principal in-kind programs is given in Table 9.10.

The Insurance Approach

Between the market system, through which households meet their needs through earnings and savings, and the assistance system, through which the government and private charities care for those who would otherwise be destitute, lies an enormous social insurance system. Though there are others, the principal social insurance programs in the United States are OASDI and unemployment insurance. The income schemes were devel-

TABLE 9.10 **EXPENDITURES FOR MEDICAID, FOOD STAMPS, AND PUBLIC HOUSING: 1975–1995** (In billions of nominal dollars)

Year	Medicaid	Food Stamps	Public Housing
1975	$ 12.6	$ 4.6	$28.6
1980	25.7	9.2	27.4
1985	40.9	12.6	11.1
1990	72.5	16.5	10.5
1995	168.8[1]	24.8[1]	19.4[1]

[1]Projected amount

Source: Calculations made from tables in the U.S. Congress, House, Committee on Ways and Means, *Overview of Entitlement Programs*, 103rd Cong., 2nd Session, Committee Print 103–27 (Washington, D.C.: U.S. Government Printing Office, 1994).

oped in Europe in the late nineteenth century and incorporated in this country in the 1930s. Medicare (our system for financing the medical care of the aged and disabled) and Medicaid (our system for financing the care of our poorest children and families and, increasingly, elderly people whose health needs are not covered by Medicare) are discussed in Chapter 11, "Health Care."

Unemployment insurance developed as a joint responsibility of the states and the federal government. The OASDI program is a total federal program. The Social Security Act of 1935 provided retirement benefits only to retired workers themselves. In 1939, the first of numerous extensions to the system provided benefits for survivors and dependents. Over the years, the program has been expanded to include all who work or are dependents of a person in the labor force. In 1956, the age at which women become eligible for some benefits was lowered from 65 to 62, and in 1961 men were given the option of retiring at age 62 with a reduced level of benefits. In 1957, the government added the **Disability Insurance** (DI) program, which established a separate fund to provide cash benefits to workers over age 50 who become totally and permanently disabled. In 1960 the age limit for disability was removed. In 1965, Medicare was introduced, providing medical benefits for those over 65 and creating yet another Social Security fund to finance them. (In 1965, Congress also established the separate Medicaid program to provide medical benefits for certain categories of the needy poor: children and their caretakers, the elderly, and the disabled).

Between now and 2020, the Social Security tax will exceed the Social Security benefits. The excess of income over outgo goes into a trust fund, which ideally will pay the benefits from 2020 to 2050 when claims will be larger than then-current taxes (see Figure 9.2). The problem is that the trust fund does not automatically make the resources available. They do give the Social Security Administration a valid claim on the federal government, but for the government to pay that claim it will have to collect other tax revenue to do so. If, according to one argument, the government reduces its deficit now and invests in the infrastructure of our economy over the next twenty years, then the enhanced productivity will yield tax revenue high enough to pay off the obligations without burden. Otherwise, in the near future (i.e., twenty-five years), the government will have to sharply raise tax rates or reduce public expenditures. In the short-term future (i.e., the next five years), the debate about what to do to reduce the current deficit is likely to divert attention away from the rest of the welfare system.

◥ BELIEFS AND OPTIONS FOR WELFARE

The common factor of the beliefs about welfare is that they are not easily changed. Critics on the left and the right are shouting at one another and seldom debate the same topic. Whether viewed from the left or the right, public assistance cannot be separated from its societal context. There are social problems for which there is scant evidence that the welfare system is at fault. These include the shrinkage in the number

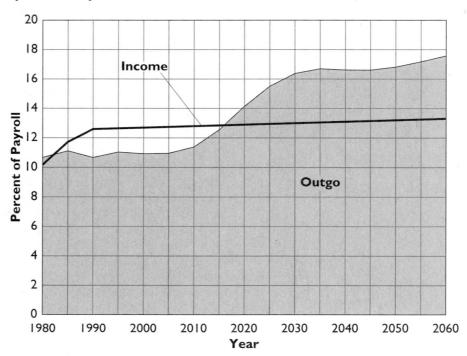

FIGURE 9.2

SOCIAL SECURITY COST RATES AND INCOME TAX RATES (1980–2060)

Tax income represents payroll tax and income tax receipts from taxing benefits. The income surplus from 1980 to 2015, invested at a nominal compound rate, should produce enough income to cover the deficit from 2015 to 2050.

Source: Social Security Administration, *1991 Trustees Report* (Washington, D.C.: U.S. Government Printing Office, 1992), 3.

of jobs for unskilled labor, discrimination, differential pay by gender, and trends that retard incentives to marriage, encourage divorce, and stimulate out-of-wedlock births. Nonetheless, the welfare system must respond to society as we find it, not as we would wish it to be.

What is the proper scope of government in our society? In our social welfare system? These are questions much debated in the 1990s. Adam Smith, the founder of classical economics, provided a short list for governmental actions: national defense, the administration of justice, and a very few public works such as roads and schools. Today, the divisive issue between Republicans and Democrats often boils down to which social problems are best dealt with by market mechanisms, which by public actions, which by a private/governmental partnership, and which by voluntary actions.

Governmental action in the economy is based on the notion that such actions promote a more efficient economy. We may, and do, debate under the rules of evidence and the cannons of logic whether a particular program is efficient. The welfare transfer programs, by contrast, are based not on efficiency concepts but justice concepts.

There is no economic proof to show that taking a dollar in taxes from Scrooge and giving it to Tiny Tim's family is efficient. There are all sorts of moral arguments for taxing Scrooge and giving benefits to Tim. As a political society, we have made a political judgment that a society which approaches equality is, on the whole, good. Many social programs are designed to promote that equality of opportunity. The more limited goal of cash transfers is to reduce the incidence and severity of poverty. There are many reasons for wanting to help the poor: we may want to aid the poor out of fear, out of a sense that "there but for the grace of God go I," out of a sense of compassion, or out of a particular conception of social justice.

The problem becomes one of determining how to promote equality and abrogate poverty without violating either economic efficiency or the elementary democratic morality that informs us that others have a sense of justice that may differ from our own. In a practical sense we have to ask, how can we help Tim without driving Scrooge into retirement and causing the resulting loss of Bob Cratchet's job? How can we help Tim get his operation without everyone wanting "free medical care"? Basically, how can we help Tim (and his family) without encouraging dependency and all of its debilitating results?

A generation ago, Henry Aaron posed a simple question: "Why Is Welfare So Hard to Reform?" (Aaron 1973). Aaron answered his question by suggesting that the simple questions hide more complex questions:

- Who should be eligible for aid?

- Can we distinguish between deserving and undeserving?

- What is the effect of welfare on incentives to work, to save, and to care for members of one's own family?

- To what extent is the deprecation in family standards traceable to welfare programs?

- What obligations do recipients of welfare owe society?

- To what extent do welfare programs dealing with the symptoms of poverty divert attention from more fundamental programs that deal with the causes of poverty?

At the time Aaron asked his question, the Nixon Administration was in its third year of efforts to gain Congressional passage of its welfare reform. It was defeated, as were the large-scale welfare reform proposals of every subsequent president except George Bush, who had none. The Clinton Administration welfare plan was designed to "end welfare as we know it." Health care reform became the primary issue in the 103rd Congress and the 1994 by-election.

The Clinton Administration welfare reform package tried to address five things: (1) "increase parental responsibility," (2) "make work pay," (3) strengthen the nation's system of child support enforcement and collection, (4) provide education and training to poor people, and (5) place limits on the length of time that people can receive welfare benefits.

House Republicans celebrated their election victory with their own plan to end welfare as we know it. The essential features of their plan were three: First, individuals in poverty who meet eligibility guidelines would no longer have a legally enforceable right to welfare, known in legislative parlance as an entitlement. Instead, specific funds would be appropriated and if funds ran out before the year end, Congress and the state legislature could either pass a supplemental appropriation or scale back benefits depending on current political and economic realities. Second, the Republican proposal would restrict eligibility for welfare for mothers unmarried and under 18 and use the funds to create group homes and child care institutions as an alternative to welfare, based on reasoning that when the family has failed the child, it makes no sense to give money to that family. Third, and according to Republican leadership most important, their proposals would shift the center of decision making out of Washington and back to the state capitols.

The "welfare debate" continues and raises these issues regarding the proper role of government, which level of government should have which responsibility, and the best way to enforce responsibilities of individuals. Views of society, inequality, dependency, and theories of causation of poverty enter the debate.

THE ROLES OF SOCIAL WORKERS IN THE FIGHT AGAINST POVERTY

Social work, more than any other profession, maintains a strong commitment to fighting poverty at all levels of the environment. Social workers provide direct services to individuals and families living in poverty; advocate for programs and policies that improve the lives of the poor and reduce poverty at the community, state, and federal levels; and develop and administer policies and programs that serve our nation's poor.

Some BSW graduates become income eligibility or public assistance workers in federal, state, and local human services agencies. They help individuals apply for public assistance programs, such as AFDC, food stamps, Medicaid and general assistance. They also help individuals apply for social insurance programs such as Social Security and Medicare and oversee the provision of both public assistance and social insurance benefit programs.

Many public assistance programs have increased the roles of social workers in the fight against poverty by mandating that all AFDC clients receiving employment services be assigned a case manager to help them obtain self-sufficiency. Case managers use a generalist approach to assess their clients' strengths and needs; work with their clients to develop appropriate goals to work toward getting off AFDC and achieving adequate employment; develop appropriate service plans with clients to accomplish their goals; assist their clients in accessing needed resources and provide support to them in accomplishing their established goals; and terminate with their clients when the plans have been completed. Case managers also assist clients in developing skills in areas such as interviewing, assertiveness, and handling stress on the job; help them enroll in job training and education programs; and help them locate appropriate resources such as transportation, housing, child care, health care, or family counseling.

Social workers also are employed by churches and other religious organizations, the Salvation Army, local social services agencies, housing programs, Head Start and other child development programs, drop out prevention and teen pregnancy and teen parenting programs, and health clinics and hospitals that provide a variety of services to adults, children, youth and families who live in poverty. Additionally, social workers work with federal, state and local agencies and governments; state legislatures and the U.S. Congress; and advocacy organizations such as the Children's Defense Fund in developing, lobbying for, and administering anti-poverty programs. The values base of the social work profession mandates that social workers treat all clients, including those in poverty, with dignity and respect and work to empower them to be in charge of their own lives.

SUMMARY

Welfare has always been a politically charged issue. The most basic questions it involves are the contradictory views that different segments of society hold about poor and vulnerable people—how to prevent the condition. As the United States evolves with increasing technological sophistication requiring more highly educated workers, along with a slack labor market and constrained public spending, the issues of welfare in general will also have to be confronted. There are no easy answers; even more importantly, there are no correct answers, and that is why it is such a problem.

KEY TERMS

Aid to Families with Dependent
  Children (AFDC)
Disability Insurance (DI)
Earned Income Tax Credit
  (EITC)
market basket concept
Medicaid
Medicare

Old Age Survivors and Disability
  Insurance (OASDI)
poverty
relative poverty
Supplemental Security Income
  (SSI)
Unemployment Compensation
  (UEC)

DISCUSSION QUESTIONS

1. Do you believe that a preference for welfare keeps AFDC recipients out of the work force?

2. How does the changing shape of the American economy change the shape of American poverty?

3. To what degree is the number (or percentage) of poor people a good measure of a society's commitment to social welfare?

4. Which level of government, state or national, is best equipped to deal with poverty?

REFERENCES

Aaron, Henry J. 1978. *Politics and the professors.* Washington, D.C.: Brookings Institution.

Heffernan, Joseph, and Kathleen Vickland. 1994. *Is there an underclass?* In H. J. Karger and J. Midgley (eds.), *Controversial issues in social policy.* Boston: Allyn & Bacon.

Herrnstein, Richard J. and Charles Murray. 1994. *The Bell Curve.* New York: Free Press.

McLanahan, Sara, and Gary Sandefur. 1995. *Growing up with a single parent.* Cambridge: Harvard University Press.

Mincy, Ronald. 1995. *The underclass: Concept controversy and evidence.* In S. Danziger et. al. *Confronting poverty: Prescriptions for change.* Cambridge, Mass.: Harvard University Press.

Orshonsky, M. 1965. Counting the poor. *Social Security Bulletin,* January, 3–29.

Steiner, Gilbert. 1966. *Social insecurity.* Chicago, Rand MacNally, p. 203.

U.S. Congress. House. Committee on Ways and Means. 1994. *Overview of entitlement programs.* 103rd Cong., 2nd Session. Committee Print 103–27, p. 1210. Washington, D.C.: U.S. Government Printing Office. (This publication is commonly known as the Green Book.)

SUGGESTED FURTHER READINGS

Danziger, Sheldon and Peter Gottschalk. 1995. *America unequal.* Cambridge, Mass.: Harvard University Press.

Garfinkel, Irwin. 1992. *Assuring child support.* New York: Russell Sage.

Handler, Joel. 1995. *The poverty of welfare reform.* New Haven: Yale University Press.

CHAPTER 10

MENTAL HEALTH, SUBSTANCE ABUSE, AND DEVELOPMENTAL DISABILITIES

Twenty-four-year old Joanna Barclay currently lives in a halfway house in the innercity area of a large northern city. She has lived there for three months, after being released from her fourteenth stay at a state mental hospital since the age of 16. Joanna and her roommates earn money for food and part of the rent by working for an industrial cleaning company. They are supervised by a social worker from the local mental health outreach center, who meets with them as a group twice a week and is available on an on-call basis whenever they need support. Joanna, with her social worker's help, is planning to enroll in a job-training program next month and to move into her own apartment with one of the other residents of the halfway house within the next six months. Joanna is excited about the opportunity to live on her own.

Joanna enjoyed a relatively stable childhood, growing up in a rural area of the South with her middle-class parents and four brothers. During junior high school, she began to experience severe headaches and what she terms "anxiety attacks." Her parents took her to several doctors, but no physical reasons could be found for these problems. At about age 15, Joanna's behavior changed from calm and stable to erratic, ranging from screaming rages to long periods of crying to fun-loving, carefree behavior. She began experimenting with drugs, ran away from home a number of times, and got into several physical altercations with other girls at school. Her family had difficulty coping with her behavior. After one serious incident when Joanna threatened her mother and her younger brother with a knife, she was hospitalized in a local private psychiatric hospital for thirty days. She was placed on medication to help stabilize her erratic behavior, and she and her family received therapy. After her release from the hospital, Joanna functioned better for several months. But she soon reported feeling overwhelmed and pressured and told her family she "could not stop the frightening thoughts that kept running through her head." Her psychiatrist wanted to rehospitalize her, but her family's insurance benefits had been exhausted during her first hospitalization, and Joanna did not want to admit herself to the state mental hospital nearby.

After continual arguments with her family and school personnel and several minor run-ins with the law, Joanna quit school and moved with a boyfriend to California, where she held a series of temporary jobs. When the boyfriend left her because he could not handle her mood swings, her behavior became even more erratic. Finally, after she was found asleep in a dumpster and unable to remember who or where she was, the police picked her up and took her to the state hospital. During the next six years, Joanna repeated a pattern of briefly holding a menial job for a short time, losing the job, living on the streets, entering the state hospital, and being released in a more stable condition. When Joanna was released from her last hospital stay, the local mental health center in Joanna's area finally had space available at the halfway house where she currently is living. ∎

The mental health needs of Americans are receiving increased attention. The National Commission on Mental Health estimates that 15 percent of the United States population at any given time is in need of mental health services, and that 25 percent of the population suffers from some type of emotional problem. But services are available to only one out of every eight individuals who need them. Because of increases in individual stress, financial pressures, divorce and marital problems, and work-related pressures, it can be expected that most individuals will experience emotional problems at some point in their lives.

Emotional problems are highly correlated with substance abuse, a related field of practice in which large numbers of social workers are employed. The systems/ecological framework can be used to understand the relationships between environmental factors at all levels that contribute to emotional problems and substance abuse. Problems with one area, such as mental illness, do not automatically mean problems with substance abuse. But researchers from the United States Department of Health and Human Services found that 30 percent of adults who had been assessed as having a mental disorder also had a substance problem during their lives. Moreover, these same researchers found that more than half of adults with drug abuse disorders had one or more mental disorders (1994).

Additionally, many individuals in the United States have some type of developmental disability, either physical or mental. Often, individuals with physical developmental disabilities abuse alcohol or other drugs as a way to cope with their disabilities. Some types of developmental disabilities are a result of drug abuse by mothers during pregnancy. The relationship between developmental disabilities and substance abuse is dramatized by recent legislation that prohibits the discrimination of persons with disabilities and includes both substance abusers and persons with emotional problems in its definition of disability.

In this chapter we focus on mental health and mental illness, the abuse of alcohol and other drugs, and developmental disabilities. Students should keep in mind that the three problems do not always overlap, and that different histories, policies, and issues surround each area. However, there are also many similarities, particularly in relation to the stigma, oppression, and discrimination experienced by each group. Social workers can play many important roles at all levels of the environment in working with individuals, families, and communities experiencing these problems. Key roles include recognizing the strengths of individuals, families, cultural groups, and communities and empowering them to use their strengths to develop a healthier environment in which to live. ■

MENTAL HEALTH

How do we determine who needs mental health services and who should receive them? The stigma placed on individuals with mental health problems and the stereotypes about the services provided them cause many individuals with mental health problems to avoid seeking services. People think of mental health services and those who receive them as portrayed in popular movies and books, such as the classic novel *One Flew Over the Cuckoo's Nest* (Kesey 1962) and the film *Rainman* (1993). For this reason, many communities are passing zoning or other ordinances to prevent moving individuals with mental health problems into their areas.

The rights of persons with mental health problems also are receiving increased attention. Should these individuals be forced to be hospitalized, receive electric shock treatments, or receive drug therapy against their

Mental health problems, including substance abuse, affect at least one-fourth of all Americans at some point in their lives. Growing up in a family with a parent who is a substance abuser has intergenerational effects if the problem is not addressed by the entire family.

wishes? Or, like Joanna, when they so desperately need treatment that is not available due to scarce resources, do they have a right to demand services, especially if it means that they will be less likely to need more intensive services, such as institutionalization, in the future? Does someone who is currently in an institution, but could function in a less restrictive environment, have the right to demand such a placement?

What about the protections for those in our society who may encounter persons with serious mental health problems? Concern is being expressed about the accountability of those with serious mental health problems and what should happen when such individuals become dangerous to themselves and others. This was exemplified by several recent court cases. The young adult who shot former President Reagan in 1981 was not sentenced for the act due to "reasons of insanity." In contrast, a young adult who killed a number of women over a period of several years was diagnosed by a number of psychiatrists as having severe psychological problems, sentenced to death in a Florida court, and executed in 1989. And a retarded young adult who aided in a murder at the age of 17—when his mental age was about 6—recently was put to death, also in Florida. Mistrials were declared in 1994 for both of the Menendez brothers, who were on trial for killing their parents and based their pleas to the court on emotional damage due to child abuse, although they were found guilty in a later trial.

Current studies also show a strong relationship between mental health problems and physical health problems. When persons do not get help in addressing their mental health problems, they are much more likely to become physically ill. For example, IBM researchers found that 50 percent of persons coming to company physicians with health-related problems were experiencing mental health problems (Comprehensive Care Corporation 1981). A study of over 40,000 persons in Hawaii, cited on 25 July 1990 in an Associated Press release, found that those who received short-term mental health services for a specific psychological problem experienced a 35 percent to 38 percent drop in subsequent medical costs. The high costs of health care could be reduced if more attention were given to the mental health needs of individuals.

Mental health problems, if left untreated, also disrupt families and increase the financial costs to taxpayers, as well as decrease productivity at the workplace. It is difficult to obtain accurate data on actual expenditures for mental health services and other related costs to individuals with mental health problems, as well as the costs to their families, workplaces, and communities. The current estimate is that expenditures for mental health services alone consume approximately 10 percent of national health care resources. In 1990, public and private costs for mental health expenditures were over $20 billion. State mental health expenditures totaled $12 billion, while expenditures were $4.6 billion for private psychiatric hospitals and $3.6 billion for general hospital psychiatric care (Lin 1995). These costs do not include all costs for outpatient or preventive care.

Over half of the individuals providing mental health services today are social workers. They are employed in state mental hospitals, private psychiatric treatment facilities, community outreach facilities, child guidance clinics and family service agencies, emergency hotlines, crisis centers, and private offices. The provision of mental health services is a rapidly growing area that offers many critical roles for social workers.

Mental Health or Mental Illness: Definitions

Societies have always developed their own systems for labeling acceptable and unacceptable behavior. What is tolerated in one society may be unacceptable in another. For each society, there is a continuum, with certain definitely unacceptable behaviors at one end and definitely acceptable and appropriate ones at the other. Typically, the behaviors at either end of the continuum are almost uniformly agreed upon by most members of that society. But the behaviors in the middle of the continuum tend to cause much debate and disagreement. For example, although murder would be considered a definitely unacceptable behavior by most, where on the continuum would continually talking to oneself fall, or being convinced that you were King Tut? Some societies tolerate little deviance from acceptable behavior. For example, for a brief period during colonial times in Salem, Massachusetts, some persons whose behavior was considered "deviant" were labeled as witches possessed by the devil, and they were tortured and burned at the stake. Later research (Mechanic 1980) suggested that many of these individuals had severe psychological problems. In other societies, those whose behavior deviates from the norm are given special roles and, in some instances, elevated to status positions within the society. For example, in many Native American tribes, nonconforming individuals often became shamans, or medicine men, assuming high-status positions within the tribes.

Historically, those labeled as mentally ill or retarded often have been isolated or punished. In colonial times, individuals frequently were locked in attics or cellars or warehoused in lunatic asylums. Today, our society is still ambivalent about how such individuals should be regarded. Attempts at deinstitutionalization or mainstreaming emotionally disturbed and disabled individuals into classrooms and communities have met with much resistance. Various people (e.g., Goffman 1961; Mechanic 1980) have suggested that for many individuals who have emotional or developmental problems, the stigma attached to the labels they are given is far more damaging to them than the extent of their problems. David Mechanic, a prominent social policy analyst in the mental health field, argues that definitions of mental illness are made at varying levels in the social structure. Early informal definitions are made in groups within which the person operates, usually family members or co-workers. Such definitions depend on the norms of the particular group and what is tolerated, as well as on the position the person occupies within the group. A boss's behavior, for example, may be defined as outside of the group norms much less quickly than a file clerk's. Definitions of this type also depend on whether the other members of the group can empathize; that is, whether they can fit that behavior into their own frames of reference. For example, a person who continually carries on an imaginary conversation with his mother while on the job is more likely to be tolerated if the group is aware that the mother recently died and the son had a very close relationship with her. But if there is no apparent context for the behavior or if the behavior persists, such individuals are likely to be labeled as strange or odd (Mechanic 1980).

Definitions of so-called abnormal behaviors typically are based on visible symptoms, such as talking to people who are not present, rather than the severity of the actual problems. Anytime you attempt to define a condition based on invisible factors, such as what is going on inside an individual's mind, specific definitions are difficult to achieve. Only those who in some way enter the mental health system are likely to be specifically defined as having some type of emotional problem. The mental health system, in spite of its problems, is likely to accept—at least for short periods of time—almost all individuals who seek its services, including the unwanted, the aged, the indigent, the lonely, and those with nowhere else to go. At times, this results in overestimates of the number of individuals defined as having emotional problems and underestimates of those who should enter the system.

Categorizing Mental Illness

Formal definitions of mental illness traditionally have followed the **medical model,** which considers those with emotional problems as sick and thus not responsible for their behavior. This model also assumes that sick people are entitled to be helped and that help or treatment should be guided by the medical profession in medical settings or settings such as psychiatric facilities directed by medical professionals. The medical model conceptualizes mental illness as severe emotional problems caused by brain dysfunction or intrapsychic causes, with little attention to systems or environmental influences. (See Chapter 3 for a comparison of the medical model and the systems/ecological perspective.) Traditionally, mental illness also has been viewed from a genetic or physiological perspective as a disease of the mind or a disturbance in the functioning of the individual.

The American Psychiatric Association has attempted to monitor the categorization and definition of various types of emotional disorders through a classification system termed the **Diagnostic and Statistical Manual of Mental Disorders,** or the *DSM.* This classification system is currently in its fourth revision and referred to informally as the *DSM-IV-R.* It uses a multiaxial system for evaluation, which focuses on the psychological, biological, and social aspects of an individual's functioning. The system incorporates information from five axes in diagnosing an individual. Axes I and II incorporate all of the mental disorders, such as schizophrenic and psychotic disorders. Axis III incorporates physical disorders and conditions. Axes IV and V rate the severity of the psychosocial stressors that have contributed to the development or the maintenance of the disorder and the highest level of adaptive functioning that the individual has maintained during the previous year (Williams 1995).

Some social work professionals believe that the *DSM* classification system is consistent with a systems/ecological perspective in assessing an individual, allowing a focus on either organic factors or environmental factors, or both, that affect an individual's condition. They believe that the *DSM* allows for the incorporation of the individual's strengths as well as problems when completing an assessment. This classification system has been used increasingly in recent years for third-party insurance reimbursement when mental health services are provided (Williams and Spitzer, 1995).

Although many social workers find the *DSM-IV-R* helpful, its use by social workers and other professionals to label conditions of clients in order to obtain third-party insurance reimbursements has raised questions about whether such labels really are beneficial in improving services. Critics suggest that such a diagnostic process may actually be more detrimental to clients, because labels such as "schizophrenia" or "conduct disorder" can negatively affect clients and the way others treat them, particularly if such labels included in clients' records are obtained and misused. More recent criticism of the *DSM* by social workers focuses on its reduced emphasis on environmental factors that affect a person's mental health and increased attention to disorders and deficits, more consistent with the medical model (Hutchins and Kirk 1995).

The National Association of Social Workers (Karls and Wandrei 1994) has published an alternative classification system, the person-in-environment system, or PIE, that provides a more holistic approach based on the systems/ecological framework. Like the *DSM,* this system can also be used to describe, classify, and code the emotional, mental, and social problems experienced by adults. The PIE system assesses clients according to four major factors:

- Social functioning (social role in which each problem is identified, type of problem, severity of problem, duration of problem, and ability of client to cope with problem)
- Environmental problems (social system in which each problem is identified, specific type of problem within each social system, severity of problem, duration of problem)
- Mental health problems (clinical syndrome and personality and developmental disorders)
- Physical health problems (diseases diagnosed by a physician and other health problems reported by the client and others)

A major difference between the two systems is that the PIE system focuses primarily on the importance of the interrelationship of the person and the environment. The PIE system

> seeks to balance problems and strengths; it delineates problems pertinent to both the person and the environment and qualifies them according to their duration, severity, and the client's ability to solve or cope with them. (Karls and Wandrei 1994, 3)

Mental Health: A Matter of Viewpoint

The traditional view of mental health and mental illness is that they exist at opposite ends of a continuum. Others, like psychiatrist Thomas Szasz (1970), suggest that mental health and emotional problems are issues that defy specific boundaries. Szasz objects to labeling the mentally ill and argues that there is no such thing as mental illness. He agrees that there are illnesses due to neurological impairment, but he believes that such illnesses are brain diseases rather than mental illnesses. Although he acknowledges the existence of emotional problems, Szasz contends that labeling nonorganic emotional problems implies a deviation from some clearly specified norm. He feels that the label not only stigmatizes individuals, but may cause them to actually assume those behaviors.

Szasz argues that instead of talking about definitions of mental illness, we should talk about problems of living—an individual's struggle with the problem of how to live in our world. He and others suggest that positive mental health is promoted by our competence in dealing with the environment and our confidence of being able, when necessary, to cause desired effects. Szasz advocates a systems/ecological perspective for viewing mental health. Within his framework, problems in living can be viewed as being due to biological/physiological, economic, political, psychological, or sociological constraints. Promoting positive interactions between individuals and their environments is viewed as congruent with the promotion of optimal mental health and social functioning for individuals. Szasz (1960) proposes a classification system with the following categories of mental health problems:

- Personal disabilities, such as depression, fears, inadequacy, and excessive anxiety
- Antisocial acts, such as violent and criminal behaviors

- Deterioration of the brain, such as Alzheimer's disease, alcoholism, and brain damage

Many mental health experts prefer this system and its emphasis on healthy functioning to a system that emphasizes mental illness. This system assumes that at some point all individuals have difficulties in negotiating their complex environments. Mental health services are viewed as available to and needed by all individuals at some time during their lives rather than as something to be avoided. Szasz's perspective is much more consistent with the systems/ecological perspective and the PIE classification system than the medical model and the *DSM-IV-R*.

The Development of Mental Health Problems

There is considerable debate on how mental health problems are created. In many instances, it is difficult, if not impossible, to say that one specific factor *caused* a mental health problem. More than likely, mental health problems are the result of a variety of factors. Research suggests a number of possible explanations:

- **Heredity, biological, and genetic factors:** Research has identified possible genetic traits that suggest that individuals' gene pools may be prone to certain mental health disorders. For example, among identical twins, if one of the twins has schizophrenia, the other is also likely to have the disorder, even if the twins were separated at birth and raised in different environments. Other researchers suggest that genetic factors alone do not cause mental health disorders, but that some individuals are predisposed to certain problems through heredity, and that under certain environmental conditions, this predisposition is triggered, resulting in the emotional problem. A variation of this position is that, due to genetic traits or physiological characteristics, some individuals are biologically less capable of coping with environmental stress.

- **Psychosocial developmental factors:** This perspective, based on the work of developmental theorist Erik Erikson and others, suggests that mental health problems result from environmental experiences during childhood. Research shows that individuals who experience severe trauma during childhood—such as physical or sexual abuse, separation from a close family member, or alcoholism or drug abuse among family members—are much more likely to experience mental health problems later in life.

- **Social learning:** The social learning perspective suggests that mental health problems are the result of learned behaviors. Such behaviors may be learned by observing parents or other role models or as survival mechanisms to cope with difficult life experiences.

- **Social stress:** This perspective, based on the work of Thomas Szasz, focuses on the relationship between environmental stress and mental health, suggesting that individuals who are under greater stress—including the poor, people of color, and women—are more likely to experience mental health problems.

- **Societal reactions and labeling:** This perspective suggests that society creates individuals with mental health problems through a societal reaction process. By establishing social norms and treating as deviant those who do not subscribe to the norms, a society identifies individuals with mental health problems. Additionally, individuals identified or labeled as somehow different will assume the role prescribed to them; that is, individuals labeled as having mental health problems will behave as they would be expected to if they had the problem. Individuals labeled as having mental health problems, even though they do not behave any differently from those without problems, may also be *perceived* as behaving differently because of how they are labeled (see Box 10.1).

• **Systems/ecological perspective:** This perspective suggests that mental health problems are the result of a variety of factors that interact in a complex fashion and vary according to the uniqueness of the individual and the environment within which he or she interacts. Within the systems/ecological framework, for example, many factors that shape a person's self-concept, competence, and behaviors can be addressed, such as the person's biological characteristics; ethnicity; gender; place within the broader environment, including family, peer groups, and the neighborhood and community in which the person functions; and cultural and societal expectations.

The Systems/Ecological Perspective on Mental Health Issues

A systems/ecological perspective can include a combination of the other perspectives identified earlier as well. For example, a person may be predisposed biologically to experience mental health problems, may have suffered as a child from sexual abuse, may have had a parent who also experienced mental health problems, and currently may be in an extremely stressful living situation (e.g., experiencing an unhappy marriage, a stressful job, or financial problems). If such an individual experienced mental health problems, it would be impossible to isolate which of those factors directly caused the problems.

A systems/ecological perspective allows us to focus on *all* of the factors within an individual's past and present environment, as well as the individual's physiological characteristics, in addressing mental health problems. If we know which factors are most important, we are much more likely to be able to intervene successfully in alleviating the problems. This focus on both the individual and the individual's environment allows the social worker and the client to "map out" the critical factors most likely to account for the problems, and then to develop an intervention plan that specifically addresses those factors.

Whether one takes a mental illness perspective or a broader perspective, how and when an individual's emotional problems are identified and defined depend on a number of factors:

1. The visibility, recognizability, or persistence of inappropriate/deviant behaviors and symptoms;

2. The extent to which the person perceives the symptoms as serious;

3. The extent to which the symptoms disrupt family, work, and other activities;

BOX 10.1

DOES LABELING SHAPE OUR EXPECTATIONS OF HOW PEOPLE WILL FUNCTION?

The identification of individuals with mental health problems and the ways those problems are defined are hotly debated issues among mental health professionals. A number of years ago, psychologist David Rosenhan and his associates conducted a study that exemplifies this concern. Rosenhan (1973) and his seven associates went separately to the admissions offices of twelve psychiatric hospitals in five different states, all claiming that they were hearing voices. In every instance, they were admitted to the hospitals as patients. Immediately upon admission, they all assumed normal behavior. At least one of the researchers did not try to hide his role as a researcher—he sat on the ward and took copious notes on legal pads of all of the events going on around him.

In spite of the fact that the researchers all behaved completely normally while hospitalized, hospital professionals were unable to distinguish them from other patients. In a number of instances, however, the other patients were able to determine that they were not mentally ill. Rosenhan and his associates remained at the hospitals as patients from time periods ranging from seven to fifty-two days, with an average stay of nineteen days, before they were discharged. The diagnosis at discharge for each of them was "schizophrenia in remission" (Rosenhan 1973).

---

4. The frequency of the appearance of the signs and symptoms, or their persistence;

5. The tolerance threshold of those who are exposed to and evaluate the signs and symptoms;

6. The information available to, the knowledge of, and the cultural assumptions and understandings of the evaluator;

7. The degree to which processes that distort reality are present;

8. The presence of needs within the family/environment that conflict with the recognition of problems or the assumption of the "sick" role;

9. The possibility that competing interpretations can be assigned to the behaviors/signs once they are recognized;

10. The availability of treatment/intervention resources, their physical proximity and costs of money, time, and effort as well as costs of stigmatization and humiliation. (Mechanic 1980, 68–69)

◪ OTHER PROBLEMS RELATED TO MENTAL HEALTH

Two other problems related to mental health—homelessness and suicide—affect many individuals and their families and have escalated in recent years.

Homelessness

Increased attention has been given to the rising number of homeless persons in the United States. The first official count was taken by the United States Census Bureau in 1990. Although the count is not completely accurate since it was based on people in shelters and located on the streets during a 24-hour period, 178,828 persons were found in shelters and 49,793 on the streets. Other estimates suggest that the number of homeless is closer to 600,000 (Johnson 1995).

In earlier times in the United States, individuals who were poor and had nowhere to live were housed in poorhouses (also called almshouses) and orphanages. But the homeless population increased significantly during the Great Depression of the 1930s. It decreased when the Depression ended, with the typical homeless person (until the 1970s) an older white male who was an alcoholic living in a ''skid row'' district in an urban area. But with increased downturns in the economy and concurrent increases in the costs of housing and decreases in available, affordable housing, the homeless population has increased both in numbers and in diversity. The homeless population today includes not only white males who have problems with substance abuse but also battered women, single-parent women with children, women who are chemically dependent, men and women of color of all ages, both married and single, with and without children, often younger than white persons who are homeless, and youth who have either run away from or been pushed out of their family homes.

Current estimates indicate that 73 percent of homeless are single men, 11 percent are families with children, 9 percent are single women, and 7 percent are unrelated persons. The average age of homeless persons was 35 in 1992 and is increasingly getting younger. People of color are overrepresented in this population, with 47 percent of homeless white, 40 percent African American, 9 percent Hispanic, and 4 percent other (Burt 1992). The majority of homeless individuals were extremely poor and lived a marginal existence before becoming homeless.

Advocates of more effective services for the mentally ill, the developmentally disabled, and the chemically dependent argue that deinstitutionalization and the lack of community services have resulted in a significant increase in homelessness among these three groups. Some advocates for the homeless also indicate that being homeless increases a person's risk to become mentally ill or chemically dependent. Recent estimates show that approximately 30 percent of the homeless are mentally ill, and about 15 percent of homeless women and 45 percent of homeless men have serious problems with alcoholism or drug abuse (Burt and Cohen 1989; Koroloff and Anderson 1989).

Many homeless persons have spent time in mental hospitals, and even greater numbers have some type of mental health problem that contributes to their being homeless. In contrast, many individuals who are homeless, because of the stress of survival and the stigma associated with being homeless, develop mental health problems *after* they become homeless. In one study, researchers who tracked individuals released from a state hospital in a large Ohio metropolitan area for a six-month

The fastest-growing group of homeless is families, as housing becomes increasingly expensive. Programs for homeless families are extremely limited. Many homeless families stay in the same shelters as other homeless people. Such shelters often lack resources appropriate for families and children.

period after their release found that 36 percent became homeless during this period. Of that group, approximately 75 percent were chronically mentally ill and 15 percent were both mentally ill and substance abusers (Burt and Cohen 1989). Another study (Sosin 1989) compared homeless persons with very poor but not homeless persons. They found that 23.4 percent of the homeless persons studied had symptoms of alcoholism compared to 15 percent of never homeless persons, and that 20 percent of the homeless had previous mental hospitalizations compared to 8.7 percent among the never homeless. But of those who were homeless and had been hospitalized in mental hospitals, over one-third had been hospitalized for the first time *after* they were homeless.

Many homeless mentally ill have serious cognitive disturbances, like Joanna (at the beginning of this chapter), and are out of touch with reality, unaware of where they are going or where they have been. Their most frequent contacts with community resources are with the police and emergency psychiatric facilities. They most often remain on the streets, extremely vulnerable, until they are unable to function and are rehospitalized. For many, their lives become a pattern of homelessness and hospitalization.

Increasing numbers of individuals are becoming homeless because they have either lost their homes or cannot find affordable housing, and they lack support systems to help them become financially stable enough to find another home. Consider the following as a typical example of this trend. A young mother with two preschool children worked at a plant assembling parts for a large company. She lived in a moderately priced apartment and was able to provide child care for her children while she worked. She was laid off from her job when the company lost a major contract. The only job she was able to find was at a cafeteria, which paid just above the minimum wage. She was able to get a friend to care for her children, but could not pay the rent for her apartment. She moved in with the friend for awhile, but discovered that the friend's husband was violent toward the friend and their children. Fearing for the safety of herself and her children, she tried to find alternative housing. She had no relatives nearby, and her other friends had no space available for her family of three. She tried to obtain public (government-subsidized) housing, but learned there was a waiting list of three years. Finally, she and her children moved to the shelter at the Salvation Army. She is presently living there hoping to save money for the $450 deposit she is required to make on an apartment, although the most inexpensive apartment she has been able to find is $350/month, her take-home pay is only $700, and child care for her two children is $300.

In addition to increased risk for mental health problems such as depression and substance abuse, homeless individuals face other problems on a daily basis. Safety issues are paramount, since the homeless are easy targets for violence, including sexual assault. Other problems include what to do with worldly possessions, bathing and cleanliness, eating, access to health care and the risk for increased health problems because of exposure to the elements and poor nutrition, and difficulty in locating employment because of the lack of a telephone or address in case an interview is warranted. Elliott Liebow, a social science researcher who studied homeless women in a Washington, D.C., suburb (1993) shows how resourceful the homeless are in developing networks for survival in their daily struggle with a myriad of social services programs whose regulations often exacerbate their being homeless, rather than help them become self-sufficient enough to obtain housing.

Individuals become homeless for a multitude of reasons: loss of jobs, eviction from housing, discharge from an institution, divorce, domestic violence, a disaster such as a hurricane or flood, mental health problems, substance problems, or serious health or medical problems. Increasing numbers of homeless are people of color. In contrast to homeless whites, homeless people of color tend to be younger, better educated, homeless for shorter periods of time, and less likely to have serious psychological or substance abuse problems. Women of color are also more likely to have children with them for whom they are responsible. Different approaches are necessary to deal with different factors associated with being homeless (North and Smith 1994).

Homeless people increasingly detach from traditional social roles, such as being a family member or an employee. They reaffiliate with new groups of individuals who are in the same situation. As they re-affiliate, they become more comfortable with this new group because of the shared stigma and discrimination. Liebow writes about one woman who met her grown children regularly, taking the bus to visit them. They had no idea she was homeless. Another woman at the shelter, who had an outstanding work record, lost her job when her employer found out that she was homeless and lived at the shelter. As time goes on, the homeless become more isolated from others, more entrenched with other homeless persons, and lose touch with other social support systems that might be of help to them in alleviating their situation, such as locating employment or housing.

In 1987, the Steward B. McKinney Homeless Assistance Act established programs for funding additional low-income housing units and for the rehabilitation of older units. These programs are not only inadequately funded, but they are extremely fragmented. The twenty federal housing programs that fall under the act are located in ten different federal agencies. Local community groups competing for funding must complete a myriad of applications and meet different requirements depending on which agency is funding the project they want in their community. In addition to the programs authorized under the McKinney act, sixteen other national programs provide assistance to the homeless in some way. Most programs for the homeless concentrate on emergency shelters and do not address underlying causes. In addition to affordable housing for low-income families, other needs include increased employment, education, and job-training opportunities, allowing the homeless to accumulate assets, comprehensive physical and mental health services and substance abuse treatment, discharge planning for individuals from institutions, child care and education for homeless children, and public laws that prohibit the criminalization of sleeping and panhandling in public places (Johnson 1995).

Suicide

Suicide is a serious mental health problem in the United States, which has a higher suicide rate than many other western countries. In 1995, suicide was the eighth leading cause of death among all age groups and the third leading cause of death among teens 15 to 19. The teenage suicide rate for white males 15 to 24 has increased significantly in recent years. Suicide rates are four times higher for males than for females and almost twice as high for whites than for African Americans. Females are more likely than males to make suicide attempts. However, male suicide attempts are more likely to succeed because their methods are usually more lethal. Suicide is also increasing among elderly males, with the highest rate among males over 85. In 1988, 21 percent of all suicides in the United States were among persons over 65 (Ivanoff and Riedel, 1995).

While the majority of persons contemplate suicide at some point in their lives, persons who make suicide attempts are likely to have experienced one or more significant losses in their lives—the loss of a parent, sibling, spouse, close friend, good health, or a job. They feel helpless and hopeless and are experiencing so much pain that they do not see any options other than ending their pain. Loneliness and isolation, and lack of a stable support system and environment, are other significant factors associated with persons who attempt suicide.

Persons at risk to attempt suicide also often abuse alcohol and other drugs as a means of reducing their pain. But because alcohol and some other types of drugs are depressants, these substances tend to make a depressed person more depressed, as well as impairing the person's ability to think rationally. Poor health, particularly among the elderly, who may not see any hope of getting better and may not want to be an emotional or financial burden to anyone, also contributes to suicide among this population. Other factors that suggest a person is serious about suicide include previous attempts, a change from a depressed, hopeless perspective to suddenly seeming to get better, and giving possessions away. Suicide threats by any person should be taken seriously. Persons dealing with someone who is suicidal should locate appropriate resources that can assess the mental health of the person and intervene appropriately.

ALCOHOLISM AND CHEMICAL DEPENDENCY

Problems of alcoholism and chemical dependency can be related not only to the area of mental health, but also to developmental disabilities, child and family issues, poverty, criminal justice, and the workplace. Vulnerable populations, including women, the elderly, people of color, and gays and lesbians, are also at greater risk to experience serious problems with alcoholism and chemical dependency than other groups.

What constitutes alcoholism and drug abuse, the ways that these problems are conceptualized, and their causes are undergoing increased debate among professionals from a variety of disciplines. Historically, most attention has been directed toward alcohol abuse and alcoholism, which were until recently considered to be moral issues. The general societal perception was that persons drank too much because they were weak, and they could stop drinking if they wanted to.

While many people still hold this view, during the 1940s and 1950s attention began to focus instead on the concept that alcoholism is a disease, and that it must be treated as one might treat a person with diabetes or another chronic illness. In 1957 the American Medical Association recognized alcoholism as a disease, and this concept is well-established today. One definition of alcoholism, for example, views it as a chronic condition, meaning it is treatable but incurable; progressive, meaning it becomes worse if the drinking does not stop; and fatal, since if it is untreated, death can result.

Although debate continues on whether alcoholism should be viewed as an individual disease, a family or societal disease, or an individual, family, or societal problem, there are some advantages to the disease model. First, persons and their families are more likely to accept the alcoholism and become involved in an intervention program if they view the alcoholism as a disease rather than as a moral weakness or a social problem. Second, conceptualizing alcoholism as a disease also allows for coverage for treatment and hospitalization by insurance companies and public health care programs. Because of recent legislation in many states, the serious abuse of other drugs also must be treated as a disease. But because use of drugs other than alcohol more often involves illegal and/or counterculture activities, there has been much more reluctance to consider the abuse of drugs other than alcohol as a disease.

Alcoholism and the abuse of other drugs are denied as problems affecting them by many substance abusers and their families, who define a substance abuser in many ways—as someone who takes one more drink or drug than they or their family member takes; as someone who only drinks excessive amounts of hard liquor and not beer or wine as they do; as someone who uses more dangerous drugs and not marijuana, which they use; or as someone who drinks and uses every morning or every day and not only evenings or weekends, as they do. More recent definitions of alcoholism and chemical dependency focus on the personal implications of the drinking or drug use rather than the amount or frequency.

Alcoholism, for example, has been defined as any use of alcohol that results or interferes with personal life—including school, jobs, family, friends, health, or the law—or spiritual life (Royce 1989, 10). Definitions of drug abuse are similar.

Although the abuse of alcohol is considered more socially acceptable than the abuse of other drugs, it is increasingly difficult to separate abuse of alcohol and alcoholism from the abuse of other drugs and chemical dependency. Some experts in the field prefer to keep the two separate to call attention to the fact that alcohol is still the most widely misused drug and that it, too, has serious individual and societal costs. But others point out that 80 percent of persons under age 20 and 60 percent of persons under age 40 abuse more than one substance. Current research on addiction also shows that many individuals treated for one type of **substance abuse** stop using that substance and "cross-addict" to another drug. Thus, persons in the field of chemical dependency often refer to the substance a person has abused as his or her "drug of choice" and to those who abuse more than one drug as "polyaddicts."

Other experts in the field of chemical dependency and alcoholism conceptualize the problem as one of **addiction,** which can be defined as a "physical and/or psychological dependence upon mood changing substances, including, but not limited to, alcohol, drugs, pills, food, sex, or money" (Parkside Medical Services Corporation 1988). Some experts believe that treatment should focus on addiction and eliminating addictive behaviors in all areas of a person's life, including food, work, and relationships as well as drugs.

Commonly Abused Substances

Alcohol, the most commonly abused substance, is most often viewed as a depressant, although it can also be a stimulant, and, for some individuals, a hallucinogen. Other depressants include sedatives, such as sleeping pills, tranquilizers, and pain killers. Women and persons who have experienced or are experiencing chronic pain are two groups more at risk to abuse depressants than other groups.

Narcotics such as opium and its derivatives, morphine and heroin, are also highly addictive. Legally, cocaine is considered a narcotic, but it often acts more like a stimulant, creating a high in its users. Crack, a relatively inexpensive cocaine-based drug, has a similar but much more euphoric and highly addictive effect. Because of its easy availability and highly addictive nature, crack has resulted in high increases in crime, overdoses, prostitution, AIDS, and homelessness. Recent publicity has also focused on "crack" babies, who are born addicted and at risk to die during the first year of their lives or to survive with serious physical and emotional problems. Stimulants that are often abused include caffeine—legal but not as safe as was once thought—nicotine found in tobacco, and amphetamines such as speed.

Illicit drugs also include the hallucinogens, such as LSD, and marijuana, the most commonly used. One group of substances that is abused and often overlooked is inhalants. Use of inhalants is especially prevalent among Latino youth, and often results in retardation or death. A wide variety of inhalants are used, including petroleum products such as gasoline, freon, aerosol products, paint, glue, and typewriter correction fluid. Amyl nitrate and butyl nitrate, commonly called "poppers," are also inhalants.

Social and Economic Costs of Substance Abuse

While it is difficult to estimate the number of individuals who are dependent on alcohol or other drugs, current estimates suggest that 36 to 43 million persons in the United States, or 15 to 18 percent of the population, will become dependent on at least one drug during their lifetime (Royce 1989). The majority of media attention is devoted to the abuse of drugs other than alcohol, primarily cocaine, crack, and heroin. Although it is difficult to obtain accurate numbers, recent national studies suggest that there are ten million regular users of cocaine and that 25 million Americans have tried cocaine at least once.

Alcohol remains the most common drug of choice for most drug abusers in the United States. It is estimated that there are 15 million alcoholics in the United States, and that 50 million Americans are affected directly by alcohol abuse by a family member. Most people's image of an alcoholic is the skid row bum—old, male, unkempt, unemployed, living on the streets, derelict. In reality, only 3 percent of alcoholics can be characterized this way. About 45 percent of alcoholics are in professional or managerial positions, 25 percent are white-collar workers, and 30 percent are manual laborers. Physicians, air traffic controllers, airline pilots, law enforcement officers, attorneys, and members of the clergy all have high rates of alcoholism (Royce 1989).

Similar patterns are also found among the family members of alcoholics and abusers of other drugs. Studies have found that 25 percent of males and 10 percent of females who grow up in families where their parents abused either alcohol or other drugs become substance abusers themselves. Even those who do not develop substance abuse problems themselves often develop other addictive behaviors or experience emotional problems. Although fewer women repeat the pattern of substance abuse, they are much more likely to select a mate who is a substance abuser. Royce (1989) surveyed alcohol-related literature and journals, which reported that alcohol was involved in 6 percent of child abuse cases, 40 percent of forcible rapes, 80 percent of spouse abuse cases, 8 percent of homicides, and 90 percent of incest situations.

As abuse of drugs becomes more widespread, the implications are becoming more obvious, more costly, and of greater concern. Costs include not only intervention for alcoholics and other substance abusers but also lost productivity, motor vehicle losses from accidents, and property losses from violent crimes. But cost estimates typically do not include personal costs such as physical and emotional injury and loss of life. The economic costs of alcoholism and alcohol abuse in the United States have been estimated at $120 billion in 1986 by the United States General Accounting Office and $142 billion in 1986 by the University of California at Berkeley School of Health. In 1987 the National Institute of Drug Abuse estimated that $80 billion was lost from the abuse of other drugs. Furthermore, Americans spent an estimated $71.9 billion on alcohol, $60 billion on cocaine, and $80 billion on other drugs in 1987 (Royce 1989). General Motors estimates that consumers pay an additional $242 for each automobile that they purchase due to workers who have problems with substance abuse. Other studies have shown that work productivity also declines for family members of the abuser: absenteeism rates have been found to be five times greater than for persons from families without substance abuse problems.

At-Risk Populations and Substance Abuse

Although substance abuse can affect anyone, some groups of people are more at risk than others. These groups include adolescents, the elderly, people of color, women, and children.

Adolescents

While alcohol abuse and chemical dependency are widespread among all age groups, their increased use among adolescents has caused concern. Recent reports show that use of drugs other than alcohol is decreasing among teens, but alcohol use continues to increase. Researchers who conducted a study in 1990 found that 40 percent of high school seniors had gotten drunk at least once within the two weeks prior to being surveyed. The study also found that 3.5 million 12 to 17-year-olds had tried marijuana at least once, and that one-third of the teens surveyed said they were regular users (Lipman 1990). Whereas the death rate for other age groups has decreased, the death rate for adolescents has increased significantly in recent years, with most deaths due to traffic accidents and suicides and related to abuse of alcohol or other drugs. Use of alcohol and other drugs by adolescents is often viewed as a way to be an adult—a "rite of passage" from childhood to adulthood—and part of the risk-taking behavior common among adolescents. Researchers who conducted a study in

1992 found a decrease in the numbers of individuals in the United States who believe that using drugs is not harmful for all age groups, but particularly for adolescents. Only 54 percent of 12 to 17-year-olds believed that there was high risk associated with trying cocaine once or twice (U.S. Department of Health and Human Services 1994).

But heavy substance abuse and addiction among adolescents is more often found among those experiencing other problems, such as survivors of child sexual abuse, gay and lesbian teens experiencing discrimination and oppression, and individuals experiencing depression. These adolescents turn to drinking and drugging to deaden their pain, as a form of self-medication so they will feel better, or as a way to relate more comfortably to peers.

The Elderly

Substance abuse, particularly alcoholism, among the elderly is also a problem. This age group, like adolescents and young adults, also has a high death rate due to alcoholism, due primarily to chronic alcohol-related diseases such as cirrhosis of the liver, digestive diseases, and hepatitis. Again, factors associated with substance abuse of this group include loneliness and isolation and use of substances as coping mechanisms to deaden the pain they are experiencing because of physical or emotional problems in their present or past.

People of Color

Some ethnic groups are more at risk to abuse alcohol and drugs and to experience serious problems because of the abuse. African Americans, for example, are three times as likely to die as a result of alcoholism than whites, even though their actual rates of alcohol use are less than for whites, because of the interactive effects of oppression on access to healthy food and health care. The situation is similar for Latinos (Johnson 1995).

Native Americans have the highest incidence of alcoholism of any ethnic group in the United States. They also have high rates of alcohol-related homicide, suicide, and serious car accidents. It has been estimated that as many as fifty percent of Native American children are born with either fetal alcohol syndrome or fetal alcohol effect, medical diagnoses of conditions at birth that usually result in serious developmental disabilities caused by the mother's consumption of alcohol during pregnancy. It is unclear whether this is due to factors associated with unemployment and poverty or different cultural patterns in the use of drugs and alcohol, or some combination of factors.

Members of marginalized groups who are outside of the mainstream of society are more at risk to abuse substances as coping mechanisms to overcome feelings of despair and hopelessness resulting from oppression and discrimination. Additionally, in some communities drug pushers can easily tempt children, often from impoverished families, to become drug runners so that they can make large amounts of money quickly. While often still too young to realize the implications of using drugs, they begin experimenting with the drugs they are delivering and become addicted themselves. The heightened risk of some ethnic groups for suffering the personal, emotional, and economic consequences of substance abuse raises a number of issues about our society, since nonmembers of these groups are most often those who oversee large-scale production and sale of drugs and reap the economic profits.

To be effective, interventions for people of color must be culturally relevant and sensitive. For example, while participation in Alcoholics Anonymous groups may be highly effective for some individuals, if group membership is largely white, people of color may not feel comfortable participating. Additionally, some cultures are reluctant to share any personal information outside of their families. Many Asians, for example, have been socialized to believe that personal problems they experience, like substance abuse, bring shame to their families, and should not be discussed with people outside the family.

Women
Recent estimates suggest that one-third of all alcoholics in the United States are women, and that six million women are addicted to drugs other than alcohol, with the largest increases among younger women. Women who abuse substances have different issues than men. They are more likely to abuse legal drugs, such as tranquilizers and sedatives, than male abusers. They are more likely to become addicted to multiple drugs and use drugs in isolation rather than in social settings. They are also more likely to have another family member who is a substance abuser and to have experienced rape, incest, or other sexual assault.

Women, however, are much less likely to seek treatment than men, even though they experience more health problems related to their substance abuse and their lives are often more disrupted (Burman and Allen-Meares 1991). Female substance abusers experience greater stigma than males. Researchers in one study found that 23 percent of women received opposition from friends and family when entering substance abuse treatment programs compared to 2 percent of men (Royce 1989). Women are also less likely to have support from family members in treatment. Other studies show that in families where alcoholism is a problem for male spouses, women remain in the relationship in 90 percent of situations. In families where alcoholism is a problem for female spouses, men, however, remain in the relationship only 10 percent of the time. Substance abuse has also resulted in increases in AIDS, prostitution, and homelessness among women.

Although there are few substance abuse intervention programs designed specifically for women, studies have found that they face different issues than men. They are more likely to experience depression and to abuse substances as a way to cope with the depression. They are also more likely to have been sexually abused, and repressed memories of sexual abuse often surface when women have been sober for a period of time. Recovery issues for women must include a recognition of client strengths and the impact of oppression on women, financial disadvantages, job skills, and setting healthy boundaries in and establishing positive and healthy relationships (Nelson-Zlupko, Kaufman, and Morrison Dove 1995). Women also often need assistance with child care, transportation, support in parenting, housing, education, and employment to escape from the pressures related to substance abuse (Finkelstein, 1994).

Children

Alcoholism and chemical dependency have serious impacts on children (see additional discussion in Chapters 12 and 13). Increased attention has been given recently to the large numbers of infants born addicted or impaired because of their mothers' addiction or misuse of alcohol or other drugs during pregnancy. Five thousand infants born each year to addicted mothers in the United States have fetal alcohol syndrome, now the third leading cause of birth defects associated with mental retardation. Thousands more babies born to mothers who abused alcohol or other drugs during their pregnancies have other less serious disabilities.

Child welfare advocates suggest that the United States has not yet begun to experience the long-term effects of having such a large number of children born to women who are drug addicts. A recent study by the Alcohol and Drug and Mental Health Administration, for example, found that 11 percent of all babies born in 28 cities in the United States were exposed to some type of illicit drug. One urban Michigan hospital identified 43 percent of infants delivered there as being prenatally exposed to drugs (Select Committee on Children, Youth and Families 1990). Estimates are that it will cost the United States $15 billion each year to care for addicts' offspring during the first five years of their lives simply to prepare them to enter the public schools (Associated Press, 1 December 1989).

Other Factors Associated with Substance Abuse

Reasons why substance abuse occurs follow the general reasons why emotional problems occur among individuals. New research suggests that there may be genetic factors associated with substance abuse. These include hereditary connections. Some researchers believe that substances are metabolized or broken down differently for some individuals, resulting in an inability of the body to eliminate some chemicals that then not only build up in the body but also serve as stimulants for even greater use when the addictive substance is used again.

Other researchers suggest that for some individuals, substance abuse is a form of self-medication, or a way for them to attempt to regulate their emotions or the pain that they are experiencing. Persons who have been sexually abused, have experienced a significant personal loss or series of losses, or are depressed may use alcohol or other drugs to moderate their moods or try to deaden the pain they are experiencing (see Box 10.2). Other substance abuse experts suggest that persons use drugs to experience excitement, fit in with peers, alleviate pressure, or improve their performance along one or more dimensions; others see it as behavior learned from family members.

BOX 10.2

A YOUNG ADULT'S STORY

Three years of drinking pushed a seemingly outgoing, good student to the depths of depression and despair. This is her story:

I began ninth grade excited about starting high school. I was like most other teenagers—I wanted to make good grades and be accepted by my teachers and peers. The peers I sought out were popular, cheerleaders, and on the student council, and they seemed to know everyone. I liked being included in their parties and other activities.

My mom asked me questions about my friends and the rules their parents had for them, but she usually let me go with them if I was waiting for her when she picked me up. At games and the other teen hangouts there was lots of drinking and it looked like people drinking were having a good time. One night I stayed over at a friend's house and we went to a party. When I was offered a beer I drank it. When the alcohol hit my body, I found I wanted more. That night I drank 7 beers. I was 14 years old.

After that, I drank almost every weekend. I drank to be accepted, escape day-to-day pressures of my home and school life, and forget the pain from some experiences I had while growing up. When I drank, I usually laughed and clowned around a lot. People told me how much fun I was and what a great sense of humor I had. I felt relaxed and accepted when I drank.

I continued to drink on weekends, and my activities with my friends usually centered around sneaking beer or other alcohol from our parents' pantries or having older friends buy it for us. We drank it at games, parties, or at each other's houses after the parents were asleep. Soon we went to the mall to meet older guys. We had no sense of risk. Our parents dropped us at the mall, then we hopped in some guy's car to go to a party where everyone was drunk. Then we were dropped back at the mall in time for our parents to pick us up. We sprayed ourselves with perfume, chewed gum, and somehow managed to hide our drinking from our parents most of the time. I often felt guilty about my drinking and worried about what my parents would do if they found out, but I also enjoyed it. I felt grown up, and my friends enjoyed telling me how hilarious I had

been with all of my antics. Boys paid a lot of attention to me and I discovered that it was much easier to relate to them when I had been drinking.

I became more popular and was elected to the student council. I rationalized that drinking even helped my grades, since the few times I decided that I was drinking too much and stopped for a week or two, I became depressed and my grades went down. I became more involved in school activities, got a part-time job at the mall, and partied even more. When my parents confronted me with their suspicions about my drinking, I either managed to convince them that everyone else was drinking except me or to tell them that I had a little bit now and then, but didn't every teenager?

During my junior year I made the dance team. I thought all my feelings of insecurity and my drive to fit in would be over, and that I could slow my drinking. To my surprise, being on the dance team meant even more pressure. I had to maintain my popularity, be more involved in school activities, and work even harder to be sure that I wasn't surpassed by the many girls who I thought were almost all smarter, prettier, and had more personality than I did. Soon I was drinking in the locker room in the morning before dance practice "just to wake me up and help me stretch better," in the parking lot or the bathroom after lunch "just to make it through the afternoon," or at my job "just to make it until closing," and always on the weekends.

I still could hide my drinking from teachers and my parents. I sat in the back of the classroom, answered questions, and did my homework and handed it in on time. I always gave my parents a plausible explanation what I would be doing when I went out and I was lucky enough to be where I said I would be when they checked up on me. When I didn't drink a lot, I came home at or before my curfew. When I did drink a lot, I stayed overnight at friends' homes. I began blacking out at parties and waking up at a friends' house and not remembering how I got there. I rode with drivers who were drunk and I would drive when I was drunk too. I also began to get involved with a lot of guys who I never would have gotten involved with if I had been sober. I got really scared about getting pregnant, since I knew someone could take advantage of me during my blackouts.

At that point my drinking wasn't fun anymore, but I couldn't stop. In fact, I began drinking more and more. It was nothing for me to drink 16 to 17 cans of beer all by myself in one night. All of my friends could still drink and enjoy it but it started getting me in trouble. My grades went down and I started skipping school. I became edgy and worried about everything. I started having fights with my friends and my family over little things. The drinking was controlling me. The more I drank, the worse I felt, and the worse I felt, the more I needed to drink to ease my pain. What had started out to be fun was now completely out of my control.

During the summer my parents suspected something was really wrong. I started seeing a psychologist, and both she and my parents tried to convince me that my drinking was a problem and that I was using it to escape the pain I had about some of the things that had happened in my life. I got angry at them and refused to see the psychologist. I began to rebel more and more. One night a party I was at turned into a brawl. I got knocked out when I tried to break up a fight. I left with a friend and a guy I barely knew. I woke up the next morning in the guy's apartment, and couldn't remember what had happened. Driving home I was still so drunk that I had to stop and get out of the car to read the street signs, and I was only a half mile from home. I told my parents we'd stayed up all night talking at my girlfriend's house and I slept the whole next day.

Gradually I stopped caring what everyone thought of me and trying to hide my drinking from my parents. Finally one weekend I stayed out all night when I had a midnight curfew. When I came home and got grounded, I ran away and stayed with a friend for 3 days, mostly drinking. When my friend went to work, I got a six-pack of beer and drank it alone. When I came home my parents grounded me for a month and took away my car. They told me I had to see the psychologist. I was going to leave home for good, but I knew that I had reached a dead end and that my life was out of control. I didn't care about myself, my parents, or anything any more. Life had no purpose.

When I was confronted with my drinking again, I decided to enter a treatment program. I was tired of fighting, and at that time I thought that anything, even treatment, would be better than living at home and being nagged about my behavior. I now realize that entering treatment was the most important risk I have ever taken. The 6 weeks that I spent there were some of the hardest days of my life, but they were also some of the best. I was able to get rid of some of the pain, hurt, and anger that I had stored up for so many years. I learned new ways to communicate, share my feelings, and how to have fun while I was sober instead of drunk. I realized not only had I hurt myself, but also my family and other people who cared about me. My whole family took part in my treatment and we all grew together. They began going to Alanon while I went to Alcoholics Anonymous.

After I got out of treatment, I continued to attend AA regularly. I had found a place where I fit in. AA members understood how I felt and where I was coming from. Each day got better for me. I became more content and gained self-confidence. I also found the peace I had never had before I got in touch with myself and met many wonderful people in the process. Today, I am a recovering alcoholic and have now been sober for two years. Finding sobriety at 17 has meant a whole new world for me. I have fallen in love with a wonderful person who understands my need for sobriety, and we are building our life together. My family and I enjoy being together. I am a college sophomore and plan to attend graduate school and work with children. I have goals and a sense of purpose I didn't have before. Although life is still difficult, I have learned to take things as they come, one day at a time. I am grateful that I had the courage to change myself.

Source: Journal entry by an anonymous student, University of Texas at Austin, 1991.

Intervention for Substance Abusers and Their Families

Initial efforts to address problems of alcoholism and substance abuse were aimed at moral rehabilitation, prohibition, and temperance. The most significant breakthrough in the alcohol field came in 1935 with the establishment of **Alcoholics Anonymous (AA),** a self-help group for alcoholics. The beginnings of AA were in Akron, Ohio, when a New York stockbroker named Bill W. and an Akron physician named Dr. Bob met and discovered they could maintain sobriety by supporting one another and following a formal program of gradual recovery, which has since been incorporated into the twelve steps of AA. During the next several decades, as AA continued to grow in numbers and in popularity, various physicians also developed research and intervention efforts that shifted attention from the moral concept of alcoholism to the disease concept. The formation of education and advocacy groups such as the National Council on Alcoholism in 1944 also aided in drawing increased attention to alcoholics' problems.

But needed federal attention to the problem of alcoholism did not occur until 1970, when Senator Harold Hughes of Iowa (a recovering alcoholic at the time of his election) advocated for the passage of the Comprehensive Alcohol Abuse and Alcoholism Prevention, Treatment and Rehabilitation Act. This act provided financial assistance to states and communities to establish treatment, education, research, and training programs and established the National Institute on Alcohol Abuse and Alcoholism. The act also provided for the withdrawal of federal funding from any hospital that refused to treat alcoholics.

Much has been learned about intervention approaches, and programs have expanded significantly since the passage of the act. Although early intervention models focused on inpatient hospitalization and participation in Alcoholics Anonymous, research has shown that these programs are not effective with all substance abusers. Different types of clients require different intervention approaches. Some clients are so entrenched in their substance abuse that they require hospitalization, often undergoing detoxification before they can effectively begin treatment. Most hospitalization programs range from 30 to 90 days. Although many experts suggest that 30 days is not long enough for many individuals to really get into a recovery program well enough to stay sober after being released from the hospital, insurance companies increasingly are limiting hospital stays for substance abuse to this time period or requiring that treatment be on an outpatient basis. Hospitalization is usually incorporated with other treatment programs, including community-based self-help groups such as Alcoholics Anonymous or Narcotics Anonymous. Individuals released from hospital programs are usually encouraged to continue attending these meetings, as well as hospital aftercare programs, usually held evenings and weekends for periods of time up to one year after leaving the hospital.

Other programs provide day or partial-day hospitalization, allowing clients to return to their homes in the evenings. Still others offer outpatient treatment programs, with intense participation several evenings during the week and often weekdays as well. These programs allow individuals to continue employment, child care, and living at home.

Proponents of outpatient and partial hospitalization programs say that clients have to deal with the pressures of day-to-day living while receiving support from the program, rather than being placed in a sheltered environment away from the previous pressures and individuals with whom they abused substances.

The majority of chemical dependence programs in which social workers are employed incorporate a family systems model and also provide psychoeducational experiences for other family members in addition to the client. These experiences involve educational and therapy sessions with other clients and their families as well as individual, group, and family therapy.

Other chemical dependence programs focus on a more cognitive/behavioral approach, particularly with adolescents and persons in the criminal justice system. These approaches focus on consequences for abusing substances and other inappropriate behaviors, and on reinforcers for appropriate actions. An increased number of juvenile and adult corrections programs, including jails and prisons, include substance abuse treatment. But services are often limited in both duration and numbers served, in spite of the large numbers of inmates who are incarcerated because of substance-abuse-related crimes, and, without treatment, are likely to be incarcerated again, often for more serious crimes. Agencies that serve clients with a wide range of problems are incorporating special programs targeted at substance abuse. Many child protective services agencies, for example, which work with abusive and neglectful parents, indicate that the substantial increase in child maltreatment is largely due to substance abuse, and have developed treatment programs for their clients. Such programs also incorporate information on parenting and the impact of substance abuse on children.

Few inpatient or residential programs exist for women with children that also provide care for the children. Several innovative programs in the United States provide treatment for both women and their children together, allowing for modeling of parenting skills, working through communication problems and other family dynamics, and providing a safe, supportive environment for both the mothers and their children with others in similar circumstances so they do not need to go through the added stress of reuniting with their children when the treatment is over. Increasingly, substance abuse programs also are having to address issues of dual diagnosis, or those clients who have other emotional problems in addition to substance abuse. Often, an individual will go through treatment for chemical dependence and, after maintaining sobriety for an extensive period of time, return to the mental health system for additional help in dealing with other emotional problems such as depression or family-of-origin issues, including sexual abuse.

DEVELOPMENTAL DISABILITIES

Generally, the term **developmental disability** refers to developmental problems, such as mental retardation or cerebral palsy, that developed before adulthood. Although in the past these persons were often referred to as ''mentally retarded'' or ''mentally handicapped,'' the terms *developmentally disabled* or *physically challenged* are preferred because they are viewed as less negative. But because individuals have specific preferences about such terms, it is best to ask the person how he or she wants to be addressed.

In 1984, the United States Congress passed the Developmental Disabilities Assistance and Bill of Rights Act (PL 98–527), which defined developmental disability as follows:

> A severe, chronic disability of a person which (a) is attributable to a mental or physical impairment or combination of mental and physical impairments; (b) is manifested before the person attains age twenty-two; (c) is likely to continue indefinitely; (d) results in substantial functional limitations in three or more of the following areas of major life activity: (i) self-care, (ii) receptive and expressive language, (iii) learning, (iv) mobility, (v) self-direction, (vi) capacity for independent living, and (vii) economic self-sufficiency; and (e) reflects the person's need for a combination and sequence of special, interdisciplinary, or generic care, treatment, or other services which are of lifelong or extended duration and are individually planned and coordinated. (PL 98–527, Title V, 1984)

This definition was expanded on in the Americans with Disabilities Act (ADA), passed in 1990, which included persons with AIDS, substance abusers, and individuals with mental disorders.

Although over 75 percent of those classified as having developmental disabilities are mentally impaired, other individuals also may be so classified due to cerebral palsy; epilepsy; autism; spina bifida; or speech, hearing, vision, or orthopedic disabilities. Other individuals may have learning disabilities, such as dyslexia (a reading disability in which symbols are perceived differently than they are) or attention deficit disorder (an inability to pay attention to an activity for a reasonable amount of time that may also include hyperactivity). Of those individuals classified as mentally disabled, 75 percent are only mildly disabled and can be educated to function fairly independently or with some supervision; 20 percent are moderately disabled; and only 5 percent are profoundly disabled and need constant care and supervision.

Factors Associated with Developmental Disabilities

The types of disabilities vary as much as the factors associated with them, and researchers still are uncertain why some types of disabilities occur. But a number of factors are associated with developmental disabilities based on current knowledge and research:

• **Hereditary and fetal development factors:** Factors such as metabolic disorders, brain malfunctions, or chromosomal abnormalities can result in disabilities such as Tay-Sachs disease and Down syndrome.

• **Prenatal factors:** Chemical and alcohol addiction, radiation, and infections such as rubella (a form of measles) can result in disabilities, as can fetal malnutrition if mothers do not receive adequate prenatal care.

• **Perinatal factors:** Premature birth, trauma at birth, and infections transmitted during birth, such as herpes, can result in disabilities.

• **Postnatal factors:** Postnatal infections such as meningitis, trauma as a result of automobile accidents or child abuse, lack of oxygen during illness or an accident, and nutritional deficiencies can result in developmental disabilities. Environmental factors, such as lead poisoning, parents with severe emotional problems, or parental deprivation, also are important factors that often lead to developmental disabilities. Children who do not receive appropriate nurturance, especially during their early years, are often developmentally delayed, and if intervention does not occur soon enough, mental retardation, learning disabilities, or other types of problems can result and may be permanent.

Specific causes of developmental disabilities often cannot be identified. Many parents who give birth to children with such problems often spend a great deal of time—sometimes their entire lives—blaming themselves because their children have disabilities. Research has enabled the early identification of many types of disabilities, such as phenylketonuria (PKU), which results in retardation. A simple test at birth can allow for immediate treatment, which has virtually eliminated this problem in most western countries. More attention needs to be given to understanding how and why such disabilities occur.

Researchers interviewing clients with disabilities who participated in social services programs found that social services providers often played a significant role in *disempowering* clients rather than empowering them to meet their own needs. For example, gainful employment and housing were identified by clients as their major needs if they were to live in a community setting rather than an institution (deinstitutionalization will be discussed later in this chapter). Yet 70 percent of clients interviewed said that the biggest obstacle they faced regarding employment was discouragement from their social service providers regarding seeking jobs (Rapp and Kisthardt 1993).

The Americans with Disabilities Act

In 1986, the National Council on the Handicapped published its report, *Toward Independence*, which provided a comprehensive national approach to addressing problems of persons with disabilities. The Americans with Disabilities Act (P.L. 101–336) passed through both the United States House and Senate with little opposition and was quickly signed by President George Bush. Prior to the passage of the ADA, almost anyone could discriminate against a person with a disability. A major problem for many persons who experience mental illness or developmental disability has been the denial of basic rights that others take for granted. The ADA bans discrimination based on disabilities among private employers with a workforce of more than fifteen persons, public accommodations, public services, transportation, and telecommunications. The act also extends protections included in the 1964 Civil Rights Act to an estimated 43 million people with physical and mental disabilities to include heart disease, diabetes, emotional illnesses, drug addiction, alcoholism, and persons with AIDS. The act requires public places—including nongovernment entities such as restaurants, hotels and motels, business places, and other facilities that are used by the general public—to provide reasonable accommodations to persons with disabilities, in terms of both service and employment. The act mandates the elimination of discrimination and establishes standards and mechanisms for enforcement.

This act significantly changed the way that persons with disabilities have been treated historically. Since the Elizabethan Poor Laws, persons with disabilities have been viewed as in need of public assistance, and definitions of who is disabled have been used primarily for determining eligibility for public assistance. The ADA empowers persons with disabilities to be less stigmatized by removing the numerous barriers that have existed and often forced them to remain isolated. Individuals with disabilities can insist on reasonable accommodations, as can their family members. For example, a mother of a child with a disability cannot be passed over for a job because the employer is worried that she will need to spend additional time with the child and miss extensive work time (Orlin 1995).

As a result of the act, states and local communities have had to establish special transportation systems, place elevators and ramps in buildings, and install special telephones for persons with hearing impairments as well as for those in wheelchairs. Still more needs to be done, and additional education is also needed. One disabilities advocate, for example, gives the following report about her trip to check out accessibility at a large mall, which the mall manager claimed met ADA guidelines:

> There were numerous parking spaces for people with disabilities. However, they were in an area of the parking lot which was poorly lighted, and the closest entrance, some distance away, had heavy doors that could only be used by someone on crutches or in a wheelchair if someone came along to open them for you. There also was an elevator to go from the first to the second floor; however, it was located on the opposite side of the mall from this entrance. The one restroom that had been remodeled to meet ADA guidelines was not close to either this entrance or the elevator. The telephone that had been installed was in still another direction from all of the other facilities. The elevator and restrooms were marked in Braille, but the signs were made so poorly that it was impossible to distinguish the markings from each other. The manager had not considered the implications of these upgrades and has agreed to make changes so they are more accessible to persons with disabilities (Barrera 1995).

The quality of life for those who are mentally or developmentally impaired increasingly rests on the fate of federal and state legislation and funding, which decreased markedly since the 1980s and is facing even more serious cutbacks during the mid-1990s. Rather than categorical funding for mental health programs that largely ensure funds for specific client groups, the current trend is toward block grants to states that allow each state to determine how it should spend its funds. It will be up to advocacy groups representing these constituents to try to ensure that resources are allocated to these groups. It is clear that we have both the technology and the capacity to maintain those with mental health problems and developmental disabilities in community settings. But it is also clear that to meet the needs of these individuals adequately, substantial and continuing resources will be required.

The Americans with Disabilities Act also advocated for supported employment of individuals with disabilities. Supported employment includes employment for wages and benefits in workplaces that integrate both persons with and without disabilities and continuous on-the-job training to reinforce job skills. Community-based programs in many areas have obtained successful employment for clients with disabilities in recycling centers, mail centers, offices, food service settings, and landscaping and park programs. One program has successfully placed its clients as child care aides in centers that mainstream children with disabilities, giving them a chance not only to work but also to be successful role models for the children (Rapp, Shira, and Kisthardt 1993).

The act has many implications for social service providers and social workers. Services must be accessible and individuals cannot be denied participation based on their disability, nor can they be required to participate in a program because of their disability. (Orlin 1995). Social workers should ensure that clients have access to individuals who can meet their needs; for example, clients with hearing problems need social workers who sign or interpreters to help them communicate. Additionally, social service agencies need to provide employment opportunities for persons with disabilities (and *not* just in agencies that work with persons with disabilities). Jobs can be structured with special equipment and accommodations such as part-time work and job-sharing. Table 10.1 suggests appropriate employment interventions, which are based on the systems/ecological framework, at levels ranging from the individual to the community. Successful programs for persons with disabilities require consistent advocacy and community support if people with disabilities are to receive the services they need.

Programs for Persons with Developmental Disabilities

Efforts to improve conditions for the developmentally disabled continued to focus on institutionalization through the 1950s. Greater attention shifted to this population when parent advocates in 1950 formed the Association for Retarded Children, which later became the Association for Retarded Citizens. This group has been instrumental in advocating for national and state legislation and improved conditions for the developmentally disabled. Additional attention to the needs of the disabled came during President John F. Kennedy's administration. Kennedy's developmentally disabled sister, Rosemary, received extensive publicity, and he established the Presidential Panel on Mental Retardation during his term, which called for additional research and the development of a system that provided continuity in caring for the disabled. The Community Mental Centers Act, passed in 1963, included funding for research and facilities for this population.

TABLE 10.1	SAMPLE EMPLOYMENT INTERVENTIONS AT MULTIPLE LEVELS FOR PEOPLE WITH SEVERE MENTAL ILLNESS

Level	Sample Interventions
Individual	Career counseling Volunteer work opportunities Job placement Supported work
Group	Fairweather Lodge Job clubs Consumer-owned and consumer-operated businesses Consumer self-help groups
Organization	Make employment the number one agency priority Include considerations of work in all case reviews Set rewards for staff who get the most people employed Convert day treatment program to prevocational program Provide vocationally oriented staff training Put aside agency funds for transportation and clothing for work
Service system	Assign vocational rehabilitation counselors to treatment teams Increase funding for supported work programs Liberalize vocational rehabilitation eligibility criteria Include vocational content in core discipline degree programs
Community	Public educational campaign to reduce stigma in employment (for example, media exposure to consumer achievement) Chamber of commerce—initiated jobs program for clients

Source: C. Rapp, W. Shera, and W. Kisthardt, "Research Strategies for Consumer Empowerment of People with Severe Mental Illness," *Social Work* 38(6): 731 (1993). Copyright 1993, National Association of Social Workers, Inc.

◢ CHANGING VIEWS TOWARD MENTAL HEALTH PROBLEMS, SUBSTANCE ABUSE, AND DEVELOPMENTAL DISABILITIES

As mentioned earlier in this chapter, the treatment of individuals with mental health problems has undergone considerable change. Historically, the fate of the mentally ill depended on their family. In most cases, individuals remained at home and were at the mercy of family members. Although in some instances individuals were treated humanely, many mentally ill and retarded persons were chained in attics and cellars, and sometimes they were killed. When there were no family members to provide for them, they were often transported to the next town and abandoned. Later, almshouses were established (see Chapter 1). Some mentally ill or developmentally disabled individuals were placed in jails if they were deemed too dangerous for the almshouse. Most alcoholics also were jailed, and their family members, unable to care for themselves, were sent to almshouses.

The Pennsylvania colony's hospital, established in 1751 for the sick poor and "the reception and care of lunatics," was the first hospital in the United States that provided care for the mentally ill, although treatment of mentally ill patients was little better than it had been in jails and almshouses. Individuals deemed mentally ill were assigned to hospital cellars and placed in bolted cells, where they were watched over by attendants carrying whips, which were used freely. Sightseers paid admission fees on Sundays to watch the cellar activities.

From Inhumane to Moral Treatment

During the late 1700s, people throughout the world began to seek better approaches to address the needs of the mentally ill. What mental health historians describe as the first of four revolutions in caring for the mentally ill actually began in France rather than the United States, with a shift from inhumane to moral treatment. Phillippe Pinel, director of two hospitals in Paris, ordered "striking off the chains" of the patients in 1793, first at the Bicetre Hospital for the Insane in Paris. Pinel advocated the establishment of a philosophy of **moral treatment,** which included offering patients hope, guidance, and support, and treatment with respect in small, family-like institutions.

The moral treatment movement soon spread to America. Benjamin Rush, a signer of the Declaration of Independence, wrote the first American text on psychiatry, advocating that the mentally ill had a moral right to humane treatment. But it was not until the 1840s, through the efforts of Dorothea Dix, a schoolteacher, that the mentally ill in the United States actually began to receive more humane treatment (see Chapter 1). Dix became aware of the plight of the mentally ill through teaching Sunday school for a group of patients in a Massachusetts hospital. Appalled by what she saw, Dix gave speeches, wrote newspaper articles, and met with government officials to bring attention to the inhumane and abusive treatment she observed in the many facilities she visited. As a result of her efforts, a bill was introduced in Congress to use the proceeds from the sale of western land to purchase land for use in caring for the mentally ill. This bill was vetoed by President Franklin Pierce, setting a precedent for the federal government's refusal to be involved in state social services programs that remained unchanged until the New Deal era.

Refusing to give up, Dix turned her efforts to the individual states. By 1900, thirty-two states had established state mental hospitals. But Dix and other advocates for the humane treatment of the mentally ill soon had additional cause for concern. What began in many hospitals as humane treatment changed as hospitals became overused and overcrowded, admitting all who could not be cared for elsewhere. State insane asylums became warehouses, commonly described as snake pits.

Dorothea Dix and her group of reformers demanded that strict guidelines be established for the treatment of mental hospital patients. Again, states responded, and expanding facilities soon were heavily bound by detailed procedures. Although abuse and neglect of patients decreased dramatically, the guidelines left little room for innovation, and until the 1960s, patients in state mental hospitals received little more than custodial care. In the years immediately following the Dix reform, nearly half of patients who had been admitted were released, often only to make room for new admissions and to alleviate overcrowding. Once the population stabilized somewhat, however, long stays in mental hospitals became the norm, with discharge rates falling to as low as 5 percent. While these state institutions had been intended to house a transitory patient population, the absence of a treatment technology forced the retention of many patients until their deaths. The desire for single state facilities to house large populations of mentally ill patients resulted in their location in rural areas, where land was less expensive, expansion of facilities possible, and the safety of the community protected. Thus, the state mental hospital became—and, in many instances, still is—the "principal industry" in the area where it is located.

Although much less attention was given to the developmentally disabled, institutionalization became prevalent for this group as well. During the 1850s, many states established state training schools for the retarded, which housed persons who ranged from profoundly to mildly retarded. Many individuals who were retarded were also often mistakenly labeled as mentally ill and were placed in state hospitals for the mentally ill as well.

More Reforms Needed

In spite of the efforts of Dorothea Dix and others, overcrowded conditions and neglect of the mentally ill and developmentally disabled still existed in many state facilities. Facilities continued to be overcrowded, with large numbers of immigrant residents. While the staff could provide moral treatment, love, and respect to some residents, it was difficult for many to transfer this philosophy to foreigners. Also it was increasingly hard to get medical staff willing to work in state mental institutions. Graduates from medical school often were repelled by the foreigners, alcoholics, and severely disturbed individuals who populated the institutions.

A second effort to reform conditions in state mental hospitals was undertaken in the early 1900s by Clifford Beers, a Yale graduate from a wealthy family who had been hospitalized in a Connecticut mental hospital for three years. After his release, Beers almost immediately suffered a relapse and was hospitalized for a second time. During this stay, he began to formulate plans for more effective treatment of the mentally ill. He kept careful notes of the maltreatment he received from physicians and the well-intended but ineffective care he received from caretakers. After his release in 1908, Beers wrote a book, *A Mind that Found Itself*, which was intended to be a parallel to *Uncle Tom's Cabin* but focused on conditions in mental hospitals. This book led to the formation of state mental health advocacy organizations, such as the Connecticut Society for Mental Health. Later, state organizations formed the National Association for Mental Hygiene, which became a lobbying force for the continual reform of state hospitals and the development of alternative systems of care.

The Introduction of Psychoanalysis

What is described as the second revolution in the mental health field occurred in the early 1900s with the introduction of Sigmund Freud's writings and the use of **psychoanalysis** in the United States. Professional mental health workers trained in Freud's techniques attempted to gain cooperation and insight through verbal or nonverbal communication with patients, seeing them at regular intervals over long periods of time.

The first social workers hired to work in state mental hospitals actually were hired before Freud's teachings were introduced into the United States. Their primary role was to provide therapy to clients, but it was based on a limited knowledge about what the therapy should entail. As psychoanalysis gained popularity in the United States, psychiatric social workers, like others working with the mentally ill, were quick to adopt a system of therapy that was reportedly much more effective than the often haphazard treatment they were using. In 1905, Massachusetts General Hospital in Boston and Bellevue Hospital in New York City hired psychiatric social workers to provide therapy to patients. But because of staff shortages and the large numbers of patients, few patients actually received psychotherapy, which requires highly trained therapists, fairly verbal patients who speak the same language as the therapist, and long hours of treatment to be effective. In most instances, psychotherapy as a treatment approach for dealing with mental health problems was used more in outpatient facilities, either private practices established by psychiatrists or child guidance centers, which were established in the United States in the 1920s and focused primarily on promoting healthy relationships among middle-class children and their parents.

The Shift to Community Mental Health Programs

The third revolution in mental health, a shift in the care of individuals with mental health problems and developmental disabilities from institutions to local communities, began in the 1940s and still continues. Public interest in mental health issues and treatment of the mentally ill remained at a fairly constant level until the 1940s and the onset of World War II. The military draft brought mental health problems to the attention of Congress. Military statistics showed that 12 percent of all men drafted into the Armed Forces were rejected for psychiatric reasons. Of the total number rejected for any reason, 40 percent were rejected for psychiatric reasons (Felix 1967). Serious questions began to be raised about the magnitude of mental health problems within the entire United States population.

Initial Postwar Developments

After the war ended, state hospitals, which had been neglected during the war, again began to receive attention. Albert Deutsch wrote a series of exposés on state mental hospitals, later published as *Shame of the States* (1949). This stimulated a series of similar books, one of which was made into a film, *The Snake Pit.* The attention resulted in widespread public outcry and created a climate for reform. In 1946, Congress passed the National Mental Health Act, which enabled states to establish community mental health programs aimed at preventing and treating mental health problems. The act also provided for the establishment of research and educational programs and mandated that each state establish a single state entity to receive and allocate federal funds provided for by the act.

In 1949, the United States Governors' Conference sponsored a study of mental health programs in the United States. That same year, Congress created the **National Institute of Mental Health (NIMH),** the first federal entity to address mental health concerns. In 1955, with impetus from a working coalition of leadership from the National Institute of Mental Health and the **National Association of Mental Health (NAMH),** university medical schools and schools of social work, and organizations of former mental patients and their families, the National Mental Health Study Act was passed. This act signified the belief among both mental health experts and government officials that large custodial institutions could not deal effectively with mental illness. The act authorized an appropriation to the Joint Commission on Mental Illness and Health to study and make recommendations in the area of mental health policy. The commission published a series of documents in the late 1950s and early 1960s calling for reform. Commission reports called for a doubling of expenditures within five years and a tripling within ten years in mental health expenditures to be used for comprehensive community mental health facilities, increased recruitment and training programs for staff, and long-term mental health research. The commission suggested expanding treatment programs for the acutely mentally ill in all facilities while limiting the numbers of patients at each hospital to no more than a thousand inpatients.

The commission also recommended that the major emphasis be placed on community programs, including preventive, outpatient treatment, and aftercare services that could reduce the numbers of institutionalized patients and allow for their successful treatment within their local communities. The group also recommended that the states play a smaller role in providing services and that the federal role be increased in addressing mental health needs. President John F. Kennedy also made mental health issues a high priority and strongly supported the efforts of the commission, becoming the first United States president to publicly address mental health concerns. Furthermore, the public was beginning to see the effectiveness of **psychotropic drugs** in the treatment of the mentally ill and consequently was becoming more receptive to the idea of community care.

Community Mental Health Initiatives
Congress passed the Mentally Retarded Facilities and Community Mental Health Center Construction Act in 1963. This act provided major funding to build community mental health centers and community facilities for the developmentally disabled. This and subsequent legislation mandated that centers built with federal funds be located in areas accessible to the pop-

ulations they serve, and that they provide the following basic service components: inpatient services, outpatient services, partial hospitalization (day, night, or weekend care) emergency services, consultation, and educational services. By 1980 there were over 700 community mental health centers in the United States partially funded with federal funds.

The intent of the community mental health care legislation was to replace the custodial care within a large-scale institution with therapeutic care within a community by providing a comprehensive array of locally available services. Emphasis was to be placed on **deinstitutionalization,** or keeping individuals from placement in hospitals whenever possible, and on a **least restrictive environment,** or providing the least restrictive environment appropriate. The 1978 President's Commission on Mental Health defined the purpose of providing a least restrictive environment as "maintaining the greatest degree of freedom, self determination, autonomy, dignity, and integrity of body, mind, and spirit for the individual while he or she participates in treatment or receives services" (44). Such programs were not only deemed cost effective, because many individuals could work at paid jobs and live in situations requiring less expense than an institution, but also were seen as increasing individual self-esteem and feelings of contributing to society.

The community health center legislation, coupled with the use of psychotropic drugs, significantly reduced the numbers of individuals in mental institutions. In 1955, 77.4 percent of all patients received inpatient services; 22.6 percent received outpatient services. By 1980, the numbers virtually had reversed themselves, with only 28 percent receiving inpatient services and 72 percent outpatient services. (Mechanic 1980). Emphasis on treatment had shifted from custodial care, shock treatment, or long-term psychotherapy to short-term treatment, group therapy, helping individuals cope with their environments, and drug treatment. The number of outpatient clients seen at community mental health centers continues to increase; the client load increased by more than one-third between 1990 and 1993 (NASW 1995).

Legal Rights of Clients and Consumer Advocacy

Mental health and developmental disabilities experts have identified clients' rights as the fourth and current revolution in the mental health/disabilities arena. The legal advocacy movement, begun in the 1960s, was part of the civil rights movement of the sixties. It received further impetus in 1971 in the landmark case *Whyatt v. Sticknesy,* in which a federal judge ruled that "extraordinary or potentially hazardous modes of treatment" (Lin 1995, 1706) used with patients in state mental hospitals in Alabama must be restricted. Another patients' rights case followed four years later when the United States Supreme Court ruled that being mentally ill and in need of treatment was not sufficient grounds for involuntary confinement.

With the increased number of options available to individuals with developmental disabilities and mental health problems, including placement in less restrictive facilities, new counseling techniques, and drug treatment, legal issues have surfaced that require serious deliberation. On one hand, do individuals have the right to refuse treatment? On the other hand, if treatment technology or knowledge about more appropriate types of treatment exists but such treatment is not available, do individuals have the right to demand treatment? In some states, class action suits have been brought on behalf of persons in institutions demanding that they be placed in less restrictive settings and receive treatment unavailable to them in the institutions.

The National Association of Mental Health and other advocacy organizations have forced the United States court system to establish a series of patients'/clients' rights, which include the right to treatment, the right to privacy and dignity, and the right to the least restrictive condition necessary to achieve the purpose of commitment. The courts also have determined that persons cannot be deemed incompetent to manage their affairs; to hold professional, occupational, or vehicular licenses; to marry and obtain divorces; to register to vote; or to make wills solely because of admission or commitment to a hospital.

Patients in mental institutions have the same rights to visitation and telephone communication as patients in other hospitals, as well as the right to send sealed mail. They also have the right to freedom from excessive medication or physical restraint and experiments and the right to wear their own clothes and worship within the dictates of their own religion. Finally, patients also have the right to receive needed treatment outside of a hospital environment (Mechanic 1980).

Most states make it difficult to commit a person to an institution involuntarily. In many states, however, law enforcement agencies can order that persons be detained in state institutions for a limited time without a court hearing. At the end of that time, a court hearing must be held, and involuntary commitments can be ordered only if persons are found to be dangerous to themselves or others. Individuals who are not really capable of functioning on their own but who are not found to be dangerous often are released to be on their own.

Because of this system, many individuals receive what some mental health experts have termed "the revolving door approach to treatment"—they are picked up on the streets because they are too incapacitated to function on their own, admitted to the hospital, given medication and food and rest, and then released quickly because they legally cannot be held any longer against their wishes.

Children's right to refuse or to demand treatment is an issue that has received even less attention. In many instances, parents commit children to institutions because they do not want to or are unable to care for them. In other instances, the child's problems are the result of family problems that the parents do not want to accept. Currently, both the rights of individuals to avoid treatment and the rights of individuals to receive treatment are unclear and need to be clarified further by the United States Supreme Court.

Consumers of services and their families, like social work professionals, are becoming increasingly concerned about these issues as well. Advocacy groups for persons with mental health problems increasingly have sought to include individuals with mental health problems and their family members. A number of groups specifically for consumers of mental health services have developed and have worked tirelessly to strengthen legislation, policies, and programs at all levels of the environment. The National Alliance for the Mentally Ill, for example, has advocated for the inclusion of family members in treatment planning (Lin 1995). The consumer movement emphasizes empowerment, independence, and recovery. Many social workers work closely with consumer groups and have become strong allies of the consumer movement and the changes they advocate.

AVAILABILITY OF RESOURCES AND RESPONSIBILITY FOR CARE

Perhaps the most overriding issue in the mental health, substance abuse, and developmental disabilities arena relates to how to manage limited resources to best address the needs of those who require services. Current estimates are that approximately 10 percent of national health care resources are spent for public and private mental health care (NASW 1995). Medicaid is the largest funding source of seriously ill people, and mental health costs continue to increase; state mental health controlled expenditures totaled $12 billion in 1990, a 100 percent increase since 1981. Other costs for psychiatric care are also high: in 1987 costs for private psychiatric hospitals totaled $4.6 billion and psychiatric care in general hospitals totaled $3.6 billion (NASW 1995). Funding patterns are changing somewhat with the trend toward community-based programs and deinstitutionalization. In 1987, 67 percent of state expenditures were for state mental hospitals, but this figure dropped to 58 percent in 1990. At the same time, state expenditures for community services increased from 29 percent in 1987 to 38 percent in 1990. Half of state mental hospitals also offer nonhospital care as part of their services.

Persons who are mentally ill and developmentally disabled, often unable to advocate well for themselves, do not always receive their just share of funding. Public attitudes that still persist in viewing alcoholism and substance abuse as moral issues also have limited funding for substance abuse programs. Many of the gains in mental health and developmental disabilities programs established in the 1960s have been eroded as governments battle over who should have the responsibility for the care of individuals who are mentally ill or developmentally disabled and what constitutes appropriate levels of service for these groups. Although attitudes have changed significantly since colonial times, additional change is required if normalization of these populations is to be achieved. In the following sections, we discuss a number of issues relating to current resources.

Deinstitutionalization

The mental health field has been subjected to considerable shock since the movement toward deinstitutionalization. Some individuals have argued that deinstitutionalization has resulted in the "ghettoization" of persons who are mentally ill and disabled, meaning that communities in many instances have neither the funding nor the commitment to accept recently released patients, forcing them to subsist in subhuman conditions in poverty areas.

In 1976, two social workers from the Mental Health Law Project visited Mr. Dixon, who had won his right to freedom in a class action suit several months after being transferred from the hospital to a boarding care facility. The workers described their observations in testimony before a Senate subcommittee:

> The conditions in which we found Mr. Dixon were unconscionable. Mr. Dixon's sleeping room was about halfway below ground level. The only windows in the room were closed and a plate in front of them made it impossible for Mr. Dixon to open them. There was no fan or air conditioner in the room. The room had no phone or buzzer. There would be no capacity for Mr. Dixon to contact someone in case of fire or emergency and this is significant in the face of the fact that Mr. Dixon is physically incapacitated. Mr. Dixon had not been served breakfast by 10 A.M. He stated that meals were highly irregular and he would sometimes get so hungry waiting for lunch that he would ask a roomer to buy him sandwiches. He can remember having only one glass of milk during his entire stay at his new home. (U.S. Senate Subcommittee on Long Term Care 1976, 715)

Shortly after this testimony, Mr. Dixon returned to St. Elizabeth Hospital and was placed in a more suitable home. Twenty years later, in 1996, a series of articles by an investigative reporter for an urban newspaper in a large southwestern state found similar or worse conditions existing among persons throughout the state who had been released from state hospitals. Although states have moved to establish regulations, including licensing or certification systems for group and boarding homes for clients of the mental health system, monitoring and sanctioning are difficult. Even if facilities are forced to close, there are often no other facilities to move the residents.

Many states and local communities have successfully moved large numbers of individuals who are developmentally disabled or mentally ill from institutions to community programs and facilities, but some are reluctant to do so. Some states are under court order, as a result of suits brought by citizen advocate groups, to move more quickly to deinstitutionalize. Reasons for resistance to deinstitutionalization include inadequate funds and other resources, economic disruption caused by shutting down institutions in areas where they are the major source of employment, and lack of appropriate facilities at the community level to house individuals who could be deinstitutionalized.

In some instances, deinstitutionalization has resulted in individuals, like Joanna in the opening vignette, falling through the cracks. Many individuals who could function well within an institutional setting do not do as well in a community setting, particularly with little day-to-day supervision. Deinstitutionalization also means decentralization and the potential for shoddy standards of maintenance and the failure to provide follow-up services to clients. This decentralization points to the necessity for a case management system in which social workers or other mental health professionals are responsible for a specific number of clients, ensuring that their living conditions are appropriate, that they are maintaining health care and taking medication, and that their other needs are met.

Some deinstitutionalization programs, however, have been extremely successful. For example, George Fairweather, a noted mental health expert, has established a series of community programs for individuals who were previously institutionalized. Called Fairweather Lodges, these facilities provide supervised living for individuals in small groups, with residents sharing housekeeping chores. Residents also work in the community, with a lodge coordinator who ensures that residents are successful in the workplace. The coordinator also facilitates support group meetings for residents' families, as well as for lodge members. The rate of recidivism for this program has been extremely low. While some communities that have established lodge programs were reluctant to do so at first, they now view the lodges and their residents as important parts of the community.

Wide-Ranging Program Alternatives

Other beneficial community programs that have been established include partial hospitalization, through which persons attend hospital day programs and receive treatment, returning to their homes at night or to work in the community, and return to the hospital for treatment and monitoring the next day. Day programs for persons who are developmentally disabled that provide education, supervision, and in some instances employment opportunities have also been successful. Halfway houses and refurbished apartment complexes, with resident supervisors who oversee and lend support to residents for persons who are mentally ill, developmentally disabled, and recovering substance abusers, have been especially successful. Many persons have been able to return to their own homes. Some go to adult or special children's day-care centers during the day while parents work, returning home at night. Respite care programs established in some communities, using trained volunteers, make it possible for family members to find substitute caregivers so they can have some time away from the person on occasion to regain their energies.

Community-based alternatives for the elderly have also received increased attention as the population continues to age. Many residents of both state mental hospitals and state schools for the developmentally disabled once were, in fact, elderly persons who could function in a less restrictive environment if they had someone to care for them. A number of elderly individuals have been successfully placed in nursing homes, often in integrated facilities that take people without mental health or disability problems. Other alternatives such as those mentioned in the preceding paragraph have also been developed for older people.

Caring for Children with Disabilities

The passage of Public Law 94–142, the Education for All Handicapped Children Act (1975), also has made deinstitutionalization more feasible for children. This law mandates that public school systems provide educational and social services for children with a range of disabilities, including emotional disturbances, mental retardation, and speech, vision, hearing, and learning disabilities. Parents and educators are required to develop jointly an individualized educational plan (IEP) for each child. The law also requires each child to be placed in the least restrictive setting possible, with the intent that children with disabilities and emotional problems be placed in regular classrooms to the extent possible and in special education classes as a last alternative. A number of early childhood programs also allow children with disabilities to remain in their own homes. Many communities have preschool programs, funded with state and federal monies to assist children with disabilities, that combine early childhood education with physical and speech therapy and other needed services. Both working and nonworking parents can bring their children to the centers, where trained staff work with the children individually and in small groups to help them progress developmentally. Some preschool programs include children with and without disabilities so that both groups of children can learn to value each other and discover and grow together.

There are still, however, large numbers of children who have disabilities that prohibit them from remaining in their own homes, and others whose parents are overwhelmed by their own needs and the added stress from having a child with a disability and cannot care for them. Advances in technology to keep children alive who are born with serious disabilities have resulted in issues about how best to care for those children if they cannot remain at home. The costs to keep such children in hospitals are extensive, and a hospital setting does not provide the kind of nurturance a child needs to develop to his or her maximum potential. As many states have closed their state schools for the mentally retarded/developmentally disabled, attention has been focused on how to care for children previously housed there. In many instances, children have been placed in nursing homes with elderly residents. Although sometimes these experiences have been positive, they are often the only child, or one of only several, in the facility, which is likely to be ill equipped to meet the special needs of children.

Much remains to be done to develop adequate community-based programs for individuals of all ages. Many deinstitutionalized individuals have difficulty adjusting to community living, particularly when adequate support programs are not available. As one former state hospital resident stated:

> At the hospital, I had hot coffee every morning, three meals a day and a warm bed every night, and people to talk to if I wanted to talk. Here, I have the street and that's about it. No food on a regular basis, no bed, and no one to talk to. I didn't have a bad life at the hospital. (Iscoe 1990)

The biggest problem with deinstitutionalization is that large numbers of individuals have been released from institutions to communities that have been unable to develop the necessary infrastructure to support these individuals in a community setting.

Prevention versus Treatment

The issue of prevention versus treatment, especially within the confines of scarce resources, is a final consideration in responding to the needs of those who are mentally ill, are substance abusers, or have developmental disabilities. Mental health experts address prevention issues at three levels:

- **Primary prevention,** or prevention targeted at an entire population (e.g., prenatal care for all women to avoid developmental disabilities in their infants, parenting classes for all individuals to decrease mental health problems among children)

- **Secondary prevention,** or prevention targeted toward at-risk populations, those groups more likely to develop mental health problems than others (e.g., individual and group counseling for family members of schizophrenics or alcoholics)

- **Tertiary prevention,** or prevention targeted at those individuals who have already experienced problems to prevent the problems from recurring (e.g., treatment groups for alcoholics or mental health programs for individuals who have attempted suicide)

Although numerous studies show that prevention programs are cost-effective ways to reduce developmental disabilities and mental health problems, it is difficult to create such programs when resources are scarce and so many individuals need treatment. Still, policy makers often focus on short-term solutions to problems, ignoring long-term and more favorable solutions. For example, although substance abuse prevention programs cost money, the costs are far less than those to house individuals in institutions, to provide other extensive treatment programs, or to pay the costs for imprisonment and services to victims if the substance abuse leads to crime.

Other mental health problems besides substance abuse also are currently in the limelight. These include homelessness and family violence. These problems, while not new, are being recognized as having significant negative impacts not only on the individuals experiencing these problems, but on the entire family. This emphasis on intergenerational, cyclical problems has focused attention on the need to provide resources not only to children and their families experiencing these problems but also to adults who grew up in such families (see Chapters 12 and 13).

Cultural and gender differences must also be considered when discussing mental health, mental illness, substance abuse, and developmental disabilities. The importance of gender and cultural differences, including both strengths and the impact of oppression and social injustice, on individuals must be considered in relation to theories used to understand human behavior and to identify "normal" and pathological behavior; the use of diagnostic classification systems such as the *DSM-VI-R;* the ways that practitioners view and relate to individuals with whom they interact; and the ways that mental health and developmental disabilities services are organized and delivered (Goldstein 1987).

◪ THE ROLES OF SOCIAL WORKERS IN THE DELIVERY OF MENTAL HEALTH SERVICES

Social workers today are involved in the total continuum of mental health and developmental disabilities services. They provide these services in a variety of settings, including traditional social services agencies—such as community mental health centers, child guidance centers, and public social services departments—as well as nontraditional settings—such as the courts, public schools and colleges and universities, hospitals and health clinics, child care centers, workplaces, and the military. While they fulfill a variety of roles, social workers presently form the largest group of psychotherapists in the United States.

The History of Social Workers in Mental Health

The first social workers credited with providing mental health services were the psychiatric social workers hired in New York and Boston mental hospitals in the early 1900s. They were responsible primarily for providing individual therapy to hospitalized mental patients and overseeing the care of discharged patients in foster homes. The mental health field expanded during the 1920s with the establishment of child guidance centers.

With the influence of psychoanalysis and the child guidance movement, social workers in mental health increasingly moved into the role of psychotherapist, with the individual as the unit of attention. Social work's unique perspective on the person-in-environment and intervention at other levels of the environment beyond the individual waned during the 1930s, 1940s, and 1950s. But the civil rights movement and Vietnam War in the 1960s increased activism among the social work profession as a whole, and emphasis was again placed on community organization, advocacy, and a return to the roots of the profession.

The focus on the systems/ecological perspective since the late sixties has broadened the roles of social workers in all fields, including mental health, although many continue working primarily with individuals. As psychiatrists have increasingly played more technical roles in the mental health system, with an emphasis on medication and biopsychological perspectives, social workers have tried to maintain leadership in the mental health arena: "As the largest group of mental health care providers in the country, . . . social workers are in a unique position to address the social context of clients' problems" (NASW 1994). They are also in a unique position to advocate for the need to look at interventions beyond the individual to other levels of the environment. Why do some communities and geographic areas have higher incidences of mental illness, substance abuse, people with disabilities, and homelessness than others? What factors constitute a healthy community—or society—that promotes mental health and values diversity? Eliminating environmental racism, oppression and discrimination; creating adequate housing and employment; and maintaining an environment that values diversity and difference, children and families, and the elderly all can improve the quality of life for individuals and families. Social workers, regardless of their field or the environment in which they practice, need to play a more active role in advocating for social change at all levels of the environment to promote positive mental health.

Career Opportunities in Mental Health

Clinical Social Workers

Many social workers in mental health settings still provide individual counseling, including psychotherapy, to clients. But instead of being referred to as psychiatric social workers, most are called **clinical social workers.** The majority of agencies who hire clinical social workers require that they meet the qualifications of the National Association of Social Workers Academy of Certified Social Workers (ACSW) certification or obtain appropriate state certification or licensing. To receive ACSW certification an individual must have a Master of Social Work (MSW) degree from an accredited graduate school of social work, two years of social work experience under the direct supervision of an ACSW social worker, and a satisfactory score on a competency examination administered by the National Association of Social Workers. State licensing and certification programs have similar requirements but vary by state.

Crisis Intervention and Child and Family Services

Many social work jobs also are available in the field of mental health and developmental disabilities for social workers with Bachelor of Social Work (BSW) degrees. BSW social workers provide such services as crisis intervention for women and their children at battered women's centers, and they operate suicide, runaway youth, child abuse, and other types of crisis hotlines (see Chapter 2). They also counsel adolescents and their families at youth-serving agencies and work as social workers in state hospitals and community living programs for the mentally ill and state schools for the developmentally disabled. In these settings, they counsel residents and serve as the primary professional involved with the individual's family.

School-Based Services and Drug Treatment Programs

Social workers also work in schools with troubled students and their families, providing individual counseling, family counseling, and family outreach and leading groups for children and their families in areas such as divorce, child maltreatment, ways of dealing with anger, techniques for getting along with adults, and substance abuse. The reauthorization of the Education for All Handicapped Children's Act in 1990 includes the use of social workers in the act's definition of social services. Many social workers are employed as counselors in alcohol and drug treatment programs. In fact, wherever mental health services are provided, social workers are likely to be employed. In the 1990s, social workers compose the largest professional group in public mental health services. Over half of the labor force employed in mental-health-related jobs are social workers, and over one-third of the federally funded community mental health centers have social workers as their executive directors.

Social Workers in Multidisciplinary Teams

Social workers in the field of mental health provide a variety of functions. Many work in direct practice, clinical settings, providing therapy to individuals, groups, and families. Many mental health programs use a multidisciplinary team approach, hiring social workers, psychiatrists, physicians, psychologists, psychiatric nurses, child development specialists, and community aides, who work together to provide a multitude of services. While social workers on multidisciplinary teams are involved in all aspects of treatment, most often they are given the responsibility of working with the client's family and the community in which the client resides. Because of their training from a systems/ecological perspective, they help other team members understand the many competing factors that can support or impede a client intervention plan. If resources from another agency are needed, usually the social worker obtains them and ensures that they are provided.

Social Workers as Case Managers

Many social workers in mental health settings provide case management services even if they are not employed in agencies that use multidisciplinary teams. Case managers are responsible for monitoring cases to ensure that clients receive needed services. A case manager does not necessarily provide all services directly but manages the case, coordinating others who provide the services.

BSW social workers who work with persons who are mentally ill, disabled, or homeless often serve as case managers. Assigned a group of clients, they fill a number of roles to ensure that their clients are following intervention plans and functioning adequately. A case manager empowers clients to become as self-sufficient as they can by focusing on their strengths and providing support and affirmation. Case managers also serve as the liaison with the client and other service providers when necessary, monitoring the provision of services and advocating for changes in services or additional services when necessary. Many individuals can function fairly well with a case manager to lend support, to ensure that they are taking medication if needed, to advocate with an employer if there is a problem, to help them access health care if they get sick, and to keep them from becoming isolated from their environment.

Many states are employing case managers at community mental health centers to oversee clients who are living in the local community, including those previously in institutions, who can function fairly independently with supervision and support. The case manager meets with the client and contacts her or his family members, employers, and other appropriate individuals on a regular basis to ensure that the client is functioning adequately.

Social Workers as Advocates

Still other social workers involved in the mental health field function as advocates. Organizations such as The Arc (formerly ARC—the Association for Retarded Citizens) advocate for persons with disabilities on an individual basis, ensuring that they receive needed services. For example, a 14-year-old girl with mental disabilities in a junior high school in an urban area was not receiving special education services and had been suspended several times for behavior problems. An advocate assigned to her arranged for the school district to provide the needed testing, saw that she was placed in a special education program that reduced her anxiety level and allowed her to function in a setting where she felt better about herself, and arranged for her to receive counseling. Advocates also work to ensure that groups of citizens are provided for, such as working within a community to ensure that housing is available to individuals with mental health problems and developmental disabilities. Advocates work within an empowerment framework, empowering the population that they work with to advocate for themselves for individual and social change.

Social Workers as Policy Makers

Social workers also function in the mental health arena as administrators and policy makers. Many direct mental health programs, and others work for government bodies at the local, state, and federal levels. They develop and advocate for legislation, develop policies and procedures to ensure that the needs of individuals with mental health problems and disabilities are met, and oversee governing bodies that monitor programs to ensure that services are provided. Increasingly, social workers are also being elected to local, state, and national office. A number of social workers at all three governmental levels have played key roles in working to get legislation passed that improves services for persons who are mentally ill, chemically dependent, and/or have developmental disabilities; or in trying to thwart the passage of legislation deemed detrimental to these groups.

New Trends in Services and Social Work Roles

Although the intent of the Community Mental Health Act was to provide services to individuals within specific geographic areas with the greatest need, particularly in poverty areas with diverse populations, studies have shown that in many instances persons receiving services largely have been middle class and white. The Commission on Mental Health, established by President Carter in the 1970s, found that people of color, children, adolescents, and the elderly were underserved, as were residents of rural and poor urban areas. The commission also found that many services provided were inappropriate, particularly for those persons with differing cultural backgrounds and life-styles. In many instances when mental health centers were first established, they were directed by psychiatrists trained in psychotherapy or influenced by educational psychologists accustomed to providing testing and working with students. As a result, the staff members often were inexperienced at dealing with nonvoluntary clients, who did not want to be seen, failed to keep appointments, and were unfamiliar with the concept of one-hour therapy sessions. Staff members often were also unequipped to deal with problems such as family violence, child abuse, and sexual abuse.

As programs developed, many centers became skilled at reaching special populations and developing more effective ways of addressing client needs. In the 1970s, centers were required to establish special children's mental health programs. Currently, many centers provide programs that address special populations such as abused children, individuals with substance abuse problems, and Vietnam veterans. Mental health professionals also assist in the establishment of self-help groups, such as Alcoholics Anonymous, Adult Children of Alcoholics, Alateen, Parents Without Partners, and Parents Anonymous (a child abuse self-help program).

Today, social workers in mental health settings provide crisis intervention, operate telephone hotlines, conduct suicide prevention programs, and provide alcoholism and drug abuse services. Mental health services increasingly are provided in settings other than mental health centers, including churches, nursing homes, police departments, schools, child care centers, the workplace, and health and medical settings. Problems addressed by mental health professionals have expanded to include loneliness and isolation, finances, spouse and child abuse, male/female relationships, housing, drugs, and alcohol. Mental health staff members have become more multidisciplinary, using teams of professionals as well as volunteers.

One of the major issues facing the mental health profession today relates to who pays for services clients receive and how long those services should be provided. Many mental health services are paid for by third-party insurance payments and, if the client meets eligibility requirements, by Medicaid (see Chapter 11). Because of the costs of services and the large numbers of individuals needing them, mental health services are also significantly influenced by the concept of managed care, which will be discussed in more detail in Chapter 11. Most insurance companies limit the numbers of sessions for which an individual can be reimbursed for mental health counseling, and the number of hospital days for mental health reasons. They also restrict the service providers available, often to a list of professionals and specific hospitals who have agreed to provide the services for that insurance company. Hospital stays, particularly for substance abuse, have been limited, and more insurance providers are mandating outpatient treatment first to determine if that is successful.

Because of these limitations, the types of outpatient services provided also are changing. More agencies are seeing clients in groups, and limiting the numbers of group and individual counseling sessions in which a client can participate. The trend is also toward case management, with an individual, sometimes from the insurance company, sometimes from the agency, monitoring the services received to ensure that they are needed. Intervention approaches that focus on "brief," or "short-term" therapy, often using a cognitive behavioral approach, are being used to attempt to stabilize clients and help them cope more quickly. One short-term intervention approach used by social workers is solution-focused therapy (de Shazer 1985). This approach focuses on the strengths of clients, empowering them to come up with effective solutions for addressing their problems. Questions such as "what worked before for you?" and comments such as "how have you managed to do as well as you have with all this going on?" use the clients' own ideas and affirm their abilities to cope. While these intervention approaches are effective for some types of mental health problems, they are not as effective for others, such as sexual abuse or substance abuse.

Another trend relates to recent breakthroughs in neuroscience and the discovery of new relationships between biological makeup and mental illness, developmental disabilities, and substance abuse. Specific genes have been identified, for example, that cause diseases associated with developmental disabilities such as cystic fibrosis. Although it was previously believed that schizophrenia was more environmentally- than biologically-related, new research is showing that factors associated with this serious illness are more likely related to genetic makeup or chemical functioning within the brain. Research suggests similar factors associated with Alzheimer's disease, and early detection of both diseases, as well as others, is likely. These discoveries are tremendous breakthroughs, because it is likely that interventions such as gene therapy or medication can be developed to change the course of, or prevent, these illnesses. A new drug is also being tested that alters an individuals' craving for alcohol and has the potential to significantly reduce problems associated with alcoholism. While exciting advances, these discoveries raise new issues for social workers. First, what are the ethical implications of such knowledge? If early detection is possible, for example, before birth, what are the choices and who should make them? No matter when problems are identified in individuals, should all individuals have affordable access to such interventions, even if they are expensive? Who should pay for such interventions? And finally, what if an individual decides not to take advantage of such interventions? The issues of right to treatment and client empowerment will surface in new areas and are important ones for social workers.

Although research and the current direction of many mental health professionals supports a systems/ecological approach to dealing with mental health, substance abuse, and developmental disabilities issues, particularly a family systems perspective, limited resources do not always support this perspective. In the short run, it may not be cost effective to intervene with the entire family, but such an approach is more likely to reduce recidivism (reoccurrence of the problem) or prevent the problem from exacerbating. Researchers and practitioners, for example, have found a psychoeducational approach, whereby individuals and their families receive education that helps them understand the problem their family member is experiencing, the roles they have played in trying to cope with the problem, and possibly more effective ways of coping, as well as family therapy to address the dynamics within their own families, to be highly successful in many situations. But with limited resources, many agencies see only the individual and do not provide additional resources to family members.

With scarce resources and persons with mental illness and developmental disabilities and in recovery from substance abuse becoming increasingly empowered to advocate for themselves, including the filing of class action suits, states that find it difficult to provide needed services may be forced to do so by court order. Social workers will continue to play major roles in these arenas at all levels—working directly with clients and their families individually and in groups, empowering them to advocate for themselves, advocating with them, administering agencies and policies, establishing new programs, and lobbying for the passage of new or continuing legislation.

Future trends in mental health include more attention to the provision of services at the community level, with local communities determining the level and type of services needed. The federal government is pressuring community mental health centers previously funded almost totally by federal dollars to become self-sufficient. Although some individuals will still need to be hospitalized in state or private psychiatric hospitals, more and more individuals will be treated in community-based programs. One study found that 80 percent of people in psychiatric hospitals could be treated in local communities if services were available, at half the cost and more effective outcomes than hospitalization (Ray 1994).

Other concepts include "one-stop mental health centers" that incorporate individual and group counseling services, day and partial-day treatment programs, social skills training, and recreation programs, as well as assistance with housing and employment. Increased attention will also be given to in-home mental health care, sending social workers in therapist or case management positions into clients' homes to provide services there, further reducing the need for outpatient and inpatient care. Intensive case management and therapy services provided in the home on a short-term basis can often stabilize situations and get the entire family working together with the client before problems escalate and hospitalization or other out-of-home services are required.

The National Association of Social Workers adopted a policy statement on mental health in 1994, which stated that mental health is a national priority for both the public and private sectors in the United States. The statement called for political action by the professional organization and social workers to increase funding for prevention, treatment and research in mental health, and for the passage of legislation that requires adequate mental health benefits for all citizens as part of any health reform. The policy also calls for social workers to be included as providers of mental health services under such legislation. Additionally, the policy calls for clients to be placed in least restrictive environments and a mental health service delivery system that allows for a continuum of care, including community-based prevention programs; both short- and long-term inpatient hospitalization; partial hospitalization; and outpatient, outreach, and emergency services, with all services involving families and including case management (Lin 1995).

SUMMARY

Services for individuals with mental health needs and developmental disabilities have changed significantly since colonial times. Four major revolutions have occurred in the area of mental health, including

- The shift from inhumane to moral treatment
- The introduction of psychoanalytic therapy
- The move from institutions to community programs and the development of psychotropic drugs that effectively treat many types of mental health problems
- A new emphasis on the rights of clients and patients

Current issues in the mental health field include

- The legal rights of clients and whether they should be able to refuse or demand treatment
- Scarce resources and conflict over the roles of federal, state, and local governments in providing services
- Attention to substance abuse and the expansion of substance abuse treatment facilities
- The need for more effective services for women, people of color, the homeless, and individuals in rural settings
- Additional services that address problems such as child maltreatment, alcohol and drug abuse, particularly for low-income groups
- The special needs of rural and ethnic populations

Social workers currently play a critical role in providing mental health services, serving as therapists, advocates, case managers, administrators, and policy makers. These roles are expected to continue and expand in the future. With increased social change and the resulting stress to all individuals in our society, it is anticipated that the mental health needs of all individuals will become an even more important area of focus.

KEY TERMS

addiction
Alcoholics Anonymous (AA)
alcoholism
clinical social worker
deinstitutionalization
developmental disability
Diagnostic and Statistical Manual (DSM or DSM-IV-R)
least restrictive environment
medical model
moral treatment

National Association of Mental Health (NAMH)
National Institute of Mental Health (NIMH)
primary prevention
psychoanalysis
psychotropic drugs
secondary prevention
substance abuse
tertiary prevention

DISCUSSION QUESTIONS

1. Discuss the problems in defining *mental illness.*
2. Identify and briefly describe at least four frameworks that can be used in understanding mental health problems.
3. Do you agree with Szasz' concept of mental health? Discuss your rationale for either agreeing or disagreeing.
4. Identify the four major revolutions in the field of mental health.
5. Identify at least three different ways that substance abuse may be conceptualized.
6. Identify at least four ways that substance abuse is costly to society.
7. What is your definition of a substance abuser? Identify at least three factors at each level of the environment that can place an individual at risk to become an alcoholic.
8. Discuss the meaning of the term *developmental disabilities.* How does this term contrast with previously used terminology to identify persons within this category?
9. Discuss the advantages and disadvantages of current efforts at deinstitutionalization.
10. Identify at least five factors associated with homelessness. Suggest a possible intervention strategy for each area.
11. How have the media portrayed persons with emotional problems, substance abuse, and developmental disabilities? Compare the portrayals in two recent popular films. What messages do these portrayals give to individuals with similar characteristics? To the general public about individuals with these characteristics?
12. Identify at least five areas in which social workers employed in mental health settings might work. What are some of the roles in which they might function?

REFERENCES

Ackerman, R. 1983. *Children of alcoholics.* 2d ed. Oshtemo, Mich.: Learning Publications

Barrera, M. 1995. Implementing the Americans with Disabilities Act: Issues for social workers. Unpublished paper, School of Social Work, University of Texas at Austin.

Burman, S., and P. Allen-Meares. 1991. Criteria for selecting practice theories: Working with alcoholic women. *Families in society: Journal of contemporary human services.* 72(7): 387–93.

Burt, M. 1992. *Over the edge: The growth of homelessness in the 1980s.* Washington, D.C.: Urban Institute.

Burt, M. R., and B. E. Cohen. 1989. *America's homeless: Numbers, characteristics and programs that serve them.* Washington, D.C.: Urban Institute Press.

Comprehensive Care Corporation. 1981. *Employee assistance programs: A dollar and sense issue.* Newport Beach, Calif.: Comprehensive Care Corporation.

de Shazer, S. 1985. *Keys to solution in brief therapy.* New York: W. W. Norton.

Deutsch, A. 1949. *Shame of the states.* New York: Columbia University Press.

Felix, R. 1967. *Mental illness: Progress and prospects.* New York: Columbia University Press.

Finkelstein, N. 1994. Treatment issues for alcohol-and-drug-dependent pregnant and parenting women. *Health and Social Work* 19(1): 7–15.

Goffman, E. 1961. *Asylums: Essays on the social situation of mental patients and other inmates.* Garden City, N.Y.: Doubleday.

Goldstein, E. 1987. Mental health and illness. *Encyclopedia of social work,* 18th ed., vol. 2: 102–109. Silver Springs, Md.: National Association of Social Workers.

Hutchins, H., and S. Kirk. 1995. Should DSM be the basis for teaching social work practice in mental health? No! *Social Work Education* (31)2: 159–65.

Iscoe, I. 1990. Personal communication with author, summary of interviews with previous mental hospital patients. Center for the Study of Human Development, University of Texas at Austin.

Ivanoff, A. and M. Reidel. 1995. Suicide. *Encyclopedia of Social Work,* vol. 3, 2358–2372. Washington, D.C.: NASW.

Kesey, K. 1962. *One flew over the cuckoo's nest.* New York: Basic Books.

Johnson, A. 1995. Homelessness. *Encyclopedia of Social Work,* vol. 2, 1338–1346. Washington, D.C.: NASW.

Journal entry by anonymous student. 1991. University of Texas at Austin.

Karls J. M. and K. E. Wandrei. 1994. *Person-in-environment system: The PIE classification system for social functioning problems.* Washington, D.C.: NASW Press.

Koroloff, N. and S. C. Anderson. 1989. Alcohol-free living centers: Hope for homeless alcoholics. *Social Work,* 34: 497–504.

Lipman, L. 1990. Study finds U.S. youth on dangerous track. *Austin American Statesman,* 8 June 1990, sec A, p. 1.

Lex, B. 1994. Women and substance abuse: A general review. In *Addictive Behaviors in Women,* ed. R. Watson, p. 279–327. Totowa, N.J.: Humana Press.

Liebow, E. 1993. *Tell them who I am: The lives of homeless women.* New York: Free Press.

Lin, A. 1995. Mental health overview. In *Encyclopedia of Social Work,* 19th ed., vol. 2: 1705–1711. Silver Springs, Md.: National Association of Social Workers.

Mechanic, D. 1980. *Mental health and social policy.* Englewood Cliffs, N.J.: Prentice-Hall.

NASW. 1995. Community mental health centers grow. *NASW News* (January). Silver Springs, Md.: Author.

Nelson-Zlupko, L., E. Kaufman, and M. Morrison Dove. 1995. Gender differences in drug addiction and treatment. *Social Work* (40)1: 45–95.

North, C., and E. Smith. 1994. Comparison of white and non-white homeless men and women. *Social Work* (39)6: 639–47.

U.S. Department of Health and Human Services. 1994. *Addictive and mental disorders found together.* SAMHSA News, (2)2. Washington, D.C.: Author.

Orlin, M. 1995. The Americans with Disabilities Act: Implications for social services. *Social Work* (40)2: 233–39.

Parkside Medical Services Corporation. 1988. *Participant handbook.* Parkridge, Ill: Parkside Medical Services Corporation.

Rapp, C., W. Shera, and W. Kisthardt. 1993. Research strategies for consumer empowerment of people with severe mental illness. *Social Work* (38)6: 727–33.

Ray, C. 1994. *Managed care workshop notes.* Adelphi, Md.: Vesta, Inc.

Rosenhan, D. 1973. On being sane in insane places. *Science* 179: 250–57.

Royce, J. 1989. *Alcohol problems and alcoholism: A comprehensive survey.* New York: Free Press.

Select Committee on Children, Youth and Families. 1990. *Women, addiction, and perinatal substance abuse fact sheet.* Washington, D.C.: U.S. House of Representatives Select Committee.

Sosin, M. 1989. Homelessness in Chicago. *Public Welfare* (47)1: 22–27.

Szasz, T. 1960. The myth of mental illness. *American Psychologist* (15 February), 113–18.

_____. 1970. *The manufacture of madness.* New York: Harper and Row.

U.S. Department of Health and Human Services. 1994. *Perception of drug risk drops.* SAMHSA News, (2)2. Washington, D.C.: Author.

U.S. Senate Subcommittee on Long-term Care. 1976. *Hearings on long term care.* Washington, D.C.: USDHEW.

Williams, J. 1995. Diagnostic and statistical manual of mental disorders. *Encyclopedia of Social Work,* vol. 1, 729–739. Washington, D.C.: NASW.

Williams, J. and R. Spitzer. 1995. Should DSM be the basis for teaching social work practice in mental health? Yes! *Social Work Education* (31)2: 148–53.

SUGGESTED FURTHER READINGS

Bickenbach, J. 1993. *Physical disability and social policy.* Buffalo, N.Y.: University of Toronto Press.

Black, C. 1987. *It will never happen to me.* New York: Ballantine.

Green, Hannah. 1964. *I never promised you a rose garden.* New York: Holt, Rinehart and Winston.

The President's Commission on Mental Health. 1978. Washington, D.C.: Government Printing Office.

Scheff, Thomas. 1966. *Being mentally ill.* Chicago: Aldine.

Schwartz, D. 1994. *Crossing the river: Creating a conceptual revolution in a community and disability.* Cambridge, Mass.: Brookline.

HEALTH CARE

Alice and Ruben Mendoza and their 2-year-old daughter, Carmen, live in a rural community in the Southwest. Until two years ago, Alice and Ruben owned a family restaurant; however, because of a downturn in the economy, they were forced to declare bankruptcy. Since then Ruben has worked seasonally as a farm worker and as a construction worker, and Alice has worked as a waitress in a neighboring town. Three years ago, Alice became pregnant. Because she and Ruben did not have health insurance, Alice waited until she was five months pregnant to see a doctor. Two months later, she gave birth prematurely to a daughter. Shortly after the birth, the baby began experiencing severe respiratory and cardiac problems, and the doctors decided to fly her to the regional neonatal center 300 miles away. The baby remained at the neonatal center for three months, requiring intensive care and heart and lung surgery.

When Carmen finally was allowed to return home, she required extensive care, and Alice was unable to return to work. Already financially strapped, the Mendozas were now faced with a $50,000 medical bill for the delivery and Carmen's care. A visit to the local human services department to seek Medicaid was unsuccessful. Although Alice and Ruben's income was less than $10,000 per year, they earned too much to qualify for the medical assistance. Alice's boss and other friends held a dance to raise money for the family, which netted $4,000.

At this point, Alice and Ruben are overwhelmed with medical bills and are unsure if they will ever be able to pay them all. Doctors say that Carmen is developmentally delayed and is likely to need extensive physical therapy and possibly more surgery later on. Although Ruben and Alice had hoped to have a larger family, they have decided they cannot afford to have any more children. Over the last six months, Ruben has developed kidney problems and has already missed five days of work. But he feels that he can't afford to see a doctor with the already-extensive medical bills and so is hoping that whatever is wrong will clear up by itself. ■

At the present time, **health care,** care provided to individuals to prevent or promote recovery from illness or disease, in America is in a crisis state. On one hand, many of America's citizens, like Ruben and Alice Mendoza, are faced with the payment of mammoth medical bills as a result of life-threatening situations. Thirty-seven million Americans, or about 15 percent, do not have any health insurance at all; an additional sixty million are underinsured, with only limited coverage (NASW 1995).

On the other hand, national expenses for health care have increased at incredibly high rates—from $12.7 billion in 1950 to $251.1 billion in 1980 to $884.2 billion in 1993. Health care expenses currently make up 14.1 percent of the U.S. gross domestic product, or a per-capita cost (cost per person) of $3,299; see Figure 11.1 (*Statistical Abstract* 1995). The health care industry is the third largest in the United States, preceded only by agriculture and construction.

Debates over national health care issues focus on two primary concerns: First, how much of our country's resources should be allocated to health care? And second, how should those resources be allocated? As our knowledge and technology in the health care arena continue to expand, decisions in the area of health care increasingly will become moral and ethical. Given scarce resources, for example, should an infant who requires tens of thousands of dollars to be kept alive be given maximum treatment to save its life, particularly when the child may live a life continually fraught with health problems and possibly retardation? And what about organ transplants and kidney dialysis—should these be made available to everyone? And if not, who should get them? Given the growing numbers of persons with AIDS, how many dollars should be allocated to research, education, and treatment, and who should pay what costs? Does the government have the right to mandate good health practices for women drug users who are pregnant or to impose penalties on persons with AIDS who do not practice safe sex? With more U.S. citizens living longer, to what extent should resources be allocated toward health care for older persons? And to what extent should attention be given to environmental concerns, such as nuclear power, sanitation, and pollution and their impact on personal health? Finally, given the high costs of health care, who should pay for health care for the indigent—the federal government, states, local communities, or individuals and their families themselves? And if individuals cannot afford health care, should it be denied to them?

Increasingly, social workers are playing a central role in helping policymakers, medical practitioners, and family members make these critical decisions. Social

FIGURE 11.1 **U.S. HEALTH CARE COSTS AS PERCENTAGE OF GROSS DOMESTIC PRODUCT**

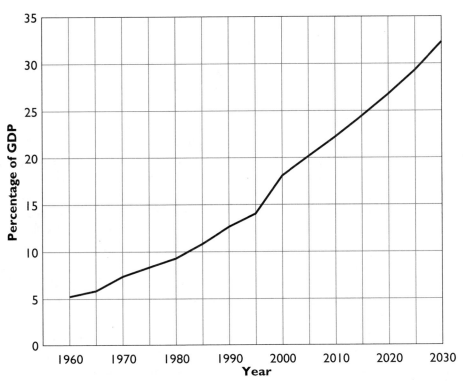

Sources: *Statistical Abstract of the United States* (Washington, D.C.: U.S. Government Printing Office, 1995), 109; D. Rice, "Health Care: Direct Practice," *Encyclopedia of Social Work* (Washington, D.C.: NASW, 1995), 1169. Copyright 1995, National Association of Social Workers, Inc.; and C. Lenkefeld and R. Welsh, "Health Systems Policy," *Encyclopedia of Social Work* (Washington, D.C.: NASW, 1995), 1207.

workers provide services in a variety of health-related settings, ranging from traditional hospitals to family planning clinics, rape crisis centers, home health care programs, and hospice programs for dying individuals and their families. Studies project that the area of health care, particularly as it relates to the elderly, is the fastest-growing area of employment for social workers today.

In this chapter, we give an overview of our country's current health care system, the problems it faces, and the types of health care policies and programs currently available. We also discuss the roles social workers play in making those policies and programs possible. ■

A SYSTEMS/ECOLOGICAL APPROACH TO HEALTH CARE

Because the systems/ecological perspective was first introduced as a mechanism to explain the functioning of the human body, this perspective has a longer history within the health care arena than other arenas in which social workers function. As early as the Greek and Roman eras of civilization, it was observed that many health problems were precipitated by changes in the environment. An ancient Greek medical text entitled *Airs, Waters, and Places,* said to be authored by Hippocrates, explained health problems in terms of person-environment relationships. This work attributed human functioning to four body fluids: blood, phlegm, and black and yellow bile. As long as these body fluids were in equilibrium, an individual was healthy. But Hippocrates attributed changes in the balance of these fluids to ecological variations in temperature, ventilation, and an individual's life-style in relation to eating, drinking, and work. Negative influences in the environment caused these fluids to become unbalanced, which in turn resulted in illness to the individual.

Other early works subscribed to germ theory, which is based on the premise that illness is a function of the interactions among an organism's adaptive capacities in an environment full of infectious agents, toxins, and safety hazards. The Greeks and Romans also were cognizant of the relationship between sanitation and illness. Early Roman writings suggested that people could predict and control their health through the environment and prevent epidemic diseases by avoiding marshes, standing water, winds, and high temperatures. Public baths, sewers, and free medical care were all ways that early civilizations used to promote health and reduce disease (Catalano 1979).

The focus on the relationship between individual health and the environment continued during later centuries. Frank's medical treatise, *System of a Complete Medical Policy* (written in 1774–1821), advocated education of midwives and new mothers, a healthy school environment, personal hygiene, nutrition, sewers and sanitation, accident prevention, collection of vital statistics such as births and deaths, and efficient administration of hospitals to care for the sick.

Numerous studies throughout the years have attributed incidence of infant mortality, heart disease, and cancer to environmental influences. A number of studies, such as Dohrenwend and Dohrenwend's well-known research (1974), show strong relationships between stressful life events and the subsequent development of physical disorders, supporting Hippocrates' earlier theories of the ways that a negative life-style can affect health. Brenner (1973) demonstrated the relationships between health problems such as heart disease, infant and adult mortality rates, and other health indicators and national employment rates between 1915 and 1967. He found that when employment rates were high, health problems were low, and that low employment rates were associated with higher incidences of health problems.

The interactions between environmental factors, such as unemployment, and mental health significantly affect individual health. Increased attention began to be paid to the relationship between health problems and mental health problems in the late 1970s with the release of the surgeon general's national health report, *Healthy People* (1979), which emphasized the important link between physical and mental health, noting the "importance of strong family ties, the assistance and support of friends, and the use of common support systems" in promoting healthy individuals (U.S. Surgeon General 1979).

Lazarus (1991) takes a somewhat different systems perspective, presenting research findings that show that persons who perceive their environments as stressful, such as those living in highly urban or highly rural areas, place their psychological systems in jeopardy and develop ways to cope that are tied to their perception of the situation. For example, an elderly man living in a rural area who perceives himself as being extremely isolated and without the resources to get him to a hospital quickly if he becomes ill is more likely to experience health problems than an elderly man who perceives that he is living in an area where health care is more readily available to him. As can be seen in Table 11.1, the greatest contributions to premature death are not individual hereditary factors, but environmental and life-style factors. Studies show that the following factors affect health status significantly.

TABLE 11.1   MAJOR FACTORS CONTRIBUTING TO PREMATURE DEATH, ESTIMATED PERCENT CONTRIBUTION TO CAUSE OF DEATH

Leading Causes of Death	Age-Adjusted Death Rate*	Life-Style	Environment	Inadequacy of Health Care Services	Genetic/ Hereditary Factors
Cardiovascular disease	281.4	54%	9%	12%	25%
Cancer	204.1	37%	24%	10%	29%
Strokes	56.1	50%	20%	10%	22%
Pulmonary diseases	36.0	50%	22%	7%	21%
Non-motor vehicle accidents	34.0	51%	31%	4%	4%
Motor vehicle accidents	16.1	69%	18%	12%	1%
Influenza/ Pneumonia	29.7	23%	20%	18%	2%
Diabetes	19.6	34%	0%	6%	60%
HIV	13.2	NA	NA	NA	NA
Suicide	12.0	60%	35%	3%	18%
Homicide	10.0	63%	35%	0%	2%
Total					
All ten causes together	852.9	51%	19%	10%	20%

*Per 100,000 population
NA = Data not available

Source: Data compiled from U.S. National Center for Health Statistics, *Statistical Reports* (Hyattsville, Md.: author, 1995), and U.S. Department of Health and Human Services, Centers for Disease Control, *Ten Leading Causes of Death in the U.S.*, 1995.

The major causes of death vary significantly by age. Although tremendous gains in preventing some major causes of death have taken place, many deaths are not related to major physical illness, particularly in youth. Accidents are still the leading cause of death for people under 25 years of age (see Table 11.2). Increased violence in our society has also affected causes of death, with homicide one of the three leading causes of death for youth 5 to 25. HIV also surpassed other causes of death for persons 25 to 44 for the first time in 1995.

Disability

Individuals with both permanent and temporary disability are much more at risk to have serious health problems than nondisabled persons. The fact that they may be less resilient due to their disability is often compounded by the lack of affordable, accessible, appropriate health care that allows them to maintain good preventive health practices.

Rural and Urban Areas

Individuals living in extremely rural or highly populated urban areas are more at risk to have health problems. This can be attributed to the increasing environmental hazards such as pollution and increased stress from living in a highly populated urban area, and to the lack of medical facilities for prevention and early medical care found in extremely rural areas. Over half of all people at the poverty level live in rural areas, and individuals in rural areas are more likely to suffer from emotional disorders than people in urban areas (see Chapter 16).

Applying a Systems/Ecological Perspective

It is vital that a systems/ecological perspective that focuses on the interaction and interdependence between person and environment be

TABLE 11.2   **TOP CAUSES OF DEATH IN THE UNITED STATES BY AGE IN 1995**

Age	#1 Cause	#2 Cause	#3 Cause
1–4	Accidents	Congenital anomalies	Cancer
5–14	Accidents	Cancer	Homicide
14–24	Accidents	Homicide	Suicide
25–44	HIV	Accidents	Cancer
45–64	Cancer	Heart disease	Strokes
65 and older	Heart disease	Cancer	Strokes

Source: U.S. National Center for Health Statistics, *Statistical Reports* (Hyattsville, Md.: author, 1996).

used in understanding **health risk factors,** or those factors that affect individuals' health and place them at risk for serious health problems and health conditions (see Table 11.1).

The current emphasis on holistic health care stems from a systems/ecological approach to health care. This perspective views all aspects of an individual's health in relation not only to how that individual interacts with family members, the workplace, and the community but also to how the environment, including community quality of life as well as legislation and funding available to support quality of life, affects a person's health. This perspective slowly is replacing the more traditional medical model used by health practitioners, which often focuses on symptoms and malfunctions of only one part of the body without focusing on other body systems or the environment within which the individual interacts. The World Health Organization defines **health** as "a state of complete physical, mental, and social well-being and not merely the absence of disease or infirmity" (Schlesinger 1985). This definition reflects the systems/ecological perspective in viewing health as clearly dependent on a combination of environmental, physiological, sociological, and psychological factors.

◪ THE EVOLUTION OF HEALTH CARE IN AMERICA

Early emphasis for health care in the United States focused on keeping people alive. Persons born in the United States 200 years ago had only a 50 percent chance of surviving long enough to celebrate their twenty-first birthday. One-third of all deaths were of children less than 5 years old. Even then, people of color had higher death rates. In the late eighteenth century, the death rate was 30 per thousand for whites and 70 per thousand for slaves (U.S. Public Health Service 1977). Health practitioners at that time were limited in number and in training and faced great difficulties in keeping their patients alive due to environmental constraints, such as poor sanitation and extreme poverty. Many illnesses resulted in catastrophic epidemics, which claimed the lives of entire families. In 1793 during a yellow fever epidemic in Philadelphia, three physicians were available to care for 6,000 patients stricken with the disease. Thus, early attempts to improve health care in the United States included national and state legislation relating to control of communicable diseases, sanitation measures such as pasteurization of milk, and education for midwives, physicians, and young mothers (U.S. Public Health Service 1977).

Although more recent legislation and programs have focused on control of chronic, degenerative diseases such as heart disease and cancer, on self-inflicted illnesses such as cirrhosis of the liver, and on other health problems such as accidents and violence, most efforts are still directed to restoring health after illness has occurred. The health care system in the United States still allows large numbers of U.S. citizens to remain unserved or underserved, and mortality rates remain higher than in many developed countries (Rice 1995).

◢ CRITICAL ISSUES IN CURRENT HEALTH CARE DELIVERY

Many domestic policy experts believe that the United States is experiencing a crisis in health care. While health care costs are increasing significantly, greater numbers of Americans are finding health care inaccessible to them. Health care statistics show that more infants are dying at birth, and other people are experiencing serious health problems that are often treatable.

Funding and Costs of Health Care

The rapidly increasing cost of health care at all levels of our society—for consumers, local health care practitioners, community hospitals and local governments, and state and federal programs—is considered one of the most critical issues facing the United States today. The United States spends over $1 billion a day on health care alone, with present predictions that this amount will increase to almost $5 billion a day by the year 2000, or $1.7 trillion per year and 18.1 percent of the gross domestic product; see Table 11.3 (Rice 1995).

Individuals like the Mendozas, whom we introduced at the beginning of this chapter, are not the only ones experiencing financial bankruptcy because of health care costs; physicians are leaving independently owned practices, particularly in rural and poverty areas; hospitals are closing; insurance companies are going out of business; communities and states are in the red due to increased costs of indigent health care; and the federal government's Medicaid and Medicare systems are not supporting themselves. Medicaid is being cut significantly by the U.S. Congress, and proposals are being considered to cut Medicare funding as well. In spite of the costs, services are increasingly fragmented, inaccessible, and unattainable for many U.S. residents and not well-matched to the needs of those receiving them when they are provided. In fact, the health care system in the United States unfortunately is an excellent example of how lack of planning and funding has created an ineffective, narrowly focused, fragmented, and expensive approach to a major social welfare problem.

Emphasis during the 1950s and 1960s was on providing the best possible health care to all Americans and improving health personnel, services, and research. But as costs for health care have skyrocketed, attention has shifted to ways to control costs and to determine who should pay for what expenditures. In 1993, the U.S. health care system provided over 1 billion examinations in physicians' offices; treated over 30 million persons in over 6,000 hospitals; provided care to over 1 million persons, mostly elderly, in over 19,000 nursing homes; provided over 435 million examinations during outpatient visits to hospitals; and provided home health and hospice care to over 5 million people (*Statistical Abstract* 1995).

Health Insurance Plans and Managed Care

In 1991, **private insurance,** or insurance purchased by individuals on their own or through their employers from companies such as Blue

TABLE 11.3	GROSS DOMESTIC PRODUCT (GDP) AND NATIONAL HEALTH EXPENDITURES BY SOURCE OF FUNDS (1929–2030)

| | NATIONAL HEALTH EXPENDITURES | | | |
| | PUBLIC FUNDS | | PRIVATE FUNDS | |
Year	Amount (billion $)	% of Total	Amount (billion $)	% of Total
1929	$ 3.2	86.4%	$ 0.5	13.6%
1950	9.2	72.8	3.4	27.2
1955	13.2	74.3	4.6	25.7
1960	20.5	75.5	6.7	24.5
1965	31.3	75.3	10.3	24.7
1970	46.7	62.8	27.7	37.2
1975	77.8	58.5	55.1	41.5
1980	145.0	58.0	105.2	42.0
1985	248.0	58.7	174.6	41.3
1990	390.0	57.8	285.1	42.2
2000	859.9	49.4	879.9	50.6
2010	1,819.2	48.0	1,968.8	52.0
2020	3,776.1	48.2	4,063.2	51.8
2030	7,753.0	48.5	8,216.7	51.5

Cross/Blue Shield, paid for 37 percent of the costs of this care. Consumers paid for 19 percent of the care directly, either to cover health costs if they did not have health insurance at all, or to cover costs not covered by their personal health insurance if they had it. **Public insurance** funds, both state and federal, paid for 44 percent of care, mostly through Medicaid and Medicare programs. Medicare costs in 1991 totaled $102.2 billion, while Medicaid costs totaled $96.5 billion (Rice 1995).

One factor that has contributed to the increased costs for both private and public health care has been the shift from retrospective to prospective payment systems. In the past, with the exception of insurance for hospitalization, most health care was paid for after you used it—you went to the doctor, and you paid the full amount after your visit. Today most health care is paid for in advance through premiums to private insurance companies or federal programs such as Medicaid, because the health care industry is trying to contain costs and promote preventive health care.

Most current health care plans are based on a **managed care system,** a system of health care delivery that limits the use and cost of services and measures performance. Health care professionals are hired by health insurance companies and large employers to review specific health care needs and determine the most cost-effective ways to provide for them. After review, limited options are presented to consumers. Some plans include preferred provider organizations, which offer health

	TOTAL		
GDP (billion $)	**Amount (billion $)**	**$ per Capita**	**% of GDP**
$ 103.1	$ 3.6	$ 29	3.5%
284.8	12.7	80	4.5
398.0	17.7	101	4.4
513.4	27.1	143	5.3
702.7	41.6	204	5.9
1,010.7	74.4	346	7.4
1,585.9	132.9	592	8.4
2,708.0	250.1	1,064	9.2
4,038.7	422.6	1,711	10.5
5,522.2	675.0	2,601	12.2
9,637.0	1,739.8	6,148	18.1
17,238.0	3,787.8	12,522	22.0
29,594.0	7,839.4	24,278	26.5
49,936.0	15,969.6	47,891	32.0

Sources: S. T. Bruner, D. R. Waldo, and D. R. McKusick, "National Health Expenditures Projections through 2030," *Health Care Financing Review* 14(1), 1–29; National Center for Health Statistics, *Health, United States, 1991* (DHHS Publication No. PHS 92–1232, Table 112), Hyattsville, Md.: U.S. Public Health Service, 1992; National Center for Health Statistics, *Health, United States, 1992* (DHHS Publication No. PHS 93–1232, Tables 114, 122), Hyattsville, Md.: U.S. Public Health Service, 1993; and D. Rice "Health Care: Financing," *Encyclopedia of Social Work*, p. 1169 (Washington, D.C.: National Association of Social Workers, 1995). Copyright 1995, National Association of Social Workers, Inc.

care through a network of specific providers. An individual who chooses other providers than those in the network usually must get specific permission from the health care plan to do so, pay additional costs to use other providers, or not have those health care costs covered by the plan at all.

Another important group in the health care industry is **health maintenance organizations** (HMOs), which consist of prepaid medical group practices to which individuals pay monthly fees and receive specific types of health care at no cost or minimum costs per visit. Payment of a monthly amount to a health insurance company or HMO entitles a person—and, if insured, the person's family—to either needed health care on demand at no additional cost or a limited cost, for example, 15 percent of the cost with the insurance or health care company paying the additional 85 percent.

Such managed care plans try to stress more preventive services, reduce hospital stays, and allow fewer expensive medical tests. But concern has been expressed about some of these efforts, in particular reduced hospital stays for both health and mental health care. Some plans, for example, allow women who give birth under normal situations to remain in the hospital only twenty-four hours. Termed "drive-through birth" by some opponents, this practice has raised issues about the increased risk to infants and their mothers during the first forty-eight hours after birth without being in a hospital setting where they can be closely monitored and any serious complications addressed quickly.

Although prospective health care has been an attempt to promote early preventive use of care to create a nation that is physically healthier and to reduce costs, it has not been highly successful at either task. Administrative costs alone to manage such a complex system have escalated over the years. In Canada, which has a government-supported system, administrative costs for health care in 1990 were 6 percent of the total health care budget. Administrative costs for health care that same year in the United States were 22 percent (Scuka 1994).

Health care costs continue to escalate at rapid rates in spite of efforts of cost containment. Increases can be seen at every level: the average cost of health care per person per year in the United States is now $3,299, the highest rate of any industrialized country—38 percent more than Canadians pay and 49 percent more than the Swedish pay. Between 1980 and 1987, employees' share of health insurance premiums increased 50 percent. When someone buys a Chrysler or General Motors car, $700 of the amount provides health care coverage for employees and their families, compared to $200 when buying a Japanese car (Edwards 1990).

Comparing Health Care Costs to Outcomes

Although the United States currently spends more on health care than any other country, its health care system does not produce superior outcomes in comparison to other countries (see Table 11.4). In 1995 the United States ranked twentieth in life expectancy and seventeenth in infant mortality among twenty countries of the Western world.

In 1995, infant mortality rates in 21 countries ranged from 4.3 per thousand live births in Japan to 45.6 per thousand in Turkey. The U.S. rate was 7.9, or the fifth highest. The life expectancy in 1995 ranged from 80.2 in Hong Kong to 71.5 in Turkey. The U.S. average life expectancy was 76.0 or a ranking of twentieth among the 21 countries cited. It is understandable that Turkey's infant mortality rate would be so high and its life expectancy so low, since Turkey spends the lowest amount of any country cited on health care, an average of $146 per person. However, it is more difficult to understand why the United States' infant mortality rate is much higher than most western countries and its life expectancy for both males and females is much lower, since the United States spends more than any other country per capita on health care (*Statistical abstract of the United States* 1995). When comparing significant health care indicators, the U.S. investment in health care has failed to achieve its intended outcomes.

Almost one-fourth of all U.S. women who deliver babies at public hospitals have received no prenatal care. Although studies show that as much as $14 a day can be saved for every dollar invested in immuni-

TABLE II.4   **COMPARISONS OF HEALTH CARE COSTS, LIFE EXPECTANCY, AND INFANT MORTALITY RATES**

Country	Percent of GDP Allocated to Health Care (1993)/Rank	Health Care Costs per Capita (1993)/Rank	Infant Mortality Rate* (1995)/Rank	Average Life Expectancy (1995)/Rank
United States	14.1/1	$3,299/1	7.9/17	76.0/20
Canada	10.2/2	1,971/3	6.8/10	78.3/6
Switzerland	9.9/3	2,283/2	6.3/6	78.4/3
France	9.8/4	1,835/4	6.5/8	78.4/3
Austria	9.2/5	1,777/6	6.9/12	77.8/10
Finland	8.8/6	1,363/12	5.2/2	76.2/18
Netherlands	8.7/7	1,532/8	6.0/5	78.0/8
Germany	8.6/8	1,814/5	6.3/6	76.6/17
Australia	8.5/9	1,494/11	7.1/15	77.8/10
Italy	8.5/9	1,523/9	7.4/16	77.4/13
Belgium	8.3/11	1,601/7	7.0/13	77.2/14
Sweden	7.5/12	1,266/14	5.6/3	78.4/3
Japan	7.3/13	1,495/10	4.3/1	79.4/2
Spain	7.3/13	972/16	6.7/9	77.9/9
United Kingdom	7.1/15	1,213/15	7.0/13	77.0/16
Denmark	6.7/16	1,296/13	6.8/10	76.1/19
Greece	5.7/17	500/17	8.3/19	77.8/10
Cuba	NA	NA	8.1/18	77.1/15
Hong Kong	NA	NA	5.8/4	80.2/1
Israel	NA	NA	8.4/20	78.1/7
†Turkey	2.7	146	45.6	71.5

*per thousand births

†Turkey is included for comparison purposes only; it is not ranked in the top twenty of any category

NA = Not available

Source: Data compiled from *Statistical Abstract of the United States* (Washington, D.C.: U.S. Government Printing Office, 1995), 849 and 853.

zations, large numbers of children in the United States remain unimmunized: 60 percent of infants do not receive the immunizations they need by the age of 7 months (NASW 1995). In 1990 a number of children died because of a large measles outbreak in the United States, and increasing numbers of children are getting whooping cough and other illnesses that had declined significantly in recent years.

Although costs of health care, like costs in other areas, have increased due to inflation, other reasons for rising health expenditures also must be considered. Some attribute increased costs to more extensive use of medical resources by a more educated population interested in preventive health care. They argue that accessibility to group insurance plans

More than 37 million individuals in the United States do not have health insurance. Although this mother works full-time, her workplace does not provide health insurance. She is constantly worried that her children will get sick and she will not be able to pay for their medical care.

through the workplace and the increase in HMOs and other health programs aimed at reducing health costs actually increase costs because of more extensive use. Statistics show, however, that many Americans, particularly poor persons—people of color, single-parent females, and the elderly—work for employers who do not offer health insurance or are paid such low wages that they cannot afford the health insurance offered. Thus, they are less apt to use health care resources; but when they do, they are more likely to need more costly services because they have not sought preventive care.

Even with today's emphasis on wellness and public awareness about the potential damages of smoking, alcohol and other drug consumption, and lack of exercise, few dollars are spent on prevention by private citizens and by all levels of U.S. government. This trend continues even though studies show that dollars spent for prevention pay for themselves as much as eight times over in the long run (Van Den Bergh 1995).

An Increasing Elderly Population

There are other, more reliable explanations for the extreme costs of health care in the United States. First, because of increased access to health care, improved knowledge and technology, and a better quality of life, people are living longer, resulting in increased need for medical care for those 65 and older. Composing approximately 11 percent of the population and more likely to be poor and unable to pay for health care than other groups, persons over 65 have three times more health problems and needs than persons in other age groups. Between 1990 and 2030, the population of people over 65 will more than double, increasing from 30 to 65 million, or one out of every five people in the United States (Scuka 1994).

As this population continues to increase, costs will also increase. Few insurance premiums cover the costs of nursing home care, and those that do are rapidly increasing their premium charges. The insurance system, particularly in care for the elderly, is also fragmented, with separate systems paying for home health care, medical equipment, nursing homes, and transportation to and from health care facilities (Ford Foundation 1989). It is estimated that by the year 2040, persons 65 and older will account for more than half of the total personal health care expenditures in the United States.

Medicare and Medicaid costs are also expected to increase significantly. Medicare costs in 1994 were $147 billion; they are expected to increase at an annual growth rate of 10 percent; Medicare costs in the year 2040 are projected to be six times greater than they were in 1990 (Scuka 1994). Medicaid costs, which were 82 billion in 1994, are also expected to increase significantly as the elderly population increases. Although only 12 percent of the Medicaid population in 1992 was 65 years and older, this group accounted for 32 percent of Medicaid expenditures. In contrast, AFDC recipients and their families made up 71 percent of the Medicaid population but accounted for only 30 percent of expenditures, while persons with disabilities made up 14 percent of the population and accounted for 37 percent of expenditures (Rice 1995).

Increased Knowledge and Availability of Technology

A second explanation for the increased costs of health care is the greater availability of knowledge and technology for saving lives: neonatal procedures for infants born prematurely; heart, lung, and other organ transplants; and heart surgery to restore circulation and reduce incidence of heart attacks and other cardiac problems. Currently, the extent of and knowledge about technology exceed the dollars necessary to support such sophisticated systems and make them available to everyone in need (see Box 11.1). In many instances, heroic procedures are covered by health care policies, whereas preventive care, such as long-term care, rehabilitative services, and health education, are not (Ford Foundation 1989). Although values issues are inherent when discussing health care, our current health technologies have become very costly. Current studies suggest, for example, that persons who receive heart transplants live an average of four years longer than persons who do not receive transplants, at a cost of $100,000 per transplant or $25,000 for every additional year of life.

Additionally, with increased numbers of private hospitals and the difficulties public hospitals face in remaining solvent, health care has become increasingly competitive. Many private hospitals are now owned by large corporations with real estate subsidiaries and their own insurance divisions. In many instances, the increased competition has resulted in duplicative purchases of expensive equipment by hospitals in

BOX 11.1

ETHICAL DILEMMAS THAT BALANCE HEALTH CARE COSTS AND HUMAN LIFE

BRACKENRIDGE TO PAY $15,300 FOR EQUIPMENT TO MOVE GIRL

Patty Carnes' special wish to have a family of her own is closer to coming true.

Brackenridge Hospital officials Tuesday decided to buy the $15,300 worth of medical equipment the 6½-year-old girl needs to stay alive in the home of a Portland, Ore., family who plan to adopt her.

"We don't want Patty to wait any longer," said Sandra Bockelman, an assistant city attorney. Brackenridge is a city-owned hospital.

Patty, who was left paralyzed and unable to breathe on her own by a spinal cord inflammation when she was an infant, has been in the hospital for six years—longer than any other Brackenridge patient. A ventilator breathes for Patty, but it does not prevent her from talking, laughing, or making wishes like any other child.

Patty's move from Children's Hospital of Austin at Brackenridge to the home of Diane and Ken Stacy in Oregon will cost nearly $45,000—$15,300 for a ventilator and other equipment, $20,000 for a van with a wheelchair lift, and $9,600 for an air ambulance.

Brackenridge's decision to buy the equipment came one day after Travis County commissioners voted to pay for the air ambulance, which doctors say is the safest way to transport Patty.

The van, which the Stacys need to take Patty to school and to the doctor, "is the only thing that stands in her way" of moving, said Stephanie Crowell, a pediatric social worker at Brackenridge. "That's the glitch."

"If we can get this money for the van, I think this little girl is going to go home," said Crowell, who has spent years trying to locate a family to adopt Patty.

Patty is a ward of the state because her mother gave up her parental rights when she realized she could never properly care for her daughter. Last week, a state judge ordered the Texas Department of Human Services to have Patty moved to the Stacy's home by Feb. 15. During a hearing before State District Judge Jeanne Meurer, representatives of the state, county and city argued that the other governmental entities should pay for Patty's move.

City officials decided to buy the medical equipment because it appeared that DHS and the county have not found any money for equipment, Bockelman said.

"We'll buy the equipment and put it on (Patty's) bill," she said, but "we're all hoping somebody will drop out of the sky with the money" to reimburse Brackenridge.

Patty's unpaid hospital bill totals more than $2 million, and charges of more than $1,500 are added each day, officials said.

Source: Denise Garnino, "Brackenridge to Pay $15,300 for Equipment to Move Girl," *Austin American Statesman,* 24 January 1990, sec. B. Reprinted with permission.

close proximity. While hospitals struggle to compete with each other for paying clients, the number of persons who are unable to pay hospital bills continues to increase. The limits on public insurance (i.e., Medicare and Medicaid) reimbursements to hospitals also have created serious financial problems for many hospitals that are unable to provide services at reimbursement levels. In Texas, for example, 105 hospitals have closed since 1980, 73 percent in rural areas. Eighty percent of rural hospitals in Florida were leased or sold between 1982 and 1987. During the third quarter of 1989, Texas hospitals lost $1.6 billion in uncompensated care, or an average of $619 for each Medicare patient and $601 for each Medicaid patient. One in ten patients was indigent and could not pay for medical costs at all.

Emphasis on Third-Party Payments

A third reason that has been suggested for escalated health care costs is the use of third-party billing by many medical practitioners (billing an insurance company directly rather than billing the patient). Many physicians and hospitals charge the maximum amount allowable under an insurance system, whereas they might otherwise be reluctant to charge individual clients the same amount if they knew the clients would be paying for the services directly.

Faced with rapidly increasing costs, the 1,500 private insurance companies in the United States that cover about half of the population are now minimizing their risks by reducing benefits covered, requiring second opinions in many instances, and excluding the chronically ill. At the same time, insurance premiums continue to increase, with high costs to employers who pay portions of employees' premiums as well as to employees themselves. In 1965, 9 percent of corporate profits was spent on employee health care, while in 1989 it was 46 percent. As a result, many employers, particularly smaller ones, are now either no longer covering employees or their families or are covering a smaller percentage of premiums, so that employees are paying much larger shares. Increasing numbers of people who carry health insurance on an individual rather than an employee policy are being forced to cancel their policies because they cannot afford them, requiring local communities to pick up the rising costs of their health care when they become ill and cannot pay their bills.

Increased Costs of Health Care for the Poor

A fourth reason for the increased costs of health care is the number of poor individuals who need health care and cannot afford to pay for it. As this number continues to increase, federal and state governments are struggling with the high costs of health care. But efforts to reduce Medicaid and Medicare expenditures by setting ceilings for reimbursable costs have led some physicians and nursing homes to refuse to accept clients under these health care assistance plans, claiming they lose too much money because the actual costs are much higher than the ceilings allowed.

Even though there are problems with the Medicaid system of health care for the poor and with group insurance programs, of greater concern are the large numbers of persons who have no health coverage at all. Over half of the poor in the United States are either not covered by Medicaid or do not use the system. Those persons who have neither Medicaid nor other health insurance coverage often become destitute immediately when they or members of their family suffer health problems. Few families can afford even several thousand dollars in health care costs, and many health problems can easily cost a family over $10,000. Unfortunately, when individuals and other available health care programs cannot pay for health care, local communities and tax-payers must bear the costs. One study (Kingston et al. 1988) was of poor persons aged 50 to 64 who received services at a New York City shelter for the homeless and did not qualify for federal health care programs. The researchers found that 75 percent of this group had had some type of medical treatment during the past year, 30 percent had been hospitalized, and 76 percent had received emergency room services. The city had to pay for the health care.

Many local public hospitals that must accept all patients are operating in the red; one local hospital spent over $2 million on a young child with serious health problems, because the girl was not covered by any type of private or public health care plan. Thus, the hospital—and the local taxpayers—absorbed the costs of her care. The story had a happy ending; the child was adopted and moved to a home with parents equipped to provide for her special needs at a cost much, much less than the $1,500 per day cost for her hospital care (see Box 11.1).

But the costs of indigent health care to local communities are increasing. Many state legislators and citizens do not understand the complicated reimbursement system for government programs such as Medicare and Medicaid. For every dollar of Medicaid money spent, for example, the state contribution is forty cents and the federal contribution is sixty cents. But conservative legislatures limit dollars allocated for state health care, not always understanding that limiting state costs reduces the number of federal dollars available to the state and ultimately results in more money, not less, paid by that state's citizens.

One large state, for example, consistently limits its legislative authorization of state dollars for health care coverage for the poor, particularly dollars to draw down federal Medicaid and Medicare funds. As a result, less federal money comes into that state and more goes to other states. In one recent year, for example, for every $3.00 that a citizen of the state paid in federal income taxes, only $1.89 was returned to the state. The other $1.11 went to other states for their programs. Yet because the state authorized only a limited Medicaid program, large numbers of women and children were not eligible to receive Medicaid benefits. When they became ill, they went to local government hospitals, funded by local tax dollars, with the hospitals having to absorb the costs of their unpaid care. Thus, from a cost standpoint, the health care the women and children received that could have cost state citizens forty cents per dollar if they had been covered by Medicaid ultimately cost the citizens the entire dollar—and this does not include the extra tax money the state citizens are paying in federal taxes that is going to other states.

Increased Numbers of Malpractice Suits

Our society's encouragement of lawsuits is another cost-raising factor. Many medical practitioners fear the increasing number of malpractice suits being filed. One study found that all practitioners face at least one suit during their careers, no matter how competent they are. This has resulted in extremely high costs for malpractice insurance, and practitioners who feel compelled to order numerous tests, exploratory surgery, and other medical procedures when they are not sure what is wrong with an individual, to eliminate the risk of a lawsuit for a wrong decision.

CURRENT MAJOR HEALTH PROBLEMS

Although many health problems that faced Americans in the past have been all but eliminated, new ones arise upon which attention must be focused. Current major health problems facing the United States and its citizens include heart disease, strokes, cancer, AIDs, and catastrophic illnesses.

Heart Disease, Strokes, and Cancer

Heart disease, strokes, and cancer remain the three leading causes of death in the United States. Although heart disease and strokes are declining because of the increased attention to personal health, including fitness and diet, it is estimated that almost 50 percent of U.S. citizens will die from heart disease. Cancer rates continue to rise, and are increasingly associated with environmental factors. Cancer will eventually strike one out of every three persons. Breast disease is the leading cause of death for women, and rates of breast cancer are increasing in the United States. While new technology and medications have made treatment of these diseases more effective, they remain major causes of death. When all federal monies, including Medicaid and Medicare, are taken into account, federal annual expenditures for heart disease total $36.3 billion and for cancer $16.9 billion (Seelye 1995).

AIDS

Acquired immunodeficiency syndrome (AIDS) is the greatest tragedy to strike the world in the health area in decades. AIDS has affected all of our social institutions and most communities in the United States. Although people who are diagnosed with HIV infection often live ten years or more after the diagnosis, the disease is always fatal and continues to spread to all segments of the population. Because the method of transmission of the virus is tied to culturally sensitive topics, including the use of illegal drugs, sex, and sexual orientation, AIDS is often viewed at all levels of society in political and moral contexts rather than as a serious public health issue (Lloyd 1995).

AIDS first came to the attention of health authorities in the early 1980s. Through June of 1994, a total of 401,749 cases of AIDS had been identified, including more than 6,000 among children. According to the National Centers for Disease Control and Prevention, more than 250,000 people have died from the disease or related causes. A new definition adopted by the National Centers for Disease Control and Prevention broadened conditions from those previously associated with the virus. Based on more research and the inclusion of additional populations experiencing the virus, including women, this new definition will allow for earlier detection of persons infected with the virus, double the numbers of persons known to have it, and lengthen their survival time (Lloyd 1995).

When a person is referred to as being **HIV-positive,** it means that the person has tested positively for AIDS, is infected with the virus, and has HIV (human immunodeficiency virus) antibodies present in his or her blood. HIV is an intracellular parasite that binds to molecules in the body, causing the destruction of cells that help maintain the immune system and leading to a gradual but progressive destruction of the entire immune system (McGrath 1990). During the primary HIV infection period, 50 to 90 percent of individuals develop a mononucleosis-like infection that begins one to three weeks after infection and continues for one to two weeks (Lloyd 1995). But most individuals will not recognize HIV-related symptoms at this point, and test results are usually not accurate until approximately six months after getting the virus. Although persons who test positive for AIDS may not show symptoms of AIDS for many years, they are carriers of the virus and can infect others with it.

Previously, AIDS-related conditions were viewed in three stages: infection with the virus, AIDS-related complex (ARC), and clinical AIDS. But these conditions are now seen on a continuum from the point of infection to clinical AIDS. Conditions related to AIDS include fever, weight loss, swollen lymph nodes, diarrhea, fatigue, and night sweats. In addition, laboratory tests show a low white blood cell count, low red blood cell count, low platelet count, or elevated levels of serum globulins. Other conditions include a low number of T-helper cells and a low ratio of T-helper to T-suppressor cells. This condition moderately damages the body's immune system.

As the disease progresses, the body's immune system begins to collapse. This results in the recurrent development of otherwise treatable infections, which continue to break down the body's resistance and stress the entire system. Kaposi's sarcoma, a rare skin cancer, is a common disease associated with AIDS. As more women are diagnosed with AIDS, cervical cancer and chronic yeast infections have been added to the list of conditions associated with AIDS. About half of persons with AIDS die from a rare form of pneumonia caused by the organism *Pneumocystis carinii* (Rothstein 1989).

Little is known about how the disease can be treated effectively, and current research efforts have yet to find a cure or vaccine to prevent its spread. AIDS is transmitted by exchange of body fluids, primarily blood and semen. To date, there is no evidence that AIDS is transmitted by casual contact such as shaking hands, sharing drinks from the same glass, getting an insect bite, sneezing, or living or working with a person infected with the virus. Persons at the highest risk to be exposed to AIDS are homosexual and bisexual men, intravenous drug users who share needles, persons who are exposed to the virus through blood transfusions, and babies born to mothers who are infected with the AIDS virus.

Although AIDS originally hit the populations of gay men and substance abusers hardest, the highest rates for newly infected individuals are among women through heterosexual transmission of the virus.

Seventy-eight percent of the cases reported to the Centers for Disease Control and Prevention through June of 1994 were men and women 20 to 39 years of age. AIDS is now the leading cause of death among all Americans 25 to 44 years of age. Although when causes of death are separated by gender, AIDS is first for males and fourth for females, it is expected to rise to second place for females within the next several years.

AIDS experts have suggested that because it takes several years for AIDS symptoms to show up, instead of looking at data relating to the numbers of persons with full-blown AIDs, we should focus on the numbers of persons who have the HIV virus in their blood. Recent projections of blood testing of persons in the military and from other studies are consistent with new AIDS cases reported to the Centers for Disease Control and Prevention. These projections suggest that whereas rates among homosexual and bisexual men have stabilized, rates among the heterosexual population, particularly intravenous drug users, women, and children, are increasing. One recent study of two inner-city hospitals in the East found that 6 percent of persons tested carried the AIDS antibody. In one of the hospitals, in an area with a high number of drug users, 30 percent of African American males ages 25 to 44 carried the antibody. Heterosexuals, drug users and their partners, and children born to persons with AIDS now make up over 25 percent of new cases. Pediatric AIDS cases make up 2 percent of all cases, with the average age of diagnosis six months and the average life span two years. Many of these children never leave the hospital after birth, and their care is expensive both in dollars and emotional costs to hospital employees who work with the children and their families.

Because of the long incubation period for AIDS, most of those who will die of the disease do not know that they have it. Once the AIDS antibody is discovered, estimates are that it costs $80,000 to cover all health care costs of a person with AIDS. Most persons with AIDS eventually have to quit their jobs if they are employed and often lose their health insurance before the disease takes their lives. Persons with AIDS and their families face not only serious financial problems, but also discrimination both in communities and the workplace and problems in obtaining health care, housing, employment, social services, and emotional support. Although the Americans for Disabilities Act (see Chapter 11) specifically mentions persons with AIDS in its listing of groups of persons with disabilities covered under the act, oppression and discrimination still are major issues faced by persons with AIDS and their families (see Box 11.2 for the NASW policy statement on AIDS). Additionally, it is estimated that by the year 2000, there will be approximately 100,000 children whose parents have died of AIDS. Developing permanent plans for them is another difficult issue that parents with AIDS are forced to address. While many of their children are going to live with relatives, increasing numbers of children will need foster care and adoption placement (Conover 1994).

Currently, only limited funding has been made available for research, treatment, or public education. In contrast to the other major life-threatening diseases that strike most U.S. citizens, federal expenditures for AIDS are much less, totaling about $6 billion annually (Seelye 1995).

BOX 11.2

HUMANE TREATMENT FOR PERSONS WITH AIDS: THE NATIONAL ASSOCIATION OF SOCIAL WORKERS POLICY STATEMENT ON AIDS

Because of the complex biopsychosocial issues presented by AIDS, ARC, and HIV infection, social workers, with their special knowledge, skills, and sensitivity, can make a unique contribution to the management of this crisis by pursuing action in eight areas:

1. **Research:** Basic research, including epidemiological, clinical, and psychosocial studies, is imperative. Social workers, particularly in the area of psychosocial research, have a special contribution to make. They have been at the forefront of issues relating to AIDS and have demonstrated significant leadership in identifying critical issues and needs and have a responsibility to continue in these research efforts.

2. **Public Education and Dissemination of Information:** Accurate information about AIDS; HIV infection control measures; prevention; treatment; and medical, financial, and psychosocial resources available should be widely distributed. The fears of caregivers and the general public must be addressed with appropriate education and interventions. Adequate public funds must be authorized for educational efforts among the general public to reduce the fear of AIDs, ARC, and HIV infection and the stigmatization of persons assumed to be at risk for infection. Adequately funded public education programs should encourage prevention, early treatment, and formulation of new behaviors to reduce the risks of HIV infection. Professional health care organizations, training programs, and continuing education programs should incorporate the latest information and address especially the needs of minority groups, adolescents, women, infants and children, the

developmentally and physically disabled, and the chronically mentally ill. Education and training programs must accommodate differences in culture and ethnicity among people. Program materials must be clear and explicit and targeted to individuals of all sexual orientations. Social workers should work cooperatively with existing AIDS-related educational, treatment, and research organizations. Especially important, social workers should be educated and updated on all AIDS-related issues, including prevention strategies, and should play major roles in reducing public hysteria and prejudice.

3. **Psychological and Social Support:** Comprehensive psychological and social support is necessary to help persons with AIDS, ARC, and HIV infection and all individuals close to them. Extended families, including domestic partners and significant others, represent rich resources of emotional and social support, just as they represent a network of persons likely to be affected by the disease-related changes, including death, of persons with AIDS and HIV infections. All care providers should respect the individuality of people with AIDS, ARC, and HIV infection and the importance of the individual's relationships with family, domestic partners, and close friends.

    The diversity of interpersonal relationships and support systems should be recognized, nurtured, and strengthened. Supplemental services, including support groups, counseling, and therapy, should be made available to people with AIDS and AIDs-related conditions and their loved ones as well as to others who feel vulnerable. In addition, all providers of care should have access to support groups and related services to alleviate the stress inherent in assisting persons with AIDS-related conditions. All AIDS-related service organizations should provide for support, supervision, respite, and recognition of social workers engaged in the emotionally demanding work of serving people with AIDS.

4. **Service Delivery and Resource Development:** A comprehensive service delivery system to respond to AIDS based on a case management model must include suitable housing, adult-child foster care, home health and hospice care, appropriate, affordable health care, access to legal services, and transportation services. Children needing foster care should be provided care at the least restrictive level in nonsegregated settings. Traditional health and social welfare agencies including income maintenance programs must become responsive; eligibility requirements and coverage by health insurance and income maintenance should be adapted to meet the rapid onset and catastrophic effects of AIDS. The health status of people with AIDS-related disorders may vary daily. Currently, service delivery systems do not take health care needs and work requirements into consideration. Systems should be more flexible in providing services for individuals with AIDS-related disorders.

Adequate funding both from public and private sources should be provided to assist alternative health and social services that deal with AIDS and AIDS-related conditions in various communities. Such services, many of which are complementary to and cooperative with mainstream services, help broaden and strengthen the range of traditional supports available to persons with AIDS and AIDS-related conditions. Social workers should be encouraged to be involved in the initiation of—and serve as membership on—local, statewide, regional, and national AIDS task forces.

5. **Civil Rights:** No person should be deprived of civil rights or rights to confidentiality because he or she has been diagnosed as having contracted AIDS, is infected with HIV, or is assumed to be at risk for infection. Nondiscrimination laws should be extended and existing legal protection should be vigorously enforced to protect individuals with AIDS, ARC, and HIV infections from being presumptively deprived of health care, employment, housing, and immigration rights.

6. **HIV Testing:** Social workers should be concerned particularly with the violation of human rights and the psychosocial consequences to people taking HIV antibody tests. Given the potential for serious discrimination, all testing should be voluntary, anonymous, and conducted with informed consent. Social workers should make certain that the limits of the predictive value of such testing are known in advance by clients. Appropriate pre- and post-test counseling must be offered by social workers or other skilled professionals. Social workers are mandated to protect client confidentiality.

7. **Professional Accountability:** The helping professions and appropriate

continued

BOX 11.2   concluded

licensing authorities should use their full range of persuasive and regulatory powers to assure that people with AIDS, ARC, and HIV infection and their significant others are not discriminated against in their eligibility for or receipt of services because of their illness or lack of financial or social resources.

8. **Political Action:** Social workers, individually and organizationally, should participate with other groups to lobby actively at local, state, and federal levels on behalf of people with AIDS in order to improve their quality of life; protect

their civil liberties; and to advocate for increased funding for appropriate education, prevention, interventions, treatment, services, and research.

The National Association of Social Workers (NASW), as the organizational arm of the profession, must help coordinate a response to AIDS, ARC, and HIV infection by pursuing the multifaceted strategy outlined in this policy statement.

Source: National Association of Social Workers, *Social Work Speaks: NASW Policy Statements*, 3rd ed. (Washington, D.C.: NASW Press, 1994). Copyright 1994, National Association of Social Workers, Inc.

Other Illnesses and Health Problems

Other illnesses receiving increased attention are diabetes, musculoskeletal diseases such as arthritis and osteoporosis, and respiratory diseases. These problems are much more likely to be experienced by the poor, people of color, and the elderly, who are less likely to be able to afford both preventive and rehabilitative health care.

Recent research is finding that some life-threatening diseases, such as Huntington's disease and cystic fibrosis, are genetically linked. Researchers indicate that within the next several decades, prenatal genetic screening will most likely be able to indicate the presence of hypertension, dyslexia, cancer, sickle cell anemia, manic depression, schizophrenia, Type 1 diabetes, familial Alzheimer's disease, multiple sclerosis, and myotonic muscular dystrophy (Rothstein 1989). Others predict that genetic screening will also show a predisposition for addictions to alcohol and other drugs.

These discoveries will increase the level of debate regarding moral and ethical choices in relation to birth, fetal and parental rights, abortion, and emotional and dollar costs to individuals and society. If it is certain that a child will be born with multiple sclerosis, AIDS antibodies, or cancer, who should decide the outcome? If the child is born, who should pay the costs for care? Present pregnancy termination rates for women who decide to have genetic screening are nearly 100 percent for muscular dystrophy and cystic fibrosis, 60 percent for hemophilia, and 50 percent for sickle-cell anemia. But what if the disease is one that occurs much later in life, such as Huntington's disease; is not fatal, such as Down syndrome; or reveals a "predisposition" to a disease, such as cancer, heart disease, or schizophrenia? The field of **bioethics** is a fast-growing one in which social workers can play a major role.

Another health concern is the increased numbers of persons with serious head or spinal injuries who are brain injured, multiply disabled, or both. Many require years of rehabilitation, and some require institutional care for the remainder of their lives. As technology enables many more persons who experience such injuries to remain alive more often than in the past, costs for their care also increase. Because large numbers of persons have received head and spinal injuries because of motorcycle accidents when they were not wearing helmets, or had alcohol- or drug-related accidents or car accidents when they were not wearing seat belts, additional concerns are raised about who should pay for health costs and how much should be paid.

Catastrophic Illness

Increased national attention is also being given to the problems encountered by families when a **catastrophic illness** occurs. A catastrophic illness is a chronic and severely debilitating condition that results in high medical costs and long-term dependence on the health care system. Although many families can provide health care for themselves during typical, less serious bouts of illness, a catastrophic illness most often can wipe out the savings of even a fairly wealthy family. To date, proposals have failed for national legislation to provide national health insurance for individuals and families who experience a catastrophic illness when their available health insurance is exhausted and the costs for the care have reached a certain limit. The Catastrophic Health Care bill, passed by both the U.S. House and the Senate in 1988, provided coverage for families and the elderly who experienced catastrophic illness or disability. But it was repealed in 1989 after a strong lobby by middle- and upper-middle-class elderly persons, who protested against increased Medicare premiums included in the legislation. The bill provided Medicare benefits at full coverage after one year of hospitalization, but increased the deductible for benefits as well as the costs for premiums. The bill also did not cover long-term nursing home care. Although many national groups and health care lobbyists continue to advocate for a national health insurance program that provides some type of health care coverage for all individuals in the United States, coverage limited only to catastrophic health care is a compromise measure more likely to be approved. Thus, it is likely that some sort of catastrophic health care bill will pass in the near future.

Teenage Pregnancy

Attention has been directed toward at-risk groups that generate additional health problems. Recently, the group most publicized has been teenage parents. Studies show that pregnant teens receive little or no prenatal care, poor nutrition during pregnancy, and limited services (USDA 1990). As a result, they are at more risk of miscarriages, and of giving birth to premature and low-birth-weight infants and ones with congenital problems.

Although availability of family planning and other preventive services, as well as prenatal health care, is viewed by many as a moral issue because such services supposedly promote teen pregnancy, such services are cost effective and more likely to result in healthy infants better able to grow up to become healthy adults. A one-year study by the U.S. Department of Agriculture found, for example, that low-income pregnant women who participated in the food and nutrition education program saved an estimated $573 for every newborn. Birth weights increased and the number of premature births declined among program participants.

Environmental Factors

Increased attention also is being paid to environmental factors and their impact on the health of individuals. These include hazardous household substances and other poisons, as well as the quality of household building materials, such as lead-based paints and formaldehyde in insulation. Workplaces also present risks to health, and increased attention is being given to environmental protections for employees from dangerous chemicals, pollutants in the air, and hazardous jobs. An estimated one-fifth of all cancer deaths are associated with occupational hazards. A recently publicized environmental hazard, associated with increased incidence of cancer and respiratory diseases, has been the discovery of harmful asbestos in many older buildings. Yet in spite of the known health risk, workers hired to remove asbestos in many instances have not been given needed protection to avoid exposure to the substance. Fifty percent of persons who have long-term exposure to asbestos die. Other environmental risks associated with some occupations also receive little attention. For example, 30 percent of uranium miners develop lung cancer (U.S. Senate Committee on Labor and Human Resources 1994).

For all persons living in the United States, regardless of occupation, the environment is an increasing health hazard. The rising amount of ozone in the air and other pollutants in the air, the soil, and food products has resulted in significant increases in heart disease, cancer, and respiratory diseases in the United States in comparison to other countries. States and communities are paying increased attention to road and traffic safety; unsafe housing; contaminated food, meat, and dairy products; pest and animal control; biomedical and consumer product safety; and other public health risks, such as inappropriate disposal of chemical and human wastes, storage and treatment of water, and control of nuclear energy plants.

Smoking is increasingly being seen as an environmental hazard. New studies suggest that smoking poses a health threat not only to smokers, but to those who also inhale their smoke. Recent federal and state legislation, local community ordinances, and workplace policies limit smoking to specially designated areas or prohibit it completely. For example, smoking is not allowed on airline flights.

Prevention and Wellness Programs

Increased attention is also being given to preventive aspects of health care, although prevention is still secondary to intervention after a health problem has occurred. The 1979 surgeon general's report, *Healthy People*, stated that the United States spends only about 5 percent of health care

Preventive health care is far more cost effective than medical problems that arise when preventive services are not provided. This young infant's mother received no prenatal care and he was born prematurely, requiring intensive care and a hospital stay of several months.

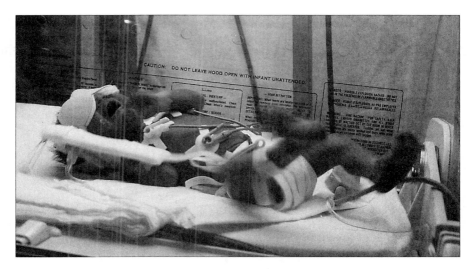

dollars on promotion of preventive measures. But some businesses have established wellness programs, with exercise and fitness programs, nutrition and weight control programs, smoking cessation workshops, and other health prevention efforts. A number of employers are working with insurance companies to offer incentives to employees who are low health risks, such as salary bonuses or reduced insurance rates. Problems in the workplace and the broader society due to substance abuse have also led employers and insurance companies to establish substance abuse prevention programs in the workplace.

Ethical Issues

As health care costs continue to increase, more people need health care, and new technology and knowledge make it possible to keep people alive who previously could not have been helped. For these reasons, ethical dilemmas in the area of health care continue to increase. Many of these issues are already before our courts. When infants born three and four months premature can be saved, at what point, if at all, should abortion be prohibited? When infants require extensive neonatal care in order to survive, should such care be made available, even if the parents cannot afford the costs? Should the circumstances change to provide such care if the infant can survive but with serious mental and/or physical disabilities? (See Box 11.1.) If technology for heart and lung transplants is available, should everyone of all ages and income groups have equal access to these procedures? If genetics testing reveals that a fetus has a serious illness or disability, what choices should be considered, and who should be involved in the considerations? If persons can survive with medical care or special procedures, should they have a right to decide whether to receive the care or to be allowed to die? Do persons have the right to choose unsafe behaviors, such as riding motorcycles without helmets, not using seat belts, or using drugs or alcohol heavily, when injuries or other health problems may result in high costs to others—taxpayers, state, and local governments, others in the same insurance group? Does a pregnant woman have the right to drink alcoholic beverages, use other drugs, or smoke if it can compromise the survival of her child? Who makes such decisions? What are the rights of the individual? Of the parents if the person is a child? Of the state or local governments if they are to pay for the care? (See Box 11.3.)

Several recent court cases have attempted to address some of these issues. In the early 1980s, the so-called Baby Doe case received national attention. This case involved an infant born with serious health problems who would have been seriously disabled—physically and mentally—with surgery, and who would have died immediately without surgery. The parents did not want the child to have surgery or to suffer, but instead to die a peaceful death. Some members of the hospital staff wanted the child to have the surgery, and others wanted the child to die. Concern has been raised in similar situations throughout the country. In some instances, it was reported that infants had been starved to death or had experienced great pain when life supports were removed from them before they died. Special legislation was introduced that would have required local child welfare agencies to handle all such situations as child protective services cases and conduct investigations before medical decisions were made to ensure that children were being protected. The legislation was changed before it passed so that this did not happen, but it did mandate that hospitals establish special review boards to deal with such cases.

Some states have also made legislative decisions that have addressed serious ethical issues. In 1987 the state of Oregon voted to stop using its Medicaid funds to pay for liver, heart, bone marrow, and pancreas transplants and to use the $2.3 million saved to provide prenatal care for women in poverty. Other states, including Alabama, Arizona, Texas, and Virginia, have set limits on what they will pay for organ transplants. Illinois passed transplant legislation allowing funding for transplants, but appropriated only a limited amount to pay for them. The California legislature decided to pay for transplants, but then reduced its Medicaid funding shortly thereafter, cutting health care benefits to 270,000 Californians. Citizens groups throughout the United States are forming to address such ethical decisions. One of the first, Oregon Health Decisions, formed in 1983 and has held meetings throughout the state to determine and then advocate for priorities for health funding.

Another major ethical issue relates to decisions surrounding the right to die. The Karen Quinlan case (and other similar cases involving persons who are kept alive only because of life support systems, but are in a coma or not in touch at all with their surroundings) generated increased debate over the issue. Other situations involving persons who have serious health problems and decide themselves that they wish to die are also receiving attention. Ethical issues are also raised regarding the role of others in aiding those who decide they want to die. Dr. Jack Kevorkian, a physician and a vocal proponent of the right to choose to die, has generated extensive controversy and been arrested several times for successfully helping a number of individuals to die, including those who are terminally ill and have a short time to

BOX 11.3

BIOETHICS: THE CHALLENGES OF GENETIC DISCOVERIES

The medical system is the core around which other institutions build their use of new diagnostic techniques. Their acceptance in medical settings is encouraging their use outside the clinical context: in insurance companies, in schools, in the workplace, in the courts. The accumulation of diagnostic information about individuals can indicate preventive actions or therapeutic procedures. On the other hand, nonclinical institutions may use the tests in ways that the medical profession did not intend, with devastating results.

Imagine, for example, a small electronics firm planning to manufacture an intricate navigational system. Part of the system must be assembled manually, and the company must carefully select an individual for the arduous training this new job requires. One of the company's employees seems ideal. Dependable, bright, and particularly quick with her hands, she is thirty-five years old and has worked for the company for eight years. This company routinely uses the latest diagnostic tests to screen its employees, and has her biological profile on record. The company physician does a computer scan of it, searching for disabilities that could affect her motor coordination in the future. He discovers an unexpected problem: the woman's DNA markers show, with a high degree of certainty, that she will develop Huntington's disease, an inherited degenerative neurological disorder that results in loss of motor control, depression, personality changes, and death. Symptoms may begin to develop when she is about forty, and soon after she may be unable to work. Her condition would eventually become debilitating and require costly medical care. Thus she would be an economic drain on worker's compensation and the corporation's health insurance and long-term disability policies. From the employer's perspective it would hardly be rational to promote and to train this person. But for the individual, the consequences of this information are disastrous. Her employer might begin to question her ability to function in her current job. If she is terminated, who else would employ her? And who would pay her costly medical bills?

Sophisticated diagnostic tests serve many useful and humane purposes: in clinical settings they may point the way to particular therapeutic measures. They can provide families the opportunity to avoid the anxiety and cost of bearing a child with an untreatable disease; they can identify potential health or behavioral problems for remedial or preventive action. In nonclinical contexts, they can help in the early recognition of learning-disabled children, protect vulnerable workers from exposure to harmful toxic substances, and provide solid evidence for legal decisions about a person's criminal responsibility or competence to stand trial. The language used to describe diagnostic techniques speaks mostly of such benefits. The tests emerging from research in the neurosciences will "generate clinical successes" and provide "answers to disabling mental illness," claims the National Institute of Mental Health. "New genetic clues to heart disease, cancer, AIDS, and other killers could save your life," reports a journalist. "We'll achieve the ideal in medical care, the prevention of disease," predicts the director of a biotechnology firm.

Yet information from tests is not always beneficial or even benign, for in many cases nothing can be done to prevent the predicted disease. What will happen to a twenty-year-old who discovers that he is likely to develop a fatal disease in middle age? The genetic flaws detected by tests will not necessarily translate into functional impairment; yet knowing about the potential problem without being able to prevent it will be a source of extreme anxiety for him. Moreover, it could subject him to considerable discrimination. He may be denied a job, and his insurance costs will surely increase. Even if something can be done to prevent the manifestation of a predicted condition, awareness of the predisposition can be used in ways that harm the individual. A diagnosed genetic vulnerability to heart disease may encourage a preventive life-style, but the prediction itself could affect a person's career. After all, tests have often been abused, serving, for example, as a means to justify racial or gender bias, to legitimate arbitrary exclusionary practices, and to enhance institutional power with little regard for the rights or personal fate of individuals.

Source: D. Nelkin and L. Tancredi, "The New Diagnostics," *National Forum* 69(4): 2–4 (1989). Reprinted with permission.

live and those who have been in constant pain for years from debilitating diseases.

Although those situations obviously involve some degree of choice, the American Medical Association estimates that 70 percent of the 6,000 deaths that occur each day involve some sort of negotiation regarding life or death. A recent U.S. survey found that 80 percent of persons interviewed approved of laws allowing medical procedures withheld if the patient wishes (Malcolm 1990).

In many instances, such ethical dilemmas can be avoided, and dollars saved, by providing accessible and affordable health care before the problem occurs. For example, pregnant women who do not receive care during the first three months of pregnancy are 30 percent more likely to deliver infants with low birth weights. Costs for providing such infants with neonatal intensive care average $20,000 per child. Not only is $772 saved for each day that an infant remains in its mother's uterus between the twenty-ninth and thirty-fourth week of pregnancy, but the ethical dilemmas that often occur with such cases are also avoided (Metropolitan Council 1985).

Ethical issues will also continue to occur as knowledge and technology about health-related issues increase. For example, geneticists have identified specific genes that are responsible for diseases such as cystic fibrosis. Gene therapy, a procedure in which healthy new genes are introduced to interact with other healthy genes or to suppress production of abnormal cells, is resulting in breakthroughs in treating such diseases. Researchers are also beginning gene therapy trials with various types of cancer. As geneticists discover new relationships, futurists suggest that scientists will have the capability to change characteristics such as eye color, complexion, temperament, and possibly gender and sexual orientation. This raises numerous ethical issues, such as who decides what is changed and under what conditions. Obviously, most individuals would agree that gene therapy is ideal in treating such life-threatening conditions as cystic fibrosis. But the potential for "genetic engineering" to create a homogeneous society also exists. This potential means that social workers and others with a strong values base that embraces human diversity will need to play major roles in advocating for the appropriate use of such technologies.

◢ HEALTH PLANNING

To eliminate problems in costs of health care, duplication of care in some areas and gaps in others, and interface of public and private sector health care delivery, several important pieces of legislation have been passed. These include the following.

Hill-Burton Act

Passed in 1946, the Hill-Burton Act funded construction of a number of rural hospitals. Amendments in 1964 authorized the development of areawide hospital planning councils and the concept of areawide hospital planning. The act also specifies that hospitals that receive funding through this legislation cannot refuse to serve clients if they are unable to pay for services.

Medicare and Medicaid

National legislation has also established Medicare and Medicaid programs, which provide the majority of federal financing for health care. Medicare is a special health care program for the elderly, to be used as a supplement to their other insurance programs (see Chapter 17); whereas Medicaid is available only to low-income individuals and families (see Chapter 9). The growth of both programs has been extensive.

In 1994, Medicare was funded at a cost of $160 billion and served 37 million elderly and disabled persons. Medicare is now experiencing a serious financial crisis. Current estimates predict that the Medicare trust fund will not be able to pay for services shortly after the year 2000. Although Medicare pays many costs, it does not provide long-term care for chronic needs, particularly nursing home care, or for other costs such as special wheelchairs that might enable more elderly to be cared for in their own homes. Because of increases in premiums for Medicare, in 1990 it paid for less than 50 percent of the total costs of health care for senior citizens. Analysts predict that significant reductions in federal spending of Medicare programs will occur during the next five years.

Medicaid was funded at $125.2 billion in 1993, with 57 percent, or approximately $81.3 billion, coming from the federal government. Approximately 10 percent of Americans were covered by Medicaid, including 3.7 million elderly, 4.9 million persons with disabilities, 7.4 million adults in families, and 16.1 million children. Fourteen percent of health care in the United States is funded by Medicaid, including one in three births and health care for one in four children (NASW 1995).

Although costs for Medicaid have increased, many of the poor do not qualify for coverage; in 1990, for example, only 37 percent of our nation's poor were covered by Medicaid. The Omnibus Budget Reconciliation Act of 1989 mandated states to increase the number of pregnant women and children covered under Medicaid from those at or below 130 percent of the poverty level to those at or below 133 percent. This 3 percent increase cost the state of Texas alone $26 million in state dollars, with the federal government paying the remainder of costs. In 1992, federal legislation extended Medicaid coverage to families who are at or below 185 percent.

The 1988 Family Support Act also extended Medicaid coverage to AFDC (Aid to Families with Dependent Children) recipients for up to one year after they become employed. Although more expensive initially, it is hoped that this plan will actually reduce government health care costs, since large numbers of recipients who leave the AFDC rolls have been forced to return when they or their children experience health problems and they have not been able to become financially stable enough to afford health insurance. It is hoped that the employment programs for public assistance recipients in states required by the Family Support Act will result in human services agency staff helping more recipients find long-term jobs that offer health insurance, and that the extension of Medicaid as a transitional benefit also will help recipients to remain off AFDC once they obtain employment.

Although Medicare was intended to provide the bulk of health care for the elderly, with Medicaid intended to serve children and families, increasing amounts of Medicaid dollars are being used to pay for nursing home care that is not provided under Medicare. In 1994, for example, two-thirds of all nursing home residents in the United States were covered by Medicaid (NASW 1995). State and federal budget crises in Medicaid are not because of increased costs to serve families, but to cover nursing home and other extensive health care costs for the increased numbers of elderly persons who cannot afford to pay for health care not provided by Medicare.

Like Medicare, Medicaid is also likely to be cut significantly by the federal government in the next five years. But because Medicaid is viewed as health care for poor people rather than for the elderly, the program lacks a powerful constituency to advocate on its behalf and may be more vulnerable to significant cuts (NASW 1995).

Maternal and Child Health Act

Title V of the Maternal and Child Health Act, through the Supplemental Food Program for Women, Infants, and Children (WIC), provides screening, counseling, and food supplements for pregnant women and children up to 5 years old who are at nutritional risk due to low income. Studies show that WIC reduces infant deaths, low birth weight, and premature births and increases good health and cognitive development among preschoolers. Since the Reagan administration significantly reduced funding for the program, some states have been able to document that infant deaths, low birth weight, and premature births are on the increase and can be tied to the reduction in WIC programs. Additionally, because states have the option of offering the program, only half of eligible women and children in the United States were receiving WIC services in 1990.

Comprehensive Health Planning Act

Passed in 1966, the Comprehensive Health Planning Act expands on the concept of local health planning districts to coordinate services and also requires review of other factors affecting the health of area residents, such as life-style and environmental conditions. The National Health Planning and Resources Development Act of 1974 further mandates the establishment of health systems agencies and statewide health coordinating councils to monitor hospital bed supply and occupancy rates, obstetric and neonatal special care units, pediatric beds, open heart surgery, and availability of expensive technological equipment such as megavoltage radiation equipment. The focus of this legislation is to increase availability of services in rural or other underserved areas and eliminate duplication in other areas, as well as to provide high-quality care at reduced costs by requiring rate review panels and professional standards of care.

Health Maintenance Organization Act

Passed in 1972, the Health Maintenance Organization Act allows the development of health maintenance organizations (HMOs) to reduce health care costs for individuals. Most HMOs require a monthly fee, which allows free or low-cost visits to a special facility or group of facilities for health care. HMOs are intended to reduce health costs and encourage preventive health care.

CARE Act

The Ryan White Comprehensive AIDS Resources Emergency (CARE) Act of 1989, named in honor of 18-year-old Ryan White (who died of AIDS in 1989) authorizes emergency funds to metropolitan areas hardest hit by AIDS, grants to states for comprehensive planning and service delivery, early intervention with HIV-infected infants, and the development of individual pilot projects to serve children with AIDS and to provide AIDS services in rural areas. This act was reauthorized by Congress in 1995 but without a significant funding increase.

Future Legislation: Health Care Reform

The absence of universal access to health care is creating a two-track system in the United States: (1) health care for those persons who are employed in organizations that offer adequate health care coverage who can afford to pay health care premiums and are healthy enough to be covered, and (2) those persons who are either receiving government health care benefits, most likely Medicaid and/or Medicare, or have no options for health care because they are unemployed, underemployed, or employed by employers that do not offer adequate benefits or offer benefits that are too expensive to purchase. Many individuals are caught in the middle as health care providers and employers grapple with ways to reduce quickly escalating health care costs. For example, some health care plans restrict benefits that cover previous health problems, often denying benefits to those who need them most. Thus if an individual changes jobs or an employer changes benefit plans, new rules may force reduced coverage or no coverage at all. These individuals then may not obtain preventive health care or may end up with health care problems so serious they are forced to leave the workforce, possibly becoming eligible for Medicaid or other government health care.

Efforts continue to be made through legislation and other policy arenas to balance health care costs with quality of care. It appears likely that some sort of mandated universal health care program will be established at some point. Currently, the United States and South Africa are the only two industrialized countries that do not have some type of government-funded universal health care system.

Because of the complexity of reasons for increased health care costs and the many groups concerned about health care in the United States, tackling health care reform is difficult. President Bill Clinton made health care reform the single most important issue when he first took office. But his administration's efforts to oversee the overhaul of the health care system met with resistance from a wide range of sources. While most individuals and constituency groups agree that reform is needed, there is a great deal of diversity in suggestions about the types of reforms that should be adopted.

Many advocates for a universal health care system in the United States are calling for a national health insurance program for all types of health care, not just catastrophic illness. Those in favor of such a program argue that costs for health insurance are too high for large numbers of individuals to afford, that many local hospitals are going in debt because they are having to pay health care costs for the increasing numbers of indigent persons, and that health costs are higher because persons are not seeking preventive health care, which would be more likely were there a national health insurance program with such an emphasis. Those against such a program argue that it means going to a system of socialized medicine, that the costs would be too high, that individuals would lose their freedom of choice regarding which health care provider they want, and that people would clog the health care delivery system with trivial health problems that do not require medical attention.

Proponents of government-funded health care programs have proposed a variety of alternatives. Many, including the National Association of Social Workers, call for a universal access, single-payer system with national standards. They want to eliminate the relationship between health care and employment so that those unemployed, employed by employers without available or affordable health care, or not covered because of previous health conditions can still receive health coverage. Some plans call for the federal government to collect funds for a national health care program from various taxes, with the program administered by private insurance companies instead of by a single government system. Others advocate for a "pay or play" proposal, with employers providing health care to their employees contributing to a public fund to pay for those without insurance or underinsured. Critics of this plan say that it is a punitive system that does not guarantee universal coverage and still creates a two-track system. Other plans call for having persons claim a tax credit on their income tax form if they use health care and providing health coverage only for catastrophic illnesses.

Changes in the Congressional makeup in the fall 1994 elections seem to have put health care reform on the back burner. The Republicans' Contract with America in 1995 did not mention health care reform at all. Current plans call for eliminating federal bureaucracy and channeling health funds to the states to administer directly. Many state leaders, including a number of governors, are concerned that such efforts merely pass the burden of complex issues and astronomical costs to them.

Some states have already begun to implement health care reforms. Minnesota, for example, funds a program to provide health care to all children who fall below a certain income level and are not covered by other programs. Oregon, realizing that most health care dollars are spent on long-term care for the elderly and persons with disabilities, has shifted its focus on long-term care from institutions to less expensive home and community-based options. Termed "aging in place," with services delivered to the individual rather than requiring the individual to go to the services, the number of nursing home beds per 1,000 population has been reduced by 25 percent, with 27 beds per thousand senior citizens compared to 42 nationally; the per capita cost for long-term care is $448 compared to $693 nationally; and the state has saved $400 million from 1981–1994; see Box 11.4 (Concannon 1995).

Local states also are passing other health care legislation, limiting the amounts that can be collected in malpractice suits in an attempt to keep medical costs down; mandating availability of health care for indigent persons and reducing the burden on local hospitals in poor areas of states; and establishing procedures for decision making about organ transplants and life-threatening situations. More states will follow the path set by Oregon and California, passing legislation limiting the types of health care allowed with state dollars.

Proposals will continue to be made and debated at all levels of government. Scuka suggests the following criteria for evaluating proposals for health care reform (1994, 582):

- Does the proposal provide universal coverage so no U.S. citizen or legal resident is deprived of access?

- Does it eliminate the link between employment status and health insurance coverage?

- Does it eliminate cost-sharing such as copayments and deductibles that could impede access because of out-of-pocket costs?

- Are preexisting medical conditions prohibited as a condition for restricting or excluding individuals from coverage?

- Is universal access given priority over specialty care services for a limited population so that no one gets extraordinary care until everyone gets minimal care?

- Are there controls on purchase of expensive technology to limit duplication?

- Is there a nationwide system of standard fees to control rising costs?

Legislation, planning, and service delivery at all levels will need to focus on reducing the costs of health care while increasing the accessibility. Other critical issues in the next decades include reducing the fragmentation of care, developing private and/or government insurance for long-term health care for the elderly, and increasing the availability of funding for home health and respite care. More resources will be devoted to outpatient community-based care and case management. Greater attention will also be given to prevention, including teen pregnancy and violence as well as AIDS education, and to the promotion of life-style changes such as improved diet and the elimination of substance abuse and smoking.

BOX 11.4

LIVING IN THEIR OWN HOMES

Ella Nelson, of Eugene, Oregon, was 105 years old January 19 and still lives in her own home. She is surrounded by familiar furniture and knickknacks. Photographs of family and friends—from her childhood in turn-of-the-century Sweden to the latest great-grandchild—cover walls and shelves.

She is able to live at home and maintain her independence because of Oregon's home- and community-based care program. She employs a live-in provider, who is paid by the state, and also has a lift chair and a quad cane, both purchased by the state. Mrs. Nelson's family provides respite care on the weekends. SDSD estimates that the cost of her in-home care is about half of what it would be in a nursing facility.

Of course, Ella Nelson is one of only eight Medicaid-eligible centenarians living at home in Oregon. More typical are Herb and Martha Sweeny (not their real names), who live in Woodburn in Oregon's mid-Willamette Valley. He is 73, and she is 62 and has a heart condition that prevents her from performing household chores such as vacuuming or scrubbing. They are nevertheless able to live in their own home because the state pays for two hours of housekeeping a week.

"It's better to be here in our own home together," she says, "than to have to be put into a home that would take care of us."

That has been Oregon's thinking for a dozen years. Caring for older citizens in their homes saves money, keeps them healthier, and is responsible for Oregon's being the only state with fewer Medicaid-eligible seniors living in nursing homes today than 10 years ago.

These seniors are among more than 25,000 statewide whom the state helps—about two-thirds of them with nursing, housekeeping, cooking, laundry, and other services in home- and community-based care. They have in common that they are poor. Three-fourths are women. But by keeping people in community-based care—in their own homes, in adult foster care, or in assisted-living facilities—nearly three people can receive services for every one living in a nursing facility.

Note: *Ella Nelson died at home of natural causes February 26, 1995—Ed.*

Source: K. Concannon, "Home and Community Care in Oregon," *Public Welfare* 53, no. 2 (1995): 13 (Washington, D.C.: American Public Welfare Association).

◢ SOCIAL WORK ROLES IN THE DELIVERY OF HEALTH SERVICES

Today, social workers play many roles in a variety of health care settings. In fact, social work in health care, particularly in working with the elderly, is one of the fastest-growing occupational areas today. Health care is the third largest field of social work practice, with 14 percent of social workers employed in health care settings. Recent developments have expanded the social work profession's involvement in health care. In 1989, federal legislation relating to nursing homes mandated that by October 1990 all nursing homes in the United States with 120 or more beds must have a social worker with a BSW or MSW degree. Changes in legislation relating to Medicare also now require that social workers with an MSW degree who also have professional social work certification should be reimbursed for providing outpatient mental health services to the elderly. Previously, only psychiatrists or psychologists could be reimbursed under Medicare for these services. As the number of home health care agencies expands, the role of social workers in assessing mental health needs and providing intervention and case management services will also expand. Social workers will also need to pay increased attention to the strengths of the family members of persons with health needs as greater demands are placed on natural caregivers (Poole 1995). As individuals with serious physical and mental injuries continue to live longer due to increased technology, the role of social workers in rehabilitation hospitals will also increase. Additionally, for the first time, federal legislation providing training monies for persons interested in health care includes social workers as well as nurses and physicians.

Both roles and settings have increased significantly since social workers became involved in health care issues. As early as 1888, social workers were advocating for some sort of insurance coverage for all U.S. citizens. Jane Addams and other social workers focused on health care prevention and community action relating to concerns such as poor sanitation, malnutrition, unsafe housing, and poverty (Poole 1995).

The first known hospital social worker was employed at Massachusetts General Hospital in Boston in 1905. At that time, hospitals and general physicians were the major sources of health care. The social worker worked with the physician, other hospital staff, and the patient's family to ensure that high-quality care and attention continued after the patient returned home. Although responsibility for care after a patient leaves the hospital is still a major one for many social workers in health care settings, today social workers in these settings provide a variety of other tasks as well. Social workers often serve as a liaison between the patient's family and health care staff. They help the staff understand family concerns and how family constraints and other environmental factors may affect a patient's ability to recover. They also help patients and their families understand the implications of illness and issues relating to recovery and care. In many instances, the social worker provides support to the family when a death occurs or a patient's condition worsens.

Social workers in health care settings provide a number of other functions, including

- Conducting screening and assessments to determine health risk factors, particularly those involving the family and the broader environment

- Offering social services to patients and their families, such as individual counseling to help a patient deal with a major illness or loss of previous capabilities due to accident or illness, helping family members grieve over a dying individual, or helping a teenage mother accept her decision to place her child for adoption

- Providing case management services, including working with other social and health services agencies regarding patient needs, such as helping arrange for financial assistance to pay hospital bills, nursing home or home health care for patients when they leave the hospital, or emergency child care for a single parent who is hospitalized

- Serving as a member of a health care team and helping others understand a patient's emotional needs and home or family situation
- Advocating for the patient's needs at all levels of the environment, including the patient's family, hospital and other health care settings, social services agencies, school, workplace, and community
- Representing the hospital and providing consultation to other community agencies, such as child protective services agencies in child abuse cases
- Providing preventive education and counseling to individuals relating to family planning, nutrition, prenatal care, and human growth and development
- Making health planning and policy recommendations to local communities, states, and the federal government in areas such as hospital care, community health care, environmental protection, and control of contagious diseases

Whereas many social workers function in agencies administered by and hiring primarily social workers (called **primary settings**), health care settings are considered **secondary settings** because they are administered and staffed largely by health care professionals who are not social workers. Social workers in health care settings must be comfortable with their roles and be able to articulate their roles and functions clearly to other health care professionals. A strong professional identity is important for health care social workers. Additionally, social workers in health care settings must be able to work comfortably within a medical setting. Knowledge and understanding of the medical profession and health care are important for social workers, as is the ability to function as a team member with representatives from a variety of disciplines. Social workers in health care settings, particularly hospital settings, must be able to handle crisis intervention, and they most often prefer short-term social work services rather than long-term client relationships. They must be able to work well under pressure and high stress and be comfortable with death and dying.

Hospital Settings

The American Hospital Association requires that a hospital maintain a social services department as a condition of accreditation. Social workers in hospitals may provide services to all patients who need them, or they may provide specialized services. Larger hospitals employ emergency room social workers, pediatric social workers, intensive care social workers, and social workers who work primarily on cardiac, cancer, or other specialized wards. M. D. Anderson Hospital in Houston, Texas, for example, has over twenty social workers. It is a large hospital that specializes in treating cancer patients. A number of large hospitals have added social workers who provide social services primarily to AIDS patients. Other hospitals use social workers in preventive efforts, providing outreach services, including home visits to mothers identified during their hospital stay as potentially at risk to abuse or neglect their children. Still others use social workers to coordinate rehabilitative services, serving as a case manager to ensure that occupational, physical, recreational, speech, and vocational therapy services are provided. Social workers work in both public and private hospitals, providing both inpatient and outpatient care. Many are employed by Veterans Administration (VA) hospitals, which have a long-standing tradition of using social workers to work with persons who have served in the armed forces. Many VA social workers provide specialized counseling relating to physical disabilities and alcohol and drug abuse. A number of VA social workers now specialize in post–Vietnam stress syndrome and provide services to Vietnam veterans and their families.

Because of accreditation standards, most hospital social workers must have master's degrees in social work. Many graduate schools of social work offer specializations in medical or health care.

Long-Term Care Facilities and Nursing Homes

Many persons who suffer from illness or disability do not need the intensive services of a hospital, but cannot care for themselves in their own homes without assistance. For some individuals, particularly the frail elderly, **long-term care facilities,** programs that provide medical care and other services to individuals including the elderly and the disabled, such as nursing homes, are most appropriate. There are various levels of care facilities, with licensing and accreditation requirements for each. From 1965 to 1972, social work services were mandated for all nursing homes that cared for residents covered by Medicare. Beginning in 1990, all nursing homes with 120 or more beds must employ a social worker. Social workers in these settings help residents adjust to the nursing home environment, help families deal with their guilt and feelings of loss after such placements, serve as liaisons to other social services and health care agencies, provide individual and group counseling and other social services for nursing home residents and their families, network with others interested in services for the elderly at the local and state levels, and advocate for improved services for the clients they serve.

Provision of social work services to the elderly in health care settings is probably the fastest-growing area of social work, and many schools of social work are offering specializations at the master's degree level in health and gerontology and special courses at the BSW level in these areas to meet the demand.

Community-Based Health Care Programs

Many social workers, both at the BSW and MSW levels, are employed in local community-based health care programs. Most state health departments operate local health clinics, which provide a variety of health services available to low-income residents as well as community education programs for all residents. Such programs include immunizations, family planning services, prenatal care, well baby and pediatric services, nutrition and other types of education programs, and basic health care. Many health clinics employ social workers to work with patients and their families as other health care services are provided. For example, some clinics operate high-risk infant programs, which include social services for parents of infants at risk for abuse, neglect, or other serious health problems or those who already have serious health problems and whose parents need monitoring and support. Social workers also work with local community groups and schools, providing outreach programs to publicize and prevent such problems as sexually transmitted diseases and teen pregnancy.

Social workers are also employed in family planning clinics, such as Planned Parenthood, providing counseling and help in decision making regarding pregnancy prevention or intervention, such as planning for adoptive services in an unwanted pregnancy. With new technology that can diagnose problems in embryos in the uterus, many health providers also are employing social workers to offer genetic counseling, helping clients to understand possibilities of giving birth to infants with potential problems, and to make appropriate decisions regarding whether to become pregnant or to terminate a pregnancy.

Many social workers are employed in community health care settings that provide services to persons with AIDS and their families. Social workers perform individual, family, and group counseling; serve as case managers assisting clients and their families in accessing community resources; provide advocacy for clients and their families; and offer community education programs.

Increasingly, other health care settings are recognizing the impact of environmental factors, such as unemployment, on mental and physical health. To help address the relationship, previously traditional health care settings increasingly are employing social workers. In many areas, for example, local physicians' clinics, usually operated by a small group of physicians who share a practice, are hiring social workers to provide counseling to patients in an effort to improve mental health and reduce stress. HMOs are also hiring social workers to perform similar functions.

Home Health Care

Many states and communities are recognizing the need for **home health care,** or services that enable persons with health problems to remain in their own homes. Home health care services most often preserve self-esteem and longevity for the individual and are far less costly than hospital or nursing home care. Trained nurses and home health aides, as well as social workers, make home visits to perform health care in a person's home. Social workers provide counseling to both the client and family, help clients cope emotionally, and serve as case managers, ensuring that appropriate resources are provided to deal with client needs. Home health care allows the elderly, persons with AIDS, and other persons who do not need to be hospitalized the right to have greater control over their lives. Such care also offers them dignity and emotional support they might not receive in a hospital or other institutional setting. Because home health care programs are more cost effective than hospitalization or other institutional care, these programs will be expanded during the next several decades, and more social workers will be needed to work in them.

State Department of Health and Health Planning Agencies

Many social workers at both the BSW and MSW levels are employed in health care policy and planning jobs. They help make critical decisions regarding funding, policies, and programs for state legislatures, federal officials, and state and local health departments and planning agencies. A social worker might determine how many more elderly could be served by Medicaid if the income eligibility requirements were changed from 130 percent to 150 percent above the poverty line, develop plans to implement a community-wide AIDS education program, or suggest ways that a local hospital can be more responsive to the needs of the primarily African American and Latino population it serves. In one state, for example, planners in the state health department recommended that the agency solicit bids for infant formula for infants served by the WIC program instead of contracting with the same company the agency had always used. The bids received were much lower than the amount the department was paying for the formula, enabling the department to serve many more clients while still saving money.

The impact of environmental changes on individuals, disease prevention and control, monitoring of solid waste and water facilities, and emergency and disaster planning are other areas in which social workers in these programs become involved. Many social workers have become heavily involved in policies and studies relating to the impact of AIDS in the United States, for example. State health departments provide services relating to dental health, family planning, nutrition, and teenage pregnancy; nutrition programs for pregnant women and young children; periodic health screening programs for infants and young children; substance abuse programs; and teenage parent services. Health departments and other federal, state, and local agencies also develop policies and implement plans for the provision of emergency and disaster services. Social workers from a number of federal, state, and local public and private agencies, for example, were involved in planning and overseeing emergency services after the hurricane and subsequent flooding in California in 1994 and the bombing of the federal building in Oklahoma City in 1995.

The national Public Health Service provides health and health-related services to indigent populations in areas with few medical practitioners, such as Native American reservations and migrant areas. The service also monitors communicable diseases and provides research in a variety of health areas. Many individuals who receive federal funds to attend college or professional schools in health-related areas, including social work, are required to return to devote a set number of years of service to the Public Health Service after graduation. Other federal programs such as the National Institutes of Health (NIH) also provide research and policy alternatives. Both the Public Health Service and the National Institutes of Health employ social workers at the BSW and MSW levels. The NIH, for example, employs social workers in direct-care settings established to develop new techniques in health care, such as its pediatric AIDS program in Washington, D.C.

Other Health Care Settings

Social workers are involved in numerous other health-related programs. Many work for the American Red Cross, for example, providing emergency services to families when disaster strikes. Recently developed health programs that often employ social workers include women's health clinics, which currently number over 1,000 and provide gynecological and primary care using a holistic health approach; genetic counseling centers; and rape crisis centers. Many EMS (emergency medical service) programs in large cities are employing social workers to assist in crisis intervention during family violence, child maltreatment, rape, and homicide.

Hospices are multiplying throughout the country and employing social workers in their agencies. Originally begun in England, hospice programs allow terminally ill persons to die at home or in a homelike setting surrounded by family members rather than in an often alien hospital environment. Using the stages of grief described by Elizabeth Kubler-Ross as a framework, many hospices employ social workers to work with families and the dying person or to supervise a cadre of volunteers who provide similar services. As more elderly persons and persons with AIDS continue to live longer, the need for hospice programs will increase. As critical issues in health care continue to be identified, the functions of social workers in health care settings will continue to expand.

SUMMARY

The state of health care in the United States has been declared a national crisis by many policymakers and health care experts. Issues relating to health care continue to be controversial and complex. As health care costs continue to rise, new technology and medical discoveries continue to be made. Ethical issues in health care—such as who should receive services at what cost, who should be allowed to make decisions about the right to refuse medical care, and who should be held accountable when a person's health is jeopardized by that person or another individual—are becoming increasingly complex and arising more often than in the past.

Addressing issues of diversity in health care are also critical. Understanding how individuals' cultures shape their views about health and wellness, illness, health care providers and interventions, birth and death, and their own roles in preventing and dealing with health-related concerns and helping empower persons to communicate those views to others involved in their care are essential and important roles for social workers in health care settings.

The AIDS epidemic has focused additional attention on the health care system. With more persons living longer, concerns about health care will become increasingly evident. The relationships between environmental factors and health need additional exploration. Finally, the large numbers of Americans, particularly children and the poor, who receive inadequate health care, if any, and the long-term implications for these individuals in all areas of their lives and for our country as a whole must be addressed.

Finding a balance of health care that is available, accessible, acceptable, and affordable, yet accountable to funding sources, is the highest priority for the United States in this decade. Whatever the balance established, social workers will play an ever-increasing role in both the planning and the delivery of health care services. Social work in health care settings is one of the fastest-growing areas of social work today.

KEY TERMS

acquired immunodeficiency
   syndrome (AIDS)
bioethics
catastrophic illness
health
health care
health maintenance organizations
   (HMOs)
health risk factors
HIV-positive

home health care
hospices
infant mortality rates
long-term care facilities
managed care system
primary setting
private insurance
public insurance
secondary setting

DISCUSSION QUESTIONS

1. Discuss some changes in the focus of health care that have taken place in the United States since colonial times.

2. Identify at least three reasons why health care costs have increased over the last decade.

3. Which groups of persons in the United States are most at risk to experience problems with their health? Why?

4. What are some of the ethical issues faced by health care providers and policymakers? Who do you think should receive priority in access to health care if costs prevent it being available to everyone?

5. Select one of the recent proposals for health care reform. Using Scuka's criteria, evaluate the proposals. Which proposals do you think have the most merit, and why?

6. What are some preventive programs social workers can implement to reduce the need for health care in the United States?

7. Identify at least three roles social workers might play at various levels of the environment in dealing with the AIDS epidemic. Why is AIDS such an important issue for the world today?

8. Identify at least five roles social workers can play in the delivery of health care services. How do careers for social workers in health care compare to careers in other areas in terms of availability and opportunity? Why?

REFERENCES

Astrachan, A. 1991. Research links hypertension, racial stress. *New York Times Service*, 6 February.

Brenner, M. H. 1973. Fetal, infant and maternal mortality during periods of economic stress. *International Journal of Health Sciences* 3: 145–59.

Bruner, S. T., D. R. Waldo and D. McKusick. 1992. National health expenditures projections through 2030. *Health Care Financing Review* 14(1): 1–29.

Catalano, R. 1979. *Health behavior and the community: An ecological perspective.* New York: Pergamon Press.

Concannon, K. 1995. Home and community care in Oregon. *Public Welfare* 15(2): 10–16. Washington, D.C.: American Public Welfare Association.

Conover, T. 1994. Finding a new mother. *New York Times Sunday Magazine*, 8 May 1994, pp. 27–36, 58–63.

Dohrenwend, B. S., and B. P. Dohrenwend, eds. 1974. *Stressful life events: Their nature and effects.* New York: Wiley.

Edwards, R. 1990. Health system's crisis calls for a cure. *NASW News* 35:6, 2 and 4.

Ford Foundation. 1989. *The common good: Social welfare and the American future.* New York: Ford Foundation.

Kingston, E., C. S. Petersen, J. Magaziner, E. D. Lopez, C. Joyce, E. Kassner and S. Sowers. 1988. Health, employment and welfare histories of Maryland's older general assistance recipients. *Social Work* 33(2): 105–109.

Lazarus. R. S. 1991. *Emotions and adaptation.* New York: Oxford University Press.

Lloyd, G. 1995. HIV/AIDS overview. *Encyclopedia of Social Work*, pp. 1257–90. Washington, D.C.: NASW.

Malcolm, A. 1990. Whose right to die? *Austin American Statesman*, 10 June, D1, D4.

McGrath, M. 1990. HIV: Overview and general description. In *The AIDS knowledge base.* ed. P.Cohen, M. Sande, and P. Volberding. Waltham, Mass.: Medical Publishing Group.

Metropolitan Council/Metropolitan Health Planning Board. 1985. *Prescription for health.* St. Paul, Minn.: Metropolitan Council.

National Association of Social Workers. 1995. *Health and mental health care in the 104th Congress.* Washington, D.C.: Author.

Nelkin, D., and Tancredi, L. 1989. The new diagnostics. *National Forum*, Phi Kappa Phi Journal, Fall, pp. 2–6.

Poole, D. 1995. Health care: Direct practice. *Encyclopedia of Social Work*, pp. 1156–65. Washington, D.C.: NASW.

Rice, D. 1995. Health care: Financing. *Encyclopedia of Social Work*, pp. 1168–75. Washington, D.C.: NASW.

Rothstein, M. 1989. AIDS rights and health care costs. *National Forum*, Phi Kappa Phi Journal, Fall, pp. 7–10.

Schlesinger, E. 1985. *Health care social work practice: Concepts and strategies.* St. Louis, Mo.: Times Mirror-Mosby.

Schoenborn, C., and Marano, M. 1988. Current estimates from the national health review survey: United States, 1987. *Vital and Health Statistics*, Series 10, No. 166, p. 115. Washington, D.C.: Public Health Service.

Scuka, R. 1994. Health care reform in the 1990s: An analysis of the problems in three proposals. *Social Work* 39(5): 580–87.

Seelye, K. 1995. Reduction urged in AIDS funding. *Austin American Statesman*, 5 July, A-7.

Statistical abstract of the United States. 1995. Washington, D.C.: U.S. Government Printing Office.

U.S. Department of Agriculture. 1990. *Five state study of women, infants and children program.* Washington, D.C.: U.S. Government Printing Office.

U.S. National Center for Health Statistics. 1995. *Statistical reports.* Hyattsville, Md.: Author.

U.S. Public Health Service. 1977. 200 years of child health. In *200 years of children*, ed. E. Grotberg. Washington, D.C.: U.S. Department of Health, Education, and Welfare.

U.S. Senate Committee on Labor and Human Resources. 1994. *Oversight of the Radiation Exposure Compensation Act: Hearing of the U.S. Senate Committee on Labor and Human Resources.* Washington, D.C.: U.S. Government Printing Office.

U.S. Surgeon General. 1979. *Healthy people: The surgeon general's report on health promotion and disease prevention.* Washington, D.C.: U.S. Department of Health, Education, and Welfare, Public Health Service.

Van Den Bergh, N. 1995. Employee assistance programs. *Encyclopedia of Social Work*, vol. 1, 842–49. Washington, D.C.: National Association of Social Workers.

SUGGESTED FURTHER READINGS

Aday, L. 1993. *The health and health care needs of vulnerable populations in the United States.* San Francisco: Jossey-Bass.

Biomedical ethics and the bill of rights. 1989. Special issue. *National Forum: The Phi Kappa Phi Journal.* Baton Rouge, La.: Louisiana State University.

Bayer, R. 1989. *Private acts, social consequences: AIDS and the politics of public health.* New York: Free Press.

Bracht, N. 1978. *Social work in health care.* New York: Haworth Press.

deVita, V. T., S. Hellman, and S. A. Rosenberg, eds. *AIDS: Etiology, diagnosis, treatment and prevention,* 3rd ed. Philadelphia: J. B. Lippincott.

Dougherty, C. 1988. *American health care: Realities, rights and reforms.* New York: Oxford University Press.

Estes, R. 1984. *Social work in health care.* St. Louis: Green.

Germain, C. 1984. *Social work practice in health care: An ecological perspective.* New York: Free Press.

Health & Social Work journal.

Holosko, M. and P. Taylor. 1992. *Social work practice in health care settings.* Toronto: Canadian Scholars' Press.

Kerson, T. 1982. *Social work in health settings.* New York: Longman.

Lee, P. and C. Estes. 1994. *The nation's health,* 4th ed. Boston: Jones and Bartlett.

Lynch, V. J., Lloyd, G. A., and Fimbres, M. F. 1993. *The expanding faces of AIDS: Implications for social work practice.* Westport, Conn.: Auburn House.

Marmor, T., and Christianson, J. 1982. *Health care policy: A political economy approach.* Beverly Hills, Calif.: Sage Publications.

Nacman, M. 1977. Social work in health settings: A historical review. *Social Work in Health Care* 2 (Summer): 407–417.

O'Brian, M. 1992. *Living with HIV: An experiment in courage.* New York: Auburn House.

Schlesinger, E. 1985. *Health care social work practice.* St. Louis, Mo.: Times Mirror-Mosby.

Shilts, R. 1987. *And the band played on: Politics, people and the AIDS epidemic.* New York: St. Martin's Press.

Social Work in Health Care journal.

Vourlekis, B. and C. Leukefeld, eds. 1989. *Making our case: A resource book of selected materials for social workers in health care.* Washington, D.C.: NASW.

CHAPTER 12

THE NEEDS OF CHILDREN, YOUTH, AND FAMILIES

Divorced for two years, Ernestine Moore is struggling to survive. Her five children are in a foster home while she tries to stabilize her life. Ernestine is looking forward to the day when she and her children can live together as a family again.

Ernestine came from a large family. Her father drank often and beat her mother, her siblings, and her. Pregnant at age 16 and afraid of what her father would do, she eloped with the father of her child, a 19-year-old high school graduate named James Moore who worked at a fast-food restaurant. The first year was fairly peaceful for the new family, although money was a continual problem. Lacking health insurance, they took several years to pay the bills for the birth of the baby. But both the Moores were excited about the baby, and Ernestine worked hard to provide a good home for her husband and baby. She wanted desperately to have the kind of home and family she had not had as a child.

Ernestine and James had three more children during the next six years. Because one of the children had a number of health problems, financial pressures continued to mount, and life became increasingly stressful. James began to drink heavily and beat Ernestine often. He also physically and verbally abused the middle child, a boy who was diagnosed as mildly developmentally disabled. When Ernestine became pregnant again, her husband left her. Since that time, he has only paid child support for six months.

After James left, Ernestine moved in with a sister, who had three children. To support her children and help contribute to the rent her sister was paying, she got two jobs, one in a fast-food restaurant and one at night cleaning a bank. Shortly after her new baby was born, this arrangement ended because of continual arguments between the two sisters over money, space, and child rearing.

At that point, Ernestine applied for food stamps and medical assistance and moved into a two-room apartment. She applied for low-income housing, and although she was eligible, she was told there was a two-year waiting list. Ernestine hired a young teenage girl to babysit for her children while she worked. Tired and overwhelmed, Ernestine had little time to spend taking care of the children or the apartment. She became increasingly abusive toward the children. The older children did poorly in school and were continually fighting, stealing, and vandalizing. Neighbors in the apartment complex saw the younger children outside at all hours, unsupervised, often wearing only diapers. They often heard screaming and the baby crying throughout the night.

The babysitter quit because Ernestine was behind in paying her. When she missed two days of work while she tried desperately to find another sitter, Ernestine was fired from her fast-food job. Afraid that she would also lose her cleaning job, she began putting the younger children to bed at six o'clock and leaving the oldest child (age 8) in charge until she returned home. Finally, the Moores were evicted from the apartment because Ernestine was unable to pay the rent. For two weeks the whole family slept in a friend's car. Finally, when the oldest child came to school with multiple bruises and complaining of a sore arm and revealed the family's living situation to her teacher, the local child protective services agency was called. The social worker discovered all of the children badly bruised and malnourished, and the oldest girl had a broken arm. Ernestine was overwhelmed and angry, and she felt extremely guilty about what had happened to her children.

The children were placed in foster care with an older, nurturing couple. With more structure and a stable living situation, the children began doing better in school and were able to develop some positive relationships with others. Ernestine visited the children often and began to see the foster parents as caring individuals who seemed almost like parents to her.

She enrolled in a job-training program and was hired as a health care aide for a local nursing home. She enjoys her job and is talking about getting her high school equivalency certificate and going to nursing school. Her social worker encouraged her to join Parents Anonymous, a support group for abusive parents. For the first time, Ernestine Moore has developed positive, trusting relationships with others. She has located an affordable duplex, and she and her social worker are making plans to have the children return home on a permanent basis. ■

For all individuals, the family is probably the most significant social system within which they function. Within the family we first develop trusting relationships, a special identity, and a sense of self-worth. Traditionally, despite difficulties in society, the family has been looked upon as a safe, protective haven where individuals can receive nurturing, love, and support. It is increasingly difficult for children and their families to grow up in today's complex and rapidly changing world. Daily, children are confronted with family financial pressures, the need for one or both parents to work long hours, or the physical or mental illness or loss of a family member.

Unable to cope with these pressures, family members often turn to alcoholism or drug abuse, resort to violence, or withdraw from other family members and do not respond to their needs. Sometimes, because they did not receive love and nurturing when they were children, the parents are unable to provide this for their own children. Other parents do not know how to provide for their own children because they have never learned what children need at certain ages or what to expect from them. Other families, although generally functioning well, may be unable to adequately meet the needs of family members during some type of crisis, such as death or a serious illness.

How well a family is able to meet the needs of its members also depends on other systems within the family's environment. The workplace, the neighborhood, the community, and the society with which that family interacts have a tremendous impact on its well-being. Uri Bronfenbrenner (1979) and James Garbarino (1992), two researchers interested in the development of children and families, suggest that more attention should be given to intervention in these broader systems than in the past, rather than just providing services to individual family members. A family that functions within an unsupportive environment is much more susceptible to family problems than a family functioning within a supportive environment. If the family lives in a community that has no programs available to family members, that also may threaten the family's well-being.

Consider Ernestine Moore's situation. Her children were at risk for many reasons. Abused as a child, she learned to distrust others and failed to have her emotional needs met during her childhood. This left Ernestine feeling worthless and inadequate. Individuals with low self-esteem are more likely to get pregnant during their teenage years. They also are more likely to abuse their children than other parents. Parents like Ernestine also have learned from their own parents that anger is dealt with by hitting. Like Ernestine, they may be used to living with an alcoholic and may have learned many behavior patterns that they carry into their own lives.

In this chapter, we discuss general issues and trends that must be considered when focusing on the needs of children, youth, and families; the types and extent of problems that can have an impact on children and their families; and factors that place families more at risk to experience those problems. In Chapter 13 we focus on services and policies that prevent or alleviate problems experienced by children, youth, and families. The roles that social workers play in providing these services and developing and implementing policies are also discussed in Chapter 13. ■

▨ ISSUES TO CONSIDER WHEN ADDRESSING CHILD AND FAMILY NEEDS

Many issues must be considered when discussing children and their families. All families have strengths and many diverse ways of coping to survive and stay together. However, no matter how many strengths a family has, past and present impacts from the broader environment may make it difficult, if not impossible, for families to meet their own needs without additional support. In fact, all families need support beyond the family to survive and to reinforce their internal strengths. The African saying, "It takes a village to raise a child," is perhaps more true in today's modern world than ever before.

What Is a Family?

The typical American family in the 1950s, 1960s, and 1970s included a husband, a wife, and 2.6 children. Today, fewer than 10 percent of American families are of this type. Twenty-five percent of all families are headed by only one parent, usually a woman, although an increasing number of men are assuming responsibility for raising children following a divorce or separation. Many families have extended-family members such as grandparents, aunts, uncles, or cousins living with them. Others are gay or lesbian couples with children. Still others have adopted or foster children either taken in informally or by legal agreements with the court system. It is also becoming more and more common for individuals to live together who are not related by blood or marriage.

During the 1970s, a program was funded by the federal government to develop a national policy that supported families. The program's first task was to define a **family.** The program staff determined that this task was impossible. Others, however, provide a broad definition of a family exemplified by the following: Any group of individuals who are bonded together through marriage, kinship, adoption, or mutual agreement (Goode 1964). When discussing the needs of children and families, a family is referred to within the context of a parent figure or figures, and at least one child. Perhaps the most important issue in relation to what constitutes a family is that although all children and families have similar needs—to be loved, wanted, accepted, fed, clothed, given shelter, and protected—no two families are alike. Each family may be viewed as its own system, and each family system must be viewed as unique.

How Are Families of Today Viewed?

Many frameworks are used in studying the family. Two of the most relevant when considering the family in the context of the social welfare system are the systems/ecological framework and the life-span development framework. The systems/ecological framework allows researchers to explore interactions and relationships between family members as well as between the family and other levels of the environment, such as extended-family members, other families, the neighborhood, the school, the church or synagogue, the workplace, the community, the state, and other larger systems such as the economic system and the political system. Ernestine Moore's family was discussed briefly using the systems/ecological framework.

A second framework that can be used is the life-span development framework, previously discussed in Chapter 3. The family as a social system has more impact on the individual throughout the life cycle than any other system. Even before birth, the physical and emotional health of the family in which the child will be born and the environment in which the family functions significantly affect the child's future. How well individuals learn to trust others, to develop autonomy, to take initiative, to be industrious, to have a positive identity, to be intimate with others, to give something of themselves back to others, and to face death with integrity are all shaped extensively by relationships within the family.

Families also go through stages of development. Carter and McGoldrick (1989) identify six stages of family life, each with emotional transition and changes in status: the unattached young adult, early marriage, the birth and care of young children, raising adolescents, launching children, and aging. Although these stages are most likely to be experienced in this way by more traditional families, every family will experience changes throughout its duration as its members grow and change, and the family's needs and interactions with the social welfare system will differ according to its stage of development. Carter and McGoldrick have also identified specific changes that are characteristic of divorced families and families who experience the remarriage of a parent.

What Is a Healthy Family?

Unfortunately, much of the literature about families focuses on family problems without considering what constitutes a healthy family. The perfect family portrayed in television situation comedies does not exist, and all families experience some type of problem at some point during their family life cycle. But some families are better able to cope with family problems because of the availability of financial resources and social support systems, and the physical and mental health of family members. A major crisis—no matter how healthy the family is—will have a serious impact on the family and is likely to result in at least temporary need for assistance from the social welfare system in some way.

Studies show that a number of factors are associated with healthy families. These include the opportunity to express all ideas and feelings, no family secrets, a valuing of everyone's opinions and feeling, rules that are flexible yet enforced with consistency, positive energy, and opportunities for growth and change. Children are more likely to grow up to be successful adults able to develop intimate relationships, maintain employment that allows self-sufficiency, and experience relatively good health and mental health if they experience nurturing and a positive relationship with at least one caregiver; consistent parenting, particularly during their first year of life; well-balanced discipline; are two years or more apart in age from any siblings; and have access to others who can provide emotional support if their immediate families cannot do so (Werner and Smith 1982).

How Are Family Problems Defined?

What constitutes a family problem depends a great deal on the perspective of the individual defining the problem. How a problem is defined depends on a variety of factors, including the social and historical context within which the problem takes place, the attitudes and values of the culture or society of the family; the attitudes and values of the community in which the family resides and the norms of the community; the attitudes, values, culture, previous life experiences, and professional background of the person defining the problem; legal definitions of the problem; and the availability of resources to address the problem.

Cultural Attitudes

Cultural attitudes, values, and practices shape how family problems are defined. For cultures in which women become sexually active as soon as they reach menses, teenage pregnancy is not likely to be considered a problem. Some cultures think it abusive that we make young children sit in a dental chair and force them to open their mouths and have their teeth pulled out. Some family policy experts suggest that the United States as a society is less supportive of children and families than other countries, when legislation and programs supportive of families are considered. In many Scandinavian countries, for example, the government provides free health care to children, subsidies for working parents to stay home when their children are young, and free child care. Other policy experts suggest that our country's fascination with violence as exemplified through the media and sports events has a strong impact on the high incidence of violence within the family, and that the emphasis placed on sex in the media contributes to the high incidence of teenage pregnancy.

Community Norms and Values

The norms and values of the community also shape the way family problems are defined. If everyone within a community is unemployed and lives in housing without plumbing and with dirt floors and all children are poorly fed and clothed, the families in that community living under those circumstances are not likely to be seen as neglecting their children. But a family living like that in a wealthy community with high employment and stability most likely would be considered neglected. Whipping a child with a belt is not as likely to be considered child maltreatment in some communities or parts of the country as in others.

Attitudes and Values

The attitudes, values, personal life experiences, and professional background of the person defining the problem also influence how a problem is defined. A person raised in a conservative family, for which drinking of any alcoholic beverages was considered taboo, might define alcoholism differently than a person raised in a family for which drinking alcoholic beverages was commonplace. A physician may be more likely to define child abuse only as bruises or broken bones, whereas a social worker may be more likely to argue that emotional neglect or harassment also constitutes an important form of child abuse.

Legal Definitions

Legal statutes also provide definitions of some types of family problems. These definitions vary by country and state and often leave a great deal of room for interpretation at the personal, professional, and community levels. For example, child maltreatment has been defined in the Child Abuse Prevention and Treatment Act of 1974 as

> the physical or mental injury, sexual abuse or exploitation, negligent treatment, or maltreatment of a child by a person who is responsible for the child's welfare, under circumstances which indicate that the child's health or welfare is harmed or threatened. (42 Section 5016g)

Terms such as *mental injury, threatened,* and *negligent treatment* often are difficult to interpret. At the same time, they allow leeway for additional protection of children who may be subject to just as much risk as a child in a more easily defined situation. For example, a child who is constantly threatened with a knife or gun, even though never actually hurt physically, is likely to suffer serious emotional problems.

Availability of Resources

The availability of resources to address the problem may be the most important factor in how a problem is defined. The broader the definition, the more children and families will be identified as having the problem and needing assistance; the narrower the definition, the fewer identified as having the problem and needing assistance. The legal definition just given, for example, allows for the inclusion of neglected and emotionally maltreated children. In fact, when a similar state definition was first implemented, three times as many cases of child neglect were reported as cases of child abuse. Twenty years later, due to scarce resources and significantly more cases reported, physical abuse and neglect cases are investigated and substantiated about equally, and only the most serious cases are defined as such. Resources are so stretched to their limits in many states that more narrow definitions of child mal-treatment are being used. During the Kennedy and Johnson administrations, when resources to address domestic social problems were considered to be abundant, the emphasis was on developing programs "to achieve the maximum potential of all children." The emphasis shifted under the Nixon, Reagan, and Bush administrations to "meeting minimum levels of care for children and their families," thus significantly narrowing the numbers of families and children who fit within the definition of needed services. The debate between the Clinton administration and the more conservative congressional majority in the mid-1990s exemplifies the debate relating to the role of government and how social problems are defined. As the debate continues, children in the United States are faring less well than they did in the 1980s (see Table 12.1).

What Causes Families to Have Problems?

Families have problems for many reasons—and some families experience similar problems but for different reasons. There is no single cause for a given problem, which is why it is important to use a systems/ecological perspective in addressing family problems. It is also more appropriate to say that certain factors are associated with specific family problems, rather than saying that factors cause those problems. This means that a family experiencing a problem may have other problems as well, but it is often difficult to determine which problem caused the other.

We know that problems often go together. You are likely to find child abuse, spouse abuse, alcoholism, and teenage pregnancy within the same family. Individuals with these problems are more likely to be under stress, to be worried about financial pressures (whether rich or poor), to have low self-esteem, and to come from families in which similar problems existed when they were children than are individuals in families without these problems.

Services for children and families often are provided by problem area—for example, specialized services for alcoholism, child abuse and neglect, and spouse abuse—rather than as services that focus on the family as a system. This is due largely to the categorical basis on which state and federal funding generally is allocated. This categorical funding system has resulted in fragmented and duplicated services, as well as gaps in services in which client groups "fall through the cracks."

How Do Cultural and Gender Differences Affect Family Problems?

While statistics show that more children and families who experience family problems in the United States are white and headed by two parents, that is only because there are more white, two-parent families than other types of families (Children's Defense Fund 1994). Thus, it is important to consider not only raw counts, but rates; that is, numbers of individuals of a certain group experiencing problems compared to the

| TABLE 12.1 | **HOW AMERICAN CHILDREN ARE DOING** |

Millions of children thrive in America. However, a profile of U.S. children developed by KIDS COUNT, a project of the Annie E. Casey Foundation, reveals a nation failing to keep pace with the needs of its youngest citizens. Over the 1980s, we made no progress or slipped backwards in seven of nine measures of child well-being. Child poverty expanded. Births to unmarried teens climbed. More children are living in families with only one parent. More babies are being born at-risk because they are underweight. We made no progress in graduating young people from high school on time. The chances that a teenager, particularly an African-American teen, will die as a result of an accident, suicide, or murder rose. And, more young people are required by juvenile courts to spend formative years away from their families and communities because they are in trouble. Our only advance has been in reducing the death of infants and young children, though that progress has not been shared equally by all children. The 1990s offer us a choice—to do nothing and consign our children to rising risk and in so doing be complicit in their eclipsed futures, or to rise to the occasion and reverse these results.

KIDS COUNT Benchmark	National Trends over the 1980s	State Trends
Percent low birth weight babies	3% worse	35 states worse*
Infant mortality rate (per 1,000 live births)	22% better	51 states better*
Child death rate ages 1–14 (per 100,000 children)	18% better	48 states better*
Teen violent death rate ages 15–19 (per 100,000 teens)	11% worse	34 states worse*
Percent all births that are to single teens	14% worse	42 states worse
Juvenile custody rate ages 10–15 (per 100,000 youths)	10% worse	32 states worse*
Percent graduating high school	0% no change	28 states better
Percent children in poverty	22% worse	40 states worse
Percent children in single-parent families	13% worse	44 states worse

*Includes the District of Columbia.

Source: *Kids Count Data Book* (Greenwich, CT: Annie E. Casey Foundation, 1992), 7.

total population of that group. Such comparisons show that some groups are more vulnerable, or at risk, to experience certain problems than other groups.

Single women and people of color with children are more at risk to experience family problems in the United States than men and whites. Do not infer from this statement that women and people of color are in any way less competent, genetically impaired, more prone toward violence, or interested only in themselves.

There are a number of very critical reasons why women and people of color are more at risk than other groups. In 1993, the poverty rate for African Americans was 33.1 percent, or almost three times as high as it was for whites, whose poverty rate was 12.2 percent. The rate for Hispanics was 30.6 percent. In 1993, the poverty rate for married couples was 6.2, while for female-headed households it was 38.7 percent. Over half of all poor families in 1993 were headed by single-parent females. That same year, 22.0 percent of all children, or about one in five, were growing up in poverty. When focusing only on children under age 6, the ratio increases to one child in four (U.S. Bureau of the Census 1995). It is estimated that by the year 2000, 70 percent of African American families will be headed by single-parent women and 30 percent of African American men will be unemployed (Moyers 1986).

Because individuals who experience poverty are far more likely to experience stress, they are far more at risk of experiencing other family problems. Thus, women and people of color, by the very nature of their positions within the socioeconomic hierarchy, are more likely to experience family problems. Additionally, these groups traditionally have had less power than other groups and not only are more vulnerable to being ignored or blamed for causing problems but also are unable to advocate for solutions and resources to address the problems they face. Women, for example, are often paid less and hired into lower-level jobs than men. Those who reenter the workplace after or while in more traditional marriages where they have not been employed outside the home ("displaced homemakers") are at a disadvantage in getting jobs that allow them to adequately support their families. They also most often must bear the brunt of child care and other child-related needs. Traditional attitudes about women and people of color are changing, but because of a scarcity of resources available to address their needs, they continue to be at the bottom of the social structure in our country.

Children growing up in families where social support is not available are more likely to experience problems in development, have low self-esteem, drop out of school, become pregnant at an early age, and have difficulty in finding adequate employment. Because they often lack appropriate role models and have been raised in an environment of hopelessness and despair, having children is often the only way they feel competent as people. With few skills and even fewer resources and opportunities, the cycle of the at-risk family often is repeated with their own children.

Although some attention is being given to the special needs of women and people of color and their families, this attention does not always address the problems from a broad context. For example, with the increased divorce rate and the growing number of people having children out of marriage, women have been targeted as "America's new poor," and much attention has been given to the **feminization of poverty** (DiNitto and McNeese 1990). However, in addition to providing more social supports to women and their families, the problem needs to be addressed from a systems/ecological perspective—women alone are not responsible for pregnancy or divorce, and men's responsibility in such situations also must be addressed.

Additional factors must be taken into account when considering the relationship between family problems and people of color and women. While such families also are more likely to experience poverty and stress, and thus are more likely to experience alcoholism or spouse or child abuse, or be too overwhelmed by these pressures to parent their children adequately, they are also more likely to be labeled as having such problems. An African American or Latino parent who abuses a child, for example, is much more likely to take the child to a public hospital or clinic for treatment, where the case is likely to be reported to authorities. A white parent, however, is much more likely to take the child to a private physician, and perhaps to a different private physician if the child is reabused. Families of color and single-parenting women also are more likely to seek help for family problems at public services agencies, such as local mental health centers, than at private psychological counseling programs. White parents having problems with children are far more likely to be able to afford to send them to residential treatment facilities for therapy, whereas children of color are much more likely to be sent to juvenile detention centers, where such treatment usually is not available.

Families of color and female-headed families have many strengths, and we must be careful not to stereotype such families. But individuals studying social welfare systems need to be aware that children who grow up in families headed by people of color and women are more vulnerable than children growing up in other families. Family problems must be considered within the context of the broader environment, including the impacts of oppression and discrimination, and these considerations are important as we work to shape the environment to make it more supportive for children and their families.

CHANGING FAMILY SITUATIONS

The increasing diversity of families has created a number of issues that social workers need to consider when working with children and their families. Many families today experience changes in composition due to divorce and separation, often requiring difficult transitions for all family members. An increasing number of children are being raised in single-parent families, necessitating additional effort from these parents to provide for their children. Many single parents who marry or remarry already have children, creating additional transitions and the development of new relationships for children as well as adults. Some children are being reared by gay or lesbian parents, often in the face of oppression from the broader environment. While each of these situations often strengthens the family, family members may face specific issues that are helpful to understand when working with them.

Divorce and Separation

The divorce rate in the United States has increased dramatically during the past several decades. One of every three marriages ends in divorce, with each marriage involving an estimated two children. Current projections suggest that over half of today's children will spend at least some time in a single-parent household (Children's Defense Fund 1994).

Divorce and separation often result in crises for family members. For adults, the separation or divorce signifies the loss of an intimate relationship that also brought security and support. Separation or divorce also signifies a loss of hopes and dreams as well as feelings of failure. Although there may be relief over the divorce, being alone also brings fear, anxiety, loneliness, and guilt, especially if there are children involved. Initially, parents are usually so caught up in dealing with their own emotions that they have little energy left to help their children cope. Thus, at a time when their children need them most, many adults find themselves unable to function adequately as parents.

For children, the initial aspect of the divorce almost always is traumatic. If a great deal of fighting existed in the family, children may feel a sense of relief. But they, too, experience anger, guilt, fear, and sadness. Often, children blame themselves for their parents' divorce. Many times, they try to change their behavior, either acting overly good or overly bad in the hope that this will bring their parents back together. Parents often fail to say anything to their children about an impending divorce, because of their own grieving and the belief that their children will cope better if they are not burdened with adult problems.

Studies suggest that the most important factor that helps children get through a divorce is having someone to listen and provide support to them. Parents need to explain that they are divorcing each other and not the child, and that both of them will continue to love and spend time with the child. Some children may not react visibly when they are informed that their parents are separating or divorcing. However, if children do not react immediately after the divorce, they are likely to hold their feelings inside and express them at a later age (Wallerstein and Blakeslee 1989).

Talking about the divorce and giving them a chance to express their feelings are important aspects in helping children cope with divorce. Children experiencing a divorce in their family usually regress at the time of the divorce. They may exhibit such behaviors as nightmares and bed wetting, thumb sucking, behavioral problems at school and at home, drop in academic performance at school, listlessness and daydreaming, changes in eating habits, increases in illness, and, if preadolescents or adolescents, experimentation with alcohol, drugs, sexual activity, and other risk-taking behaviors. Particularly if one parent has much less contact than in the past, children may develop extreme fears that they will be abandoned by the other parent or worry about what will happen to them if the parent they are living with dies (Wallerstein and Kelly 1980).

Although children are likely to cope better with divorce if the adults cope well, it usually takes them longer to recover, primarily because they have no control over the situation. Various studies (Wallerstein and Kelly 1980; Wallerstein and Blakeslee 1989) show that it takes children at least three and a half years to work through a divorce. In some cases, individuals may still be struggling ten to twenty years later to achieve equal footing again. Children fare better after a divorce if they maintain a positive relationship with both parents and if the parents do not speak negatively about each other through the children or use the children to fight their battles with each other.

Custody and visitation problems often have a negative impact on a child following a divorce (see Figure 12.1). Although the situation is changing, mothers are much more likely to obtain custody in a divorce, with fathers, as the noncustodial parents, having children visit them on holidays and during summer vacations. Courts have emphasized a long-held doctrine that, in a child's "tender years," the mother is more important in the child's life, and unless totally unfit, she should receive custody of children in a divorce. Although in many instances today fa-

FIGURE 12.1   A NINE-YEAR-OLD GIRL WHOSE PARENTS ARE INVOLVED IN A CUSTODY BATTLE DEPICTS HER FEELINGS IN A DRAWING

thers want custody and are equally and often more capable of caring for children, less than 10 percent of divorces result in children living with their fathers. Because the average woman's income decreases significantly following a divorce, whereas the average man's income increases, children of divorce often view their fathers as "Santa Clauses." Their fathers may buy them presents and take them special places, let them stay up later, and let them have fewer rules than their mothers, who are buying the necessities and maintaining the daily routine, which usually requires more discipline. Mothers may resent that they cannot give their children the same fun aspects of life, whereas fathers often find visitation time with their children artificial and awkward and don't know what else to do with them.

Parents also often expect the child to decide where to live and where to spend holidays, creating undue pressure on the child, who knows he or she will be forced to hurt one parent no matter what the decision. Experts recommend that children be allowed to give input in such decisions, but that final decisions be made either by the parents or, if they cannot agree, by a trained mediator skilled in divorce conflicts or by the court (Wallerstein and Blakeslee 1989).

Increasingly, parents are opting for joint custody, where both parents equally share custody and, often, time spent living with the child. Some parents alternate the child's living with them every three or four days, whereas others have the child with them for six months and then switch the living arrangements. In some instances, to maintain stability for the child, the parents move in with the child, who remains in the same home, one at a time for a specified period of time. Studies conflict as to the benefits of different types of custody. Many experts suggest shared custody if the parents have a positive relationship with each other, since this provides the child with two strong role models who love and pay attention to the child and communicates that the child is wanted and loved by both parents equally. Other experts suggest that shared custody, particularly if it involves a great deal of moving back and forth on the child's part, creates instability and a lack of permanence, and that the child has no place to truly call his or her own.

The need for support to families experiencing divorce, particularly for children, is receiving increased attention. Many cities have established family **mediation** centers, where a team of social workers and attorneys work together with families in the divorce process. This helps parents maintain positive relationships with each other in an adult way, resolving conflicts together rather than forcing them to take adversarial roles, as is often the case when individuals have separate attorneys and a court action. Public schools and family service agencies also have established special programs and support groups for children experiencing divorce and their parents.

Single Parenting

Currently, 25 percent of families in the United States are headed by a single parent, either because of divorce or separation or, increasingly, because of unmarried women giving birth to children. There is no evidence that suggests that growing up in a single-parent family is inherently positive or negative. Researchers have found that when socioeconomic status is eliminated as an intervening variable, children in single-parent families fare as well as those in two-parent families. Factors that have a greater impact on how children fare are poverty and conflict between parents (Quinn and Allen 1989; Wallerstein and Kelly 1980). Single-parent families, like other families, need to be viewed from a strengths perspective, with attempts to eliminate environmental barriers that place such families at risk and to build on family strengths (see Table 12.1).

There are, however, a number of barriers that affect the well-being of single-parent families. The major barrier for most is income; a single-parent woman is more likely to be poor and, if not within the poverty definition of poor, experiencing financial stress. Whereas the median income for all married households was almost $36,959 in 1993 it was $13,472 for single-parent, female-headed households. Incomes for white female-headed households was significantly higher than for households headed by women of color (U.S. Bureau of the Census 1995).

These families, with a single income most often earned by a woman, are more likely to be poor and, if not within the poverty definition of poor, experiencing financial stress. In addition to financial pressure, single parents must maintain sole responsibility for overseeing the household and child rearing. As a result, children growing up in single-parent families often are used to different life-styles than others. It is a paradox of children growing up in single-parent families that, on one hand, they are likely to have more freedom than other children, and on the other hand, they must take on much more responsibility. Children of single parents often have increased freedom because they must spend more time by themselves while their parents are working. Because child care is so expensive, many children of single parents, especially school-age children, become "latch-key" children, responsible for themselves until their parents get home from work. Others must be responsible for younger siblings. It is not unusual for a child of a single parent to come home from school alone, do homework and household chores, and prepare the evening meal. Single-parent children also must assume more responsibility for themselves because of the unavailability of supervision.

Single-parent children who are the same gender as the parent who has left the home also may assume many of the roles of the absent parent, for example, mowing the lawn and doing household repairs. They also may serve as companions to their parents, who may be lonely or too busy or hurt to establish adult relationships. Parents may confide in children about money, relationships with their ex-spouse, and other adult matters, and expect children to accompany them on activities such as shopping trips, meetings, or parties. They also may place children in a situation of role reversal, expecting children to comfort them and meet their needs. Other parents become overly protective, worrying that since they have lost a significant relationship with an ex-spouse, they also may lose the relationship with the child.

Children in single-parent families may experience inconsistent discipline. A parent may be too tired to discipline at some times or stressed and likely to overdiscipline at others. Parents' dating and development of opposite-sex relationships also can be stressful to children in single-parent families. Many children, particularly if they feel abandoned by the absent parent or do not have a positive relationship with that parent, may be anxious for the parent with whom they reside to remarry. Other children, particularly older children who have been in a single-parent family for a longer period of time, may see any dating by their parent as a threat to their own relationship and may do everything possible to destroy such relationships. Such issues as how much to tell children about dating, how involved they should be in decision making about serious relationships or remarriage, whether to have "overnight" guests and live-in partners, and how to help children handle a relationship that has ended are of concern to single parents and their families.

Children growing up in single-parent families also may have fewer options regarding long-range plans for their future. Income and time limitations of such families may preclude college or other post-high school education.

Other issues children growing up in single-parent families may face include kidnapping or fear of being kidnapped by the noncustodial parent, sexual abuse or other types of child maltreatment by the parent or parent's friends, alcoholism or drug abuse by one or both parents, and concerns about the child's own sexuality and ability to establish long-term opposite-sex relationships.

Increasingly, schools, child guidance centers, and community mental health centers are offering special programs for children growing up in single-parent families. Programs include individual and group counseling, family counseling, and the development of self-help groups for children. Big Brother and Big Sister programs, which match adult role models in one-to-one relationships with children, also help children in single-parent families develop healthy relationships with adults of the opposite sex of the custodial parent figure to ensure that children experience positive relationships with both male and female adults. A number of books and other materials are also available to help both children with single parents and their families. Longitudinal studies of children growing up in single-parent families are also helping to identify strengths of such families, as well as problem areas, to be better able to help children growing up in this type of family constellation.

Gay and Lesbian Parenting

Many homosexuals have children; studies show that many gays and lesbians have been married before declaring their homosexuality. In addition, many gays and lesbians may decide to have children while they are in same-sex relationships or as single parents. Difficulties may arise, however, when gay and lesbian parents seek custody of children through the courts; both men and women in recent years have had difficulty gaining custody in some instances if they are gay or lesbian in spite of research findings regarding their parenting capabilities.

Studies show that there are few differences between gay or lesbian families and nongay or lesbian families. Children born and/or raised in families where one or more parents is gay or lesbian are no more or less likely to be gay or lesbian themselves than children born and/or raised in families where both parents are heterosexual. Studies also have found that gay and lesbian parents do not influence their children to become gay or lesbian, and that children raised by homosexual parents are not emotionally impaired. Although a number of individuals suggest that children are at risk to be molested by gay or lesbian parents, researchers have found that a child is more at risk to be molested in a heterosexual household than in a homosexual one. There is supportive evidence that gay and lesbian parents are just as effective at parenting as heterosexual parents (Moses and Hawkins 1982; Laird 1995).

There are some specific issues that families with gay and lesbian parents must address, however. For example, homosexual parents may not want their employers to know that they are gay or lesbian because they fear being fired. Thus, children may have to keep the homosexuality a secret from others. Many gay and lesbian parents also worry about how their children's friends and their parents will react to their being homosexual, and, as children grow older and more aware, they may fear this as well. Gay and lesbian parents may also fear that their children will be ridiculed or discriminated against. As in any family, children who are dealt with honestly and have open communication with their homosexual parents usually are better adjusted than children who find out about the homosexuality from others or sense the homosexuality but are not allowed to discuss it with their parents.

Stepparenting and Blended Families

With increased numbers of single-parent families, second marriages also are on the increase. Eighty percent of divorced adults remarry, and 60 percent of remarriages involve at least one child. In 1990, over 15 percent of children in the United States were living in a stepparent family (Children's Defense Fund 1994). A number of these families involve marriages between partners who each have children from previous marriages. Such families are often referred to as **blended families.**

Remarriage typically generates a number of strong feelings among both children and adults involved. Whereas adults may feel a sense of joyousness and security, children are likely to feel a sense of loss in relation to the parent, who must now be shared with the spouse, as well as anxiety over what the addition of another adult will mean to their own well-being. They also may experience concern about balancing the stepparent relationship with that of the absent birth parent. If the new marriage brings other children, relationships between stepsiblings may bring forth feelings of competition and jealousy.

The development of stepfamily relationships can be a difficult process, and time and effort are required on the part of all family members to make the new family constellation work. Children frequently feel distant from their new stepparent and may see that parent as a replacement for their absent parent. Even if they like the stepparent, conflicts over loyalty to their birth parent may prevent them from establishing a positive relationship. If the child functioned as more of a "partner" in the family than a child prior to the new marriage, feelings of displacement and jealousy toward the stepparent can occur. Additionally, many children, no matter how old, still have fantasies of their birth parents reuniting, and the remarriage represents a threat to these fantasies. Stepsiblings also may mean less attention for birth children, as well as possible competition outside of the family boundaries regarding friends, sports, and school.

In addition to the development of emotional bonds among family members, adjustments to changing family roles, responsibilities, and family identity must be made in a blended family. Rules often are readjusted, and many times are more strict than they were in the single-parent household. If children are still in contact regularly with their own birth parent, they are now essentially members of two households, each with its own distinct culture and rules. Problems regarding multiple role models and parental figures can create confusion for children. Some experts in stepparent family relationships suggest that the stepparent should not in any way undermine the absent birth parent relationship but should establish himself or herself as a parental figure in the family and take an active role in immediate family issues such as rules and discipline. Other experts argue that the parenting should be left completely to the child's parents, with the stepparent working to establish a positive bond with the child, but as an adult friend rather than a parental figure, staying out of decisions regarding rules and discipline.

Although remarriage can increase the stability, security, and financial resources for children, working through the implications of such changes takes a great deal of time before there is acceptance. Special parent education classes for stepparents; support groups for stepparents, spouses, and children in stepparent families; and family counseling programs are available in many communities to help focus on strengths of such families and provide support in working through problem areas.

◢ FAMILY PROBLEMS AFFECTING CHILDREN

Families today face increasing pressures from the broader environment. They often live in communities that are not as supportive of families and their needs as they could be. Today's families are also more diverse, which means that the issues to consider when addressing their needs are more complex than in the past. An increasing number of children and families need social support beyond the family because of serious problems such as substance abuse, spouse abuse, and child maltreatment. Additionally, as increasing numbers of children grow up in communities rife with poverty and violence and do not receive the positive nurturance and guidance they need for healthy development, they are more likely to enter adolescence angry, depressed, and searching for positive attention and acceptance wherever they can find it. Thus, problems associated with adolescence, including youth crime, membership in or pressure from gangs, violence, and teenage pregnancy and parenthood are rising and receiving national attention. Suicide is not only a serious problem for adolescents, but is also on the rise among younger children.

Substance Abuse

Current evidence indicates that over 10 percent of individuals in the United States are being raised or were raised in alcoholic homes. An increasing number of children are being raised in homes where abuse of other substances is common. There are 30 to 50 million children of alcohol and drug abusers in the United States (Ackerman 1983). Until recently, substance abuse has been viewed as an individual disease rather than a family problem. But recent studies have found that individuals raised in such families are five times as likely to become substance abusers themselves. Twenty percent of juvenile delinquents and children seen in child guidance and mental health clinics come from families where alcohol abuse is a problem. Other studies show high correlations between substance abuse and family violence. The U.S. Advisory Board on Child Abuse and Neglect (1990) cited increased use of substance abuse as the most important factor in the rise in incidence and severity of child maltreatment. Researchers in one study found that two-thirds of reported cases involve substance abuse. Seventy percent of infants abandoned in hospitals have parents who are addicts; many of these children are born addicted to drugs as well.

Children who manage to "survive" in substance-abusive families seldom escape unscathed. Experts in substance abuse suggest that adult children of alcoholics manifest coping characteristics they developed as children within their own families, including a compulsion to control, a need to overachieve, and a need to please others continually (Black 1981). They also have many fears—they worry about being abandoned, physical and emotional harm, and personal violence to themselves or other family members. They also experience feelings of loneliness, guilt, anger, shame, and sadness. Because of messages they receive in their families and the resulting feelings of guilt and shame, they maintain as secrets not only what is going on in the family, but their own feelings as well.

In looking at a substance-abusive family from a systems/ecological perspective, the family develops a way of functioning with the abuser as the central family member that, although dysfunctional to outsiders, is functional to the family in that it facilitates survival. Family members or others who facilitate continuation of substance abuse are called **enablers.** For example, a spouse may assume the major responsibility for maintaining the family, protecting the children from the substance abuser, and making excuses for his or her behavior. An older child may take on a "hero" role, believing that by being a perfect child and pleasing the parents, the substance abuse will stop or be less likely to disrupt the family. This child is likely to get excellent grades in school, take care of younger children, nurture both parents, and work toward keeping family members happy no matter what the costs to the child. Another child in the family may take on a "scapegoat" role, subconsciously believing that negative attention directed at him or her will take the attention away from the parent who is the substance abuser. Conflict between the parents over the substance abuse may instead be directed at the child, who is always getting in trouble at home, at school, and in the neighborhood. Yet another child may assume the role of the "lost child," believing that the family is better able to cope if he or she is out of sight. These children are always in their rooms, under the table or in the corner, or at friends' homes. They seek little attention and, in fact, go out of their way not to call any attention to themselves at all. A final role a child in such families may assume is the "mascot" role. These children, often the youngest, become the pets or clowns of the family, always available to be cuddled when cuddling is demanded or to entertain when entertainment can alleviate some of the family's pain (Ackerman 1983).

Some experts in the substance abuse field take issue with the term *enabler,* because although it describes many characteristics typical of individuals in families where there is a substance abuser, it still places the focus of attention on the abuser. Instead, they prefer to use the term **codependent,** or "a person who lets someone else's behaviors affect him or her and is focused on controlling others' behaviors" (Beattie 1987), in describing relationships between family members and the abuser. These individuals suggest that the term *codependence* defines the problem more clearly as belonging to the codependent person and indicates a need for individual recovery for that person separate from the substance abuser (Schaef 1986). Although definitions and models of codependence range from those that support a disease model of substance abuse to those that are more family-systems based, they all focus on the impact of the behavior on the codependent individual and the long-term consequences, regardless of whether the person remains in a relationship with the substance abuser.

Ackerman and others who have studied relationships in substance-abusive families point out the enormous costs these roles have played on the individual family members throughout their whole lives, as well as on the total family. Such roles actually promote the substance abuse, and family members are seen as unknowingly encouraging the substance abuse. This is why current substance abuse intervention strategies view the abuse as a family-systems problem; if communication patterns and roles within families are not changed concurrently with treatment for the substance abuser, the substance-abusive behavior is likely to return quickly, reinforced by the behaviors of other family members.

The ways that families typically cope with substance abuse can be divided into four phases. The first phase is the reactive phase, in which family members deny that the substance abuse exists and develop their own coping strategies around the substance-abusive parent, usually—sometimes intentionally—enabling the abuse to continue. These strategies range from nagging to making excuses or covering up abuse (often without directly confronting the fact that there is a substance abuse problem) to staying at home and trying to prevent the substance abuse to denying emotional feelings. Children in such families may be victims of birth defects as a result of the substance abuse, may be torn between parents wondering why one is angry or feeling sorry for or angry at the abuser, may avoid activities with peers because of fear and shame, may not trust others, and may learn destructive and negative ways to get attention (Ackerman 1983).

The second is the active phase, in which family members become aware that there is a substance abuse problem, that this is not a normally functioning family, and that help is available. Family members begin to realize that the abuser does not control the family and that they have the power to make changes in their own behaviors and cannot assume responsibility for the substance abuser. At this point, members may join self-help groups such as Al-Anon or Alateen, where others going through similar experiences within their own families can lend support.

The third phase in a substance-abusive family is the disequilibrium phase. This phase is difficult for all family members but must be experienced if the problem is to be alleviated. This phase occurs after family members are aware that a problem exists, but all efforts to change the abuser or the family dynamics have been unsuccessful. During this phase, family members consider openly whether disruption is the only alternative. This often leads to polarization among family members. This phase often ends in divorce, with subsequent separation of family members if the abuser still will not seek help. Although usually better in the long run, at the time it is often doubly traumatic for children, who then have to experience the problems of both alcoholism and divorce. It is estimated that divorce occurs in approximately 40 percent of family situations that reach this phase (Ackerman 1983). For those families who do not choose separation, the traditional family communication patterns may be shaken enough that the family begins to change actively. Whether disruption occurs or the family member who is the substance abuser agrees to make a concerted effort to change, the family is forced to reorganize. This requires new and different roles for family members (Ackerman 1983).

The final phase that families involved in substance abuse experience is the family unity phase. Many families with substance abuse problems either disrupt or maintain the substance abuse problem and never reach this phase. Being free of substance abuse is central to this phase; however, it is not enough. Acceptance of the family member as a non-substance abuser and lasting changes in family communication patterns must take place if the family is to remain free of recurring substance abuse problems.

Spouse Abuse

Although definitions of **family violence** differ across state lines, a general definition often used is "an act carried out by one family member against another family member that causes or is intended to cause physical or emotional pain or injury to that person." Family violence typically has been separated into two major categories: spouse abuse (also referred to as "domestic violence," "battering," or "relationship abuse") and child abuse. Recent attention also has focused on elder abuse and children battering their parents.

Although spouse abuse has received extensive attention due to the well-publicized O. J. Simpson trial, most attention up until that time focused on the abuse of children. Child abuse first received attention as a major national issue in the 1960s, with impetus from the medical profession and other professionals and concerned child advocates, but spouse abuse did not gain attention until a number of years later. Attempts to combine forces by women's advocates were met with resistance from child abuse advocates. Early attempts to develop programs and secure legislation for spouse abuse were spin-offs from rape crisis centers, which often were run by feminists at the grassroots level.

Professionals, particularly those from the medical profession, were concerned that joining forces with feminists might place child abuse programming in jeopardy. Thus, currently there are only limited legislation and centralized programs to deal with spouse abuse, although significant efforts in both legislation and federal programs exist for child abuse. More important, very limited federal dollars have been appropriated for spouse abuse programs. Some states have allocated funding for spouse abuse programs; however, of these programs many are either small adjuncts to child welfare/child abuse departments or under the auspices of special women's commissions, implying that spouse abuse is a woman- or child-related problem rather than a family problem of concern to everyone. Some child abuse programs have funded spouse abuse programs only by suggesting that children raised in a home where spouse abuse is present are emotionally abused.

Although men are sometimes abused in partner relationships, the majority of the abuse is perpetrated on women; studies indicate that women are the individuals abused in 95 percent of spouse abuse situations; men, in 5 percent (Davis 1995). Thus, an additional reason why attention to spouse abuse was late in developing relates to ways men and women are viewed in our society: men are regarded in power positions both within and outside of the home. Although men are seen as having power over children as well, it is much easier for the general public to become concerned about abused children than abused women. Many individuals still subscribe to the myth that women who are beaten somehow deserve it, or that they must enjoy it or they would not put up with it.

Although it is difficult to determine the exact incidence of family violence because it happens behind closed doors, it is estimated that half of all women will be hit at least once while in a marriage or long-term relationship. (Although most family violence research has focused on heterosexual couples, violence also occurs in homosexual relationships.) Incidence of family violence among couples is thought to be about one in every four marital, heterosexual relationships. A recent study determined that over 1.5 million women experience serious violence inflicted by their male partners each year (Gelles and Straus 1988). Domestic violence can result in serious injuries: 22 to 35 percent of women seen at hospital emergency rooms have injuries related to domestic violence (Davis 1995), and hundreds of persons are killed each year. Violence between heterosexual couples extends beyond the marital relationship. A recent study found that between 22 and 67 percent of dating relationships involve violence of some sort. Milder forms of violence, such as slapping, pushing, and shoving, are more common; but more severe types of violence, including kicking (commonly done in the stomach to pregnant women), biting, punching, and threatening with a knife or gun also are surprisingly common. A sad commentary on the implications of family violence is that more than 25 percent of the victims of the violence and more than 30 percent of the abusers interpreted the violence as a sign of love.

While the majority of attention in the media has focused on physical violence, there are other types of spouse abuse. Susan Schecter, a researcher and expert in the field of spouse abuse, classifies emotional spouse abuse in five major categories (cited in Davis 1995, 782):

- Isolation, which includes behaviors such as not allowing a partner to go anywhere without the partner, monitoring and questioning telephone calls, and trying to keep the partner from being involved with anyone else other than the abuser

- Economic abuse, which denies access to resources, such as education, clothing, medical care, and the ability to work for pay

- Humiliation and degradation

- "Crazy-making" abuse, which includes placing responsibility for the abuse on the person who is being abused, changing interpretations of the person's reality, and other erratic behavior that leads the abused person to begin to believe that she is crazy

- Suicidal and homicidal threats

A number of factors commonly are associated with spouse abuse. Men who assault their wives generally have low self-esteem and feel inferior. Feeling powerless outside of the family, they exert their power within the domain of their homes. It is more difficult to interpret factors associated with women who are abused. Lenore Walker has identified "learned helplessness" as a common trait among abused women (1983). She suggests that women have learned to act passive and helpless as a way of coping with their violent spouses and have been conditioned to believe that they are powerless to get out of the violent situation. Others (Frieze and Browne 1989) suggest that battered women exhibit symptoms consistent with post-traumatic stress syndrome, a diagnosis commonly given to persons who have suffered severe trauma. Earthquake victims, persons involved in accidents where they have witnessed deaths or serious injuries, and Vietnam veterans are often given this diagnosis. Frieze and Browne suggest that women in violent domestic situations react emotionally to their experiences, and are often paralyzed and unable to act to defend themselves or their children. They exhibit the characteristics of learned helplessness identified by Walker, blaming themselves for their abuse because they did such things as not getting dinner ready on time; or they redefine the event, rationalizing that it wasn't that serious or that it was a rare occurrence.

Many times, abused women are reluctant to leave violent situations. They often have no employable skills and are concerned about being able to survive, particularly if they have children. Other studies show that battered women are not always passive—they often seek help in dealing with the abuse, but love their husbands in spite of the violence and believe they will reform. In many violent situations among spouses, the period following the violence is almost like a honeymoon period, with the abusive spouse often crying, being extremely sorry for the violence, threatening suicide if he is deserted, promising never to be violent again, and being extremely loving and supportive. It is difficult for a woman who loves her husband not to be taken in by this Jekyl and Hyde personality, at least initially.

Other studies show that women with low self-esteem, particularly those who were physically or sexually abused as children, feel so worthless that they believe they deserve the violent treatment. Such women are more at risk to be abused than other women. While in some situations, the woman is passive and the man abusive, in other situations both spouses are violent. But because of size differences, it is most often the woman who is hurt. Other factors that place couples more at risk for spouse abuse include substance abuse, financial stress and poverty, and the male's unemployment or underemployment. Persons of all ethnic backgrounds are both perpetrators and recipients of spouse abuse. Studies show that differences between ethnic groups are based more on socioeconomic status than ethnicity (Davis 1995).

Spouse abuse and the lack of policies and programs that address the problem are tied to the oppression of women in our society. Working toward eliminating the oppression of all groups will reduce spouse abuse. Several federal policies have been passed that support spouse abuse programs. The Family Violence Prevention and Services Act of 1984 provides funding for shelters for abused persons, but the funding is limited and does not come close to meeting the demand for shelter. The Victims of Crime Act, also passed in 1984, gives priority to abused spouses in receiving compensation for crime-related costs. Although programs that address spouse abuse are extremely limited, many communities have established safe houses and battered women's shelters, where battered spouses and their children can seek refuge. These programs also provide counseling for both women and children, and assist them in legal issues, locating housing and employment if they decide not to return to the batterer, and in developing support networks. Sadly, an estimated three out of every four women seeking shelter at such a program were turned away because of lack of space. Additionally, while community outreach programs have been established that provide counseling and other services to survivors of spouse abuse, and some programs have been developed that focus on helping the batterer to learn to control anger and on improving communication patterns in couple relationships, most programs usually begin to treat the violence after it has reached an intolerable point and change is difficult.

Child Maltreatment

Child maltreatment has received far more attention, and far more resources, than spouse abuse. But reported cases of child abuse continue to increase at epidemic rates, and current resources are unable to serve the many abused and neglected children and their families who come to the attention of available programs. In 1992, there were 1.9 million reported cases of child abuse and neglect in the United States, involving 2.9 million children—more than double the number of reported cases in 1980 (National Center on Child Abuse and Neglect 1994). A recently conducted national study (National Center on Child Abuse and Neglect 1988) suggests that reported cases of child maltreatment represent less than one-third of children who actually are maltreated (see Figure 12.2). Exact figures on numbers of abused and neglected children do

FIGURE 12.2   **KNOWLEDGE ABOUT MALTREATED CHILDREN: THE TIP OF THE ICEBERG**

This figure depicts the estimated incidence of actual cases of child maltreatment and who in the community knows about these cases. As the figure shows, the child protective services (CPS) agencies that are mandated to provide services in such cases actually know about only 33 percent of cases that other professionals know about. This percentage does not even include those cases that only neighbors or immediate family members know about, suggesting that known cases of maltreatment are only the "tip of the iceberg" when it comes to how much child maltreatment actually exists.

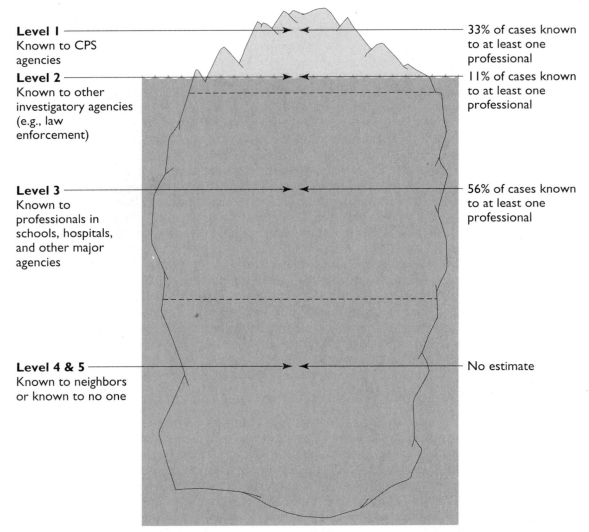

Level 1 — Known to CPS agencies — 33% of cases known to at least one professional

Level 2 — Known to other investigatory agencies (e.g., law enforcement) — 11% of cases known to at least one professional

Level 3 — Known to professionals in schools, hospitals, and other major agencies — 56% of cases known to at least one professional

Level 4 & 5 — Known to neighbors or known to no one — No estimate

Source: Figure adapted from *National Study of the Incidence and Severity of Child Abuse and Neglect* (Washington, D.C.: U.S. Department of Health and Human Services, 1988).

not exist because most maltreatment happens within the confines of family privacy, and when cases are known to others, they are often not reported.

There are four categories of child maltreatment: physical abuse, sexual abuse, child neglect, and psychological maltreatment, which includes psychological abuse and neglect. Neglect is the most frequently reported type of maltreatment, with almost half of all reports of this type. Reports of sexual abuse, however, have increased most in recent years. This is probably because of increased awareness about sexual abuse, which has eliminated some of the secrecy that previously surrounded the problem. Children of all ages are maltreated. While infants are most at risk to be abused or neglected severely, most abused and neglected children are school age. Large numbers of adolescents are also maltreated; however, because of scarce resources, these cases are least likely to gain the attention of authorities. The distribution across both genders is fairly equal: in 1991, 53 percent of children whose cases were substantiated as child maltreatment cases were female and 46 percent were male. Fifty-five percent of those children were white; 26 percent were African American, and 9 percent were Hispanic (National Center on Child Abuse and Neglect 1993).

Physical Abuse

The National Center on Child Abuse and Neglect's national child abuse reporting system indicates that 2.2 of every one thousand children in the United States was severely injured as a result of physical abuse, while 15.4 per thousand children received less serious physical injuries and 4.1 per thousand received unspecified physical injuries. Of substantiated reports received in 1991, 24 percent were cases of physical abuse (National Center on Child Abuse and Neglect 1993). Most children who are **physically abused** receive bruises, welts, or abrasions. These injuries are caused by parents whipping or spanking children with objects such as belts, extension cords, hair brushes, or coat hangers. Often, imprints of the objects can be seen on the child's body. When these types of injuries occur on the face or head of an infant (unlikely places for infants to bruise themselves), or on more than one plane of a child's body (such as the back and arms), and are in various stages of healing (for example, bruises in varying colors), child abuse is suspected.

Children also receive broken bones and burns, as well as internal injuries, as a result of physical child abuse. Physicians can use x-rays to determine the types of breaks and when they occurred. Children with spiral fractures, for example, may have experienced the break when a caretaker became angry and twisted one of their limbs. Children who are physically abused and brought to the hospital with one suspected broken bone or other serious injury will often have fractures or other injuries in various stages of healing in several areas of the body. This condition, termed **battered child syndrome** by C. Henry Kempe, is a diagnosis now recognized by medical professionals. One of the most serious types of child maltreatment is an internal injury to the head, which results in internal bleeding and often brain damage or death. Shaking a child severely can also result in serious injury, including blindness (due to detached retinas), brain injury, and death.

Physical child abuse occurs most often among school-age children. This young boy just brought home his report card; studies show that reports of abuse increase when report cards are distributed.

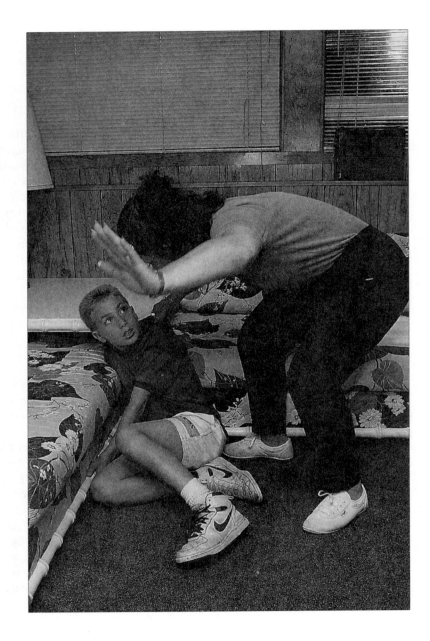

Burns are another type of physical injury. Children may be burned on their hands, feet, and other parts of their bodies with cigarettes or lighters. Parents with unrealistic expectations about toilet training often burn children by placing them in extremely hot water when they have soiled themselves.

Physical abuse is a result of beating, kicking, spanking too severely, slapping, biting, punching, throwing, burning, or shaking a child. Many times, parents lose their tempers and do not intend to harm the child severely. Many factors are associated with families who physically abuse children, including economic problems (with unemployment and poverty), isolation, unrealistic expectations about child developmental milestones and about children's abilities to meet parental needs for love and attention, alcoholism and drug abuse, abuse or maltreatment of the parent during childhood, lack of education about nonphysical alternatives to discipline, low impulse control and inability to cope well with stress, and marital problems. Studies show that only about 10 percent of parents who maltreat their children are seriously psychologically disturbed.

Studies also show that some children are more at risk to be physically abused than others. Children who were born prematurely or with congenital problems, children who somehow do not meet parental expectations or are perceived as different by their parents, and children who are the result of unwanted pregnancies are more at risk to be abused physically than other children. Many parents who abuse children begin with role reversal within the family system, expecting the child, even as an infant or toddler, to meet their emotional needs. When the child resists or is unable to do so because she or he is too young, the parent may feel rejected, become angry and frustrated, and abuse the child.

Using a systems/ecological perspective, we can also see that children who grow up in communities with few economic resources and few support systems available to families also are more at risk to be abused (see Box 12.1). Cultural conditions also have an impact on physical abuse. Studies show that cultures that value children and share parenting among extended family members or others beyond the nuclear family have less child abuse than other cultures (Korbin 1982).

Sexual Abuse

Sexual abuse, more than any other type of child maltreatment, has received increased attention in recent years. Reported cases of sexual abuse have increased significantly, for two reasons: (1) with increased public awareness, many more individuals, including the children themselves, are reporting cases; and (2) with children today exposed to more adults than in the past, including child care providers, stepparents, and other adults, the likelihood of being abused is increased.

Child **sexual abuse** can be defined as "any childhood sexual experience that interferes with or has the potential for interfering with a child's healthy development" (National Center on Child Abuse and Neglect 1985, p. 3). Thus, child sexual abuse can include acts such as fondling in addition to sexual intercourse. Recent legislation also mandates that state child abuse laws include child pornography and sexual exploitation in definitions of sexual abuse. This expands the definition to include acts such as taking pictures of children in sexual poses or for purposes of sexual gratification. Although the true incidence of sexual abuse is not known, the National Center on Child Abuse and Neglect reports that 11.7 of every thousand children in the United States were found to be sexually abused in 1989. Many individuals are unaware until later in life that they have been sexually abused, either because they repress the experience since it is so horrifying to them or because they have no idea of what are not healthy interactions, assuming all children experience such treatment. Others are reluctant to report the abuse because they are ashamed, embarrassed, have been threatened,

BOX 12.1

INDICATORS OF RISK FOR CHILD ABUSE AND NEGLECT

1. **Child previously reported:** There have been previous founded or unfounded reports of abuse or neglect of the victim or his or her siblings in the family system.
2. **Parent abused as a child:** The parent remembers having been abused as a child, or this fact is documented in the parent's history.
3. **Age of the parent:** The parent was under age 18 at the time of the reported child's or the first child's birth.
4. **Age of the child:** There are differences in the occurrence and type of abuse of infants, young children, or adolescents.
5. **Family composition:** This factor generally refers to a single parent raising children alone, including a never-married, separated, or divorced parent and children living in an extended family household.
6. **Domestic violence in the home:** In a home where violence frequently occurs, a child may be injured accidentally or purposely; emotional abuse is a factor.
7. **Separation of a parent or child for a long period:** The child may

have been raised by a grandmother or other family member or have been in foster care.

8. **Parent or caretaker's abuse of substances:** The parent or the caretaker may be abusing drugs or alcohol to the extent that parenting is affected or distributing drugs, both of which affect the child's safety and healthy development.
9. **Physical, mental, or emotional impairment of the child:** The child has been diagnosed or observed to be mentally retarded, cognitively limited, physically or emotionally disabled, or chronically ill.
10. **Physical, mental, or emotional impairment of the parent:** The parent or other caretaker has been diagnosed and treated for mental illness or has a physical or emotional disability or a chronic physical or mental illness.
11. **Low socioeconomic status:** The family is dependent on or eligible for public assistance.

Source: R. Herring, Ph.D. diss., 1992, in "Child Abuse and Neglect: Direct Practice," by S. Brissett-Chapman, *Encyclopedia of Social Work*, vol. I (Washington, D.C.: NASW, 1995), 361–2. Copyright 1995, National Association of Social Workers, Inc.

or are worried about possible repercussions for themselves and their families. Thus, the National Center's incidence study is much lower than other studies, which suggest that 27 percent of women and 16 percent of men were sexually abused before reaching the age of 18 (Finkelhor, et al. 1990). It is estimated that only 6 to 12 percent of cases are reported to law enforcement agencies at the time that they occur (Berliner 1995).

While most individuals think of sexual abusers as strangers who accost children in the park, the majority are known and trusted by the children they abuse. The first category of abusers consists of parents. Sexual abuse by birth parents, commonly referred to as incest, is considered by many to have the most serious personal and social consequences. Abusers also may be other parent figures, such as stepparents. The second category of abusers consists of family members other than parent figures. This includes siblings, grandparents, and uncles or aunts.

Sexual relationships between siblings are reported to be the most common. The broadest definition of **incest** includes sexual relationships between any family members. The third category of sexual abusers includes trusted adults. These may be teachers, babysitters, neighbors, coaches, leaders of children's groups, or other adults. The last, and least frequent, types of sexual abusers are strangers or remote acquaintances. It is estimated that only about 40 percent of reported abuse is perpetrated by someone outside of the child's family (Tower 1996).

Although all children are at risk to be sexually abused, those who are seen as most vulnerable are often singled out by perpetrators. Children living without their birth fathers, living in stepparent families, having their mothers employed outside of the home, having a mother who is ill, observing violence between parents, or having a poor relationship with parents are characteristics that make children more likely to be sexually abused (Finkelhor 1986). Boys are most likely to be abused by nonfamily members and girls by family members, and 95 percent of girls and 80 percent of boys who report being sexually abused indicate that their abuser was a male. Ethnicity is not clearly associated with differences in rates of sexual abuse, but it is associated with differences in related factors such as age of child and type of perpetrator (Berliner 1995).

The reasons why adults sexually abuse children are complex and vary according to the individual abuser. Characteristics of perpetrators of sexual abuse include poor impulse control, low frustration tolerance, low self-esteem, denial, manipulation, social and emotional immaturity, abuse of alcohol and other drugs, and isolation (Tower 1996). About one-fourth of male offenders report being sexually abused as children, and about half began sexually abusing others during adolescence (Berliner 1995).

Most abusers engage in a seductive, power role with children with whom they become involved. Children, wanting affection and too young to know how to draw boundaries themselves between positive affection and sexual abuse, initially may become involved and then be too afraid to tell anyone what is going on. Although the sexual abuse acts themselves may not involve physical force on the part of the adult, the child is trapped in the situation because adults are in power positions with children. Some abusers tell children that the relationship is the only thing keeping the family together, or the abuser is the only one who really loves and understands the child. Other abusers threaten physical harm to the child or to other family members if the child refuses to cooperate or tells anyone what is going on. For example, they say that their mother will "go crazy," the child will be taken out of the home, or the adult will sexually abuse a younger sibling.

Studies on the effects of sexual abuse show that it is extremely harmful to children emotionally and that many individuals who have been sexually abused suffer long-term effects. The impact of sexual abuse on children depends on factors such as the age of the child when the abuse occurred, the type of sexual abuse that took place, the relationship of the abuser to the child, the length of time the abuse occurred, how long it was between the time the abuse occurred and someone found out that it was going on, other characteristics of the child's family and available positive support to the child, and the reactions from family members and professionals when the sexual abuse finally is discovered (Sgroi 1982).

Issues faced by survivors of sexual abuse include lack of trust and feelings of betrayal, powerlessness, isolation, blame, and loss (Conte 1995). Many persons who have been sexually abused see themselves as victims due to the trauma of the abuse and have extremely low self-esteem; difficulty in establishing intimate, trusting relationships with others; and problems with their own families and marriages when they become adults. Without intervention for the sexually abused child and the family, persons who have been sexually abused are more at risk than others to turn to alcohol, drugs, or suicide to ease their pain. Many communities have established programs that promote public awareness of sexual abuse and early intervention with families once cases are reported to attempt to address such long-term effects.

Child Neglect
As opposed to child physical abuse, in which damage to a child is inflicted, neglect is characterized by acts of omission; this usually means that something that should have been done to or for a child was not done. **Child neglect** can be defined as

> a condition in which a caretaker responsible for the child either deliberately or by extraordinary inattentiveness permits the child to experience available present suffering and/or fails to provide one or more of the ingredients generally deemed essential for developing a person's physical, intellectual and emotional capacities. (National Center on Child Abuse and Neglect 1980)

Many states include specific categories in their definitions of child neglect, including failure to provide adequate food, clothing, or shelter for a child, often termed physical neglect; failure to provide adequate supervision for a child, for example, leaving young children alone for inappropriate periods of time, often termed lack of supervision; leaving a child alone or not returning when expected to care for a child, often termed abandonment; failure to provide medical care for a child, often termed medical neglect; failure to provide an education for a child, often termed educational neglect; and failure to provide for a child's emotional needs, often termed emotional neglect. The National Center on Child Abuse and Neglect's national reporting system determined that 55.7 per thousand children were deprived of necessities for survival in 1989, while 5.7 per thousand were abandoned.

Although some individuals view neglect as less dangerous to a child than abuse, this is not the case. Studies have shown that just as many children die each year from neglect as from abuse. Many are burned in fires while left alone or with inadequate supervision, some drown in bathtubs while left unsupervised, others die because their parents did not obtain medical care for them soon enough when they became ill. Other studies show that neglected children, in fact, may suffer from more long-term consequences of their maltreatment than abused children. Adults who did not have their physical or emotional needs met as children are much more likely to have problems in finding and maintaining jobs, developing positive relationships with other individuals and remaining in marriages, and parenting their own children adequately.

Failure to Thrive

One type of neglect that is receiving increased attention is **nonorganic failure to thrive,** a form of parental deprivation. Failure to thrive has been medically defined as describing a child who is three percentiles or more below the normal weight for his or her particular age. The child seems to be being fed on a regular basis by its caretakers, and nothing organically wrong can be found with the child, yet it does not gain weight and literally "fails to thrive." When placed in a hospital and given nothing more than regular feedings of its normal diet, coupled with love and attention (e.g., holding and cuddling), the child begins to gain weight immediately. Bowlby's studies of maternal deprivation and children raised in orphanages in Europe without love and attention found a high death rate and significant differences in intelligence quotient (IQ) and physical and emotional development when compared to children raised in environments where they received love and attention (1951). Similar findings are evident among children diagnosed with failure to thrive syndrome.

Neglectful Parents

Parents who neglect their children differ from other parents at the same socioeconomic level. While there is a strong relationship between poverty and neglect, not all parents who are poor neglect their children. Research studies have shown that the typical neglectful parent, as compared with non-neglectful parents also living in poverty, is more isolated, has fewer relationships with others, is less able to plan and less able to control impulses, is less confident about the future, and is more plagued with physical and psychological problems. Neglectful parents also are more likely to say that they have never received love and were unwanted by their parents. Many have been raised by relatives or in foster care. Neglectful parents often began life lonely, and continue to live in isolation. Polansky, Ammons, and Gaudin (1985) found that neglecting parents had difficulty identifying neighbors or friends with whom they could leave their children if they needed emergency child care or from whom they could borrow five dollars in an emergency. They are extremely isolated from both formal and informal support networks; many neglecting parents describe their social workers as being their best or only friends.

Polansky, et al. (1991) classify five types of neglecting parents.

• **Apathy-futility syndrome:** The first type suffers from what they term **apathy-futility syndrome.** These neglecting parents have all but given up on life. They see little hope for the future and view all efforts to try to relate to either their children or others as futile. They convey an attitude of hopelessness and despair. Usually neglected themselves as children and in many instances in the past, beaten down whenever they tried to make a go of life, they lack the physical or emotional energy to relate to their children. A neglectful parent with apathy-futility syndrome is likely to be found lying on the couch in a chaotic household that hasn't been cleaned or cared for, with children unkempt and uncared for, left largely to fend for themselves. Children raised by this type of neglectful parent suffer from physical, medical, educational and/or emotional neglect, as well as lack of supervision.

• **Impulse-ridden behavior:** The second type of neglecting parent characterized by Polansky, et al. (1991) is one with **impulse-ridden behavior.** This type of parent may be loving and caring and may provide adequate food, clothing, and medical care most of the time. But this parent has trouble making appropriate decisions and often behaves impulsively. Such parents suddenly may decide to go to a party and leave their children alone, or they may answer the telephone and become so engrossed in the telephone conversation that they forget that their child is unattended in the bathtub. They often get in trouble with employers over impulsive behavior at work, with creditors because of impulsive spending habits, and with friends because they make commitments and then impulsively change their minds and go off with others instead. Neglectful parents with impulse-ridden behavior are restless, intolerant of stress, and lacking in consistency. Their children never know exactly what to expect and, in fact, may be abandoned for long periods by an impulsive parent who suddenly decides to go off somewhere on a trip. Such parents can be seen by their social workers as making great progress in being more consistent in their child care, and then ask their social worker to babysit for their children so they can go off to the beach, or go to the beach and seem to forget completely that their children are left unsupervised. Children of neglecting parents of this type are likely to suffer from abandonment, lack of supervision, and emotional neglect. Additionally, because of the inconsistency they experience, they are likely to have difficulty trusting others, developing positive relationships, and being consistent themselves.

• **Mental retardation:** The third type of neglectful parent is mentally retarded. Although only a small percentage of neglectful parents are mentally retarded, neglect can occur if parents do not receive, or cannot comprehend, parenting information or adequate supervision to help them care for the child.

• **Reactive-depressive behavior:** The fourth type of neglectful parent is characterized as **reactive-depressive.** These parents are so depressed they cannot parent adequately. They may be depressed because of the death or loss of a significant person in their lives, the birth of a child, or ending a love relationship.

• **Psychotic behavior:** The fifth, and smallest percentage, of neglectful parents are psychotic. These parents may be in such a delusional state that they cannot adequately parent the child.

Neglecting parents often are more difficult to help than abusive parents, particularly those who are apathetic and feel hopeless. Unlike abusive parents, who still have enough spirit to be angry, many neglecting parents experience feelings of despair and futility. These feelings are much more difficult to change. By helping neglecting parents develop trust in other individuals and increase their self-esteem, particularly through links with supportive individuals, social workers can help them begin to care adequately for their own children. Neglect is also more affected by environmental factors than other types of maltreatment. Because of its relationship to poverty, some experts note that it may be more appropriate to talk about the unmet needs of the child, rather than the inappropriate actions of the parents (Zuravin 1992) and focus on the community and societal responses to meeting the needs of children. Most of the attention and resources in the area of child maltreatment have gone to child physical and sexual abuse rather than to neglect. Because studies show that neglect is just as detrimental to children as abuse—and in some instances, more so—increased concern needs to be given to this type of child maltreatment.

Psychological Maltreatment

Psychological maltreatment, also often referred to as "emotional maltreatment," is the most elusive form of child maltreatment. It is the most difficult to define, the most difficult to substantiate, and the most difficult to obtain resources for. It probably, however, also is the most common type of child maltreatment, and like other types of child maltreatment, it can result in serious long-term consequences for the child. Experts suggest that there are two types of emotional maltreatment: emotional abuse and emotional neglect (Garbarino, Guttman, and Seeley 1986). Definitions parallel those of abuse and neglect. Emotional abuse is viewed as acts of commission, or emotional acts against a child. Emotional abuse is often verbal; it includes being told continually how bad the child is, perhaps that parents wish the child had never been born, and being blamed for all the parents' and family's problems.

Almost all parents psychologically abuse their children at some times; one child development expert notes that children receive six negative messages about what they do for every one positive message (Ginott 1965). Continual psychological abuse can lower self-esteem and undermine a child's feelings of competence. Parents also psychologically abuse children in other ways; some parents, for example, give away children's prize possessions to "another child who will appreciate it," telling children that they don't deserve special things because "they are bad." Less often, parents psychologically abuse children by shaving their heads or cutting their hair or doing other humiliating things as forms of punishment. Children who are forced to watch parents or others in the family being beaten or otherwise abused are also experiencing psychological abuse. Children forced to experience sexual abuse are psychologically abused; in fact, some experts suggest that the psychological abuse has just as severe, if not more severe, consequences for the sexually abused child than the sexual abuse (National Center on Child Abuse and Neglect 1980).

Psychological neglect, like neglect itself, relates to acts of omission involving a child and includes the failure to meet the child's emotional needs. Parents who psychologically neglect children may provide for their physical needs, but they usually interact very little with their children in an emotional sense. Common parent-child activities such as cuddling, holding, reading or singing to, going places with, or just talking together are nonexistent for children who are emotionally neglected. Children who do not have their emotional needs met are likely to become

Emotional maltreatment is probably the most common type of child maltreatment. The National Committee for the Prevention of Child Abuse and other programs have developed media campaigns to focus attention on this problem.

"You're pathetic. You can't do anything right!"
"You disgust me. Just shut up!"
"Hey stupid! Don't you know how to listen."
"Get outta here! I'm sick of looking at your face."
"You're more trouble than you're worth."

"Why don't you go and find some other place to live!"
"I wish you were never born!"
Children believe what their parents tell them. Next time, stop and listen to what you're saying. You might not believe your ears.
Take time out. Don't take it out on your kid.

 Write: National Committee for Prevention of Child Abuse, Box 2866E, Chicago, IL 60690

adults who cannot give emotionally to their own children. Such adults may not only psychologically neglect their own children but also subject them to other types of maltreatment.

James Garbarino, Edna Guttman, and Janis Seely (1986, p. 8) provide a broader conceptualization, using the term *psychological maltreatment,* which they define as "a concerted attack by an adult on a child's development and social competence, a pattern of psychically destructive behavior." They suggest that psychological maltreatment takes five forms:

- Rejecting, where the adult refuses to acknowledge the child's worth and the legitimacy of the child's needs
- Isolating, where the adult cuts the child off from normal social experiences
- Terrorizing, where the adult verbally assaults the child, creating an environment of fear and terror

- Ignoring, where the adult deprives the child of essential stimulation and responsiveness
- Corrupting, where the adult stimulates the child to engage in destructive antisocial behavior and reinforces deviance

The conceptualization offered by Garbarino and colleagues is based on a systems/ecological perspective, which suggests that emotional deprivation or emotional trauma in one domain of children's lives increases their vulnerability to similar experiences in other domains.

Problems Associated with Adolescents

Until recently, little attention has been given in the literature about children and family problems to the special needs of adolescents. Problems associated with adolescents—including youth crime, gangs, violence, and teenage pregnancy—have currently escalated and drawn extensive media attention. Many family development experts are quick to point out that prevention and early intervention efforts aimed at young children and families would quite likely have eliminated many of these adolescent problems. They note that adolescents who come through the juvenile justice system as delinquents, gang members, runaways, or due to pregnancy most often come from families who have experienced many of the problems discussed in this chapter, but have not received appropriate services and support.

Although delinquent adolescents are required by law to be treated differently than adults, the present juvenile justice system does not have the resources to address the numerous family problems and provide the extensive treatment that many juveniles need. Many who are released from the juvenile system quickly enter the adult criminal justice system. But as juveniles commit more severe crimes at younger ages, how to effectively address their needs and protect them, as well as those they harm, is becoming a more pressing issue. Many states are changing laws relating to juveniles to make the system tougher on them; for example, in one large southwestern state, children as young as 12 can now be certified to stand trial as an adult.

In the United States today, because of the scarcity of resources available to address family problems, most resources are targeted toward younger children, who are more vulnerable than adolescents. In one state with few resources, school personnel find themselves agreeing with teenagers when they determine that their only recourse to escape a serious family situation is to run away from home. Because youth shelters and services are limited, a youth advocate in another state suggested that her only alternative to ensure that teens had safe shelter was to suggest that they get arrested so they could be booked into the juvenile detention center.

Adolescents labeled as delinquent often should more appropriately be considered "throwaways" or "push-outs," as more and more families fail to provide for the needs of their children and find themselves with emotionally damaged adolescents (Children's Defense Fund 1994). Estimates suggest that 1 to 1.3 million children and adolescents run away each year; most of these are teenagers who are gone only a night or two, but many never return to their homes. Most runaways are running in an attempt to cope with serious problems, including physical and sexual abuse, family alcoholism or drug abuse, divorce or spouse abuse, other family problems, or failure in school. A study of youth agencies found that two-thirds of teens who came to them for help had been abused or neglected and did not feel that they had a home to return to (Bass 1992). Although the Runaway and Homeless Youth Act of 1974 provided funding for emergency shelters for runaway youth, resources are limited and numbers continue to increase. Children served are also increasingly younger: in 1994, 42 percent of youth served at shelters were age 14 and under, while 54 percent were ages 15 to 16 (de Anda 1995). Runaway youth are also at risk for other problems. They are at risk for crime, assault, rape, robbery, prostitution, and participating in the development of pornographic materials, as well as for getting sexually transmitted diseases, including HIV.

Many adolescents experiencing problems also suffer academically. Family problems often result in learning disabilities and other learning problems, and young persons who do not feel good about themselves and are faced with daily problems at home are not likely to do well in school. Increased concern is being expressed about dropout rates of youth and the high illiteracy rate of both young and older adults. In 1991, 35 percent of Hispanic youths dropped out of school before reaching age 18, while 14 percent of African Americans and 9 percent of whites did so. [Rates for whites and African Americans declined somewhat from recent years, but not rates for Latinos. But it may be that Latinos finish school later, since 82 percent of those in school in 1982 had finished by 1986 (de Anda 1995).] Even with a high school education, increasing numbers of persons in the United States are illiterate. A recent study found that 56 percent of Latino adults, 44 percent of African American adults, and 16 percent of white adults in the United States are illiterate.

Youths who do not complete high school suffer in their ability to locate suitable employment. Researchers have found that there is a strong positive relationship between the number of years of school completed and getting and keeping jobs, as well as between socioeconomic status and school achievement (de Anda 1995). There is a serious lack of employment available for young adults, particularly those who are African American and Latino, even when they do graduate from high school. In 1993, more than half of all African American high school graduates not enrolled in college were unemployed, whereas only approximately 25 percent of white high school dropouts were unemployed (Children's Defense Fund 1994). The increasing dropout and illiteracy rates, especially for Latino and African American populations, have raised serious questions about the ability of the United States to maintain qualified workers, since the demand for employees requires a minimum of a high school education and technological skills. The limited availability of job skills training and adequate employment suggests that poverty rates, particularly for African Americans and Latinos, will continue to increase.

Another major problem facing our country today is teen pregnancy. Birth rates of children born to teen mothers have increased significantly in recent years, particularly rates of children born to unmarried females. The rate increased from 27.6 per thousand in 1980 to 44.8 per thousand in 1991. The rates differ significantly by ethnicity: they were 32.8 per thousand for whites (including Hispanics) and 108.5 per thousand for African Americans. Increased proportions of teen parents make up the population of new mothers: in 1990, 20 percent of first births to white mothers were to teen parents, while 40 percent of first births to African American mothers were to teen parents. Over 20 percent of the births to teen parents were to mothers 15 years old and younger (Williams 1995).

In 1990, demographic studies showed that by age 20, 20 percent of white and 45 percent of women of color become pregnant at least once. Of those females who become pregnant, 48.1 percent give birth to live infants while 38.5 percent have legal abortions. Fewer than 10 percent place their children for adoption. There are also ethnic differences in relation to decisions made about what to do when a pregnancy occurs; white females are much more likely to have an abortion, while African American females are much more likely to give birth and raise the child. Becoming a parent when a teenager is not developmentally prepared interrupts, sometimes permanently, the teen's successful transition into adulthood.

Teens today are faced with a great deal of pressure from many sources—peers, the media, advertising—to see their primary self-worth in terms of their sexuality. With limited opportunities to be successful in other arenas, such as the family, school, and the workplace, many male and female teens feel that their sexuality, and producing a baby, are the only ways they can feel good about themselves and have someone to love them. The United States has one of the highest pregnancy rates in the Western world, and the number of younger teens, age 12 to 14, becoming pregnant is increasing each year.

Many factors are associated with teen pregnancy, including poverty, low self-esteem, lack of information about reproduction, school failure, lack of appropriate health care and other services, and poor family relationships. Additionally, emphasis on pregnancy prevention and intervention has focused on teenage girls, and little has been done in regard to prevention and intervention with teenage boys. A survey regarding the use of condoms by adolescents, for example, found that 2.1 to 38.0 percent used them when they had intercourse (de Anda 1995).

Even more important, attention to pregnancy prevention often begins only when teens (girls) reach age 13. Developing positive self-esteem, effective decision-making skills, a strong value system, and a sense of responsibility for one's self and others—all major deterrents to teen pregnancy—are characteristics shaped from birth on.

Whereas in the past, most teens who became pregnant relinquished their babies for adoption, either formally through agencies or informally through relatives, today the majority of teens are choosing to keep their babies. This places tremendous pressure on both the teen mothers and their children. Infants born to teenagers are much more likely to have low birth weight, be premature babies, or have congenital or other health problems. Their mothers also are more likely to drop out of school, remain un- or underemployed, and raise their children in poverty than parents who are not teenagers.

The cycle often repeats itself. Teen pregnancy is both a cause and a result of poverty. In 1994, teens of color, more likely to grow up poor, constituted 27 percent of the teenage population, about 50 percent of poor adolescents, and about 40 percent of teenage mothers (Children's Defense Fund 1994). Teen pregnancy is viewed by many concerned about family problems as the hub of the cycle of poverty in the United States.

Increased concern is also being raised about youth violence and crime. Arrest rates for violent crimes have increased for both males and females under age 18. More whites (data includes Hispanics in this category) are arrested than African Americans, but the arrests for violent crimes are more equally divided (de Anda 1995). Table 12.2 shows the increases in arrest rates of youth under the age of 18 in 1992. As the table indicates, the most significant increases have been in the more serious crimes, including violent crimes, and for violations relating to the carrying and possession of weapons. There was a 79 percent increase in the frequency with which guns were used in murders committed by youth (de Anda 1995).

Increased numbers of youth are also joining gangs. A major reason why many youth join gangs is to belong; many gang members indicate that gangs are "like families to them" and for many youth, gangs replace the nurturing and support and sense of belonging that they find lacking in their own families. Gang members often commit crimes or violent acts as part of initiation rites or other gang-related activities. Peer pressure is considerable for youth who join gangs, and it is difficult for members to say no to their peers when they become involved in inappropriate and/or illegal activities and to leave gangs once they join them (McWhirter, et al. 1993).

TABLE 12.2   **INCREASES IN ARREST RATES OF ADOLESCENTS UNDER 18**

Offense	Percentage Increase in Arrest Rate
Burglary	1.5
Property damage	7.6
Larceny/theft	8.5
Running away from home	12.9
Disorderly conduct	24.4
Vandalism	27.9
Violent crimes (murder, forced rape, robbery, aggravated assault)	47.4
Other assaults	49.1
Weapons violations	66

Source: FBI, 1992, in "Adolescent Overview," by D. de Anda, *Encyclopedia of Social Work* (Washington, D.C.: NASW, 1995), 27–28. Copyright 1995, National Association of Social Workers, Inc.

Suicide and Children's Mental Health

Changes in society, communities, and the family have resulted in increased instability of many children and adolescents in the United States. Children are too often the victims of divorce, family and community violence, substance abuse, and other types of family, community, and societal dysfunction. In one recent study, researchers found that 12 percent of all U.S. children suffer some type of emotional illness, but fewer than 28 percent of those children receive treatment. Many children and adolescents become involved in substance abuse, becoming alcoholics or addicts, often at young ages, or suffering serious physical and emotional injuries as a result. In 1994, drinking and driving was the number one cause of death among adolescents. Suicide was the third leading cause of death for adolescents and the sixth leading cause of death for children 5 to 14 years of age (Allen-Meares 1995).

Suicide rates among children and adolescents of all ages are higher in the United States than in most other countries. Ten percent of all boys and 18 percent of all girls attempt suicide at least once before they reach age 18, but boys are more successful because their methods are more lethal. Suicidal individuals often try other ways to stop their pain first, frequently with drugs and alcohol, before turning to suicide. Children and adolescents who attempt suicide feel helpless, hopeless, and powerless, and they are often experiencing or have experienced a series of losses in their lives. When they are in an environment over which they feel they have no control, sexual experimentation, use of alcohol and drugs, suicide attempts, eating disorders, and other risk-taking behaviors become ways to either gain control over what they perceive as an uncontrollable environment or to escape from it.

Several experts in working with adolescents believe that mattering, or the degree to which a person believes he or she is important to others, is an important aspect in the prevention of mental health problems among children and youth. They identify three aspects of mattering that are significant: (1) feeling that you command attention from others; (2) feeling that you are important to others; and (3) feelings that others depend on you (Rosenberg and McCullough 1981).

Homelessness

There is a strong relationship between other problems discussed in this chapter and homelessness (see Chapter 10). As rents and purchase prices of homes throughout the United States continue to escalate, and federal funds to build low-income housing continue to be reduced, more and more families and their children are becoming homeless. Although it is impossible to determine the exact incidence of the homeless in the United States because they cannot be readily located, in 1994 it was estimated that more than 500,000 children were homeless. Families are the fastest growing group of homeless. The average homeless family consists of two parents with an average age of 27 and three children with an average age of 6. Many families are forced to live in welfare hotels in unsafe neighborhoods, tents, or automobiles.

Depression and suicide are common among adolescents, particularly those who feel helpless and hopeless about their lives and have experienced a recent loss. This young teen lived with his grandmother, who recently died.

Without a permanent address, it is difficult for parents to locate employment and for children to attend school. The psychological consequences of being homeless can be developmentally devastating to children, who may then repeat the same patterns with their families.

SUMMARY

There are many reasons why children, youth, and families in the United States experience problems. Many families experience a number of problems, and families who are at risk to experience one type of problem are likely to be at risk to experience others as well. From a systems/ecological perspective, factors associated with family problems are complex and interactive.

Societal and cultural factors, as well as the level of support available to families from the communities in which they reside, have an impact on the nature and extent of problems experienced by families. Finally, all families have strengths that can be used to draw from when they do experience problems. Effective intervention and prevention programs can capitalize on these strengths when working with children, youth, and families. But effective intervention and prevention efforts must be undertaken within the broader context of understanding the complexities of the family problems discussed in this chapter. In Chapter 13, we address programs and policies that help families in need and the roles that social workers play in providing these policies and programs.

KEY TERMS

apathy-futility syndrome
battered child syndrome
blended family
child neglect
codependent
custody
enabler
family
family violence

feminization of poverty
impulse-ridden behavior
incest
mediation
nonorganic failure to thrive
physical child abuse
psychological maltreatment
reactive-depressive behavior
sexual abuse

DISCUSSION QUESTIONS

1. Identify and discuss at least three of the issues that must be considered when defining a family problem.

2. Discuss briefly at least three issues that often surface in families who experience divorce.

3. Describe at least four roles family members might play where substance abuse is a problem.

4. Describe the dynamics that are found in a violent spousal relationship.

5. Identify and briefly describe the four types of child maltreatment.

6. Identify at least five factors likely to be associated with families who abuse or neglect their children.

7. Briefly discuss at least four reasons why teenagers today are likely to become parents.

8. Why are children, youth, and families of color more likely to be at risk of serious problems than white children, youth, and families?

REFERENCES

Ackerman, R. 1983. *Children of Alcoholics.* Holmes Beach, Calif.: Learning Publications.

Allen-Meares, P. 1995. Children: Mental health. *Encyclopedia of Social Work,* vol. 1. Washington, D.C.: NASW.

Bass, D. 1992. *Helping vulnerable youths: Runaway and homeless adolescents in the United States.* Washington, D.C.: NASW Press.

Beattie, M. 1987. *Codependent no more.* Center City, Minn.: Hazelden Foundation.

Berliner, L. 1995. Child sexual abuse: Direct practice. *Encyclopedia of Social Work,* vol. 1, 408–17. Washington, D.C.: NASW.

Black, C. 1981. *It will never happen to me.* New York: Ballantine.

Bowlby J. 1951. Maternal care and mental health. *Bulletin of the World Health Organization* 3:355–534.

Brissett-Chapman, S. 1995. Child abuse and neglect: Direct practice. *Encyclopedia of Social Work,* vol. 1, 361–2. Washington, D.C.: NASW.

Bronfenbrenner, U. 1979. *The ecology of human development.* Cambridge, Mass.: Harvard University Press.

Carter, E., and M. McGoldrick. 1989. *The changing family life cycle: A framework for family therapy.* 2nd ed. Boston: Allyn and Bacon.

Children's Defense Fund. 1994. *Children's defense budget: An analysis of the FY 1994 federal budget and children.* Washington, D.C.: Children's Defense Fund.

Conte, J. 1995. Child sexual abuse: Overview. *Encyclopedia of Social Work,* vol. 1, 402–8. Washington, D.C.: NASW Press.

Davis, L. 1995. Domestic violence. *Encyclopedia of Social Work,* vol. 1, 780–89. Washington, D.C.: NASW.

de Anda, D. 1995. Adolescent overview. *Encyclopedia of Social Work,* vol. 1. Washington, D.C.: NASW.

DiNitto, D., and A. McNeese. 1990. *Social work: Issues and opportunities in a challenging profession.* Englewood Cliffs, N.J.: Prentice-Hall.

Finkelhor, D. 1984. *Sexual abuse: New theory and research.* New York: Free Press.

———. 1986. *A sourcebook on child sexual abuse.* Newbury Park, Calif.: Sage.

Finkelhor, D., G. Hotaling, I. Lewis, and C. Smith. 1990. Sexual abuse in a national survey of adult men and women: Prevalence, characteristics, and risk factors. *Child Abuse and Neglect* 14:19–28.

Frieze, I., and A. Browne. 1989. Violence in marriage. In *Family violence,* ed. L. Ohlin and M. Tonry. Chicago: University of Chicago Press.

Garbarino, J. 1992. *Children and families in the social environment.* 2nd ed. New York: Aldine Press.

Garbarino, J., E. Guttman, and J. Seeley. 1986. *The psychologically battered child.* Lexington, Mass.: Lexington.

Gelles, R., and M. Straus. 1988. *Intimate violence.* New York: Simon and Schuster.

Ginott, H. 1965. *Between parent and child.* New York: Avon Books.

Goode, W. J. 1964. *The family.* Englewood Cliffs, N.J.: Prentice-Hall.

Herring, R. 1992. Ph.D. diss. In child abuse and neglect: Direct practice by S. Brissett-Chapman. *Encyclopedia of Social Work,* vol. 1, 361–2. Washington, D.C.: NASW.

Korbin, J. 1982. *Cross-cultural perspectives on child abuse.* Berkeley: University of California Press.

Laird, J. 1995. Lesbians: Parenting. *Encyclopedia of Social Work,* vol. 2, 1604–16. Washington, D.C.: NASW Press.

McWhirter, J., B. McWhirter, A. McWhirter, and E. McWhirter. 1993. *At-risk youth: A comprehensive response.* Pacific Grove, Calif.: Brooks/Cole.

Moses, A., and R. Hawkins. 1982. *Counseling lesbian women and gay men: A life issues approach.* St. Louis: C. V. Mosby.

Moyers, W. 1986. "The Vanishing Black Family." New York: ABC Television.

National Center on Child Abuse and Neglect. 1980. *Neglect: Mobilizing community resources.* Washington, D.C.: U.S. Department of Health and Human Services.

————. 1988. *Study findings: Study of national incidence and prevalence of child abuse and neglect.* Washington, D.C.: U.S. Department of Health and Human Services.

————. 1993. National child abuse data system: Working paper 2–1991. Washington, D.C.: U.S. Government Printing Office.

————. 1994. *Child abuse and neglect fact sheet.* Washington, D.C.: Author.

Polansky, N., P. Ammons, and J. Gaudin. 1985. Loneliness and isolation in child neglect. *Social Casework* (January): 38–47.

Polansky, N., M. Chalmers, E. Buttenwieser, and D. Williams. 1991. *Damaged parents: An anatomy of child neglect.* 2nd ed. Chicago: University of Chicago Press.

Quinn, P., and K. Allen. 1989. Facing challenges and making compromises: How single mothers endure. *Family Relations* 38:300–395.

Rosenberg, M., and B. McCullough. 1992. Mattering: Inferred significance and mental health among adolescents. *Research in Community and Mental Health* 2:163–182.

Schaef, A. 1986. *Co-dependence: Misunderstood-mistreated.* San Francisco: Harper & Row.

Schechter, S. 1982. *Women and male violence: The visions and struggles of the battered women's movement.* Boston: South End Press.

Sgroi, S. 1982. *Handbook of clinical intervention in child sexual abuse.* Lexington, Mass.: Lexington.

Tower, C. 1996. *Understanding child abuse and neglect.* 3rd ed. Boston: Allyn and Bacon.

U.S. Advisory Board on Child Abuse and Neglect. 1990. *Child abuse and neglect: Critical first steps in response to a national emergency.* Washington, D.C.: Government Printing Office.

U.S. Bureau of the Census. 1995. *Current population reports.* Washington, D.C.: Author.

U.S. Department of Health and Human Services. 1981. *National study of the incidence and severity of child abuse and neglect.* Washington, D.C.: Department of Health and Human Services.

Walker, L. 1983. The battered women's syndrome study. In *The Dark Side of Families,* ed. D. Finkelhor, R. Gelles, G. Hotaling, and M. Straus, pp. 31–48. Beverly Hills, Calif.: Sage Publications.

———. 1988. The battered women's syndrome. In *Family Abuse and its Consequences,* ed. G. Hotaling, D. Finkelhor, J. Kirkpatrick, and M. Straus. Newbury Park, Calif.: Sage Publications.

Wallerstein, J., and S. Blakeslee. 1989. *Second chances: Men, women and children after a decade of divorce.* New York: Ticknor and Fields.

———. 1980. *Surviving the breakup: How children and parents cope with divorce.* New York: Basic Books.

Wallerstein, J., and J. Kelley. 1979. Children and divorce: A review. *Social Work* (November): 468–75.

Wells, S. 1995. Overview of child abuse and neglect. *Encyclopedia of Social Work,* vol. 1. Washington, D.C.: NASW.

Werner, E., and R. Smith. 1982. *Vulnerable but invincible: A longitudinal study of resilient children and youth.* New York: McGraw-Hill.

Williams, C. 1995. Adolescent pregnancy. *Encyclopedia of Social Work,* vol. 1. Washington, D.C.: NASW.

Zuravin, S. 1992. Child-neglecting adolescent mothers: How do they differ from their nonmaltreating counterparts? *Journal of Interpersonal Violence* 7(4): 471–90.

SUGGESTED FURTHER READINGS

Gelles, R., and Cornell, C. 1990. *Intimate violence in families.* 2nd ed. Newbury Park, Calif.: Sage Publications.

Kozol, J. 1995. *Amazing grace: The lives of children and the conscience of a nation.* New York: Crown Publishers, Inc.

McNeece, C. A., and D. DiNitto. 1994. *Chemical dependency: A systems approach.* Englewood Cliffs, N.J.: Prentice-Hall.

CHAPTER 13

SERVICES TO CHILDREN, YOUTH, AND FAMILIES

Juanita Kingbird, a social worker with the local family services agency, is involved in a number of activities that prevent families from becoming dysfunctional, as well as activities that help families when they have special needs. Her agency provides a variety of programs: parenting programs teach child care to teenage parents; an outreach program and parent groups seek out and help parents who are under stress or need help parenting their children; and the agency provides individual, family, and group counseling for children and family members of all ages. Recently, the agency has developed a shelter for adolescents who cannot remain in their own homes and a respite care program for families of children with developmental disabilities. The agency also provides homemaker services, child care, and employment services to help families remain economically self-sufficient and able to stay together.

On a typical day, Juanita begins by returning a crisis call from a mother whose son ran away from home the night before, after a family argument. She calls the school social worker and arranges for her to try to locate the boy if he is in school and talk with him. After two counseling sessions with adolescents who are staying in the shelter, focusing on their feelings about becoming independent and separating from their families, Juanita leaves for the local high school, where she leads a support group for teenage parents. After the group, she meets individually with several of the girls and helps one of them obtain an appointment with a specialist for her developmentally delayed infant. She has a quick lunch with the school social worker to coordinate services both are providing to some of her clients, and then she meets with the runaway boy, who did come to school, getting him to agree to meet with her and his mother later on in the day. On the way back to her office, Juanita stops off to make a home visit to one of her clients who has been emotionally abusing her two young children. Juanita interacts with the mother and her children, role modeling good communication patterns and ways to give feedback and set limits positively. She returns to the office in time to attend a staffing on another family with social workers from the five other agencies involved. Although the family has many serious problems, the coordinated intervention plan developed by the agencies with the family seems to be effective, as everyone reports the family is making progress. Juanita then meets with the runaway boy and his parents. They negotiate family rules and boundaries and agree to try to live together without major conflicts, returning in a week for another family counseling session. Juanita leaves the agency to go home, glad that she has a supportive family waiting for her that will help her so that she does not burn out from getting too emotionally involved with her clients.

Juanita enjoys her job a great deal. Although she finds it difficult to deal with the many needs of the families with whom she is assigned to work, especially when children are suffering, she has learned to share small successes with family members. "If I can make things better in some small way each day for one child or one parent, my job is more than worthwhile," she stated in a recent newspaper interview. ▪

Programs and policies that address the needs of children, youth, and families are as diverse as the types of needs experienced. Traditionally, the system that has provided programs and policies that address child and family concerns has been called the **child welfare service delivery system.** This system includes the "network of public and voluntary agencies in social work practice that specializes in the prevention, amelioration, or remediation of social problems which are related to the functioning of the parent-child relationship network through the development and provision of specific child welfare services" (Kadushin and Martin 1988, 30)

In this chapter, we focus on services provided that address the children, youth, and family-related needs discussed in Chapter 12. We also discuss the roles that social workers play in providing services to children, youth, and families. ▪

CURRENT PHILOSOPHICAL ISSUES

All policies and programs that address the needs of children, youth, and their families must consider not only the social and cultural context of the child's family, the community, and the broader environment but also a number of current philosophical issues.

The Right to a Permanent, Nurturing Family

The first assumption is that every child has a right to grow up in a permanent, nurturing home, and that every attempt must be made to provide such a home whenever possible. This assumes that the child's own home should be seen as the best option for that child whenever possible. Such a philosophical position dictates that services should be provided first to the child's family, and that every attempt should be made to keep the child and the family together. This position has led to the development of **family preservation programs,** or services provided to a child and family while they remain together, as opposed to placing a child in a foster home or other type of substitute care. Increasingly, special attention is being given to those services that will keep families together rather than quickly removing children from their family settings.

In the past, many children receiving services in an overloaded service delivery system became lost in the system, with no chance to either return home, be adopted, or become emancipated. There was no way of determining exactly how many children were in substitute care, and in some instances, children were sent to other states because care was less expensive and responsibility for their care could be shifted elsewhere. Although foster care was, and still is, supposed to be temporary, many children placed in foster care at young ages needed extended care and left only because they reached age 18 and the system did not provide care for adults. Children often lived in five or more foster homes and had five or more social workers. Some children moved around so much they never went to the same school for an entire school year.

Concern among many individuals and advocacy organizations has led to legislation at both the state and federal levels that mandates **permanency planning.** This concept ensures that when a child and family first receive services, a specific plan is developed that states what is planned to help that family remain together if possible and, if not, what will be done to provide a permanent, nurturing home for the child. Specific plans are developed to take place within time limits and are monitored by the court and/or a citizens' review panel. This way, if a family receives services without making enough progress to provide for a child's most basic needs, the parents' rights can be terminated and the child placed in an adoptive home, rather than the child remaining in limbo in the foster care system. Such planning assists agencies to make more realistic decisions about helping children and their families and ensures that families know specifically what they need to do in order to be allowed to continue to parent their children.

The Best Interests of the Child

Decisions about needs of children and families should be based on what is in the **best interests of the child.** Sometimes, even with the most appropriate intervention, it is questionable whether it is best for children to remain with their own families. In such circumstances, should decisions regarding where a child is placed (i.e., remain with his or her own family or be placed elsewhere) focus on the child's best interests, the parents' best interests, or the family's best interests? Although experts agree that the rights of both the parents and their children need to be considered carefully, current trends give attention first to the best interests of the child. This means that before any decision, careful attention must be given to what the most beneficial outcome will be for that particular child. In *Before the Best Interests of the Child* (1979) and *Beyond the Best Interests of the Child* (1973), Goldstein, Freud, and Solnit give careful consideration to this issue. They argue that in considering what is best for a child, the **least detrimental alternative** for that child must be considered. In other words, if it is detrimental for a child to remain with his or her family, we must then ask what the least harmful alternative would be.

Legislation now requires that courts appoint a guardian *ad litem* (one who advocates for the minor on a limited and special basis) in certain child welfare situations, such as hearings when a parent's rights are being terminated. The guardian ad litem's sole purpose is to represent the best interests of the child and to make a recommendation to the court with those interests in mind. This is especially important in situations where the parents have an attorney advocating one decision to a judge, such as returning a child to the parents, and the state child welfare agency has an attorney advocating another decision, such as placing the child in substitute care or terminating parental rights.

Goldstein and colleagues (1973) also focus on considering who is most significant and should be involved in planning changes in a child's life. Until recently, decisions regarding where a child should be raised usually involved the child's biological mother, and then father. But the early rearing of many children is by a relative or a foster parent rather than their biological parents. Goldstein, Freud, Solnit, and others stress the importance of considering the child's **psychological parent** rather than biological parent, who might not always be the same individual.

Considerations before State Intervention

Another important philosophical issue is determining under what circumstances the community or state should intervene in family matters. As indicated previously, in the past, families were considered sacred, and intervention in family matters seldom took place. Such intervention when allowed has been based on the doctrine of *parens patriae.* This doctrine is based on the concept that the state is a parent to all of its children and has the obligation, through regulatory and legislative powers, to protect them and, when necessary, provide them with resources needed to keep them safe.

Now, with increased attention to such family problems as child abuse, child neglect, domestic violence, and substance abuse, many children are growing up in unsafe and unnurturing environments. Many family advocates argue that early intervention is necessary to keep a family together, as well as to protect the child from growing up with severe emotional damage. Recently, other advocates have suggested that intervention in families should take place less often, because there are too many instances when the intervention—especially when limited resources do not often allow for the family to be rehabilitated—is more harmful than no intervention at all. These advocates suggest that intervention in families should take place only when requested by a parent, such as child custody disputes; when a parent chooses to relinquish the rights of a child and place that child for adoption; or when a parent is seriously maltreating a child and the effect of the maltreatment on the child can be visibly observed.

The issue of when a government entity has the right or the obligation to intervene is increasingly before the courts. Many child advocacy groups have filed class action suits against state agencies mandated to provide child protective services, charging failure to provide needed services to protect children from serious maltreatment. But in 1990 the Wisconsin State Supreme Court ruled that a state cannot be expected to protect all children in the state who are at risk from serious injury or death. This issue is likely to come to the attention of the United States Supreme Court at some point.

Preventing Family Disruption and Dysfunction

Another major issue is whether scarce resources should be targeted toward preventing family problems. And, if prevention is chosen, should it be primary, secondary, or tertiary? All three are important in strengthening families.

Most intervention with families today occurs after problems have already occurred rather than before, and even those programs are not available to many parents and families in need of such services (see Box 13.1). Because resources are scarce, little attention is given to any type of prevention at all. Of the few prevention programs available, the focus is tertiary in nature. For example, the current focus is on family preservation; however, in many instances children must be severely abused or families must experience a serious crisis before services are available, and by that time family preservation is not as likely to be a realistic option.

How Accountable Are Parents?

A final issue receiving increased attention is the extent to which parents should be held accountable in regard to caring for their children, and what should be done to parents who do not give children adequate care. A number of specialists in family dynamics suggest that punishment is more likely to make parents angry and less likely to teach them how to be better parents. These specialists hold that effective intervention programs and the availability of resources are much more optimal for

BOX 13.1

TASHA AND FAMILY DESERVE A GOOD CHANCE

Tasha loves her children. This is not in question. Tasha holds Patik and Felicia, ages 2 and 4, close to her, pulling their heads to hers, smiling, singing the Barney song. "I love you . . . you love me . . ."

Her two older children, Robert and Honree ("I was 13 when I had him," says Tasha. "What did I know about spelling a French name?"), are helping women lay out doughnuts, sandwiches and loaves of bread on a table set up on a sidewalk in inner-city Baltimore.

The food is for giving away to hungry people. It has been donated to an organization that does that, and more. For four days, Tasha and her children have stayed in a shelter operated by this organization. While food is being laid out, a taxi pulls up, carrying a woman and a little boy. Both have been beaten by the boy's father. They, too, are looking for shelter. And more.

Honree, at 8, the oldest of Tasha's children, watches the women giving away food, then asks if he, too, may have a pair of the thin, white rubber gloves the women wear to handle food. The next time someone approaches the table, Honree is right there.

"May I help you?" he says. "You can have one sandwich, a doughnut and three loaves of bread, if you want to. May I get it for you? Here, will you sign this?" A man takes a second sandwich. "Please," says Honree, "there isn't enough. You can only have one sandwich." The man faces down this dignified boy and, after a couple of beats, returns the second sandwich.

For several hours, Honree runs the free food table. He is polite and firm. . . . He means to do it right.

Tasha has laid Patik down for his nap. Patik sleeps, curled on a blanket on the sidewalk. His sweet baby face carries in it all the possibilities in the world. He does not yet know how limited his are.

Meanwhile, Tasha answers questions from the white, middle-class women who have come to help distribute food, only to find an 8-year-old boy doing it better.

"My own mother was a junkie," says Tasha. "She's been clean for six years now. She made me go to a parenting program for a year. My children's fathers? Two are dead from drugs. The other two, they don't do anything for the kids. Nothing at all. Yea, I did drugs. I'm in the program now. AA, you know?"

Tasha looks at Felicia, who, at 4, already is beautiful. "I got to do what I can to make sure her life is different. I don't want her to be 13 and make the choices I made. Or only have the choices I had. But it's hard. I can't get a good job because I can't get my GED because I can't get child care. Actually, I can't get any kind of job until I can work out the child-care thing. I'm getting a place to live next Monday. The social worker called and said we'd go look at it. I told her I don't have to look at it. If it's got a roof and walls and locks on the door and windows and a toilet that flushes, I'll take it."

Tasha's children play with one another, and with others. Robert and Felicia sing a song about a rabbit and smile at everybody. Their smiles can light a whole day. They hug people, too, probably because they have been hugged. Honree works the food table. It seems clear he's been helping his mother take care of the smaller kids. This is an intelligent boy, alert, interested, quick, kind. One wants to do something. Something that will give Honree his chance. Something that will give Tasha an opportunity to give Honree—and Robert and Felicia and Patik—a chance.

Something.

One thinks of politics. But politics is theory and politicians take too long to do anything. Tasha, Patik, Felicia, Robert and Honree are not theory—they are people—and they don't have too long.

Two men, old and wasted, approach the free food table. The sandwiches are all gone, Honree tells them. Tasha looks up and seeing the old men, takes two sandwiches that had been given to her children and says, "Here. Take these. My kids got fed last night. They're not as hungry as you."

And so it goes.

Source: Written by award winning TV producer and best-selling author, Linda Ellerbee. From "Tasha and Family Deserve a Good Chance," *Austin American Statesman,* 23 June 1995, p. A15.

children than punishment of their parents and likely separation from them. Other experts suggest that a compromise is most effective: that parents whose family problems pose severe consequences for their children be brought before the court and ordered to receive help, with punishment ordered if the help is refused.

The relationships between parents' problems and consequences for a child are also being debated increasingly and coming before the courts for decisions. Should a woman who fears for her own life if she intervenes to protect her child be held accountable for the injury of the child, for example? In two recent child abuse fatality cases, one in New York and one in Texas, a battered woman was charged with failing to protect her child from her violent husband. In the New York case, the mother was found not guilty. In the Texas case, the woman received a prison sentence that, because she was tried separately from her husband by a different jury, was longer than he received. The court also terminated her parental rights. The 1995 case of the woman from South Carolina who drowned her two young sons also resulted in extensive debate. Should parents who have experienced severe maltreatment themselves as children and/or who have serious emotional problems be held accountable for their actions? If so, should those experiences be considered when penalties for their actions are assessed? When the South Carolina woman was a young child, her mother committed suicide, her stepfather molested her when she was a young teenager, and she had a history of psychiatric problems. Although the prosecuting attorney asked that the woman receive the death penalty, the jury recommended that she receive a life sentence. Unfortunately, if efforts are not increased to prevent problems such as domestic violence and child maltreatment from occurring, and to intervene quickly and effectively when they do, many more tragic situations such as these are likely to occur.

◢ DEFINING SERVICES TO CHILDREN, YOUTH, AND FAMILIES

Traditionally, services to children, youth, and families have been defined as **child welfare services.** Initial definitions of child welfare, promoted by child welfare experts such as Alfred Kadushin, focused on residual services, appropriate when the normal institutional arrangements for meeting social needs of children and youth—primarily the family—break down. In his 1980 child welfare book, Kadushin suggests that the goals of child welfare services are "to reinforce, supplement or substitute the functions that parents have difficulty in performing; and to improve conditions for children and their families by modifying existing social institutions or organizing new ones" (p. 5).

The Social Security Act, the most significant piece of national legislation ever passed in relation to providing support to children and families, has a specific section (Title IV–B) that mandates states to provide a full range of child welfare services, defined as follows (Section 425):

[P]ublic social services which supplement, or substitute for parental care and supervision for the purpose of:

1. preventing or remedying, or assisting in the solution of problems which may result in the neglect, abuse, exploitation or delinquency of children,

2. protecting and caring for homeless, dependent, or neglected children,

3. protecting and promoting the welfare of children of working mothers and

4. otherwise protecting and promoting the welfare of children, including the strengthening of their own homes where possible or, where needed, the provision of adequate care of children away from their homes in foster family homes or day care or other child care facilities.

Because of negative connotations associated with the term *welfare* and the current emphasis on the importance of strengthening the family in order to support the child, child welfare services today more often are referred to as services to children, youth, and families (or as child and family services). They also are viewed in a broad sense, not only focusing on the more traditional child welfare services of child protection for maltreated children, foster care, and adoption to keep children safe but also emphasizing family preservation and supportive services to families, such as child care and parenting programs.

THE HISTORY OF SERVICES TO CHILDREN, YOUTH, AND FAMILIES

Some historians argue that societal attitudes toward children and families have improved significantly since the settling of the United States, as have policies and programs that are supportive of children and families. Others argue that little has changed for the better and that history has had a tendency to repeat itself. They suggest that a review of debates about the needs of children and families in the 1880s and early 1900s includes many of the issues discussed today—youth crime, family violence, and substance abuse. Regardless of whether today's children and families are better or worse off than in the past, reviewing the history of services to children, youth, and families shows clearly the historical base of our present child welfare service delivery system.

Colonial Times

In colonial times, children were considered to be the responsibility of their families, and little attention was given to children whose families were available to provide for them, no matter whether the family actually met the child's needs. Children usually came to the attention of authorities only if they were orphaned and relatives were not available to provide for them. Churches and a few private orphanages cared for some dependent children; however, prior to 1800, most orphans were placed in almshouses, or indentured, that is, given to families to function as servants. The focus during this time period was on survival, since death often occurred at early ages; fewer than half of all children born in the United States prior to the 1800s lived to reach the age of 18.

The Nineteenth Century

During the 1800s, increased attention began to be given to the negative effects of placing young children in almshouses along with insane, retarded, and delinquent persons and those with disabilities. In 1853, Charles Loring Brace founded the Children's Aid Society of New York, which established orphanages and other programs for children. Brace and others felt that such programs were the most appropriate way to "save" many children from the negative influences of their parents and urban life (Bremner 1974). Brace viewed rural Protestant families as ideal parents for such children, and he recruited many foster families from the rural Midwest to serve as foster parents. During the mid-1800s, "orphan trains" carrying hundreds of children stopped at depots throughout the Midwest, leaving behind those children selected by families at each stop (Bremner 1974). By 1880, the Children's Aid Society of New York had sent 40,000 children to live with rural farm families (Bremner 1974). A number of individuals and organizations strongly criticized this move. Although some called attention to the negative effects of separating children from their parents, the greatest criticism targeted religious conflicts. The majority of children placed in foster homes were from Irish immigrant families who were predominantly Catholic, whereas their foster families were primarily German and Scandinavian Protestants. The outcry led to more emphasis on the development of Catholic orphanages and foster homes.

Still, little attention was focused on children living with their own families or with other families as a result of informal placement by their families, and no standards or any system of intervention existed to address the needs of abused and neglected children and their families. This changed in the 1870s as the result of a now-famous case involving a young girl in New York named Mary Ellen. Abandoned by her parents at birth, Mary Ellen was living with relatives who beat her severely, tied her to her bed, and fed her very small amounts of food from a bowl—like a dog. A visitor to Mary Ellen's neighborhood was appalled at the abusive treatment she was receiving from her caretakers and reported the situation to a number of agencies in New York City. When none would intervene, the visitor, reasoning that Mary Ellen fell under the broad rubric of "animal," finally got the New York Society for the Prevention of Cruelty to Animals to take the case to court and request that the child be moved from the family immediately. As a result of the Mary Ellen case, New York established the Society for the Prevention of Cruelty to Children, and other northeast cities followed suit. These organizations, however, focused primarily on prosecuting parents rather than on services to either children or their families. The establishment of Charity Organization Societies (COS) and settlement houses in the late 1800s gave increased attention to children and families, as well as to the environments in which they functioned.

The majority of other efforts in the 1800s and early 1900s focused on the health needs of children. This was because illness was frequent and the death of children was commonplace during this time period. It was also because middle- and upper-middle-class families saw prevention of disease as a way to keep the diseases of immigrants from spreading to their own children (Bremner 1974). Immunization laws, pasteurized milk legislation, and other sanitation laws passed early during this period. Other relevant legislation focused on child labor laws and compulsory school attendance legislation. Increased attention began to be given at both state and national levels to the responsibilities of government to provide for children and families, and many states passed legislation establishing monitoring systems for foster care and separating facilities for dependent, neglected, and delinquent children from those for adults.

The Early Twentieth Century

The most significant effort toward the establishment of a true service delivery system for children, youth, and families during the early 1900s was the creation of the **U.S. Children's Bureau** in 1912. This was a result of the first White House Conference on Children, held in 1910, and a coalition of child advocates from the settlement houses, COS groups, and state boards of charities and corrections. The legislation establishing the U.S. Children's Bureau was significant, because it was the first national legislation recognizing that the federal government had a responsibility for the welfare of its children. Julia Lathrop was appointed the first chief of the bureau, and its first efforts were aimed at birth registration and maternal and child health programs, in an attempt to reduce the high infant mortality rate and improve the health of children. One of the bureau's first publications, *Infant Care,* a booklet for parents, has undergone over twenty revisions and remains the most popular document available from the Government Printing Office. Today, the Children's Bureau is responsible for a number of federal programs for children, youth, and families and is a part of the U.S. Department of Health and Human Services.

During the first thirty years of the 1900s, states continued to become more involved in services to children, youth, and families, particularly in the South and West, where strong private agencies did not exist. Many states established public departments of welfare that also were responsible for child and family services, including protecting children from abuse and neglect, providing foster homes, and overseeing orphanages and other institutions for children. The establishment of the American Association for Organizing Family Social Work (which later became the Family Service Association of America) in 1919 and the **Child Welfare League of America** in 1920 gave further impetus to the provision of child and family services. Both of these organizations stressed the role of the social work profession and established recommended standards for the provision of services. During the 1920s, attention turned to parenting and facilitating the development of healthy parent-child relationships. Child guidance centers were established and the emphasis on psychoanalysis led to increased attention to child therapy. Establishment of adoption as a formal child welfare service and subsequent adoption legislation also occurred during this period.

The Social Security Act of 1935

Services to children, youth, and families became more formalized with the passage of the **Social Security Act** in 1935. This act established mothers' pensions, which later became the AFDC program, and also mandated states to establish, expand, and strengthen statewide child welfare services, especially in rural areas. The definition of child welfare stated earlier in this chapter incorporated the following trends currently seen in state and federal child welfare services:

- Recognition that poverty is a major factor associated with other child and family problems

- A shift from rescuing children from poor families and placing them in substitute care to keeping children in their own homes and providing supportive services to prevent family breakup

- State intervention in family life to protect children

- Increased professionalization and bureaucratization of child welfare services

- An emphasis at the federal level that it is the responsibility of the federal government to oversee the delivery of child welfare services within states to ensure that all children and families in the United States have access to needed services

In spite of the Social Security Act, there continued to be problems with the delivery of services to children, youth, and families. Access to services remained unequal, and many children continued to grow up in poverty. Some child welfare services, such as adoption, were provided primarily to white middle-class families, and few child welfare services adequately addressed the needs of African American, Latino, and Native American children and their families. Many children, particularly children of color, spent their entire childhoods in foster care. What initially was meant to be temporary care until families stabilized enough for their children to return became a permanent way of life for many children.

The 1960s and 1970s

In the 1960s the Kennedy and Johnson administrations took a strong interest in children, youth, and families. Services during these administrations were broader and were targeted at prevention and elimination of poverty. Many of these programs were based on then-new studies that suggested that children could be shaped by their environment and that heredity played only a minimal role in individual outcomes. The focus became to "maximize the potential of all individuals" and to help them become productive adults. As a result, programs were implemented—such as infant care centers and **Head Start** (a preschool program focusing on physical, social, emotional, and cognitive development)—and increased emphasis was placed on education, as well as on job training and employment programs for youth and their parents. With this broad-based focus, traditional child welfare services received less attention in favor of strengthening families and preventive services.

When President Nixon took office, resources were perceived as being more scarce. The focus shifted from providing maximum resources to meeting minimum standards in regard to child and family services. With only a few exceptions that Congress actively advocated, services to children, youth, and families narrowed. In addition, funding, programs, and policies shifted back to more traditional child welfare services, including protective services to abused and neglected children and their families, foster care, and adoption.

During the Nixon administration, because of increased concern about the high costs of child care and the number of children left alone because their parents could not afford child care, Congress attempted to pass legislation that would give states funding for child care subsidies for low-income working parents. It was reasoned that this not only would keep more children safe but also would reduce the number of women on AFDC and the number of families living in poverty. But it was not until 1990 that child care legislation—the A Better Child Care (ABC) Act—was introduced in Congress with a wide base of support. That legislation, which was not supported by the Bush administration, also failed, as has most other child and family services legislation since the Carter administration.

Other significant legislation that did pass in the 1970s includes the 1974 Juvenile Justice and Delinquency Prevention Act, which establishes limited funding for runaway youth programs; the Indian Child Welfare Act (1976), which attempts to prevent disruption of Native American families; and the Education for All Handicapped Children Act (1975), which mandates, through public school systems, the provision of educational and social services to children with disabilities.

Child Abuse Legislation

The most significant child welfare legislation of the seventies provided services in the area of child abuse and neglect. In 1974, attention to the battered child syndrome—a medical diagnosis given to a child who comes to a medical setting with an injury such as a broken bone, and whose x-rays reveal previously broken bones or other internal injuries throughout the body in various stages of healing—resulted in strong advocacy from the medical profession and key Congressional leaders. As a result, Congress passed the Child Abuse Prevention and Treatment Act. This act mandated the establishment of the National Center on Child Abuse and Neglect as part of the Department of Health, Education, and Welfare (now the Department of Health and Human Services). It required states receiving federal dollars to strengthen child maltreatment programs to meet a number of mandates, including state definitions and reporting laws regarding child maltreatment. It established research and technical assistance programs to assist states in developing child maltreatment prevention and intervention programs. And it established special demonstration programs that could later be adapted by other states. When the act was renewed three years later, a new section was added to strengthen adoption services for children with special needs, or those children who were waiting to be adopted and were considered difficult to find homes for because of ethnicity, age, or developmental disabilities.

Adoption Assistance and Related Child Welfare Legislation

In 1980, Congress passed the Adoption Assistance and Child Welfare Act. For many years advocates had been urging that legislation of this type be passed, because they had become increasingly concerned about the large numbers of children "drifting" in the foster care system and about those who were legally free for adoption but for whom homes were not being found. A number of studies (Maas and Engler 1959; Vasaly 1976) indicated that the child welfare services delivery system perhaps was doing more harm to children than they would experience if they had remained in their own homes. Researchers in one study (Shyne and Schroeder 1978) found that although foster care philosophically was (and is) intended to be short-term (six months or less) while parents prepare for family reunification through counseling and other types of assistance, this was not the experience of many children. The average age of children studied in foster care was approximately 13; the average number of years a child had been in foster care was approximately 5; the average number of social workers managing the child's case while in foster care was approximately five; and the average number of different foster homes in which the child had lived was approximately five.

The Adoption Assistance and Child Welfare Act changed the thrust of services to children, youth, and families. Through ceilings on funding allowances, it encouraged the establishment of own-home services and reductions in the number of children in foster care; it required case plans and six-month reviews for all children receiving child welfare services so that they do not languish in foster care; and it provided federal funding to subsidize the adoption of special-needs children.

Unfortunately, however, the act did not receive the funding appropriations needed to successfully implement what it was legislated to do. Because the act offered financial incentives to states if they reduced the number of children in substitute care and strengthened services to children while they remained in their own homes, foster care rates dropped nationwide during the early 1980s, from an estimated 500,000 to an estimated 270,000. But as child abuse and neglect reports have increased and funding for services has decreased, more children have been seriously injured or have died when they have remained in their own homes. Although the act put no ceiling on federal payments for foster care of children who qualify for AFDC benefits, it severely restricted funding for in-home services such as family counseling. The more frequently required court hearings have also overloaded an already overextended court system, making it difficult for legal proceedings to take place that can free children for adoption.

In spite of the legislation, substitute care rates are again on the increase, with an estimated 442,000 children in foster care nationwide in 1992 and rates showing no signs of decreasing. Furthermore, funding for in-home services and other programs that keep families together is seriously lacking. In 1990, for example, funding under the authorization of the act was $1.5 billion for foster care and $252 million for prevention programs. Still, child and family advocates point to important gains in philosophy, practice, and management of cases since the passage of the act. There is now increased recognition given to children's right to remain in their own homes or to return to their homes as soon as possible, more special-needs children have been adopted, and innovative family preservation programs have been developed in many parts of the country (NASW 1995b).

The Mid-1980s and the 1990s

Legislation also passed during the late 1980s and early 1990s focusing on services to children with disabilities and teenage pregnancy. The Developmentally Disabled Assistance and Bill of Rights Act (1990) requires states to establish services in the least restrictive settings possible. The Special Education for Infants and Toddlers Act (1989) provides special identification and intervention for developmentally delayed infants and toddlers. The Public Health Act (1987) authorized the establishment of adolescent family life demonstration programs to prevent teenage pregnancy and to serve pregnant and parenting teens and their families.

One of the drawbacks to these legislative acts, in addition to the limited funding authorized to implement the requirements of each act, has been the continued categorization of legislation. Such categorical legislation, targeted more recently toward areas such as child abuse, alcoholism and drug abuse, runaway youth, school dropouts, adolescent pregnancy, pediatric AIDS, and increased gang activities and serious crimes against juveniles, leads to the establishment of programs limited to narrow populations and reinforces the fragmentation of services rather than a holistic approach. Recent sessions of Congress also have placed additional ceilings on amounts available for child and family services. Thus, even attention to a newly publicized area deemed important, such as legislation establishing programs targeted at gangs and youth crime, has usually not meant increased funding.

Support to Get Families Off Welfare

The federal legislation that had the potential to be the most significant for children and families since the Social Security Act of 1935 was the Family Support Act of 1988, commonly referred to as the "welfare reform act." Proponents of the legislation believed that the provision of transitional benefits for AFDC recipients such as health care, child care, and transportation; the emphasis on education, job training, and placement in a job that leads toward self-sufficiency; and the case management approach, which views the client and family from a holistic perspective, would reduce some of the problems with previously fragmented services created by categorical legislation. But funding to provide such massive changes has been limited, and implementation of the act at the state and local levels required extensive coordination and services provided by human services agencies, school districts, community colleges and universities, employment and job training programs, child care programs, health care providers, transportation programs, and private and public sector employers. Because of the costs of efforts to initiate or strengthen welfare reform programs, many states were unable to provide sufficient resources to address the needs of AFDC recipients wanting to get off welfare. In a number of instances, often-disappointed clients were placed on waiting lists for education, job training, and child care programs. Other clients were placed in jobs that paid the minimum wage so that states could meet federal requirements to maintain funding for their programs; however, these jobs did not pay enough or provide benefits that allowed clients to become self-sufficient.

Issues relating to welfare reform are currently being reexamined at both the federal and the state levels. If increased numbers of families are to be able to achieve self-sufficiency and get off welfare, they will need support systems in place to assist them in the process. Although there is much room for debate about the type and extent of assistance that should be provided, the long-term benefits to future generations of present public assistance recipients, as well as to the national economy and the well-being of our society, will be far more substantial than the initial costs. The Children's Defense Fund (1995), Lindsey (1994), and other child welfare advocates maintain that the elimination of children living in poverty is the most important aspect of a child welfare service system.

During Bill Clinton's presidential campaign, he made strengthening services to children, youth, and families a high priority, stressing the need for welfare and health care reform as key components to improving the lives of children and their families. Clinton's wife, Hillary, was the former head of Arkansas Advocates for Children, a statewide coalition of groups concerned about children's needs, and a member of the board of the Children's Defense Fund, one of the major national child advocacy programs in the United States. The Clinton administration's initial efforts were targeted largely at health care reform, and that and its other legislative plans met intense resistance from the Republican-dominated Congress.

Moving into the Twenty-First Century

During the 1995 session of the United States Congress, Republicans pushed plans to eliminate much of the federal legislation that provided for specific child welfare programs to states and collapse them into large noncategorical block grants, giving states the freedom to decide how and under what conditions they wanted the monies to be spent. Proponents of the Republican plan, publicized as the Contract with America, indicated that administrative costs would be reduced and programs more effective because they could be holistic in approach rather than based on fragmented narrow pieces of legislation, and they also could be tailored to specific geographic needs. Opponents of the plan were concerned that advocates of specific causes would garner most of the funding, leaving the needs of less vocal constituents—including the most at-risk children and families—undermet or unmet. Plans for block grants also called for reducing the amount of funding given to states from what they would have received under the more categorical pieces of legislation, with child welfare dollars scheduled to be reduced over $5 billion from 1995 to 2000.

A newspaper cartoonist captures the essence of the systems/ecological framework and the need for giving attention to children at all levels of the environment.

Republican proposals called for the elimination of twenty-three federal programs designed to protect at-risk children and their families, including three child care programs: child care for mothers on AFDC, child care for the working poor, and child care for parents moving from welfare to work. Proposals also call for the elimination of legislation that provided funding of programs under the Adoption Assistance and Child Welfare Act; and the Child Abuse Prevention and Treatment Act, including the Family Violence Prevention and Services Program, the Adoption Opportunities Program, foster care and independent living programs, family preservation and support services, and other programs funded to states at the federal level. The proposed Child Welfare Protection Block Grant, which consolidates all of these programs and gives funding directly to the states in large blocks of money, removes the leadership role in child welfare efforts from the federal government and eliminates most of the funding of special federal demonstration and research projects.

A major concern of child advocates is that the block grant plan also proposes to eliminate foster care services as an entitlement program, meaning that states would get specific lump sums of funding based on state population estimates rather than actual reimbursement for the exact numbers of children in foster care. States anticipate that since they will need to spend more of their own monies for foster care, there will be fewer dollars for prevention and intervention efforts that keep families together. Some states indicate that abused and neglected children in need of foster care may need to be placed on waiting lists until care becomes available (NASW 1995a).

PREVENTIVE SERVICES TO CHILDREN IN THEIR OWN HOMES

Although preventive services receive less attention than other types of services, there are many programs that strengthen families and reduce chances for family dysfunction.

Natural Support Systems

Given the scarcity of resources, increased attention is being given to the strengthening of **natural support systems** to assist families. Many families develop social networks of friends, relatives, neighbors, or co-workers who provide emotional support; share child care, transportation, clothing, toys, and other resources; offer the opportunity to observe other children, parents, and family constellations and how they interact; and provide education about child rearing and other family life situations. But studies show that many families who experience problems are isolated and lack such support systems. Many social services agencies, churches, and other community organizations are assisting communities in the establishment of support systems for new families and other families who lack natural support systems to help them meet their needs. Some communities have established telephone support programs for various groups, such as a Parents' Warmline or Teen Help Line, where individuals can receive support and information about appropriate resources.

Home-Based Services

Recently in the United States there has been increased attention given to the provision of **home-based family-centered services,** or services delivered to children and families in their own homes, with a focus on preserving the family system and strengthening the family to bring about needed change. Comprehensive services, which are usually overseen by a single case manager assigned to the family, include homemaker services, respite care, child care, crisis intervention, financial assistance, substance abuse treatment, vocational counseling, and help with various concrete services, such as locating housing or transportation. Most home-based service programs include the following features:

- A primary worker or casemanager who establishes and maintains a supportive, nurturing relationship with the family;
- Small caseloads of 2–6 families with a variety of service options used for each family;
- A team approach with team members providing some services and serving as a back-up to the primary worker/case manager;
- A support system available 24 hours a day for crisis calls or emergencies;
- The home as the natural setting, with maximum use of natural support systems, including the family, extended family, neighborhood, and community;

- Parents remaining in charge of and responsible for their families as educators, nurturers, and primary care givers;
- A willingness to invest at least as much in providing home-based services to a family as society is willing to pay for out-of-home care for their children (Lloyd and Bryce 1980).

Most families receiving home-based family-centered services are families with multiple needs who have received fragmented services for long periods of time from a number of agencies. Many children from these families have also spent previous time in substitute care. But due to the chronic and severe problems experienced by such families, and the repeated crises they often experience, past efforts have been largely ineffective.

Home-based family-centered services are based on a systems/ecological approach to family intervention, viewing the entire family as the focus of help. Intervention is short-term and goal-oriented, focused on behavioral change. Intensive services are usually provided to families for sixty to ninety days, which averages out to the same number of families a worker providing traditional child welfare services carries during a one-year period. But the ability to focus on a limited number of families intensively has important benefits. First, it gives workers a chance to stabilize more families so that they can function either independently or with fewer services while allowing children to remain in their own homes. Second, it allows workers to make a better determination more quickly and with more documentation if the family cannot be stabilized, allowing children to be placed more quickly in adoptive homes rather than remaining in limbo in either a dysfunctional life-threatening family situation or the instability of foster care.

Studies comparing home-based family-centered service programs to more traditional child welfare services show that when 18 percent to 20 percent of children who would otherwise enter substitute care can be maintained safely in their own homes, the home-based services pay for themselves. Evaluations of home-based family-centered programs show that 75 percent to 90 percent of children are able to remain in their own homes when such services are provided (Lloyd and Bryce 1980).

Parent Education

While most people are required to learn math and English in school, little attention is given to one of the most important roles they are likely to play as adults—that of being a parent. Many communities offer parenting classes aimed at a wide range of parents: prenatal classes for parents before the birth or adoption of their first infant, classes for parents of toddlers and preschoolers, classes for parents of school-age children, and classes for parents of adolescents. Such programs not only offer education about basic developmental stages of children and adolescents and alternative methods of child rearing and discipline, but they also encourage the development of mutual support systems among participants, who often relax about their roles as parents when they realize that other parents have similar concerns and struggles.

One successful parent education prevention program is Healthy Families in America, launched by the National Committee for the Prevention of Child Abuse in partnership with Ronald McDonald Children's Charities in 1992. The goal of the program is to provide early intervention and home visits to new parents during pregnancy and after birth to provide parenting information, information about community resources, and opportunities for parents to talk with staff about their hopes, concerns, and stresses. The program has been effective in Hawaii, and over 100 programs have now been established in twenty-two states (National Committee for the Prevention of Child Abuse 1995).

Child Development and Child Care Programs

Accessible and high-quality child care programs that are affordable for working parents, particularly single parents, also can be seen as preventing family breakdown. Such programs help parents ensure that their children are happy and safe in a comfortable, nurturing environment while parents work, thus reducing parental stress. Many child care programs offer additional opportunities for parents, including parenting education classes, babysitting cooperatives, social programs, and the opportunity to develop support systems with other parents and children. But affordable, high-quality child care programs often are unavailable to working parents, particularly in rural areas. Child care for infants, for children with disabilities or other special needs, for school-age children during vacations and holidays, and when children are sick also is not widely available in the United States. An additional gap in services is the availability of evening and night child care for parents who must work late shifts.

Special programs are available for low-income parents, but they are often limited in the hours and in the number of children they can serve. Head Start, perhaps the most successful program established under the Office of Economic Opportunity in the 1960s, provides not only a developmental learning program for preschool children but also health care, social services, and parent education. Infant-parent centers, which allow parents the opportunity to learn how to interact and play with their children in order to stimulate their development, also are available to some parents on a limited basis.

Recreational, Religious, and Social Programs

Often when services for children, youth, and families are discussed, no attention is given to the major roles that community resources other than social services agencies play in meeting family needs. From a systems perspective, the broader social, recreational, and religious programs must also be included when discussing programs that strengthen the welfare of children and their families. Religious organizations such as churches and synagogues meet the spiritual, emotional, social, and recreational needs of many children, youth, and families. They often play a major role in establishing special preventive services, such as child care programs, outreach centers, and parent education programs. Increasingly, the business community is providing preventive services through the workplace, including bag lunch programs for working parents, recreational facilities and programs for employees and their families, and the facilitation of co-worker support systems. Many communities offer substantial recreational programs for families that are free and provide family entertainment. Serious gaps exist in most communities, however, in providing appropriate recreational programs for adolescents. Some experts attribute increases in adolescent problems, including teenage pregnancy and delinquency, to the lack of available programs for this age group.

Health and Family Planning Programs

Early screening of health problems also reduces child and family problems. Health problems place increased stress on families, and access to affordable health care from prenatal care to adulthood is an important aspect of preventing family breakdown. Additionally, access to programs that provide help in responsible decision making about becoming a parent, through family planning clinics, churches, and other community resources, reduces the risk of unwanted children and assists families in exploring options when pregnancy occurs.

A number of programs have successfully reduced infant mortality and developmental disabilities through the provision of comprehensive prenatal care. In California, for example, state-funded health programs that had not previously paid for health education, nutrition, counseling, or vitamins for pregnant women began to do so in the early 1980s. Such efforts cut the percentage of very low birthweight babies more than in half when compared to a similar group that did not have access to the program, and saved an estimated $1.70 to $2.60 in neonatal care costs for every dollar spent on the program. Other programs involved storefront operations located in accessible areas and "resource mothers" who provide mentoring and support for pregnant teens (Schorr 1989).

Education about Family Problems

Finally, education about the various types of family problems—and, should they occur, about resources available—is a significant form of prevention. Many communities provide programs that focus on preventing sexual abuse of children by teaching them about types of touch and what to do when they find themselves in an uncomfortable situation with an adult or older child. Other communities provide alcohol and drug awareness programs.

Appropriate Educational Opportunities

Most studies identify strong relationships between difficulties in school and individual and family problems. Programs that give children an opportunity to learn in ways that help them feel good about themselves and develop a sense of competence prevent family- and child-related problems in the long run. Such children are less likely to have children themselves, drop out of school, and live their lives in poverty. School-based social services allow for close cooperation between children and adolescents, teachers and school administrators, parents, and the community.

SCHOOL SOCIAL WORK

One specialized field that focuses on services to children, youth, and families is **school social work,** or social work services offered in a school-based setting. Such services provide an opportunity to identify needs of children and their families early and to facilitate early intervention before problems become more serious. Social workers in school settings perform preventive services such as parent education and facilitate the development of positive mental health for children through special outreach programs in the school. School social work includes individual, family, and group counseling, as well as crisis intervention services. School social workers deal with suicidal students; with students and their families and friends after a serious injury or death has occurred; and with students in conflict with family members, peers, or school authorities. (See Box 13.2 for an account of a school social worker in an inner-city elementary school.) School social workers serve as members of intervention teams who work with children with developmental disabilities or other special

School social workers are an integral part of many schools. They provide individual, family, and group counseling, help students and their families access community resources, and advocate for the needs of children and their families. School social workers work closely with many other professionals, including teachers and school administrators, psychologists, religious and community leaders, and other social workers.

BOX 13.2

A DAY IN THE LIFE OF A SCHOOL SOCIAL WORKER

- 8 A.M.: A student is in my office waiting to talk. He is 7 years old and is crying. Last night his 16-year-old brother took his gun, drove to the park, and shot himself dead. The little boy knew his brother was upset and had tried to talk to him. The family had hidden the gun. The little boy thought he could have stopped it from happening.

- As I was talking with this student, a frantic call came in from the school office. A 7-year-old girl is bruised and battered. The secretary says the little girl is shaking like a leaf. I ask a social work intern to help the little boy find a quiet place to try to rest as he had not slept the night before. The girl got in the middle of a domestic violence episode the night before. Her drunk stepfather came over in the middle of the night, beat her mother, trashed the place, tore out the phone, battered the child, and vowed to return. After comforting the child I asked her to draw pictures of her feelings. I went to check on the boy.

- Another call from the office. An 8-year-old's father had overdosed the previous weekend. He is dead. The little girl had just returned to school.

- The 7-year-old girl had drawn a 6-page "story" of the night's events. She expressed terror about him returning. Together we came up with a plan for her:
  1. Crawl out of her bedroom window.
  2. Wake the neighbors by screaming "HELP! HELP!!! CALL 911!!"
  3. Pound on their door.

- A regular student in the CIS Program* dropped by. She is 7 years old and is very sad. She and her mother and sister have been homeless for months. She has not seen her older sister since spring break.

Her mother is using again. They are staying at a man's apartment. His name is "Killer."

- A child protective services worker arrived to interview the 5-year-old boy who had been found "having sex" with a 7-year-old boy at the baby-sitter's place over the weekend.

- The 4-year-old girl I had just begun to work with was not at school. The day before I made a CPS† report for medical neglect. She has open sores all over her head. She is developmentally delayed; her height, weight, and head circumference are all below the 10th percentile. She comes to school dirty and in inappropriate clothing. She has never seen a doctor. Mom refuses to come to any appointments, even for immunizations provided at the school. The other six children appear to be healthy and well fed.

- And finally I made time to talk with the 10-year-old CIS student who the afternoon before had picked up her little brother out of a pool of blood and called 911. She had been watching him outside; he was hit in the crossfire by two bullets. As of this writing he is in a coma. The 10-year old is in two of our "pre-employment" groups: the "child care club" and the "nurse assistants."

- 7 P.M.: I end the day by writing this to process these events so that I might be able to sleep tonight.

*CIS Program—the Communities in Schools Program directed by the school social worker
†CPS—Child Protective Services

Source: Written by Deborah Selbin, a school social worker and program manager of an inner-city, social services program at the elementary level. The program is part of Communities in Schools–Central Texas, a dropout prevention program that works with at-risk children and their families.

needs, often serving as the liaison to parents and the community when special services are needed. The Education for All Handicapped Children Act has been updated to specify that schools may hire social workers to provide social services to special-needs children, and dropout prevention legislation in some states also suggests the hiring of social workers.

School-based social work services are advantageous for many reasons. First, the social worker gets to see the child or adolescent in a natural setting, interacting with peers, teachers, and school administrators, which gives the social worker a different perspective than seeing a client in an office or an agency. Second, the social worker has access to large numbers of children and families in need of services; most children aged 5 to 18 attend school. Third, the social worker can help parents and school personnel use a systems/ecological approach to better address the child's needs, focusing on the relationships between the child, the home, the school, and the broader community. Often, in school, the focus of staff is on academic performance and school behavior. A social worker with a systems/ecological perspective can help school personnel understand the importance of family and community variables in relation to the child's capacity to function in the school setting.

◪ SERVICES TO CHILDREN AND FAMILIES AT RISK

Although, because of a scarcity of resources, it is sometimes easier to locate community resources for children and families already at risk than to find preventive services, such services are also limited and fragmented. Many studies of child and family services find that coordination among service providers is a problem identified by both service providers and recipients. Some communities have made special efforts to increase coordination, avoid duplication, and reduce gaps in services available to at-risk children and families. Efforts include developing computerized databases and information and referral systems, which can provide instant information about the type of services available, location, eligibility requirements, and costs of available services.

Other efforts involve "first-stop" resource centers where families at risk can receive thorough assessments, identifying needs so that they can be referred to appropriate agencies rather than going from agency to agency only to learn that services are not available to them or do not meet their needs. In some communities multiservice agencies have been established, in which a number of agencies are located in the same facility with a single assessment point and agency staffings to share information about families and determine which agencies can best meet a family's needs. At-risk families, often reluctant to trust service providers and without transportation to access services, can receive individual and family counseling, complete forms to receive public assistance, get help in finding employment and housing, and attend parenting classes and parent support groups—all at the same location. A variety of programs are available, particularly in urban areas, to help meet the needs of at-risk children and families.

Health and Hospital Outreach Programs

Many health clinics and hospitals have established special programs to address the needs of children and families who are at risk of family disruption or dysfunction. (These and other services to families at risk are shown in Box 13.3.) Some clinics have high-risk infant programs, for example, that provide intensive services to teenage parents; parents of low-birthweight or premature infants or infants with disabilities; parents with substance abuse problems; and parents who never seem to have established appropriate relationships with their children. Clinics offer a variety of services, such as weekly outreach programs conducted by a public health nurse, individual counseling, play groups for children and support groups for parents, role modeling of appropriate child care, and assistance in obtaining other resources as needed.

Hospitals offer similar programs. In some hospitals, specially trained nurses identify at-risk mothers in the delivery room and work with hospital social workers to give those mothers intensive care and support during their hospitalization, in addition to outreach services for both parents after the hospital stay. In a number of instances, such programs help parents realize they do not wish to be parents and help them relinquish children for adoption or place them in foster care while they receive additional help. More often, such programs prevent child abuse or neglect and help parents establish positive relationships with their children. Pediatric-AIDS programs have also been established in many major metropolitan-area hospitals. Such programs attempt to stabilize the health of infants and older children infected with the AIDS virus. Because many parents do not want to or cannot care for children with AIDS and it is difficult to locate foster families willing to do so, many children with AIDS remain in the hospital for extended periods of time, sometimes longer than a year.

In some areas, special health clinics have been established to provide services for adolescents. Clinics offer basic health care, information on adolescent development and puberty and sexually transmitted diseases; and in some instances, pregnancy tests, contraceptive information, and prenatal care. Some clinics are located in public high schools. Although this has caused some controversy, studies show that physical and emotional problems, sexually transmitted diseases, and pregnancies have decreased significantly in these schools.

One successful family-planning approach began with a health clinic connected to a St. Paul, Minnesota, high school, which paved the way for health clinics attached to other city high schools. Thirty-five percent of female students who came to the clinic came for family-planning services, reducing the numbers of children born to students by more than half and the number of second pregnancies to less than 2 percent. Other health clinics established in high schools have found that rather than increased sexual activity, girls became sexually active later instead

BOX 13.3

SUPPORT SERVICE OPTIONS FOR FAMILIES AT RISK

Family Relationships Support Services: Casework with individual parents or couples; family groups; family life education discussions; marriage seminars; pastoral counseling; AA or special counseling, etc.

Housing: Tenant advocacy linkage; maintenance and repairs planning; landlord-neighbor tension resolution; housing relocation for improved space and environmental supports; mortgage financing; other.

Parenting Assistance: Respite provisions; homemaker services; foster grandparent role modeling and support; release of possibilities for extended family involvement; other, such as family day care.

Socialization Matrix of Parents: Adult and family recreational and social opportunities enhancement; direct services or linkage; adult education and advancement groups; programs that support and enhance the parent's and family's culture and ethnicity.

Socialization of Children: School-, agency-, or community-based programs of recreation, camping, trips, interest and hobby building,

shared homework, part-time work experiences; programs that support and enhance the child's culture and ethnicity.

Income and Economics: Advocacy and/or escort job-finding; or training stipend; on-the-job training program linkage; help with income supports such as food stamps, Medicaid, SSI; budget management assistance; other advocacy.

Health: Child and adolescent health clinic services; family physician, outpatient or inpatient resources; public health nursing or other in-home consultation; adaptive equipment and prosthetic devices, etc.

Remediation of Behavioral Problems: Individual or group approaches to problem modification by direct involvement of worker with child; linkage with special school; tutoring; activity group; etc.

Source: Adapted and reproduced by permission of the publisher, F. E. Peacock Publishers, Inc., Itasca, Illinois. From B. McGowan and W. Meezan, *Child Welfare: Current Dilemmas, Future Directions*, 1993 Copyright, p. 179. Originally appeared in Sr. Mary Paul Janchill, *Guidelines for Decision-Making in Child Welfare* (New York: Human Services Workshops, 1981), p. 13.

of earlier when they could talk honestly about sex with a trusted adult. Additional opportunities for teens, such as school success and job training and employment opportunities, also must be provided so that self-esteem and adulthood can be tied to factors other than having a child (Schorr 1989).

Child Care

Although attention usually is given to child care for working parents, child care also is used as a service for at-risk parents to enable children to remain in their own homes. Many parents need respite from their children and cannot attend to their needs twenty-four hours a day. Child care gives parents time to meet their own needs and gives children the emotional support they may not be getting at home. It allows families to stay together and is less costly than foster care and less traumatic for the child. In many states, some child care providers receive special training to enable them to work more effectively with at-risk parents and children. In some instances, child care providers develop surrogate-parent or positive role relationships with parents, giving them and their children much-needed emotional support.

Many times, parents under stress reach a point where they need a break from their child or they will abuse or neglect the child. Other times, emergencies occur and parents lack natural support systems to help them during a crisis. In other situations, families with children with severe developmental disabilities need time for themselves but must cope with their children's needs twenty-four hours a day. Many communities have established various forms of crisis or respite-care programs for such families. Some agencies have respite-care programs for children with developmental disabilities, where specially trained adults care for children evenings or weekends so parents can have time to themselves. Other communities have established crisis nurseries or shelters, where parents under severe stress or in a serious emergency can leave their children for a limited amount of time. Some programs even provide emergency transportation for the children; most require counseling for parents under extreme stress while their children are in crisis care.

Some communities offer respite care for adolescents who need time away from their parents. Emergency shelter facilities for teens also most often provide crisis and family counseling to help stabilize the situation so the teen can return home. But special services for teens are lacking in many areas. In some communities, the only resource available for children as young as 12 or 13 is the Salvation Army's general shelter.

Increased attention is also being given to child care for working parents, particularly under the provisions of the Family Support Act of 1988. The inability to access affordable child care can often be the last straw that creates an additional crisis for families who are already at risk and under severe stress. Many at-risk working parents lose or are forced to quit their jobs because of a lack of child care.

Homemaker Services

Many agencies provide homemaker services to families who are at risk or who have abused or neglected their children. Homemakers are specially trained individuals, often indigent persons from the community who have been parents themselves and can serve as a nurturing, supportive role model for the parents and children in the home. Homemakers offer practical suggestions and education about housekeeping, child care, nutrition and cooking, health and safety, shopping, budgeting, and access to community resources. Additionally, they may serve as surrogate parents to both parent and children in the family and often develop positive, trusting relationships with family members who may have been previously isolated. Homemaker services are far more cost effective than foster care and often prevent the necessity to separate children from their parents.

Crisis Intervention Programs

Various community agencies provide **crisis intervention** services to families in crisis, which de-escalate the crisis and often result in a subsequent referral for additional help, such as counseling. Law enforcement agencies in many communities have crisis intervention teams that handle domestic disputes, including situations of spouse and child abuse. Some youth shelters have crisis intervention for adolescents and their parents. Hospitals also provide crisis intervention services in emergency rooms, dealing with child maltreatment, family violence, and other serious family problems. From a systems/ecological perspective, intervention often can be more effective in a crisis situation than in a noncrisis situation, because the family system is thrown into disequilibrium. Studies show that families are more receptive to change and to agreement to services such as counseling during disequilibrium, because regular defenses and the family balance are no longer intact.

Counseling

Individual, marital, and family counseling services are available in many communities for families experiencing problems. Mental health centers, social services agencies, child and family services agencies, child guidance clinics, employee assistance programs, churches, schools, youth services programs, and hospital outreach programs often provide various types of counseling services. Unfortunately, services often are available on a limited basis, due to scarce resources and the large number of persons needing services, and may not always be available at no cost or on a sliding scale. Additionally, specialized counseling to address family problems (such as family violence or sexual abuse) often is unavailable in many communities. For example, only $5 per child was available for counseling services for the large number of sexually abused children in one large city, when one hour of counseling cost $50–$100 and children needed long-term counseling in most instances.

Studies show that for many problems, group counseling is more effective than individual counseling, or a combination of both is more effective than individual counseling alone. For example, when dealing with sexual abuse, children who have been sexually abused need to hear from other children that they are not the only ones who have had such an experience. Sexual and physical abusers, as well as others with family problems, often deny that there is a problem, and group therapy sessions with others in similar situations typically break down their defenses more quickly than in individual counseling.

Increased attention by helping professionals is being given to family counseling as an effective way to strengthen individual functioning and address needs. Family counseling is effective in helping families understand behavior and coping patterns, establish more productive communication patterns, identify needs and resolve problems, and support each other as family members. In almost all situations where a family member is experiencing a problem or undergoing a stressful change— for example, substance abuse, family violence, rape, a serious illness or disability, death of a family member, divorce, or remarriage—family counseling can help the entire family reinforce positive changes and address negative patterns appropriately, and also serve as a source of support to each other.

Some agencies have initiated multifamily groups, or groups of families that receive therapy jointly. Many times individuals can see their own issues and family dynamics more clearly while watching other families interact, because they are too involved when such interactions occur within their own families. Teenagers, for example, may be more likely to listen to another parent who offers feedback than to their own parents, and parents are often more likely to listen to other teens or parents than to family members.

Social workers, because of their emphasis on a systems/ecological perspective, have played an important role in this shift in focus from individual to family counseling. Social workers in particular focus on the strengths of family members and of the family as a total system, building on those strengths to make the system more supportive of its individual members.

Support and Self-Help Groups

Support groups and **self-help groups** also are effective ways of helping children, youth, and families cope with family problems. Such groups help individuals realize that they are not the only ones coping with a given problem. Support and self-help groups also help members develop new ways to cope as they learn from each other. Perhaps most important, persons who may see themselves as being inadequate have a chance to reach out and give something to someone else. Types of self-help groups include twelve-step programs such as Alcoholics Anonymous for alcoholics, Al-Anon for family members of alcoholics, Alateen for teen family members of alcoholics, Narcotics Anonymous, and Adult Children of Alcoholics; Parents Anonymous for abusive or potentially abusive parents, Parents United for sexually abusive parents, Tough Love for parents of out-of-control adolescents, and Parents Without Partners for single parents.

Many communities have established support groups for adults, children, or teens dealing with divorce, stepparenting, death of a loved one or other type of loss, or those living with a family member with a physical or emotional disability. Schools have established support groups for students experiencing difficulty functioning within the school setting, coping with family problems such as divorce or abuse, and recovering from substance abuse, as well as for students who are teen parents. As resources become more scarce, social service agencies are realizing that in many instances more individuals and families can be served effectively through support and self-help groups.

Volunteer and Outreach Programs

Many traditional social services agencies are overloaded with cases and can provide only limited services—and those only to families with the most severe problems. A number of agencies have established volunteer components, whereas other agencies have been established that use only volunteers. In many instances, because they can spend more extensive time with families, volunteers can be highly successful in intervention and prevent family disruption. Most volunteer programs have established effective screening mechanisms that recruit volunteers with good nurturing skills who can relate well to clients. Many have been parents themselves, some are grandparents, and others are students or already involved in human services. Volunteers usually receive extensive training and are supervised by a social work case manager.

Many communities and states have successful volunteer programs. SCAN (Suspected Child Abuse and Neglect) of Arkansas, and Family Outreach Centers (established by the National Council of Jewish Women) both use highly trained volunteers to work on a one-to-one basis with abusive and neglecting families. The SCAN model is based on a reparenting framework, which focuses on developing trust and then helps parents work through all the stages of psychosocial development that they missed during childhood. Volunteers in such programs visit often and converse with parents and children, assist in problem solving and accessing community resources, and serve as a surrogate parent/role model/friend to the parent and family members. Similar programs have been developed that pair volunteers with teenage parents and abused and neglected children. The national Big Brothers/Big Sisters program uses volunteers as friends and role models to children from single-parent families. Studies show that volunteer programs can keep families together. Given the continuing increase in the number of families needing services and the lack of resources, volunteer programs are likely to increase.

Programs for at-risk families are funded by federal, state, and local governments as well as the private sector. The United Way funds numerous programs for families at risk in many communities. Churches, foundations, and private contributions fund other programs. Increasingly, public-private partnerships are being developed with funding from a variety of sources. In many instances, state and local governments contract with private agencies to provide services, and many private agencies receive funding from multiple sources, both public and private. Which entity should pay for what type of services is an increasingly complex issue at all levels in the United States. As the number of at-risk families continues to increase and as federal and state funding continues to be limited, more emphasis is being placed on local communities to fund such programs. But local governments, employers, and private contributors are also becoming financially strapped as inflation continues and recessions are predicted. New ways of providing services and more effective cost-sharing are issues that will have to be explored in more depth as we move into the twenty-first century.

◪ CHILD PROTECTIVE SERVICES

The federal Child Abuse and Neglect Prevention and Treatment Act mandates that all states must designate a single agency that is in turn mandated to oversee services to abused and neglected children and their families. Such services are usually termed **child protective services.** Families reported to state human services agencies with child protective services divisions as being abusive or neglectful must be investigated by the agency to ascertain if the maltreatment report can be substantiated if initial screening indicates that the situation is likely to be one of abuse or neglect. Legislation in all states, although often vague, establishes a minimum standard of care that caretakers are expected to provide to their children. If the child protective services worker investigating the case finds that abuse or neglect is a problem, and the minimum standard of care is not being met by the parent, the family receives protective services. This is an involuntary program—that is, the parents did not request or volunteer to receive the services.

Investigations of Child Maltreatment

In implementing the mandated services, child protective services workers cooperate closely with other professionals, including law enforcement officers, attorneys, health care providers, and educators. Child protective services workers assume a variety of roles in providing protective services, in cooperation or jointly with other agencies. They may offer intake services, where they screen reports of child maltreatment, interviewing persons reporting cases over the telephone to obtain appropriate information needed to make a preliminary determination about how serious the report is and if it needs to be investigated immediately. Most states require life-threatening situations to be investigated immediately or within twenty-four to forty-eight hours and less serious cases to be investigated within ten days.

Child protective services workers, by themselves or jointly with law enforcement officers, also conduct investigations of child maltreatment, interviewing children, parents, other family members, and collateral contacts such as teachers and neighbors to determine the nature and extent of the reported maltreatment. Investigations involve examining and interviewing the child, attending to the child's immediate emotional needs during the investigation, and making a preliminary assessment about whether maltreatment is occurring. If it is, investigators determine whether the maltreatment is causing or could cause permanent damage to the child's body or mind, how severe the maltreatment has been, and whether the situation is life-threatening and warrants immediate removal to a safer environment. In some instances other resources, such as physicians, may be used to assist in gathering needed information. Investigations of child maltreatment require knowledge and skill in the identification of various types of maltreatment, interviewing techniques appropriate with children and adults who may be apprehensive and reluctant to cooperate, and a balance of compassion and firmness. Striking a balance between use of authority and the use of compassion, or between the ability to confront and the ability to be empathic, is one of the challenges of being a child protective services worker (Maidman 1984).

Determination of Intervention Approach

The outcome of an investigation of child maltreatment is an assessment of the situation and the most appropriate actions to take. Child protective services workers are not expected to prove that the maltreatment is a criminal offense or to determine who perpetrated the maltreatment— those actions are within the domain of the courts. Their role is to determine if the child needs to be protected and what is needed to provide the protection. Workers must assess a number of risk factors to determine if the child is at risk and how severe the risk is. They have four options when assessing a possible situation of child maltreatment: to determine that the child is not being maltreated and withdraw from the case; to offer help to the family; to determine that the child is at serious risk and/or that the parents are uncooperative and make arrangements to take the family to court; and with the court's permission to remove the child from the home immediately and place the child in emergency care and later, usually foster care.

Child protective services workers most often determine that, although services are required, it is safe to leave the child in the home while the services are being provided. When children are removed, it is most often because the child or a sibling has been seriously injured or abandoned, the parent/caretaker states that he/she is going to kill or injure the child, evidence suggests that the child has experienced sexual abuse and the perpetrator is still in the home or has easy access to the child, there is a current crisis such as a psychotic parent or a parent in jail because of substance abuse, or there is little or no cooperation from parents and the child is at serious risk for substantial harm.

Child protective services workers, like other helping professionals, are most effective if they operate from a strengths perspective, identifying strengths in their clients and the clients' environment and working to empower clients to make choices that keep the children safe. But if, after trying to provide mandated services to families, the protective services workers believe that the families are resistant to the services and are not making choices that keep the children safe, they may take such cases to court and request that the court order services, such as counseling. This way, if the family does not comply, the worker can bring the case back into court and request more serious options, such as placing the child in foster care. Some states mandate court involvement with all families receiving child protective services.

The issue of when to involve the court in child protective services cases is often debated, with advocates for early involvement indicating that it gives workers leverage in dealing with families because the authority of the courts is present immediately. Advocates for limited involvement, and only when necessary, believe that most families are more receptive to services without court action because they feel more empowered and thus can maintain a less adversarial relationship with their workers. A number of states are developing two-track child protective services programs, with those clients who can be charged with criminal charges under the auspices of an investigative unit and the majority of other clients under the auspices of an assessment/intervention unit. Proponents of this approach think that it will remove the adversarial relationship that occurs when a law enforcement investigation is done for those families who need family preservation or other supportive services (APWA 1995).

Child protective services workers provide a variety of services to the families with whom they work. Their primary goal is to keep children safe, and they make every effort to ensure that children can be safe in their own homes. They often serve as case managers, arranging for community resources such as housing, employment, transportation, counseling, health services, child care, homemaker services, or financial assistance. They provide counseling, parent education, and support. They may assist a client in getting involved in a church or other support group, or they may suggest (or require) that the client attend Parents Anonymous or be assigned a volunteer. Often, they develop a contract with a parent delineating specific goals the family must accomplish in order to be removed from the child protective services caseload.

Child protective services is challenging work because of the emotional aspects of working with abused and neglected children and the multiple roles that child protective services workers must play. Increased attention is being given to the importance of child protective services staff, and a number of national organizations, including the Child Welfare League of America, the American Association for Protecting Children, and the American Public Welfare Association have established specialized training programs for staff and worked with states to explore new ways to provide protective services. Many states have developed computerized risk management systems that help workers assess family situations and needs and the safety of children involved. Some systems, for example, use a checklist of factors, then analyze the factors associated with a specific family based on previous knowledge about how likely each factor is to be associated with serious child maltreatment cases. Although the systems are used as part of a broader assessment by

Here, a CPS social worker takes an abused child to a children's shelter. After a short time in foster care, the family became involved in a family preservation program, the child returned to his family, and the family has worked hard to provide a safe, nurturing home for him with the new skills they have learned.

workers, families with many factors or the factors most likely to be associated with serious maltreatment are usually most at risk and given high priority in regard to intervention, services, and monitoring.

Child protection agencies are also increasing collaboration efforts with other systems that come into contact with abused and neglected children. Increased attention is being given to the need to develop collaboration between child welfare and domestic violence programs. Domestic violence and child abuse often occur within the same families, and programs targeted at each serve overlapping populations. Collaborative training, shared use of resources, and coordinated case management efforts can remove many barriers that may prevent women from being harmed when their children are under protection or vice versa. Such programs strengthen the concept of family preservation. One battered women's shelter, for example, had a family preservation worker assigned to the shelter to work onsite with the program's clients and their children (Schecter and Edleson 1995).

As reports of child maltreatment continue to increase and often involve children more severely injured than in the past, the role of child protective services as part of the child and family service delivery system is undergoing extensive debate. Due to the scarcity of resources, child protective services is the dominating child welfare service in many communities. Although child protective services agencies once publicized their role as providing services to children and families to prevent child maltreatment from occurring or recurring, their current message is that they protect children. Because of staff shortages, many agencies can barely respond to all reports received and are unable to investigate all but the most serious reports. With increases in child maltreatment due to more extensive crack and cocaine use, poverty, and homelessness, the emphasis of child protective services is more often one of "damage control" rather than intensive services. This shift in philosophy leaves other community organizations to prevent child maltreatment and often to provide the extensive services needed to keep it from recurring, while child protective services must monitor to ensure that children are protected and refer cases to the courts for action when they are not (Kamerman and Kahn 1990).

◪ FAMILY PRESERVATION SERVICES

Keeping families together is also being emphasized for families who in the past would have been separated, with children placed out of the home in foster care, residential treatment, or juvenile detention facilities. In one type of own-home, family-based program, family preservation services are targeted for families at imminent risk of having a child removed from the home. Such families usually have complex needs, with family members experiencing (in various combinations) child abuse, child neglect, sexual abuse, and substance abuse; or exhibiting oppositional behavior in the home, school, and community, often including delinquency (Tracy 1995). Goals of family preservation programs are:

1. To allow children to remain safely in their own homes

2. To maintain and strengthen family bonds

3. To stabilize the crisis situation that precipitated the need for placement

4. To increase the family's coping skills and competencies

5. To facilitate the family's use of appropriate and informal helping resources. (Tracy 1990, 973).

Efforts geared toward family preservation have built on the earlier permanency planning emphasis of the late 1970s, after a number of studies found that many children were remaining in foster care with little attention given to other alternatives.

As increasing numbers of children, particularly children of color and those living in poverty, were removed from their own homes and placed in foster care, more attention began to be given to finding ways to keep families together or to reunite them, rather than having children languish in foster care. In most instances, due to scarce resources and negative beliefs about biological families, only limited efforts were made to work with them, since they were often viewed as a large part of the problem rather than the solution.

The Adoption Assistance and Child Welfare Act of 1980 required that reasonable efforts be made to avoid family disruption, to reunify families after separation, and to place children in permanent settings if they could not be reunited. Although the number of family preservation programs increased rapidly in the 1980s, these programs are based on traditional social work practice, which includes home visits and intensive approaches with high-risk families. Currently there are more than 400 family preservation programs in the United States (Tracy 1995).

The Child Welfare League of America delineates three types of family preservation programs (Tracy 1995):

1. Family resource programs, which are usually community based and provide support and education services

2. Family-centered services, which provide case management, counseling, and education for families with problems that threaten their stability

3. Intensive family crisis services, which are designed for families in crisis when removal of the child is imminent or reunification with the family is taking place

Although programs vary, they offer crisis intervention, staff members available to provide around-the-clock services if needed, low caseloads, and highly intensive, time-limited services, similar to other own-home services previously described.

Family preservation programs use interventions based on a systems/ ecological perspective, working with all relevant levels of the environment. Such programs incorporate a family systems perspective in working with families as well, viewing the family as a dynamic system with equilibrium out of balance due to the unmet needs of various family members. Emphasis in family preservation programs is on empowering family members to get needs met and to develop new skills in problem solving and communication to stabilize the family system. Family preservation social workers do not blame families for failure. The model is based on the assumption that the family is an important influence on children, and that separation has detrimental effects on both parents and children. Through role modeling, counseling, and interactions with family members, the program focuses on values, respect, listening rather than giving advice, and helping with goal-setting, coping, and problem-solving skills. Social workers try to connect with and get to know all family members in a nonjudgmental way. The first stage of services is often spent addressing concrete needs such as housing or food. As the social worker develops a relationship with the family, emphasis is consistent with good social work practice—not on diagnosis and labeling, but on understanding the day-to-day reality of the family and how it functions. Interventions often include contracts, encouragement, and reframing of issues (Tracy 1995).

Evaluation of family preservation programs is difficult because families' needs and how they are addressed vary, as do strategies of interventions used. Programs are also finding that while the original program goal was to prevent out-of-home placement of a child or adolescent, the program may not be able to prevent such a placement from occurring; and that in fact some placements are necessary (Barth et al.). Other outcome measures that measure additional change, such as an increase in positive communication among family members, also need to be studied. Family preservation programs are used in a number of instances, including preventing foster care and adoption disruptions, reunifying family members after a family member has been out of the home, identifying families who are high risk before maltreatment has been confirmed, keeping children and youth from juvenile detention placements, and assisting families undergoing intervention for substance abuse (Tracy 1995; Schuerman, et al. 1994).

◪ SUBSTITUTE CARE

Although every attempt is made to keep children in their own homes, sometimes this is not possible. Parents may have too many unmet needs of their own, serious health or emotional problems, or be too uninterested in parenting to care for their children adequately. In such situations, substitute care is located for the children involved. Unless the situation is an emergency—which many state laws define as a life-threatening situation—a child protective services worker cannot remove a child from a family without a court order. Even with emergency removals, court orders must be obtained, usually within twenty-four hours, and hearings held with parents present.

Types of Substitute Care

There are a number of different types of **substitute care.** Many communities have established crisis shelters, available to take children twenty-four hours a day until a family situation can be stabilized or other care that best meets a child's needs can be located. Although attempts are made to place children with relatives or neighbors so that they can remain in their immediate environment, this is not always possible. Other types of substitute care include foster homes, group homes, residential treatment facilities, and psychiatric treatment facilities. Once a child is placed in substitute care, social workers, in collaboration with the family if possible (and with the child depending on the child's age), must develop a plan for the child, focusing on either returning the child home or, less often, on terminating the parental rights and placing the child in an adoptive family. Each case must be reviewed by the court every six months to ensure that the child is not in limbo in the child welfare system.

If a child does need to be placed in substitute care, every effort should be made to ensure that the placement is the least restrictive option, although this is not always done. Thus, relatives, neighbors, and others with whom the child is familiar should be considered first if they meet criteria to be positive substitute parents for the child. Consideration also should be given to finding care for the child consistent with his or her cultural background, preferably in the same neighborhood or school area. Since it is important that the birth parents visit the child, if this is in the best interests of the child, attention also needs to be given to accessibility of the parents as well.

Foster Care
If appropriate relative placements or other suitable arrangements cannot be made, the child most often is placed in foster care with a foster family. **Foster care** means that children live in homes with families other than their birth parents and are nurtured until they can return to their birth parents or be adopted. Foster parents are recruited and trained to relate to children and their birth parents. They are often parents already and may take in more than one foster child. Many foster parents keep in touch with their foster children after they leave, and some adopt the children if they become available for adoption.

All states have strict standards regarding foster care, including training that individuals must complete before becoming foster parents and in order to continue as foster parents, the number of children foster parents can take, appropriate discipline and treatment of children, and supervision of foster parents. A number of states train foster parents to parent certain types of children, for example, adolescents, children with AIDs, or children who have been sexually abused. Foster parents also develop support systems, and many belong to local and national foster parent organizations. Although foster parents are paid a limited amount each month to care for each child, they often spend more than they receive and in almost all instances give large amounts of love and attention to the children they parent, who are often needy and may take out their frustrations on the foster family.

Currently, almost all children who require foster care have been abused or neglected. Because more children whose safety is threatened are being removed from their homes, there is a need for additional foster parents nationwide. Many localities are having difficulty finding foster parents willing to parent adolescents and younger children with serious emotional problems that often have resulted from child maltreatment.

Some children have difficulty handling the intimacy of a foster family, particularly if they have been seriously abused or neglected. In other instances, a foster family may not be found for a particular child—it is difficult to find foster homes for adolescents, for example. Group homes, which usually have a set of house parents to care for five to ten children or adolescents, are an alternative to foster care. Such homes attempt to maintain a homelike atmosphere and provide rules and structure to children and adolescents. They also may include regular group counseling sessions for residents.

A major problem with the foster care system is the lack of adequate foster homes. As the number of children needing care has increased, the number of foster parents has decreased. As a result, children often remain for long periods of time in emergency shelters and institutions, and many foster homes have more children than they can adequately handle. Children still continue to be moved frequently: in a 1990 study conducted by the American Public Welfare Association, more than half of children in substitute care had been moved at least once, 27.5 percent had had two foster care placements, 23.6 percent had had 3–5 placements, and 6.1 percent had had six or more placements (Center for Law and Social Policy 1994).

Residential Treatment

Children and adolescents who need more structure than foster care or group homes can provide may be placed in **residential treatment** programs. Such programs, more expensive to maintain than foster care and group homes, provide consistent structure for children and adolescents, as well as intensive individual and, usually, group counseling. Most residential treatment programs help the child establish the boundaries that may be missing from home, focus on building self-esteem and competence, and help the child resolve anger and other issues from his or her family experience.

The goal of residential treatment is to develop enough coping skills that the child can return home better able to deal with the family situation. Ideally, the family also has undergone counseling, so they do not enter into old roles that may force the child back into previous behaviors in order to survive. Family counseling does not always occur, however, and it is often up to the child to cope on returning to the family and community. In situations where returning home or living with a nonparent relative is not possible, a child may be placed in a less restrictive setting, such as a group home or foster care. Children and adolescents with more serious problems may be hospitalized. In hospital settings, more restrictions are usually placed on the child (i.e., leaving the unit or the hospital), more intensive therapy is usually provided, and it is more likely that medication will be used. In other instances, children or adolescents, primarily delinquent adolescents, are placed in juvenile detention facilities. Studies suggest that white, middle-class children are more likely to be placed in residential treatment or hospital programs, while poor children and children of color are more likely to be placed in juvenile detention facilities.

Although recent attempts have been made to strengthen the substitute care system, problems remain. Perhaps the greatest problem is the lack of resources available to birth parents to enable them to reunite with their children. Overloaded service delivery systems often thwart social workers from providing needed services to parents. As a result, social workers are reluctant to terminate parental rights and free children for adoption. On the other hand, because they cannot provide needed services, they are also reluctant to return children to unsafe homes. Thus, children languish in the foster care system. Emlen (1977) shows, however, that when intensive services are provided to parents, even those who have multiple problems and have been separated from their children for long periods of time can be reunited successfully with them.

◪ ADOPTION

When parents choose not to or cannot provide for their children, parental rights are terminated by the court and the child becomes legally free for **adoption.** But many children in the United States, particularly African American children, are adopted informally by relatives without a formal court hearing ever taking place. The focus of adoption has changed significantly in recent years. In the past, the emphasis was on finding a perfect child for a couple who biologically could not have children, with an attempt to match the child to the parents according to physical features such as hair and eye color. Today, the emphasis is on finding an appropriate parent for a child—that is, one who can best meet the child's needs.

Adoption Issues

The types of adoption that are taking place in the United States have also changed. Until the 1970s, most formal adoptions in the United States were couples who adopted healthy infants. But most adoptions that take place today are adoptions by stepparents, which is a result of the increasing rates of divorce and remarriage. Today there are also fewer infant adoptions. This is because many young women of all ethnic groups are choosing to keep their babies rather than place them for adoption. But traditional maternity homes/adoption agencies still provide residential and health care and counseling services before birth and, in some instances, postadoption counseling as well.

A major issue relating to adoption is the length of time it takes to move children through the child welfare services system once they are removed from their homes. Because of the priority given to family preservation, efforts are made first to ensure that parents are given the opportunities and resources to provide safe, supportive homes for their children. If children are in substitute care, the initial plan whenever possible is to return them to their birth parents. Making the decision to terminate parental rights and sever the parent-child relationship is one of the most difficult decisions anyone has to make. Even though parents may not be able to provide for their children's needs, most children have to deal with separation and loss issues throughout their lives if they are not raised by their parents. The extent that they have to address these issues depends on many factors; but all children, no matter how exceptional their adoptive and foster parents are, still have to struggle with the impact of not being raised by their birth parents. Unfortunately, there is no perfect way to predict if and when parents will be able to change enough to provide for their children, or the best type of placements for children if their parents are unable to care for them.

Most children who become legally free for adoption because their parents' rights have been terminated due to abuse or neglect spend a number of years in foster care. Sometimes they go back and forth between their birth parents and foster parents before they move into an adoptive family. Social workers in child placement agencies work with children before placement, preparing them for what adoption is like and helping them to address grief and loss issues surrounding their birth parents so they can begin to attach more readily to adoptive parents. Many children in foster care have parents whose legal rights have not been terminated and have to wait for that legal process to occur. In 1990, there were 442,000 children in foster care in the United States. Almost 70,000 were being prepared to be adopted, but of that number parental rights had been terminated for only 20,000.

Adoption of Special-Needs Children

The majority of children legally free and available for adoption in the United States are considered **special-needs children.** Such children, while traditionally considered by many to be unadoptable, have been placed successfully in a variety of family settings. Special-needs children are those who are children of color, are older, have physical or emotional disabilities, or are members of sibling groups. Of the 20,000 children legally free for adoption in 1990, 55 percent were white, 43 percent were African American, and 7 percent were Hispanic. Most were between the ages of 6 and 12 (NASW 1995b).

Adoption agencies also have focused on parents they had not previously considered. In the 1960s and 1970s, emphasis was on transracial adoption; currently most agencies focus on finding parents who are of the same ethnic or cultural background as the child, if possible. Advocacy by groups such as the Association of Black Social Workers and the passage of the Indian Child Welfare Act—which mandates that when placing Native American children, efforts must first be made to place a child with a family of the child's same tribe, then with another Native American family, and only then with a non-Native American family—have given impetus to the emphasis on ethnicity when placing children for adoption. A number of agencies have established special outreach programs to African American and Latino communities to recruit adoptive parents. In the 1980s Father George Clements, an African American priest in Chicago, worked to establish the "One Church, One Child" campaign, based on the premise that if each church in the United States, particularly churches with primarily minority congregations, could work to have one child adopted by a member of its congregation, the adoption of special-needs children would no longer be so critical. This campaign has spread throughout the United States and has been one of many successful efforts; however, many special-needs children still need adoptive families.

Concern about waiting children of color has raised a number of issues about how and when ethnicity should be considered in child placement. Several states have passed or have considered legislation from various perspectives relating to this issue. Minnesota, for example, passed legislation mandating that children be placed in settings that reflect their heritage whenever possible. Other states, criticized by white parents who want to adopt children of color, developed laws and policies stating that race and ethnicity are important factors in child placement, but not the only factors. In 1994, Congress passed the Howard M. Metzenbaum Multiethnic Placement Act, which prohibits any federally funded program from denying the opportunity to become a foster or adoptive parent based solely on the ethnicity, race, or national origin of either the foster or adoptive parent or the child involved, or to deny or discriminate in a placement decision on the basis of ethnicity. This act further states that race, ethnicity, or national heritage can be used as one of a number of factors in making placement decisions, but not as the only factor (Barth 1995). The act does specify that states need to continue efforts at recruiting families of color as adoptive and foster parents. If agencies shift trends and begin to make transracial placements, attention must be paid to the adoptive parents' willingness to address issues of racial identity of the child and to ensure that the child is raised in an environment that not only supports the child's heritage, but allows the child to develop friends and relationships with role models representative of that heritage (see McRoy and Zurcher 1983).

Unfortunately, many children have become caught in the middle of arguments about the importance of ethnicity in regard to placement, with psychological damage done to them no matter what the decision has been. In several situations that have received national attention, children of color have been placed with white foster parents, remaining with them for extensive periods of time. Later, when the foster parents have tried to adopt the child, children have been placed in adoptive homes with parents of the same heritage as the child. Any very young child, regardless of ethnicity, experiences separation trauma when removed from a psychological parent who has been the primary caretaker for that child. One key aspect in avoiding such conflicts is to use the same criteria, including ethnicity, when placing children in temporary settings that are used when placing children in permanent homes.

In addition to trying to recruit more families of color, adoption agencies are recruiting single parents, working parents, foster parents, and parents with large families already. Experience is showing that all of these families can successfully parent. An additional emphasis is on placing siblings together in the same adoptive family. Previously, many siblings were separated, often forever.

The Adoption Assistance Act, previously discussed, allows monthly living allowances and medical expenses for families who could not otherwise afford to adopt special-needs children. More assertive outreach efforts—such as Father Clements' "One Church, One Child" program, television's "Wednesday's Child" programs that portray children available for adoption, and national computerized services listing waiting children and waiting parents—have resulted in children being adopted who were previously considered unadoptable, including many who in the past would have been relegated to a life in a state institution.

Other current adoption trends include foreign-born adoptions and open adoptions, which allow the birth parent(s) to be involved in the selection of the adoptive parents, and, in some instances, to be able to maintain contact with the child as the child grows up. While adoption services have been strengthened, there are still barriers to successful placements, particularly of special-needs children. Agencies and individuals still consider some children unadoptable, and some agencies are reluctant to work on placing children across state lines, even when parents (or children) in other states can be located.

As the number of special-needs adoptions has increased, agencies and adoptive parents have also recognized the need for postadoption services for children and their adoptive families. Children who have experienced not only the loss of their birth parents, but extensive child maltreatment, have special needs that often continue or do not surface until long after the adoption is final. Adoptive parent groups have been instrumental in advocating for legislation, in establishing adoption programs, and in supporting other adoptive parents. Currently, they provide the primary support after placement in many communities.

An additional issue relating to adoption that has gained recent attention is what should be decided when birth parents want to reclaim their children after they have been placed for adoption. Such incidents are traumatic for everyone involved and, like the conflicts with ethnic placements, can usually be avoided if good child welfare practice is followed and licensed adoption agencies are used. But if the system fails in some way, the courts are required to decide who obtains custody of the child. In many instances, Goldstein, Freud, and Solnit's concept of the psychological parent and the extensive research on attachment and the impact of separation on children have not been considered, and children have been moved into new settings with complete strangers.

This issue and others will continue to be raised in the next decade, including who has priority in gaining custody of children in an adoption dispute after an adoption has taken place, how important ethnicity is in determining child placement and at what point ethnicity should be considered, to what extent adopted children should have contact with birth parents and siblings, ethics of paying young pregnant girls large amounts of money for their unborn children without going through an agency, and what rights surrogate parents should have.

CHILD WELFARE AND CULTURAL DIVERSITY

Whatever the types of child welfare services provided, they must be responsive to meet the day-to-day realities of diverse populations. Ideally, this means that all aspects of the child welfare service system should be culturally competent: federal, state, and local entities as well as individual social workers who provide child welfare services must understand the impact of culture on individuals, families, and communities; recognize that while some factors may be more typical of one ethnic group than another in general, there is vast diversity within groups and they should not assume specific factors just because someone is from a given group; value the diversity of individuals and cultural groups and view the diversity as a strength rather than a deviation; and at the same time recognize the impact of oppression and social and economic injustice on at-risk populations.

Child welfare workers need to learn as much as possible about the cultures of the diverse populations with which they work, including history, family structure, family dynamics, religion, language, music and art, traditions, communication patterns, and views about seeking help and about social work and social welfare (Prater 1992). For example, strengths of African American families identified by various researchers include strong kinship bonds that go beyond the nuclear family, flexibility of family roles, a strong work ethic, and a strong religious orientation (Hill 1989). These strengths are seen from a child welfare perspective in the informal kinship system regarding children's living situations; many African American children live with relatives other than their birth parents or nonrelatives considered kin without going through a formal foster care or adoption process. Until recently, child placement agencies did not consider relative or kin placements, which meant that African American children were often placed with nonrelatives when there were close family members who could serve in parental roles for them. The church was also often overlooked by child welfare agencies as a resource in keeping African American families together or helping children when families could not care for them. In one southern city recently, a church was awarded custody of a sibling group.

Many Asian persons, particularly first-generation immigrants, hold traditional Asian values, which emphasize the needs of the family above the needs of the individual. Another value emphasizes the importance of bringing honor to a family. Thus, if outsiders know about family problems, it can be viewed as bringing shame to the family. Asian family members may be reluctant to share information with social workers about how children are being cared for or what is needed to help them (Mass and Yap 1992). They also may be reluctant to disagree with individuals they view as authority figures, including social workers. This cultural pattern may be seen when clients would seem to agree with a social worker but then not follow through on what was agreed to.

Latino cultures also value family, not only as a means of socializing family members about culture but also as sources of social support and coping. Many Latino persons will leave jobs and immediate family members to travel long distances to help other family members in need. Males also play important roles in most Latino cultures, and view protecting and supporting their families as critical. Mothers in Latino families are also important and respected. Social support systems in many Latino families include not only parents and extended family members, but also godparents who can often be looked to as a resource. The church is also a viable resource for many Latino families (Delgado 1992).

Just as there is diversity within the African American, Asian, and Latino cultures, there is vast diversity within Native American cultures. Some tribes are matrilineal, meaning that the mother's family is looked to first when legal issues such as adoption are addressed, as well as for other types of social support, while other tribes are patrilineal. The family is also valued by Native Americans, with an emphasis on cooperation and respect for the elderly. Native Americans may seek out elderly members of the family or the tribe for consultation about child welfare issues, and may remain quiet or defer to these persons when interacting with them (Red Horse 1988).

We have presented just a few examples of ways that culture can shape interactions with social workers and child welfare agencies. These examples must be placed in the context of the rich heritage of each cultural group—and not be taken as fact out of that context. The critical issue is to view the client from his or her day-to-day reality, and from the way that person's culture shapes that reality, rather than to overlook culture completely, misunderstand it, or to assume an "expert" role and stereotype without looking at the uniqueness of each individual. To be culturally competent when dealing with children, youth, and families, social workers must be self-aware and in touch with their own culture and the ways that their culture shapes their beliefs about and interactions with others; knowledgeable about other cultures, and willing to learn from clients and see the clients as the experts in regard to their lives and needs.

Because of oppression and discrimination, children, youth, and families of color are overrepresented in the population needing child welfare services. Understanding and embracing diversity must be high priorities for social workers in child welfare settings if services are to effectively enhance individual and family functioning.

◩ CHILD WELFARE AND THE FUTURE

A major debate in the child welfare field relates to what direction should be taken in providing services to children, youth, and families. Some experts indicate that much more knowledge is needed before significant changes can be made. Others indicate that the problems are too overwhelming and will require wide-scale change. Lisbeth Schorr, in her book *Within Our Reach: Breaking the Cycle of Disadvantage* (1989), has a different perspective. Schorr's premise is that we already know enough to prevent many of the "rotten outcomes" facing today's children and youth (p. xvii). In a nationwide review of current child welfare programs, she found many programs that were effective. Schorr indicates that programs that work best for children and families in high-risk environments take comprehensive and intensive approaches, are flexible, and meet a wide range of needs. Schorr also calls for intervention at macro levels of the environment as well as at lower levels, advocating for economic and welfare reform. Consistent with the systems/ecological framework, she identifies three themes in relation to reduction of environmental risk factors (1989, 29):

1. Risk factors leading to later damage occur more frequently among children in families that are poor, especially if they are persistently poor and live in concentrated areas of poverty

2. The needs of at-risk children are not just individual, but need a societal response

3. The knowledge to help is available; the problem is a commitment to resources rather than a lack of knowledge.

Programs cited by Schorr as successful include vans that provide health care to rural areas, also delivering clean drinking water and lumber to build outdoor bathroom facilities where none exist; using high school students in a health professions program to track and work with young parents of high-risk children; quality child care programs with well-trained caregivers; and public school programs that value active learning and parent and community participation. Schorr (1989) identified the following characteristics in those programs she studied that were working:

• They provided a broad spectrum of services, including social and emotional support as well as concrete services such as food, housing, employment, and transportation

• They were flexible in collaborations with a wide range of social services and other providers in regard to funding, policies, and program structure

• They used a systems/ecological focus, seeing the child in the context of the family and the family in the context of the broader environment and working with all levels as needed

• Social workers and other staff members were regarded as caring and individuals who could be respected and trusted

• Services were regarded as coherent and easy to use

Another well-known child welfare expert takes a different approach. Duncan Lindsey, editor of *Children and Youth Services Review,* a major research journal in the child welfare field, takes issue with the more narrow view of child welfare services advocated in the past by experts such as Kadushin. In his book *The Welfare of Children* (1994), Lindsey advocates for comprehensive reform of the current child welfare system, suggesting that it abandon its residual focus and instead turn its attention to the economic security of children, youth, and families. Lindsey notes that in the past several decades, the vast amount of attention to child welfare services has been devoted to child abuse and neglect. He points out that in spite of that attention, reports continue to rise and the child welfare system continues to be overloaded with critical cases. Lindsey makes the argument that reporting systems and services dedicated to child abuse and neglect have become a red herring ("a highly charged issue that devotes attention away from the real and more difficult problem"), when the broader issues are economic structure and poverty (157). He cites a report from the advisory board to the National Center on Child Abuse and Neglect, which indicated (123):

> It is not a question of acute failure of a single element of the system. Instead, the child protection system is plagued by "chronic and critical multiple organ failure." No matter which element of the system that the Board examined—prevention, investigation, treatment, training, or research—the Board found a system in disarray, a societal response ill-suited in form or scope to respond to the profound problem facing it. . . . The system the nation has devised to respond to child abuse and neglect is failing.

Lindsey calls for a complete overhaul of the child welfare system, transferring all responsibility for investigation and handling of child protective services cases to the criminal justice system and focusing attention on the root causes of problems such as child maltreatment. He suggests that until the United States moves from a residual system to a preventive system that focuses on economic structure, the physical and mental health of children, youth, and families in the United States will continue to decline, with serious consequences not only for them, but for the country as a whole.

As part of his broad-based approach, Lindsey advocates for a number of innovative but controversial options. He proposes a Universal Child Support Collection system, in which noncustodial parents would be placed under a "child support" tax table with money for child support withheld from their paychecks based on earnings and the number of children they are supporting. Their employer would withhold the determined amount along with other withholding taxes, with the monies going indirectly to the custodial parent through a central collection system (239). Lindsay also advocates for a universal Guaranteed Child Exemption. Similar to the current child exemption allowable under federal law for employed parents, this system would be extended to those individuals who are either unemployed or not in the labor market. All children would be guaranteed a monthly allotment regardless of their parents' employment status. Another idea proposed by Lindsey is the establishment of a "social savings account" for children (309). Like social security, a system would be set up that would provide funding for each child annually from birth until the child reaches age 18. Parents could also contribute to the account, which could be used for approved career program expenditures.

Other advocates for changes in the child welfare service system also call for a broader approach. They call for an exploration of issues relating to teen pregnancy and parenting, including the role of males; declining economic opportunities for people of color, particularly African American males; the relationship between divorce rates and women on AFDC; and cultural diversity issues and the need for a more culturally competent delivery system. Social workers at all levels of the environment—agency, community, state, nation, and world—are advocating in various ways for improving services to children, youth, and families.

THE ROLE OF SOCIAL WORKERS IN PROVIDING SERVICES TO CHILDREN, YOUTH, AND FAMILIES

Social workers play many roles in providing services to children, youth, and families. In fact, this is the most traditional area of social work practice. The "child welfare worker," first a volunteer during the 1800s and then a trained social worker in the 1900s, is most often the stereotype of social workers. But the roles of social workers in this area have expanded significantly, and social workers at the BSW, MSW, and PhD levels all are actively involved in providing services to children, youth, and families. At the BSW level, social workers are involved as child care workers in group homes and residential treatment centers, as women and children's counselors at battered women's shelters, as counselors at youth shelters, as crisis counselors in law enforcement agencies, and as child protective services and foster care workers in public social services agencies.

An entry-level position in the area of child and family services usually offers broad-based experience that gives workers a great deal of flexibility to move to other jobs in working with children and families (either in direct services or supervisory positions) or in other areas of social work. Some states require a minimum of a BSW for certain child and family positions, such as child protective services and foster care staff. A growing number of social workers specialize in child protective services, investigating reported cases of abuse and neglect and intervening when necessary. They work closely with the courts, law enforcement agencies, and community-based family intervention, self-help, and volunteer programs. Foster care staff recruit foster families and oversee their training, and they often work with the child and foster family while the child is in foster care, helping the child to adjust (see Box 13.4).

Many BSW graduates work as child care workers in residential treatment and psychiatric care facilities, serving as members of treatment teams and working directly with children and adolescents to implement the team's plan. Such experience is valuable in learning skills in working with emotionally disturbed children and their families. Other social workers are employed in agencies such as Big Brothers and Big Sisters of America, assessing children and potential volunteers and monitoring the matches after they are made. Increasingly, BSW graduates are being hired as social workers in family preservation programs, family support programs that assist families in getting off public assistance, and programs that provide services to children with developmental disabilities and their families. Social workers at the BSW level are also hired to

BOX 13.4

DO YOU HAVE THE CHARACTERISTICS TO BE A COMPETENT SOCIAL WORKER?

The Child Protective Services Training Institute at the University of Texas at Austin recently reviewed client satisfaction research to understand what constitutes an effective client-worker relationship. According to the research, child protective service clients want social workers who show they are

- Willing to listen and help
- Accurately empathic
- Genuine and warm
- Respectful and nonjudgmental
- Fair

- Accessible
- Supportive and practical
- Experienced and competent

Child protective services programs, like most other social service programs, provide training after hiring. But many of these characteristics relate to social work values and skills learned in BSW social work programs.

Source: Charlene A. Urwin, ed., "What Clients Want from Workers," *Child Protection Connection*, vol. II, no. I (Austin, Tex.: CPS Training Institute, University of Texas at Austin, 1994).

work as substance abuse counselors in inpatient and community-based adult and adolescent treatment programs. Special certification in the area of substance abuse is often required for such jobs.

School social workers also often require special state certification, which varies from state to state. In some states, BSW graduates can be hired as school social workers, whereas in other states you must have teaching experience and graduate-level courses or an MSW degree. With increased attention to school dropouts and increases in such problems as teenage pregnancy, school social work is a rapidly growing area. School social workers work closely with teachers, school administrators, and other school support staff, including school counselors, nurses, and psychologists. They provide individual, parent, and family counseling; lead groups of students who are teen parents, on probation, recovering from substance abuse, experiencing family problems such as divorce or abuse, or having problems relating to teachers and peers; provide crisis intervention services such as suicide intervention; organize parent education and parent support groups; advocate for the needs of children and families within the school system and the community; and network with other social services agencies in the community to assist parents and their children in accessing appropriate services. The National Association of Social Workers has a school social work division, and two school social work journals are published nationally.

Some BSW graduates also become employed in advocacy or policy-related positions, as legislative assistants or staff members of state or federal child and family services organizations or agencies, such as the Children's Defense Fund. An MSW degree may be required for some of these positions, particularly those related to policy analysis.

A number of other social work jobs in the child and family services area require an MSW degree. This is due partly to the standards established by the Child Welfare League of America, which many agencies follow, and partly to the fact that some child and family services are highly specialized. In almost all instances, an MSW is required of an adoption worker. Most child guidance centers and child and family service agencies also require MSW degrees. Many social work or therapist positions in residential treatment centers require an MSW, as do clinical social work positions in adolescent and child psychiatric treatment programs. Most schools of social work have child and family or child welfare specializations at the graduate level, which provide special coursework in this area, as well as field placements in child and family services settings. With the implementation of the PhD degree in social work, some child guidance or child and family services agencies are attempting to hire agency directors at this level. Additionally, persons who want more highly specialized clinical experience are earning PhD degrees, enabling them to do more intensive therapy with children, youth, and families.

If students are interested in a social work career in the area of child and family services, a number of child welfare and child and family journals, as well as numerous books on all areas discussed in this chapter, are readily available. In addition, because many child and family services programs have volunteer programs, volunteer experience not only helps students determine if they are interested in this area but also provides sound social work experience.

SUMMARY

Policies and programs that focus on the needs of children, youth, and families are developed and implemented within the context of society and community attitudes and values, awareness about needs, and the availability of resources. The presently preferred focus is prevention and early intervention, keeping families together, and making decisions based on the best interests of the children. But the lack of resources places large numbers of children, youth, and families in jeopardy of disruption and serious dysfunction. Because individual and family needs are diverse, as are available programs to address them, there are many opportunities for social workers interested in children, youth, and family services.

KEY TERMS

adoption
best interests of the child
child protective services
Child Welfare League of America
child welfare service delivery
  system
child welfare services
crisis intervention
family preservation programs

foster care
Head Start
home-based family-centered
  services
least detrimental alternative
natural support systems
permanency planning
psychological parent
residential treatment

self-help group   special-needs children
school social work   substitute care
Social Security Act   U.S. Children's Bureau

DISCUSSION QUESTIONS

1. What is meant by the concepts *in the best interests of the child, least detrimental alternative,* and *psychological parent?*

2. Describe briefly at least three prevention programs used with children and their families.

3. Compare home-based family-centered services with substitute care and adoption. What are the advantages and disadvantages of each?

4. Identify at least two areas in which social workers at the BSW and MSW levels might be employed in a child and family services position.

5. What is meant by *special-needs adoption?*

6. Select one of the "family problem areas" discussed in Chapter 12. Identify at least one prevention and one intervention program you would suggest to address that problem area.

7. Identify at least three problems with the current children, youth, and families service delivery system. What are some possible solutions?

8. Debate the following arguments, giving a rationale for both pro and con positions:
   a. Child abuse is a "red herring" that has directed attention away from the more critical child welfare issue of poverty.
   b. The knowledge to make things better for children and families is within our reach; we just have to begin to put the tools in place to do so.

REFERENCES

American Public Welfare Association. 1995. *W Memo,* vol. 7, no. 5. Washington, D.C.: Author.

Barth, R. 1995. Adoption. *Encyclopedia of Social Work.* 19th ed. Washington, D.C.: NASW, pp. 48–59.

Barth, R., M. Courtney, J. Duerr Berrick, and V. Albert. 1994. *From Child abuse to permanency planning.* New York: Aldine de Gruyter.

Bremner, R. 1974. *Children and youth in America.* Cambridge, Mass.: Harvard University Press.

Center for Law and Social Policy. 1994. Child welfare: A system in crisis. *Family Matters* vol. 6, no. 1. Washington, D.C.: Author.

Children's Defense Fund. 1995. *Children's defense budget: analysis of the FY 1994 federal budget and children.* Washington, D.C.: Children's Defense Fund.

CPS Training Institute. 1995. What clients want from workers. *Child Protection Connection*, vol. II, no. 1. Austin, Tex.: Author.

Delgado, R. 1992. Generalist child welfare and Hispanic families. In *Child welfare: A multicultural focus,* ed. N. Cohen. Boston: Allyn and Bacon.

Ellerbee, L. 1995. Tasha and family deserve a good chance. *Austin American Statesman,* 23 June, p. A15.

Emlen, A. 1977. *Overcoming barriers to planning for children in foster care.* Portland, Ore.: Portland State University.

Goldstein, J., A. Freud, and A. Solnit. 1973. *Beyond the best interests of the child.* New York: Free Press.

_____ . 1979. *Before the best interests of the child.* New York: Free Press.

Hill, R. 1989. *Research on the African-American family: A holistic perspective.* Boston: University of Massachusetts Press.

Janchill, M. 1981. *Guidelines for decision-making in child welfare.* New York: Human Services Workshops.

Kadushin, A. 1980. *Child welfare services.* 3rd ed. New York: Macmillan.

Kadushin, A., and J. Martin. 1988. *Child welfare services.* 4th ed. New York: Macmillan.

Kamerman, S., and A. Kahn. 1990. Social services for children, youth and families in the United States. Special issue, *Children and Youth Services Review,* vol. 12, nos. 1–2. New York: Pergamon Press.

Lindsey, D. 1994. *The welfare of children.* New York: Oxford University Press.

Lloyd, J., and M. Bryce. 1980. *Placement prevention and family unification: Planning and supervising the home-based family centered programs.* Oakdale, Ia.: National Clearinghouse for Home-based Services, School of Social Work, University of Iowa.

Maas, H., and R. Engler. 1959. *Children in need of parents.* New York: Columbia University Press.

McRoy, R. and L. Zurcher. 1983. *Transracial and inracial adoptees: The adolescent years.* Springfield, Ill.: Charles Thomas.

Maidman, F. 1984. *Child welfare: A source book of knowledge and practice.* New York: Child Welfare League of America.

Mass, A., and J. Yap. 1992. Child welfare: Asian and Pacific Islander families. In *Child welfare, a multicultural focus,* ed. N. Cohen. Boston: Allyn and Bacon.

National Association of Social Workers. 1995a. *Government Relations Update,* 28 February. Washington, D.C.: Author.

_____ . 1995b. The adoption equation, minus race. *NASW News* 40, no. 7 (July): 3. Washington, D.C.: Author.

National Committee for the Prevention of Child Abuse. 1995. Healthy Families America . . . Stopping child abuse before it starts. *Memorandum,* vol. II, no. 6. Chicago: Author.

Prater, G. 1992. Child welfare and African-American families. In *Child welfare: A multicultural focus,* ed. N. Cohen. Boston: Allyn and Bacon.

Red Horse, J. G. 1988. Cultural evolution of American Indian families. In *Ethnicity and race: Critical concepts in social work,* ed. C. Jacobs and D. D. Bowles, 86–102. Silver Springs, Md.: NASW.

Schecter, S. and B. Edleson. 1995. In the best interests of women and children: A chance for collaboration between child welfare and domestic violence. *Prevention Report* (Spring): 3–4. Iowa City, IA: National Resource Center on Family Based Services, University of Iowa School of Social Work.

Schorr, L. 1989. *Within our reach: Breaking the cycle of disadvantage.* New York: Anchor.

Schuerman, J., T. Rzepnicki, and J. Littell. 1994. *Putting families first: An experiment in family preservation.* New York: Adline de Gruyter.

Shyne, A. and A. Schroeder. 1978. *National study of services to children and their families.* Washington, D.C.: U.S. Children's Bureau, Department of Health, Education, and Welfare.

Social Security Act. 1935. Title IV–B, Section 425. Washington, D.C.: U.S. Congressional Record.

Tracy, E. 1995. Family preservation and home-based services. *Encyclopedia of Social Work,* 19th ed., pp. 973–82. Washington, D.C.: NASW.

United States Advisory Board on Child Abuse and Neglect. 1991. *A caring community: Blueprint to an effective federal policy on child abuse and neglect.* Washington, D.C.: Author.

Vasaly, S. 1976. *Foster care in five states.* Washington, D.C.: U.S. Department of Health, Education, and Welfare.

Whittaker, J., and E. Tracy. 1990. Family preservation services and education for social work practice: Stimulus and response. In *Reaching high-risk families: Intensive family preservation services,* ed. Whittaker, J., Kinney, J., Tracy E., and Booth, C. New York: Aldine de Gruyter.

SUGGESTED FURTHER READINGS

Algate, J., A. Malucio, and C. Reeves. 1990. *Adolescents in foster families: Child care policy and practice.* Chicago: Nelson-Hall.

Billingsley, A. 1992. *Climbing Jacob's ladder: The enduring legacy of African-American families.* New York: Simon and Schuster.

Child Welfare. A bimonthly journal published by the Child Welfare League of America, New York.

Children's Defense Fund. Published annually. *Children's defense budget: analysis of the federal budget and children.* Washington, D.C.: Children's Defense Fund.

Cohen, N., ed. 1992. *Child welfare: A multicultural focus.* Boston: Allyn and Bacon.

Gambril, E., and T. Stein, eds. 1994. *Controversial issues in child welfare.* Boston: Allyn and Bacon.

Garbarino, J. 1992. *Children and families in the social environment.* New York: Aldine de Gruyter.

Gustavsson, N., and E. Segal. 1994. *Critical issues in child welfare.* Thousand Oaks, Calif.: Sage.

Kamerman, S., and A. Kahn. 1990. Social services for children, youth and families in the United States. Special issue, *Children and Youth Services Review,* vol. 12, nos. 1–2. New York: Pergamon Press.

CHAPTER 14

CRIMINAL JUSTICE

Joe is a thirty-two-year-old man whose current address is Huntsville State Prison. He is serving a twenty-year sentence for armed robbery. This is not Joe's first term in prison, but he hopes that it will be his last.

Joe first came to the attention of the criminal justice system when he was 14 years old. He was arrested for stealing a car. The third child in a family of six children, Joe grew up with his mother and siblings in a poverty-stricken area in a large eastern city. He was abused physically during his childhood and received little positive attention from his mother. From first grade on, Joe had difficulty in school. He had a short attention span, disrupted the classroom, and rarely completed his schoolwork.

At the time of his first arrest, Joe was in the seventh grade for the second time. He was placed on probation, and his family was referred for counseling. However, because his mother worked long hours, she was never able to arrange the sessions. Joe became more of a problem in school and the neighborhood. He began skipping school, experimenting with drugs, and committing a series of burglaries. His mother could not handle his frequent bursts of anger nor get Joe to respond to her limits.

When Joe was 16, he spent three months in a juvenile detention facility, where he did well with the structure provided by the program. When he left the program, he was assigned a probation officer and returned to his family. His conditions of probation stipulated that he attend school on a regular basis, maintain a specified curfew, and report to his probation officer monthly. Joe followed these conditions for several months; however, he continued to have difficulty in school and dropped out four months after he returned home. He held a series of jobs at fast-food restaurants but had difficulty coming to work regularly and became frustrated because he was not earning very much money. Increasingly, he gravitated toward older young adults who hung out on the street and seemed to have the freedom and the money he yearned for. They liked Joe, and he felt accepted by them and enjoyed being with them. Joe soon became involved with them in selling drugs and committing burglaries.

Joe then began a series of arrests for drug dealing, burglary, and assault, which resulted in several stays in various detention facilities.

Just before his last arrest, Joe married a 19-year-old, who recently had their baby. He is anxious to get out of prison and begin to get to know his son and support his family. He is frustrated by the limited work programs and the lack of counseling available at the prison. He has enrolled in a prison education program to try to earn his high school equivalency certificate and hopes to be released to a community halfway house and enroll in a job-training program. He knows that he will need job skills and help in dealing with his anger and frustration if he is to maintain a successful marriage and job and to stay out of prison. ∎

In this chapter we look at the four components of the criminal justice system: legislative, law enforcement, judicial, and corrections. Although social workers play some role in all of these, the focus of our attention is on the corrections component and social work roles in rehabilitation. Consistent with the overall focus of this text, we will look at the rehabilitation strategies in light of the competing views of criminal behavior. ∎

THE CRIMINAL JUSTICE SYSTEM

The criminal justice system in its broadest sense refers to the means used to enforce those standards of conduct required to protect individuals and property and to maintain a sense of justice in the community. In broad terms, a system of criminal justice creates the laws governing social behavior, attempts to prevent violations of these laws, and apprehends, judges, punishes, and makes efforts to rehabilitate those who violate the laws. Crime is a legal concept with political origins. Crimes are acts that some dominant groups in the society see as a threat to individual or community well-being. Some acts are more horrible than others. No modern society allows citizens to roam about and kill one another at random. Yet we do not agree on what it is to kill in a criminal sense. At this writing (1995), it is a crime to request or perform an abortion in the Republic of Ireland, but not so in the United States. Some Irish citizens and some American citizens would like the law of their country changed to reflect their personal values regarding abortion. As individuals we applaud or abhor laws depending on our own sense of justice.

There are two principal restraints on criminal behavior: (1) morality, enforced by an individual's social conscience; and (2) law, enforced by the police and the courts. If society is to control crime, any decline in the former must be matched by a rise in the latter. If family and other traditional restraints on behavior are eroded, it becomes necessary to increase the legal restraints. Suspicion of the state, as the moralizer for society, makes it more difficult to use the criminal justice system to achieve what custom and morality once produced. This is a modern dilemma (Wilson 1994).

The criminal justice system has four components:

- The *legislative component,* which deems certain acts to be criminal

- The *law enforcement component,* which seeks to deter crime and to catch and prosecute lawbreakers

- The *judicial component,* which determines if the laws are valid under our constitution (if a law has truly been broken, the individual charged is guilty) and prescribes penalties for the illegal behavior

- A *corrections component,* which administers the penalties and performs the rehabilitative functions

In the United States, these components do not form a "system" in any functionally organized sense.

Legislative Component

Criminal codes define the types of conduct that are criminal and establish a range of penalties for such behavior. In the United States, each state is empowered to legislate its own criminal statutes, within the restrictions laid down by the U.S. Constitution. Crime definitions are specific to legislative acts. Since social change is a constant the federal Congress, the state legislature, and the local legislative bodies are constantly at work criminalizing, decriminalizing, or recriminalizing behavior.

As a social worker, and as a citizen, you are likely to engage in political action to persuade legislative bodies to criminalize certain allowed behaviors and to decriminalize certain prohibited behaviors. You may even decide that you were wrong and go back and ask the legislature to recriminalize the behavior they have just decriminalized at your request. Certainly you should not be surprised to find that other decent citizens are working the other side of the street. Your sense of crime is different from their sense of crime. Our political/legislative system attempts to define and enact a consensus criminal code. The ideal is that the criminal codes forbid, or at least extract penalties for, behavior that most of us find threatening to the community—while protecting the rights of the minority to express their own life-styles.

Enforcement Component

When a police officer has probable cause to believe that a certain individual has violated a law, the officer is legally "empowered" to make an arrest. Arrested persons are generally taken into police custody until arraignment. Then a trial judge or a grand jury determines whether there is probable cause for the arrested person to stand trial. As shown in Figure 14.1, there are many "stops" in the system from suspicion to trial. The officer often turns away or gives a warning; cases are pleaded away at arraignment, and so forth. Social workers play significant roles and have strong beliefs about how the enforcement component should proceed. Should spousal abuse, for example, be covered by mandatory arrest laws to reduce the discretion of the police officer or even the spouse? Despite our desire for certainty on such matters, the evidence on this and other questions pushes us in both directions: mandatory arrests do reduce the incidence of spousal abuse, but carry a cost to the community in arrest and arraignments that are not always sustainable in court.

Judicial Component

Between the enforcement strategies of a society and the judicial strategies of a society, there is need for discretion so that the justice component of the criminal justice system is effectively and efficiently served. Our system of justice is based on the notion that it is better to let a criminal go free than to convict an innocent person. In all criminal proceedings, state attorneys have the power to dismiss cases without proceeding to trial. Trial judges can set or withhold bail. Critics of the bail system point out that large numbers of defendants are imprisoned solely because they cannot afford bail, while dangerous persons (child abusers, for example) are allowed to go out on bail and commit the crime that they were prevented from performing with their first arrest. What principles should govern these choices?

Regardless of the disposition of bail, more than 90 percent of all criminal cases never reach the formal trial stage. They are adjudicated by way of guilty pleas in a process known as plea bargaining, which involves

FIGURE 14.1   **THE PATH THROUGH THE CRIMINAL JUSTICE SYSTEM**

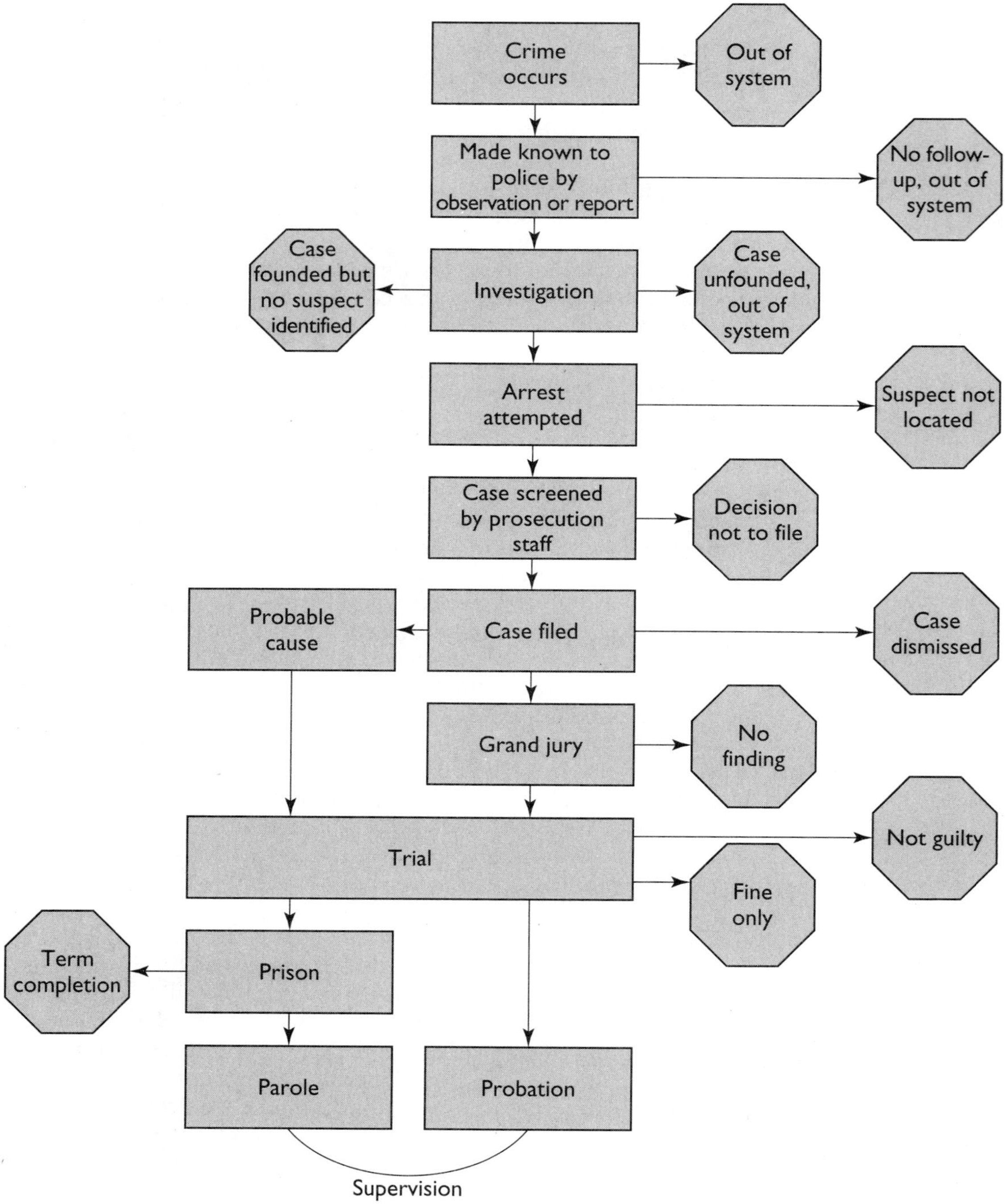

Note: The stop signs show how a crime drops out of the system. Rectangles represent stages in the system.

negotiations between the prosecutor, the defendant, and the defendant's counsel that lead to the defendant's entering a guilty plea in exchange for a reduction in charges or the prosecutor's promise to recommend a more lenient sentence. The process may take place at the arraignment, at the preliminary hearing (if there is one) or during the trial itself. A defendant who plea bargains and pleads guilty may not receive the trial to which he or she has a constitutional right. Guilty pleas, however, do relieve the courts, which could not possibly handle the trials of all accused persons. Prosecutors are often willing to accept plea bargaining, particularly when the case against a defendant rests on weak evidence or less than credible witnesses, and a trial may therefore result in an acquittal.

About 90 percent of cases that do proceed to trial are under the jurisdiction of the minor, or lower, trial courts. Under various names in the various states, the lower courts are generally empowered to hear *misdemeanor* cases—crimes punishable by a maximum sentence of a fine or one year in jail. Major trial courts, called district courts in the federal system, hear *felony* cases—more serious crimes punishable by a sentence of at least one year in a prison.

In the criminal courts, social workers play a wide variety of roles, for example, serving as an information witness in child abuse cases. They also are often asked to serve as expert witnesses in a wide range of cases. After the verdict, social workers from the state attorney's office often are asked to prepare a presentencing report for the judge.

Corrections Component

Imprisonment rates rose far more sharply in the 1980s than in any previous decade in American history. Since 1980, the number of inmates confined in federal, state, and local correctional facilities has nearly tripled. By year-end 1992, inmates in federal and state prisons numbered 883,593 as compared to 329,821 at year-end 1980 (Bureau of Justice Statistics 1993). This has produced a serious shortage in prison and jail capacity and a rush to build more prisons.

Longer sentences and more frequent incarceration were expected to reduce crime by deterring would-be offenders from committing crimes because of the growing threat of a prison sentence and by causing their incapacity—physically preventing increasing numbers of offenders from committing new crimes because they are behind bars. Criminal sentences are also imposed because society wants to revenge the crime; you have done the crime, now you will do the time.

The incarceration policy has not reduced crime levels. It is difficult to detect any overall relationship between incarceration and violence rates, or to show that incarceration is a cost-effective means of reducing crime. Why hasn't the incarceration strategy worked?

- The penalties are already in place, with longer sentences used as a deterrent effect on violent crime. However, there is little research evidence to suggest that longer terms reduce recidivism.

- Violence in crime is systemic. It is often linked to participation in other criminal activities such as drug use. Thus the incarcerated offenders are replaced quickly on the streets by others. Incapacitation of the one offender does not necessarily reduce the propensity of others to commit the offense itself.

- Older offenders (e.g., late 20s, early 30s), who already are "aging out" of crime and represent the bulk of the prison population, are replaced continuously on the streets by fresh cohorts of youth entering the high-crime-prone ages (18 to 24).

- We have used prison time as an expression of moral outrage with little thought to its deterrent or incapacitation effect on other criminals.

THE JUVENILE JUSTICE SYSTEM

How to handle youthful offenders has been an issue debated throughout the history of the United States. Until the late 1800s, youth were treated in the same way as adult offenders, imprisoned with adults and even sentenced to death. The juvenile courts in this country were first established in Cook County, Illinois, in 1899. The philosophy of the juvenile courts has been that the courts should be structured to act in the best interest of the child. In essence, juvenile courts thus have a treatment and rehabilitation orientation that sometimes dominates their adjudicative function. In adult criminal proceedings, the focus is on a specific crime. In contrast, the focus of juvenile courts is often on the psychological, physical, emotional, and educational needs of the defendant, as opposed to the child's specific guilt in a unique case. Of course, not all juvenile court judges live up to these principles, and there is the ever-present danger that the juvenile court process can be subverted.

In the 1960s, Gerald Gault (a fifteen-year-old youth) was tried in the Arizona juvenile court for allegedly making an obscene phone call to a neighbor. Neither the accused nor his parents were given advance notice of the charges against him. He was not informed of his legal rights and, if found guilty, could have been held within the criminal justice system until he reached the age of majority. The procedures used by the Arizona officials in the Gault proceeding were not unreasonable. They were in accord with the thinking of the times, namely, that advance notice and formal trial are likely to stigmatize a child and violate many confidentialities. The focus of concern was on the state as a parent rather than the state as the embodiment of a social conscience. Thus, Gault was brought before the juvenile court and tried without proper safeguards.

In 1967 the case went to the Supreme Court. The majority opinion, written by Justice Abe Fortas, vehemently criticized the juvenile correctional establishment and made it clear that regardless of intent, juveniles should not be deprived of their liberty without the full set of due process rights available to an adult. This case restored to juvenile procedures safeguards that often had been ignored, including notification of charges, protection from self-incrimination, confrontation, cross-examination, and the like (Niger 1967).

The wisdom of the Gault decision is still disputed. There is no doubt that it gives minors the same basic constitutional rights enjoyed by adults. They should never have lost them. However, the return to a focus on whether or not a young person has committed a crime often masks the need for help exhibited by young persons caught up in the court processes. This case has brought about a critical reassessment of juvenile procedures and has suggested that the treatment and rehabilitative role of the juvenile correctional system must be secondary to the process of protecting the rights of the juvenile before the criminal justice system. Youth crime is a particularly troublesome problem to society. The way in which we have addressed this in the past has been either to treat juveniles as though they were adults or to treat juveniles in such a fashion that their basic rights were not protected.

The necessity to reassess our responsibility to youths is one of the most challenging problems that social work is facing in the 1990s. As youth crime has increased both in incidence and severity, many states have adopted a much tougher stance toward young offenders, including more arrests, stricter sentences, and a higher incidence of sentencing to juvenile detention facilities.

CRIME PREVENTION

Prevention is everyone's first choice. It would be wonderful to live in a society in which no one would want to commit a crime. To some persons, a second-best society would be one in which enough police were on the streets that criminals would be too afraid of being caught to commit a crime. Prevention has its clear limits; it would cost enormously to have that many police, and they might (when not catching criminals) interfere with our legitimate fun.

Rehabilitation

Rehabilitation has merit. The problem is that even the best-evaluated programs on rehabilitation show that such programs, despite their merits, have only minimal effects on the collective crime rate (Bureau of Justice Statistics 1993).

Regarding crime, the argument is often made that you pay now or you pay later. Joseph Califano, former Secretary of Health, Education, and Welfare under President Carter and now chairman of the Center on Addiction and Substance Abuse at Columbia University, makes such an argument in an article from the *New York Times*, 30 December 1994. Early intervention costs roughly $5,000 per child per year, he admits, but adds, "you give us $5,000 per kid per year and you'll never have to spend $40,000 or $60,000 per year per kid for prison later on."

If we take a figure between Califano's high and low estimate for a year in prison at $50,000, it appears that the $5,000 investment in a rehabilitation/prevention program now saves $45,000 in some future year. Truly a wonderful investment. It assumes that every youth in the program would have gone on to a life of crime if the program were not

These kids are participants in a diversion program for youth who have already been involved in delinquent activities. It is hoped that early intervention will prevent future problems with delinquency and crime.

in place, and that every child touched by the program is diverted from that criminal path by dint of the program. This is clearly not so. The **deterrence factor** of a social program is the "no program incidence" of some unwanted occurrence divided by the "program incidence" of that occurrence. The problem is that evaluations of rehabilitation/prevention programs under careful research guidelines show low deterrence factors. The Perry School experiment in Ypsilanti, Michigan (one of the best known, best evaluated) showed a criminal deterrence factor of only 5.0. Future program costs ratio is the ratio of no program to program for, in this case, criminal behavior. Califano says that factor is 9.0. The cost-benefit ratio is thus 9/5, or 1.8. For every $5,000 invested in crime prevention now, we save $9,000 in the future.

If crime prevention based on rehabilitation is to be widely accepted, its detractors will have to be convinced that the programs do work. To do that, program proponents will have to stop overpromising the program impacts.

Using data from the Perry School, this problem can be shown for a hypothetical example: If a crime rehabilitation program for 100 children were funded at $5,000 per child per year, the total yearly cost would be $500,000. Without the program, 35 children will end up in prison; with the program, only 7. Thus if we restrict our consideration to only these factors for a random 100 children at risk for a life of crime, we reach the conclusions shown in Table 14.1.

TABLE 14.1   **COST AND BENEFIT OF PROGRAM INTERVENTION TO REDUCE CRIME**

	Program	No Program
Investment now	$500,000/year	No cost
Future prison costs	$350,000/year	$1,750,000/year
Total cost	$850,000/year	$1,750,000/year
Savings	$900,000/year Cost-benefit ratio = 1.8	

Even in the meanest of mean neighborhoods, what you must realize is that two-thirds of the children will not choose a life of crime—with or without the program. The problem is that we cannot identify which 35 are crime prone and which are not. But since it is that 35 or so we wish to affect, we have to provide the program to all 100. Even so, cost-benefit ratio of 1.8 looks very good; but it has to be compared with other public programs that might have higher cost-benefit ratios. The economic rule is never to invest in a social program with a savings ratio of less than one; and when comparing programs, select the program with the highest cost-benefit ratio.

It is hard, and perhaps politically impossible, to invoke economic reasoning in the crime debate. Economic reasoning artificially restricts the debate, and our beliefs about crime and what to do about it are almost always subjects of much passion. The question is, does this country have the will to address its crime problems? We could in theory make justice swifter and more certain, but we will not accept the restrictions on liberty and the weakening of procedural safeguards that this would entail. We could vastly improve the way in which our streets are policed, but some of us will not pay for it and some of us will not tolerate it. We could basically alter the way in which at-risk children experience the first few years of life, but some say this is too costly and others say it is too intrusive into family life-styles.

Crime has many faces. The crimes that drive the demands for reform of the criminal justice system have three elements:

- The crime is violent, involving homicide, rape, or serious bodily assault.

- The victims are selected at random; their only role in the crime is being in the wrong place at the wrong time.

- The criminal has committed prior crime and has been released from prison early or given a furlough in preparation for prison release.

The implication is that if the criminal justice system had done its job, the crime would never have occurred. In fact, such crimes represent a tiny share of all crimes and such inmates a tiny share of all prisoners.

A "three strikes and you are in" approach would solve the problem of such crimes, but at an enormous cost in dollars and lost liberty of former offenders.

The question is, can we reduce the incidence of these types of crimes while preserving a sense of justice at a reasonable cost?

Deterrents to Crime

Public social problems are specific conditions in the society that are perceived as sufficiently bothersome to merit intervention by government. Crime is clearly such a condition. Citizens have a right to expect government protection from crime. Society has a need to apprehend suspended offenders, to convict the guilty and free the innocent, and to appropriately punish and rehabilitate the convicted. These steps constitute the ordered processes of the criminal justice system.

The criminal justice system is expected to act as both a specific and a general deterrent to crime. A **specific deterrent** is structured to prevent crimes very directly. In capital cases, for example, the execution itself is obviously a specific deterrent; the fear of capital punishment serves as a further **general deterrent.** This does not mean a society can impose capital punishment without cost.

In our society the criminal justice system is evaluated not only by its capacity to contain crime but also by the justice meted out by the system. That is why we refer to the *criminal justice system* rather than the *criminal containment system.* The system's dual responsibility to protect the citizenship rights of criminals as well as their victims constitutes the core of the criminal justice system. The constitutional safeguards of our society are expected to follow criminals from their first apprehensions by police, through their arraignments, trials, imprisonments, and reentries into society. That these constitutional safeguards increase the costs and perhaps lower the effectiveness of police, courts, and prisons in containing crime is seen as one of the costs of democracy.

All systems of public policy face policy dilemmas, but the dilemma of the criminal justice system is particularly acute. This is reflected by the rise of vigilantism, a public expression of discontent with the balance that has been struck within the criminal justice system. This system is charged with the deterrence of crime and the maintenance of justice. Its desired goals include (1) efficient, but not intrusive police work; (2) fair and impartial trials for the accused, and an awareness of the rights of the victims; (3) safe, yet secure and humane, prisons; and (4) parole programs that provide reentry into the free society for ex-offenders but protect the community at large.

Law-abiding citizens want to be protected from criminal behavior but also want protection from unwarranted intrusion of the criminal justice system into their private lives. The duality of these demands imposes costs and constraints on police, court officers, and prison and parole officials. Since in the final analysis "law and order" exponents and "civil libertarians" want the same things, where does the policy problem lie? It lies in the question of emphasis and balance, and the latter seldom seems to exist.

◿ VIEWS OF CRIMINAL BEHAVIOR

A number of views of criminal behavior compete to explain why people commit crimes. Crime can be viewed as psychologically aberrant behavior, as socially induced behavior, as a consequence of rational thought where criminals simply see crime as just another way to make a living, or as a complex interactive process of an individual's personal characteristics and the many factors that constitute his or her environment. The explanation accepted by various citizens constitutes the structure upon which they wish the criminal justice system to be built.

Psychological Views of the Criminal Personality

One school of thought suggests that criminals differ from noncriminals in some fundamental way, other than the obvious one of having been convicted. The distinguishing trait has been thought over the years to be reflected in body or head shape, skull size, chromosome structure, specific patterns of response to projective tests, or in the complex labeling process of psychiatric diagnosis. Of course, there is a circular reasoning process in all of the psychological-physiological attempts to establish a criminal type. There also is a kind of satisfaction in the notion of a criminal type, because crime policy then becomes, simply, segregation of the criminals from the rest of society.

A second psychological interpretation of the **etiology of crime** is only slightly more sophisticated. Crime is seen simply as a manifestation of a compulsion derived from unresolved conflicts between the superego and the id. Someone with a criminal personality—by definition a defective ego—is unable to overcome the desire to defy social taboos, yet the conflict reflects itself in an unconscious desire to be caught.

Anecdotal evidence suggests that criminals do operate this way—they may deliberately, albeit unconsciously, leave the clues that lead to their arrests. Were it not for the seriousness of the incidents, this behavior often would be truly comic. One young criminal brought a pair of slacks to the cleaners and, after being presented with the claim check, he pulled a gun and robbed the attendant. He returned three days later with the stub of the claim check to pick up his slacks and was patient enough to wait when the same attendant said the slacks were on the way. The young man waited calmly for the police to come and arrest him. Another pair of criminals left the motor running in the getaway car, but because they had failed to check the fuel gauge before the robbery, their car ran out of gas while they were holding up the bank. Anecdotal, but not systematic, evidence suggests such a pattern in all crime (Silberman 1980). If there is any basis for such a theory of crime, it leads to the conclusion that punishment is not a deterrent to crime but, in fact, is a stimulant.

A more sophisticated psychological theory of the etiology also contains in its assumptions the prescription for a proper anticrime policy. The following is a summation of what can be classed as a psychosocial theory of crime:

- Criminal behavior is learned.
- There is a relationship between the type of criminal behavior learned by individuals and their socioeconomic status in society. Certain classes of persons will learn different ways of crime.
- The processes involved in learning criminal behavior are the same as those in learning other behavior that involves learning a technique as well as values.

This view of criminality is less encompassing than the more simple etiological-psychological views of crime. It does not attempt to explain which people will commit crimes—an impossible task—but rather why and how those who have committed crimes are systematically different from those who do not.

Social Views of Criminal Behavior

Another perspective suggests that crime is not caused by individual physical or mental deficiencies but by societal breakdown. Proponents of this perspective focus on industrialization, racism, poverty, and family breakdown as major factors that create social disorganization, and, in turn, increases in crime. Discussions of crime and society too often are presented as a conflict between straw men. As an illustration, the journalist Charles Silberman and the political scientist James Q. Wilson, both popular writers on crime policy, are portrayed as prototypical advocates of extreme positions. In fact, both see the relationship between crime and social conditions as inordinately complex. Whereas Wilson believes that criminal sanctions would deter crime, Silberman places more faith in indirect social reforms. Both would argue that we need more carrots (job opportunities, antipoverty programs, etc.) and more sticks (swift and certain prison terms as a deterrent), but they would disagree on mix and emphasis.

Sociological inquiries into crime frequently are based on statistical correlates, such as the increasing breakdown of the traditional family or variations in unemployment and crime rates. The more sophisticated inquiries fall short of establishing a direct path of causation. Crime is seen as a result of many factors within the context of the offender's society. Street crime and white-collar crime are seen as very different expressions of social maladjustment. Regardless of specifics, the essence of the sociological perspective is that general deterrence, rehabilitation, and reeducation of offenders constitute the best safeguards against repeated crimes.

The social view of crime advocates a criminal justice system that offers a variety of social intervention strategies (Cullen 1982). One such strategy of importance to social work practitioners is collaboration between social worker and police officer at the earliest intervention point. When the suspected offender is first in police custody, social workers and police officers are expected to concur on the case disposition. The argument is made that, despite their disparate professional orientations, both social workers and police officers are experienced in dealing with troubled people at crisis points in their lives. Individualization of response is seen as critical (Treger 1975).

No one sociological perspective is seen as dominant. Rather, a number of theories are offered, depending on the type of crime committed. Marshall Clinard (1967) suggests the following classification of crimes:

1. Violent personal crimes (i.e., murder)
2. Sexual offenses
3. Occupational/white-collar crimes
4. Political crimes
5. Organized crimes
6. Professional crimes
7. Crimes without victims

Each of these types of crime has its own sociological pattern, and each crime type places a unique set of demands on the criminal justice system.

Economic Rationale of Crime

A final perspective is that crime is simply another form of entrepreneurship, which happens to be illegal. Proponents of this view see the criminal as an amoral person who calculates the costs and benefits of a particular crime, much as a businessperson calculates the costs and benefits of opening a new store. In the economic formulation, potential criminals assess the costs of getting caught and sentenced against the probable benefits of successful completion of the crime. They decide to be criminal or not, depending on the outcomes of their calculations. People who are not poor commit fewer crimes because the costs of going to prison (in lost wages, deprivation of status, amenities of life, etc.) are higher for them than for others. If we subscribe to this theoretical perspective, then to contain crime all we need to do is increase the probable chances of being caught, sentenced, and sent to jail. There is little or no empirical evidence to suggest a valid basis for this theory (Hillman 1980).

Each of these views of crime—and we have listed only three—provides a policy paradigm for the criminal justice system, from the role of the arresting officer to the responsibilities of the parole and probation workers. One's beliefs about why some people commit crimes are the obvious source of ideas about how to contain crime.

PROGRAM ALTERNATIVES

For every thirty-six crimes committed, one person is sentenced to prison. Only one crime in every four reported results in an arrest of a suspected offender. There is roughly one arraignment for every three arrests, and although nearly 95 percent of all criminal arraignments result in criminal conviction or guilty pleas, only one in three results in a prison term. These numbers mislead as much as they reveal, for tracking a particular crime (acknowledging that crimes are greatly underreported) to a particular sentence is a Herculean statistical task. One thing that is unambiguous in these numbers is the enormous amount of discretion that operates within the criminal justice system. Figure 14.1, presented earlier, portrays the complex pathways in the criminal justice system. At each new stage (represented by the rectangles) an opportunity exists for diversion out of the criminal justice system. Only a small percentage of all crimes result in criminal convictions.

The American criminal justice system is largely an English invention, but it includes some important innovations that are the peculiar products of the United States. These innovations are the elements of the system in which social work is most explicitly and importantly involved; these are the programs of probation, parole, and juvenile procedures. The American system is perhaps more fragmented than the criminal justice system in most countries. The criminal justice system can be seen first as composed of three parts: police, courts, and correctional arrangements. With federal, state, and local involvement at each level and a separation into adult and juvenile divisions, a multipartite system emerges. More dramatic is the fact that no subsystem views the criminal problem from a total perspective. Each entity is busily resolving its own problems. The result is a highly fractured system that is difficult to describe, evaluate, or control.

Despite the lack of cohesion and the internal tensions, actions within one subsystem clearly have reverberations throughout the entire system. "Success" or "failure" in one part may generate significant problems for another part. Should state and local police, by virtue of more personnel or better investigation, apprehend 25 percent more offenders, both the courts and the correctional system would have to absorb more defendants and prisoners. If the prison system released a higher proportion of recidivists, police and the courts would have to deal with a larger population of criminals. On the other hand, overcrowded prisons generate backups in local jails. All elements of the criminal justice system must respond to the factors in the larger society that accelerate criminal behavior. Because the criminal justice system is not examined or funded as an entity, each component accepts and adopts its own strategies. The fundamental adaptation for one part often produces particular problems for another entity within the system.

◪ THE ROLE OF SOCIAL WORK IN THE CRIMINAL JUSTICE SYSTEM

The role played by the social work community in the criminal justice system has been relegated almost exclusively to the correctional components of the system. Police agencies only recently have begun to use social workers; these social work functions have low priority in the police budgets and often fall quickly to budget cuts. Adult courts have made relatively little use of professional social workers. Social workers most frequently work in the criminal justice system in the juvenile courts, rehabilitation centers, prisons, and parole programs. Such uses of social workers, however, need to be assessed in a systemwide context.

Some law enforcement experts suggest that the majority of police calls are family or crisis oriented rather than crime related. When crimes occur, they often are the result of family problems—many homicides, for example, occur among family members rather than outside of the family. Increasingly, crime is associated with other social problems, such as alcohol or drug abuse.

Social workers play various roles in police departments. Many departments have crisis intervention teams, consisting of both police officers and social workers, that respond to domestic violence calls or calls to assist victims of rape or other violent crimes. Some police departments have established special victim assistance programs. Often staffed by social workers, these programs provide follow-up services to victims of crime, helping them work through their feelings. They also help victims locate emergency funding, shelter, employment, counseling, and other needed services.

Many police departments also have special child abuse or sex crimes units, which sometimes include social workers on their staffs. The social workers assist in investigating suspected cases, interviewing children and other individuals involved, contacting other agencies such as child welfare departments and hospitals, and arranging for emergency services when needed. A number of police departments also hire social workers to work in youth programs. In Pittsburgh, for example, social workers operate inner-city recreation programs. In Austin, Texas, the police department has had a social worker managing a dropout prevention program in the public schools. Such social workers provide counseling and drug and alcohol education, and serve as positive law enforcement role models to youth at risk of becoming involved in crime.

The role of the social worker in prison and prison life is very much peripheral. The social worker most likely is involved only when convicts enter or leave prison. The classification and assignment process at entry point is heavily influenced by social work practice. The pardon and parole recommendation also is influenced by social workers. Many BSW graduates become probation or parole officers, helping youth and adults learn new skills and behaviors that will deter them from committing additional crimes and recommending stricter penalties to the court if they violate probation or parole. Others work in youth correction facilities, including half-way houses and community-based programs. Although social services in prisons for problems such as substance abuse are limited, some BSW graduates work within prisons as well.

SUMMARY

In the sad history of crime and punishment, reform is always just beyond the horizon. As the chapter shows, a dreary picture is drawn from practice and current procedures. Police practices do not deter crime, the courts do not dispense justice, the corrections system does not correct, and the parole system does not facilitate ex-prisoners' reentry into society as law-abiding citizens. Clearly, part of the problem is that insufficient funds are spent on the criminal justice system. Too much is expected for too little expended.

Funds alone are not the problem. Despite a considerable and growing body of knowledge of what works and what does not work in police, court, and correctional settings, there is insufficient attention to integration within the system. Each unit of the system seeks to improve its operation and to clarify its mission, but at the expense of other components within the system. A more effective integration of police, court, and prison practices is required.

The failure of the criminal justice system also is due to uncertainty about what it is expected to deliver: Is it safe streets, a just system, effective rehabilitation, or simple containment? Effective policies require clarity, choice, commitment, and closure. The segmented structure of the criminal justice system precludes all of these. As a consequence, during some periods society throws money at certain aspects of the overall problem; during other periods, other aspects are funded. Clearly, careful diagnosis and prescription are needed.

KEY TERMS

deterrence factor   general deterrent
etiology of crime   specific deterrent

DISCUSSION QUESTIONS

1. To what extent is the policy dilemma of the criminal justice system reflected in the juvenile justice system? To what extent does the juvenile justice system have its own unique policy dilemma?

2. Which of the three views of crime, if any, is most consistent with social work practice theory?

3. If systems integration is the central problem of the criminal justice system, how can the contemporary social worker enhance the probability of that integration?

REFERENCES

Bureau of Justice Statistics. 1993. As reported in *New York Times,* 10 May 1993, p. A20.

Clinard, Marshall. 1967. *Criminal behavior systems.* New York: Holt, Reinhart & Winston.

Cullen, F. T. 1982. *Rethinking crime and deviance.* Totowa, N.J.: Rowman & Allanheld.

Davis, Liane V. 1992. The problem of wife abuse: The interrelationship of social policy and social work practice. *Social Work* 37, no. 1 (January): 15.

Hillman, Darrell. 1980. *The economics of crime.* New York: Routine Press.

Niger, Allen. 1967. The Gault decision, due process and the juvenile court, *Federal Register* 31(4): 8–18.

Schmidt, Janell D. 1993. Does arrest deter domestic violence? *American Behavioral Scientist* 36, no. 5 (May–June): 601.

Silberman, Charles. 1980. *Criminal violence and criminal justice.* New York: Random House.

Treger, H. T. 1975. *Police and social work teams.* Springfield, Ill.: Thomas.

Wilson, James Q. 1994. What to do about crime. *Commentary* 98, no. 3 (September): 25.

SUGGESTED FURTHER READINGS

Brake, Mike. 1992. *Public order and private lives: The politics of law and order.* London: Routledge.

Friedman, Lawrence. 1993. *Crime and punishment in American history.* New York: Basic Books.

Masters, Ruth. 1993. *Counseling criminal justice offenders.* Lewiston: E. Mellen Press.

Neely, Richard. 1994. *Tragedies of our own making.* Urbana: University of Illinois Press.

Raynor, Peter. 1985. *Social work, justice, and control.* Oxford: Blackwell.

CHAPTER 15

OCCUPATIONAL SOCIAL WORK

Bill and Meredith Hunt, both 32 years old, live in a small house in a rapidly deteriorating part of the city with their three children, ages 2, 4, and 8. Bill works at a large manufacturing plant, as one of several workers who monitor a largely automated assembly line. Meredith works as a computer programmer for a large company. The Hunts' two youngest children attend a child care center, and their oldest child attends school. Until recently, Bill's job has been the most important aspect of his life. He is well liked as an employee, and in the neighborhood, his job is viewed as desirable. But Bill is finding that his job is a lot less meaningful to him than it has been in the past. His raises are less frequent and are not enough to pay even for necessities. Last year, Bill and the other assembly-line workers were laid off for two months due to a production slowdown. Most manufacturing companies in the area are buying their parts from abroad, and Bill's company increasingly is automating its operations, reducing the need for employees. There is even talk of shutting down the plant and moving it to Mexico. Bill is frustrated about the recent layoff and the lack of pay and concerned about how long his job will last. Although he knows that his wife has to work in order to make ends meet, Bill resents the fact that she has less time for him and feels bad because he can't provide for his family on his own.

Within the last two years, Bill has begun drinking heavily. He has beaten Meredith several times, and he yells at the children and spanks them more often. Bill's supervisor has noticed a change in his job performance and is ready to give him formal notification that he needs to improve or risks being fired. Bill feels tired, financially pressured, and emotionally defeated. Meredith also finds herself strained emotionally. In addition to her job, Meredith maintains primary responsibility for taking care of the house and the children. She gets up at 5:30 a.m. and it is always after midnight before she has everything done and can collapse into bed. Because the child care for the Hunts' two children costs over half of Meredith's take-home pay, they can't afford child care for their oldest son before and after school. Meredith worries about him being at home alone and makes several telephone calls to him each afternoon. Additionally, neither of the companies the Hunts work for allows employees to take sick leave when the children are sick, and all three children have been sick a lot lately. Meredith has missed six days of work in the last two months to care for her sick children. On three other occasions, Meredith has kept her oldest son home from school to take care of the younger children.

Meredith's mother, who lives in a neighboring city, recently was diagnosed with cancer and is scheduled to have surgery. Meredith would like to spend several days with her mother during and after the surgery since her other siblings live out of state. But she has used all of her vacation days for her children's illnesses, and her company has no policies that provide for leave in such situations.

Recently, Meredith has been having difficulty sleeping and has had stomach problems. Her doctor prescribed tranquilizers, which she takes more often than the prescription calls for. Meredith's coworkers are worried about her, but resent having to do extra work when she is absent or not able to work as quickly as she usually does. Her boss has commented on her slip in job performance. Meredith likes her job very much but also is very worried about her husband, her children, and her mother. She feels guilty because her working places extra pressures on her family. Her oldest son is not doing well in school, and Meredith is too tired to help him. All of the children vie constantly for her attention. Both Meredith and Bill feel caught between the pressures of work and their family, and they are becoming increasingly overwhelmed by the demands of both. ■

Most individuals over the age of 18 have two major domains in which they interact: the family and the workplace. While attention to social problems and individual needs usually includes an emphasis on the family, rarely is there any focus on the relationship between the individual and the workplace. This omission has caused us to help individuals and their families less often and not as effectively as we could.

Consider again the systems/ecological perspective to understanding problems discussed in Chapter 3—the way systems overlap and interact with each other and the individuals who function within those systems. Think about this perspective in relation to the Hunt family. Though until recently the Hunts have been a close-knit family, work is a primary focus in their lives. It produces the economic resources needed to provide food, clothing, shelter, and the recreational activities affordable to them. When someone meets Bill or Meredith, a frequent first question asked is not "to what family do you belong?" but rather "where do you work?" In our society, a person's status in life is defined largely by occupation. Much of our self-respect, self-fulfillment, identity, and status is defined by the type of work that we do. Until recently, both Bill and Meredith received positive fulfillment from their workplaces. They got along well with co-workers and received raises, recognition for jobs well done.

At first, their two jobs allowed the Hunts to support their family adequately. The positive aspects of work spilled over into the family, and they also maintained positive support within the family. But the overlaps between the two domains began to create additional pressures for both Bill and Meredith. Conflicts began about which came first—home or work—when there didn't seem to be enough energy for both; what to do when children or relatives were sick; how much money to spend on child care, on eating out when tired or cooking meals at home, and on other items; and what types of jobs and career paths to pursue when the type of work available seemed to be changing. All these had an impact on Bill and Meredith's relationships and ability to function, both at home and at work.

For both Bill and Meredith, work currently has many negative implications. Ideally, they will seek help from some type of social service program before either their family or their jobs become jeopardized further. A social worker or other helping professional who becomes involved with the Hunts' problems cannot help them effectively if work issues are not taken into consideration.

In this chapter we explore current and projected demographics regarding the workforce; the changing nature and meaning of work; problems within the family and at the workplace created by work and family tensions; and the roles the workplace and social workers can play in attempting to prevent such problems from occurring or recurring. ■

A HISTORICAL PERSPECTIVE ON WORK AND FAMILY RELATIONSHIPS

In most Western countries, particularly in the United States, much of the basis of society can be traced to the Protestant work ethic, which stems from the Protestant Reformation of the seventeenth century. The work ethic suggests that work is an expectation of God, and that laziness is sinful. Attitudes toward paupers during the early colonization of the United States and toward welfare recipients today stem from the impact of the work ethic on our society.

For women, however, the emphasis was different; the primary role of women was to maintain the family and to support the ability of men in the family to work outside the home. Until the 1970s this pattern changed only during wartime, when women were needed in the factories because men were away at war. But as soon as peace returned, women returned home and men to the workplace. Those women who did work outside of the home—because of either necessity, interest, or both—often were considered to be outside of their appropriate role. It is interesting to note, for example, that until the 1970s most studies regarding work focused on the negative impact of the unemployed male on his family, or on the negative impact of the employed female on her family (Bronfenbrenner and Crouter 1982).

In recent years, much has changed in regard to the relationship between the individual and the workplace. Probably the biggest change has been due to the large number of women who are working, including those with children. Other changes have taken place as well. Workplaces are more diverse, not only in regard to gender, but also ethnicity. Increasing numbers of African Americans, Latinos, and other people of color are joining the workforce. By the year 2000, the typical employee will be a person of color and/or a female, and only 45 percent of the workforce will be white males (Ginsberg 1992).

Employees' expectations about work have also changed. Individuals today expect more from the workplace than just a paycheck: recognition, a say in decision making, benefits, and flexible working hours. Numerous studies have focused on the alienation of some workers and the fact that many workers today put other priorities ahead of their jobs. Additional problems receiving increased attention from the workplace include substance abuse; increased costs of health care and other benefits; maternity, paternity, and sick leave; and the overall increase in employees' stress. Because work for pay is such an important aspect of our society, fluctuations in the United States economy in recent years have raised added concern about the unemployment and the underemployment of many individuals. The unemployed and underemployed are much more likely to be women and people of color, most often with children. Unemployment and underemployment—and the fear of both—cause added stress not only to individual employees, but to their families as well.

A growing number of experts view the relationship between work and family life as one of the most critical policy issues to be addressed during the next decade. In many instances, special social services and other programs have been established in the workplace to assist employees and their families in order to maintain or increase productivity. Increasingly as well, social services programs in the workplace are helping workers deal with layoffs and business closings.

Occupational social work (sometimes called "industrial social work") has emerged as a growing field for social workers. By applying a systems/ecological perspective, social workers have the potential to play a major role in strengthening relationships between the individual, the family, and the workplace.

◪ THE CHANGING NATURE OF THE WORKFORCE

Today's workforce is considerably different from what it was even a decade ago. In the past, most employees were white males who were employed in business and industry and who often stayed with one company until retirement. The current workforce is much more diverse. Employees today are much more likely to be women and people of color employed in service-related jobs. Additionally, because of technological and economic changes, many workplaces have either closed, downsized their operations, or changed the nature of their work and the type of resources needed, including personnel. Employees today not only are more likely to change jobs frequently, but also will probably experience at least one major career shift before they retire. Being terminated from a job for reasons other than job performance will also become much more common as global changes that affect the workplace continue to occur.

More Women in the Workforce

The majority of today's work-related programs and policies are based on work and family demographics as they existed during the 1950s: an almost totally male workforce and a male breadwinner supporting his stay-at-home wife and 2.6 children (an average figure). But currently, fewer than 10 percent of American families can be classified this way. Over 50 percent of two-parent families have both parents employed full time. Over 75 percent of all working women have children under 18, and over 60 percent have children under 6 years of age. More than half of all women with children under 1 year of age are employed outside the home. (U.S. Bureau of Labor Statistics 1995)

The increase in the number of women employed outside of the family has been fairly sudden, leaving both employers and families unprepared to deal adequately with the resulting implications. Many individuals argue that the reason for this phenomenon has been primarily economic—that the majority of women work as an economic necessity rather than by choice. Others argue that the women's movement and the realization that women have choices open to them other than remaining at home have created this shift. Still others argue that the women's movement occurred because women were forced by economics to enter the workforce, and once there, they faced unfair conditions and began lobbying for changes and more options. Still others counter that more women are working because of the increased emphasis on self-fulfillment (the "me" generation) and consumption among both genders. Although studies indicate that some women work because of choice, most women who are mothers want to work less than they do now.

Whatever the reason or reasons for the increased number of women in the labor force, this factor more than any other has focused attention on the relationship between work and family. As sociologist Rosabeth Kanter (1977) explains, when only one family member left the home each day and operated within the work system, there was less necessity for overlap or interaction between the work and family systems, and it was fairly easy to keep them separate. But when two family members become involved in the work system, it is impossible to keep the two systems separate.

Single-Parent Families

Other demographic shifts require special attention as well. In 1994, 31 percent of all families in the United States were one-parent families, most headed by women (U.S. Bureau of the Census 1995). Nationally, women in general earn less than their male counterparts in the work force. Real wages have fallen in recent times. The weekly paycheck for the lowest 10 percent of workers according to wage averaged $225 in 1994, a 10 percent decrease in wages since the '70s if inflation is accounted for. Low wages make survival for individuals, particularly those with families, extremely difficult. While experts recommend that no more than 30 percent of take-home pay be spent on housing, many poor families spend 70 percent. Many also cannot afford health insurance, even if it is available through their place of work. Two-thirds of the nearly forty million U.S. families without health insurance have full-time jobs (Gibbs 1995).

The median income in 1993 for all married households was about $43,000. For all single-parent, male-headed families, it was $29,849, compared to $31,177 for white male-headed families, $22,000 for African American male-headed families, and $25,013 for Hispanic male-headed families. For all single-parent, female-headed families, median income was $18,545, compared to $21,583 for white female-headed families, $12,423 for African American female-headed families, and $13,223 for Hispanic female-headed families (Strand 1995). When both ethnicity and gender are accounted for, white males earn the highest wages and African American women, the lowest (see Figure 15.1).

Emerging Issues

For women and their families, issues such as patterns of child rearing and affordable child care, flexible working hours, transportation to and from work, and job training, in addition to salary, benefits, pensions, and compensation, are crucial. For their employers, absenteeism and tardiness, sick leave, and employee stress become factors no matter how competent and hard-working their employees are. Johnston and Packer (1987) indicate that the increased numbers of working women will lead to more heavily subsidized and regulated child care; readjustments to tax systems such as the "marriage penalty," which penalizes families where both spouses are employed outside the home, and child care deductions; decreased flexibility of the workforce as two-career families become less willing to relocate; fewer distinctions between males' and females' jobs and wage rates; an increase in part-time, flexible, and stay-at-home jobs and a decrease in total work hours per employee; a restructuring of private benefit policies to reflect the needs of two-income

FIGURE 15.1 **FULL-TIME WORKERS' MEDIAN WEEKLY EARNINGS BY ETHNICITY AND GENDER**

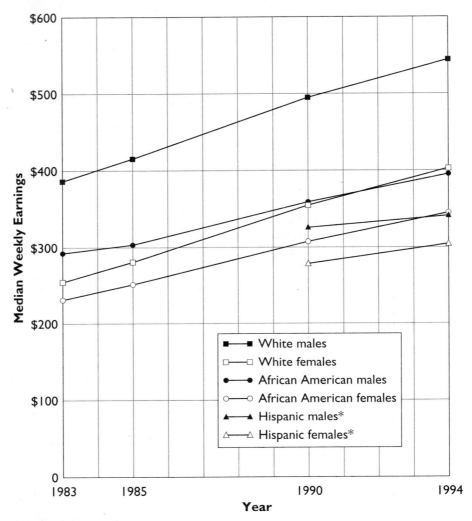

*Data not available for Hispanics until 1990

Source: U.S. Bureau of Labor Statistics, *Current Employment Statistics* (Washington, D.C.: Author, 1995).

families and single workers; and more stringent public programs, with access to benefits more segregated between those available to wage earners and those available through government to low-income earners and the unemployed.

A Smaller, Aging Workforce

As a result of the decrease in the number of babies being born, the work-force is expected to decrease in size and will also grow older. Between 1985 and 2000, the labor force is projected to grow by about 22 percent, a slower gain than at any time since the 1930s. This in turn will decrease the national rate of economic growth. Economic growth also will depend more heavily on the increased demand for products such as travel and tourism, restaurant meals, luxury goods, and health care.

Whereas the overall population between 1985 and 2000 is projected to grow by only 15 percent, the number of persons age 35 to 47 will increase by 38 percent and the number of persons age 48 to 53, by 67 percent. The average age of the workforce, which was 35 years of age in 1984, will reach 39 by the year 2000. The increased aging of the workforce and of society is likely to have the following impacts:

- A more experienced, stable, and reliable workforce should increase U.S. productivity.

- A continuing decrease in the number of workers available to assume responsibility for those not in the workforce will have long-term implications for areas such as Social Security.

- Although initially, jobs in areas such as fast-food service may be plentiful due to the decreasing number of younger workers, the labor market for younger workers may actually tighten as companies initially forced to raise wages to attract young workers develop other strategies such as increased automation.

- If workplaces continue the trend to reduce middle-management positions and develop less hierarchical work organizations, there will be more competition among workers to move up within organizations, and those workers who leave or lose jobs will have a difficult time seeking new jobs at their previous levels.

Greater Ethnic Diversity within the Workforce

During the next decade, African Americans, Latinos, and other people of color will continue to enter the workforce in greater numbers. Nonwhites will make up over 30 percent of new work entrants and more than 25 percent of the workforce in the year 2000 (see Figure 15.2). African Americans will make up 12 percent of the workplace; Latinos, 10 percent; and Asians, 4 percent (Ginsberg 1992).

The number of immigrants in the workforce will also continue to increase. Estimates suggest that if immigration patterns continue, even under the most conservative estimates Latino and Asian populations in the United States will double by the year 2000. This shift in population will be most significant in the South and the West, particularly in California. Recent legislation in California indicates that immigrants will have an even more difficult time finding work that pays enough to make ends meet, particularly if they are unable to access education and job-training programs.

The increase in ethnic diversity in the workforce is likely to have a number of implications:

- People of color will continue to be discriminated against, to be in lower-paying jobs, and to be promoted to management positions less often than whites. A recent study, for example, found that

FIGURE 15.2   **PROJECTED NEW ENTRANTS TO THE LABOR FORCE**

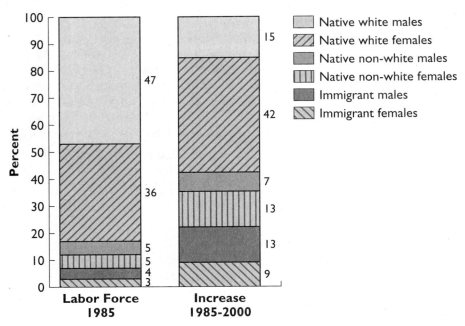

Source: Hudson Institute, *Workforce 2000: Work and Workers for the 21st Century* (Indianapolis: Author, 1987), 95. Reprinted with permission.

although women of color represent 10 percent of the workforce, only 2 percent are employed in managerial positions. African American males are employed in 3 percent of management positions, while white females are employed in 23 percent of such positions (Alexander 1990).

- People of color will continue to earn less than whites, and unemployment rates and earnings may actually worsen for them. In 1993, the median household income for African Americans was 59.3 percent of the median household income for whites, while the median household income for Hispanics was 69.4 percent of that for a white household (U.S. Bureau of the Census 1995).

- Unemployment rates will continue to be higher for people of color in comparison to whites. The unemployment rate for African Americans was 2.04 times higher than for whites in 1993, while the rate for Hispanics was 1.87 times higher during that same time period; see Figure 15.3 (U.S. Bureau of the Census 1995).

- African Americans and Latinos will continue to be overrepresented in dead-end jobs and in declining occupations. An Equal Employment Opportunity Commission study found that both African Americans and Latinos were 35 percent more likely to be employed in occupations projected to lose the most employees (Johnston and Packer 1987).

- Over 50 percent of African Americans and Latinos, compared to 25 percent of whites, will continue to live in inner-city areas with severe problems that place their residents more at risk for unemployment (Johnston and Packer 1987).

- Immigrants will represent the largest share of the increase in both the population and the workforce since World War I and will also often experience barriers due to language and lack of education (Johnston and Packer 1987).

Employment experts are concerned that unemployment and low earnings rates will worsen for people of color, because they also have disproportionately high drop-out rates and more problems with literacy than whites. These issues indicate that the changing nature of the workforce will have significant implications for employers and employees alike, particularly for those companies that have previously hired primarily young white males.

Debates about affirmative action going on nationally will also have implications for workplaces. If affirmative action legislation is changed, some worksites may not hire as many women and people of color. Those women and people of color who are hired may find less support available because employers and employees may be less inclined to provide fair treatment when some policies emphasizing such treatment are eliminated, even though there are other, often less well known policies (e.g., civil rights legislation) that still require fairness.

FIGURE 15.3   **UNEMPLOYMENT RATES BY GENDER AND ETHNICITY**

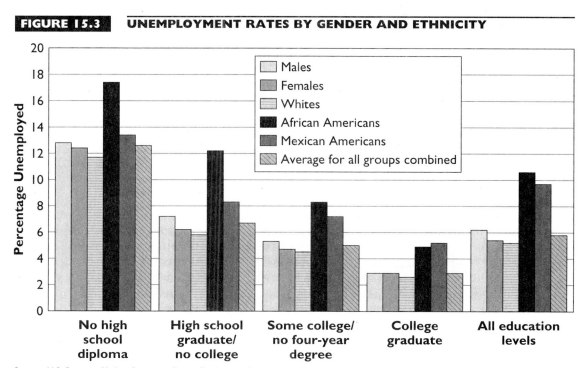

Source: U.S. Bureau of Labor Statistics, *Current Employment Statistics* (Washington, D.C.: Author, 1995).

Types of Jobs Available

The types of jobs in which workers are employed also have changed. Through the 1960s, the majority of workers have been employed in blue-collar jobs. But as the United States has shifted from a manufacturing-based society to a services-based society, more and more workers are employed in white-collar jobs. In 1993, over half of the workforce was in white-collar jobs (U.S. Bureau of the Census 1995). Jobs in the least-skilled job classifications will continue to be eliminated, while the number of white-collar and skilled professional jobs will continue to grow. Most new jobs will require higher levels of education and greater skills in mathematics and language. As high school drop-out rates increase, the number of jobs requiring less than a high school education continues to decrease. It is estimated that by the year 2000, only 10 percent of jobs will require less than a high school degree.

Shifts in the types of jobs available are likely to lead to a dual work-force—more jobs available in the white-collar and skilled areas, primarily in services, requiring high levels of education, and a limited number of jobs available in manufacturing and low-level service jobs requiring less education and skill. Such changes are likely to make the workforce even more segregated, with more people of color, immigrants, and women in the less-skilled, lower-paying jobs and more white males in the higher-paying jobs requiring greater education and skill.

The shift in jobs away from major industrial centers in the North and East to the Sunbelt and West Coast states, as well as the move away from small agricultural production, also has had a significant impact on workers and their families. Many individuals and families who have remained in industrial centers or farm areas have been forced to take lower-paying jobs or to seek financial assistance for the first time in their lives. They often have lost their homes, farms, and businesses and face an unpredictable future.

◢ THE CHANGING NATURE OF WORK

During the 1990s, workplaces of all types have continued to shift their emphasis to remain competitive in a world marketplace that is changing rapidly. Workplaces that have been able to survive have had to be increasingly flexible, shifting direction and staff creatively and quickly. As a result, many workers have lost jobs, have been shifted to new roles within the organization, or have had to become individual contractors or employees of an organization that contracts for goods or services with the organization with which they were previously employed. Most workplaces have eliminated much of the hierarchy in organizations and shifted to a task team approach. They form a team of workers to meet one organizational goal, then dismantle that team and form another team, which may have a different configuration of employees to meet the next goal. In some workplaces, salaries and raises are based on the performance of the entire team rather than on individual performance.

These shifts have significantly affected employees in many work-places. The key to being a successful employee is to be flexible and willing to work at multiple tasks, changing to new tasks quickly. Inter-personal skills are more important than in the past, as is knowledge of new technology. Today's workers have to find new ways to measure their job performance, since salary increases often occur less frequently due to the need of organizations to remain economically competitive. Promotions are also much less frequent, since hierarchies and many middle management positions have been eliminated. Additionally, be-cause the costs of employee benefits have increased at such a rapid rate, many workplaces are eliminating benefits or requiring workers to pay a much greater share of benefits such as health insurance. The trend to add new benefits to keep employees on the job has also stopped in most workplaces as more and more applicants are applying for positions when they become vacant. These changes have created additional stress for employees at all levels of work organizations, including top-level man-agers, as job security becomes an increasingly valid concern.

Such issues have important implications when addressing employee concerns and the roles social workers and others can play in dealing with them. Because there have been so many changes in the workplace and the nature of work, it is difficult to predict accurately the future needs of employees and their families, how those needs will surface in the workplace, and which strategies are most likely to meet them (see Box 15.1).

Unemployment and Underemployment

Although employed individuals often bring numerous problems to their families, and vice versa, the ramifications of unemployment are far more serious. Layoffs and unemployment are expected to increase as the na-ture of work continues to change. In 1994, twenty four and a half mil-lion workers lost jobs due to plants either closing, moving overseas or abolishing positions (U.S. Bureau of Labor Statistics 1995). An increas-ing number of jobs are being lost due to **outsourcing,** or the contracting out of production of parts of complete products by U.S. companies to plants in countries other than the United States. For example, many major companies operate twin plants (*maquiladoras*) in U.S. and Mexi-can border cities. The major production takes place in the Mexican plants, where labor is relatively inexpensive compared to the costs to hire workers to complete the same tasks in the United States.

Because work not only provides economic support to families, but is a basic definition of an individual's self-worth, increased unemployment is an issue of national concern. Studies show that unemployment and low economic status are associated with poor family cohesion and family deterioration (Rubin, 1994).

Although official unemployment rates have remained at 6 percent to 6.5 percent during the past few years, some employment experts suggest that they have actually increased as much as 25 percent, because the rates do not reflect those individuals who are not actively seeking

BOX 15.1

THE CHANGING WORK PARADIGM

WHAT IT USED TO BE (PRE-1970s)

- The workforce is predominantly white and male—few women and people of color
- Companies are paternalistic, yet don't always act in the best interests of employees
- Companies meet the most basic needs of employees
- Employees have little say in the workings of the organization
- Benefit programs are traditional and limited
- Most employees work for the same organization for their whole work lives. In many instances, generations of families work for the same organization
- Employees do what they are told to get ahead—the company comes first
- Organizations are highly structured with a rigid chain of command
- The only talk about families is to ensure that top executives have one (marriage is assumed to be a virtue)
- Big is definitely better
- The only economy is the U.S. economy

WHAT IT BECAME (1970s AND 1980s)

- The "new breed worker" replaces the "organization man"; quality of worklife becomes more important than simply getting ahead
- Women and people of color enter the workforce in increasing numbers
- Employees begin to demand more say in what happens at work
- The dual wage-earning family is common
- Employee loyalty to the company is no longer unquestioned
- The global economy emerges—companies can no longer be concerned only with what goes on at home
- New "perks" are created to retain highly sought after employees
- Leveraged buyouts become popular
- Average employee tenure drops significantly
- Many companies falter because they do not adapt to the global economy or can not change quickly enough to meet new and different markets

employment. Unemployment rates for African Americans are double those for whites. Underemployment, or persons placed in jobs that are at a lower level than they are qualified for, is also an increasing problem. A recent study found that one-third of Americans reported that they were underemployed in their present jobs (Foster and Schore 1989).

When faced with unemployment or underemployment, many individuals and their families relocate to a supposedly more opportune area. Such areas, however, usually are largely unprepared to address the many needs created by a rapidly expanding population. Housing and other necessities are unavailable or more expensive than anticipated; the availability of work for certain types of workers is inflated or exaggerated; and transportation, utilities, and education are often lacking or underdeveloped. The absence of support from family and friends also plagues those relocating; and social services agencies, overwhelmed by the population influx, are unable to provide resources to meet many employee and family needs.

For employees and their families who remain in unproductive areas, as well as for those who relocate to new areas, stress increases signifi-

- The information age explodes
- Increasingly, companies merge, downsize, or do both to become more competitive
- The service industry grows by leaps and bounds
- Workers with limited skills and little education are increasingly displaced
- Companies start to realize that past success guarantees nothing

WHAT IT IS NOW (1990s)

- Women and people of color constitute more than 50 percent of the workforce, although their presence in executive and management positions is still disproportionate
- Successful organizations are flexible and able to change focus quickly
- Advances in information technology make the global marketplace the only marketplace
- Traditional employee benefits are replaced with a menu of benefits, many of which require significant employee contributions
- Organizations are flatter and leaner

- Even current success guarantees nothing
- Only those organizations that can adapt to constantly changing market conditions are able to survive
- Having satisfied customers is not enough—organizations must provide additional value to their customers to retain them
- Increased use of contract labor and outsourcing displaces many traditional employees
- Strategic planning is redefined
- Outside of legal protections, employee entitlements no longer exist
- There are no job guarantees
- Employees are asked to "give at the office" in new ways
- Faster is better
- Product development cycles decline significantly
- What makes sense today may have no relevance tomorrow

Source: R. J. Ambrosino, *The Changing Work Paradigm* (Austin: University of Texas at Austin, 1995). Reprinted with permission.

cantly. Social services agencies in these areas report significant increases in suicides, family violence, substance abuse, marital problems, juvenile delinquency, and other mental health problems. They also report significant increases in family financial problems and pressures. For example, as a result of increased economic stress to farm families in the Midwest during the mid-1980s and 1990s, rates of spouse abuse and suicide increased significantly, and depression was the most common mental health problem in the rural Midwest (U.S. Congress 1989).

 ## THE CHANGING WORKFORCE: ATTITUDES AND VALUES

Demographic changes in the workforce have had a considerable impact on changing attitudes and values toward work. Although most employees continue to be fairly satisfied with their jobs, there is a growing discontent among certain segments of the labor force over the nature and meaning of work. Employees today are experiencing a new type of worker, described by one policy analyst, Daniel Yankelovich (1979), as the new breed worker. Yankelovich contrasts today's worker with the "organization man" described by Theodore Whyte in the 1950s (1956). (This term would be considered sexist today, but was appropriate at that time since the workforce was primarily male.) Whyte's organization man was one who put the needs of the organization for which he worked above all else. He came to the company intending to remain there for his entire career, worked long hours, willingly traveled and relocated for the company, and viewed his paycheck as his primary reward for his loyalty and hard work.

Today's worker is much different from Whyte's organization man. Concerns about quality of life and a willingness to express such concerns to employers have forced an emphasis on additional incentives beyond the paycheck. An insistence on individual accomplishment and self-fulfillment, priorities given to interests outside of the workplace, and personal recognition on the job suggest that employees expect work to have additional meaning beyond the extrinsic rewards of a paycheck. Not only is the meaning of work changing, but it must be viewed differently for different individuals. A study conducted by Yankelovich for *Working Woman* magazine found that men viewed the meaning of work and satisfaction with their jobs along two dimensions, salary and a say in decisions. Women, however, viewed job satisfaction among six different dimensions, primarily related to relationships with and recognition from co-workers and supervisors (Kagan 1983).

Bureaucratization of the workplace resulted in a lack of clarity regarding the self-identity of individuals and what should be valued most in a person's life: job, as was true for individuals in the past; family; or one's self and one's own needs. Less support from family members and lack of time to develop supportive relationships with others have resulted in a growing number of individuals who maintain a strong identity with the workplace and expect the majority of their needs to be met by their work. One study found that employees were more likely to seek help when dealing with problems, including marital and other family problems, from co-workers than from neighbors or family members (Anderson 1985).

In addition to the increased expectations that the workplace should meet personal needs, a growing number of younger, more educated workers expect high salaries, rapid promotions, and challenging jobs. Because of increased acceptance of alternate life-styles and the large number of families in which more than one individual is employed, Yankelovich and others suggest that for many workers, the traditional work ethic has diminished significantly.

The changes in the types of workers in today's workforce and their attitudes toward work have occurred so rapidly that the workplace, for the most part, has been unable to adjust at a comparable pace. Many workplaces still expect the loyalty of the organization man, to which they were accustomed, and also the willingness of the employee's wife and children to remain at home and out of the realm of the workplace.

◢ IMPLICATIONS FOR EMPLOYEES AND THEIR FAMILIES

Most of the attention relating to changes in the types of individuals now in the workplace has been directed toward the impact on the family rather than on the workplace. The majority of this attention has been focused on two-parent families, although these conflicts are also experienced, perhaps more so, by employees who are single parents. As suggested earlier, when work and family domains begin to overlap, in many instances this overlapping creates conflict. Such conflicts result in lack of time for individuals for themselves and family members; stress caused by balancing work and family schedules and priorities; problems in obtaining adequate child care and other parenting issues; feelings of isolation due to lack of time and energy to develop friends and support systems; and financial difficulties (Kamerman and Hayes 1982; Rubin 1994).

Several studies focusing on the impact of work on family life have stemmed from Wilensky's (1960) suggestion that people experience a **spillover effect,** in which feelings, attitudes, and behaviors from the workplace spill over into leisure life and vice versa. Evans and Bartolome (1980) suggest five possible work-family relationships:

1. Spillover effect, where one domain affects the other in either a positive or negative way—for example, if you really like your job, this will add satisfaction to your family life.

2. Independent, where work and family life exist side by side but are independent from each other, making it possible to be satisfied and successful with your job but not your family, for example.

3. Conflict, where work and family are in conflict with each other and cannot be reconciled. In a conflict relationship, sacrifices are required in one area in order to be satisfied and successful in the other—for example, spending less time at home with family members in order to be successful at your job.

4. Instrumental, where one domain is primarily a means to obtain something for the other—for example, a job is seen only as a way to earn money to maintain a satisfying family life.

5. Compensation, where one domain is a way of making up for what is missing in another—for example, a recently divorced man puts all of his energies into his job, works long hours, and socializes only with co-workers.

In helping both employees and their family members understand how they can better balance work and family life, it is useful for social workers and other helping professionals to help them look at how they view their work-family relationships.

One researcher (Yamatani 1988) surveyed employees at a number of worksites regarding problems that they think affect their job performance (see Table 15.1). While almost 30 percent indicated that frustration

TABLE 15.1	PROBLEMS THAT EMPLOYEES THINK MOST AFFECT JOB PERFORMANCE

Problem	Percentage of Employees
Frustration and stress about the job	27.8%
Problems of family members and other relatives	16.2
Unsafe working conditions	14.0
Employee's personal/family financial problems	6.4
Problems with co-workers	5.3
Employee's personal health problems	4.2
Employee's personal emotional problems	3.9

Source: H. Yamatani, "Client Assessment in an Industrial Setting: A Cross-Sectional Method," *Social Work* 33(1): 34–37, 1988. Copyright 1988, National Association of Social Workers, Inc.

and stress about the job itself affected their performance the most, 16 percent indicated that problems related to relatives and family members, such as substance abuse and marital problems, were their greatest sources of stress.

When examining the impact of work on the individual and family, one additional perspective that deserves attention is the importance of life events. Rapoport and Rapoport (1980) advocate the use of a **life-span model,** in which the meaning of work and family changes as individuals move through childhood, adolescence, youth, adulthood, midlife, and old age. Individuals often are pressured to give full attention to both work and family life at the same period of life—for example, learning and beginning a successful career at the same time that they have recently married and are beginning to have children. Some policy analysts suggest that companies should consider not focusing on promotions and moves up the career ladder for their employees until they are middle-aged and have already dealt with the child-rearing years. The importance of looking at life span can also be seen when focusing on the large number of individuals who make midlife career changes, not because they are necessarily unhappy with their jobs, but because they are dealing with personal developmental issues that are age related.

The majority of attention given to the impact of work on the family has been devoted to working wives and mothers. For all families in which mothers work, the impact on the family, particularly the children, is an issue that has been well researched. Current findings indicate that, taken by itself, a mother's employment outside the home has no negative effects on the child. Factors that may affect children of working mothers include the quality of child care that the child receives while the mother is working; the overall stability of the family itself; the type of employment; the socioeconomic status of the family; and the quality and quantity of time that either parent spends with the child (Bronfenbrenner and Crouter 1982).

Increased Stress

Not surprisingly, the majority of studies focusing on work and family issues find that increased stress on the employed family member and the family itself is the issue most often identified by those individuals studied. Some mental health experts suggest that the tremendous increase in the number of individuals seeking mental health services can be attributed to increased pressures faced by more and more individuals trying to balance the demands of job and family.

Recent studies have also focused on **dual-career families,** which are families that have both spouses pursuing their own careers, particularly in relation to the changes in family roles and responsibilities when both parents work. Although most studies find that both parents in dual-career families experience stress and less time for themselves and family members, it is the wives and mothers who feel these pressures the most. Although in many dual-career families, husbands share more in child-rearing responsibilities, the majority of child-rearing responsibility still falls on the wife. Studies also show that although husbands take on more of the parenting tasks, housekeeping responsibilities fall almost totally on the wives, even among families in which both husbands and wives view themselves as being less traditional in the division of household tasks than other couples. Both men and women from dual-career families list strengths as being additional income, greater opportunities for meaningful communication and growth because both individuals are stimulated by jobs, and more sharing in parenting roles. But women in such families face numerous role conflicts, citing lack of time to accomplish tasks both at home and at work, lack of time for self, lack of time

Quality child care is a concern for all working parents, particularly mothers. Many children are left in unsafe child-care settings or at home alone because parents cannot afford the high cost of care, which is usually more than $300 a month for one child.

for spouse, and lack of time for children as major concerns. Furthermore, some studies find that partners in dual-career families are not having as many children as in the past. When families do have children, childbearing occurs within a shorter span of years so that parents can continue working (Gilbert 1993).

Relocation

Increases in the numbers of dual-career families have also resulted in problems when one spouse has a job opportunity in another geographic location. Which spouse's job should prevail and under what conditions presents conflicts in many marriages when such opportunities arise. These dilemmas have resulted in more employers providing relocation services that include help in finding employment for spouses, as well as an increase in the number of commuter families, or families in which spouses are employed in different locations, often in different parts of the country. Many more workers are also refusing promotions that require relocation.

Financial Problems

Individual and family finances is another area of work-family problems. In many families, both parents are employed outside of the home, but their incomes are below or barely above the poverty level. Financial pressures are especially great for women, people of color, and other workers less likely to be well educated or trained—and, as a result, more likely to be employed in low-paying jobs. Those individuals who are single parents (also most likely to be women and people of color) are especially vulnerable to financial pressures. Increasingly, the majority of poor in the United States are working. In 1993, almost 1.3 million (16.6 percent) of families whose incomes were below the poverty level had at least one family member working full time or more on a year-round basis, while over half of all families below the poverty line had at least one family member who worked during the calendar year (U.S. Bureau of the Census 1995). Because of the low minimum wage, even those persons who work full time at that rate find it difficult to support themselves and their families. A full-time worker earning the minimum wage in 1993 and supporting a household of three persons earned a salary that fell $2,682 below the poverty level (U.S. Bureau of the Census 1995). Advocates for the working poor suggest that continuing to ignore the working poor will result in substantial costs to families as well as to the U.S. economy. Suggested options to aid families include restoring the minimum wage to an adequate level that would lift a family of three out of poverty, expanding allowable income tax credits for working parents, and establishing future security accounts for all children that can be used for education or job training once they reach age eighteen (Shapiro and Greenstein 1987; Lindsey 1994).

Additionally, 25 percent of the U.S. workforce is not covered by employee health insurance. These employees, more likely to be women and people of color, have eight times as many dependents as individuals who are covered by insurance. When these families do have health crises, they are likely to face severe financial problems. Many employers continue to hire workers as temporary or part-time workers so that they will not have to pay part of their health insurance and other benefits. For women employees who become pregnant, maternity leave (without pay) is available only 60 percent of the time. Paid sick leave, taken for granted by many employees, is unavailable to 35 percent of the workforce (U.S. Bureau of the Census 1995).

One of the most important pieces of legislation in regard to work and family issues, the Family and Medical Leave Act, was passed by Congress in 1993 after several previously unsuccessful attempts. (Similar legislation was passed by Congress in 1990 but vetoed by President George Bush.) The act requires employers with more than fifty employees to provide up to twelve weeks of unpaid leave to eligible employees for certain medical or family reasons, such as the birth or adoption of a child or the serious illness of a child, spouse, or parent. The act also specifies that most employees must be able to return to their original jobs or equivalent positions with equivalent pay, benefits, and other conditions of employment (U.S. Department of Labor 1993).

Accidents and Other Occupational Hazards

Accidents and other on-the-job health hazards create additional stresses for employees and their families. Coal miners whose daily contact with coal dust results in black lung disease, workers in chemical plants who contract cancer and miscarry or produce children born with congenital deformities, and construction workers who may be hurt by heavy equipment place themselves and their families in jeopardy. A number of individuals have successfully sued employers for mental anguish that they or their family members experienced as a result of such situations.

The United States continues to have a much higher rate of industrial health and safety accidents than other countries. In 1970 the federal Occupational Safety and Health Act was passed to address this problem. The act sets health and safety standards in industrial workplaces through onsite inspections and citations for violations. The regulatory function is through the Department of Labor, while research and technology are addressed through the National Institute of Occupational Safety and Health (NIOSH), housed within the Department of Health and Human Services. NIOSH also sets standards that relate to hazardous materials. But cutbacks in staff and the fact that anonymous reports from workers are less likely to be investigated than those that are from companies and relate to immediate danger have jeopardized the effect of the act. Approximately 25 deaths each workday, or 6,000 each year, result from industrial accidents. African Americans and Latinos are most likely to be employed in the most dangerous jobs and occupations, and are most at risk to suffer accidental injury or death while on the job. Although increased publicity has been given to occupational hazards such as exposure to asbestos and other dangerous chemicals, efforts to deal effectively with such concerns have been limited at both state and federal levels (Lewis 1989).

Violence in the Workplace

Workplace violence is an increasing problem identified by employers and their employees. Some employees are bringing their family problems to work, or are harassed by others, often family members, while at work. Each year, an average of 750 reported deaths occur in the United States due to actual violence. But this number is underreported. In 1994 the U.S. Justice Department conducted a survey relating to workplace violence. The department reported that nearly one million employees are victims of violent crimes at work each year, and that an estimated 8 percent of rapes, 7 percent of robberies, and 16 percent of assaults occurred while victims were at work. Over 30 percent of the situations involved armed perpetrators; 30 percent of them were armed with handguns. The total number of victimizations cost about half a million employees an average of 3.5 days of missed work per crime and more than $55 million in lost wages (Justice Department 1995).

Sexual Harassment

Sexual harassment is another concern in the workplace, both to employers and their employees. The costs of sexual harassment can be extremely damaging both emotionally and from a cost perspective to employees, and employers are legally responsible to ensure that sexual harassment does not occur. It is difficult to obtain accurate figures about the actual incidence of sexual harassment in the workplace, because half of all people who are harassed never report it. They may fear that they will lose their jobs or experience other retribution, that they will not be taken seriously, or that they have somehow contributed to the harassment. Title VII of the Civil Rights Act of 1964 specifies that discrimination that violates individual rights occurs if

1. Individuals are offered rewards in return for sexual favors or threatened with punishment if they do not provide them

2. A hostile environment is created that interferes with employees' ability to concentrate on their job tasks because of behaviors such as making lewd comments and telling inappropriate sexual jokes, displaying inappropriate art work and other materials, and touching or threatening to touch individuals in inappropriate ways

3. An employee's job or job opportunities are jeopardized because of another person who is responding positively to requests for sexual favors. (Petrocelli and Repa 1992)

Social workers in the workplace often provide employee training regarding what constitutes sexual harassment and how to handle it if it does occur, assessment and conflict resolution if such incidents are reported, and counseling to individuals who are sexually harassed. They also advocate and encourage employee empowerment to ensure that the workplace culture does not support such behavior.

Lack of Dependent Care for Working Parents

Nationally, an estimated 5.2 million children under the age of 14 are without adequate child care while their parents work. Often, infants and toddlers are left sleeping alone at night by working parents. It is not unusual for children ages 4 and 5 to be left at home alone for long periods of time, and children as young as 8 are often left in charge of much younger children. Increased numbers of children are being injured, often fatally, as a result of fire or other accidents while left unsupervised by working parents. In New York recently, five children 5 years old and younger died in a fire; they had been left alone in a locked apartment while their mother worked as a waitress. The same day in Texas, a 12-year-old girl, left in charge of her 10-year-old brother while her parents worked, heard a noise in the front yard and, becoming scared, got out her father's gun. The gun went off accidentally, killing her younger brother. (The noise was being made by the family dog.) Increases in vandalism and other youth-related delinquent acts, as well as increases in teenage pregnancy, are being attributed partly to the lack of supervision provided to adolescents while their parents work. Even when parents leave children in supervised settings, they have concerns about both the costs and quality of care. Over 50 percent of working mothers indicated that they were unable to find satisfactory child care while on the job (Vinet 1995).

Care of elderly parents is another problem increasingly affecting employees, particularly because the over-65 age group is the fastest-growing population in the United States. More than seven million Americans, mostly women, care for dependent adults, usually aging parents. Forty-two percent of these women have full-time jobs. Women caring for dependent adults report health problems, emotional disorders, and problems with absenteeism and tardiness (Pritikin 1995).

New attention has also been given to the increased number of elderly and the need for members of the workforce to care for them. In one recent study, researchers found that 20 percent of workers 30 years of age and older provide some type of care for older persons, usually parents, who are not in institutions. Many middle-aged women are projected to have dual responsibilities for dependent children and elderly parents, a situation described as the "sandwich phenomena" (Anastas, Gibeau, and Larson 1990). The stress to these caregivers is considerable.

Changing Expectations about Balancing Work and Family Life

Changing expectations regarding what is important in life have also had implications for both families and the workplace. Researchers in one recent study found that increasing numbers of individuals are reassessing tradeoffs between work and family life. The investigators found that 50 percent of persons surveyed would reduce their salaries by 25 percent to have more personal or family time. Forty-five percent of persons surveyed indicated that they would turn down a promotion if it seriously jeopardized the amount of time they could spend with their families (Stanush 1990). The term **downshifting** has been used to refer to the voluntary limiting of job demands so employees can devote increased time to their families or to themselves.

Implications for Mental Health of Employees and Families

Escalating divorce rates and numbers of individuals living alone have left the affiliational needs of many individuals largely unmet. Increasingly, employees and their families, lacking a support system and unable to cope with life's pressures, succumb to divorce, family violence, substance abuse, suicide, or other health or emotional problems. Researchers who conducted a study for the IBM Corporation found that 50 percent of individuals seen by the company's medical department had problems that were emotional or psychological in nature (Compucare Corporation 1981). For workers and their families facing such pressures, however, options are often limited. Many individuals work because they have to in order to support their families, often as the sole source of support for those families. For those who earn low wages and cannot rely on other family members to offer emotional support or to meet family needs such as child care, the toll on them and their families can be extensive. Consider again the Hunts, the family described at the beginning of the chapter. Even for those who have more options, such as being able to afford child care or rely on relatives, or who work different hours than other family members, balancing work and family pressures is still difficult.

◤ IMPLICATIONS FOR THE WORKPLACE

The problems that have an impact on the individual employee and his or her family also have a significant effect on the workplace. The United States is currently ranked eighth in productivity among Western countries. Job turnover, absenteeism, and other costs created by employee and family problems are expensive to both the workplace and the consumer, who ultimately is forced to absorb these costs.

Costs of Substance Abuse

Although child care problems have received much attention in relation to the workplace in recent years with the increased numbers of mothers in the workforce, other employee problems are even more costly. Alcoholism cost the United States $142 billion in productivity in 1986, with an additional $80 billion lost because of the misuse of illegal drugs. That same year, Americans spent $140 billion to purchase these substances (Royce 1989). Because of related costs paid out of federal, state, and local government funds, it is estimated that employees who have alcohol problems cost taxpayers $694 per employee each year (Van den Bergh 1995). Forty percent of industrial fatalities and 47 percent of industrial accidents are related to alcohol use, and the average cost of one employee grievance relating to poor job performance due to alcoholism is over $1,500. At General Motors Corporation, absenteeism costs $1 billion each year, and costs related to substance abuse and other mental health problems add hundreds of dollars to the costs of each automobile. In one study, investigators found that consumers pay an additional $237 per automobile because of alcohol-related costs alone (Compucare Corporation 1981). Such costs are not only attributed to the individual with the problem; one study found that individuals from families in which one person was an alcoholic were absent from work ten times more often than persons from families for which alcohol was not known to be a problem (Royce 1989).

Other Problems That Cost Employers

Other health and mental health problems also are expensive, particularly if they are not addressed early. Health care costs one dollar for every ten the United States spends, or $1 billion a day. Mental illness results in $17 billion in lost productivity each year. Eighty-five percent of industrial accidents and 32 percent of worker-related accidents and heart attacks are attributed to employee stress each year (Van den Bergh 1995). A study conducted by the Massachusetts Institute of Technology found that depression, a common but serious emotional illness, cost $23.8 billion in absenteeism and lost productivity, with direct costs for treatment and rehabilitation costing $12.4 billion and lost earnings due to depression-induced suicides costing $7.5 billion (Simple math 1995).

Increased Demands on Employers

Many studies suggest that increased individual and family problems that are emotionally based exact a heavy toll on both the individual and the workplace in relation to health care costs. In 1992, more than $800 billion was allocated to fringe benefits (U.S. Department of Commerce 1993). More than 100 labor unions cover 17.4 percent of the U.S. workforce, and their collective bargaining powers also obtain additional benefits that support workers and their families. The high cost of health care is a major issue for employers. Many are not only increasing employee-paid costs of health care but also reducing the extent of benefits available.

Because more and more workers are looking to the workplace to meet affiliational needs, there are additional problems on the job. Co-workers and supervisors find themselves spending increased amounts of work time listening to employees' problems, ranging from marital disputes to more serious problems such as substance abuse and family violence. A supervisor for a large company who oversees fifteen employees recently noted that in one day she had helped find temporary shelter for a woman employee who had been beaten the previous night by her spouse, listened to another employee whose son was in jail for cocaine abuse and theft and referred him to a counseling center, confronted an employee regarding a job error and learned that he was in the midst of a divorce from a twenty-five-year marriage, and covered for another worker who had to leave early because she had a sick child.

◩ ADDRESSING WORK AND FAMILY PROBLEMS: WHOSE RESPONSIBILITY?

Given the serious costs to workers of employee- and family-related problems, their families, and the workplace, many groups have become involved in developing strategies to address these problems. Social services counselors are much more likely to address factors related to the job when working with individuals and family members than they have in the past. Many communities have developed task forces and programs to provide affordable child care and transportation for employees. A number of public schools have established before- and after-school child care programs, and some schools schedule parent-teacher conferences and other events during evening hours so that most working parents can attend. Social services agencies in some communities have come into the workplace to provide noon-time seminars and other programs relating to topics such as coping with divorce, substance abuse, and parenting.

A growing number of employers have also realized that they have a social responsibility to address such problems. Today, many employers have replaced their personnel departments with human resources departments that have expanded roles, including a more holistic approach to employee needs. Human resources departments oversee personnel, social services, and health and wellness, along with other employee-related programs. Some employers have used social workers as consultants to assist managers in determining how they can better meet the needs of their employees. Using a systems/ecological approach, appropriate interventions can be directed at all levels of the workplace, from the total corporate environment to the individual employee.

Some companies have established **employee assistance programs (EAPs),** which provide counseling and other social services to employees, and often their families, through the company. Others have expanded health coverage to cover treatment for substance abuse, mental health counseling, and dental care. A number of both public and private employers have established flexible working hours for their employees, also called **flextime,** which allows employees to work hours that vary from a typical 8 a.m. to 5 p.m. workday. For example, a worker could work four 10-hour days each week or work a different set of hours from other employees, perhaps 6 a.m. to 3 p.m.

Other employers allow **job sharing,** a system that allows two people to share the same job, which means each person usually works half time. Another alternative for employers is to create permanent part-time positions. Some employers also allow employees to work in their homes. For example, workers with disabilities and workers with children can access employers' computer networks to complete word processing and other tasks without leaving their homes. This practice is sometimes referred to as **flexiplace.**

Still other employers have stress reduction and health promotion programs, including onsite fitness centers where employees and their families can exercise. Some employers also provide onsite child care for employees, or have established other programs that offer child care; several companies have even established special programs that provide care for school-age children during the summer or when the children are sick.

◪ EMPLOYEE ASSISTANCE PROGRAMS

A number of organizations have established formal employee assistance programs (EAPs) to provide counseling to their employees. A survey of EAPs conducted by the American Society for Personnel Administration found that 79 percent of organizations who responded to the survey had EAPs, and of those who did not have them, 55 percent planned to establish them shortly. EAPs are mandated in federal government agencies, including the military, and in most state, county, and city governments as well. A related group of programs known as MAPS (membership assistance programs), under the auspices of labor unions, offer similar social services to union members (Van den Bergh 1995).

Originally, EAPs were established to provide counseling and treatment for employees with alcohol problems; a recovering alcoholic, often one of the company's own employees, usually worked as the program coordinator. Today, a wide variety of EAPs are available. Although many are still primarily alcohol related, others are ''broad-brush'' programs, addressing a wide range of employee problems, including divorce, child-rearing, family violence, and financial problems. Many innovative programs have been developed for employees and their families through EAPs. Kennecott Copper Company's INSIGHT Program operates a twenty-four-hour hotline. Other EAPs provide computerized networks that locate services such as child care. An increasing number of EAPs are offering services relating to the care of elderly parents. One EAP, for example, was able to locate a nursing home in a distant state for an employee's elderly father. EAPs are also called on when workers are relocated or laid off, or when companies close. Social workers employed in EAPs become involved in a wide range of situations involving employees—discrimination, including unfair treatment of people of color, women, new immigrants, and persons with AIDS; the needs of workers with disabilities, the effects of toxic chemicals and pollutants on employees; and the effects of the physical and emotional demands of the workplace on employees.

There are four major types of EAPs (Van den Bergh 1995):

- *Internal* programs, or those provided in-house by professional staff who are employees of the organization

- *External* programs, those provided through referral to an outside contractor that actually provides the services, usually off the workplace site (This model has seen the most growth in recent years.)

- *Consortium* programs, in which several employers pool resources together to provide "group coverage" (This model is less expensive for its members, who can share the costs of operating an EAP with other consortium members, and also may work better for smaller organizations).

- *Association* programs, whereby an occupational association (such as the Association of Airline Pilots) or professional organization (such as state bar associations or NASW) provides EAP services (Advantages of this model are the EAP's sensitivity to the unique aspects of the profession/occupation served and possible reduced stigma because the EAP is not directly connected with the employee's workplace).

Most workplaces that use models other than the internal model have a full- or part-time coordinator (employed by the company) who trains supervisors in how to recognize troubled employees and make referrals and publicizes the program within the company. This coordinator provides the initial screening of employees to ensure that the EAP services are appropriate; however, a referral is then made to a contracting social services agency or trained professional outside of the company that provides the services.

Studies have found that such programs reduce employee absenteeism as well as health care costs, and increase employee productivity. General Motors Corporation found that it saved $3,700 per year for each employee successfully enrolled in its EAP, or a total of $37 million in a single year alone (Compucare Corporation 1981). One company spent $65,000 to establish an EAP and saved $750,000 in sick leave alone. ITT estimates that it has saved $30 million dollars over a ten-year period since establishing its EAP (Royce 1989). Kennecott Copper Company estimated that it saved six dollars for every dollar spent on its EAP. Equitable Life Insurance found that absenteeism of alcoholic employees was cut in half after EAP referral to and treatment by alcohol programs; 3M Company data suggest that 80 percent of employees who used the EAP showed improved attendance, greater productivity, and improved family relations; and Illinois Telephone saved $1.2 million over a nine-year period as a result of its EAP (Van den Bergh 1995). The American Society for Personnel Administrators surveyed 409 employers that had EAPs in 1989; the society found that 98 percent of respondents said the benefits of their EAPs outweighed the costs and 46 percent said that having an EAP had improved their employees' morale (Van den Bergh 1995).

Increasingly, with the rise in health and mental health care costs, EAPs also oversee managed health and mental health care for employees, attempting to reduce inadequate and ineffective services. EAP staff in this role assess employee needs, determine the most appropriate type of care needed, and refer the employee or family member to the most appropriate resource. EAP personnel also often serve as case managers in such situations, ensuring that the services are received and monitoring the case until it is terminated. Employees receive an incentive in reduced co-payments for using these services. This role has raised ethical issues for social workers in some instances if the emphasis is on saving costs for the employer at the expense of providing the most appropriate services for the client.

Another critical issue that EAP workers find themselves confronted with is confidentiality, with increasing numbers of EAPs adopting clear guidelines about the circumstances under which information about employees is given to management. Most programs advocate total confidentiality between the EAP and employees unless a crime has been committed or the employees are dangerous to themselves or others.

◢ DEPENDENT CARE PROGRAMS

Companies are responding to the needs of employees in other ways. Many organizations have helped to establish a variety of child care programs. Over 5,600 employers in the United States offer some type of child care support. Of these, 1,400 work sites have onsite child care programs. Nine hundred of these sites are hospitals and nursing homes, which employ primarily women and need to have a workforce operating around the clock. Such sites often have evening and night-time child care available as well as child care during the day. Onsite child care programs allow parents to bring children to the program on their way to work, to see them during their lunch periods, and to be close by if a child should become sick.

Other companies have worked with communities in establishing child care referral systems, helping employees to locate appropriate child care that best meets individual needs, or they offer flexible spending packages in which employee benefits can be designed for the care of elderly dependents. Some companies provide vouchers for child care, allowing parents to contribute a portion of their employee benefits for child care of their choice. Others provide a variety of after-school and summer child care programs and programs for sick children. Some companies, realizing the amount of money lost every time a child is sick, provide nurses to go to parents' homes and care for children, paying a portion of the cost for this service (Vinet 1995).

While not yet well documented, child care programs appear to be cost-effective to employers. The turnover rate for one company was 1.8 percent for those employees with children in its child care program compared to 6.4 percent for employees who did not enroll children in the program. One company in Houston, Texas, reported saving 3,700 hours in absenteeism in one year after its child care program was established. The company had a waiting list of potential job applicants, whereas a similar company without child care was having difficulty recruiting workers (Center for Social Work Research 1983).

Because so many employers were finding that their employees were having problems with dependent care for both children and the elderly, a number have expanded their efforts to include this population as well. For example, the IBM Corporation served as a catalyst to establish the American Business Collaboration for Quality Dependent Care, joining with ten other corporations to provide funding to improve the quality and availability of dependent care for children and the elderly. The group provided $25.4 million during a two-year period in the early 1990s for training of providers and to give employees priority care in communities where services have been developed (Vinet 1995).

Although a limited number of worksites have special provisions for sick children, most organizations do not allow employees to take personal leave time when children are sick. In 1993, only 21 percent of U.S. companies provided personal leave time when children were sick (U.S. Bureau of Labor Statistics 1995).

Some firms have implemented other programs to increase productivity, including flexible work schedules, health and wellness programs, transportation systems, recreation teams, and employee work groups that work together to improve the workplace and its environment. Co-workers also play an important role in lending support to other employees and their families. Many co-workers are turning to their fellow employees for support during times of crisis. Help with child care and transportation and advice about coping with teenagers or divorce are all types of assistance increasingly provided by co-workers rather than neighbors, friends, or relatives.

In spite of this assistance, the need for affordable, accessible child care for working parents was recently identified as the most critical need for families in the United States. Twenty-nine million children currently need child care, but many parents—particularly those at or near the poverty level—cannot afford the costs of good care. Child care costs are less than ten percent of total expenditures for the average family, but often over one-third of total expenditures for the working poor (Lindsey 1995).

◪ SOCIAL WORK IN THE WORKPLACE

One area in which the profession of social work is expanding is in providing social services in the workplace. This area is known as industrial or **occupational social work.** Many view this specialization in social work as relatively new; however, this is not the case. In fact, it is interesting to note that the profession of social work owes its name to industry. The term *social work,* introduced in the United States in the early 1890s apparently as a direct translation of the German phrase *arbeiten sozial,* was used to refer to housing, canteens, health care, and other resources provided to employees by Krupp munitions plants to support the industrial workforce (Carter 1977). Although in many other countries, industry is the largest field in which social workers practice, in the United States industrial social work developed and was practiced between 1890 and 1920, then was largely dormant until the 1970s.

Historical Developments

The development of welfare and social work programs in industry began with mutual aid societies and volunteer programs established as a result of many of the progressive reform movements during the late 1800s and early 1900s. Positions of "social secretary," "welfare manager," or "welfare secretary" existed in many American industries, including textile mills in the south, Kimberly Clark, and International Harvester. Welfare secretaries had backgrounds primarily in religious or humanitarian work, with little previous experience in either social work or industry. In general, they were responsible for overseeing the physical welfare (safety, health, sanitation, and housing), cultural welfare (recreation, libraries, and education programs), economic welfare (loans, pensions, rehabilitation, hiring, and firing), and personal welfare, which included social work (then called case work) with employees and their families (Carter 1977).

According to a Bureau of Labor Statistics survey, by 1926, 80 percent of the 1,500 largest companies in the United States had at least one type of welfare program and about half had comprehensive programs. Sociologist Teresa Haveren reviewed old records and conducted a historical study of work and family relationships at the Amoskeag Textile Mill in New Hampshire in the late 1800s and early 1900s. The company, like many other industries during that time, provided corporate housing close to the mill for working parents; boarding houses for young single employees; English, sewing, cooking, and gardening classes; nurses who provided instruction in housekeeping, health care, and medical aid and visited the sick and elderly regularly to provide food and assistance; a charity department to provide needy families with clothing, food, and coal and assistance to widows with large families if their husbands died or were injured on the job or were former employees; a hospital ward for employees injured on the job; a dentist for employees' families; a child care program and kindergarten; a children's playground with attendants to supervise the children; a swimming pool and ice skating rink; an Americanization program; an athletic field and showers; lectures, concerts, and fairs; and a Boy Scouts program (Haveren 1982).

Although many companies were generous with assistance, services were denied if an individual refused to work. Thus, the system was designed to encourage loyalty to the organization. Since many industries employed entire families, often in the same work unit, it can also be argued that this system made it less difficult for workers to make the transition from family to factory, with many family members seeing little difference between work life and family life.

During the late 1920s, opposition to these programs came from a number of fronts, including employees themselves. Many employees were immigrants, including women. As they became more acculturated within the United States, they saw such welfare programs as paternalistic. The rise of the labor movement also increased negativism toward corporate welfare programs. Labor leaders considered such programs anti-union, believing that the welfare secretary diffused employee unrest without bringing about changes that would improve working conditions for employees. The emergence of scientific management of the workplace turned the focus to improving efficiency of workers. Later, scientific management and welfare work merged into a new field, personnel management. At the same time, public and private social services agencies became more prevalent, decreasing the need for businesses to offer the many services they had previously. Thus, corporate welfare programs declined.

During World War II, the National Maritime Union and United Seaman's Service operated an extensive industrial social work program, providing assistance to the families of the more than 5,000 union members who had been killed during the war. Because unions feared social workers hired by companies would not be sympathetic to unions, other unions initiated industrial social work programs. Until recently, unions were responsible for the majority of industrial social work programs in the United States (Carter 1977).

Social Workers' Roles

With the decline in manufacturing and other industries and the shift to a service economy, the term *industrial social work* has been replaced by the term *occupational social work*. Historically, occupational social work has served a variety of functions in business and industry. Profit often has been a major motivation of employers who provide social work services, in hopes that these services would increase productivity and morale much as fringe benefits have.

But social workers have affected the workplace in ways other than providing social services to employees and their families. Social workers have also played a role in integrating new groups of inexperienced workers (such as women, people of color, and immigrants) into the work world; in consulting with businesses on how to increase diversity in the workplace and to be sensitive to the needs of diverse groups; in strengthening relationships between the corporate world and the community; and in organizational development through redesign of work to make the workplace more humane for employees.

In addition to expertise in working with troubled individuals and families, social workers also are trained in the art of effective communication and negotiation, skills that lend themselves well to advocating for employee needs or working to improve conditions within a workplace, and increase the understanding between employees and employers.

It seems logical that social workers should become more actively involved in the workplace. Occupational social work lends itself to the provision of services within a natural setting—the majority of adults, after all, are employed. The opportunity for a universal service delivery system that goes beyond services to the poor, the elderly, and the sick also is ideal for the provision of preventive services, an area that is almost negligible from the broader perspective of total services provided.

While individuals with specializations in fields other than social work, such as personnel management and industrial psychology, also are employed in human relations capacities in business, such as in personnel or employee counseling positions, social work as a profession is strengthening its interests and capabilities in the area of industrial social work (see Box 15.2). The two major professional bodies that guide the profession, the National Association of Social Workers and the Council on Social Work Education, have established task forces, developed publications, and held conferences that focus on occupational social work. In some

---

BOX 15.2

THE OCCUPATIONAL SOCIAL WORKER

A job description for an occupational social worker might include the following:

- Counseling and carrying out activities with troubled employees and their families to assist them with their personal problems and to achieve maintenance of their productive performance
- Advising on the use of community services to meet client needs and establishing linkages with such programs
- Training front line personnel to enable them to (1) identify when changes in job performance warrant referral to a social service unit and (2) carry out an appropriate approach to the employee that will result in such referral
- Developing and overseeing the operation of a management information system, which will record service information and provide data for analysis of the unit's program

- Developing a plan for future programmatic direction and staffing of the industrial social work program
- Offering consultation to management decision makers concerning human resource policy
- Helping to initiate health, welfare, recreational, or educational programs for employees
- Advising on corporate giving and on organizational positions in relation to pending social welfare legislation.

Source: S. Akabas and P. Kurzman, "The Industrial Social Welfare Specialist: What's So Special?" In *Work, Workers and Work Organizations: A View from Social Work,* ed. S. Akabas and P. Kurzman, © 1982, pp. 201–202. Reprinted by permission of Prentice-Hall, Englewood Cliffs, N.J.

---

instances, university education programs are interdisciplinary in nature and operate jointly with other departments such as business administration. All programs provide future industrial social workers with knowledge and skill in dealing with substance abuse, marriage and family problems, and other individual and family problems. They also offer courses relevant to working in organizations and the corporate world. To be successful in the workplace, social workers need additional knowledge and skill in business principles, planning and management, marketing, financial management, personnel administration, family counseling, and organizational behavior. Students in occupational social work programs also are placed in field internships in corporations and unions, where they work directly with troubled employees and their families or are involved in administration and planning activities.

Much of the focus of occupational social work to date has been on the client as a worker. Although it is important that social work as a profession recognize the importance of work within the individual's life, the emphasis of occupational social work has been primarily at the individual casework level through employee assistance programs and other forms of one-to-one counseling or information and referral services. The central focus appears to be on the relationships of work to emotional problems. Social workers have also played a role in addressing work-related social policy issues such as the appropriate division between corporate and social welfare sectors in the provision of social services; the relationships between work and family roles for men and women; the impact of affirmative action programs on women, people of color, and individuals with disabilities; and unemployment. But little attention has been given to the role social work might play from an organizational change perspective.

Social Workers and the Changing Workplace in the Decade Ahead

Many workplaces in the 1990s reflect changes that are not new to social workers. An emphasis on empowering employees to take responsibility for initiative and product design and completion, for example, is consistent with the social work focus of empowering clients at all levels of the environment. The use of task groups, rather than a hierarchical structure, to make decisions and complete projects is also not new to social workers. They are skilled at understanding group dynamics, leadership styles, and the use of a systems/ecological perspective in achieving synergy among systems, including groups. The need for occupational social work continues to be supported by legislation relating to the civil rights and equal opportunities of employees, safe work conditions, and the financial and legal protection of at-risk populations through programs such as Workmen's compensation, unemployment insurance, and income support programs (Akabas 1995).

Social workers can play key roles at all levels of the workplace in incorporating these new directions into the workplace culture to ensure that they are effective from both employer and employee perspectives, and that they balance both individual and organizational interests.

Applying a Systems/Ecological Perspective

Because social workers operate from a systems/ecological perspective, focusing on the interaction between the individual and his or her environment, they are well equipped to develop strategies of intervention at various levels of the systems within which the individual functions (see Box 15.3). Consider again, for example, the Hunt family discussed at the beginning of this chapter. Social work intervention could include individual counseling for Bill and Meredith Hunt relating to their respective jobs. But because the problems that the Hunts face are associated with their relationship to each other, a social worker might propose marital counseling for the couple, seeing both of them together. Remember, though, that the Hunt children also were having difficulties in the family. It also might be appropriate for a social worker to provide counseling for the entire Hunt family.

Other individuals within the systems in which the Hunts operate may need to be involved, too. Co-workers and supervisors with whom the Hunts interact may be exacerbating their problems. The oldest son's teacher also might be helpful in offering insight into the boy's problems. A social worker might wish to work with these individuals in addition to the Hunts, helping others with whom they interact to be more supportive

---

BOX 15.3

ASSESSMENT OF PROBLEM(S)

A comprehensive social worker's assessment of a worker's problem(s) should include the following:

I. Worker
   a. Work History
   b. Current Position—Occupation, Hours, Salary, Fringe Benefits
   c. Job Duties and Responsibilities
   d. Adequacy of Job Performance
   e. Degree and Type of Autonomy and Control in Work Role
   f. Relationships with Colleagues, Supervisors, Subordinates
   g. Specific Work Strains and Satisfactions
   h. Career Goals
   i. Self-Concept as a Worker

II. Work Organization
   a. Size, Location, Function, Physical Setting
   b. General Ambiance
   c. Organizational Structure
   d. Opportunities Provided to Worker for Advancement
   e. Expectations Regarding Loyalty, Performance, etc.

III. Interface between Work and Family
   a. Mesh between Worker's Time and Family Time
   b. Adequacy of Income to Meet Personal and Family Needs
   c. Degree to which Work Role and Responsibilities Intrude on Family Life
   d. Degree to which Family Roles and Responsibilities Intrude on Work Life
   e. Degree to which Work Role Meets Expectations of Significant Others, e.g., Spouse, Children, Family of Origin, Friends
   f. Overlap between Worker and Leisure Activities

Source: J. Cohen and B. McGowan, "What Do You Do?" An Inquiry into the Potential of Work-Related Research. In *Work, Workers and Work Organizations: A View from Social Work*, ed. S. Akabas and P. Kurzman. © 1982, pp. 126–27. Reprinted by permission of Prentice-Hall, Englewood Cliffs, N.J.

---

of the Hunt family's needs. There may also be other resources within the community that the social worker might refer the Hunts to, such as a low-cost after-school child care or recreational program for the son; parenting classes; Alcoholics Anonymous; or a family violence program.

The role of a social worker can go beyond the individual and family intervention level. The social worker might realize that there are numerous individuals at the workplace experiencing the same kinds of problems as the Hunts, so he or she might establish support groups for employees with similar concerns and needs. An additional role of the social worker could be to advocate with management for company policies that better support the needs of employees like the Hunts. The social worker might work with others within the workplace to implement child care programs, flexible work hours, and adequate sick leave policies. The social worker might also work with others beyond the workplace in developing state and federal legislation to mandate policies that are more supportive of employees and their families, such as expanding family leave and sick leave policies that allow leave for family-related issues beyond the employee's illness to include all workplaces.

Service Models

The University of Pittsburgh School of Social Work has developed three models of service for occupational social workers that incorporate a variety of roles inherent to the profession of social work. The first model, the employee service model, focuses primarily on the micro level of the systems within which employees and their families function. In this model, social work functions include counseling employees and their families; providing educational programs to employees; referring employees to other agencies; implementing recreational programs; consulting with management regarding individual employee problems; and training supervisors in recognizing and dealing appropriately with employee problems.

The second model, the consumer service model, focuses on intervention at a broader level within the same systems. This model views employees as consumers and assists them in identifying needs and advocating to get those needs met. Social workers work with consumers-employees in assessing their needs; developing strategies to best meet the needs identified; identifying and providing community resources to meet the needs; serving as a liaison between consumer-employee groups and social services agencies; and developing outreach programs to meet employee needs.

The third model, the corporate social responsibility model, focuses on intervention at the exo and macro levels within the various systems in which employees and their families function. Social workers operating within the realm of this model work with the workplace, community, and society in general in developing and strengthening programs that support individual employees and their families. They provide consultation about human resources, policy, and donations to tax-exempt activities within the workplace and to community organizations such as the United Way; analyze relevant legislation and make recommendations for additional legislation; administer health and welfare benefits; conduct research to document needs and evaluate programs and policies; and serve as community developers, providing a link between social service, social policy, and corporate interests (Akabas and Kurzman 1982).

These models often overlap in actuality, with social workers in workplace settings providing tasks that fall within more than one model. The majority of social work activity in the workplace to date has been with the employee service model. It is anticipated that as a growing number of social workers practice in an occupational setting, more of their activity will fall within the other two models.

SUMMARY

A systems/ecological approach to social problems focuses on the interactions between individuals and their environments. Until recently, little attention has been given to the interactions between the individual, the individual's place of employment, and the individual's family. But as more women, both with and without children, enter the workplace, and as rapid social change continues to negatively affect many individuals, the relationship between the workplace and the family can be ignored no longer. Individuals experiencing stresses at the workplace invariably bring their stresses home. Conversely, individuals experiencing stresses at home bring their stresses to the workplace. The costs of employee and family substance abuse, marital problems, parenting problems, and other mental health problems are extensive to both the family and the workplace.

A number of communities and workplaces have developed programs that assist individual employees and their families to better balance work and family pressures. These include employee assistance programs as well as child care, transportation, and health and wellness programs. Studies show that these programs are effective in preventing family and workplace dysfunction. The field of occupational social work is emerging as an area where some impact can be made through intervention in the workplace to improve family functioning and promotion regarding the consequences of change, as well as increasing profitability and productivity for the work organization. It is anticipated that social work as a profession will begin to play a more major role in developing programs within the workplace, as well as advocating for appropriate policies and legislation, that provide increased support to employees and their families.

KEY TERMS

downsizing
dual-career family
employee assistance programs
  (EAPs)
flexiplace
flextime

job sharing
life-span model
occupational social work
outsourcing
spillover effect

DISCUSSION QUESTIONS

1. List four ways that the composition of the workplace has changed over the past thirty years. What effect have these changes had on the workplace?

2. Using a systems/ecological perspective, discuss the relationships between an individual, his or her workplace, and his or her family.

3. Name three types of employee- and family-related problems and describe how these problems affect the workplace.

4. Name three types of work-related problems that an employee might experience. In what ways might these problems affect the employee's family?

5. Describe five types of programs employers have established to address employee and family needs.

6. Describe the three models on which an industrial social work program might be based. List at least three of the roles an industrial social worker employed in a workplace setting might play.

REFERENCES

Akabas, S. 1995. Occupational social work. *Encyclopedia of Social Work,* vol. 2, 1779–86. Washington, D.C.: NASW Press.

Akabas, S., and P. Kurzman. 1982. The industrial welfare specialist: What's so special? In *Work, workers, and work organizations: A view from social work,* ed. S. Akabas and P. Kurzman. Englewood Cliffs, N.J.: Prentice-Hall.

Alexander, K. 1990. Minority women feel race, sexism are blocking the path to management. *Wall Street Journal,* 25 July 1990, p. B1.

Ambrosino, R. J. 1995. *The changing work paradigm.* Austin: University of Texas at Austin.

Anastas, J., J. Gibeau, and P. Larson. 1990. Working families and eldercare: A national perspective in an aging America. *Social Work* 35(5): 405–411.

Anderson, R. 1985. *Employer-based support to employees and their families.* Austin: University of Texas.

Bronfenbrenner, U., and A. Crouter. 1982. Work and family through time and space. In *Families that work: Children in a changing world,* ed. S. Kamerman and C. Hayes. Washington, D.C.: National Academy Press.

Carter, L. 1977. Social work in industry: A history and a viewpoint. *Social Thought* 3: 7–17.

Center for Social Work Research. 1983. *Work and family life issues: A report of a series of corporate forums held with selected work-related organizations in Texas.* Austin: University of Texas Center for Social Work Research.

Cohen, J., and B. McGowan. 1982. "What do you do?" An inquiry into the potential of work-related research. In *Work, workers, and work organizations: A view from social work,* ed. S. Akabas and P. Kurzman. Englewood Cliffs, N.J.: Prentice-Hall.

Compucare Corporation. 1981. *Employee assistance programs: A dollar and sense issue.* Newport Beach, Calif.: Author.

Despite economic upturn, employee job insecurity still high. 1995. *EAP Digest* 15(2): 16.

Evans, P., and F. Bartolome. 1980. The relationship between professional life and personal life. In *Work, family, and the career: New frontiers in theory and research,* ed. C. Derr. New York: Praeger.

Foster, B., and L. Shore. 1989. Job loss and the occupational social worker. *Employee Assistance Quarterly* 5(1): 77–98.

Gibbs, N. 1955. Working harder, getting nowhere. *Time* 166, no. 1 (3 July 1995): 16–21.

Gilbert, L. 1993. *Two careers, one family: The promise of gender equality.* Newbury Park, Calif.: Sage.

Ginsberg, L. 1992. *Social work almanac.* Washington, D.C.: NASW Press.

Haveren, T. 1982. *Family time and industrial time.* Cambridge, England: Cambridge University Press.

Justice department reports on workplace violence. 1995. *EAP Digest* 15(2): 17.

Johnston, W., and A. Packer. 1987. *Workforce 2000: Work and workers for the 21st century.* Indianapolis: Hudson Institute.

Kagan, J. 1983. Survey: Work in the 1980's and 1990's. *Working Woman* (April 1983): 26–28.

Kamerman, S., and C. Hayes. 1982. *Families that work: Children in a changing world.* Washington, D.C.: National Academy Press.

Kanter, R. M. 1977. *Work and family in the United States: A critical review and agenda for research and policy.* New York: Russell Sage Foundation.

Lewis, B. 1989. Social workers' role in promoting occupational health and safety. *Employee Assistance Quarterly* 5(1): 99–118.

Lindsey, D. 1994. *The welfare of children.* New York: Oxford University Press.

Petrocelli, W., and B. Repa. 1992. *Sexual harassment on the job.* Berkeley, Calif.: Nolo Press.

Pritikin, E., and T. Reece. 1995. The not-so-golden years: Eldercare issues at work. *EAP Digest* 15(3): 33–35.

Rapoport, R., and R. Rapoport. 1980. Balancing work, family and leisure: A triple helix model. In *Work, family and career: New frontiers in theory and research,* ed. C. Derr. New York: Praeger.

Royce, J. 1989. *Alcohol problems and alcoholism.* New York: Free Press.

Rubin, L. 1994. *Families on the fault line: America's working class speaks out about the family, the economy, race, and ethnicity.* New York: HarperCollins.

Shapiro, S., and R. Greenstein. 1987. *Making work pay: A new agenda for poverty policies.* Washington, D.C.: Center on Budget and Policy Priorities.

Simple math: Better care leads to better outcomes and lower costs. 1995. *EAP Digest* 15(3): 16.

Stanush, M. 1990. An executive decision: Family life taking top priority. *Austin American Statesman,* 16 September 1990, p. E1, E13.

Strand, V. 1995. Single parents. *Encyclopedia of Social Work,* vol. 3, pp. 2157–63. Washington, D.C.: NASW.

U.S. Bureau of the Census. 1995. *Current population reports.* Washington, D.C.: Author.

———1995. *Statistical abstract of the United States 1995.* Washington, D.C.: U.S. Government Printing Office.

U.S. Bureau of Labor Statistics. 1995. *Current employment statistics.* Washington, D.C.: Author.

U.S. Chamber of Commerce. 1993. *Employee benefits, 1992.* Washington, D.C.: U.S. Chamber of Commerce.

U.S. Congress, House. Select Committee on Children, Youth, and Families. 1989. *Hearing summary: Working families at the margins:*

The uncertain future of America's small towns, 11 April 1989. Washington, D.C.: U.S. House of Representatives.

U.S. Department of Labor. 1993. *Family and medical leave act.* Washington, D.C.: U.S. Government Printing Office.

Van den Bergh, N. 1995. Employee assistance program. *Encyclopedia of Social Work,* vol. 1, pp. 842–49. Washington, D.C.: NASW.

Vinet, M. 1995. Child care services. *Encyclopedia of Social Work,* vol. 1. 367–375. Washington, D.C.: NASW Press.

Whyte, W. 1956. *The organization man.* New York: Doubleday.

Wilensky, H. 1960. Work, careers and social integration. *International Social Science Journal* 7(4): 543–60.

Yamatani, H. 1988. Client assessment in an industrial setting: A cross-sectional method. *Social Work* 33(1): 34–37.

Yankelovich, D. 1979. Work, values, and the new breed. In *Work in America: The decade ahead,* ed. C. Kerr and J. Rosow. New York: Van Nostrand Reinhold.

SUGGESTED FURTHER READINGS

Akabas, S., and P. Kurzman. 1982. *Work, workers, and work organizations: A view from social work.* Englewood Cliffs, N.J.: Prentice-Hall.

Emener, W., and W. Hutchison, eds. 1988. *Employee assistance programs.* Springfield, Ill.: Charles Thomas.

Googins, B., and J. Godfrey. 1987. *Occupational social work.* Englewood Cliffs, N.J.: Prentice-Hall.

Masi, D. 1993. Occupational social work today. *Employee Assistance Quarterly* 5(8): 42–44.

Occupational social work today. 1989. Special Issue. *Employee Assistance Quarterly* 5(1).

Social Work. 1988. 33(1). Entire journal is devoted to workplace issues.

CHAPTER 16

SOCIAL WORK IN RURAL SETTINGS

Melinda Herrara recently lost her husband, Juan, in a farm-related accident. Juan had been the sole source of support for his wife and their 7-year-old son, Ramon. Without Juan's income, Melinda and Ramon were destitute. Melinda had dropped out of school in the ninth grade and had few employable skills.

Juanita Gonzalez, the local social worker for the Department of Human Services, worked with Melinda to secure limited support through the AFDC program, and to procure food stamps to enable the family to meet minimum basic needs. Although Melinda lived in a rural area where resources were limited, she expressed strong views about getting a job and becoming self-sufficient. Ms. Gonzalez contacted the local community college, which, although small, did have a vocational training program. Through the efforts of Ms. Gonzalez, Melinda was able to secure a small grant to attend the college, where she was enrolled in a program to obtain her GED and pursue a Licensed Vocational Nursing certificate. ∎

Today, approximately 27 percent of the nation's population live in rural areas. Although the majority of our citizens reside and work in urban areas, the population of small towns and outlying areas has increased over the past decades. According to Offner, Seekins, and Clark, rural America is a "mix of elderly people, children, miners, timber workers, veterans, service providers, industrial workers, self-employed workers, urban escapees, the persistently poor, federal land managers, people with disabilities, and an array of many others" (1992, 6). Strikingly, only 12 percent of the rural population are directly engaged in agriculture. In addition, as more individuals and families become disenchanted with the high crime rates, fast pace, and overcrowded conditions of cities, it is likely that rural populations will continue to expand.

Rural areas, with their characteristic small towns, farms, and ranches of varying sizes, offer an appreciably different environment and life-style than that found in cities. Although automobiles and airplanes have given many rural residents access to the resources of major cities, isolation and long distances to the cities' resources continue to pose problems for others. On the average, people living in rural areas have more limited resources than do urban residents. For example, it is estimated that over half of America's substandard houses, half of our poor, higher percentages of the unemployed, and the majority of the untreated ill live in rural areas.

In this chapter, we will review some of the more salient characteristics of rural America and identify social welfare and social work resources available in rural communities. ■

◪ RURAL: AN OPERATIONAL DEFINITION

Arriving at a universally agreed upon definition of **rural** is more difficult than you might think. Generally, such definitions are based on population counts (the census) of a specified area rather than upon the behavioral traits and customs of people. For example, the "hillbillies" from Tennessee, Arkansas, and West Virginia who migrated into many northern cities brought with them their customs, values, and traits. Disadvantaged and unsophisticated in the ways of urban life, they had a great deal of difficulty adapting to the demands of urban life. Uneducated and unskilled, they were relegated to poverty and a continual struggle for survival. Although their customs and habits positioned them clearly as rural transplants, once in the urban environment, they were no longer considered rural. Urban dwellers moving into rural areas have experienced similar **culture shock.** The point is that definitions of *urban* or *rural* are not subject to the behavioral attributes of population groups, but to population size. Seemingly, such definitions should constitute a rather simple task, yet it is complex.

The U.S. Census Bureau classifies as rural communities those that are composed of 2,500 or fewer people. This classification has limited utility in that it only enables us to separate those communities statistically identified as rural from those that are not. For example, in terms of access to resources, is a small, isolated rural community of 2,500 in Utah the equivalent of a similarly sized, incorporated, "bedroom" community twenty-five miles from Houston? Probably not.

In addition, millions of Americans live on farms or ranches that are some distance from villages, towns, or cities. In many of these areas, small farms are close together, whereas in others, miles may separate. families from each other. Rural inhabitants often are identified as *rural-farm* or *rural-nonfarm* to further clarify and differentiate the nature of rural residency. Clearly, there are differences and distinctions in the daily living requirements and patterns of the small-town resident and those of the farm dweller.

Farley et al. (1982) have suggested that rural life might be conceptualized as ecological, occupational, and sociocultural. Each conceptual aspect provides a basis for differentiating among rural towns and outlying areas. Many of these characteristics are reflected in the discussions that follow. As you read these discussions, be aware that the life of a small farmer in Georgia may be appreciably different from that of a goat rancher in West Texas.

◪ CHARACTERISTICS OF RURAL POPULATIONS

Data are available that enable us to gain an overview of rural life. Approximately 70 million Americans are living in rural areas, and that number is increasing. Table 16.1 illustrates the age and gender distribution of the rural population in 1988. Many of the areas in which they live

| **TABLE 16.1** | **AGE AND GENDER OF THE RURAL POPULATION, 1988** (In thousands) | | |

Age	Both Genders	Male	Female
All Ages	64,798	32,152	32,646
Under 15	14,935	7,641	7,295
15 to 19	5,131	2,622	2,508
20 to 24	4,097	2,091	2,006
25 to 29	4,869	2,358	2,511
30 to 34	5,431	2,659	2,772
35 to 39	5,196	2,610	2,586
40 to 44	4,525	2,270	2,255
45 to 49	3,802	1,922	1,881
50 to 54	3,145	1,595	1,550
55 to 59	3,047	1,490	1,557
60 to 64	2,976	1,438	1,538
65 to 69	2,693	1,308	1,385
70 to 74	2,087	967	1,120
75 and Over	2,864	1,181	1,683
Median Age:	33.1	32.6	33.6

Source: U.S. Department of Agriculture and U.S. Census Bureau, "Rural and Rural Farm Population: 1988," *Current Population Reports*, ser. P-20, no. 439 (Washington, D.C.: GPO, 1988).

are predominantly agricultural, with crops, poultry, cattle, sheep, or goats as the main sources of livelihood. Inhabitants may live on small acreages and be self-sufficient or work for large commercial farms. Many attempt to do both. Increasingly, major industrial developments are seeking out rural areas to establish plants or factories, thus providing opportunities for employment. Jennings (1990) has further described rural communities as characterized by the following:

- Basic trust
- Basic friendliness
- Isolation
- Resistance to change
- Suspicion toward newcomers or outsiders
- Tendency for children to take on the identity of their parents
- Independence of spirit, yet vulnerable
- Similarity to a family system, especially regarding roles
- Financial and experiential poverty
- Reliance on informal and/or natural helping systems first for assistance
- Concrete thinking and more reserved behaviors
- Traditional values and conservatism
- More holistic, less compartmentalized lives

• Multilevel relationships

The strength and intensity of any (or all) of these characteristics may vary, depending on the organization and density of the population of the rural area as well.

SOCIAL ORGANIZATIONS OF RURAL COMMUNITIES

Unlike major metropolitan areas, rural communities have social networks that are more personalized and informal. Many of the prominent and powerful community leaders are descendants of early settlers, are often large landowners, and are leaders in community affairs. Residents, both affluent and poor, tend to be known by many people in the community. Privacy and anonymity are seldom achieved. Good, as well as bad, news travels through the informal community network with amazing speed. Reputations are routinely established for residents and are changed only with great effort. Newcomers often find themselves in an "out-group" category and, regardless of their interest or endeavor, find it difficult to be accepted fully into the inner circles of community life. Judgments concerning the character, ability, and competency of individuals tend to be based on subjective assessments. The success or failure of community residents usually is considered to be the result of personal effort and motivation. Hence, the poor, unemployed, or downtrodden are viewed as individuals who lack the determination to achieve. Divorce and poverty typically are classified as personal failures, and strong negative sanctions serve as constant reminders that deviation from the norm is accompanied by increasing social distance and exclusion from free and full participation in community life.

On the other hand, responses to people in need are often quick and personal. A death in the family or a farm failure stimulates neighbors to respond with goods and services designed to assist the needy through the crisis situation. Droughts, floods, tornadoes, and other natural disasters create a bond among farmers and ranchers and a unity of purpose with shared concern. People often show reciprocity by sharing labor for the harvesting of crops, assisting others in times of need, and organizing to counteract threats to community life. Often politically conservative, rural communities are characterized by resistance to innovation and skepticism concerning modern technological innovations. City slickers are viewed with disdain and are not to be trusted until proven worthy of trust. They are considered to be uninformed as to the needs of rural residents. Honesty and strong character are valued as desirable traits.

The action hub of rural communities centers around the church, the local bank, the county extension office, small businesses, the feed store, and the local school system. As a consequence, the local banker, ministers, the county agent, store owners, and school administrators usually hold powerful influence over community life. County government is typically relegated to the county judge and county commissioners. The sheriff's office handles law enforcement, although many small towns also have a police force. Violations of the law are considered to be a personal offense against the community, and mitigating circumstances are usually downplayed or viewed as irrelevant. The social organization of rural communities is as varied as the locations in which they occur. Although there are common threads of roles and relationships that knit the community together in any setting, each locale has its own character.

SUPPORT SERVICES IN THE RURAL COMMUNITY

Many of the **support services** that urban residents take for granted are often scarce or nonexistent in rural communities. It is not uncommon to find an absence of doctors, nurses, social workers, dentists, or attorneys in small rural towns. Adequately staffed hospitals with up-to-date equipment are expensive to develop and maintain, and small communities lack the resources to finance them. As a consequence, many health-related problems go unattended, or people rely on traditional cures or folk medicine. Resources for the treatment of mental illness are particularly lacking. But individuals exhibiting ''peculiar'' behavior often find acceptance in rural areas, and their families may experience considerable understanding and social support from neighbors. Social work and social services are distributed sparsely in rural areas, often because of the community's mores or limited financial support capabilities.

As noted earlier, the church is a significant institution in rural life. Congregations are quick to respond to those in need and set the pace for community action in time of crisis. The church also is the center for community activities, sponsoring various social get-togethers and recreational opportunities. Religion typically plays a vital role in setting the moral tone and in meeting the spiritual needs of rural residents. Ministers are viewed not only as spiritual advisors but also as community leaders.

In agricultural areas, the county extension office, funded by the **U.S. Department of Agriculture,** provides many services valued by the farm community to assist rural areas, and the county liaison office provides a variety of community and family services. Technical assistance is made available for crop planting and harvesting, ranch management, disease control, care of livestock, food preparation, home canning, and other activities related to farm, ranch, and home management. Informally, the **county agent** often becomes aware of personal problems and serves as counselor, case manager, and resource finder. The county agent also often functions as an advocate or broker (with the local banker or other lending agencies) for farmers experiencing financial disaster.

Recreational activities are often limited in rural areas. The absence of a local movie house, skating rink, park, library, and other outlets for children and teenagers severely restricts opportunities for leisure-time activities. Many small communities literally ''roll up the sidewalks'' at dark. As a consequence, the local school often is a prominent source for recreational get-togethers and sponsors dances and holiday programs.

Athletic events are usually well attended and serve as the central focus for young people and adults to meet and socialize. The school, along with the church, is among the primary institutions for social organization in the rural community.

The importance of **natural helping networks,** many of which have been mentioned in the preceding paragraphs, should not be minimized in **rural social work.** Historically, those networks of friends, relatives, congregations, clubs, civic groups, and related entities have constituted the "backbone" of assistance to those in need. The rural culture of values and mores that gave rise to assisting each other in times of crisis and need to a large extent remains intact today—particularly in the more isolated areas. Social service workers who understand this phenomenon and are skillful at identifying relevant natural groups often find that their efforts to provide assistance are abetted by incorporating natural helping networks into the helping process.

◢ SOCIAL PROBLEMS IN RURAL AREAS

The romantic view that rural areas are peaceful, serene, and devoid of the types of problems found in large cities and metropolitan areas fails to portray the reality of rural life. Unfortunately, rural areas are not devoid of social problems, and the impact of those problems is often far greater on rural residents than those living in cities because of the distance or absence of support services. In the following paragraphs, we examine a few of the more prominent problems.

Mental Health in Rural Areas

Although mental health problems have always existed in rural environments, considerable concern has been expressed over what appears to be an increase in dysfunctional mental health problems since the 1980s. J. Dennis Murray (1990), president of the National Association of Rural Mental Health (NARMH), has pointed out that (1) the prevalence of mental illness in rural America at least equals, if not exceeds, that in cities; and (2) rural areas have higher rates of emotional disorder (especially depression). Murray has expressed concern over the limited resources that are available to address these problem areas. It is also commonly known that the suicide rate in rural areas is similar to that found in cities.

In addition to these more severe and traumatic problems, the psychological and emotional anguish associated with marital discord and parent-child conflicts has intensified as a result of the frustration and insecurity related to the unsettled farm economy. Child abuse, for example, once thought to be a primarily urban problem, is also found in rural areas in ever-increasing numbers. Many view such problems as a reflection of the ecological instability of rural life as it exists today. The abuse of alcohol and other drugs, often viewed as a symptom of economic and social unrest, has also become a more significant problem in rural areas.

The availability of mental health resources to meet the needs of the rural constituency varies with population density, but it is generally considered woefully inadequate. Some reasons for the lack of service availability and the limited use of available resources are described in the *Rural Health Reporter* ("Mental Health Services" 1989) as follows:

- Artificially configured service areas
- Very large service areas
- Stigma and the lack of privacy
- Staff shortages
- Inadequate facilities
- Absence of support services
- Few treatment alternatives

In addition to these problems, inadequate financial resources and community resistance present barriers that must be overcome if individuals and families in need of mental health services are to receive them. As discussed later in this chapter, resources necessary to assist rural families are very limited.

Health Care Problems

Problems associated with health care are also of concern to rural Americans. Health indicators, for example, reflect that infant mortality and chronic disease rates are higher in rural areas than in urban ones. It is generally concluded that the rural aged suffer from chronic illness and poor health in far greater numbers than their urban counterparts. Resources such as rural hospitals are being curtailed with increasing frequency, leaving the rural residents with little access to health care treatment centers that are nearby. This results in either postponing necessary care or traveling great distances in order to secure it—often beyond the means of the patients or their families to manage.

Although most rural areas have emergency medical services (EMS), these services are not prepared to handle life-threatening diseases or severe traumatic injuries. In addition, the recruitment of doctors, nurses, and other health care professionals for practice in rural areas has been relatively unsuccessful. For instance, as of 1988 one Texas county consisting of over 960 square miles with a rural population of over 6,000 had only one medical doctor, with the closest hospital forty miles away. Solutions to rural health problems are difficult to achieve, but the health needs of rural residents must become a priority for policymakers. The **1989 Omnibus Health Care Rescue Act (H.B. 18)** was designed to provide some relief in the form of additional health care resources, although even with its implementation, major gaps in service continue to exist. Some of the more recent health care concerns such as AIDS create even more demand on rural health resources. A California study reported "409 cases of AIDS in the rural areas, and 588 cases in eleven cities," thus dispelling any myths that AIDS is a manifestly urban phenomenon (Wooten 1989). The demands on rural health providers will continue to escalate while resources to meet the needs are limited.

The shortage of medical doctors and medical specialists also imposes limited choices and available resources from which to select treatment options for diseases and illness in many rural areas. Patients requiring kidney dialysis or other complicated health problems often must travel long distances for treatment or, in some cases, move to a location where treatment facilities are easily accessed. Furthermore, turnover rates among medical practitioners tend to be higher in rural areas and attracting and retaining qualified medical personnel poses no small problem (Winslow 1990).

In recent years, one innovative approach to improving the quality of care for rural residents is the product of our high-tech society. Through the vehicle of **telecommunications,** rural practitioners have immediate access to large medical centers where consultation is available for both diagnostic and treatment regimens. "Telemedicine" has rapidly expanded throughout rural areas of the United States and has the capacity to enhance the quality of care for those clients who lack the capacity to receive care in a major medical center.

Poverty

Lower incomes and erratic employment opportunities contribute to higher rates of poverty and disease in rural areas. Among the rural population, which makes up slightly more than 26 percent of the total U.S. population, the poverty level is slightly higher than 38 percent—a percentage that has increased over the past decade (Watkins and Watkins 1984). Gore (1995) points out that poverty rates are 21 percent higher than those found in urban areas, while income is 27 percent lower for rural residents than that of their urban counterparts. Numerically, whites "constitute a majority of the rural poor, but persons of color are overrepresented: about 41% of all rural Blacks and 26% of all rural Hispanics live in poverty" (Uhr and Evanson 1984, 5). The rural poor tend to work primarily at menial jobs; however, their ability to achieve higher-paying jobs is affected by the fact that they are less well educated. The income-earning capacity of the rural poor is also affected by seasonal employment, illness, and injury (Morrissey 1985).

The majority of the rural poor are engaged in crop harvesting, which is often unpredictable, pays poor wages, and often requires that families move from place to place to secure employment. Although many of these families no longer travel great distances to harvest crops, they are generally referred to as migrant workers.

Other types of employment such as working in a feed store, as a nurse's aide, clerking at a hardware or department store, or similar types of jobs generally pay only minimum or near minimum wages—hardly sufficient income to enable one to meet family financial needs, as the wages are often at, or slightly above, the poverty level. Career mobility is severely limited, and it is common to find workers who, with twenty or thirty years of experience, continue to earn only a minimum wage.

Poverty is found frequently in rural areas. Because resources are sparse in rural areas, social workers must often provide most services themselves rather than making referrals to other resources.

As mentioned earlier, the children of these workers, like their parents, receive less education than their counterparts who live in urban areas. Disease rates and higher infant mortality rates reflect the substandard conditions under which the majority live. Small-town school systems, already strained for financial resources, are not diligent in enforcing mandatory school attendance laws. As a result, many children are not encouraged to pursue an education and, instead, work alongside their parents to help the family make enough income to survive. Consequently, a vicious cycle is set in motion, perpetuating intergenerational patterns of farm laborers who are poor and lack the necessary resources to break out of poverty.

Rural communities are also more segregated than urban areas. Morrison (1976) reports that racial segregation, limited political participation, and impoverishment continue to characterize the plight of people of color in rural communities. Attempts to organize farm labor and implement civil rights legislation have met with only limited success due, primarily, to the resistance of large landowners and commercial farmers who seek to maintain the status quo and exert sufficient power to assure that reform does not occur. In states that border Mexico, such as Texas, New Mexico, Arizona, and California, the many undocumented persons are often viewed negatively, because they are seen as compounding problems in the farm labor market through their willingness to work for lower wages. However, experience has shown that they do jobs that otherwise go unfilled or that otherwise would not be filled. Since most undocumented persons are concerned with being detected by federal immigration officials (and returned to Mexico), they are vulnerable to exploitation by landowners who seek cheap labor. The recent decline in the value of the peso has further exacerbated the problem and prompted large numbers of undocumented persons to cross the border to seek work and better living conditions.

Poor white farm workers experience many of the same problems. Typically less educated than urban whites, they are viewed stereotypically as people with less incentive and motivation to succeed. Limited resources and skill levels keep them on the farm. Illiteracy rates are higher and poverty more pervasive among rural whites than urban whites. When rural whites do migrate to cities, they are relegated to low-paying jobs and often experience considerable difficulty in becoming assimilated into the urban environment.

Migrant workers are some of America's most poor and vulnerable people. Often the most recent immigrants move from rural area to rural area, usually with their families, and face substandard living conditions that jeopardize their physical and mental health and opportunities for education.

Perhaps the conditions of the poor are best described in an article by Colby, who cites an anonymous poor rural resident:

> Poverty is dirt. You say in your clean clothes coming from a clean house, "Anybody can be clean." Let me explain housekeeping with no money. For breakfast I give my children grits with oleo, or cornbread with no eggs or oleo. . . What dishes there are, I wash in cold water with no soap. . . . Look at my hands, so cracked and red. . . . Why not hot water? Hot water is a luxury. Fuel costs money. . . . Poverty is . . . remembering quitting school in junior high because "nice" children had been so cruel about my clothes and my smell. . . . Poverty is a chisel that chips on honor until honor is worn away. (1987, 9–10)

The problems of the rural poor are compounded by the lack of community support services—public water and sewage, fire and police protection, transportation, employment opportunities, and related services (Bedics 1987).

The Rural Family

The notion that rural families experience a high degree of harmony, are problem free, and enjoy high levels of life satisfaction is not necessarily borne out by fact. This idyllic view, while desirable, is an illusion that may serve to filter out the reality of existing conditions. Just as in urban areas, negatives related to strained relationships, alcoholism, substance abuse, divorce, child abuse and neglect, sexual exploitation, and a myriad of related problems are not uncommon in rural areas. Certainly the rural environment has much to offer its residents, and the majority of them find contentment and satisfaction within the context of family solidarity. Unlike urban families, however, for rural families when problems do emerge, finding solutions may become more problematic. Many rural children with special problems such as physical, mental, or learning disabilities often find that needed support programs are lacking. Marital discord and related interpersonal relationship issues may go unattended. Teenage pregnancy has become more prevalent, as have single-parent families. Among the poorest (although not limited to them), early marriage, coupled with limited education, serves to lock younger couples into a life with low wages and insurmountable barriers to career mobility.

Even where limited support services are available, rural families tend to be reticent about using them. For example, one small Southwest town of 3,500 people seldom used a mental health service except for court-ordered substance abuse cases. Careful community analysis reflected strong value ties to self-help and self-management of problems. Anonymity was also treasured and served to deter residents from using available mental health assistance. Only after an innovative plan was implemented in which a social worker was housed in the local medical clinic did matters change. Prospective clients first visited the medical center, where they were referred by the doctor to the social worker when mental health or family-related problems were detected. Within a relatively short period after the plan was implemented, the social worker had a full caseload including marital conflict problems, spousal

alcoholism, family violence, depression, and related dysfunctional behaviors (Shuttlesworth 1993).

This brief discussion suggests that regardless of the environment in
which human beings live, problems can and do emerge. How these
problems are managed, however, is a function of values, skills, community support systems, and opportunity structures for finding satisfactory solutions.

◪ SOCIAL WELFARE IN RURAL COMMUNITIES

There are many more small communities and towns in the United States
than cities or major metropolitan areas. These communities vary in size
and in their proximity to major metropolitan areas. For example, Tilden,
Texas, a county-seat town of approximately 350 residents, is situated in
a county that covers approximately 1,400 square miles. It is the largest
town in the county. What type of organized social welfare programs
would one find in this community? What is needed? To what extent
could the community support social welfare services?

You should be wary about generalizations concerning the nature and
extent of organized social welfare programs in small towns and rural
areas, because they vary greatly in size, nature, and ability to finance
needed services. Many rural areas have very few services, and those
available tend to be basic ones. Typically, public welfare services, mental
health and developmental disabilities outreach centers, and public
health services are found in rural areas, although they usually are minimally staffed, offer only limited assistance, and often may be reached
only by a drive of several hundred miles. It is not unusual for counties
to offer a limited welfare assistance program and for county administrative officials (usually the county judge) to administer benefits, along
with their other duties. A few rural communities have Community Action Agencies (a residual of the War on Poverty programs), although
attempts to organize rural areas, in general, have been unsuccessful
(Morrison 1976). Senior citizens' luncheon programs may be provided
by a branch of an areawide agency on aging. Employment agencies,
family planning services, and family counseling agencies and related
services are not typically found in rural areas. Ginsberg suggests some
innovative changes that would increase the service capacity to meet the
needs of rural populations:

1. The public, basic services must often expand their activities to
   include functions that they might not carry in cities. For example, a
   public welfare office might be charged with much more responsibility
   for family counseling, community development, and social welfare
   planning simply because it exists, is staffed with knowledgeable
   people, and needs to help meet problems that occur, despite the
   absence of agencies. Similarly, a community mental health program
   may be required to carry some youth services activities that its urban
   counterparts would leave to other agencies.

2. Many activities are voluntary and depend, therefore, on the good
   will and interest of their supporters rather than upon full-time

professional staff. This is particularly true of social welfare planning efforts, which are often the result of social welfare professionals working together without additional compensation to create and sustain a structure for coordination and planning. Some direct service and community development activities are conducted in a similar manner.

3. Although formal structures may not exist, many informal services are offered in rural communities. In fact, it is the nature of communities, both rural and metropolitan, to develop services for overcoming human problems. For example, the functions carried by Travelers' Aid agencies in large cities may be performed in rural communities by the police or the sheriff's office. A single individual may carry out a program serving children. Churches may assume responsibility for everything from food baskets to family counseling. It is important for social workers in all communities to understand the nature of the service delivery system. In rural America that structure may be hard to identify because of its informal nature.

4. Some formal agencies in rural areas may carry expanded functions. Youth-serving programs such as 4-H, the Boy Scouts, Girl Scouts, and Campfire Girls may be the only resource for activities that in a larger area would be handled by the YMCA, YWCA, and other programs.

5. The importance of individuals and families in serving social welfare needs should not be overlooked. As has already been suggested, one public spirited woman may function almost as effectively as an agency or office. Knowing about such people and gaining their assistance is crucial for the rural worker.

6. Perhaps most important is the fact that some formal organizations exist in rural areas that are important but different from those one finds in urban settings. The best example is probably the cooperative extension services, which are sponsored by each state (along with Department of Agriculture standards and funds), usually under the supervision of state land-grant universities. The traditional function of such programs is to provide consultation on agricultural activities to farmers and ranchers as well as homemaking information to rural women. However, they have expanded their functions dramatically, with many cooperative extension programs now heavily committed to community improvement and development programs in areas as diverse as housing, drug abuse treatment, and social welfare planning. Working with such organizations, which are most prominent in rural areas, is essential for the rural worker. (1976, 7–8)

As suggested earlier, public social services are generally extended to rural areas through the auspices of state agencies. For example, state mental health programs generally have satellite offices in rural areas that are implemented through regional offices, as do state departments of human services which offer public assistance programs. Regional Education Service Centers provide resource assistance for rural schools. Ironically, "per capita spending for rural human services programs is substantially lower (than in urban areas) despite the fact that rural areas have a significantly larger proportion of poor people" (Offner, Seekins and Clark 1992, 6; Cordes 1989).

In general, however, organized social welfare services in rural areas are not as well developed, well organized, or efficiently staffed as those that serve urban populations. Additional resources must be developed in rural areas if services equivalent to those in urban areas are to exist. In the past decade, efforts have been made to update and improve rural social services. Projects such as the Great Plains Staff Training and Development for Rural Mental Health in Nebraska, the information and advocacy efforts of the NARMH, and the caucus of national rural social workers and rural human service workers are all active in promoting higher levels and quality of service in rural areas.

◪ SOCIAL WORK IN RURAL SETTINGS

The practice of social work in rural communities is both similar and different from that practiced in urban areas. The core of knowledge, methods, and skills of social work practice undergirds practice in both environments. The nature of rural settings, the problems experienced, discussed earlier, and the lack of resources converge to confront the social worker with a unique set of challenges. Creativity and the ability to innovate and influence community members to mobilize in meeting needs are crucial skills for successful practice in rural settings. Bruxton states:

> No other environment compares with rural practice in carrying out the dictum of the "total individual" in the "total environment." The rural social worker by her- or himself must often provide the rural dweller with services, support, and hope while simultaneously helping to change the environment in order to provide better transportation, increased medical care, and a more responsive community. (1976, 32)

Unlike urban social workers, the worker in a rural area may feel frustrated by the absence of fellow professionals and a social service network. Opportunities for consultation and feedback are limited, so decision making is often difficult and problematic.

Social workers who both live and practice in rural areas find that they are seen as neighbors as well as professional practitioners. Almost everyone in the community knows who they are, and they may be called on at home as well as the office to provide a wide range of services. Their service constituency may consist of children, adults, the mentally ill, the incarcerated, the bedridden, the distressed, and the abandoned (Bruxton 1976). At any one time, the worker may be assisting a family in securing a nursing home placement for an older parent, securing resources for a child with a disability, counseling with a pregnant teenager and her family, collaborating with local ministers in developing leisure-time activities for youth, assisting school personnel in developing management techniques for a hyperactive child, or working with the court in securing rehabilitation resources for a delinquent child. These varied demands require that the social worker be flexible, have good communication skills, engage both private and public resources, and have a basic understanding of community values and practices.

As Fenby (1978) suggests, practicing social work in a rural setting subjects the social worker to a life in a "gold-fish bowl." Everyone tends to know the social worker both professionally and personally. The private life of the social worker is closely scrutinized. Since social workers, like other community people, have problems, the way they are managed becomes a matter of community concern. Like ministers, their work is expected to meet high personal and moral standards, and any deviation may lower community esteem. In rural communities, the ability to separate personal life from professional competence is difficult. Often, the credibility of the social worker is at stake should personal problems go unresolved.

Maintaining client confidentiality is difficult. Neighbors may become clients. Community residents typically know when problems are being experienced and when professional assistance has been sought. A casual encounter at the grocery store may prompt a resident to inquire as to how a client is progressing. As Fenby has indicated:

> At times a client will be open about his or her knowledge. "I hear you had oil burner problems this morning and Art sent his truck out." At times there is a subtle change in the therapy hour, and the therapist cannot discount the fact that information from the "outside" is affecting the interaction "inside." For example, a client who had been working well in therapy became evasive and distant, although nothing discernible had caused the change. Probing uncovered that the woman had discovered that my husband was on a yearly contract at the college, and had surmised that therefore I would not be staying in the area. She thought that therapy would end in failure, uncompleted. In a small world it is essential to be aware of contamination from outside information in the process of therapy. (1978, 162)

Social workers who have periodic assignments in the rural area but do not reside there encounter other problems. Typically, they are viewed as outsiders. In some instances, they have not had the opportunity to become aware of community priorities and values. Often, they are viewed as having little vested interest in the community and, as a result, respond to special client problems out of context. Community resistance may become an additional barrier to problem solving. Sensitivity to the importance of interpersonal relationships with community leaders is essential in gaining support for change efforts.

An old social work axiom suggests that "change comes slow." While this premise is open to debate, it is valid in rural social work practice. Timetables and the pace of life tend to be slower. Urgency is offset by practicality and patience. Waiting matters out may be given more credence than intervention. Social workers must learn to stifle their frustration and impatience, yet retain their persistent efforts in the helping process. As the credibility and competence of the worker become more established, community resistance will turn into support, and the contribution made to the community as a problem solver will become enhanced.

By now you should be aware of some of the more salient differences between social work practice in rural areas as compared with urban areas. The models of intervention used in urban areas are generally not effectively transportable to rural areas due to the nature, culture, diversity, and resource limitations of rural areas. Urban areas—due to their characteristic population density, opportunity structures, and re-source bases—serve to challenge social planners in a manner quite different from the models needed for effective application in rural environments.

◢ RURAL SOCIAL WORK AS GENERALIST PRACTICE

By now it should be apparent that the variety and diversity of the tasks inherent in rural social work practice can best be accomplished by the generalist practitioner. Social workers in rural communities are called on to work with individuals, families, and groups, and in community organization. Administrative and management skills are essential in rendering needed services (see Box 16.1). The abilities to define problems operationally, collect and analyze data, and translate findings into practical solutions are requisites for enriched practice. The rural practitioner is a multimethod worker who appropriately facilitates in the problem-solving process. Knowledge of resources, resource development, methods of linking clients with resources, and case management is required of the rural social worker. We discuss other essential requirements for generalist social work practice in Chapter 2.

◢ THE BACCALAUREATE SOCIAL WORKER AND RURAL SOCIAL WORK PRACTICE

Social work in rural communities is both challenging and rewarding. Self-reliance and the ability to work apart from social work support systems are attributes that rural social workers must have in order to function effectively. Many undergraduate social work programs are located in small cities or large towns adjacent to rural areas and specialize in rural social work practice. Field placements typically utilize rural agencies to familiarize students with skills essential for practice in those settings.

The baccalaureate social worker's generalist practice perspective will prove invaluable in working with rural populations. The opportunity to engage existing formal and informal organizations in extending or developing resources to meet community needs is a continuing challenge the BSW worker can address competently. The worker also will find that individuals and families in rural areas often have problems and need assistance in problem solving. The knowledge and expertise of the worker in problem identification, outreach, linking of target systems with resources, resource development, education, and problem solving help enrich the lives of rural inhabitants as well as strengthen community support systems. The abilities to understand community value systems and to experiment with innovative techniques in working with community residents are essential assets for productive practice.

BOX 16.1

SOME CHARACTERISTICS OF EFFECTIVE RURAL SOCIAL WORKERS

1. They are especially skillful in working with a variety of helping persons who are not social workers or who may not be related to the profession of social work, as well as with peers and colleagues.

2. They are able to carry out careful study, analysis, and other methods of inquiry in order to understand the community in which they find themselves.

3. They utilize their knowledge of the customs, traditions, heritage and contemporary culture of the rural people with whom they are working to provide services to the people with special awareness and sensitivity.

4. They are able to identify and mobilize a broad range of resources which are applicable to problem resolution in rural areas. These include existing and potential resources on the local, state, regional and federal levels.

5. They are able to assist communities in developing new resources or ways in which already existing resources may be better or more fully utilized to benefit the rural community.

6. They are able to identify with and practice in accordance with the values of the profession and grow in their ability and effectiveness as professional social workers in situations and settings where they may be the only professional social worker.

7. They are able to identify and analyze the strengths and/or gaps and shortcomings in governmental and nongovernmental social policies as they affect the needs of people in rural areas.

8. They accept their professional responsibility to develop appropriate measures to promote more responsiveness to the needs of people in rural areas from governmental and nongovernmental organizations.

9. They are able to help identify and create new and different helping roles in order to respond to the needs and problems of rural communities.

10. They initiate and provide technical assistance to rural governing bodies and other organized groups in rural communities.

11. They are able to practice as generalists, carrying out a wide range of roles, to solve a wide range of problems of individuals and groups as well as of the larger community.

12. They are able to communicate and interact appropriately with people in the rural community, and adapt their personal life-style to the professional tasks to be done.

13. They are able to evaluate their own professional performance.

14. They are able to work within an agency or organization and plan for and initiate change in agency policy and practice when such change is indicated.

15. On the basis of continuous careful observation, they contribute knowledge about effective practice in rural areas.

Source: Statement on "Educational Assumptions for Rural Social Work" by Southern Regional Education Board, Manpower Education and Training Project Rural Task Force, Atlanta, Georgia.

Until recently, social workers have not been inclined to engage in rural social work practice. Fortunately, this attitude is changing. Job opportunities in rural communities are increasing, and the potential for a satisfying and rewarding career in rural social work practice is greater now than ever before.

SUMMARY

Rural environments are both like and unlike urban ones. In this chapter we have identified characteristics that tend to differentiate between rural and urban areas in social organization, life-styles, informal and formal helping networks, and the types of problems that are more likely to be experienced by rural residents. We also reviewed the unique issues related to social welfare delivery systems as they related to diversity and availability in meeting human need. Of particular importance, we examined the role of natural helping networks within the context of their viability as a resource in problem solving. We identified the methods and functions of social work practice in terms of the varied demands placed on the rural social worker, highlighting the relevance of generalist practice to addressing rural problems along with the ideal "fit" for the BSW. Job opportunities are increasing, and the challenges of a successful social work career in providing needed services for rural communities are attracting social workers in greater numbers into rural communities.

KEY TERMS

county agent

culture shock

natural helping networks

rural

rural social work

support services

telecommunications

U.S. Department of Agriculture

1989 Omnibus Health Care
  Rescue Act (H.B. 18)

DISCUSSION QUESTIONS

1. Identify some of the issues involved in defining rural populations. What are the implications of these definitions?

2. What does the concept of "natural helping network" imply? Describe some of the natural helping networks in rural areas.

3. What types of problems are likely to be found in rural areas? How are those problems addressed?

4. Identify and contrast the differences between social work practice in urban vs. rural settings. How are they alike? Different?

5. Why are formal welfare programs less available in rural areas? What are some of the problems in accessing them?

6. What are some of the special skills needed by the rural social worker? Why do generalist social work methods appear to be more compatible with rural practice?

REFERENCES

Bedics, Bonnie. 1987. The history and context of rural poverty. *Human Services in the Rural Environment* 11(1): 12–14.

Bruxton, Edward B. 1976. Delivering social services in rural areas. In *Social work in rural communities: A book of readings,* ed. Leon H. Ginsberg, 29–38. New York: Council on Social Work Education.

Colby, Ira. 1987. The bottom line: a personal account of poverty. (Anonymous author). *Human Services in the Rural Environment.* 11:1, 9–11.

Cordes, S. M. 1989. The changing rural environment and the relationship between health services and rural development. *Health Services Research* 23(6): 757–84.

Farley, O. William, Kenneth A. Griffiths, Rex Skidmore, and Milton G. Thackery. 1982. *Rural social work practice.* New York: Free Press.

Fenby, Barbara L. 1978. Social work in a rural setting. *Social Work* 23(2): 162–63.

Ginsberg, Leon H. 1976. An overview of social work education for rural areas. In *Social work in rural communities: A book of readings,* ed. Leon H. Ginsberg, 6–8. New York: Council on Social Work Education.

Gore, A. 1995. Issues in Rural Life. Presentation made to the National Rural Conference, Washington, D.C.

Jennings, Mary. 1990. Community mobilization. Presentation made to the National Association of Rural Mental Health Workers, Lubbock, Texas.

Mental health services not meeting needs of rural residents. 1989. *Rural Health Reporter.* (Fall): Austin, Tex.: Texas Rural Communities, Inc.

Morrison, Jim. 1976. Community organization in rural areas. In *Social work in rural communities: A book of readings,* ed. Leon H. Ginsberg, 57–61. New York: Council on Social Work Education.

Morrissey, E. S. 1985. Characteristics of poverty in nonmetro counties. Department of Agriculture Rural Development Research Report 52. Washington, D.C.: GPO.

Murray, J. Dennis. 1990. Written testimony submitted to the Regional Field Hearing on Mental Illness in Rural America, 12 April.

Offner, R., T. Seekins, and F. Clark. 1992. Disability and rural independent living: setting an agenda for rural rehabilitation. *Human Services in the Rural Environment* 15(3): 6–8.

Shuttlesworth, G. 1993. The rural medical social worker: a pilot project. *Journal of Human Services in the Rural Environment,* 15(4): 26–29.

Watkins, J. M., and Watkins, D. A. 1984. *Social policy and rural settings.* New York: Springer.

Winslow, W. 1990. Reducing turnover among rural mental health specialists. Presentation made to the National Association of Rural Mental Health Workers, Lubbock, Texas.

Wooten, Donald B. 1989. AIDS in rural California. *Human Services in the Rural Environment* 13(1): 30–33.

Uhr, E., and E. Evanson. 1984. Poverty in the United States: Where do we stand now? *Focus* 7(1): 13.

U.S. Department of Agriculture and U.S. Census Bureau. 1988. Rural and rural farm population: 1988. *Current population reports,* ser. P-20, no. 439. Washington, D.C.: U.S. Government Printing Office.

SUGGESTED FURTHER READINGS

Coward, R. T., and S. Cutler. 1989. Informal and Formal Health Care Systems for the Rural Elderly. *Health Services Research* 23(6): 785–806.

Dwyer, J. W., G. R. Lee, and R. T. Coward. 1990. The health status, health services utilization, and support networks of the rural elderly: A decade review. *Journal of Rural Health* 6(4): 379–98.

Journal of Small Town. Small Towns Institute: Ellensburg, Washington.

Martinez-Brawley, E. E. 1981. *Seven decades of rural social work.* New York: Praeger.

———. Beyond cracker-barrel images: the rural social work specialty. *Social Casework* 67: 101–107.

Munson, C. E. 1980. Urban-rural differences. Implications for education and training. *Journal of Education for Social Work* 16: 95–103.

Poole, D. L., and J. M. Daily. 1985. Problems of innovation in rural social services. *Social Work* 30: 338–44.

Pratt, D. S. 1990. Rural occupations and health. *Journal of Rural Health* 6(4): 399–418.

Summers, A., J. M. Schriver, P. Sundet, and R. Meinert, eds. 1987. *Social work in rural areas.* Batesville: Arkansas College.

Weber, G. K. 1976. Preparing social workers for practice in rural social systems. *Journal of Education for Social Work* 12: 110–111.

Whitaker, W. H., ed. 1985. *Social work in rural areas.* Proceedings of the Ninth National/Second International Institute on Social Work in Rural Areas. Orono: University of Maine.

York, R., R. Denton, and J. R. Moran. 1989. Rural and urban social work practice: Is there a difference? *Social Casework* 70: 201–209.

CHAPTER 17

OLDER ADULTHOOD
Issues, Problems, and Services

Mabel (age 76) and Charles (age 77) have been married for 53 years. They consider their marriage to have been very good and rewarding. They live in an older neighborhood of a mid-sized midwestern city (population 250,000). They have no children, although Mabel has two living sisters and Charles has one living brother. These siblings all live on the West Coast and have limited contact with Mabel and Charles. They also have a number of nieces and nephews, all of whom are scattered throughout the United States. None of their relatives lives within 500 miles of them.

Before retirement, Charles was an auto parts dealer and Mabel was a homemaker. Charles recently had a major stroke that left him bedfast, and while Mabel has been attempting to care for him at home, it has become increasingly difficult for her to do so. Her arthritis makes it hard for her to lift and turn Charles, and she has also become homebound due to the caretaking needs related to Charles' condition. Her social activities have become curtailed, and demands related to grocery shopping and home maintenance have become major hurdles to overcome. Although the home health nurse and visiting social worker have been very helpful in providing resources, Mabel feels that her inability to care for Charles has increased and, coupled with her own declining health, will force her to place Charles in a nursing home—a decision that creates considerable stress and guilt for her. ∎

The experience that Mabel and Charles are undergoing is not typical of the majority of older adults, although far too many share similar experiences. In general, most older adults experience high levels of life satisfaction, purpose in life, good health, and contentment. For those who experience problems similar to those of Mabel and Charles, however, the struggle to survive often limits their ability to enjoy life. Unfortunately, the myth that all older persons are alike tends to obscure the reality that there is as much variation among the older population as there is between the young and the old.

The number and percentage of people reaching old age are greater than they have ever been throughout recorded history. This is in part because life expectancy has increased dramatically since 1900. For example, in 1900, life expectancy was approximately 47 years; by 1990, it was slightly over 75 years. Viewing this phenomenon from the perspective of age distribution, in 1900 only 3 of 100 Americans were over age 65—in 1990, 12 of each 100 were 65 or over. Not only are more individuals reaching age 65—they are also living longer (see Table 17.1). As the data indicate, in 1990, one-third of all persons 65 or over were between ages 75 to 84, and an additional 10 percent were over age 85. Overall, 43 percent of the over-65 population was over age 75 (Hooyman and Kiyak 1993). To many experts, this suggests that there are really two groups of older adults—the old and the old-old (elderly). One unanticipated consequence of extended longevity is that many adults in their sixties are caring for their parents who are in their eighties and nineties.

While living a long life is a goal to which most of us aspire, the consequences to society have the potential of being catastrophic. Assuring that essential resources are available to meet the needs of the older population places a heavy burden on government and private resources, including families. More and more, middle-aged Americans are becoming the "sandwich generation," having to provide for their children while they also are providing for their elderly parents. But many families cannot provide such support, especially when major health problems occur, and many elderly people do not have families available to give even emotional support. Thus, there is an increasing reliance on federal and state government to provide for such needs. For example, it is estimated that one-fourth of the federal government's expenditures are allocated to meeting the needs of the older population. With continually increasing numbers

TABLE 17.1 **POPULATION PROJECTIONS BY AGE: 1995–2080** (In thousands)

Year	65 & Over*	85 & Over	100 & Over
1995	33,764	3,912	76
2000	34,882	4,622	100
2010	37,162	5,321	144
2020	48,212	5,397	186
2040	58,835	9,165	228
2080	49,532	9,796	438

*Age ranges in the table represent overlapping categories; the figure for those aged 65 and over includes those 85 and over and 100 and over. The figure for those aged 85 and over includes those aged 100 and over.

Source: U.S. Census of Population, 1988–2080; and Projections of the Population of the United States, by Age, Sex and Race, 1989, *Current Population Reports*, ser. P-25, no. 1018 (Washington, D.C.: GPO, 1990).

of older adults in our society, even larger government allocations will be necessary in the future (see Figure 17.1).

In this chapter, we examine the more salient issues and problems an older population creates for society, review their problems of adaptation, and identify resources that have been developed to create physical and social support systems designed to meet their needs. ■

◢ PHYSIOLOGICAL AGING

Most people are very much aware of physical changes they have experienced in their lives. The process of change through growth and physical maturation is not fixed, but continues throughout the life cycle. During midlife (around the age of 45), we go through a stage of physical change that is called senescence. Senescence is generally defined as the onset of the degenerative process. It is at this stage that adults develop an awareness of significant bodily changes—the graying or loss of hair, wrinkling of the skin, a slowing down of the pace, and an awareness that old age will soon be a reality.

Old age may be accompanied by sensory losses. Visual acuity may decrease, and bifocals may become necessary. Hearing problems may increase, and many older adults need hearing aids. In very late life, tactile (touch) and olfactory (taste) senses may lose their fine-tuning. These changes do not, of course, happen at any particular age, nor do they affect the aged to the same degree. Losses may be minor and hardly detectable in some but be major dysfunctions in others. Unless sensory losses are profound, they seldom limit the older adult's ability for social interaction and maintenance of a normal and fulfilling life-style. Even when more serious sensory debilities exist, proper prosthetic supports often allow the older person to maintain a normal life.

FIGURE 17.1   **U.S. POPULATION GROWTH (1960–1990)**

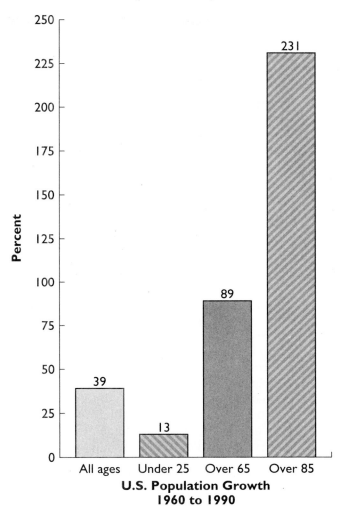

U.S. Population Growth
1960 to 1990

Source: *Time* 142, no. 9 (6 March 1995): 85. © 1995 Time Inc. Reprinted by permission.

Although sensory losses are noticeable, even more significant changes occur internally. Changes in the cardiovascular system are often reflected in elevated blood pressure and loss of elasticity in the lungs. Renal capacity is reduced, and the bladder loses approximately one-third of its capacity. There is a loss of brain weight as well as muscular strength. Estrogen and testosterone levels are reduced, and other hormonal changes occur. With the exception of disease factors, however, none of these changes reduces older adults' ability to maintain an active, well-balanced life.

As incredible as it may seem, scientists have not yet determined why we age. A number of theories—including those regarding wear and tear (external stress causes organisms to wear out), autoimmune responses (organism's immune system becomes less effective in throwing off challenges to the system), cellular (cells are reduced in number as well as the ability of the organism to replicate lost cells) and cross-linkage (changes in collagen with subsequent loss of elasticity in body tissue)—have been put forward as viable theories of aging (Hooyman and Kiyak 1993). Students who hope to work with older adults should familiarize themselves with these theoretical perspectives.

Social workers who specialize in working with older adults should be sensitive to physiological changes that are normal processes of growing old. When placed in the proper perspective, these changes should not be viewed negatively but rather as part of the normal life-development continuum.

◪ BEHAVIOR AND ADAPTATION TO OLD AGE

Although in this chapter we do not discuss in detail the developmental processes of later life, we do offer a few observations to dispel some of the myths that many individuals believe regarding the aging process. First, be aware that **aging** is a normative process and not a fixed dimension of the life cycle. Young children age, as do older adults. All societies attach significance to various stages of the life cycle. Aging is not only a chronological process; it has symbolic meaning as well. Cultures determine, for example, the age at which their members should enter school, marry, begin careers, enter the military, have children, become grandparents, and retire. Norms for behavior are prescribed at various developmental stages of the life cycle. Old age has been viewed too often as a period of dramatic decline. Thus, older adults are expected to be less active, need fewer resources, contribute less to society, and become more content and serene.

Scientific data buttress many of the symbolic definitions assigned to old age. Physiological changes, including the loss of muscular strength, sensory losses, and reduced lung elasticity, are but a few of the measurable differences between older adults and the young. On the other hand, many of the presumed losses associated with cognitive functioning have been demonstrated to have little substance in fact. Intelligence and intellectual functioning, once thought to decline appreciably in old age, are not measurably affected by the process. Behavior in old age is an individual matter and not attributable to the aging process alone. Any accurate assessment of adaptation in late life must take into consideration the effects of the environment on behavior, as well as the physiological and cognitive characteristics present within the behavioral context.

In recent years, several theories of aging have emerged that seek to explain or describe adaptation in late life. Among the more prominent ones are **disengagement theory** (Cumming and Henry 1961), **activity theory** (Havighurst 1968), **exchange theory** (Dowd 1975), and **developmental theory** (Newman and Newman 1991).

• *Disengagement theory* assumes that biological degeneration and social withdrawal are coterminous and functional for the individual and society. This theory contends that as older adults decline physically, they have less need and desire for social interaction and progressively become "disengaged" from social roles. But more penetrating analysis reveals that it is societal discrimination against older adults that limits the social contexts (and thus opportunities) for social interaction. Social barriers, such as mandatory retirement, constrain the opportunities for participation in society. For some this means limited income resources and fewer friendship networks.

• *Activity theory* "implies that social activity is the essence of life for all people of all ages," who must maintain adequate levels of activity if they are to age successfully (Barrow 1992, 69). Presumably, more active older adults will achieve greater satisfactions and thus age more adaptively. Activity theory has provided the basis for a number of programs developed for older adults, such as the Retired Seniors Volunteer program (RSVP), Senior Luncheon programs, the Foster Grandparents program, the Green Thumb program, and activity programs in nursing homes.

• *Developmental theory* emphasizes positive adaptation and life satisfactions based on mastering new tasks as the individual moves through the life cycle, including old age. Life-span development is viewed as a normal process that encompasses new challenges, new tasks, and flexibility in incorporating changes into the repertoire of behaviors. Older adults must accept the physiological changes they experience, reconstruct their physical and psychological life accordingly, and integrate values that validate their worth as older adults (Clark and Anderson 1967).

Developmental theory postulates that the psychological crises of late life are "integrity versus despair" and "immortality versus extinction" (Newman and Newman 1991). Integrity, according to Newman and Newman, is "not so much a quality of honesty and trustworthiness . . . as it is an ability to integrate one's sense of past history with one's present circumstances and to feel content with the outcome" (551). Despair suggests that the opposite of integrity will occur, that is, the inability to integrate past history with the present or to achieve contentment with the outcome. Confrontation with the psychosocial crisis of immortality versus extinction occurs in very late life. Immortality refers to the extension of one's life through one's children, contributions to social institutions, spirituality, and positive influences one has had on others. Extinction suggests the lack of connectedness and attachment and the fear that death brings nothingness (Newman and Newman 1991).

• *Exchange theory* attributes social withdrawal of the aged to a loss of power. Having once exchanged their expertise for wages, the aged must comply with mandatory retirement in exchange for pensions, Social Security payments, and Medicare. Thus, the power advantage has shifted from them as individuals to society (Dowd 1975). The effect of this power loss results in withdrawal from meaningful social interaction and greater dependence on those holding power over them.

Society's role in creating the behavioral and value context for older adults must be examined in order to gain insights into the problems and issues implicit in understanding adaptation in later life. Our society, for example, stresses productivity and distributes varying degrees of rewards and power in relation to it. Retirement serves to disengage older adults from socially recognized productive efforts. Instead of being consumers of products from their own current productive efforts, older adults are forced to be consumers of the products from the efforts of others. As we now turn our attention to the problems and issues confronting older adults, you should keep in mind that there are no simple solutions to problems. Social work with older adults who have problems may bring some relief to those individuals helped, but it does not address the causes of those problems. Changing the social systems that produce the problems is a more tenable solution, albeit more difficult.

ATTITUDES TOWARD GROWING OLD

Negative attitudes toward the aged are among many of the harsh realities people face in old age. Although there has been a pronounced positive shift in attitudes toward aging in recent years, negative attitudes persist (Butler and Lewis 1977). Our society often has been characterized by its emphasis on youth and productivity. Independence is stressed and is enabled by financial supports gained through employment. Retirement often drastically reduces available income and may contribute to dependency. As a result, older adults are often viewed as being of less value to society.

Negative attitudes also are expressed through the process of exclusion. Media, for example, have avoided the use of older adults in television commercials, while advertisements in newspapers and magazines use younger persons to convey messages. Until recently, older adults, when used in film or advertising, were portrayed as dependent, irascible, or sickly. Fortunately, there is evidence that the media are beginning to present a more accurate portrayal of older adults, such as in the movie *Cocoon*.

Collectively, many societal practices have reinforced negativism toward old age. Many of these practices, such as mandatory retirement, have supported the idea that older adults are less capable of making contributions through work and to society. Various rules and regulations governing employment limit the opportunity for them to make such contributions. The discrimination or differential treatment based on age alone is called **ageism.** Like other forms of discrimination, ageism is institutionalized and, as a result, is often subtle. Individuals are often unaware that they reinforce it through their attitudes and practices. Unfortunately, negative attitudes toward older adults may be expressed by professional practitioners as well as the general public. In a classic study, Riley (1968) identifies nurses, medical doctors, attorneys, the clergy, and social workers, among others, as giving preference to younger individuals as clientele. There is little evidence that this has changed.

Negative attitudes toward older adults often result in the loss of social status, with the accompanying diminished self-concept. Also, real-life issues further compound the problem. For example, as adults grow older, they invariably lose significant others through death, and they must deal with their own physical decline, which may limit activities and opportunities for mobility. Although the majority of older adults are independent and experience high levels of life satisfaction, these changes (or losses) invariably affect their quality of life.

As we review other problem areas experienced by older adults, keep in mind that attitudes, although not always directly linked with behavior, tend to shape our priorities and practices. Viewing the older population as "excess baggage" is not the bedrock upon which positive responses to the needs of older adults will be achieved.

RETIREMENT

The impact of **retirement** on human behavior continues to be a topic of major interest. Although retirement often has been viewed as synonymous with old age, that scarcely is the case in our society today. Data indicate that more and more Americans are electing to retire at earlier ages while, on the other hand, many older citizens continue to work either full- or part-time in the labor force. This mixture of age and work (either full- or part-time) clouds our ability to arrive at a precise definition, or line of demarcation, that clearly separates those among us who are retired from those who are not. When, for example, is an individual considered to be retired? Is the military "retiree" receiving a full retirement pension from the military, yet working full-time in a civil service position, considered retired? Or the 72-year-old person receiving full Social Security benefits from the federal government who works full-time as a court bailiff? And what about the 69-year-old homemaker receiving Supplemental Security Income (public assistance for the aged)? Certainly, many other examples would further muddy the already murky waters of the definitional dilemma.

As a result, researchers use operational definitions that seldom are accepted universally. Some view individuals as retired if they receive a pension from their employer for past work performed, regardless of their present work status. Others identify retirees as those individuals who receive retirement pension benefits that exceed any monies earned through present work, and many identify a person in retired status who receives a pension and works half-time or less. Obviously, the retiree living on a pension and not working presents us with far fewer definitional problems. There is agreement that the retired status is achieved only in relation to benefits earned through employment of one type or another.

Although it is difficult, primarily due to the definitional problems just described, to ascertain how many individuals are added to the retirement pool each year, it must be large, although 55 percent of those age 65 and over continue to participate in the labor force (U.S. Department of Labor 1990). Table 17.2 indicates the percentage of those in the labor force by age, gender, and ethnic status. For many retirees, income resources often are reduced drastically upon retirement. Few would disagree that the quality of life is related to available spendable income, and that for many retired individuals meeting basic survival needs is often difficult. Luxurious life-styles and world cruises often portrayed in magazines targeted for the retired "over-fifty" population and sponsored

TABLE 17.2 **PERCENTAGE OF THOSE IN THE LABOR FORCE BY AGE, GENDER, AND ETHNIC STATUS, 1989**

	AGE		
	60 to 64	**65 to 69**	**70 & Over**
Total male	54.8%	25.0%	10.9%
Total female	35.5	14.3	4.6
White male	55.7	25.3	10.7
White female	33.1	14.3	4.1
Black male	45.9	21.0	7.2
Black female	33.3	13.9	4.6

Source: U.S. Department of Labor, Bureau of Labor Statistics, Employment and Earnings, vol. 37, no. 1 (January 1990).

by associations such as the American Association of Retired Persons are options available only to a relatively small percentage of retirees. Understandably, many retirees remain concerned about the stability of the Social Security system, which, incidentally, has been the catalyst for retirement on a grand scale.

Income, of course, is not the only factor affecting positive adjustment to retirement. Health is a matter of great importance and concern. As the retired population grows older, good health becomes more problematic. Few survive beyond their seventies without some debilitating health problem, such as arthritis, high blood pressure, poor digestion, or related problems. For most, such problems do not severely restrict mobility or daily activities. For others with more severe conditions, the role of patient tends to eclipse preferred retirement activities. Concerns over meeting medical expenses, or anticipated expenses, may lead to conservative spending patterns that, in turn, reduce options and activities. Most older adults rely primarily on Medicare, a federal health insurance program available to individuals 65 and older. For the retiree in poor health, health-related problems may diminish satisfactions in the world away from work. Future-oriented retirees who have developed interests and activities also seem to achieve greater gratification.

The need for research on retirement continues to be crucial. Although social scientists have made great strides in the last several decades, the potential value of retirement-related research becomes more manifest as the number of retirees in this country grows. From past efforts, we have developed an emerging body of knowledge and understanding of the effects of retirement on individuals. Obviously, there is much more to learn. Appropriate and valid social policies must be undergirded with a sound knowledge base.

In the past decade considerable emphasis has been given to preparation for retirement. So-called preretirement planning is based on the notion that people who prepare adequately for retirement adjust better to the life-style changes that accompany it. Many major corporations as well as public agencies have developed preretirement training programs for their employees. These programs usually emphasize estate planning; forecasting of income; identification of federal, state, and private resources for older adults; and strategies for dealing with such issues as relocating, living alone, and planning for leisure-time activities. Although there is no compelling evidence that participation in preretirement planning positively affects adaptation to retirement, there is a mounting consensus that it does. Logic alone would suggest that life changes can best be successfully managed when adequate preparation has been made.

Retirement is emerging as a desirable goal for more Americans as it becomes more commonplace and publicly accepted. Our attention will now be directed in more detail toward the social and adaptive issues related to growing old in our society.

◪ OLDER ADULTS AND THEIR FAMILIES

Facts refute the myth that older adults are abandoned by their families, because family members continue to be the primary source of emotional support and, in times of illness, care for their elderly members (Shanas 1979). Less than 5 percent of the older population is without family members. As Table 17.3 illustrates, the majority of older men are married, but the majority of older women are widowed. As women grow older (75 and up), the likelihood increases that they will become widows and must rely more on family members other than their spouse. Most older married couples express general satisfaction with their marriage and the mutual emotional support that it brings. The majority have adult children with whom they maintain contact. Few older adults live with their children—and most do not want to, preferring instead to remain as independent as possible. Grandchildren also play important roles such as offering companionship and emotionally gratifying interaction, reducing loneliness, and often accepting caretaking responsibilities.

If older adults become debilitated with health problems, they often turn to their adult children for support. As a consequence, adult children may find the situation stressful, particularly because of the increased time demands. Middle-aged children of older adults have the responsibility of providing physical and emotional support to their own children while also giving support to their parents. Because of this dilemma, middle-aged people have been called the "sandwich generation." This strain may push these middle-aged children to their emotional and

TABLE 17.3

MARITAL STATUS OF OLDER ADULTS AGE 65 AND OVER

Marital Status	Male	Female
Single	5%	4%
Married	77	43
Widowed	13	47
Divorced	5	6

Source: American Association of Retired People, *A Profile of Older Americans, 1995* (Washington, D.C.: AARP, 1996). Reprinted with the permission of the American Association of Retired Persons.

physical limits. As older adults live longer, they may need familial support for a number of years. Although most families manage the demands adequately, the potential for intergenerational conflict is ever present.

Families continue to be a viable resource for older adults, giving them both comfort and identity. Although research continues to provide inconclusive findings about the overall quality of intergenerational relationships, it does suggest that most older people maintain regular contact with their family members, who are the primary source of assistance when needed.

DYING AND DEATH

Death can occur at any point in the life cycle; however, death rates increase dramatically among those aged 50 or over (see Table 17.7, later in this chapter). Occurrences of death in later life tend to be the product of disease rather than accidents.

Every culture shapes attitudes toward death as well as life. Our society tends to overemphasize a rational view of death as being a natural, yet highly individualized event. Most of us are not engaged with the dying and consequently have little experience that prepares us either for coping with the death of others or for our own death. Consequently, most people are uncomfortable when confronted with dying individuals, and we are apprehensive about our own death.

In a classic work, Elisabeth Kübler-Ross (1975) laid the groundwork for helping dying persons come to grips with the remaining part of their lives. Her contribution, along with others, created a framework for social workers and other professionals to provide assistance for the dying as well as their families, often through the aid of a hospice. **Hospices** are

> dedicated to helping individuals who are beyond the curative power of medicine to remain in familiar environments that minimize pain, and to maintain personal dignity and control over the dying process. (Hooyman and Kiyak 1993, 389)

The hospice movement originated in England, and the first U.S. hospice was established in Connecticut in the 1970s. This movement has grown rapidly since that time and now hospices are located in major cities as well as in some rural areas. Be aware, however, that the vast majority of dying persons are not served by a hospice due to the lack of resources or knowledge that such services are available.

In recent years controversy has been introduced into the dying process in the form of "voluntary" or "involuntary" euthanasia. The medical community has long embraced the philosophical tenet that life should be preserved as long as medically possible, even through the technique of artificial means such as respirators. Taking a contrary position, supporters of the "right to die" movement feel that the individual should have the right of choice in governing the time and circumstance under which death should occur. Proponents of the right-to-die position emphasize the importance of the **living will,** a legal device that enables an individual to delineate the conditions under which they would refuse artificial means to maintain life. Organizations such as the Hemlock Society support not only the concept of the living will but also the right of individuals to induce their own death under circumstances in which they are experiencing great pain and suffering without hope of recovery.

Social workers who work with older adults will invariably work with the dying. Through the application of their skills, social workers can assist individuals and families in handling interpersonal losses and protect the dying person's dignity, integrity, and right to choices.

AGING AND MENTAL HEALTH

The state of mental health among older adults is not appreciably different from that of the population in general. Unfortunately, adaptive problems such as disorientation, memory loss, excessive dependency, and senility are assumed to be inherent to the aging process. The pervasiveness of these myths results in the view that older adults, in general, experience mental health problems. Like individuals in other stages of the life cycle, older adults may experience problems of a mental nature that result in dysfunction. And, as with younger people, these problems generally are responsive to treatment. In some instances, these adaptive problems have been present throughout the life cycle. Other individuals have managed to function adequately and do not develop mental health problems until late in life, often as a result of interpersonal loss, organic deterioration, or some traumatic event. On the other hand, activity and future orientation appear to be associated with good mental health. Maintaining enthusiasm and working toward goals are antithetical to the development of dysfunctional behavior.

Problems experienced in old age also may be analyzed using a systems/ecological perspective. The way that an individual interacts within the environment strongly influences that individual's mental health. Many of the symptoms of dysfunctional behavior that appear in old age may be attributable to environmental factors. Social isolation and loneliness often appear to produce maladaptive behaviors. Overmedication often results in memory loss, disorientation, loss of vigor, or loss of appetite. Depression, one of the more common mental health problems in late life, may be caused by bereavement, anxiety related to income security, a limited social friendship network, health concerns, relocation, and related factors. Ageism and lack of attention to problems of the elderly have led to increased concern about this group's high suicide rate. In 1986, for example, the suicide rate for the population in general was 12 per 100,000 people. For adults 65 and over, the rate was 21.5 per 100,000 people—considerably higher. While older adults constitute only 12 percent of the population, 25 percent of all suicides occur in the older population (Meehan, Saltzman, and Sattin 1991).

Alzheimer's disease has emerged as one of the more publicized types of organic brain syndromes in later life. Given the nature of the disease, it is difficult to ascertain precisely the extent to which it occurs in the older population; however, it is estimated that 2 percent to 4 percent of adults over 65 may have this disease (American Psychiatric Association

1993). Alzheimer's is typically an insidious progressive disease that results in increasing maladaptation. Disorientation, memory loss, wandering, and inappropriate (and often bizarre) behavior are among the symptoms. In the later stages the person requires total care, including feeding, bathing, and all routine maintenance activities. Alzheimer's disease imposes heavy demands on family members, who are the primary caretakers in the initial stages. Both physical and emotional demands related to caring for a disabled loved one increase as the disease progresses. Alzheimer's support groups have been formed in many communities to provide emotional support for caregivers as well as an opportunity to share ideas related to effective techniques in caring for the person.

Dramatic changes in the mental health of individuals are seldom caused by the aging process alone. Individuals possessing well-integrated personalities who prepare themselves for changes related to retirement, develop leisure-time interests, and plan for the future are less vulnerable to age-related stress factors.

◢ INCOME SECURITY

One of the more persistent anxieties experienced by older adults relates to income security. As one grows older, the ability to secure income through employment tends to become more problematic, and the reliance on pensions, savings, investments, and social security increases. For the majority of older adults, income available after retirement is generally below what they received while working full time. For some, it may be less than half. Few of our present-day older adults earned sufficient income to allow them to "put away" money for retirement. Also, retirement incentive plans such as IRAs, tax-deferred annuities, and Keogh plans were nonexistent during the time of their employment. As a result, many retirees are forced to live on Social Security payments alone. Table 17.4 illustrates the sources of income for retirees in 1992.

As Table 17.4 reflects, only 17 percent of the retirees' income is derived from pensions. This suggests that the majority of older Americans are not

TABLE 17.4   **RETIREMENT INCOME SOURCES**

Sources	Percentage of Total Income
Social Security	40%
Assets	21
Pensions	19
Earnings	17
Other	3

Source: American Association of Retired People, *A Profile of Older Americans, 1995* (Washington, D.C.: AARP, 1996). Reprinted with the permission of the American Association of Retired Persons.

Many elderly are becoming more vocal about their rights and are advocating for their needs at all levels of government.

covered by pension plans. This, coupled with the fact that Social Security was not designed to be a "complete" retirement system, serves to create a financial dilemma for many retirees. Fortunately, the overall financial picture is improving. The average household income for adults over 65 has risen, as has the median income for individuals (see Table 17.5).

Along with the slight increase in overall income, there has been a corresponding decrease in the poverty level for older adults. For example, the poverty rate for people 65 and over in 1970 was approximately 25 percent. In 1994, it was near 12 percent—a dramatic decrease. The plight of the older poor and near-poor should not be minimized. As Table 17.6 shows, the poor are characterized as being primarily female and African American.

TABLE 17.5 **MEDIAN INCOME OF ADULTS OVER AGE 65 BY ETHNICITY**

Ethnicity	Median Income
White	$19,661
Black	12,069
Hispanic	12,379

Source: Bureau of the Census, unpublished data from the March, 1990 *Current Population Survey.*

For many social security recipients who fall in the lower to lower-middle income brackets, working to supplement their income is often not an option. (Please refer to Table 17.7 for 1995 benefits and charges of Social Security and Medicare.) The Social Security Act serves as a clear disincentive to work. For example, recipients who are between the ages of 62 and 65 find that any earnings through work over $8,160 are taxed at the rate of $1.00 for every $2.00 earned—a 50 percent tax rate. For those aged 65 to 70, the rate of taxation is 33 percent (or $1.00 for every $3.00 earned over $11,280). This "tax" comes through a reduction in their Social Security check. After age 70, earnings are not taxed. Although federal regulations clearly prohibit discrimination based on age, the Social Security system clearly does so, as evidenced above.

Recent debates concerning the future of Social Security benefits have raised the concern of many older citizens. The Social Security "trust" fund has long been "tapped" by Congress to assuage general budget expenditures. Recently, under the auspices of the "Contract with America," the proviso that relates to balancing the budget and reducing the national debt has left Social Security benefits vulnerable to being lowered, and stricter limits are placed on eligibility. Obviously this concerns beneficiaries whose benefits are already meager. Furthermore, it is conceivable that those older adults with higher levels of non-Social Security income assets would receive little or no benefits at all.

While money does not always produce happiness, it is related to satisfaction in later life. The common myth that older adults need less in-

TABLE 17.6 **PERCENTAGE OF THE AGED BELOW THE POVERTY LINE AND BELOW 125 PERCENT OF THE POVERTY LINE, 1986**

INCOME	WHITE			BLACK		
	Married	Nonmarried		Married	Nonmarried	
		Men	Women		Men	Women
Below Poverty Line	5%	13%	19%	18%	35%	43%
Below 125% of Poverty Line	9	23	32	29	55	57

Note: Categories in the table are divided into race, marital status, and gender. In 1986, the poverty line was $6,630 for a two-person unit aged 65 or older and $5,255 for one person aged 65 or older.

Source: Adapted from Susan Grad, "Income of the Population 55 and Older, 1986," SSA publication no. 13–11871, Table 54 (Washington, D.C.: U.S. Department of Health and Human Services, 1988).

| TABLE 17.7 | **SOCIAL SECURITY AND MEDICARE CHANGES** (How 1995 benefits and charges stack up) |

1995 cost-of-living adjustment (COLA)	2.80%
Tax rate for employees (unchanged)	7.65%
Social Security portion	6.20%
Medicare portion	1.45%
Tax rate for self-employed	15.30%
Maximum taxable payroll earnings	
Social Security	$61,200
Medicare	no limit
Retirement earnings-test exemption amounts	
Under age 65	$ 8,160
Age 65–69	$11,280
Maximum Social Security monthly benefit for worker retiring at age 65 in January 1995	$ 1,199
Average monthly Social Security benefits	
All retired workers	$ 698
Couple, both receiving benefits	$ 1,178
Widow(er)	$ 656
Maximum SSI monthly payments	
Individual	$ 458
Couple	$ 687
Maximum allowable assets for SSI (unchanged)	
Individual	$ 2,000
Couple	$ 3,000
Medicare Part B monthly premium	$ 46.10
Part A deductible for hospital stay—first 60 days	$ 716
Copayment for days 61–90	$ 179/day
Copayment for lifetime reserve days	$ 358/day
Copayment for skilled nursing facility, days 21–100	$ 89.50/day
Buy-in monthly premium (less than 30 quarters)	$ 261
With 30 quarters of covered employment	$ 183

Source: Department of Health and Human Services.

come to meet their living needs is hardly buttressed by fact. The need for food, clothing, shelter, recreation, transportation, and the ability to buy gifts for grandchildren and family members does not decline with age, while the cost of health care usually increases, often significantly. Lowered standards of living, unmet needs, and the inability to adequately meet those needs may result in feelings of inadequacy, despair, loss of self-esteem, and poor health. Income is an enabling resource that affects the options available in life. As income declines, so do those options with the resulting loss of independence.

Many of the support and social services designed to assist older adults with their unmet needs might not be necessary if retirement income were sufficient to enable the nonworking aged to meet those needs at the marketplace. Unfortunately, the United States continues to lag behind other industrialized nations in replacement (retirement) income for its aged, ranking fourth in payments to couples and eighth in income benefits for the single older adult (Wilson 1984).

◢ HEALTH AND HEALTH CARE SERVICES

In later life the probability of developing health problems becomes more pronounced. Unfortunately, this condition has led many observers to conclude that aging and poor health are synonymous. Such is not the case, if you consider that health problems in old age are treatable and correctable, just as they are at earlier stages in the life cycle. Older adults are more prone to develop illnesses such as pneumonia, influenza, and gastrointestinal complaints than the population in general. Also more common in old age are chronic diseases, including heart disease, hypertension, cancer, arthritis, diabetes, emphysema, osteoporosis, and visual impairments (Barrow 1992). Table 17.8 shows the health problems that are the leading causes of death for older adults.

Only 5 percent of the older adult population is affected by health problems so severe that their mobility is limited. The majority are able to move about the community even though they may have one or more disease symptoms.

Health care resources are provided primarily through Medicare and Medicaid. **Medicare** is a government health insurance program designed to pay for hospital care and related medical expenses for persons over 65. Because of the costs of medical care, the amount of benefits paid by Medicare has decreased to approximately 50 percent of the total cost of the care. The inability of older adults to pay the portion of medical fees not covered by Medicare has resulted in large numbers not seeking necessary medical attention.

Both Medicare and **Medicaid** (health insurance for the poor) have made it possible for many older adults to obtain needed medical treatment. Due to personal cost-related factors, however, many older adults often are forced to delay seeking treatment until health conditions become severe or life-threatening. Neither of these health insurance programs is designed to provide funding for preventive health care. Doubtless, many serious

TABLE 17.8   **LEADING CAUSES OF DEATH FOR AGES 65 AND OVER BY AGE, 1987** (Deaths per 100,000 population)

Cause of Death	65 to 74	75 to 84	85 & Over
Heart diseases	2171	5573	14,801
Malignant neoplasms	1745	2800	3,737
Cerebrovascular diseases	333	1170	3,461
Pulmonary diseases	311	673	957

Source: Statistical Abstracts of the United States, 1990, 110th ed. (Washington, D.C.: U.S. Government Printing Office, 1991).

health problems could be averted or become less problematic if attention were given to preventive health measures.

As with other government-funded benefit programs, Medicare and Medicaid funds are rapidly approaching deficit spending levels. Various solutions to the financing of health care have been proposed. These include a reduction of benefits, more stringent eligibility requirements, and an expansion of government coverage for catastrophic cases. Solutions to financing must be found if the health needs of our older population are to be met.

ABUSE AND NEGLECT

Because of limited research, little is known about the form and pervasiveness of abuse and neglect of the elderly. Neglect is the failure to perform the needed activities or tasks essential for meeting one's daily needs. Abuse is a physical or psychological act intended to inflict harm. As is the case with battered children or spouses, the knowledge that old persons are the victims of abuse and neglect is antithetical to our social morality.

Self-neglect is perhaps the most common. Many older adults lack the necessary resources or skills to provide adequate nutrition or to maintain daily household living tasks, such as washing dishes, cleaning the house, and securing proper health services. Self-neglect is more frequent when older persons are socially isolated and have little involvement with family or friends. Caretakers, usually family members, also may be involved in the neglect of elderly people's physical and emotional needs. Neglect often occurs when an older adult lives with a son or daughter and is dependent. Ignoring daily and special needs, denying transportation, failing to include aged persons as members of family households, ignoring their desires to contribute, and providing improper clothing and diet are among the more common forms of neglect of the aged.

Like neglect, abuse usually occurs when the older adult is living with a relative. Abusers often are overtaxed mentally and emotionally and lash out when demands are made on them by older family members. Physical abuse takes the form of slapping, shoving, punching, or placing the older adults in restraints. Psychological or emotional abuse results from threats (of sending the older adults to nursing homes, etc.), ignoring, ridiculing, taking their Social Security or other income and giving them no spending money, cursing, and reminding them that they are a burden.

It is estimated that 10 percent of the older population experiences abuse or neglect. The rates may actually be higher, since many victims are reluctant to report experiences for fear of retaliation or placement in a nursing home. Many states have enacted legislation to protect older adults from abuse and neglect. Family violence is an unfortunate and dehumanizing product of our society that generally is directed toward those dependent on others for some aspect of their care. Protective services are designed to shield victims from further harm. Unfortunately, such services do little to alleviate the causes of the problem.

NURSING HOME CARE

Most older Americans enjoy reasonably good health, with only 5 percent experiencing health problems so debilitating that they require nursing home care. The contemporary nursing home industry has emerged primarily as a result of Medicare and Medicaid legislation, which allows third-party payments to the providers of health care services. Nursing homes typically are licensed by state health departments, which have the responsibility of periodically reviewing the homes to ensure that minimal standards of care are maintained. In addition, all states require that administrators of homes be licensed, although there is considerable variation in administrator-licensing requirements among the states.

The media quite often portray nursing homes as dehumanizing warehouses where residents are neglected and abuse is common. Staff are often characterized as being incompetent, uncaring, and disinterested in providing high quality of care for the residents. Unfortunately, there are some nursing homes for which these allegations are valid. Even though the majority of nursing homes make every effort to provide quality care, caring for debilitated, aging residents is both physically and emotionally demanding. High rates of staff turnover are common, placing further stress on homes in the selection and training of nursing care staff. In recent years, however, more stringent state standards and skillful investigation and evaluation techniques by state regulatory agencies have resulted in a higher level and quality of services. The **Omnibus Budget Reconciliation Act of 1987 (OBRA)** introduced major nursing home reforms, including strengthening residents' rights, establishing written care plans, providing required staff training, and requiring that only certified social workers be employed. These efforts were designed to create a safe and secure environment for residents in which appropriate medical and nursing care would be administered by a caring staff.

The majority of nursing homes in this country are proprietary; that is, they are private, profit-making businesses. Some homes are nonprofit and are usually operated through the auspices of religious organizations or units of state or local governments. There appears to be little difference in the quality of care between the private profit-making homes and nonprofit ones. Privately owned facilities are more vulnerable to "shaving" services in order to maximize profit. Strict enforcement of standards, however, minimizes any significant differences in the services provided for residents.

Nursing homes will continue to be the most viable resource for the debilitated elderly. Alternatives such as home health care, visiting nurses, and personal care homes enable the older adult to reside in the community for a longer period of time; but they tend to defer, not replace, the need for nursing home care (see Figure 17.2). As the need for additional nursing home beds increases (400,000 more by the year 2000), financing the needed care will become more critical. Government financing plans are strained already; and should forecasted budget reductions become a reality, alternative financing or other more cost-effective plans must be developed to assure that the debilitated elderly receive

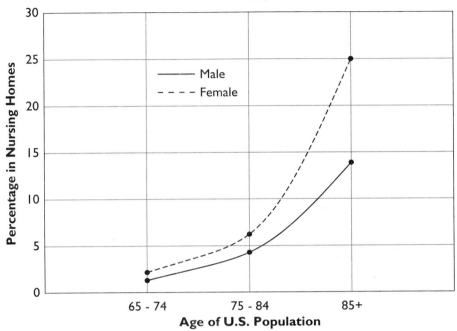

FIGURE 17.2   **PERCENTAGE OF RESIDENTS IN NURSING HOMES AMONG THE U.S. POPULATION AGE 65 AND OVER**

Source: National Center for Health Statistics, The National Nursing Home Survey: 1985, *Vital and Health Statistics*, series 13, no. 97, 1989.

essential health care services. In a number of communities, churches, unions, and private profit-making organizations are developing residential facilities for the elderly.

◪ HOUSING AND TRANSPORTATION

Although the majority of older adults are homeowners, housing often is a major concern for them. The rate of substandard homes among the elderly exceeds those for other age groups. Many of their houses become dilapidated over the years, and in later life the ability of older adults to maintain or repair them is often limited by low incomes. In addition, older adults find it very difficult to secure home repair loans. They must be content with progressively deteriorating housing, which often results in inadequate protection from the heat, cold, and other threatening climatic conditions.

Government housing for the aged typically is difficult to secure because of the high demand for low-cost housing units. Even when available, low-cost housing often appears unattractive, impersonal, lacking in privacy, often has high crime rates, and is too noisy. The advantages include low rent and adequate protection from weather extremes. More units are needed for older adults but are not likely to be forthcoming due to government budgetary limits.

Housing alternatives for the more economically secure aged have recently expanded. High-rise, self-contained apartment complexes have been developed through the auspices of both religious organizations and private sponsorship. These facilities are typically attractive, provide all the amenities for comfortable living, and assure peer interaction and essential social supports. Many of these facilities also provide differing levels of medical care, nursing services, and meals, should individuals become unable to care for themselves in their own apartments. Such facilities, however, are much more costly, and many require substantial down payments before an individual is accepted as a resident. Although housing communes are not abundant, they are growing in popularity and provide a family-type living experience for older participants. This type of housing arrangement develops when several older adults pool their resources to rent or purchase a dwelling and share in its upkeep. Basic living costs for such things as food and utilities are shared, thus enabling each participant to spend less on basic living needs.

Transportation is essential for grocery shopping, attending church services, keeping appointments with doctors and dentists, visiting friends, and maintaining contact with the family. Most older adults must travel some distance in order to procure the necessities for daily living, but it often is very difficult for them to do so. Many who once owned an automobile find the hazards of driving and the cost of vehicle maintenance and insurance beyond their capacity to manage. As a result,

Because they lack transportation, many elderly people are forced to shop in expensive stores or to go without much-needed items, including food. Here, a social work student volunteer takes a woman shopping after she was found living in a small efficiency apartment with no furniture.

they depend on alternate sources of travel. Public transit systems usually are not satisfactory. Bus routes typically are developed for employed workers who regularly use this type of conveyance. Scheduling often results in long walks to bus stops, transfers, and prolonged riding time. In addition, it is extremely difficult for older adults to carry grocery bags onto the bus and walk several blocks from the stop to their residences. A few transit systems have developed specialized services for the handicapped and aged and operate on a door-to-door basis by appointment. Few are available to serve the elderly on an on-call basis. Users must anticipate needs (often as long as two weeks in advance), make the appointment, and hope that they are not forgotten.

Volunteers have been engaged in providing transportation services for the elderly in some communities. Although only a small minority who need such services are able to get them, this option has enabled many older adults to gain mobility for securing needed goods and services. Nutrition programs also have provided transportation to luncheon programs, and some have been able to extend their transportation services to include shopping and social visits. This type of transportation alternative is available only to a comparatively few older adults in need.

The absence of transportation has resulted in many older adults becoming home-bound. Often the result is social isolation, which leads to the loss of incentive, decreased activity, self-deprecation, and eventually psychological and physical deterioration, thus confirming the stereotype that older adults elect not to participate in the mainstream of life.

Unfortunately, little has been accomplished in addressing transportation needs of the aged. Indeed, government budget cuts have significantly reduced transportation programs designed for the elderly in many communities. How do we expect older adults to be independent, shop for themselves, attend meetings, and remain engaged with societal institutions if they lack the transportation resources to do so? Such is the case for many of our aged today.

◪ PEOPLE OF COLOR AS OLDER ADULTS

The problems of adaptation discussed earlier in this chapter are also experienced by older people of color, but to a much greater extent. Life expectancy for African Americans is appreciably less than for whites (see Table 17.9). In fact, only 8.3 percent of the African American population and 10.7 percent of the Hispanic American population are 65 or over, compared with 12.8 percent of the total U.S. population (U.S. Bureau of the Census 1995). Since neither genetics nor heredity has been a factor contributing to a shorter life expectancy for these groups, social and cultural factors are more likely to account for this differential in longevity. As a result of social discrimination, larger proportions of non-white populations experience lower incomes, more physically menial and demanding work, and fewer opportunities to achieve essential life-support services. This has resulted in more severe and unattended health problems, inadequate nutrition, fewer opportunities for social advancement,

TABLE 17.9

LIFE EXPECTANCIES OF WHITE AND AFRICAN AMERICAN POPULATION AGES 65 AND OVER (In years of continued life)

Age	Mean of White and African American	White	African American
65	16.0	16.8	15.2
70	12.6	13.4	12.3
75	10.6	10.4	9.9
80	7.7	7.8	7.1
85 and over	5.9	5.7	6.1

Source: Statistical Abstracts of the United States, 1990, 110th ed. (Washington, D.C.: U.S. Government Printing Office, 1991), 74.

near-poverty wages, and an oppressive cultural environment. Growing old under these adverse conditions has to be difficult.

While retirement income benefits for all older adults are relatively low, they are even less for the non-white aged (see Table 17.10). For example, in 1990, the percentage of aged white families living below the poverty level was 10 percent, compared to 32.2 percent for aged African Americans and 22.4 percent for aged Hispanics. The percentage of white women family heads living below the poverty level was 7.0 percent, compared with 26.4 percent for African American women family heads. The data are even more revealing when comparing white and African American men living alone (18.5 percent and 45.0 percent, respectively). For aged white women living alone, the percentage was 24.5 percent, compared with 63.4 percent for their African American counterparts (Grad 1988). Accurate income data for aged Hispanics are more difficult to ascertain, but all estimates are that the percentage living below the poverty line is somewhat less than that for African Americans.

Many of the necessary support services often are not available to aged people of color because of discrimination, language differences, lack of information concerning eligibility requirements, limited entitlement, pride, and less-than-vigorous outreach services. Unfortunately, for many elderly people of color, poverty, limited options, and discrimination mean that they cannot attain the security, contentment, and life satisfaction that most other older Americans do.

TABLE 17.10

POVERTY LEVEL OF PERSONS AGE 65 AND OVER BY ETHNICITY

Ethnicity	Percentage at or Below Poverty Level
White	10.0%
Hispanic	22.4
African American	32.2

Source: Statistical Abstracts of the United States, 1990, 110th ed. (Washington, D.C.: U.S. Government Printing Office, 1991), 460.

◢ SERVICES FOR OLDER ADULTS

In recent years a wide array of social, health, and related support services have either been developed or extended to provide for the needs of the aged. On the federal level, the majority of these programs have their legislative base in either the Social Security Act or the Older Americans Act. Social Security Act programs cover both income maintenance through social insurance and Supplemental Security Income and health services through either Medicare or Medicaid. The Older Americans Act of 1965 provides supplementary services through funding of nutrition programs, transportation, social services, and the coordination of services for the aged.

Through both governmentally and privately sponsored sources, such older-citizen participation programs as Foster Grandparents, Green Thumb, and the Retired Seniors Volunteer Program, as well as a variety of self-help programs, have been developed within the past decade. Older adults in the Foster Grandparents program, for example, are employed part-time to work with children in state schools, hospitals, and child-care centers, as well as with pregnant teenagers and with abusive and neglectful parents. Senior centers provide a site in many communities where older adults can interact, eat nutritious meals, participate in recreational activities, and pursue hobbies or crafts. Through the auspices of the Older Americans Act, areawide agencies on aging (AAAs) have been established throughout the country that coordinate services to the aged. Among their many functions are such activities as assessing the needs of the older population, providing or contracting for congregate-meals programs, developing transportation services, serving as information and referral resources, and acting as advocates for the aged in assuring that communities will be attentive to their needs.

Meals-on-wheels programs provide hot meals for the home-bound aged and attempt to provide essential social contact with older adults who find it difficult to leave their homes because of limited mobility related to a variety of physical debilities. Adult day-care centers enable older adults to remain in the community. Often participants live with a working son or daughter who cannot provide the required daily monitoring for the older person. Day-care centers assume caretaking responsibilities during the periods when their children are away at work. These centers usually have a variety of activities and provide health checkups and supervision for participants. Mental health services are provided through mental health–mental retardation outreach centers, and counseling services usually are available to the aged and their families through many local social services agencies. Older adults living in rural areas often are disadvantaged in that many of these services are not readily available to them, although nutritional and transportation resources usually are offered.

Although community services are helpful in meeting the needs of manyolder adults, they are not widely available in proportion to the numbers in the community that could potentially benefit from them. Outreach efforts have been reasonably successful in securing participation;

however, resources are limited and funding levels limit the number that can be served. Often, agencies are not located strategically, and therefore the participation of many older adults is limited. Also, outreach efforts would be more effective if older adults could be employed as care providers.

The need for support services for the aged will continue to grow with the expansion of our older population. New funding sources must be developed to accommodate this growing need. Social, health, and related services are essential in promoting the well-being of the older population.

◪ SOCIAL WORK WITH OLDER ADULTS

In recent years, social work practice with the aged has intensified. In 1982 the Bureau of Labor Statistics estimated that 700,000 new jobs would be available in services to the elderly by the year 2000 ("Growth Industries of the Future" 1982). The U.S. Bureau of Labor Statistics lists home health aides as the fastest growing occupation, with a projected 138 percent increase from 1992 to the year 2005 (1993). Gerontologists expect most of these jobs to require skills at the BSW social work level or below (McCaslin 1985). Many schools of social work have developed specializations in **gerontology** (the scientific study of aging, the aging process, and the aged), and social work research has focused on problems of adaptation and life satisfactions in old age. As a result, research and literature on this topic have developed rapidly, and a beginning knowledge base for intervention is being established. It is now recognized that older adults experience many of the same problems evident at other stages of the life cycle: personal adjustment problems, marital problems, relocation, family conflict, adjustment to separation and loneliness, anxiety over limited income, mental illness, and interpersonal loss, among others. Growing along with this recognition is the acknowledgment that the aged are responsive to social work change efforts.

Direct practice is the most common form of social work intervention with the aged. This type of practice includes working with older adults and their families on specific problems, such as enhancing personal adjustment, securing resources to meet their needs, providing emotional support in decision making, dealing with death and dying, and managing family conflict. Direct practice employs a counseling and guidance approach, stresses problem clarification and the development of options and priorities, and provides an opportunity for the client to express anxiety and emotion.

Community-based practice focuses on exo-level community systems as targets for creating a more responsive opportunity structure for the aged. Using an advocacy approach, the social work function is to "identify issues such as poor housing, lack of transportation, health needs, economic needs, and . . . to mobilize community resources to help bring about change through the development of resources to meet these needs" (Johnson 1983, 234).

Social workers with an older-adult clientele must be aware of the special problems they encounter. Many of the aged have been self-sustaining members of society and have developed problems of adaptation only after reaching old age. Accumulated, interpersonal losses (e.g., loss of spouse, friends, familiar environment, job, income, physical health) often produce behavior patterns that inhibit the achievement of life satisfactions and the fulfillment of daily living needs.

Social workers are employed currently in a variety of agencies that serve the elderly, including mental health centers, family service agencies, nursing homes, nutrition programs, recreational centers, hospitals, health and nutrition centers, volunteer programs, transportation and housing programs, protective services programs, and community planning agencies. Social work activity with older adults will continue to be intensified and interventive techniques refined as the theoretical knowledge base expands, resulting in more effective services to the ever-increasing older population in need of them.

SUMMARY

In this chapter, we have described some of the more salient characteristics of the older adult population, along with many of the issues and problems that are of particular concern to individuals who are age 65 or over. Social workers who work with older adults must be aware of the physiological, psychological, and social changes that occur through the process of aging in order to form effective interventive efforts. Of particular concern are problems that relate to income inadequacies, health care costs, housing and transportation, abuse and neglect, family support and the availability and efficiency of various community programs that assist older adults with their living needs and that are culturally sensitive, recognizing the diversity that exists among the elderly.

While the majority of older adults experience few problems of sufficient magnitude to deprive them of life satisfactions, far too many suffer from deprivation that relates to limited resources and unattended health problems. Social workers can assist in meeting this challenge by developing their understanding, knowledge, and skill in working with older individuals. Social workers can also work with the community in developing and utilizing resources that will enrich the quality of life for vulnerable elderly people.

KEY TERMS

activity theory
ageism
aging
developmental theory
disengagement theory
exchange theory
gerontology

hospice
living will
Medicaid
Medicare
Omnibus Budget Reconciliation
   Act of 1987 (OBRA)
retirement

DISCUSSION QUESTIONS

1. What impact will the rapidly increasing numbers of older adults have on support networks? How will these networks be funded?

2. Activity theory tends to be favored by social workers in intervening with older adults. Why? Do you agree?

3. Describe both the positive and negative factors associated with retirement.

4. Identify the factors that converge to create higher poverty levels and shorter life expectancies among the non-white elderly.

5. As the older population continues to expand, what impact will this growth have on the social work profession?

REFERENCES

American Association of Retired People. 1996. *A profile of older Americans, 1995.* Washington, D.C.: AARP.

American Psychiatric Association. 1993. *Diagnostic and statistical manual of mental disorders (DSM-III).* Washington, D.C.: Author.

Barrow, Georgia M. 1992. *Aging, the individual, and society.* 5th ed. St. Paul, Minn.: West.

Butler, Robert N., and Myrna I. Lewis. 1977. *Aging and mental health.* 2d ed. St. Louis, Mo.: Mosby.

Clark, Margaret, and Barbara Anderson. 1967. *Culture and aging.* Springfield, Ill.: Thomas.

Cumming, Elaine, and W. E. Henry. 1961. *Growing old: The process of disengagement.* New York: Basic Books.

Dowd, James J. 1975. Engaging as exchange: A preface to theory. *Journal of Gerontology* 30 (September): 589–94.

Garvin, R. M., and Robert C. Burger. 1964. *Where they go to die: The tragedy of America's aged.* New York: Delacorte.

Grad, Susan. 1988. Income of the population 55 and over, 1986. 55A Publication no. 13–11871, Washington, D.C.: U.S. Department of Health and Human Services.

Growth industries of the future. 1982. *Newsweek* (October 18): 83.

Havighurst, R. J. 1968. A social-psychological perspective on aging. *The Gerontologist* 8 (2): 67–71.

Hooyman, Nancy R., and H. Ausman Kiyak. 1993. *Social gerontology: A multidisciplinary perspective.* 3rd ed. Boston: Allyn & Bacon.

Johnson, H. Wayne. 1983. *The social services: An introduction.* Itasca, Ill.: Peacock.

Kübler-Ross, Elisabeth. 1975. *Death: The final stage of growth.* Englewood Cliffs, N.J.: Prentice-Hall.

McCaslin, Rosemary. 1985. Substantive specializations in master's level social work curricula.

Meehan, P. J., L. E. Saltzman, and R. W. Sattin. 1991. Suicides among older U.S. residents: Epidemiologic characteristics and trends. *American Journal of Public Health* 81: 1198–1200.

National Center for Health Statistics. 1989. The national nursing home survey: 1985. *Vital and health statistics* 13(97).

Newman, Barbara M., and Philip R. Newman. 1991. *Development through life: A psychosocial approach.* 5th ed. Chicago: Dorsey.

Riley, Mathilda White. 1968. *Aging and society.* New York: Russell Sage.

Shanas, E. 1979. The family as a social support in old age. *The Gerontologist* (April) 19:2 169–74.

Statistical Abstracts of the United States, 1990, 110th ed. 1991. Washington, D.C.: U.S. Government Printing Office.

U.S. Bureau of the Census. 1995. *Current population reports.* Washington, D.C.: GPO.

U.S. Bureau of Labor Statistics. 1993. *Monthly Law Review* (November). Washington, D.C.: GPO.

U.S. Department of Labor. 1990. *Manpower report to the president, 1983.* Washington, D.C.

Wilson, Albert J. E. III. 1984. *Social services for older persons.* Boston: Little, Brown.

SUGGESTED FURTHER READINGS

Beaver, Marion L., and Don Miller. 1985. *Clinical social work practice with the elderly.* Homewood, Ill.: Dorsey.

Bould, Sally, Beverly Sanborn, and Laura Reif. 1989. *Eighty-five plus: The oldest old.* Belmont, Calif.: Wadsworth.

Burnside, Irene. 1984. *Working with the elderly: Group process and technique.* Monterey, Calif.: Wadsworth.

DeCalmer, Peter, and Glen Denning. 1993. *The mistreatment of elderly people.* Thousand Oaks, Calif.: Sage.

Estes, Carroll L., and James H. Swan. 1993. *The long term care crisis.* Thousand Oaks, Calif.: Sage.

Foner, Anne. 1986. *Aging and old age.* Englewood Cliffs, N.J.: Prentice-Hall.

Kelly, John R., ed. 1993. *Activity and aging.* Thousand Oaks, Calif.: Sage.

Lowy, Louis. 1979. *Social work with the aging.* New York: Harper & Row.

Margolis, Richard J. 1990. *Risking old age in America.* Boulder, Colo.: Westview.

Moody, Harry R. 1994. *Worlds of difference: Inequality in the aging experience.* Thousand Oaks, Calif.: Pine Forge Press.

Roff, Lucinda L., and Charles R. Atherton. 1989. *Promoting successful aging.* Chicago: Nelson-Hall.

Turner, Barbara F., and Lillian E. Troll. 1993. *Women growing older: Psychological perspectives.* Thousand Oaks, Calif.: Sage.

PART FOUR

WHAT DOES THE FUTURE HOLD?

In the final chapter, Chapter 18, "The Future of Social Work and Social Welfare," we review the history of changes that characterize the social work profession and the field of social welfare, emphasizing the impact of technological and economic changes on the individual, the family, and the community. We also attempt to forecast the probable nature of the profession and of social welfare as they are influenced by future changes at the broader societal level. As you read this final chapter, we hope that you will reflect on what you have learned about our social welfare system, the profession of social work, the diversity of our society, and the many challenging issues we face at all levels of our environment.

In these eighteen chapters, we show the need for social services for individuals from birth through death in a variety of settings. We suggest that some individuals, by the nature of their age, ethnicity, and social class, are more at risk to need social services than others. We also illustrate the many settings in which social workers are employed—government poverty programs, mental health clinics, hospitals, prisons, schools, churches, rural areas, and nursing homes—and suggest that opportunities for social work practitioners in different settings and populations are almost limitless. As you reflect on these chapters and the issues we have raised, we hope that you will develop your own sense of vision about the future of our world, the social work profession, and your role as an individual and as a professional in making our world a better and more humane place.

CHAPTER 18

THE FUTURE OF SOCIAL WORK AND SOCIAL WELFARE

George Swain recently retired after forty-five years as a social worker in a variety of settings. His first job was as a case worker in a settlement house, where he earned a yearly salary of $2,000. An active member of the state and local chapters of the National Association of Social Workers, George has been involved in many changes in the social work profession over the years. "In those early years, we did everything for our clients, since there were very few social service agencies," George stated in a recent interview. "In my first job, I led groups of teenagers, ran programs for senior citizens, set up a child care center, set up a rat control program in the neighborhood, transported people's belongings when they moved, and took kids into my house when they had nowhere else to go. When I retired as the director of a family services agency, there were forty-seven other social service agencies in the community, and most of my time and my staff's time were spent coordinating and linking resources for our clients with those other agencies."

"Today," George continued, "services are much more specialized—and we are more aware of human problems. I'm sure, for example, when I look back, that lots of kids I worked with when I was younger were sexually abused, but social workers in those days were relatively unaware of how extensive a problem that was."

George is especially excited because his granddaughter Jessica is a senior in the Bachelor of Social Work program at the state university and will graduate as a social worker this year. Jessica is completing her field internship at the local rape crisis center. When she graduates, she hopes to work for the state human services agency, providing services to help families on public assistance become self-sufficient. Both grandfather and granddaughter agree that social work has grown as a profession and that many challenging opportunities are ahead for Jessica. ■

As we move into the twenty-first century, the United States faces a serious domestic crisis. As more attention is given nationally to our social welfare system—and the roles various segments of society should play in meeting ever-increasing unmet human needs—increased recognition is being given to the importance of the social work profession in the process. The future of social work is a challenging one with numerous opportunities for the profession.

Social work has a historical commitment to help people cope with change, and the challenges of the rest of the 1990s and the next century suggest that our society will face major changes. The national ambiguity and strain that have existed in the United States since its founding regarding how the unmet needs of our society should be addressed have intensified during recent years. Many Americans are content with the way things are and uneasy about the future direction of the United States and the implications for them. As a nation, we continue to be generous and compassionate when it comes to helping an individual in need, but limiting and suspicious when it comes to helping large numbers of individuals systematically. How our country balances individual freedom versus collective responsibility is a theme that has become a major one during the 1990s and will continue into the next century.

Any attempt to forecast future trends must be tentative. Technological and social change does not always progress at an even rate, nor is the direction of change always predictable. Nevertheless, some trends can be identified that enable us to suggest what factors will have an impact on the profession of social work and the social welfare system within the near future. In this chapter we briefly identify the major issues relating to the future of social welfare in our country and probable directions that the profession of social work will take in addressing these issues. ■

THE RELATIONSHIP BETWEEN PAST AND PRESENT

For us to comprehend the difficulty of predicting the effects of social change upon social work and social welfare, it is helpful to review the earlier chapters of this book. The history of the social work profession is related integrally to the unpredictable nature of the world in which we live. The social work profession is called to respond as social change alters the economic base of society, as well as other basic social institutions such as the family and education, religion, and political and related social organizations. The rapid growth and development of the social work profession in the latter part of the nineteenth century were related directly to the emergence of large urban communities and the accompanying problems associated with increased numbers of displaced persons, detachment from means of production, high rates of unemployment, migration, slums, the rise of a subculture of poverty, increasing health-related problems, and other conditions associated with urban blight. To remediate or eliminate the sources of these problems and to provide support for these displaced persons and their families, "trained" helpers had to become an integral part of the solution. Thus, the profession of social work was born from the need to ensure that a cadre of professionals armed with an understanding of human behavior, awareness of how social organizations function, and sensitivity to the effects of the environment as a determinant to individual growth and development would emerge as society's first line of remediation.

As the technological and industrial revolution erupted, the stability inherent in a primarily agrarian society began to disintegrate rapidly. The structure and function of the family, once stable and secure, were affected by the stresses and tensions produced by the economic marketplace, which called for greater mobility, division of labor outside of the home, and a consequent restructuring of family priorities. As a result, families have become less stable, the divorce rate has increased dramatically, multiple marriages are more common, and child abuse, spouse abuse, and various forms of neglect at all levels of society have emerged as more visible problems.

As the economy has become more unpredictable, the long-sought goal of financial security has become more difficult to achieve for many people. The poor have continued to be victimized by the lack of opportunity and are often blamed for their condition. Increasingly, health and mental health needs of individuals have not been met. The spread of the HIV infection and the large number of AIDS-related deaths have had far-reaching effects on all segments of our society. As our population has grown older, greater numbers of older adults have become detached from means of production, and they often lack sufficient supports to provide for their maintenance and health-related needs. In addition, violence, crime, delinquency, substance abuse, homelessness, and a variety of related problems have become sources of constant societal concern.

The organization of social welfare services is far different today from that of the Poor Law days. Gone are the almshouses, the poor houses, and "indoor" relief as solutions of first choice. The social welfare system has expanded dramatically to meet the proliferation and magnitude of new needs, and it now requires substantial societal resources to maintain.

Social workers and others within the social welfare system have responded with diversification in order to meet a variety of needs expressed by individuals whose personal resources cannot provide an adequate level of social functioning and life satisfaction. This diversification has emerged as essential in the delivery of social welfare services (see Box 18.1). Today, social workers are skilled in working with the displaced, the poor, substance abusers, single parents, and criminal offenders, but also with persons experiencing marital conflict, family violence, mental illness, problems associated with later life, and a myriad of other related personal and social problems. In addition, the roles of social workers as promoters of social and economic justice and as advocates for disenfranchised populations—the poor, women, people of color, gays and lesbians, people with disabilities, and related groups—have become increasingly important, as society continues to become more complex and tends to overlook these groups. As new problems have emerged, the capacity of the social work profession to incorporate the knowledge and skills essential to providing assistance always has been forthcoming.

◪ SOCIAL WELFARE AND THE FUTURE

Increased world competition and politics, changing family roles and structure, our expanding aging population, gaps in health insurance, changing needs of the workplace, and the need for long-term care have serious implications that have left or will leave large numbers of individuals unable to care for themselves without assistance. Unfortunately, our present social welfare system has not adapted to address these changes. Today's system is fragmented, with one group in need pitted against equally needy ones, all vying for resources often insufficient to address the needs of even one group. Our social welfare system is fast approaching a crisis state and needs serious refinement and rethinking.

We are only now beginning to recognize that poverty and related problems are related more to structural problems with the economy than with individual failure, but as a society we still have a great deal of ambivalence toward poor people. Because the largest group of poor in the United States is children—and in particular, children of color—the impact of poverty will reach far into the next century and beyond if the cycle is not broken somehow. Additional issues relate to immigration; our country historically has been a bastion of hope to oppressed individuals from other countries seeking a better way of life, yet the needs of current citizens who are oppressed and living marginal lives must also be considered. Violence has become a major issue in our society at all levels and one that affects individuals of all ages. Children are increasingly victims of both family, community, and societal violence; and even if they are not victims directly, growing up in a country where violence is an everyday norm is likely to significantly affect their views of the future and of the environment surrounding them.

BOX 18.1

PROFESSIONAL LEVELS OF PRACTICE

The National Association of Social Workers has developed a hierarchy which delineates four levels of professional social work practice and their respective job responsibilities. The hierarchy also identifies the knowledge, skills and values that social workers are expected to demonstrate at each level:

Basic Professional Level represents practice requiring professional practice skills, theoretical knowledge, and values that are not normally obtainable in day to day work experience but that are obtainable through formal professional social work education. Formal social work education is distinguished from experiential learning by being based on conceptual and theoretical knowledge of personal and social interaction and by training in the disciplined use of self in relationship with clients.

Specialized (Expert) Professional Level represents the specific and demonstrated mastery of therapeutic technique in at least one knowledge and skill method, as well as a general knowledge of human personality as influenced by social factors, and the disciplined use of self in treatment relationships with individuals or groups, or a broad conceptual knowledge of research, administration, or planning methods and social problems.

Independent Professional Level represents achievement by the practitioner of practice, based on the appropriate special training, developed and demonstrated under professional supervision, which is sufficient to ensure the dependable, regular use of professional skills in independent or autonomous practice. A minimum of two years is required for this experiential learning and demonstration period following the master of social work program.

This level applies both to solo or autonomous practice as an independent practitioner or consultant and to practice within an organization where the social worker has primary responsibility for representing the profession or for the training or administration of professional staff.

Advanced Professional Level represents practice in which the practitioner carries major social or organizational responsibility for professional development, analysis, research, or policy implementation, or that is achieved by personal professional growth demonstrated through advanced conceptual contributions to professional knowledge.

The educational standards for the four levels of Social Work Practice are:

- **Basic Professional Level:** Requires a bachelor's degree (BSW) from a social work program accredited by the Council on Social Work Education (CSWE).

- **Specialized (Expert) Professional Level:** Requires a master's degree (MSW) from a social work program accredited by the CSWE.

- **Independent Professional Level:** Requires an accredited MSW and at least two years of postmaster's experience under appropriate professional supervision.

- **Advanced Professional Level:** Requires proficiency in special theoretical, practice, administration or policy or the ability to conduct advanced research studies in social welfare; usually demonstrated through a doctoral degree in social work or a closely related social science discipline.

Source: *NASW Standards for the Classification of Social Work Practice* (Silver Springs, Md.: NASW, 1981), p. 9. Copyright 1981, National Association of Social Workers, Inc.

Our country's increased political polarization has also significantly affected social welfare policies and programs that are attempting to address these problems. With more attention being paid to lobbyists for various issues rather than to citizens themselves, it is increasingly difficult for positions that truly advocate for the common good to be heard. The current debate about critical issues often turns into one of "buck-passing," with politicians who are concerned about their futures at the national level trying to pass expensive and controversial programs on to the states to administer, and states trying to pass them on to the local level.

Our short-sightedness only results in a society of persons increasingly unable to provide for themselves or others, which has serious implications for all of us. We cannot expect people to take responsibility for themselves if they have no opportunities to escape from inadequate living situations that promote failure. The poorly prepared student of today is the marginal or unemployed worker of tomorrow. The neglected preschoolers of today are those on whom we will depend to maintain the U.S. position in the world economy, keep our Social Security system intact and pay for our care when we are old, and run our society. If unmet needs are addressed effectively, we all benefit. If unmet needs are not addressed, we all pay.

Our social welfare system must be one that focuses on our strengths and on individual diversity. It must be one that encourages self-sufficiency, yet provides humane services for those who are unable to be self-sufficient, or those who need help from the system in order to function independently. It must be a system that invests in our nation's children—focusing on the preservation of the family but protecting and nurturing children when this is not possible, providing prenatal care, adequate nutrition, preschool programs, and child care. It must be a system that works with other systems to provide increased opportunities for adolescents and young adults—reducing school drop-out rates, increasing literacy, providing employment training, reducing teen pregnancy, and providing comprehensive health and mental health services. It must be a system that helps adults achieve and maintain self-sufficiency—reducing poverty, providing adequate housing and employment, assuring coverage for health and mental health care. It must be a system that attends to the needs of the elderly—providing housing and health and long-term care.

For most individuals in our society, personal needs can no longer be met throughout the entire life cycle by family alone. Government participation is essential to assist those in need. Private and citizen participation is also essential. The issue should not be whether the public or the private sector should meet human needs, but how they can work cooperatively to support each other. Both sectors are interconnected and interdependent parts of the social welfare system. Although the question of the most effective ways to provide social welfare to meet individual unmet needs requires substantial debate, most Americans agree that our society is a caring one and that the nation's future rests on how well it responds to the needs of its members. Each of us, private citizens with public responsibility, needs to examine what roles we can play in strengthening our social welfare system and providing a supportive society for ourselves and future generations.

CURRENT ISSUES IN SOCIAL WORK PRACTICE

The positions members of society take toward social problems and the resolution of those problems invariably relate to the resources available.

Social workers are increasingly becoming involved politically at the exo- and macro levels of society. Social worker Barbara Mikulski of Maryland is an outstanding advocate for the profession and the needs of at-risk populations it serves. She was elected to the U.S. House of Representatives and then to the U.S. Senate.

Unfortunately, members of society do not always take an unequivocally progressive stance. For example, fiscal concerns are currently paramount in society. Federal indebtedness has resulted in massive reductions in funds available for solving social problems. As a result, monies for social welfare services have been reduced significantly, and populations at risk have not received the assistance essential for even the most minimal level of functioning.

In response to the reduction of public monies for social welfare services, considerable emphasis has been directed to encouraging the private sector to "take up the slack" and provide both funds and extend assistance through volunteerism. Although noble, private efforts have fallen far short of success because of the magnitude of the need. As indicated earlier, a society inevitably must take a position relative to its commitment to those in need. The position taken and the ways it is expressed are influenced by values, morality, and the availability of resources. In a materialistically oriented society such as ours, it is paradoxical that the definition of *need* is invariably related to the "amount" of resources that society is willing to allocate. Thus, in times of monetary scarcity, or when demands are made upon individuals to share (through the taxing process) more of their earned incomes, the tendency to redefine need levels is inevitable. This redefinition, of course, does not always address the "real" need that is apparent. Today, as a society, we stand at a crossroads: Do we continue to reduce allocations for resolving the problems of our members at risk; or do we reorganize our priorities to assure that all of our members are guaranteed access to the best of our problem-solving abilities, and hope that at least their minimal needs will be met?

Related challenges facing future social work professionals include determining which of the myriad of societal and individual problems fall within the domain of the social welfare system. A traditional view of the social welfare institution is that its services should be residual—that is, incorporating those areas that cannot be served by other societal institutions. Increasingly, however, the social welfare system is seen as a panacea to address all needs not being met by other systems—that is, a system that should be all things to all people. There is a need to define and to limit the boundaries that encompass the social welfare system so that its services can be effective and retained with available resources. At the same time, however, social workers are faced with serious value conflicts over not addressing human needs that fall beyond social welfare boundaries when no one else is meeting them and they are critical for individual and societal survival.

As technology continues to generate new knowledge, the social work profession increasingly will also have to grapple with ethical issues relating to genetic engineering and surrogate parenting. Assisted death, environmental concerns and pollution, and technological measures to prolong life will also be ethical issues of growing concern that will need to be addressed by many professions, including social work.

With scarce resources, ethical decisions about types of services to be provided and who should get them will increasingly fall to the social worker. How do you say no to a woman with four children under age 6 with no housing, no food, and a temporary part-time job, who makes five dollars more each month than the income eligibility guidelines for receiving AFDC allow? If the federal government or states decide that federal and state funds cannot pay to provide for certain groups of children—those of teen parents, those whose mothers have received benefits for six months or a year and are still not self-sufficient, those whose mothers gave birth to them while they were already receiving benefits—who should provide for those children and in what ways? Should cities and counties provide funding and services such as child care and housing? Should the children be removed from their parents' care and placed in other settings, in spite of the information we have about the long-term emotional costs of separating children from their parents? How do you determine whether limited funding should be allocated to the elderly, to children, or to persons with disabilities? How do you decide who should have first priority for heart and other organ transplants, whether limited dollars should be spent on neonatal care for premature infants who may live only a limited time, or at what point resources should no longer be provided to families with little potential to be rehabilitated and the children placed in foster care or adoption?

If limited resources do not allow for a full range of preventive and remedial/rehabilitative services, which do you choose? Do you try to prevent problems such as child maltreatment, knowing that in the short run this may limit your resources for those already abused, but in the long run it may prevent more abuse? Or, instead, do you help those in immediate crisis, knowing that the lack of preventive services will mean even more crises for families in the future? One social welfare advocate told his state governor and legislature that social workers were being asked to take positions similar to that in the popular novel *Sophie's*

Choice, in which a mother in occupied Poland under Hitler's regime was forced to decide which of her two children would be spared the gas chamber and which would be sent to death.

Limited resources, rapid social change, and the influx of additional social problems such as AIDS, the increase in an underclass of people of color and women, the health care crisis, and the shift to a technocratic society suggest new opportunities for social work professionals willing to accept these challenges. Leaders of the social work profession point to a number of critical issues that the profession will face as we move into the twenty-first century. First, the profession needs to define itself more clearly. Harry Specht and Michael Courtney, two social work educators and leaders of the profession, wrote a thought-provoking book shortly before Specht's death. In *Unfaithful Angels: How Social Work has Abandoned its Mission* (1994), the authors chastise the profession for its attention to clinical issues that focus more on the micro level of the environment and related professional concerns such as managed health care; licensing, certification, and standards for the profession; and private practice. Specht and Courtney argue that social work is unique as a profession because of its commitment to work at all levels of the environment to advocate for social and economic justice and the elimination of oppression and discrimination. They believe that social work has abandoned this commitment and is ignoring the poor, abused and neglected children, the homeless, and other vulnerable populations. They also believe the profession has not given enough attention to empowering individuals, families, groups, and communities to improve their own lives. The authors advocate for the future of the profession to give more attention to community-based programs that educate individuals about how to solve problems, so that they are empowered to address their own needs, and the community's problem-solving capacity can also be increased.

Others, while perhaps not as dire in their statements as Specht and Courtney, also believe that social work will lose ground as a profession if it abandons its previous perspective and its uniqueness as a profession (Hopps and Collins 1995). They raise similar questions and suggest that because social workers will function in an even more diverse and complex environment in the coming years, more attention must be paid to exo and macro level interventions. Hopps and Collins also note that the use of the systems/ecological framework by more members of the profession has significantly expanded the many roles that social work can play in society and has the potential to increase attention to and respect of the profession.

The societal shifts that will continue into the next decade call for social workers who can apply critical thinking to social issues at all levels of the environment, embrace diversity, and promote and expand the values, skills, and knowledge bases of the profession. A recent survey of professional social workers (NASW 1990) suggested that the most critical issues facing the profession in the near future include health care, substance abuse, AIDS, the aging of our society, homelessness, violence, persistent poverty, and the provision of services that are culturally relevant. In 1995, the president of the National Association of

Social Workers, Jay Cayner, called for a "profession-wide effort to bring social work leaders, educators and practitioners together" with experts in related fields to take a "long-term view of social policy in the profession in a historical context . . . to consider how to appropriately balance individual rights with community needs in responding to social problems." (2). Cayner envisions that this effort will address national issues including

> the devolution of programs to states and cities; the push for deficit reduction . . . ; preclusion of unfunded mandates on states and localities, rather than provision of federal funds to support the mandated tasks and the implications . . . ; welfare changes and the accompanying issues . . . ; health care reform; and urban issues—violence, gun control, teen pregnancy, children's services. (2)

The social work profession and the issues it faces are challenging at all levels of society—whether the work is with individuals, families, groups, the community, or at the state, national, or international level. Social work practitioners need to increase their involvement at the legislative and policy levels and become more involved in the political arena, where key social welfare decisions are made. As society becomes increasingly complex, the number of social workers will continue to grow and their roles will broaden at all levels of practice.

TRENDS IN SOCIAL WORK CAREERS

As we indicated in earlier chapters, social workers today function in a variety of job settings and fields of practice and hold degrees at the undergraduate (BSW), masters' (MSW), and doctoral (PhD or DSW) levels. In 1992, a total of 35,000 students were enrolled in BSW programs throughout the United States. Since the late 1980s, enrollment in schools of social work at both the undergraduate and graduate levels has increased substantially as more young people commit themselves to helping others.

Social workers held approximately 484,000 jobs in 1992 (Ginsberg 1992). A survey by the National Association of Social Workers of its members that year found that social workers were employed in a variety of roles (see Table 18.1), with 68 percent in direct service roles (Ginsberg 1992). The largest number of social workers were employed in social services settings, hospitals, and outpatient health and mental health facilities (see Table 18.2). Within those settings, practitioners were most likely to be providing mental health-related services, followed by services to children and youth, medical and health services, and family services (see Table 18.3).

BSW graduates, who make up only 7 percent of NASW's membership, were most likely to be employed in public assistance programs and working with the elderly, children, substance abusers, and persons with developmental disabilities. Conductors of the survey indicate that a much stronger presence by social workers is needed in public assistance and other public social services, corrections, and working with persons

TABLE 18.1 **TYPES OF SERVICES PROVIDED BY NASW MEMBERS (1992)**

Practice Area	Number	Percentage
Direct services to clients	64,888	67.8%
Management administration	15,354	16.1
Supervision	5,582	6.2
Education-training	4,302	4.5
No social work function	2,430	2.5
Consultant	1,554	1.5
Research	478	0.5
Policy development analysis	412	0.5
Planning	347	0.4
Total	**95,609**	**100.0**

Source: L. Ginsberg, *Social Work Almanac* (Washington, D.C.: National Association of Social Workers, 1992), p. 201. Copyright 1992, National Association of Social Workers, Inc.

with developmental disabilities (Gibelman and Schervish 1993, cited in Hopps and Collins 1995).

A valid question asked by social work students is whether the supply of social workers will exceed the demand, particularly during fiscal cutbacks. Even with funding cutbacks, funding for social welfare programs has increased. The U.S. Department of Labor identifies social work as one of the professions that will continue to expand during the coming decade; the Department projects that by the year 2005 over 575,000 social workers will be employed in the United States. Projections indi-

TABLE 18.2 **PRACTICE SETTINGS REPORTED BY NASW MEMBERS (1992)**

Setting	Number	Percentage
Social services agency	21,506	23.4%
Hospital	18,429	20.0
Outpatient/health and mental health	15,181	16.5
Private practice, solo	11,259	12.2
Elementary or secondary school	6,023	6.5
College or university	4,227	5.0
Private practice, group	4,152	4.5
Institution	2,648	2.9
Nursing home or hospice	2,319	2.5
Group home or residence	2,299	2.5
Non-social services organization	1,999	2.2
Courts or criminal justice	1,269	1.4
Member organization	697	0.8
Total	**92,008**	**99.6**

Source: L. Ginsberg, *Social Work Almanac* (Washington, D.C.: National Association of Social Workers, 1992), p. 201. Copyright 1992, National Association of Social Workers, Inc.

TABLE 18.3   **PRACTICE AREAS REPORTED BY NASW MEMBERS (1992)**

Setting	Number	Percentage
Mental health	29,941	32.0%
Children and youths	15,476	16.6
Medical and health care	11,435	12.2
Family services	10,541	11.3
Combined areas	5,275	5.6
School social work	4,650	5.0
Services to the aged	4,511	4.8
Substance abuse	4,326	4.6
Developmental disabilities	2,554	2.7
Corrections/criminal justice	1,124	1.2
Community organization/planning	1,075	1.2
Public assistance and welfare	842	0.9
Occupational social work	706	0.8
Other disabilities	525	0.6
Group services	444	0.5
Total	**93,426**	**100.0**

Source: L. Ginsberg, *Social Work Almanac* (Washington, D.C.: National Association of Social Workers, 1992), p. 201. Copyright 1992, National Association of Social Workers, Inc.

cate that by that time, 31.3 percent of all service-related jobs will be in social services and 29.2 percent will be physical and mental health services, including inpatient and outpatient services, long-term care facilities, and home health care.

As the population continues to age, fewer younger social workers will be available to replace retirees. Additionally, more social work jobs will become available, particularly in the areas of child protective services, criminal justice, substance abuse, health care, mental health, and gerontology. Although the number of social workers employed in the public sector, particularly government agencies, has declined in recent years, many government programs are contracting out their services to private nonprofit and private for-profit organizations that are employing social workers to provide services and oversee programs. In 1992, approximately 40 percent of all social workers were employed by state, county, or municipal government agencies. Most in the private sector were in nonprofit services agencies, community and religious organizations, nursing homes or home health programs, and hospitals (U.S. Department of Labor 1994). As states have passed licensing requirements for social workers and insurance companies include social workers under third-party reimbursement agreements, an increasing number of social workers are establishing private practices and seeing clients for psychotherapy, marriage and family counseling, and other types of clinical services. This trend is likely to continue in spite of the emphasis on managed care and pending health care reform.

At the same time as social work services in the private sector are increasing, new attention is being given to the need to encourage social workers to seek jobs in public social service settings, particularly state social service agencies. NASW and other organizations such as the American Public Welfare Association are working together to increase awareness about the challenges of public social services and the commitment that social work as a profession has to the indigent, who are most likely to come to the attention of a public agency. The welfare reform debate provides a number of challenging opportunities for social workers to develop or strengthen programs that assist families in becoming self-sufficient. The emphasis on family preservation and national attention given to child maltreatment have also resulted in the increased professionalism of child and family services workers employed within public human services agencies. The Education for All Handicapped Children Act also provides for the hiring of social workers in school settings to work with children with disabilities. Many more schools are hiring social workers to work in a variety of school programs, and NASW recently established a special membership division for school social workers.

The social work profession's commitment to the promotion of social and economic justice also provides opportunities for social workers to play major roles in helping entities at all levels of society become more culturally competent and in empowering diverse groups to advocate for their share of resources to get their needs met. This challenge means that social workers, both individually and collectively, most continue to educate themselves about different cultural groups, and to advocate for the hiring of more social workers who reflect the diversity of the populations that the profession serves. In 1992, 88 percent of all social workers were white, 6 percent were African American, 3 percent were Hispanic, 2 percent were Asian, 0.5 percent were Native American, and 1 percent represented other ethnic groups. Seventy-seven percent were women, indicating a need for the profession to embrace a feminist perspective that values equality while at the same time working to ensure that social work is not seen as a "women's" profession. The profession is also younger and less experienced as many long-term social workers enter retirement (Hopps and Collins 1995). Currently, schools of social work and social work employers are attempting to recruit more diverse student bodies and workforces.

Whatever the field of practice or the setting, social workers today and in the future face many challenges—and many opportunities for professional and personal growth. We hope that you will consider joining us as members of the social work profession.

SUMMARY

In this book, we address the current state of the art in social work and social welfare. Throughout each chapter, the effects of social problems upon various segments of our population are identified and the societal responses through the social welfare system are described. The many roles social workers play in addressing social welfare problems are also explored. The significant and dramatic modifications in both the social welfare system and the social work profession since the early days of organized helping efforts are apparent. Armed with knowledge and understanding of human behavior and complex organizations, and bringing a systems/ecological perspective to bear, the contemporary professional social worker is uniquely capable of skillful intervention in the resolution of problems. The social worker of the future will have many challenging opportunities to make major contributions to society.

KEY TERMS

advanced professional level of
  social work practice
basic professional level of social
  work practice

independent professional level of
  social work practice
specialized (expert) professional
  level of social work practice

DISCUSSION QUESTIONS

1. What do you see as the three major social welfare issues the United States will face in the year 2000? What major issues do you feel will have the most impact on the social work profession? What will your role be in addressing these issues?

2. Identify the four levels of social work practice and describe each briefly.

3. In which settings are social workers employed most often? In which fields of practice are social workers employed most often? Where are most BSW social workers employed?

4. Discuss some of the future employment opportunities for social work professionals. Which career areas interest you most, and why?

5. What can the profession of social work do to promote social and economic justice? What can you do, both individually and as a social work professional?

REFERENCES

Cayner, J. 1995. Times call for precise policy compass. *NASW News* 40(7): 2. Washington, D.C.: NASW.

Gibelman, M., and P. H. Schervish. 1993. *Who are we: The social work labor force as reflected in the NASW membership.* Washington, D.C.: NASW.

Ginsberg, L. 1992. *Social work almanac.* Washington, D.C.: NASW.

Hopps, J. G., and P. Collins. 1995. Social work profession overview. *Encyclopedia of Social Work,* vol. 3, 2266–82. Washington, D.C.: NASW.

National Association of Social Workers. 1981. *NASW standards for the classification of social work practice: Policy statement 4.* Silver Spring, Md.: NASW Task Force on Sector Force Classification.

———. 1990. *Strategic Plan.* Washington, D.C.: NASW.

Social workers. 1994. *Occupational Outlook Handbook,* 1994–95 Edition. Washington, D.C.: U.S. Department of Labor Bureau of Labor Statistics.

Specht, H., and M. Courtney. 1994. *Unfaithful angels: How social work has abandoned its mission.* New York: Free Press.

SUGGESTED FURTHER READINGS

Gambrill, E. and R. Pruger, eds. 1992. *Controversial issues in social work.* Boston: Allyn and Bacon.

Gibelman, M. 1995. *What social workers do.* Washington, D.C.: NASW Press.

Hartman, A. 1994. *Reflection and controversy: Essays on social work.* Washington, D.C.: NASW Press.

Macarov, D. 1991. *Certain change. Social work practice in the future.* Washington, D.C.: NASW Press.

Mahafey, M. and J. Hanks. 1982. *Practical politics: Social work and political responsibility.* Washington, D.C.: NASW Press.

Martin, E. and J. Martin. 1995. *Social work and the black experience.* Washington, D.C.: NASW Press.

National Association of Social Workers. *Social work speaks: NASW policy statements,* 3rd ed. Washington, D.C.: NASW Press.

The new social worker, magazine published by WhiteHat Communications, Harrisburg, Pa.

Professional social work practice in public child welfare: An agenda for action. 1987. Portland: University of Southern Maine Center for Research and Advanced Study.

Reid, N. P. and P. R. Popple. 1992. *The moral purposes of social work: The character and intentions of a profession.* Chicago: Nelson-Hall.

GLOSSARY

Acquired immunodeficiency syndrome (AIDS) a fatal disease that attacks the body's natural immune system.

Activity theory theory relating to aging based on the premise that social activity is the essence of life for all ages, and that all people must maintain adequate levels of activity if they are to age successfully.

Addiction a physical and/or psychological dependence upon mood-altering substances or activities, including but not limited to alcohol, drugs, pills, food, sex, or gambling.

Adoption a process by which a child whose birth parents choose not to or cannot care for is provided with a permanent home and parents who are able to provide for the child; legal adoptions can take place only when the court terminates the parental rights of the birth parents, but many adoptions, particularly in minority communities, are informal and do not involve the court.

Advanced professional level of social work practice a level of practice in which the practitioner carries major social or organizational responsibility for professional development, analysis, research, or policy implementation; usually requires a doctoral degree in social work or a closely related discipline.

Affirmative Action programs usually legally mandated programs established within education, business, and industry to improve opportunities for members of ethnic minority groups and women.

Ageism discrimination against the elderly because of their age.

Aging the process of growing old.

Aid to Families with Dependent Children (AFDC) a public assistance program that provides cash assistance to families with children in need because of the loss of financial support as a result of death, disability, or the continued absence of a parent from the home.

Aid to Families with Dependent Children— Unemployed Parent (AFDC-UP) a supplemental AFDC program for two-parent families in which financial need is due to specific unemployment conditions.

Alcoholics Anonymous self-help group for alcoholics based on abstinence and a 12-step philosophy of living. Similar programs exist for family members of alcoholics and addicts and for persons with other types of addictions.

Alcoholism use of alcohol that interferes with personal life, including family, friends, school, job, health, spiritual life, or the law.

Apathy-futility syndrome term used to describe a set of behaviors exhibited by a neglecting parent who is severely depressed and apathetic toward her/his immediate environment, including her/his children.

Association a relationship between two or more factors that occur together but are not necessarily causative (e.g., alcoholism and child abuse).

Basic professional level of social work practice a level of practice representing professional practice skills, theoretical knowledge, and values; requires a bachelor's degree (BSW) from a social work program accredited by the Council on Social Work Education.

Battered child syndrome a medical term used to describe a child with physical injuries in various stages of healing, indicating the child has been physically abused on a number of occasions.

Behavior modification an action intervention, based on the assumption that all behaviors are learned and can be changed, that focuses on reinforcing present positive behaviors to eliminate inappropriate behaviors.

Best interests of child a standard of decision-making used by courts and child welfare agencies that emphasizes what is best for a specific child as opposed to what is best for other family members or persons.

Bioethics moral and ethical decisions associated with advanced technology in the health-care field.

Blended family a family formed by marriage or long-term relationship between partners in which at least one partner brings children from a previous relationship into the new family system.

Boundary the limit or extent of a system; the point where one system ends and another begins.

Broker a social worker who assists clients in locating appropriate resources.

Casework services provided to individuals, groups, and families to strengthen social functioning, based on assessing the client situation, identifying client needs, determining appropriate interventions to address identified needs, and monitoring and evaluating the process to ensure that outcomes address needs identified.

Catastrophic illness a chronic and severely debilitating illness that results in high medical costs and long-term dependence on the health care system.

Categorial assistance cash assistance programs given to individuals and families under the provision of the Social Security Act, which established specific categories of persons in need of cash assistance, including the aged, blind and permanently disabled (Supplemental Security Income) and children (Aid to Families with Dependent Children).

Cause/effect relationship a relationship between factors where one or more factors can be shown to directly cause a change in an additional factor or set of factors

Charity Organization Society (COS) the first relief organization in the United States that developed a systematic program to help the needy, promoting "scientific philanthropy," which incorporated individual assessment and development of coordinated service plans before providing services.

Child neglect a condition in which a caretaker responsible for a child either deliberately or by extraordinary inattentiveness fails to meet a child's basic needs, including failure to provide adequate food, clothing, shelter, medical assistance, or education, and/or to supervise a child appropriately.

Child protective services mandated services provided by state social services agencies to families who abuse or neglect their children, for the purpose of protecting children whose safety is seriously endangered by the actions or inactions of their caretakers.

Child welfare delivery system a network of agencies and programs that provide social services to children, youth, and families.

Child Welfare League of America (CWLA) a national organization consisting of agencies, professionals, and citizens interested in the well-being of children and families; CWLA promotes standards for services, advocates for child welfare policies and programs, conducts research, and provides publications related to child welfare issues.

Child welfare services social services that supplement or substitute for parental care and supervision when parents are unable to fulfill parental responsibilities and that improve conditions for children and their families.

Civil Rights Act federal legislation passed in 1964 and amended in 1965 that prohibits discrimination based on race, gender, religion, color, or ethnicity in public facilities, government programs or those operated or funded by the federal government, and employment.

Client system individuals, families, groups, organizations, or communities at whom intervention is directed in order to enhance social functioning.

Clinical social worker a person whose major focus is to provide clinical social work services— usually individual, group, or family counseling— often in a psychiatric, hospital, residential treatment, or mental health facility. An MSW is usually required (also called *psychiatric social worker* in some settings).

Closed system a system with a boundary that is difficult to permeate; such systems are usually unreceptive to outsiders.

Codependent person who lets someone else's behaviors control her/his functioning and focuses on meeting that person's needs/controlling that person's behaviors instead of his/her own.

Community a group of individuals who usually live near each other; who share a common environment, including public and private resources; and who identify themselves with that community.

Community development a social work approach to working with communities that considers and respects the diversity of a community's population and uses those differences to achieve community betterment for all of its citizens.

Community organization a method of social work practice that involves the development of community resources to meet human needs.

Comparable worth the concept that persons should receive measurably equal pay for the same type of work, regardless of their gender.

Competencies skills that are essential to perform certain functions; social workers must have competencies in a number of areas to be effective professionals.

Consumer price index (CPI) measure of the average change in prices over time for a fixed "market basket" of goods and services purchased by a specified group of consumers.

Contracting process of formulating a verbal or written agreement with a client system of established goals based on identified needs, usually including the steps that will be taken to meet those goals, the entities involved, and target dates for completion.

Council on Social Work Education (CSWE) the national organization of schools of social work that focuses on social work education and serves as the accrediting body for professional social work undergraduate (BSW) and masters (MSW) programs.

Crisis intervention intervention provided when a crisis exists to the extent that one's usual coping resources threaten individual or family functioning.

Cultural pluralism the existence of two or more diverse cultures within a given society where each maintains its own traditions and special interests within the confines of the total society.

Culture shock feelings that may occur when moving to an unfamiliar cultural environment; often results in temporary or longer-lasting effects such as anxiety or depression.

Custody legal charge given to a person requiring her/him to provide certain types of care and to exercise certain controls in regard to another individual, as in parent-child custody.

Deinstitutionalization a philosophy that advocates care of individuals with mental health problems and developmental disabilities in local community outpatient programs, whenever appropriate to the client's needs, as opposed to hospitalization in an institution.

Developmental disability severe, chronic disability resulting from physical or mental impairment, usually prior to age 21, which results in substantial limitations of the individual's social, emotional, intellectual, and/or physical functioning; 75 percent of those with developmental disabilities are mentally retarded.

Diagnostic and Statistical Manual of Mental Disorders (DSM) a classification system of types of mental disorders that incorporates both organic and environmental factors, developed by the American Psychiatric Association for assessment and intervention purposes.

Direct practice a method of social work involving face-to-face contact with individuals, families, groups, and actual provision of services by the social worker for the purpose of addressing unmet needs; also referred to as casework or social casework.

Disability insurance government fund established by the U.S. government in 1957 that provides cash benefits to workers who become totally and permanently disabled.

Disciplinary research research designed to expand the body of knowledge of a particular discipline; also called pure or basic research.

Disengagement theory theory related to aging based on the premise that as adults decline physically, they have less need and desire for social interaction and progressively become disengaged from social roles.

Diversion a process by which persons coming to the attention of the criminal justice system are diverted to other programs such as social services, community services, or educational (defensive driving) programs, rather than going through the court process.

Downshifting the voluntary limiting of job demands that allows a person to devote more time to family or to himself or herself.

Downsizing reduction in workforce and/or scope of goods and services produced or delivered to remain economically competitive and/or manage decreasing resources.

Dual-career family a family in which both partners/spouses have careers outside of the family.

Dysfunctional impaired or abnormal functioning.

Earned Income Tax Credit provision of federal income tax system to give cash supplements to working parents with low incomes; parents file a tax statement and if their taxable earnings are below a specific amount, they receive a check for a percentage of their earnings regardless of whether they paid that amount or less in taxes.

Educational group a group formed for the purpose of transmitting knowledge and enabling participants to acquire more complex skills, such as parenting.

Ego psychology a theoretical perspective that emphasizes ego growth and development.

Emotional maltreatment acting out against a person emotionally, such as verbally belittling or attacking a person constantly, or failing to meet emotional needs through acts of omission, such as not providing love, attention, and/or emotional support to a person.

Employee Assistance Program (EAP) workplace-sponsored program providing mental health and social services to employees and their families; services may be provided directly at the workplace, or through a contractual arrangement by a social services agency.

Empowerment process of helping others increase their personal, interpersonal, or political power so they can take action themselves to improve their lives.

Enabler a person whose behavior facilitates another person's behavior to continue; used most often to describe situations in families where substance abuse is a problem and other family members enable the substance abuse to continue by their reinforcing behaviors.

Encounter group a group oriented toward assisting individuals in developing more self-awareness and interpersonal skills through in-depth experiential activities and extensive group sharing.

Entitlement social welfare programs that any individual is entitled to if certain eligibility requirements are met; such programs are based on numbers of individuals in need of the services rather than other limitations, such as resources available or caps put on funding by government bodies.

Entropy unavailable energy in a closed system that creates dysfunction within that system and eventually results in the system's inability to function.

Equal Rights Amendment (ERA) a proposed amendment to the U.S. Constitution to assure the complete and equal rights of all citizens without regard to race, color, creed, or gender; the amendment was not ratified by the number of states necessary for its adoption.

Equifinality the idea that the final state of a system can be achieved in many different ways.

Ethics a framework for determining what is right and wrong and how specific situations should be handled; the National Association of Social Workers Code of Ethics relates to the moral principles of social work practice.

Etiology of crime theories relating to the origins or causes of crime, including physiological, psychological, and sociological perspectives.

Evaluation method of showing how a client system or a program has achieved or failed to achieve established goals.

Evaluative research research undertaken to show how a program achieves (or fails to achieve) its goals.

Exchange theory theory based on the premise that relationships are exchanges of goods and services, with those in power having the goods and services. In relation to aging, this theory attributes the social withdrawal of the elderly to a loss of power as they lose their income and move to pensions and Medicare.

Exosystem level the level of social environment that incorporates community factors in which an individual does not participate directly, but that affects the individual's functioning, such as school board and city council actions.

Family a group of individuals bonded together through marriage, kinship, adoption, or mutual agreement.

Family preservation programs family intervention programs whose goal is to keep families together by increasing the coping skills and competencies of family members.

Family roles roles taken on by family members as a way to cope with the behaviors of other family members and to maintain the family system's patterns of functioning.

Family violence use of force, or threatened use of force, by one family member against another, usually by a family member who is more powerful against a member who is less powerful.

Feminization of poverty a term used to describe the result of the increasing numbers of single-parent women being classified as poor.

Flexiplace a system that allows employees to work at alternate work sites as opposed to a standard workplace (e.g., working in their own homes).

Flextime a system that allows employees to have varied work hours as opposed to standard work hours (e.g., working from 6 a.m. to 3 p.m. rather than from 8 a.m. to 5 p.m.).

Food stamps in-kind assistance program funded by the U.S. Department of Agriculture, designed to supplement the food-purchasing power of eligible low-income households in order to allow families to maintain nutritious diets and to expand the market for agricultural goods.

Foster care a form of temporary substitute care in which children live with a family other than their birth family until they are able to be returned to their birth family, adopted, or placed in a more permanent setting that best meets their needs.

General assistance (GA) public assistance programs that provide financial aid to persons who are in need but do not qualify for federally authorized programs; such programs are usually administered by county and local governments and are also referred to as relief programs.

General deterrent deterrent toward committing inappropriate/illegal acts targeted at the total population by specifically punishing those who commit such acts; imprisoning persons who commit crimes deters others from committing the same crimes.

Generalist practitioner social worker who operates from a systems/ecological perspective, using multiple interventions in working with client systems at the individual, family, group, organizational, community, or societal level and using the strengths of those systems to empower them to change their environments.

Generalizable the ability of a theory to use what happens in one situation to explain what happens in other situations.

Gerontology the study of aging and the aging process.

Goal setting process used by social workers and other helping professionals with client systems to identify ways to meet their needs; usually includes the identification of specific goals, steps to be taken in meeting those goals, resources needed, and a time frame for completion.

Great Society a social reform program proposed by the Johnson administration in the 1960s to improve the quality of life for all Americans, with emphasis on the poor and disenfranchised; the War on Poverty was one of the major Great Society programs.

Gross domestic product (GDP) the total monetary value of a nation's annual output of goods and services.

Group a social unit consisting of individuals who define status and role relationships to one another. A group possesses its own set of values and norms and regulates the behavior of its members.

Group work a process that seeks to stimulate and support more adaptive personal functioning and social skills of individuals through structured group interaction.

Head Start a comprehensive early childhood education program initially established as a Great Society Program that provides developmental learning for preschool children with health care, social services, and parent education components.

Health a state of complete physical, mental, and social well-being that is not merely the absence of disease or infirmity.

Health and welfare services programs providing services that facilitate individual health and welfare, such as maternal health and child care, public health, family planning, and child welfare services.

Health care services provided to individuals to prevent or promote recovery from illness or disease.

Health maintenance organization (HMO) prepaid medical group practice for which individuals pay monthly fees and receive specific types of health care at no cost or minimum costs per visit.

Health risk factors factors that affect a person's health and place her/him at risk for serious health problems (e.g., smoking).

HIV-positive the first stage of acquired immunodeficiency syndrome (AIDS), also called the seropositive state, that occurs when a person has tested positively for AIDS and has HIV (human immunodeficiency virus) antibodies in his or her blood.

Home-based family services services delivered to children and families in their own homes, with a focus on preserving the family system and strengthening the family to bring about needed change in an effort to prevent family breakup.

Home health care health care provided in a person's home as opposed to a hospital or other institutional health care setting; made available through outreach visits by social workers, nurses, physicians, and other health practitioners.

Homophobia a fear of homosexuals and homosexuality.

Hospices programs for terminally ill individuals and their families that enable them to die with dignity and support, often away from a hospital setting.

Hypothesis a tentative assumption derived from theory that is capable of empirical verification.

Implementation strategy plan for carrying out the steps required to put a program or plan into practice.

Impulse-ridden behavior behavior exhibited by a neglecting parent with low impulse control, including inconsistency, leaving a child alone or in an unsafe situation without realizing the consequences to the child, or because a new activity is given a higher priority.

Incest sexual abuse between family members.

Inclusive the ability of a theory to consistently explain events in the same way each time they occur.

Independent professional level of social work practice a level of practice based on academic training and professional supervision that ensures the regular use of professional skills in independent or autonomous practice; requires a master's degree from an accredited social work

program and at least two years of post-master's experience under appropriate professional supervision.

Indoor relief assistance given to the poor and the needy through placement in institutions, such as poorhouses, orphanages, and prisons.

Infant mortality rate the number of infants who die at birth or before they reach a certain age compared to the total number of infants, both living and not living, within that age range, within a specified geographic location and a specified time frame.

Intervention planned activities that are designed to improve the social functioning of a client or client system.

Job-sharing the sharing of one full-time job by two or more individuals; this practice is increasingly being allowed by employers and is advantageous to women with young children who do not want to work outside the home on a full-time basis.

Laissez faire an economic theory developed by Adam Smith that emphasizes persons taking care of themselves and limits government intervention.

Least detrimental alternative a decision-making premise that places priority on making decisions regarding children based on which decision will be least damaging or upsetting to the child.

Least restrictive environment selecting a living environment for an individual that maintains the greatest degree of freedom, self-determination, autonomy, dignity, and integrity for the individual while he or she participates in treatment or receives services.

Life-span model a framework that focuses on relationships between individuals and their environments with major emphasis on where persons are developmentally and what transitional life processes they are experiencing (e.g., marriage, retirement).

Living will formal written statement made by an individual specifying the individual's wishes about how her/his death should be handled, including delineation of which medical procedures and life support systems, if any, should be used and under what conditions.

Long-term care facility a program that provides long-term care to individuals, including the elderly and the disabled; state and federal regulations have established specific requirements facilities must meet to be classified as long-term care facilities.

Macrosystem level the level of social environment that incorporates societal factors affecting an individual, including cultural ideologies, assumptions, and social policies that define and organize a given society.

Managed care system system of health care delivery that limits the use and cost of services and measures performance.

Market basket concept way of measuring the number of people in poverty based on a formula that includes the estimated costs a family spends to provide a minimum nutritional diet, with adjustments for family size, and a set proportion of income families generally spend for food; families spending less than this proportion of their income are considered below the poverty line.

Mediation intervention between a divorcing or divorced couple to promote settlement of child custody and property issues in order to reconcile differences and reach compromises; mediation teams usually include an attorney and a social worker.

Medicaid federal- and state-funded public assistance program that provides health care to low-income individuals and families based on a means-test using strict eligibility guidelines.

Medical model a model that considers those with emotional problems as sick and thus not responsible for their behavior. This model also focuses on deficits and dysfunction of the client and family rather than their strengths. Little attention is given to environmental aspects.

Medicare federal health insurance program for the elderly.

Mental retardation a type of developmental disability attributable to mental or physical impairment that results in below-average intellectual functioning.

Mesosystem level the level of social environment that incorporates interactions and interrelations among those persons, groups, and settings that comprise an individual's microsystem.

Microsystem level the level of social environment that includes the individual, including intrapsychic characteristics and past life experiences, and all the persons and groups in his or her day-to-day environment.

Minority group a category of people distinguished by physical or cultural traits that are used by the majority group to single them out for differential and unequal treatment.

Moral treatment a philosophy among professionals and advocates working with the mentally ill in the late 1700s and early 1800s that advocated a caring, humane approach, as opposed to a punitive, repressive environment.

Multidisciplinary team approach an approach to working with clients that involves the shared expertise of professionals from a variety of disciplines, such as social workers, health professionals, educators, attorneys, and psychologists.

National Association of Mental Health a national association of professionals and organizations concerned about mental health issues and care of persons with mental health problems; provides education, advocacy, and research.

National Association of Social Workers (NASW) the major national professional organization for social workers, which promotes ethics and quality in social work practice; stimulates political participation and social action; and maintains eligibility standards for membership.

National Institute of Mental Health federal agency created by Congress in 1949 to address mental health concerns; now a part of the U.S. Department of Health and Human Services.

Natural group a group in which members participate as a result of common interests, shared experiences, similar backgrounds and values, and personal satisfactions derived from interaction with other group members (e.g., a street gang).

Natural helping networks informal system of support available to individuals as opposed to professional service delivery system; includes individuals such as family members, friends, neighbors, co-workers, and members of organizations in which an individual may be involved, such as a church or synagogue; also called natural support systems.

Nonorganic failure to thrive a medical condition that results when a child is three percentiles or more below the normal range for height and weight and no organic reason can be determined; placing a child in a hospital and providing an adequate diet and nurturing will cause the child to gain height and weight, suggesting parental deprivation as the cause.

Occupational social work social work services provided through the workplace; also called industrial social work. Such services allow for focus on the relationships between work stresses and other systems within which individuals function.

Official poverty a way of measuring poverty that provides a set of income thresholds adjusted for household size, age of household head, and number of children under 18 years old.

Old Age Survivors Insurance (OASI) a Social Security insurance program established as part of the Social Security Act of 1935 that provides limited payments to those eligible elderly persons and/or their dependents who have been employed and have had taxes deducted from their wages matched by their employers paid into a funding pool.

Ombudsman a public or private official whose function is to assist citizens in dealing with a bureaucracy.

Omnibus Budget Reconciliation Act of 1987 federal legislation that mandated major nursing home reforms, including increased rights for residents, written care plans, training for staff, and the employment of certified social workers.

Open system a system in which the boundaries are permeated easily.

Opportunity structure the accessibility of opportunities for an individual within that individual's environment, including personal and environmental factors such as physical traits, intelligence, family, and availability of employment.

Outdoor relief cash or in-kind assistance given to persons in need, allowing them to remain in their own homes (e.g., public assistance payments for food and fuel).

Outsourcing the practice by U.S. businesses of having portions or all of their production carried out outside of the United States and its territories.

Pastoral counselor a person who provides counseling services under the auspices of a religious organization, which usually includes an emphasis on spiritual well-being; usually members of the clergy.

Permanency planning idea stating that all child welfare services provided should be centered around a plan directed toward a permanent, nurturing home for that child.

Person-environment fit fit between a person's needs, rights, goals, and capacities and the physical and social environment within which the person functions.

Physical child abuse a physical act of harm or threatened harm against a child by a caretaker which results in physical or mental injury to a child, including beating, hitting, slapping, burning, shaking, or throwing.

Policy research research that focuses upon evaluating the effects of proposed or existing social policy on constituent populations.

Poor Law legislation passed in England in 1601, established categories of the poor, including the deserving poor (orphans, widows, etc.) and the nondeserving poor (able-bodied males) and the treatment they were to receive from national and local governments. This law established precedents for policies toward the poor in the United States.

Poverty a determination that a household's income is inadequate judged by a specific standard.

Prejudice an irrational attitude of hostility directed against an individual, a group, a race, or their supposed characteristics.

Primary prevention a program targeted at the total population to prevent a problem from occurring.

Primary setting a setting in which the types of services a professional provides match the primary goals of the setting (e.g., a hospital is a primary setting for a nurse but a secondary setting for a social worker).

Private insurance insurance programs available to individuals and families through the workplace or through purchase of policies with private insurance companies.

Private nonprofit social agency nongovernmental agencies that provide social services, spending all of their funds to meet the goals of the agency with no financial profit earned by agency owners, directors, or employees.

Private practice in social work, the delivery of client services for pay on an independent, autonomous basis rather than under the auspices of an agency; social workers in most states must have an MSW degree, supervision by an advanced practitioner, and pass a licensing or certification examination before establishing a private practice.

Private sector includes programs and agencies funded and operated by nonpublic entities (e.g., voluntary and proprietary agencies and private businesses).

Problem-solving approach a common intervention used by social workers, based on client's motivation and capacity for change and opportunities available to the client to facilitate the change. Client and worker assess needs, identify problems and needs to be addressed, develop a plan to address problems and needs, and implement and monitor the plan, revising as needed.

Psychiatry a branch of medicine that deals with mental, emotional, or behavioral disorders.

Psychoanalysis a method of dealing with emotional problems that focuses on intrapsychic functioning (internal conflicts within the individual).

Psychobiological approaches that focus on the interactions between biological and environmental factors in understanding human behavior.

Psychological parent a person viewed by a child as being his/her parental figure from a psychological or emotional standpoint as opposed to a birth relationship; if a boy were being raised by his grandparents and rarely saw his mother, they would be his psychological parents. Many court decisions are being made based on the concept of psychological as opposed to biological parent.

Psychology a science based on the study of mind and behavior; involves many subspecialties.

Psychometric instruments tests used to measure psychological functioning.

Psychotropic drugs types of drugs used in the treatment of mental health problems, including depression and psychoses, which have resulted in major reductions in numbers of individuals with emotional problems needing long-term hospitalization.

Public (social) assistance programs that provide income, medical care, and social services to individuals and families based on economic need, paid from state and local taxes, to provide a socially established minimum standard usually set by the state; Aid to Families with Dependent Children (AFDC), food stamps, and Medicaid are public assistance programs.

Public insurance insurance programs provided by the public sector to those in need who are not covered by private insurance programs and meet eligibility requirements, such as Medicaid.

Public sector programs and agencies funded and operated by government entities, including public schools, agencies, and hospitals.

Reactive depressive behavior behavior resulting from depression, often due to a loss, that can affect the ability to parent and lead to child neglect.

Reality therapy an intervention, based on the assumption that people are responsible for their own behavior, that affects change by confronting individuals about irresponsible behaviors and encouraging them to accept responsibility for their behaviors and to develop positive self-worth through positive behavior.

Relative poverty poverty measured by comparing the unit being measured (e.g., individuals or families) to a set standard for that unit, such as income, with those falling below that standard identified as being in poverty.

Residential treatment center a facility that provides 24-hour care with a treatment component for persons with mental health problems or developmental disabilities such as alcoholism; such programs are usually considered less restrictive than psychiatric hospitals.

Retirement leaving paid employment, usually based on age; retirees may receive a pension or Social Security benefits depending on their work history and eligibility for such programs.

Rural a social, occupational, and cultural way of life for persons living in the country or in rural communities with less than 2500 persons.

Rural social work social work provided in rural areas, usually based on a generalist practice model that involves the actual provision of many services rather than linking individuals with other social service resources.

School social work a social work approach that involves working with children, youth, and their families within a school setting: school social workers deal directly with children, youth, and their families as well as teachers, school administrators, and other community resources.

Secondary prevention targeted at specified groups within a larger population that are determined to be "at risk," or more likely to experience a specific problem than the larger population, to prevent the problem from occurring.

Secondary setting a setting in which the types of services a professional provides differ from the primary focus of the setting (e.g., a social worker in a hospital works in a secondary setting, while a social worker in a social services agency works in a primary setting).

Self-concept the image a person has of her or himself in relation to appearance, ability, skills, motivation, and capacity to react to the environment; derived primarily through feedback from others.

Self-help group a group of individuals with similar problems that meets for the purpose of providing support and information to each other and for mutual problem-solving; Parents Anonymous and Alcoholics Anonymous are examples of self-help groups.

Sexism discrimination against an individual because of gender.

Sexual abuse the use of a child by an adult for sexual or emotional gratification in a sexual way, such as fondling, exposure, sexual intercourse, and exploitation, including child pornography.

Single-parent family a family headed by one parent, usually a female.

Single-subject designs research designs that evaluate the impact of interventions or policy changes on a single client or case.

Social action a social work approach to working with communities that stresses organization and group cohesion in confrontational approaches geared to modify or eliminate institutional power bases that negatively impact the community.

Social agencies organizations whose primary focus is to address social problems.

Social casework a social work method involving face-to-face contact with individuals, families, or groups, by which the social worker provides services directly to clients for the purpose of addressing unmet needs; also referred to as direct practice.

Social group work a social work method involving intervention with groups of individuals that uses structured interaction to promote individual and group functioning and well-being.

Social inequality unequal treatment of social groups based on factors such as economic and social status, age, ethnicity, sexual preference, or gender.

Social insurance financial assistance for those whose income has been curtailed due to retirement, death, or long-term disability of the family breadwinner; paid to former working persons or their dependents through a tax on earned income.

Social justice fairness and equity in the protection of civil and human rights, the treatment of individuals, the distribution of opportunity, and the assurance of personal and economic opportunity.

Social planning a social work approach to working with communities that emphasizes modification of institutional practices through the application of knowledge, values, and theory; a practical, rational approach.

Social Security an insurance program established as part of the Social Security Act that provides limited payments to eligible elderly persons or their dependents who have been employed and have had taxes deducted from their wages, matched by their employers, and paid into a funding pool.

Social Security Act major social welfare legislation passed by Congress in 1935, establishing social insurance programs based on taxes paid by working persons; public assistance programs to provide for those who do not qualify for social insurance programs and cannot provide for themselves or their families financially; and health and welfare services for children, families, the disabled, and the aged such as child welfare services, maternal and child health services, and services for the disabled.

Social welfare efforts organized by societies to facilitate the well-being of their members, usually focused on activities that seek to prevent, alleviate, or contribute to the solution of a selected set of social problems.

Social work the major profession that implements planned change activities prescribed by social welfare institutions through intervention with individuals, families, and groups or at community, organizational, and societal levels to enhance or restore social functioning.

Social worker a member of the social work profession who works with individuals, families, groups, organizations, communities, or societies to improve social functioning.

Socialization the process of learning to become a social being; the acquisition of knowledge, values, abilities, and skills that are essential to function as a member of the society within which the individual lives.

Specialization practice of social work focused on a specific population or field of practice requiring specialized knowledge and skill; in contrast to generalist practice.

Specialized (expert) professional level of social work practice a level of practice that includes mastery in at least one knowledge and skill area (e.g., child and family or aging) as well as general social work knowledge; requires an MSW degree from an accredited social work program.

Special-needs child a child who is available for adoption but is considered difficult to place because of special needs; special needs children are older, children of color, members of large sibling groups, and/or have physical and emotional disabilities.

Specific deterrent a program or sentence targeted at an individual to discourage him/her from repeating inappropriate/illegal behavior.

Spillover effect occurs when feelings, attitudes, and behaviors from one domain in a person's life have a positive or a negative impact on other domains (e.g., from the workplace to the family).

Steady state the constant adjustment of a system moving toward its goal while maintaining order and stability within.

Stereotyping holding a standardized mental picture of a group and attributing that mental picture to all group members.

Strengths perspective perspective embraced by social workers that focuses on the strengths of the client system and the broader environment within which it functions rather than on the deficiencies.

Substance abuse improper use of mood-altering substances such as drugs that results in detrimental effects on an individual's personal life, including school, job, family, friends, health, spiritual life, or the law.

Substitute care out-of-home care provided for children when parents are unwilling or unable to provide care in their own homes; types of substitute care include foster care, group home care, and residential treatment, and are determined based on the needs of the child.

Supplemental Security Income (SSI) a program administered in conjunction with the Social Security Program to provide cash assistance to needy aged, blind, and/or permanently and totally disabled persons who meet certain eligibility standards established by state and federal regulations.

Synergy the combined energy of smaller parts of a larger system that is greater than the sum of the energy of those parts.

System social unit consisting of interdependent, interacting parts.

Systems/ecological framework a major framework used to understand individual, family, community, organizational, and societal events and behaviors, emphasizes the interactions and interdependence between individuals and their environments.

Task-centered casework a short-term therapeutic approach to intervention that stresses the selection of specific tasks to be worked on within a limited time frame to address the needs of a client system.

Telecommunications process of communicating electronically that allows remote sites to have access to information and consultation.

Tertiary prevention efforts targeted at individuals who have already experienced a specific problem to prevent that problem from reoccurring.

Testable the ability of a theory to be measured accurately and validly.

Theory a way of organizing facts or sets of facts to describe, explain, or predict events.

Therapeutic group a group requiring skilled professional leaders who assist group members in addressing intensive personal and emotional problems.

Unemployment insurance (UI) an insurance program, established by the Social Security Act, which is funded by taxes assessed to employers and is available to eligible unemployed workers.

U.S. Children's Bureau the first federal department established by the federal government (1912) to address the needs of children and families; federal programs addressing problems of child abuse and neglect, runaway youth, adoption and foster care, and other child welfare services are currently housed within the U.S. Department of Health and Human Services.

U.S. Department of Agriculture federal department that oversees the food stamp program and houses the Agricultural Extension Service, which provides services targeted to rural areas.

U.S. Department of Health and Human Services federal department that oversees the implementation of legislation relating to health and human services, including public assistance programs, child welfare services, and services for the elderly.

Values assumptions, convictions, or beliefs about the manner in which people should behave and the principles that should govern behavior.

Voluntary sector third sector of society, along with the public and for-profit proprietary sectors; the voluntary sector includes private, nonprofit social agencies.

Workers' compensation (WC) an insurance program that is funded by taxes assessed to employers and is available to eligible workers who are injured on the job or experience job-related injuries or illnesses.

INDEX